THE UN CHILDREN'S RIGHTS CONVENTION

THE UN CHILDREN'S RIGHTS CONVENTION: THEORY MEETS PRACTICE

Proceedings of the International Interdisciplinary Conference on Children's Rights, 18-19 May 2006, Ghent, Belgium

Editors:
A. Alen, H. Bosly,
M. De Bie, J. Vande Lanotte,
F. Ang, I. Delens-Ravier,
M. Delplace, C. Herman,
D. Reynaert, V. Staelens,
R. Steel, M. Verheyde

intersentia
Antwerpen – Oxford

Distribution for the UK:
Hart Publishing Ltd.
16C Worcester Place
Oxford OX1 2JW
UK
Tel: + 44 1865 51 75 30
Fax: + 44 1865 51 07 10

Distribution for Switzerland and Germany:
Schulthess Verlag
Zwingliplatz 2
CH-8022 Zürich
Switzerland
Tel: + 41 1 251 93 36
Fax: + 41 1 261 63 94

Distribution for North America:
Gaunt Inc.
Gaunt Building
3011 Gulf Drive
Holmes Beach
Florida 34217-2199
USA
Tel: + 1 941 778 5211
Fax: + 1 941 778 5252

Distribution for other countries:
Intersentia Publishers
Groenstraat 31
2640 Mortsel
Belgium
Tel: + 32 3 680 15 50
Fax: + 32 3 658 71 21

With the support of the Belgian Science Policy (IAP Project No. P5/15 – 'Human Rights of Children')

The UN Children's Rights Convention: Theory meets practice. Proceedings of the International Interdisciplinary Conference on Children's Rights, 18-19 May 2006, Ghent, Belgium.
A. Alen, M. Bosly, M. De Bie, J. Vande Lanotte, F. Ang, I. Delens-Ravier, M. Delplace, C. Herman, D. Reynaert, V. Staelens, R. Steel and M. Verheyde (eds.)

ISBN: 978-90-5095-640-6
D/2007/7849/6
NUR 823

PREFACE

CHILDREN'S RIGHTS AS HUMAN RIGHTS

EVA BREMS

A friend who is a paediatrician once described her medical specialisation as follows: "in paediatrics, we need to be generalists because we deal with all the parts of the human body and their afflictions; at the same time we need to be skilled technicians, because the body parts we work on can be extremely small; and finally, in addition to the medical conditions that afflict both adults and children, we need to master a number of other conditions afflicting children alone. The patients are often cute, but when they suffer it is very hard; and don't forget that we have to deal also with the parents". I remember greatly admiring her courageous choice of a profession that requires an investment in specialisation yet lacks the specialist's comfort of a restriction of scope.

There are not so many people whose profession or area of specialisation is "children's rights". There are some among the authors who contributed to this book, yet other authors may be human rights specialists applying their topical specialisation (e.g. a particular right or a specific theoretical question) today to children's rights as they might apply it tomorrow to the rights of women or ethnic minorities. Or they may be practicians working with children, for whom the rights perspective is only one dimension of their work. Among the lawyers, there are those who work only with domestic law, and others who are involved exclusively with international law. As a discipline, children's rights is extremely rich and the comparison with paediatrics makes sense. A complete children's rights expert must be an expert in all 'general' human rights and all the theoretical, political and legal challenges inherent in them, in addition to the specific rights of children. Moreover, special kills are needed to deal with the rights of children. These are related not so much to children's size, but rather to their special vulnerability, their progressive capacity for autonomy and participation, and their development to adulthood under the guidance of parents, teachers and other caretakers. In legal terms, these specificities have been translated into a number of key tools or modes of reasoning that distinguish a children's rights argument from a human rights argument or a child protection argument. The best interest of the child, child participation, gradual autonomy, the triangle child – caretaker – state... handy and characteristic as they may be, these tools and concepts are also frequently contested in their application to specific situations. From the experience with general human rights, we know that transferring the consensus that exists on general rules to a consensus on solutions to concrete problems requires time: time for normative development through academic work as well as practice, and time for the change of minds that is needed for emancipation and inclusion. We also know that this consensus will never be complete, and that therefore we will need to keep debating at conferences and writing papers and books on children's rights.

In an academic work on for example women's rights, rights of indigenous peoples or rights of persons with disabilities it would not be acceptable not to include any texts written by women or indigenous persons or persons with disabilities. This is different for children's rights, as the large majority of people who acquire high-level academic skills do so only after childhood. Yet when adults write about children's rights, there is also another difference with able-bodied persons writing about disability rights or men writing about women's rights: many of the authors are parents, and all of the authors were children once. This is both a benefit and a burden. Emotional involvement is a strong work drive, but may also distract from academic objectivity. The constant availability of a reality check at home is handy, but should not obscure the enormous diversity of contexts in which the world's children live, making experiences from our own childhood and that of our children only slightly relevant for the rest of the world. And what about the tricky question of 'dealing with the parents'? I am sure that I am only one of many scholars who experienced a decrease in enthusiasm for children's rights in the family context after becoming a parent herself... Involvement can be confusing. In the school of Nathan, my six-year-old son, the children of a class choose the projects they are going to work on together. In his class, on 16 children, 'children's rights' was proposed as a project topic, but got only one vote, against 15 for 'chocolate'. I must confess I was disappointed and found it somewhat unfair: who can compete with chocolate? Yet a world in which children's rights lose from chocolate is a dream; in reality, they lose from war, poverty and adult priorities. Moreover, I am confident that the process of proposing their favourite topics and organising a vote on them has in fact taught these children the essentials of children's rights. This teacher knows children's rights, and that makes all the difference.

Adults who realise that we are actually the ones who need to learn more about children's rights will find in this book a wealth of information and thought-provoking challenges. One book cannot address all aspects of children's rights. Yet the authors of this volume have succeeded in bringing together a wide range of perspectives grouped around a number of central themes. Throughout the book, a fair balance between North and South as well as a multidisciplinary perspective are upheld. There is input from theory as well as from practice, united through the lens of a rights perspective. The book addresses children's rights vis-à-vis state authorities as well as in the family.

In general, human rights, economic, social and cultural rights still receive comparatively less attention than civil and political rights. The Convention on the Rights of the Child includes both categories of rights, and children's rights discourse generally manages a better balance between them. In this book, there is more or less an equal number of papers addressing civil and political rights (mainly in the chapters 'family' and 'juvenile justice') and economic and social rights. In addition, monitoring and implementation are extensively addressed in a series of papers encompassing different levels and mechanisms.

I hope this book will inspire your thinking and your work!

INTRODUCTION

The Conference on Children's Rights, held on 18 and 19 May 2006 in Ghent (Belgium) was the closing event of a Belgian research project on children's rights, called the IAP Research Network on children's rights (Interuniversity Attraction Poles). The network existed of researchers with different backgrounds and coming from three Belgian universities: the University of Ghent, the Catholic University of Leuven and the Catholic University of Louvain-la-Neuve, thus bringing together two language communities of Belgium. The network existed for ten years and was unique in Belgium in its set-up, its methodology and subject of research.

The researchers of the network conducted individual as well as joint research on children's rights, on a wide range of subjects and within the disciplines that are represented in the network: law, criminology, pedagogy and sociology. The network has two joint international publications. In *Participation Rights of Children* (Intersentia, 2006, 255p.), the researchers reflect on child participation in different fields, such as international criminal law, asylum- and refugee law, juvenile justice, protection against drug abuse, child mental health care, adoption, school, youth protection, and human rights education. Another important joint publication of the network is the series *A Commentary on the United Nations Convention on the Rights of the Child—CRC Commentary* (Martinus Nijhoff Publishers, Leiden/Boston, 2005-ongoing). The series entails a legal article-by-article commentary on the Children's Rights Convention, by renowned as well as young human and children's rights experts.

The researchers decided to finish their project with yet another international project: the "International Interdisciplinary Conference on Children's Rights. An appraisal of the Children's Rights Convention. Theory meets practice" – "Conférence internationale et interdisciplinaire relative aux droits de l'enfant. Une évaluation de la Convention internationale relative aux droits de l'enfant. De la théorie à la pratique". The aim of the conference was to evaluate how the UN Convention on the Rights of the Child, more than 15 years after its coming into force, has furthered children's rights, and to explore the challenges we still face in realising these rights. It did so in particular by creating an open forum where academics could meet and exchange views with other professionals, dealing with children's rights in practice.

The IAP Research Network on children's rights is pleased to say that the conference was a great success. Over 60 countries, from East and West, North and South, were represented. Over 180 people participated in the two-day event. Fascinating speeches were given and interesting debates were held, interesting stories were told and important contacts were made. The conference was truly a meeting point for children's rights advocates, both academics and practitioners, from all over the world. Several renowned human and children's rights specialists accepted to participate to the conference; to name some: Nigel Cantwell, Eva Brems, Laura Theytaz-Bergman, Eugeen Verhellen, Jean Trépanier, and Katarina Tomaševski. The network deeply regrets the death of Katarina Tomaševski only a few months after the conference. We are grateful for her presence and the very enlightening and passionate speech she gave at the conference. She was a unique human rights activist and we pay tribute to her memory.

Thanks to our sponsors, several scholarships were granted to participants coming from developing countries. The network would therefore like to thank the following sponsors, whose support made the conference and the publishing of these proceedings possible: the Belgian Science Policy Office, the Flemish Interuniversity Council, the National Lottery, the Friedrich Nauman Stiftung and the Flemish Community. The network also would like to particularly thank colleagues Marie Delplace and Charlotte Herman for their coordination role in the organisation of the conference and the editing of this conference book.

This book contains most of the keynote speeches held at the conference and a selection of the workshop papers. The IAP team hopes that this book will provide you with new information, ideas and inspiration, which in the end may make a change in the lives of children.

TABLE OF CONTENTS

III. IMPLEMENTATION OF THE CRC FROM AN NGO PERSPECTIVE

THE RIGHT TO EDUCATION IN THE REPUBLIC OF IRELAND: TEACHING THE CELTIC TIGER

VII. CHILDREN'S RIGHTS AND THE FAMILY

SILENT KNOWLEDGE: AN EXPLORATORY STUDY OF THE ISSUES IN ACTIVISM AGAINST INCEST ABUSE IN INDIA

SYNERGIES AND TENSIONS BETWEEN WOMEN'S EMPOWERMENT AND CHILDREN'S RIGHTS. A CRITICAL ASSESSMENT OF WOMEN'S SELF-HELP GROUPS IN ANDHRA PRADESH, INDIA

X. CONCLUDING REMARKS

I. CRITICAL REFLECTIONS ON CHILDREN'S RIGHTS

RIGHTS IN CONTEXT; QUESTIONING UNIVERSALITY IN THE IMPLEMENTATION OF CHILDREN'S RIGHTS USING JORDAN AS A CASE STUDY (2004)

LINA HAMMAD

1. INTRODUCTION

1. The Convention on the Rights of the Child has exerted pressure on nations to examine their current attitudes towards children, marking an ideological shift in the perception of childhood, and reconceptualising the child from being a vulnerable object in need of protection to an active subject of rights, entitled to full respect and dignity. With it also came a change in rhetoric towards putting "children first", whilst acknowledging the child as being an inclusive part of society.[1] This has also been supported by the rapid spread of globalisation, which has pushed many cultures towards a more "modern" model of childhood and children's socialisation as the archetype for childhood.[2] However, although the Convention has been argued to be "more sensitive to different approaches and perspectives than most of the principal human rights treaties",[3] this new universal image of the child has been seen as a threat to many societies holding deeply entrenched values and traditions. This is because a child is not perceived as an independent human being in many traditional societies, and Conventions such as the CRC are seen by many traditional cultures as "tools of

---

[1] E. VERHELLEN, 'Monitoring Children's Rights', in E. VERHELLEN (ed.), *Monitoring Children's Rights*, (The Hague – Boston – London: Martinus Nijhoff Publishers; The Hague: Kluwer Law International, 1996), 7–19.

[2] A. PETRÉN and R. HART, 'The Child's Right to Development', in A. PETRÉN and R. HART (eds.), *Children's rights, Turning Principles into Practice*, (Save the Children Sweden and UNICEF Regional Office for South Asia, 2000), 43–60; N. LEWIS, 'Human rights, law and democracy in an unfree world', in T. EVANS (ed.), *Human Rights Fifty Years on a reappraisal*, (Manchester: Manchester University Press, 1998), 77–104.

[3] P. ALSTON, 'The Best Interests Principle: Towards a Reconciliation of Culture and Human Rights', in P. ALSTON (ed.), *The Best Interest of the Child: Reconciling Culture and Human Rights*, (Oxford: Clarendon Press; New York: Oxford University Press, 1994), 1–25.

the imperialist", supporters of capitalism and the "new world order" and of western styled democracy.[4] Undeniably, society's attitudes towards children tend to have a substantial impact on the way children's rights are interpreted.

2. It could be affirmed that the most ongoing debate about human rights falls between that of universalism and cultural relativism. In fact, the link between rights and culture is often one of opposition. In its preamble, the CRC presents its challenge to States on guaranteeing universality irrespective of origins, while simultaneously ensuring the protection and development of the child of diverse traditions and cultural values. This poses the question as to whether it is possible to universally apply the international rights of the child in a way, which is respectful of cultural plurality while abiding by the universal principles enshrined in the Convention. It also raises the question of whether the ultimate betterment of children's lives after all needs to be approached from a "rights" perspective or whether there is a more "appropriate" and culturally sensitive way of addressing it.

3. Moreover, the impact of UN treaties in many societies can be said to be limited due to an absence of a domestic culture of human rights. In fact, it has been argued that the success or failure of any international human rights system should be evaluated based on its actual impact on people or practices on the ground, rather than just the results of processes towards systems' development.[5] Otherwise, implementation remains focused on formalities, ignoring the very essence of its principles. This is because it is in the micro-level relations, where local norms and practices are believed and practiced, that abstract ideas of rights are given meaning and content and where they play a primary role in facilitating or constraining people's ability to claim or exercise their rights.[6]

4. Many nations are thus found to be standing at a critical crossroads; do they first invest in a young generation of rights claimers so that a future culture of rights is created or do they focus on establishing an enabling macro-environment followed by the former? The challenge also lies in how to convince the local population, for many of whom the concept of rights is alien, to accept the concept and principles of rights

---

4 S. HARRIS-SHORT, 'International Human Rights law: Imperialist, Inept and Ineffective? Cultural Relativism and the UN Convention on the Rights of the Child', (2003) *Human Rights Quarterly*, (The Johns Hopkins University Press), vol. 25, no. 1, 130–181; J. ENNEW, 'The Child Business: Comments on the Management of International Policies for Children', (1996) *Journal of International Development*, (New York: John Wiley & Sons Ltd), vol. 8, no. 6, 849–858.

5 V. RAMAN, 'Politics of Childhood, Perspectives from the South', (2000) *Economic and Political Weekly*, vol. 35, no. 46, 4056–4064.

6 C. NYAMU-MUSEMBI, 'Are Local Norms and Practices Fences or Pathways? The Example of Women's Property Rights', in A. AN-NA'IM (ed.), *Cultural Transformation and Human Rights in Africa*, (London: Zed Books, 2002), 126–150.

as being "home-grown" instead of perceiving them as "tools of the West". How can such an abstract term as "rights" and the rhetoric of the CRC be translated into practical action? Simply legislating in favour of children and educating people through awareness campaigns that they must abide by the principles of the Convention, because their country is a signatory State, may not get very far. One must acknowledge that challenges generally arise when attempting to put any principled policy into practice.

5. Whilst acknowledging the detrimental impact of the external environment, globalisation and its negative effects, in realising children's well-being, this paper aims to diagnose the more *internal* issues related to implementation, the socio-cultural dynamics entrenched in the local realities. Hence, it ultimately aims to examine the extent to which an universalisation of a culture of rights for children can be established by a signatory State to the CRC, through examining some of the different obstacles towards its realisation. In doing so, the Jordanian experience, and specifically the Family Protection Project (F.P.P) in Jordan, will be used as a case study to critically diagnose issues associated with effective implementation of children's rights. The F.P.P., which specifically addresses the issue of domestic violence and child abuse, is selected due to its highly contentious and culturally sensitive nature and is a prime example of a major human rights initiative in Jordan which cannot be tackled without addressing both the public and private spheres of society. By identifying the roadblocks faced in effectively implementing such a highly charged area of children's rights, it is hoped that this critical undertaking will contribute to the effectiveness of implementation and that valuable lessons in translating policy to action in the future will be drawn.

1.1. METHODOLOGY

6. The methodology adopted for the case study primarily entailed the use of secondary literature coupled with basic primary research. The primary research, which was purely qualitative in nature, included open-ended interviews and discussions held with eleven child rights practitioners and/or managers of the F.P.P., from both the governmental and non-governmental sector, in addition to a member of the judiciary sector. These interviews sought to gain further insight on the national level into the implementation of children's rights and the F.P.P. in Jordan.

7. Primary research was also conducted with parents and children in the underprivileged community of the Prince Hasan refugee camp, located in the Jabal Al-Naser area (situated in the Eastern side of the capital Amman) in order to assess the relevance of such a project to the community and obtain further clarity and indication of the level in which a culture of rights has permeated the local level. A sample of ten households was randomly selected, consisting of eight mothers, two fathers and ten

children (males and females, aged 7–12 years). This particular location was also selected due to the presence of a renowned community centre, the Jabal Al-Naser Centre, which actively works on programmes related to children's rights and protection from abuse in that community. An interview with a social development field specialist from the centre was also conducted for further micro-level insight.

8. Finally, the short duration of the fieldwork and the limited size of the community sample selected preclude the claim of representativeness. Interviews held with parents and children primarily intended to gain insight and first-hand accounts of the usually overlooked realities at the community level. This research ultimately hopes to provide further knowledge of a reality that may require further investigation when implementing children's rights initiatives in Jordan.

2. SETTING THE MACRO CONTEXT IN JORDAN

9. Jordan has demonstrated its commitment to respecting human rights and the dignity of its citizens by joining the early group of signatory countries in the Middle East to the CRC in 1990, and ratifying it in 1991. An enabling environment for children has been supported by the political commitment and support of the Royal Family who have been at the forefront of a number of initiatives for the protection of children's rights. However, despite its prompt ratification, the CRC is not yet considered to be a national legally binding document. Until now, it has not yet been endorsed by parliament, nor published in the official gazette. This however has not stood in the way of ensuring that progressive steps have been made in translating its commitment into practice. Since the ratification, a number of concrete steps have been taken at the macro level towards incorporating the CRC into Jordan's national legislation, policy and structures.

10. As a lower-middle income developing country populated by 5.329 million people, a Human Development Index (HDI) of 0.750[7] and a Gross National Income (GNI) per capita of about US$1.760,[8] Jordan is placed amongst the better Arab countries in terms of literacy rates and school enrolment and has one of the lowest infant mortality and maternal mortality rates in the region. Jordan's considerably young population, with eighteen year olds and below comprising approximately 45% of the total population has also rendered children a social, political and economic priority for the

---

7 UNDP, *Human Development Report 2004*, <http://hdr.undp.org/reports/global/2004/pdf/hdr04_HDI.pdf>.

8 UNICEF, *The State of the World's Children 2004*, <http://www.unicef.org/sowc04/sowc04_tables.html>.

government. Conversely, Jordan's high population growth rate represents the single biggest obstacle to fulfilling children's and women's rights in the future.[9] Weakening capacities of social organisations, and increased urbanisation have not only rendered it difficult for the government to keep pace with the growing population but has also aggravated the magnitude of children in poverty and the country's ability to provide for them.[10] With poverty levels deepening and unemployment rates increasing, more hardship and stress have been placed on families' abilities to cope.

2.1. SOCIAL AND CULTURAL CONTEXT

11. Jordan has always given importance to the protection of children, stemming from a religious and cultural obligation towards their well-being. The Arab child is very much seen as the "crucial generational link in the family unit, [and] the key to its continuation..."[11] Jordan is also comprised of a predominantly Muslim population (92%) with Islamic values reflected in society's perception of children and child-rearing practices. Children have always been valued in Islam and described in the Holy Quran as being one of the valuable "riches of the world" (Surat Al-Kahf, XVII, verse 46), and by Prophet Mohammed as being "the butterflies of Paradise".[12] Parents have been called upon by Prophet Mohammed to cherish their children and to "treat children with a view to inculcate self-respect in them..."[13] Such values have facilitated the integration of the CRC into the political and social spheres of society.

The traditional structure of the Jordanian family is also fundamentally closely-knit, comprised of a hierarchical structure within a patriarchal system. The Jordanian culture is also one that puts remarkable emphasis on social reputation, shame and honour, with a woman's chastity considered to be of extreme significance. Like many Arab countries, there are strong and deep-rooted tribal notions that the welfare of the collective supersedes that of the individual, and that children are the property of the collective family.[14]

---

9 WB and NCFA, *Jordan Country Study of Disadvantaged Children 2004,* (Jordan: The World Bank and the National Council for Family Affairs, 2004).

10 UNICEF, *Integrating the Human Rights-Based Approach in the Country Programme: UNICEF's Experience in Jordan* (Jordan: UNICEF, 2003).

11 E. W. Fernea (ed.), *Children in the Muslim Middle East,* (Austin, Texas: University of Texas Press, 1995).

12 UNICEF, *Draft Childhood Act, Speech by Anne Skatvedt,* (Jordan: UNICEF Jordan, 2004).

13 E. W. Fernea (ed.), supra (note 11), 6.

14 N. Shalhoub-Kevorkian, 'The Politics of Disclosing Female Sexual Abuse: A Case study of Palestinian Society', (1999) *Child Abuse and Neglect,* (Pergamon, USA), vol. 23, no. 12, 1275–1293.

12. The delay in ratifying the Child Act Law and its publication in the official gazette for over six years is an indication of the magnitude of resistance to some of the contentious issues related to children's rights. Politicians are facing a dilemma; if they speak against having a Child Act Law they risk being criticised for their insensitivity towards a vulnerable segment. On the other hand, they are under pressure that if they support the individual and western concept of children's rights, they will be accused of being anti-Islamic, and for instilling antifamily values in society. During one of the lobbying efforts for the establishment of a children's budget, the Head of Complaints and Legal Services of Jordan's National Centre for Human Rights pointed out that "a number of ministers had laughed at the idea".

3. THE FAMILY PROTECTION PROJECT

13. Violence and abuse represent one of the most taboo and only recently debated issues in Jordan concerning children and women, with an increasing number of reported child abuse cases reaching "shocking heights" as one judge proclaimed.[15] With an approximate 20% increase from the previous year, more than 660 reported cases of child abuse were recorded in 2002 in Amman only,[16] with domestic abuse by fathers recorded as being the most common type of physical abuse[17] and girls aged 12–18 years as the most likely victims.[18]

Nevertheless, Jordan continues to work towards improving its legislative response to protecting children and women, and in comparison with other countries in the region, stands out for its serious recognition in addressing this issue. One of the unique contributions made has been the establishment of the pioneering initiative; the Family Protection Project (F.P.P.) in Jordan. This project was a recipient of the 2003 UN Prize for Human Rights as part of the UN General Assembly's commemoration of Human Rights Day, for having broken the silence on the subject of violence and opening up a debate on human rights. Despite that, many challenges and obstacles continue to be faced in effectively implementing such a highly charged area of children's rights.

The F.P.P., established in 1999, is the first of its kind in the Middle East. Through providing specialised preventative, therapeutic and rehabilitative services and support to victims, its primary aim is to build the capacity of institutions and the public, and to implement an integrated strategy for the prevention of child abuse. Its unique edge

15 D. DAJANI, 'Sharia judges to address child abuse more effectively', *The Jordan Times*, July 5, 2004, Jordan.

16 FPD, *Official statistics of child abuse victims in Jordan*, Family Protection Department, Jordan, 2004.

17 A. BOYLE, *Family Protection Project, Jordan; Mapping the Work of the Project, 1999–2002*, (2002).

18 UNICEF, supra (note 10), 10.

lies in its development of a network of relevant multi-agency working groups from both the government and non-government sectors, and which has led to the opening up of an extensive array of communication channels, which had never previously existed.

14. The Family Protection Department (F.P.D.), officially a police department and a main partner to this project, was established within the Public Security Directorate in Amman to directly deal with child and women victims of abuse. As a focal point for receiving complaints, abused victims are directly interviewed by a female police officer, medically examined by a forensic doctor if there is a need, and cases are sent to court if a crime is believed to have been committed. Social workers intervene and follow up on the case. In cases where children require temporary shelter, protection and rehabilitative support, they are sent to Dar Al-Aman, ("home of safety") the first of its kind in the region for the provision of psychological, medical, social and educational services to victims. Where it is impossible to send children back to their abusing parents, they are reintegrated into the homes of their extended family members.

15. In society, such as Jordan's, where matters of sexuality are frowned upon, and the issue of privacy is paramount, disclosing a very private matter in a venue that symbolises authority and male domination may not be the ideal approach. According to a British Social Development Expert in Jordan, allowing this system to prevail is in effect "reinforcing the status quo of male domination". She also believes that the services offered are carried out in a top-down, supply-driven manner, which does not effectively contribute to women and children's empowerment and mobilisation at the grassroots level to demand their rights.

16. Very few of the child rights practitioners interviewed mentioned the CRC as a reference point for their efforts towards protecting children from abuse. For some, it has been attested that the driving force behind such dynamism primarily stems from a response to the Royal Family's concern and interest in that field. In fact, the head of the F.P.D. very frankly pointed out that "it is royalty's leadership and interest that drive us and not the CRC exclusively. We do not need the CRC to guide us. We have religion as a reference and guide for ensuring that children have their rights. Why should the 'United Nations agreement' be our reference point?" It could be argued that such reasoning may question the likelihood of sustainable child rights initiatives in Jordan when the motive is predominantly driven by a royal decree.

17. On the other hand, the F.P.P. has been criticised by a British Social Development Expert in Jordan as taking more of a "family-based approach", which addresses the family as a whole and looks at the family as the core unit of society, rather than a "rights-based approach", which similarly to what the CRC stipulates, considers the individuality of a child as being an independent bearer of rights. This is precisely where a fundamental clash of culture arises, between eastern cultures which emphasise the collective, and particularly the family unit, as opposed to the western emphasis on individuality. In Jordan, children are not perceived as autonomous individuals with individual interests, but are part of a larger family unit and the collective interests it holds. Therefore, if a donor-enforced "rights-based approach" continues to be perceived as irrelevant to the local culture, the applicability and sustainability of such initiatives in the long run may be questionable.

18. Creating a culture of rights is not only about ensuring that systems, structures and policy are put in place at the macro level but that its trickle down effect reaches the local level too. Issues related to sustainable and effective implementation at the macro level, as well as the realities at the community level, to be covered in the following section, suggest the existence of a number of challenges that hinder effective implementation and the ultimate creation of a culture of rights for children. These will need to be seriously addressed and critically challenged if children's protection rights are to be attained.

4. REALITIES AT LOCAL LEVEL

"[One must] ensure that the spirit of the Convention and its provisions progressively work their way into... institutional life of nations, and the everyday life of individuals, families and communities".[19]

19. In ensuring the protection of children from violence and abuse, the CRC recognises the primary role and responsibility of the family as the first and ideally last line of protection and care for the child.[20] Ratifying nations are obliged to respect the rights of parents to provide guidance for their children commensurate with the child's evolving capacities, and to recognise that parents have joint responsibility for raising the child. Yet, many of the worst abuses take place within the private sphere of the family. The family unit, which is supposed to be the ideal source of nurture, is for some children a source of violence and inequality and represents the most traumatic point in their lives. The CRC therefore requires that a child can be separated from parents if the child's best interests are endangered.

---

19 J.R. HIMES, 'Monitoring Children's Rights: Cutting through the Confusion and Planning for Effective Action' in E. VERHELLEN (ed.), *Monitoring Children's Rights*, (The Hague – Boston – London: Martinus Nijhoff Publishers; The Hague: Kluwer Law International, 1996), 113–127.

20 R. HODGKIN and P. NEWELL, *Implementation Handbook for the Convention on the Rights of the Child*, (New York, UNICEF, 1998).

20. This section documents the findings of the primary research conducted with parents and children in the community of the Prince Hasan refugee camp, located in the poverty-stricken area of Jabal Al-Naser. This area, known to be burdened by multiple economic and social difficulties, is located in the eastern and relatively poorer part of Amman and is populated by 36,000 inhabitants.[21] The community has been selected to explore the different perceptions held by parents and children with regards to child rights and the principles of the F.P.P. The case study also examines how the F.P.P. has attempted to integrate the family as partners in this initiative, through exploring the different challenges imposed on these duty bearers in ensuring children's protection. This particular area was also selected due to the presence of an active local NGO – the Jabal Al-Naser Centre – that provides training sessions for parents and children on issues related to healthy child-rearing practices, and children's rights and protection from abuse. The majority of parents and children interviewed were either familiar with and/or had attended an awareness workshop on children's rights and protection from abuse. The research is also substantiated by the insight of a Social Development Field Specialist working for the centre and a key practitioner of the F.P.P., who is a Child Care Specialist and Director of Jordan River Foundation's Child Safety Programme. The following is a discussion of the main findings.

4.1. PERCEPTION AND AWARENESS OF RIGHTS

21. From the different family members and children interviewed in Jabal Al-Naser, there is an indication of a lack of true understanding of what the "rights" concept is really about. In fact, one of the main social factors recorded by UNICEF Jordan's Mid-Term Review (period 1998–2002) as contributing to the negative trends in children's situation in Jordan is a lack of understanding by parents of the child's needs and rights.[22] For many, the concept of children's rights is perceived as being a western import, penetrating the Jordanian society in an attempt to "westernise the Arab child" while others specifically referred to the CRC as an initiative "to break up and disintegrate the family unit". While the majority of parents interviewed were broadly familiar with children's rights (mainly due to their attendance at awareness workshops conducted by the centre), such knowledge was quite superficial, focused primarily on issues related to survival rights, followed by frequent reference to Islam's calling for protecting children. Their repeated reference to survival rights is perhaps an indication of what they perceive as being most fundamental given their dismal socio-economic

21 UNICEF, *Documentation and Assessment of The Community Empowerment Project In Al Naser Area*, (Jordan, UNICEF Jordan Office, 1999).
22 UNICEF, supra (note 10), 3.

situation. Little reference, if anything at all, was originally made to protection and participation rights.

22. Similarly, when children were asked about their perception of rights, the majority primarily referred to the right to education, play and protection from harm. Most children were also not aware of the F.P.P. or of the procedures for reporting abuse. However, it was apparently clear from those interviewed that none could state their rights with clarity, confidence and conviction. In fact, there was a sense that they could not really *feel* their rights or the saliency of the concept. Instead, it was simply a theoretical piece of information taught to them by the community centre and consequently recited to the public.[23] This may not be surprising as one may indeed question the extent to which Jordanian citizens as a whole are in reality familiar with their rights, let alone children are with theirs. Conclusively, this raises doubts on the likelihood of adults being able to ensure the accordance of rightful importance and respect to the rights of a segment of the population that are not held in much high regard in society.

23. In many Eastern cultures, a child is perceived to be without reason, and with that rationale, more aggressive rearing practices are justified in preparation of the child for adult life.[24] Many children living in this community are brought up within a normalised practice of child rearing; frequent hitting and spanking as a form of discipline, rather than on a foundation based on respect and the dignity of the child. A number of mothers expressed the importance of disciplining their children through such means, as UM-ABDALLAH said "how else will my child learn and be disciplined?" Such attitudes, translated into child rearing practices, are often a reflection of deeply ingrained cultural context and tradition, and usually a continuation of the way the parent him/herself was disciplined as a child.

24. Religion, according to the Child Care Specialist and Director of Jordan River Foundation's Child Safety Programme, is not necessarily practised according to the "proper" teachings of the Quran, but rather as it is personally or collectively interpreted at the local level. She also attests that it is not the teachings of Islam that call for the disempowerment of women and girls but rather the fundamentalist ideologies on religion and family values. This raises the question of how an ill-treated child at home raised to believe that this is the acceptable norm of child rearing can

---

[23] It is worth noting that the most salient difference perceived between those who expressed a relatively more abiding conviction in his/her rights was the extent to which the mother herself held a relatively stronger understanding and interest in the subject of children's rights and also to the different degrees of "poverty" seen in the different households. The poorer the household appeared, the more sceptical the family was of the concept of rights.

[24] E. W. FERNEA (ed.), supra (note 11), 8.

comprehend and accept that he/she does indeed have rights and can claim them. This is because when a child is hit, he/she is being told that hitting is acceptable behaviour and when these children grow up to be parents, they will continue the norm of what they were raised to believe is "normal" behaviour. According to PHILLIPS and ALDERSON,[25] parents' habitual exercise of authority and power over children consequently makes children's subordination seem "natural". For that reason, the Deputy Director of the British Council in Jordan strongly believes that "democracy and human rights are a *way of life* and that it is largely a matter of how democratic one is in running one's family and treating people". She emphasised the importance of children in believing in democracy and human rights, and believes the optimal strategy for infusing such ideals is through their mainstreaming into the school curriculum and especially into religion modules.

25. On the other hand, the perception of rights by children themselves has been drawn out by a Social Development Field Specialist from the Jabal Al-Naser Centre who believes that the concept of children's rights is one that is mocked by children themselves as "they do not seem to live these rights on a daily basis, either at home, school or within society itself". This raises the question of whether the current strategy adopted in educating community members of their rights is indeed an effective one. He adds that "there is something wrong with our approach that does not *simultaneously* and *collectively* involve parents, teachers and the whole community". The exclusion of these major players from this process may not very likely create a sense of participation or ownership within communities, but instead, increase their resistance. Therefore, it has been emphasised by the former Regional Protection Officer of UNICEF Middle East and North Africa region that a proper and true understanding of rights by just about *every* member of society is needed to ensure that the concept is properly instilled within society. He points out that "if we scratch the surface we will very likely still realise that there is no proper understanding of what child rights are really about. It needs several generations of changes in thinking". Interestingly also, UNICEF Jordan's Monitoring and Evaluation Officer pointed out that "we as staff cannot seem to internalise the concept of human rights and Human Rights-Based Approach to Development for us to rapidly see it in our counterparts and beneficiaries".

25 B. PHILLIPS and P. ALDERSON, 'Beyond 'anti-smacking': Challenging violence and coercion in parent-child relations', (2003) *The International Journal of Children's Rights*, vol. 11, no.2, 175–197.

4.2. THE PRIVATE SANCTITY OF THE FAMILY

"*Beyond my door knob lies my ridicule*" (Proverb)[26]

26. In traditionally "closed" society, where the private sphere is sanctified and the issue of shame and taboo are predominant, intervening into family affairs is perceived as intrusive. This is because the family is an absolutely sacred unit in Jordan. Therefore, when an act of abuse is publicly disclosed, society perceives this as not only upsetting the social equilibrium of the family, but also as being directed against the collective rather than the individual. Announcing such an act is therefore perceived as bringing shame to the collective family and a cause of tension between family and society.[27] For the community residents, the complaints procedure to an official body is unquestionably new, and for many parents, is perceived as either being "an American way of doing things" or a completely rejected idea that would "bring shame to the family and community". A child who reports abuse may very well be victimised by his/her family for bringing shame to the family's name and may indeed suffer the consequences. "We are living in a closed society where disclosing information or intervening into other people's issues is just unacceptable. We depend on family networks to solve problems and not State intervention into our private affairs" was the assertion of one of the fathers interviewed. According to SHALHOUB-KEVORKIAN,[28] when abused children in a typical Arab family seek external help beyond the family, it is also an implicit declaration of the family's inability to protect its children and is considered an act of betrayal. Therefore, the likelihood of bringing shame and consequent disintegration to the family unit has been raised, pointing out that such a procedure would indeed be "catastrophic, as the husband would definitely divorce his wife if she reported his abuse of her children". In the same vein, it was held by the majority of respondents that reporting an abused victim of a neighbour or relative would also be considered to be outside their realm of responsibility and values due to its moral unacceptability, the uncomfortable consequences of having to deal with public officials and their associated lack of trust in the governmental apparatus to maintain privacy. Conclusively, as the Director of JRF's Child Safety Programme asserts, "child rights will always conflict with family rights" and local community norms.

27. Alternatively, the idea of dealing directly with a trusted and known body from within the community, such as the Jabal Al-Naser Centre, seemed to be a more acceptable alternative by some parents, indicating that there could be a growing tendency towards disclosure beyond the household unit and into the trusted domain of a community-based organisation. This, which is principally conditioned on the

---

26 N. SHALHOUB-KEVORKIAN, supra (note 14), 1280.
27 Ibid., 1280.
28 Ibid., 1280.

confidentiality and containment of the matter, is primarily due to the relationship of trust built with the centre and its staff over a number of years.

4.3. AN ALTERNATIVE APPROACH?

28. In many cultures, children are given greater consideration for what they will become in the future rather than what they are in the present.[29] In fact, the Director of JRF's Child Safety Programme raises an interesting point stating that the primary motive behind many parents in Jordan treating their children well and ensuring that they have a proper life stems from the "benefit motive" and the issue of "belonging". She believes that the motivation behind parents' protection and care for children is not necessarily in fulfilment of their rights, but fundamentally for the concern that "they will grow up to become reputable adults with a 'decent' profession that would in effect bring good reputation to the family". She therefore believes that the best strategy for educating parents on the importance of children's protection is by approaching it from a *benefit* or *religious* angle rather than a "*rights*" perspective, as she believes many are either sceptical of or are not yet very familiar with the latter.

This view was also substantiated by a number of parents, especially by a mother who questioned "*how can I begin to think about my children's rights to not be physically or verbally abused when we cannot even meet their basic needs. Just recently, one of my daughters was forced to drop out of school by her father because we could not afford to keep her in school*". In addition, when asked whose primary role it was to ensure the protection of children, ABU-SHOROUQ responded with scepticism questioning "when children are not given their full rights by the State, how do they expect children's rights to be fulfilled by the family, especially when the State does not adequately provide for children". This questions the very essence of parents' ability to fulfil their expected roles as duty bearers, when their socio-economic conditions are unfavourable and not conducive to the materialisation of children's rights.

5. CONCLUSION

"*The CRC should not only be on paper, it has to be a belief system that drives human beings to act upon it at all times and in our everyday lives. It has to be part of our value system that directs us, whether we are parents or professionals.*"[30]

---

[29] UNICEF, *Children and Violence,* (Colombia: Regional Office for Latin America and the Caribbean, UNICEF, 1998).

[30] Extract from an interview with Director of Jordan River Foundation's Child Safety Programme.

29. The Jordanian experience has shown that effective implementation of a culture of rights for children should not only not be separated from a full understanding of the political, structural, institutional and cultural systems behind it, but must fundamentally be tackled in the context of their families and communities. Through such understanding, more appropriate, sustainable and culturally sensitive approaches can be developed. Evidently, there is a large gap between the aspirations of the F.P.P. and the reality of implementation. Despite the strong political will and support by the Royal Family, many structural, institutional, political and cultural challenges exist in translating policy into practice. If the State is to seriously address its adherence to and implementation of children's rights, it must take a revolutionary approach in re-examining structures, institutions and practices in order to make children's rights a reality.

30. Despite the awareness-raising efforts made at both macro and micro levels, there still seems to be a lack of true and sufficient understanding of rights by citizens, professionals and children alike. At the macro policy-making level where ministerial and staff turnover is high, intensified and continuous advocacy and training is still required. Sensitisation and awareness-raising efforts also need to simultaneously percolate to the local community level, involving children, parents and community members. Education is a crucial form of prevention and it is imperative that children are knowledgeable of their rights and entitlements and in turn *believe* in their right to claim them. For that reason, a robust, strategic and comprehensive communications plan is needed for more effective practical implementation of rights, bearing in mind that advocacy efforts will need ample time to create genuine attitudinal changes.

31. Further, while legislation is one of the fundamental ways of improving the situation of children, other parallel efforts are needed to catalyse stronger action for children. It takes more than legislation and National Plans of Action to change attitudes and realities. Legislation, however good on paper, is of little value if children are unable to "live" their rights in reality and are unable to claim them. Also, those working for and with children – whether lawyers, teachers, policy-makers or practitioners, as well as parents – need to be convinced of the importance and value of children's rights so that they can effectively contribute to its materialisation in practice. Law on its own may not be enough to create an inclusive society for children and positive social change.

32. KENT[31] proposes a hierarchy of responsibility for children, outlining that children must principally receive nurture from their parents, and failing that, it should be received from their local communities followed by government, international NGOs

[31] G. KENT, *Children in the International Political Economy*, (London: Macmillan Press Ltd, 1995).

and finally by international governmental organisations. We would however argue that instead of approaching it in a linear hierarchy of order, responsibilities should ideally be collectively shared through concerted efforts. Undoubtedly, there is a need for a holistic approach in dealing with children's rights, with the *simultaneous* involvement of *all* members of society at both macro and micro levels. So if the law, for example, says that children have the right to be protected from physical abuse, then that means that *everyone* concerned must realise their duty towards that goal and ensure that that right is honoured. Providing the context and enabling environment in which both children and adults are allowed to thrive, whilst ensuring that such efforts are supported at the foundation level within the family unit is paramount.

33. However, not all parents truly contribute to establishing a healthy and conducive environment for children. It is very likely that a child brought up at the household and community levels with low self-esteem or the lack of assertion to speak out, will very understandably reflect itself in the child's ability to empower him/herself to demand his/her rights legally. Empowering a child within a disempowered family or an unsupportive external environment may remain a futile effort in producing empowered rights claimers. As long as the family unit continues to reinforce patriarchal principles and traditional child rearing practices, which do not contribute to a child's self esteem, creating a generation that is convinced of the profound importance of rights may be difficult.

34. Undoubtedly, culture is strong and the universalist aspirations can in no way dominate the inevitable influence of cultural values and perceptions. Some societies like Jordan do not recognise children as full individuals and it is the collective interest of the family unit that takes precedence. While there could be universality in the situation of abuse faced by children globally, universality in the approach of tackling it does not necessarily apply in all contexts. The concept of children's rights is indeed contentious when the very crux of the ideology of the private sanctity of the family is challenged. Expecting disclosure of taboo matters, especially to distrusted government authorities in society where the preservation of family honour is highly valued, dependence on family networks is high and children are considered the property of their parents, will not likely receive widespread acceptance and will undeniably be resisted. Perhaps then, an approach that neither fully embraces an artificial universalism nor blindly and un-objectively accepts cultural relativism is required. Ultimately, the creation of a sustainable culture of rights in society must respect the social and cultural realities, whilst ensuring that the protection of children's rights is not compromised.

35. In cases where parents are not providing the nurturing environment for children, it is necessary for governments to intervene and adopt a preventive approach that ensures the fundamentals of a child's well-being. While measures such as removing abused children from their current environments are necessary for their immediate protection, longer-term and sustainable solutions are required. Reporting to an official police department for example, does not prevent the malaise of abuse and does not get to the root of the problem, especially when the legislative environment is not fully favourable for children. Emphasis should therefore be simultaneously placed on dialogue rather than prescription, prevention rather than only cure, as the Director of JRF's Child Safety Programme stresses prevention is ultimately about "healthy child rearing".[32] Supportive roles could also be provided to parents through their empowerment and education, as children's rights will only be meaningful in a context of a family environment where parents are knowledgeable of their responsibilities towards their children and do apply them.

36. It is noteworthy that evolved child rearing practices and attitudes towards children in many societies such as Jordan are often a reflection of deeply entrenched cultural traditions that have evolved in such a way where patriarchal attitudes now dominate. Often times, it is culture that supersedes religion, and religion is usually misinterpreted by many in justification of such acts. Therefore, the extent to which many traditional obstacles in realising children and women's rights are rooted in religion as opposed to culture is one that needs to be carefully debated and understood.

5.1. RETHINKING CHILDREN'S RIGHTS

"It is important that both the government and its people as well 'see' and 'feel' the rightness of these international laws if they are to make sure they are enforced".[33]

37. Undoubtedly, there is a long way to go for the establishment of a fully-fledged culture of rights for children in Jordan. As long as children's rights remain a concept that is sceptically perceived and not fully internalised, it will remain a challenge to effectively enforce these rights. If a rights discourse is to permeate all fabrics of society, its internalisation should be applied to both adults (professionals and citizens) and children alike. A culture of rights has to be carefully established and nurtured both in enforced rhetoric and in practice. In addition, a true understanding of rights must begin at home and stem from a local belief. Democratic practices must also originate

---

32 S. Saldana, 'Latest Middle East battle is one against child abuse', *The Jordan Times*, September 16, 2002, Jordan.

33 A. Vittachi, *Stolen Childhood, In Search of the Rights of the Child*, (Cambridge – Oxford – Abingdon: Polity Press, 1989).

at the household level and extend to the political sphere so that they will be ultimately reflected on children.

38. However, the deep mistrust that many Arabs presently hold towards the international community in ensuring an equitable environment of human rights in their region and the perception of the CRC as being a foreign tool of "double standards" – which selectively condemns certain violations while ignoring those inflicted upon children of war-torn neighbouring countries – represents an added challenge to the instillation of a culture of rights for children in such societies. With the wave of anti-Americanism in the region, any project calling for reform, no matter what the intentions and motives are, will not likely receive broad support. It is therefore imperative that a western view of childhood is not imposed, especially when the universal standards of the Convention conflict with the deeply entrenched values, practices and traditions of families. Perhaps then, a success story emanating from an Arab and Islamic country in protecting its children is more likely to make it a model project for the region, and less likely culturally resisted as a western imposition.

39. Further, as long as the basic needs and essentials for the survival and dignity of adults are not attained, people will continue to question the legitimacy and viability of children's rights. Talking about less prioritised issues of protecting children from abuse to communities where survival needs are barely achieved and where many families are crippled by economic hardships may not be the best way to promote a tolerant culture of rights. Perhaps the optimal approach is not to address it from an international legal perspective of "rights", which in fact is a highly politically charged word, but from a religious or moral perspective. The question then lies not only on where one must begin to address children's rights as a matter of priority but rather whether international human rights documents have any meaning for such people at all. Without acknowledging the social settings and realities in which rights as principles can be transformed into rights as practice, the concept of rights will remain a term widely used and debated in the meeting rooms of professionals, and less understood by adults and children themselves.

II. MONITORING OF THE CRC

THE APPLICATION OF THE INTERNATIONAL CONVENTION ON THE RIGHTS OF THE CHILD IN AFRICA: WHEN THE LAW IS TESTED BY THE REALITY[1]

Raoul Kienge-Kienge Intudi

1. INTRODUCTION

1. We feel ambivalent about speaking of a continent generally described as "black", as if life in Africa were "black" or "dark". Indeed, the news broadcast by television channels often refers to Africa as a continent, where endemic disease, famine, war, poverty and so on, are rife. However, if one goes there, one is struck by the immense natural resources that abound in certain African countries, and one returns positively affected by the human richness of social relationships in the middle of very real material poverty. This is the "African paradox". The introduction to this paper, will briefly set out the state of the rights of the child in Africa, the approach, described as interdisciplinary, and the focal point on which will be based the assessment that we propose to make of the application of the Convention at an African level.

1.1. STATE OF THE QUESTION OF THE RIGHTS OF THE CHILD IN AFRICA

2. The adoption by the General Assembly of the United Nations of the Convention on the Rights of the Child (CRC) on 20 November 1989, followed by its entry into force on 2 September 1990, gave the Assembly of Heads of State and Government of the Organisation of African Unity (OAU) the opportunity to adopt, in July 1990, the African Charter on the Rights and Welfare of the Child. The African Charter on the

[1] This paper, which was originally written in French, contains a great deal of detail. This is the abridged English version.

Rights and Welfare of the Child highlights certain specific features of the situation of children on the African continent and thus gives greater strength to the rights set out in the CRC.

1.2. AN INTERDISCIPLINARY APPROACH

3. Starting from a legal analysis of the provisions of the African Charter on the Rights and Welfare of the Child, our approach aims to be more empirical and attempts to understand the meaning of the ineffectiveness of the international and regional African provisions relating to the rights of the child. These provisions, which are based on socio-political, historical, anthropological and even philosophical data, can be used to call to account, those who are in power as well as the non-governmental African actors about the scope of the discourse relating to human rights in general and the rights of the child in particular.

1.3. OUR FOCAL POINT FOR ASSESSMENT: THE DEMOCRATIC REPUBLIC OF THE CONGO

4. The Democratic Republic of the Congo was chosen as a focal point for the assessment of the rights of the child in Africa, in the first place, because of its strategic position in the heart of Africa, sharing its border with several African states. Secondly, this choice has the advantage of enabling a documented, empirical assessment of the application of the CRC due to the conflicts that the country has been undergoing for around ten years, which have led to the "dramatic decay of the State", particularly in its task of guaranteeing fundamental rights. Children are obviously the biggest victims of such conflicts. Far from being particular to the Democratic Republic of the Congo, several other African States are confronted with the decay of the State.

1.4. STRUCTURE OF THE PAPER

5. This paper contains two sections. The first section is made up of an examination of the specific features of the African Charter on the Rights and Welfare of the Child compared with the International Convention on the Rights of the Child. The second section sets out the conclusion that the Convention on the Rights of the Child is ineffective in Africa, and puts forward some explanations.

2. THE SPECIFIC FEATURES OF THE AFRICAN CHARTER ON THE RIGHTS AND WELFARE OF THE CHILD

6. Before we review the specific features of the African Charter on the Rights and Welfare of the Child compared with the International Convention on the Rights of the Child, it is useful to take a closer look at the historical evolution of the representation of the child in Africa. These representations allow for an understanding of the specific provisions of the African Charter on the Rights of the Child.

2.1. HISTORICAL EVOLUTION OF REPRESENTATIONS OF THE CHILD IN AFRICA

7. In pre-colonial Africa, a child was seen as an asset of the family. It was considered a very precious valuable, as it represented the perpetuation of the life force of the tribe down the generations. Because of this, the child was born into a family structure in which it could live and thrive in harmony. The only concern was to ensure the integration of the child into the family group. The head of the family and the entire community to which the child belonged was responsible for the protection of the child.

In post-colonial Africa, the African communities were organised into States, which were initially under the dominion of the European powers and then, since their respective independence, under the authority of the Africans themselves. The protection of the child and of all the people living within the territory of the colony or the State is seen as an essential prerogative of the State, and no longer of the family community, particularly with regard to education. However, the decay of the State in post-colonial Africa has rendered the States incapable of ensuring the protection of the child, and particularly of guaranteeing the child's safety and education, although free and compulsory schooling is, in theory, constantly asserted in the constitutions of the African States.

2.2. SPECIFIC FEATURES OF THE AFRICAN CHARTER ON THE RIGHTS AND WELFARE OF THE CHILD

8. The African Charter adds the affirmation of the "welfare" of the child, to highlight the inextricable link that exists between respect for the rights of the child and its welfare. Like the United Nations Convention on the Rights of the Child, the African Charter on the Rights and Welfare of the Child is divided into two parts. The first part is dedicated to the rights and duties of the child. The second part of the charter provides for the creation and organisation of a committee on the rights and welfare of the child. The rights set out in the African Charter are generally the same as those given in the convention.

However, the specific features of the African Charter appear as early as the preamble and in its other provisions, such as those relating to the nationality and education of the child, adoption and work, the responsibilities of the parents with regard to the child, the protection of the child against negative social and cultural practices, apartheid, sale, slavery, abduction and begging, the event of armed conflict, the event of separation from parents, and the protection of child refugees and children whose mothers are in prison. The African Charter also differs from the United Nations convention since it defines, alongside these rights, responsibilities that the child must assume in order to serve the community. However, all these specific provisions provide a protection, which is more *de jure* than *de facto*.

3. THE EMPIRICAL ASSESSMENT OF THE APPLICATION OF THE RIGHTS OF THE CHILD LEADING TO A CONCLUSION OF INEFFECTIVENESS

9. In his assessment of the application of the African Charter on Human and Peoples' Rights ten years after its adoption, MUBIALA states that "*the African continent holds the sad record for violations of a number of human rights*",[2] and explains this situation by the establishment of undemocratic political systems in Africa after independence. This could be one of so many explanations for the ineffectiveness of human rights in Africa. We will cite three elements to support the conclusion that the international provisions for the protection of the rights of the child in Africa are ineffective: the African conception of the individual and his rights, which is generally tacitly superimposed onto the European conception that underlies the international conventions on human rights in general; the situation of decay of the African States, which gives rise to the instrumentalisation of the International Convention on the Rights of the Child by government authorities and actors in non-governmental organisations; and finally, the different point of view of the African actors involved, working in a context marked by the precariousness of everyday life, towards the situations legally classified as violations of the rights of the child.

---

[2] M. MUBIALA, 'La charte africaine des droits de l'homme et des peuples dix ans plus tard. Plaidoyer pour l'institution d'une cour Régionale', (1998) 322 *Congo-Afrique*, 77–82.

3.1. THE AFRICAN CONCEPTION OF HUMAN RIGHTS AND THE RIGHTS OF THE CHILD: BETWEEN APPARENT CONTRADICTION AND ATTEMPTED SUBJECTIVISATION OF THE CHILD

10. The African Charter on Human and Peoples' Rights establishes a certain "African" conception of the individual and his rights, which seems to us to paralyse any plan to promote human rights in general. The same conception also governs the foundations of the rights of the child. This conception of individual rights, which could be described as "communitarianist" draws its philosophical foundations from the community-based understanding of life in Africa, which deems that all individuals (children or adults) only reach complete fulfilment through and in their community, once centred on the family, and nowadays increasingly centred on the town, nation or State. Outside the community, the very existence of the individual as a human being would be inconceivable because awareness of existence only occurs in the individual in the light of the social existence of his fellow men. The human person in Africa is "seen as a whole indissoluble from the group".

11. Loyal to the "communitarianist" African conception of individual rights, Article 31 of the African Charter on the Rights and Welfare of the Child states, "every child has responsibilities to his family, society, the State and any other international community [...]". It would seem that by adopting this "communitarianist" African conception of individual rights, the African States are establishing both the affirmation and the negation of those rights in the same instrument.

12. Despite this contradiction, which surely reflects the mimetic tendency of African leaders to copy Europe when adopting legal principles, one could justifiably ask whether this African conception, which tends to establish responsibilities on the part of a child towards his community, nonetheless contains a positive aspect of subjectivisation of the child, as a subject of duties and responsibilities, instead of conveying an image of him as a simple object of rights for protection by the community. Perhaps Europe could gain from this African conception of the child.

3.2. THE INSTRUMENTALISATION OF THE INTERNATIONAL CONVENTION ON THE RIGHTS OF THE CHILD BY GOVERNMENTS AND ACTORS IN NON-GOVERNMENTAL ORGANISATIONS

13. The instrumentalisation of the International Convention on the Rights of the Child takes two forms: Firstly, its instrumentalisation by government authorities as a means to obtain letters of credit from European or international lenders by putting forward the ratification of the convention as proof of their commitment to the promotion of human rights in general and the rights of the child in particular; secondly, its instrumentalisation by the non-governmental institutions as a resource used to obtain means of subsistence from lenders other than the State in a context of economic crisis.

3.2.1. The parading of the International Convention on the Rights of the Child by governments as a foreign policy strategy

14. In a context of the decay of the State, the ratification of international instruments for the protection and promotion of human rights in general, such as the International Convention on the Rights of the Child, and their publication in the official journal, are one of the strategies used by African governments to create the appearance of democracy, which opens the door to cooperation with Western lenders.

15. A Congolese illustration of this parading of international instruments relating to human rights has often consisted of creating a minister within the government with special responsibility for the "rights and freedoms of the citizen" (under the MOBUTU regime) or "human rights" (under the regime of LAURENT DÉSIRÉ KABILA). Under the latter regime, a special issue was published of the official journal to the international instruments on human rights ratified by the Democratic Republic of the Congo, from the Universal Declaration of Human Rights in 1948 through to the Convention on the Rights of the Child in 1989, all at the height of the Second Congo War in 1999. The foreword to this special issue of the official journal informs the reader "*through this publication, the Democratic Republic of the Congo is reaffirming its attachment to the principles of freedom, democracy and respect for human rights and fundamental freedoms*". It was also for the purposes of external consumption (i.e. giving clear signals to Western lenders) that in 2001 the Ministry of Human Rights organised a national human rights forum, without any real political will, to promote the fundamental rights of every citizen.

3.2.2. Capitalisation on the International Convention on the Rights of the Child by non-governmental organisations

16. Capitalisation on the convention is the consequence of its instrumentalisation by the governments and forms part of the picture of the decay of the State in Africa. The actions of these NGOs on the field seem to be limited to educating the population their fundamental rights and their civic obligations and duties vis-à-vis the State. They hold numerous training and awareness seminars aimed at civil servants (police officers, magistrates, defence lawyers, educators and other civil service workers). These seminars give rise to payments to the participants of *per diem* allowances much higher than the salaries paid by the State and to the trainers. These *per diem* allowances enable them to meet the essential needs of life in a context of crisis and the non-payment of salaries. Thus, the more training and awareness seminars on human rights and the rights of the child are organised, and the more people take part in these seminars as trainers or trainees, the better the living. Yet at the same time, the number of vulnerable children living on the streets without protection is constantly increasing. However, all the actors involved (NGOs, trainers, the civil servants trained and other United Nations agencies), look on, powerless. The action of the human rights and particularly the children's rights NGOs in the application of the convention therefore seems ambiguous and helps to explain the ineffectiveness of the International Convention on the Rights of the Child.

3.3. THE POINT OF VIEW OF AFRICAN ACTORS ON THE VIOLATION OF THE RIGHTS OF THE CHILD IN AFRICA

17. The point of view of certain African actors towards the violations of the rights of the child helps to explain the ineffectiveness of the International Convention on the Rights of the Child. The lives of many African children and families are marked by great material insecurity due to the conditions of poverty and the lack of employment. The need to survive thus pushes families and children to accept, resign themselves to or throw themselves into situations that, according to the convention, are contrary to the rights of the child.

4. CONCLUSION: THE MYTH OF THE RIGHTS OF THE CHILD IN AFRICA

18. In light of the details set out above, one can only ask oneself if the rights of the child in Africa are after all a myth, despite the ratification of the Convention on the Rights of the Child by the African States, its publication in the official journal in the Democratic Republic of the Congo, and despite the adoption of the African Charter on the Rights and Welfare of the Child. If law could create the reality, the question of its ineffectiveness would doubtless not arise. However, because it results from a socio-political construction, the conclusion that the International Convention on the Rights of the Child is ineffective in Africa tends to confirm the mythical nature of the rights of the child in Africa. Would it not be more appropriate to discuss the image of the child conveyed by the Convention on the Rights of the Child or by the African

Charter on the Rights and Welfare of the Child as an object of protection rather than as a social actor with a specific point of view[3] who should not only be taken into account but also recognised in the definition of the standards relating to him or in the application of these standards by both governments and non-governmental organisations? In any case, it seems necessary to define the child differently from the definition given in the International Convention on the Rights of the Child.

BIBLIOGRAPHY

M.L. BALANDA, 'African charter on human and peoples rights', in K. CINTHER and W. BENEDEK (eds.), *New perspectives and conceptions of international law. An Afro-european dialogue*, (New York: Springer-Nerlay, 1983).

C. DEBUYST, 'Présentation et justification du thème', in *Acteur social et délinquance. Une grille de lecture du système de justice pénale*, (Bruxelles: Mardaga, 1990), 21–33.

C. DEBUYST, 'La notion d'acteur social considéré comme structure 'légère' face aux structures sociales 'lourdes'', in D. KAMINSKI et M. KOKOREF (eds.), *Sociologie pénale : système et expérience. Pour Claude Faugeron*, (Ramonville Saint-Agne: Editions érès, 2004), 67–82.

F. DIGNEFFE, 'Criminologie et droits humains en République démocratique du Congo. Une expérience de partenariat intellectuel stimulante', (April 2006) *Revue de droit pénal et de criminologie*, 407–421.

F. FENNICHE, 'Vers l'élaboration d'un projet de 'Plan national de promotion des Droits de l'homme en RDC', (1998) 322 *Congo-Afrique*, 69–76.

J. IDZUMBUIR ASSOP et R. KIENGE-KIENGE INTUDI, *L'enrôlement des enfants et leur participation aux conflits armés. État actuel des dispositions juridiques*, (Kinshasa : Éditions Universitaires Africaines, 2000).

J. IDZUMBUIR ASSOP, 'Contribution du secteur économique informel à l'insertion sociale des acteurs sociaux marginalisés', (1984) *Bulletin semestriel de Cerdas Liaison*.

J. IDZUMBUIR ASSOP, *La place de la convention relative aux droits de l'enfant en droit zaïrois* (Kinshasa: UNICEF/Zaïre, 1994).

D. KAMINSKI, F. DIGNEFFE, C. ADAM, J.F. CAUCHIE, M.S. DEVRESSE et V. FRANCIS, 'L'instrumentalisation dans les pratiques pénales. Construction et déconstruction d'un concept', (2001) vol. 18, n° 1 *Sociologie et Sociétés*, 27–51.

K. WA DONDO, *Réflexions sur la filiation hors mariage*, (Kinshasa : C. S. J., 1974).

R. KIENGE-KIENGE INTUDI, *Le contrôle policier de la « délinquance » des jeunes à Kinshasa. Une approche ethnographique en criminologie*, Phd in criminology, Catholic University of Leuven, 2005.

---

[3] We are referring here to the definition of the social actor given by C. DEBUYST, particularly at the colloquium on the *Acteur social et délinquance. Une grille de lecture du système de justice pénale*, Brussels, Mardaga, 1990, 21–33; see also C. DEBUYST, "La notion d'acteur social considéré comme structure 'légère' face aux structures sociales 'lourdes'", in D. KAMINSKI and M. KOKOREF (eds.), *Sociologie pénale : système et experience. Pour Claude Faugeron*, (Ramonville Saint-Agne: Editions-érès, 2004), 67–82.

G. MACHEL, United Nations General Assembly, *Rapport sur l'impact des conflits armés sur les enfants*, (UN Doc. A/51/306,1996), n° 43.

A. MARIE (ed.), *L'Afrique des individus. Itinéraires citadins dans l'Afrique contemporaine (Abidjan, Bamako, Dakar, Niamey)*, (Paris : Karthala, 1997).

A. MARIE, 'Du sujet communautaire au sujet individuel. Une lecture anthropologique de la réalité africaine contemporaine', in A. MARIE (ed.), *L'Afrique des individus. Itinéraires citadins dans l'Afrique contemporaine (Abidjan, Bamako, Dakar, Niamey)*, (Paris : Karthala, 1997).

A. MASSON, 'Du tomber en responsabilité à l'advenir responsable', in F. DIGNEFFE et T. MOREAU (eds.), *La responsabilité et la responsabilisation dans la justice pénale*, (Bruxelles : Larcier, De Boeck, 2006), 169–191.

M. A. NGONGO et K. ELOMBE, *L'Organisation de l'Unité Africaine, vingt ans après, des espoirs déçus ?*, (Kinshasa: Presses universitaires du Zaïre (PUZ), 1988).

T. MOREAU, 'Tomber en responsabilité et 'advenir responsable'. Un casse-tête juridique', in F. DIGNEFFE et T. MOREAU (eds.), *La responsabilité et la responsabilisation dans la justice pénale*, (Bruxelles: Larcier, De Boeck, 2006), 193–216.

M. MUBIALA, 'La charte africaine des droits de l'homme et des peuples dix ans plus tard. Plaidoyer pour l'institution d'une cour Régionale', (1998) 322 *Congo-Afrique*, 77–82.

R. NDESHIO, 'La problématique des droits de l'homme et des peuples en Afrique', in *Philosophie et droits de l'homme, Actes de la 5e semaine philosophique de Kinshasa*, (Kinshasa: Faculté de Théologie Catholique de Kinshasa, 1982), 139–157.

C. NTUMBA KABELA, 'Les droits de l'enfant, essai de fondement de la conception de la famille en milieu bantu', in *Philosophie et droits de l'homme, Actes de la 5e semaine philosophique de Kinshasa*, (Kinshasa: Faculté de Théologie catholique de Kinshasa, 1982), 197–212.

J.P. OLIVIER DE SARDAN, 'La dramatique déliquescence des Etats en Afrique', (February 2000) *Le Monde diplomatique*.

J. VAN PARYS, 'Deux philosophies de l'homme, deux notions des droits, Déclaration universelle des droits de l'homme de Ahmed Sekou Touré', in *Philosophie et droits de l'homme, Actes de la 5e semaine philosophique de Kinshasa*, (Kinshasa: Faculté de Théologie Catholique de Kinshasa, 1982), 226–227.

M. VILLEY, *Critique de la pensée juridique moderne (douze autres essais)*, (Paris: Dalloz, 1976).

Y.Y. WETSHODIMA, *Contribution à l'étude des représentations et comportements des parents face à la problématique du travail des enfants en République démocratique du Congo (cas de la ville de Kinshasa)*, paper presented at the Phd jury, Faculty of political and social sciences, research group on the third world, Ghent University, 2005.

THE DOMESTIC FULFILMENT OF CHILDREN'S RIGHTS: SAVE THE CHILDREN'S EXPERIENCE IN THE USE OF RIGHTS-BASED APPROACHES

AYE AYE TUN, GUY CAVE, DUNCAN TROTTER and BILL BELL

1. CONTEXT

1. In the last 10 to 15 years there has been a significant shift to seeing the realisation of all human rights as the end goal of development, and to accepting that human rights standards and principles should guide the means by which this goal is achieved. Two events helped to pave the way for this shift: the 1986 adoption by the UN General Assembly of the Declaration on the Right to Development and the 1993 World Conference on Human Rights in Vienna. The latter confirmed that human rights are "universal, indivisible and interdependent and interrelated" and that "democracy, development and respect for human rights and fundamental freedoms are interdependent and mutually reinforcing".[1]

2. Human rights are now being integrated into the work of all UN agencies, as part of the UN reform process and in May 2003, the UN agreed a "Common Understanding" on the meaning of a human rights-based approach to development, sometimes referred to as the "Stamford agreement".[2] Similarly, some Governmental donors (e.g.

---

1 OHCHR, *Human Rights – A Compilation of International Instruments*, OHCHR, Geneva, 2002, Volume 1, First Part, 46.

2 The UN Common Understanding:
1. All programmes of development co-operation, policies and technical assistance should further the realisation of human rights as laid down in the Universal Declaration of Human Rights and other international human rights instruments.
2. Human rights standards contained in, and principles derived from, the UDHR and other international human rights instruments guide all development cooperation and programming in all sectors and in all phases of the programming process.
3. Development cooperation contributes to the development of the capacities of 'duty-bearers' to meet their obligations and/or of 'rights-holders' to claim their rights.

SIDA) and an increasing number of International Non-Governmental Organisations[3] (INGOs) have explicitly adopted rights as the basis for their work.

3. What does it actually mean to take a rights-based approach to development work? "*The rights-based approach... means describing situations not in terms of human needs, or areas for development, but in terms of the obligation to respond to the rights of individuals. This empowers people to demand justice as a right, and not as charity. And legitimising those demands provides balance against other, less positive, forces. This also implies the direct involvement of people in decisions relating to their own development. Internationally, a rights-based approach provides the community with a sound moral basis on which to claim assistance and to advocate a world economic order respectful of human rights.*"[4]

In short, a rights-based approach is concerned with the application of human rights standards and principles to both the goal and the process of development – the means becoming as important as the end.

4. It has been said that the defining attribute of a rights-based approach is that it introduces accountability into the development paradigm. To put this in terms often used in a rights-based approach: a rights-holder has a claim on a duty-bearer who is obliged to ensure the right is realised. AMARTYA SEN has identified this as the key added value of a rights-based approach. The UNDP's Human Development Report (2000), of which SEN was one of the principal authors, states:

"*The normative connection between laudable goals and reasons for actions does not yield specific duties on the part of other individuals, collectivities or social institutions to bring about human development. This is where the human rights approach may offer an additional and very useful perspective for the analysis of human development. It links human development to the idea that others have duties to facilitate and enhance human development.*"

5. While the ultimate responsibility for the realisation of human rights rests with States Parties, the rights-based approach also implies that all non-State actors can be held accountable for their actions or inactions. This leads to an analysis at various levels of why rights are not currently being fulfilled, and a focus on the root causes for development not having occurred.

---

3 For example: Save the Children, CARE, Oxfam, and Action Aid.

4 M. ROBINSON, 'Foreword', in M.S. PAIS (ed.), *A Human Rights Conceptual Framework for UNICEF*, (Florence: UNICEF International Child Development Center, 1999).

2. A CHILD RIGHTS BASED APPROACH TO DEVELOPMENT – THE CASE OF SAVE THE CHILDREN UK

2.1. BACKGROUND

6. It is perhaps surprising to some that a child rights based approach to development came about at all – many still question whether children can even be considered as rights-holders. There have been political, philosophical, religious and legal objections to the concept of children's rights. The general discourse on rights-based approaches tends to deal with human rights in development with the unspoken assumption that "human" means "adult". Children and their human rights are still often missed out despite their significant demographic presence in most developing countries.[5]

7. However, several factors favoured the adoption of a human rights based approach to development programming by development actors working with children. The UN Convention on the Rights of the Child, adopted just as the Cold War thawed, enshrines the civil, political, economic, cultural, and social, human rights of children. Rather than being split over two Covenants and various other Conventions, it gives a comprehensive definition of children's rights which covers all five categories of rights (as well as elements normally associated with International Humanitarian Law), and thus lends itself to being the essential basis for a rights-based approach. Its almost universal ratification (192 out of 194 countries)[6] provides a common language through which the issues affecting children's survival and development can be addressed.

A further positive factor is the nature of the Committee on the Rights of the Child, widely viewed as one of the more "forward thinking" Treaty Bodies, and certainly one that is willing to involve and listen to UNICEF and (I)NGOs. Importantly, at its first session, the Committee defined four Articles of the UNCRC as providing key principles to be applied in implementing children's rights in any situation, thereby giving child-focussed development actors a framework of child rights principles within which to plan and assess their work, alongside more general human rights principles.

8. Save the Children UK, even before the UNCRC, had organisational links to children's rights. Its founder, EGLANTYNE JEBB, was the author of the first Declaration of the Rights of the Child, adopted by the League of Nations in 1924. JEBB had

---

5 For a recent example of this see P. UVIN, *Human Rights and Development*, (Bloomfield: Kumarian Press, 2004), which mentions 'children' only twice, 'kids' once, and makes no reference at all to the UN Convention on the Rights of the Child.

6 Only Somalia and the USA have not ratified – though both have signed the UNCRC.

concluded in 1922 that a new approach to working for children was needed, and declared that the answer was "*to evoke a co-operative effort of the nations to safeguard their own children on constructive rather than charitable lines. I believe we should claim certain rights for the children and labour for their universal recognition*". It was thus always likely that Save the Children UK would see the UNCRC as central to its work, and the current Mission Statement[7] declares, "*Save the Children fights for children's rights. We deliver immediate and lasting improvements to children's lives worldwide*".

Save the Children UK's shift to a rights-based approach has been gradual. Involvement in the drafting of the UNCRC marked a resurgence of interest in children's rights within the organisation, and by the mid-1990s "child rights" had become a theme within programming that often entailed raising awareness of and training on the UNCRC, and some engagement with the UNCRC reporting process.

At the same time there was a renewed "child focus" within the organisation, which included explorations of the reality of children's lives through empowerment work and participatory research with children. In the late 1990s papers circulated on a rights-based approach to all programming within Save the Children UK and were finally turned into a publication in 2001 "An Introduction to Child Rights Programming – Concept and Application". This was followed in 2002 by an International Save the Children Alliance publication entitled "Child Rights Programming – How to Apply Rights-Based Approaches in Programming" – a second edition of which has just been published.

Individual champions in head office and some country programmes led the adoption of this rights-based approach initially, but the approach is now integrated into higher-level decision-making and the new Country Planning & Review process establishes child rights programming as the framework for all programmes.

2.2. THE THEORY IN PRACTICE

9. One of the more recent definitions of Child Rights Programming within Save the Children is:

"*Child rights programming means using the principles of child rights to plan, implement and monitor programmes with the overall goal of improving the position of children so that all boys and girls can fully enjoy their rights and can live in societies that acknowledge and respect children's rights.*"

---

[7] This is also the Mission Statement of the International Save the Children Alliance.

This means that there are some key differences in applying a rights-based approach to work with children as distinct from adults, particularly in relation to concepts such as participation, empowerment, sustainability and local ownership. These differences relate to two broad categories: the status and nature of childhood, and the role and responsibilities of adults. Both have important implications for programmes as can be seen from the list below.[8]

10. Taking as a starting point the principles and concepts of human rights and in particular, the UNCRC, some of the key components of Child Rights Programming are:

- *Focus on children*: a clear focus on children, their rights and their role as social actors.
- *Holistic view of children*: considering all aspects of a child while making strategic choices and setting priorities.
- *Accountability*: a strong emphasis on accountability for promoting, protecting and fulfilling children's rights across a range of duty-bearers from the primary duty-bearer – the state, for example, the local and the central government, to the private sector, the media, child-care professionals, and other individuals with direct contact with children.
- *Supporting duty-bearers*: consideration of the ways in which duty-bearers can be helped to meet their obligations through technical assistance, budget support and other forms of partnership.
- *Advocacy*: the importance of advocacy, public education and awareness raising as programming tools in order to ensure that duty bearers are held accountable.
- *Participation*: the promotion of children's effective participation in programming and beyond, according to children's evolving capacities
- *Non-discrimination*: a commitment to the inclusion of the most marginalised children and to challenging discrimination on grounds of gender, class, ethnicity, (dis)ability, and so on.
- *The best interests of children*: consideration (with children) of the impact on children of all programme choices
- *Survival and development*: a focus on both the immediate survival of children as well as a commitment to ensuring the development of their full potential
- *Children as part of a community*: an understanding of children's place in their families, communities and societies and the role that their parents and other carers have in defending their rights and guiding children's development.
- *Root causes and broad issues*: a focus on the underlying causes as well as immediate violations.

8 G. Lansdown, 'What's the difference? Implications of a child-focus in rights-based programming', Internal Discussion Paper prepared for Save the Children UK.

- *Partnerships*: building partnerships and alliances for the promotion, protection and fulfilment of children's rights.
- *Information, and knowledge*: facilitating access to and understanding of children's rights for children themselves, their communities and key duty-bearers, including government.[9]

11. The comprehensive nature of the UNCRC and the principles of indivisibility and interdependence of rights mean that a holistic approach has to be taken in any intervention. The "whole child" must be considered even when planning and implementing a programme in a specific sector. For example, a programme intended to improve children's access to school should do more than just build a school, but would need to look at, inter alia, why children say they are not attending school; the quality of the education and its relevance to the children's lives; whether children are free from violence and abuse at school; how children's cultural rights are respected at school; the role of parents, family, and the community. It is important to promote a multi-disciplinary and cross-sectorial perspective.

12. A shift to a rights-based approach involves a shift from charity to justice, with the corresponding empowerment of rights-holders (compare the traditional view of "beneficiaries" of development as passive recipients). This is of particular importance with regard to children, and marks a significant and somewhat radical shift in the approach to child-focused development work.

13. Seeing children as rights holders involves asking oneself a whole series of questions around one's own assumptions about children and childhood. This can lead to a new way of relating to children in programmes, and a better understanding of constructions of childhood in different contexts and cultures. ROCHE makes the point that "*the children's rights project and emerging demands for 'inclusion' as citizens involves a redrawing of what it is to be an adult and a child*".[10]

2.3. CHILD RIGHTS SITUATION ANALYSIS

14. Good development programming starts with a situation analysis. The first stage of a child rights situation analysis involves mapping the child rights situation in a country (violations and gaps in provision) against the whole range of rights included

---

9 This list is taken from the second edition (2005) of the Save the Children Alliance Handbook on Child Rights Programming.

10 ROCHE goes on to conclude, "Ultimately the children's rights project is not just about making a better world for children (KING, 1997), it is about making a better world for all of us".

in the UNCRC.[11] This holistic overview of the situation of children is relatively new and often highlights the scarcity of information on children's enjoyment of their rights to protection and participation. For this reason it includes a focus on information that is coming directly from children themselves. It also links the development process to the international human rights framework – with the Committee on the Rights of the Child's Concluding Observations providing an important input.

15. The human rights principle of universality and the principle of non-discrimination in the UNCRC (Art. 2), requires that the situation analysis looks particularly at which groups of children are the most vulnerable and excluded. This calls for data to be disaggregated, for example according to age; gender; disabilities; ethnic, religious, cultural or linguistic minorities; caste; infected or affected by HIV/AIDS, and so on. It also requires analysis of legal and administrative frameworks – not only in terms of what they say on paper, but also how they function in practice.

16. A child rights situation analysis involves attempting to understand the immediate and root causes of the identified violations of children's rights. Although this causality analysis is not new, and is a part of good development practice, approaching it from a rights-basis has led to new perspectives – such as the realisation that denial of children's rights to participation[12] is often one of the root causes of violations of other rights. For example, the denial of children's rights to information – Article 17 – often has an impact on children's right to the highest attainable standard of health – Article 24.

17. The next stage of the situation analysis involves an examination of who is responsible for the violations of children's rights, including gaps in provision. Rather than child-focused development actors identifying the problem and then getting on to try and "fix" it – this is about analysing who the "duty-bearers" are in a given situation and what they (and other actors) are currently doing about it.

Finally, the situation analysis will examine internal organisational strengths and weaknesses, and the external opportunities and threats, for the realisation of children's rights. The full analysis can then inform the choice of area to work on and how best to effect change for children. Decisions normally guided by an organisation's strategic objectives and priorities; however, these decisions may increasingly be steered by children's own identification of priorities.[13]

---

11 Different frameworks can be used to map this, common ones are to use four "baskets" of rights: survival, development, protection, participation; or to organise the data available under the headings suggested by the Committee on the Rights of the Child in their Guidelines for Reporting on the UNCRC.

12 As we will define them in the section below on participation.

13 Though for UNICEF, as an intergovernmental organisation, "it is the responsibility of States to determine where to begin, what is most urgent, and what is most strategic.... (UNICEF will) assist the Government in identifying the most critical problems affecting children". UNICEF, Programming Guidelines, New York, 2003, 13.

2.4. ACCOUNTABILITY

18. The principle of accountability is fundamental to any rights-based approach. The basic understanding that the rights-holder can claim their rights from the duty-bearer (ultimately the State) with the obligation to fulfil that right, has developed to an acceptance that there are a whole series of claims and obligations involved in the realisation of a right (**diagram 1**). There is ongoing exploration of the view that a rights-based approach also implies that all non-State actors can be held accountable for the actions they take that may enhance or detract from the realisation of rights. For example, there is an increasing focus on the private sector in this regard.

Diagram 1

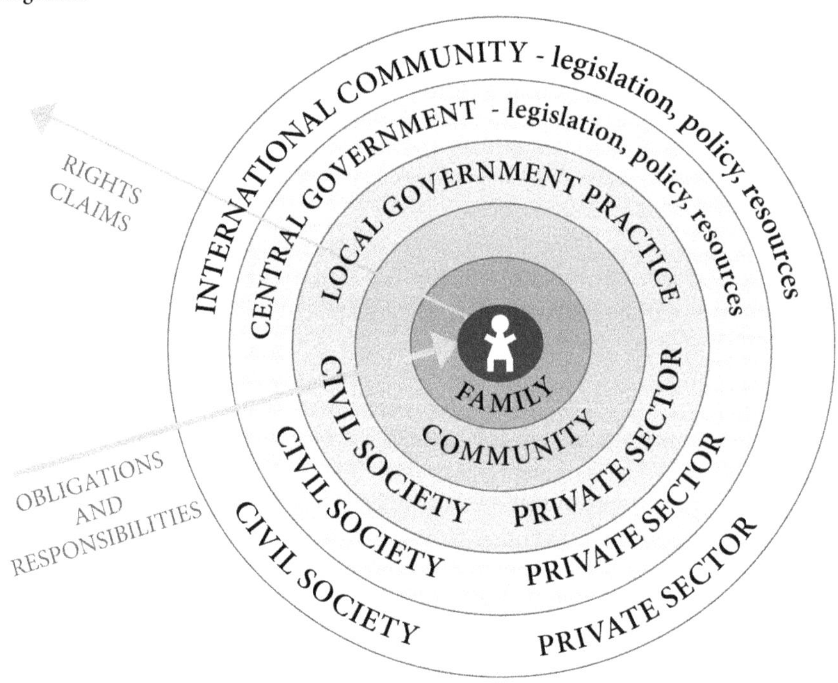

19. For Save the Children UK, the programme implications of a desire to increase accountability and advance the overall fulfilment of children's rights is captured in "The Three Pillars" of child rights programming (**diagram 2**), which aim to achieve a significant and sustainable positive impact on the realisation of children's rights by engaging in a balance of complementary and mutually reinforcing work. This approach argues that a programme that provides only services without tackling the wider policy context is incomplete, as is work that focuses on policies without ensuring that these policies and laws are translated into good practice and concrete results for children.

The intention is that by demonstrating good practice (**pillar 1**), and advocating with decision-makers to take up that good practice, and if necessary change laws and policies, and introduce new structures and mechanisms (**pillar 2**), and then the impact for children can be countrywide and sustainable. Further, by building a constituency of support – within Government, key professionals, national NGOs, the media, children themselves and so on – (**pillar 3**) the hope is that there will be, within society, people who can monitor whether the changes are being implemented, as well as forming a strong base of support for the long-term advancement of children's rights. The model does not exclude Save the Children UK from being involved in service delivery, either directly or, more often, through a partner; however increasingly this is used in pilot initiatives, and uses service delivery as an entry point and to strengthen the evidence base for the other work.[14]

Diagram 2: The three pillars of child rights programming

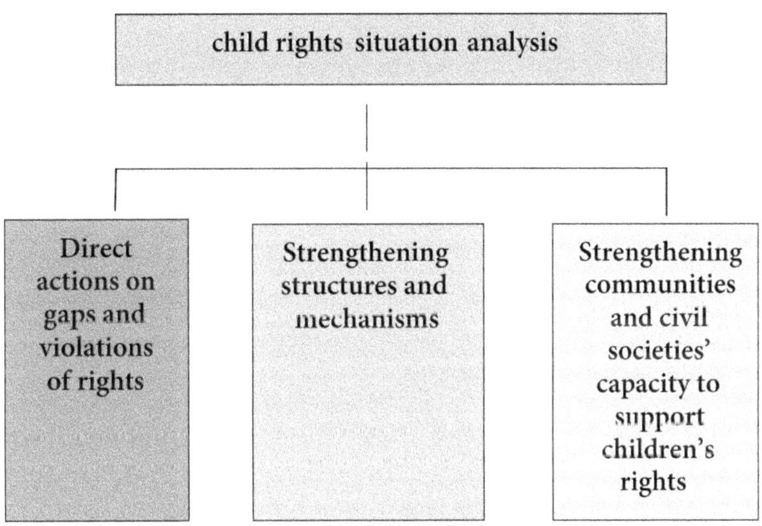

20. The shift to a child rights-based approach to programming, in parallel with a growing questioning of the legitimacy of development actors generally, is increasingly leading to child-focused organisations exploring their own accountability to children. Within Save the Children UK this has taken two forms. One is a greater focus on the

[14] In humanitarian emergencies there may well be a considerable level of work in pillar 1, but there would also be some work in the other two pillars.

actual impact that its programmes are having on children's lives (positive and negative, intended and unintended).[15]

A primary source of information for this assessment is the views of children themselves. Secondly, Save the Children UK has started a process of increasing its direct accountability to children, starting with increasing projects' accountability to children, and the involvement of children in the governance of programmes.

2.5. THE FOUR PRINCIPLES OF THE UNCRC

21. Child Rights Programming insists on the importance of considering the four principles of the UNCRC at every stage of the programme cycle and in relation to every programme intervention.

2.5.1. Survival and Development

22. The right of children to life, survival and development (Art. 6 of the UNCRC) is fundamental. Any programme should be considering and addressing the survival and development of children, with the concept of development being the UNCRC's comprehensive and holistic one.[16]

2.5.2. Best Interests Of The Child

23. "In all actions concerning children... the best interests of the child shall be a primary consideration" (Art. 3.1 of the UNCRC). In practice, this principle has aided a child focus both internally and externally.

"The inclusion of this principle in the CRC has helped crystallize the perception of the child as a real person in his or her own right, someone who must be considered autonomously. It has placed the child at the centre of the equation, on behalf of whom and because of whom decisions must be taken and taken in a particular direction."[17]

---

15 This approach aims to measure impact against five dimensions of change: 1. Changes in the lives of children and young people; 2. Changes in policies and practices affecting children and young people's rights; 3. Changes in children and young people's participation and active citizenship; 4. Changes in equity and non-discrimination of children and young people; 5. Changes in civil societies' and communities' capacity to support children's rights.

16 That is "the child's physical, mental, spiritual, moral and social development" (UNCRC Art. 27), as well as cultural development (UNCRC Art. 23).

17 M.S. Pais (ed.), *A Human Rights Conceptual Framework for UNICEF*, (Florence: UNICEF International Child Development Center, 1999), 11.

Taking this principle seriously has helped to support (and re-establish) a child-centred approach within child-focused development actors. It has served as a basis for evaluating the laws, policies, practices, and budget decisions of States Parties, which has helped to increase the visibility of children and their rights. It has also been increasingly used ensure that children's rights are taken into account in agendas where they would never have been previously considered, for example: large-scale infrastructure development projects and national budgeting.

24. The subjective nature of the concept of "best interests" entails the risk that their definition will be that of the "powerful" in any given situation. Save the Children suggest that one always asks "*How and by whom has this vision (of best interests) been defined? What are the assumptions underlying it? What have girls and boys contributed to the development of this vision?*"[18]

2.5.3. Non-discrimination (Universality)

25. The principle of universality is the foundation of all human rights treaties and is related to the principle of non-discrimination in the UNCRC (Art. 2). The implications of this article in practice are numerous, and start with the classification of data in the situation analysis so that the most vulnerable and excluded groups of children can be identified. In the past development work at times tended to aim to reach as many people as possible. However, a right is not realised until everyone enjoys it, and in a rights-based approach, this leads to a focus on the most marginalised, though not to the exclusion of others. "*Positive measures are vital to ensure that public policies benefit all children and that all children have access to basic services and other opportunities, based on, among other things, distributive justice.*"[19]

26. Within Save the Children UK a "diversity approach" to non-discrimination has been adopted as an essential part of child rights programming. Diversity is an approach characterised by recognising and valuing difference, and recognising and countering inequality and discrimination. A diversity approach also recognises multiple layers of discrimination. This means, for instance, that gender inequality cannot be tackled successfully without also taking into account ethnicity, caste or class.

2.5.4. Children's Participation – The Right To Be Heard

27. Like non-discrimination, participation is not only a principle in the UNCRC but is also a general principle of human rights. The inclusion of participation rights in the

18 International Save the Children Alliance, London, 2002, 37.
19 UNICEF Programming Guidelines UNICEF, New York, 2003, 7.

UNCRC "*provides the opportunity for international human rights law to operate as a catalyst to change the value which society places upon children's contributions*".[20] However, while there are some excellent examples of participatory and empowering work with children, this has not been mainstreamed across all the work of child-focused development actors. Despite the fact that participation of the poor and marginalised in development has been "good practice" for a long time now and certainly predates the shift to a rights-based approach. Many child-focused development actors view participation in a largely instrumental sense – with the emphasis on children's views influencing, and children themselves involved in, the design, implementation, monitoring and evaluation of programmes.[21] There is not a full enough recognition that children's rights to participation are to do with children's status in society, nor a clear commitment from organisations that they see the realisation of children's participation rights as a good in themselves.

2.6. THE UNCRC REPORTING PROCESS

28. An advantage of a child rights-based approach is that it provides an overall framework for all programming activity. PAIS refers to the importance of "international cooperation" and talks of "a universal movement of solidarity around children".[22] Experience is developing in using and promoting the UNCRC reporting process as part of a rights-based approach to programming – primarily within UNICEF but increasingly within Save the Children UK and others[23] – using the process as a tool which can create opportunities for awareness-raising, national coalition creation or development, and advocacy, rather than merely as an end in itself.

3. IMPLICATIONS AND CHALLENGES

29. Save the Children UK has certainly not finished thinking through the implications of its move to a child rights based approach to its work. There is a need for ongoing investigation into what the approach means, for example in terms of which partners to choose, how it may need to adapt in different contexts, its fuller application in humanitarian emergencies, and especially the political nature of a rights-based approach. Organisational issues also pose difficulties: staff at all levels have to be

---

20 G. VAN BUEREN, *The International Law on the Rights of the Child*, (The Hague: Martinus Nijhoff, 1995), 145.

21 This appears to be the emphasis that comes out from UNICEF's Programming Guidelines (2003) and Save the Children UK's "Introduction to CRP" (2001).

22 M.S. PAIS (ed.), supra (note 17), 11.

23 D. BARO, *A tool for change?*, (London: Save the children UK, 2002).

convinced of the benefits of the approach and they need to be supported with staff training, revised job descriptions, and improved inductions, policies and practices.

30. The child rights approach is not a blueprint but needs to be implemented in a way appropriate and responsive to context. The following case studies illustrate some aspects of the experience of applying the principles and concepts of child rights programming in the reality of three different contexts – Myanmar, a fragile state controlled by a repressive military regime; Bulgaria, a transition economy seeking EU accession; and Kenya, a developing nation. In each of the three case studies the programme was responding to rights violations highlighted as issues of concern in the Concluding Observations of the Committee on the UN Convention on the Rights of the Child in response to the relevant State Party report. The case studies highlight some of the changes introduced by child rights programming including the increased importance of advocacy, the mainstreaming of children's participation and the application of the best interests principle.

4. MYANMAR: CHILD RIGHTS PROGRAMMING IN A 'FRAGILE STATE'

31. Some development professionals have questioned the applicability of rights-based approaches in a repressive context. Referring to Burma/Myanmar, where the military regime systematically violates human rights with impunity, a Child Rights Programming (CRP) practitioner expresses doubt about the "*credibility of rights-based programming within countries where equality, freedom, accountability and fairness are meaningless words and where even moderate forms of advocacy and public awareness work are impossible*".[24] An organisation like Save the Children certainly faces challenges in adopting CRP as its main programming approach in Burma. However, below we consider an example of what has been achieved and relate this to the application of the CRC general principles.

4.1. VOICES OF CHILDREN: ADVOCACY ON ANTI-TRAFFICKING

32. Save the Children organised a national children's forum on human trafficking in Myanmar in early October 2004 as part of a joint advocacy initiative called Voices of Children within Save the Children UK's regional Cross-Border Anti-Trafficking

[24] J. THEIS, *Update on CRP Workshop in Southeast Asia, Internal report*, (London: Save the Children UK, 2001).

Project and the International Labour Organisation International Programme to Eliminate Child Labour (ILO-IPEC). Voices of Children is a response to the absence of children's participation in regional policy discussions on human trafficking and brings to the fore the views and experiences of children who have been trafficked or are at risk of being trafficked in the six Greater Mekong Sub-region (GMS) countries: China, Thailand, Laos, Cambodia, Vietnam and Myanmar.

Voices of Children facilitated a series of forums, including the one in Myanmar, for children to: share their views and experiences on trafficking in children; comment on responses to the problem in the sub-region; and advocate for policy and action, including the role that children should play in this. The forums led to a sub-regional forum in which child delegates from national forums participated in order to advocate to Coordinated Mekong Ministerial Initiative Against Trafficking (COMMIT). The Myanmar forum participants consisted of ethnic Kachin, Kayin, Mon, Pao and Shan children who had been trafficked and repatriated, who were vulnerable to trafficking and who could advocate on behalf of their peers. They were selected by other children at preliminary forums held in Save the Children UK project areas in Shan, Mon and Kayin States to reflect the diversity and patterns of trafficking. Relevant government bodies and concerned organisations such as UN agencies and international NGOs working in anti-trafficking were invited to the forum.

4.2. ACCOUNTABILITY

33. Advocacy work faces some serious challenges and threats in a context like Burma where a privileged group that systematically represses and exploits others dominates the system.[25]

These include:

- Authorities' denial of the significance of issues related to children, thereby creating sensitivity around such issues, and a lack of respect for children's rights and lack of accountability;
- Lack of political space to engage in public debate and to claim rights, and lack of freedom of expression and the media;
- Possible harm by authorities to staff, organisation, children and their communities due to advocacy work on sensitive issues;

---

[25] B. Coates and R. David, 'Learning for Change: The Art of Assessing the Impact of Advocacy Work', (2002) 3 and 4 *Development in Practice*, 530–541.

- Restricted freedom to conduct research and disseminate findings for evidence-based advocacy;
- Decision-makers' good intentions but inappropriate responses e.g. rules and regulations enforced are not in the best interests of children;
- Deliberate fuzziness and confusion arising from lack of clearly articulated policies and responsible structures/personnel among government counterparts and decision-makers;
- Limited access to decision makers;
- Uncertain political situation particularly in the light of INGO work in the country.

34. Nonetheless, Save the Children has been able to implement advocacy initiatives at different levels:

- "Project-level advocacy" with groups such as community and religious leaders, families and teachers in order to promote children's right to protection against human trafficking. Save the Children has been able to help Palaung ethnic leaders in 80 villages in northern Myanmar to develop village rules that protect children from internal and cross-border trafficking to China.
- Regional advocacy as part of the "Voices of Children" initiative against cross-border trafficking.

35. The experience and lessons learned from these initiatives indicate that:

- The government's ratification of the CRC, their other national and international commitments, and the CRC Committee's recommendations can be used for leverage. SMITH[26] notes, the language of change, reform and development is now spoken from all sides among political actors in Myanmar despite their differences in opinions. Such common language can be referred to and commonalties highlighted in advocacy and influencing.
- Skills in "quiet advocacy" can help build the confidence of decision makers in Save the Children resulting in their greater receptiveness and openness.
- Networking and collaboration with organisations with common goals is possible and strengthens advocacy efforts.
- Advocacy with other organisations and donors in and outside the country, which have more leverage with the government, such as the UN, can help address "sensitive" issues.

---

26 M. SMITH, 'Burmese Politics after 1988: An Era of New and Uncertain Change', in R.H. TAYLOR (ed.), *Political Economy Under Military Rule*, (London: Hurst and Company, 2001).

- Individuals within government bodies can be identified with whom relationships can be cultivated in support of advocacy work.
- Lessons can be learned from the experiences of others working in similar political contexts.

4.3. APPLICATION OF THE CRC GENERAL PRINCIPLES – PARTICIPATION AND NON-DISCRIMINATION

36. The Myanmar Child Law grants rights to freedom of speech, expression, thought, conscience and association and assembly but "in accordance with the law" and thus is superseded by the other stringent limitations on civil and political rights of Burmese citizens. The importance attached to hierarchy in Burmese culture also requires children to obey their elders. However, it has still been possible to create space for children's participation despite cultural and political sensitivity, starting with but later moving beyond project areas.

Save the Children has implemented several such initiatives:

- Children & youth led forum, which is a pilot initiative in some project areas. Child representatives, selected by their peers, give feedback and suggestions on Save the Children's work and raise issues of concern with staff.
- Children in community structures, which is a membership of young people under 18 in community structures such as Village Water and Sanitation Committees or Water User groups.
- National children's forum on trafficking, which is part of the regional initiative to the Coordinated Mekong Ministerial Initiative against Trafficking (COMMIT) that built on children's participation at community level and took it to national level.

37. One of the biggest challenges to applying the non-discrimination principle in Burma is limited access to the most disadvantaged, vulnerable and marginalised children such as child soldiers and those who are internally displaced (IDPs). Restrictions on accessibility can sometimes occur unexpectedly or unpredictably due to changes in authorities and regulations. However, for example, in remote communities where the government's administrative system does not reach or is not functional, Save the Children is able to work when agreement is reached with the communities concerned. Research has been conducted with children infected and affected by HIV/AIDS to understand their situation and to respond to the stigma and discrimination they are faced with as well as with children and young people most vulnerable to human trafficking.

4.4. SUMMARY

38. Although rights and development are inherently political, INGOs cannot be overtly political in Myanmar in the sense of involvement in, or even the suspicion of involvement in, partisan politics. However, they will increasingly take on the role of political actors as they become more involved in rights-based work, especially advocacy. As International Crisis Group[27] notes, many INGOs may not feel comfortable in this new role since they prefer to depoliticise their work so that it can be implemented with little scrutiny or suspicion from the authorities. INGOs that plan to apply a rights-based approach need to balance the conflicting demands of their political and technical roles.

5. BULGARIA: CHALLENGING INSTITUTIONAL CARE IN A TRANSITION ECONOMY

5.1. CONTEXT

39. Bulgaria has been going through a process of economic and political reform since 1989. The country is charting its path from a communist past towards full membership of the European Union (EU) with accession scheduled for 2007 or 2008. Largely hidden from sight, the social care institutions established under the old regime have continued into the new era. As a result, Bulgaria has the highest percentage of institutionalised children in Europe and the countries of Former Soviet Union, an estimated 31,000 children, over 2% of child population:

- The vast majority of children placed in institutions have parents: only 3% are "real" orphans.
- Children are placed in institutions and consequently abandoned for a variety of reasons including: because of stigmatisation and the lack of community-based services for disabled children; because children are considered to have special educational needs and are placed in "special schools" ,although many who are categorised as such are not; because they are "juvenile offenders"; and/or because of family poverty.
- There is disproportionate representation of ethnic minorities, notably Roma: some 9% of the overall Bulgarian population is believed to be Roma but an estimated 65–70% of children in institutions are of Roma origin.

---

[27] International Crisis Group, *Myanmar: The Politics of Humanitarian Aid,* (2002), <http://www.crisisweb.org/projects/showreport.cfm?reportid=602>.

- Alternatives to institutional care – including fostering, prevention of abandonment and re-integration services – are very poorly developed.

5.2. APPROACH TAKEN

40. The traditional strategy adopted by Save the Children from 1999 onwards, focussed around:

- Local level pilot work, modelling professional social work practice and seeking to support the reform of an institution (home for children aged 0–3).
- Bringing together all key ministries with responsibilities for child welfare.
- Supporting the development of new policy including influencing and contributing to the drafting of key national legislation – Child Protection Act and implementing regulations.

41. By mid 2002, this approach had lead to a reduction in the number of children permanently institutionalised in the local pilot site institution by over 30%. However, more widely in Bulgaria, progress on institutionalisation remained limited: numbers entering and remaining in institutions were still high; conditions in many institutions were appalling; and no government funds were earmarked for the development of community based alternative services.

Save the Children understood it was a "small fish" in terms of the bodies with whom the Bulgarian government interacted. To have real impact it needed additional "leverage" – a careful analysis suggested that this could be achieved by getting child rights more firmly onto the agenda of Bulgaria's discussions with the European Union (EU) regarding EU accession. The Bulgarian government was seen as paying attention to bodies associated with EU membership and those perceived as being influential in the process of accession. Once on their political radar screen, it was hoped that the European Commission and Members of the European Parliament (MEPs) would bring more influence to bear upon the Bulgarian government in pushing for child welfare reform than Save the Children could.

42. The Bulgarian programme advocacy work with the EU has had two major components:

Phase I, 2002–3:	lobbying for change of the EU-Bulgaria Accession Partnership agreement to sharpen its focus on children in institutions
Phase II, 2004 on:	maintaining pressure on the Bulgarian government and EU to monitor political commitment to de-institutionalisation –

using the European Commission's Regular Reports on Bulgaria's accession progress

The Accession Partnership (AP) agreement of 2002 stated only that the Bulgarian government "should fully implement the UNCRC". Because of the lobbying and advocacy efforts, the new EU-BG AP in April 2003 commits the Bulgaria government to "systematically reduce the number of children living in institutions".

As a result there was an overall increase in the profile of child welfare reform issues in the EU-Bulgaria discussions on EU accession that led to a number of positive developments:

- a Bulgarian Government de-institutionalisation plan;
- the AP commitment being debated by an EU-Bulgaria Joint Parliamentary Committee, thus raising its profile with the European Parliament;
- amendments to the Bulgarian Child Protection Act and Family Code;
- introduction of secondary legislation enabling the development of alternatives to institutional care (including foster care, measures for the prevention of institutionalisation, and criteria for standards of care).

43. Despite this considerable success in ensuring that de-institutionalisation featured explicitly in the political commitments of the Bulgarian government in relation to EU accession, it was important to maintain pressure on the government to actually implement its de-institutionalisation plan and to keep the issue alive on the EU's agenda. In addition to national level lobbying for implementation of the de-institutionalisation plan, it was decided to use the European Commission's own monitoring exercise, the annual Regular Reports on Bulgaria's progress towards accession, to maintain momentum.

In the face of government attempts to manipulate the statistics on children in institutions and present a more positive picture of its progress during 2003, Save the Children decided to submit to the European Commission in 2004 its own report on progress. Save the Children entered into coalition with four other major NGOs working in the field of social policy, another child rights organisation (EveryChild), and a disability, a minority and a human/civil rights group.

The European Commission's 2004 "Regular Report" on Bulgaria's progress towards EU accession shared our analysis of the situation and was clearly based to a large degree on the findings of the NGO report.

In addition, there were a number of other successes and indicators of impact:

- the NGO Alternative Report received considerable television, radio and newspaper coverage;
- the report continues to be quoted in public debate and used by the media and other NGOs as a reference document;
- the Head of the State Agency for Child Protection requested a meeting to discuss the contents of the report ;
- the European Commission requested a meeting, early 2005, to discuss "progress since the last NGO report", indicating that it continues to value Save the Children input on the issues covered.

6. KENYA: PROMOTING THE BEST INTERESTS OF CHILDREN IN CONFLICT WITH THE LAW[28]

44. The Kenya Diversion Project addresses the crucial role and impact that the police have on children as the first point of contact once a child is deemed to be in conflict with the law. It builds on the police's discretionary powers to avoid unnecessary criminalisation and supports them in using these powers in a positive way that recognizes children's circumstances and promotes their best interests. Crucially, it recognises not only that the police need specialised training but that there should also be a support framework for the police to call on other services to deal with each individual case. This ensures not only more appropriate and co-ordinated responses, but also better use of existing resources and better outcomes for children through appropriate case management focused on each child's best interests.

6.1. CONTEXT

45. The annual reports of the Kenyan Department of Children's Services in 1997 and 1998 estimated that 80 per cent of children in the juvenile justice system were in fact there because of failures in the arrangements for protecting children from harm and only 20 per cent had actually committed offences, of which only a few were serious. It became clear that the majority of children in remand homes in Kenya were not those who had committed offences (the age of criminal responsibility is ten years), but those who needed better ways of responding to their care and protection needs.

[28] For further details on this and other case studies of children in conflict with the law with associated policy analysis see F. Martin and J. Parry-Williams, *The Right Not to Lose Hope*, (London: Save the Children UK, 2005).

46. The Children Act 2001, like its predecessor, states that children are deemed to be in need of care and protection if they would not receive it unless the court took action. This can be applied where children are parentless, homeless, found begging, or scavenging. The law is often used to control poor urban children visible on the streets, engaged in survival behaviour by working or asking for money. Such children are arrested by the police and detained in police cells while arrangements are made for a children's officer to prosecute them. Because of delays, these children are often sent to remand homes.

Children can only be admitted to a remand home on a court order by a magistrate after a report has been received from a children's officer. Frequently, the sentence recommended to the court by these officers is to send children for approved school training, where they may stay for up to eight years or until they are 18 years old. Approved schools are intended under the law for serious offenders who require a long period of rehabilitation in order to reform. Yet children in need of care and protection are sent there and are criminalised and marginalised because they are poor and because the care and protection systems have failed them.

47. The Department of Children's Services manages the remand homes, approved schools and a children's home, which together take up two-thirds of its budget. This reflects a strong bias towards the institutionalisation of children, often in conditions that fall well below satisfactory standards and for prolonged periods of time. Interestingly, it is reported that most children go home when allowed to, undermining the impression that they are without parents or guardians.

6.2. DEVELOPMENT OF THE DIVERSION PROJECT

48. To keep children out of the justice system, especially the care and protection cases, the Department of Children's Services and Save the Children UK started a pilot diversion project in 2001 to divert children away from the courts in Nairobi, Nakuru and Kisumu. The focus was to ensure that police officers, as the earliest point of contact, were trained and competent to refer children to other agencies instead of detaining them. Specialised Child Protection Units (CPUs) were set up in four major police stations in Kisumu, Nakuru and in Nairobi (Kilimani and Kamukunji). The 17 CPU police officers were trained in child rights and the diversion process.

The CPUs were supported by a diversion framework consisting of a strategic alliance for policy level influencing, national and district level diversion teams, and community-based support systems. This support framework involved 13 government departments, 22 NGOs, three legal networks, 19 community-based organisations and four police stations in the three pilot project areas. Training on child rights and diversion was a major component of the project. From 2001–04, 290 police, 206 stakeholders including children's officers, probation officers and magistrates, 268 community members and 1,407 children received training. Seven specially designed training sessions also took place for the district diversion core teams at which an average of ten agencies attended. The publication of Guidelines for Implementation of Children and Young People's Diversion Strategy was part of the advocacy strategy used to influence the police, parliamentarians, networks and NGOs.

6.3. IMPACT OF THE MODEL

49. The project had strong impact on children's lives across the four project sites over its first four years (2001–04).

- A total of 2,800 children were diverted from the courts. Of these, around 70 per cent were reintegrated with their families, 20 per cent were taken to temporary rescue centres while work to reintegrate or place them elsewhere continued, and ten per cent were orphans sent to children's or remand homes pending further investigation.
- The district diversion core teams reported a 90 per cent drop in the number of children being referred to the children's courts in the four sites of the project.
- Two-thirds of the children dealt with by the project were boys. However, one CPU received mainly girls who had served as house girls and then run away from their employers because of mistreatment.
- Police officers were reported to treat children more humanely, pay more respect to their rights and opinions and provide better separate facilities for boys and girls.
- Decisions were much quicker with some children being resettled straight from the police station.

50. Within the project areas, there was good collaboration with civil society and communities. A wide range of groups dealing with children – children's homes, NGOs working with children, community leaders – were empowered to take a greater role in protecting children through the project. Local children's homes took in some of the children who were not immediately repatriated and provided better conditions than the remand homes.

The police, Department of Children's Services, probation service and NGOs worked together for the first time in the new collaborative structures. Training led to better practice by key stakeholders and child rights were incorporated into the police training curriculum. A Memorandum of Understanding recognising the diversion project was agreed between the Department of Children's Services, the police and Save the

Children. At the national policy level, the Ministry of Finance agreed a budget line within the Department of Children's Services on "diversion". The project was handed over by Save the Children UK to Save the Children Sweden in Kenya in January 2004 with plans for replication in a further 10 districts supported by SIDA funding.

Valuable lessons were also learned that will guide future improvements, particularly in relation to improved data collection, follow-up, ongoing police training and further change requirements to both policy and practice.

7. CONCLUSION

51. The three case studies above illustrate different experiences in encouraging national governments to accelerate their efforts to fulfil children's rights. In the Kenyan case this involved a partnership with government to develop a new approach to dealing with children in conflict with the law – one that promoted respect for children's rights and placed children's best interests at its centre. The partnership was able to demonstrate improved outcomes for children by supporting the state to fulfil its responsibility to offer effective care and protection to vulnerable children rather than criminalising them and removing them from their communities. The Bulgaria case study highlights the 'three pillars' approach to child rights programming, combining practical programmes that demonstrate the potential of new approaches with legal reform and advocacy to speed up the adoption of more child-focused policies and practices. Finally, the Myanmar case study shows how rights-based approaches can be used to advance the domestic fulfilment of children's rights even in a fragile state where respect for human rights is scarcely acknowledged.

52. The development of rights-based approaches to working with children and young people is still at a relatively early stage. But the evidence so far suggests that it is an approach that can be successfully used to encourage, persuade and support states in fulfilling their obligations to realize children's rights. A clear focus on the goal of fulfilling children's rights and the incorporation of rights-based standards into the practice of development work play important roles in delivering this result. The examples taken from Save the Children's work presented in this paper show how one organisation has tried to rise to this challenge.

CHILDREN'S RIGHTS IN ACTION: USING THE CONVENTION ON THE RIGHTS OF THE CHILD AS AN AUDITING TOOL

URSULA KILKELLY and LAURA LUNDY[1]

1. INTRODUCTION

1. The United Nations Convention on the Rights of the Child (CRC) was adopted by the General Assembly of the United Nations in 1989 and entered into force on 2 September 1990. Sixteen years later the CRC stands as the most highly ratified instrument in international law with the United States isolated as the principal dissenter from its widely accepted standards on children's rights.[2] The CRC has received considerable academic attention in its relatively short life and there is a spectrum of opinion as to its ability to transform the childhood experience. While the Convention is widely regarded as the "touchstone for children's rights throughout the world",[3] most commentators have been guarded in their praise, presenting the CRC as an important, if somewhat limited, milestone on children's rights;[4] a statement of "moderate rather than unduly ambitious standards of promotion and protection of the rights of the child";[5] and a "beginning, but only a beginning."[6] All commentators agree, however, that the issues of enforcement and implementation are the key to

---

1 This paper was published first in the *Child and Family Law Quarterly*. We are grateful to the editors of the CFLQ for permitting it to be published here also.

2 S. KILBOURNE, 'The Wayward Americans – why the USA has not ratified the United Nations Convention on the Rights of the Child', (1998) 10 *Child and Family Law Quarterly*, 243–256.

3 J. FORTIN, *Children's Rights and the Developing Law*, Second Edition (London: LexisNexis, 2003), 49.

4 D. MCGOLDRICK, 'The United Nations Convention on the Rights of the Child', (1991) 5 *International Journal of Law and the Family*, 132–169 at 132.

5 A. LOPATKA, 'The Rights of the Child are Universal: The Perspective of the UN Convention on the Rights of the Child', in M. FREEMAN and P. VEERMAN (eds.), *The Ideologies of Children's Rights*, (Dordrecht – Boston – London: Martinus Nijhoff Publishers, 1992), 51.

6 M. FREEMAN, 'Taking Children's Rights More Seriously', (1992) 6 *International Journal of Law and the Family*, 52–71 at 71.

maximise the Convention's potential to improve the lives of children and young people worldwide.[7]

2. While theoretical analyses provide an insight into the potential benefits and limitations of the CRC, it is analysis of the CRC in practice that allows its true potential to change the lives of the world's children to be understood. One use of the CRC that facilitates this understanding is its use as an auditing tool whereby its standards are used to children's rights proof law and policy at domestic level. In 2004–2005, the authors of this paper were part of a multi-disciplinary team afforded the opportunity to test the CRC heuristically across all aspects of children's lives in research conducted on behalf of the Northern Ireland Commissioner for Children and Young People. The research team was asked to conduct a children's rights audit of law, policy and practice in Northern Ireland in order to identify where children's rights were being ignored and underplayed and to assist the Commissioner in identifying the issues that should become his priorities for office. While the research has been published and its findings can be scrutinised in their own right,[8] the objective of this paper is to carry out an *ex post facto* critique of the process by which it was conducted.

The analysis begins with a description of the background to the research, focusing on its remit and the data collection methods employed. This is followed by a critique of three core, yet problematic, elements of the research process: problems with the substance of the CRC, difficulties faced in accessing detailed and current information on children's lives, and the setting of priorities for the Commissioner's office.

2. BACKGROUND TO THE NICCY RESEARCH

3. The office of the Northern Ireland Commissioner for Children and Young People (NICCY) is one of the rare and enduring successes of the currently dissolved Northern Ireland Assembly. NIGEL WILLIAMS, the first person to hold the post, took up office on 1 October 2003. In accordance with the legislation, the Commissioner's principal aim is "*to safeguard and promote the rights and best interests of children and young persons*" defined as those under 18, or those with a disability or leaving care up to the

[7] See for example, D. FOTTRELL, 'One Step Forward or Two Steps Sideways? Assessing the First Decade of the Convention on the Rights of the Child', in D. FOTTRELL (ed.), *Revisiting Children's Rights 10 Years of the UN Convention on the Rights of the Child*, (Kluwer Law International, 2000), 1; D. BALTON, 'The Convention on the Rights of the Child: Prospects for International Enforcement', (1990) 12 *HRQ*, 120 at 125–129.

[8] U. KILKELLY, R. KILPATRICK, L. LUNDY, L. MOORE, P. SCRATON, C. DAVEY, C. DWYER, S. MCALISTER, *Children's Rights in Northern Ireland*, (Belfast: NICCY, 2005). The research report can be accessed on the Commissioner's website at <http://www.niccy.org>.

age of 21.[9] From the outset, the Commissioner expressed a commitment to be guided in his work by thorough research and shortly after he took up office, he announced plans for a major study of the state of children's rights and welfare in Northern Ireland. The overarching aim of the research was to gather information relating to children's lives and to identify particular areas in which their rights were being ignored or underplayed.

4. A range of data collection methods was employed for the purposes of the analysis. These included an extensive literature review, which analysed the existing research, law and policy relating to children and children's rights in Northern Ireland. The second research method was to carry out focus groups and individual interviews with over 350 policy makers, professionals, practitioners and volunteers representing a range of child, youth and related organisations and agencies throughout Northern Ireland. The third approach was to speak to children and young people themselves; this was in keeping with the Commissioner's statutory remit and to ensure that the research itself adhered to CRC principles and was as current and inclusive as possible. In total, 1064 school children from 27 schools contributed to the research by drawing pictures, writing stories, designing posters or undertaking tasks, which were appropriate to their level of understanding. The sample included children in mainstream schools, special schools and Irish Medium schools. In view of the fact that not all children could be accessed through schools and that some pupils might be unwilling to disclose sensitive information about their lives in a classroom setting, over 100 children and young people were interviewed outside formal school environments.[10]

3. MEASURING THE IMPLEMENTATION OF CHILDREN'S RIGHTS: IDENTIFYING THE STANDARDS

5. In order to carry out the children's rights audit, it was necessary first to identify the standards to be used for this purpose. A growing body of literature now exists on the use of indicators to measure progress in areas such as child health, education and general well-being.[11] Although sophisticated, such models often rely more on

---

9 Arts. 3(2) and 3(3) of Commissioner for Children and Young People (Northern Ireland) Order, 2003.

10 For further details on the methods employed see U. KILKELLY et al, supra (note 8), vii – xiv.

11 A. BEN-ARIEH et al, *Measuring and Monitoring Children's Well-Being*, (The Netherlands: Kluwer Academic Publishers, 2001); S. HANAFIN and A.M. BROOKS, *Report on the Development of a National Set of Child Well-being Indicators in Ireland*, (Dublin: The National Children's Office, 2005) and UNICEF, *Indicators for Global Monitoring of Child Rights*, UNICEF, Division of Evaluation, Policy and Planning, New York, 2005.

quantitative than qualitative data, and generally focus on collating the statistical data necessary to measure the well-being of children on an ongoing basis and in a comparative manner. Such processes do not in themselves make substantive recommendations as to how higher standards of well-being can be secured at least not in the short to medium term.

6. Moreover, while they have many positive and important benefits, they are not necessarily either rights- or CRC-based.[12] As a result, whatever their merits, they do not offer an alternative either to a qualitative study of the extent to which children's rights have been implemented in law, policy and practice or to recommendations arising from this analysis as to what can or should be done to maximise the protection and promotion of children's rights.[13] In this regard, at least, the NICCY research was a relatively unique exercise. Nonetheless, there were broad similarities between the process used in the NICCY research and that of the Committee on the Rights of the Child (the CRC Committee) which operates the CRC's monitoring mechanism.[14] Under the CRC, State Parties are required to submit a periodic report to the CRC Committee outlining the extent to which the Convention has been implemented. The Committee then considers the report and draws conclusions as to the extent of implementation in that State Party while also making recommendations as to how greater implementation can be achieved. Given these similarities, the researchers took, as a starting point, the framework used by the CRC Committee in its monitoring role, and tailored it in order to synchronise the data collection process with Northern Ireland's local and central government structures.[15] Rights were grouped not according to the eight categories used by the Committee, therefore,[16] but under the broadly

---

12 UNICEF has been to the fore in this area. UNICEF, *Indicators for Global Monitoring of Child Rights*, UNICEF, Division of Evaluation, Policy and Planning, New York, 1998, <http://www.childinfo.org/CRind/CRCsumrpt.pdf>; UNICEF, *Implementation handbook for the Convention on the Rights of the Child*, UNICEF, Geneva, 2002; R. LEDOGAR, 'Implementing the Convention on the Rights of the Child through national programmes of action for children', (1993) *International Journal of Children's Rights*, 377–391.

13 See further S. BOYCE, *What kind of indicators can best monitor the delivery of the Children's Strategy?*, (Belfast: Children's Law Centre and Save the Children, 2005), which contrasts the conceptual underpinnings of child well-being indicators and child rights indicators.

14 On the reporting mechanism see U. KILKELLY, 'The UN Committee on the Rights of the Child – an evaluation in the light of recent UK experience', (1996) 8(2) *CFLQ*, 105–120.

15 So, for example, it made sense to group Health, Welfare and Material Deprivation together since Northern Ireland's local government structures were historically based around Health and Social Services Trusts. Likewise, Play and Leisure were addressed separately from Education as they are primarily the responsibility of the Department of Culture, Arts and Leisure, rather than the Department of Education.

16 CRC Committee, *General Guidelines regarding the form and contents of periodic reports* (UN Doc. CRC/C/5, 1996). These group CRC rights into eight categories of General Measures of Implementation; Definition of the Child; General Principles; Civil Rights and Freedoms; Family Environment and Alternative Care; Basic Health and Welfare; Education, Leisure and Cultural Activities, and Special Protection Measures.

similar headings of General Measures of Implementation; Family Life and Alternative Care; Health, Welfare and Material Deprivation; Education; Play and Leisure; and Youth Justice and Policing.[17]

7. Regarding the identification of standards within these groupings, the decision to use the provisions of the CRC was made for a number of reasons. First, it is important that the CRC enjoys legal and high moral standing in international law and that it has been ratified by the UK, which has thereby committing itself to its implementation. Moreover, it was particularly important for the purposes of a Northern Ireland based research project that, as a set of standards, the CRC provisions are relatively uncontroversial. In societies in the process of reconstruction, children's rights often enjoy a "virtually uncontested moral and political legitimacy".[18] Northern Ireland is no exception to this.[19] Thus, for example, the right of the child to health and health care in Article 24 of the CRC, to education in Article 28, and to an adequate standard of living in Article 27 are widely accepted to be of undisputable relevance and significance to children in Northern Ireland, even across Northern Ireland's infamously fractious political divide.[20] Third, the fact that the CRC's provisions are accessible, if not necessarily familiar to a wide range of people facilitated the process of ascertaining the views of those interviewed on the extent to which these rights are protected in Northern Ireland. In this regard, the general principles in Article 3 (best interests of the child as a primary consideration) and in Article 12 (children's right to have their views given due weight) were found to be well known and understood if not within the context of the CRC, then as matters of good practice within various professional contexts.

8. One of the most lauded aspects of the CRC is the wide remit of its provisions and, in particular, the fact that it encompasses civil and political rights, economic, social and cultural rights and humanitarian provisions in a single human rights instrument.[21]

17 These headings were adapted as the research got underway. For example, the heading of Civil Rights and Freedoms was absorbed in General Measures of Implementation and other areas. Education and Play and Leisure were divided into distinct categories to reflect the fact that they were the responsibility of separate Government Departments.

18 J. SLOTH-NIELSEN, 'The Contribution of Children's Rights to the Reconstruction of Society: Some Implications of the Constitutionalisation of Children's Rights in South Africa', (1996) 4 *International Journal of Children's Rights*, 323–344, at 328.

19 The widespread support for the post of Commissioner for Children and Young People, one of the rare successes of the now defunct Northern Ireland Assembly is a good example of this. See U. KILKELLY et al, supra (note 8), vi. However, on the Bill of Rights process see U. Kilkelly, 'Children's Rights in the Bill of Rights: Meeting or Exceeding International Standards', (2001) 52 (3 & 4) *Northern Ireland Legal Quarterly*, 286–295.

20 L. LUNDY, 'Mainstreaming Children's Rights To, In and Through Education in a Society Emerging from Conflict', (2006) *International Journal of Children's Rights.*

21 D. MCGOLDRICK, supra (note 4), 133.

Moreover, its comprehensive nature means that the CRC contains standards applicable in almost all areas of the child's life including school (Arts. 28, 29), family life (Arts. 3, 5, 18, 20, 21) and health and material welfare (Arts. 6, 24, 27). In addition, it contains provisions on vulnerable children and those in particularly difficult circumstances such as children whose parents have separated (Arts 3, 9), children who have been subjected to abuse and exploitation (Arts. 19, 30–34, 37) refugee children (Arts. 7, 8, 10) and children in conflict with the law (Arts. 37, 40). It contains rights of relevance to very young children (such as Arts. 7, 18) as well as those more important to older children (Arts. 13, 14, 17). It refers to the right of families to financial and other support from the state (Arts. 5, 18) and specifies the duties on the state to respect and vindicate the rights of children individually as well as members of a group (for example, Arts. 24 and 29). Overall, the coverage and scope of the CRC in recognising the rights of children and young people and setting out how they are to be both promoted and protected is unrivalled in terms of their comprehensive nature, international and national standing and relevance. For the research team, the scope of the CRC and the breadth of individual provisions was undoubtedly its most useful asset in the auditing process, insofar as it provided the researchers with standards across almost all aspects of children's lives which were widely-supported, relevant and easily understood.

9. At the same time, the process of identifying the standards and using them to evaluate the extent to which children's rights are ignored and underplayed in Northern Ireland exposed the inadequacy of some of the CRC's standards. While the broad wording of some of the individual provisions provides flexibility in terms of their application, it is clear that this allows governments some discretion to avoid the legal commitment to their implementation.[22] In measuring this implementation, gaps in the content, vagueness in its provisions and internal contradictions between its standards mean that some CRC provisions were not helpful or meaningful for auditing purposes. Other standards simply reflect a poor or low level of protection. For example, Article 23 of the CRC recognises the right of a mentally or physically disabled child to enjoy a full and decent life, in conditions which ensure dignity, promote self-reliance and facilitate the child's active participation in the community, a provision which is not only recognizably vague but places an emphasis on "welfare rather than rights".[23] Moreover, in accordance with Article 23(2), States Parties: "recognise the right of the disabled child to special care and shall encourage and ensure the extension, subject to available resources, to the eligible child and those responsible for his or her

---

[22] A. AN-NA'IM, 'Cultural transformation and normative consensus on the best interests of the child', (1994) *International Journal of Law and the Family*, 52–71 at 63; M. KING, 'Children's Rights as Communication: Reflections on Autopoietic Theory and The United Nations Convention', (1994) 57 *MLR*, 385–401 at 322–323.

[23] M. FREEMAN, 'The Future of Children's Rights', (2000) 14 *Children and Society*, 277–293 at 283.

care, of assistance for which application is made and which is appropriate to the child's condition and to the circumstances of the parents or others caring for the child".

Article 23 appears to contain more limitations than any other CRC provision and for this reason it is recognised to be grossly inadequate in terms of articulating the rights of children with disabilities to education, including special needs education, specialised health care and independent living.[24] Moreover, nothing in the CRC captures the complaint made during the NICCY research by children attending special schools about the fact that their school buses were painted yellow. The children described the stigmatising effect of the journey to school in the "banana" or "custard" bus, an intervention justified by the authorities on safety grounds. As one girl told the NICCY team: "*It is too slow the banana bus ... we are embarrassed on that bus. We hide under the seats*".[25]

10. Similarly, the broad and vague nature of Article 3 of the CRC, which provides that the best interests of the child shall be a primary consideration in all decisions taken concerning the child, was also problematic when seeking to monitor its implementation in practice.[26] What is in the child's best interests in any particular area is not defined in the CRC with the result that this principle has the potential to mean all things to all people or, at the very least, that opinions as to whether and to what extent the principle has been implemented in areas such as child care, education and youth justice, vary considerably.[27] For this reason, while the research identifies the extent to which the best interests' principle is set out in law and policy, its application in practice was far more difficult to measure effectively.[28]

11. In some areas, the problem was the tension between the best interests principle and other rights. For example, the research considered the situation of various children at risk in Northern Ireland and noted the conflict that the placing of children in "secure accommodation" creates between what is in the child's best interests and their right

[24] U. Kilkelly, 'Disability and Children: the Convention on the Rights of the Child', in G. Quinn and T. Degener (eds.), *The Current Use and Future Potential of United Nations Human Rights Instruments in the context of Disability*, (New York and Geneva: United Nations, 2002), <http://www.ohchr.org>.

[25] U. Kilkelly et al, supra (note 8), 132.

[26] The concept is regularly described as 'abstract' and 'vague'. A. Azer, 'Modalities of the best Interests Principle in Education', (1994) 8 *International Journal of Law and the Family*, 227–258; J. Herring, 'The Human Rights Act and the welfare principle in family law – conflicting or complementary?', (1999) 11(3) *CFLQ*, 223–235.

[27] This point is also made with respect to the concept of well-being. See S. Hanafin and A.M. Brooks, supra (note 11), 14.

[28] This is reflected in the Concluding Observations of the Committee on the Rights of the Child which consistently limited their recommendation with respect to Art. 3 of the CRC to encouraging states to ensure that the principle is reflected in domestic law and policy. See for example CRC Committee, *Concluding Observations: United Kingdom* (UN Doc. CRC/C/15.Add 188, 2002), paras. 25–26.

to liberty.[29] A further illustration of the tension between a "protection" right and a "participation" right arises in the area of sexual health. The inadequate access to such information by children and young people was raised as a significant concern during the research, which also noted the high rate of teenage pregnancy and sexually transmitted infection among young people in Northern Ireland. However, the fact that the CRC contains no explicit right to this information was problematic and meant that the right had to be implied from the aims of education in Article 29, the right to appropriate information in Article 17 and the state's duty in Article 24(2)(f) to take appropriate measures to develop family planning education.[30]

In other areas there were no rights, explicit or implicit in the CRC, to draw on with respect to the concerns of a group of young people and/or those who work with them. For example, an obvious gap in the Convention is its failure to accord children citizenship rights.[31] The right to vote was one example of this. Many young people criticised the fact that they had to wait until they were 18 to vote. As one girl told the NICCY team: "*I think it is so unfair the way kids do not get a say in political voting. For flip-sake, I know more about politics than some adults.*"[32]

Yet, children do not enjoy the right to vote under the CRC; nor have they any related rights with regard to having their say in the political process.

12. A further difficulty is that the CRC guarantees rights but not in a child-specific manner. This is a particular issue with regard to the civil rights and freedoms, such as the freedom of association and the right to privacy, which are recognised in the Convention in general terms only. The failure to adapt these rights and present them in an age appropriate manner undermines their potential value for children. For example, Article 15 of the CRC guarantees the right to freedom of association in almost identical terms to Article 21 of the International Covenant and Civil and Political Rights and thus does not adapt it any way to take into account the importance for young people to have the right to the company of their friends or peers. Its language bears little resemblance to the rights that young people express concern about – children and young people's right to spend time with their friends and to have their own private, safe space in which to do so.[33] While this may point towards the fact that the concerns or wishes of children – as with adults – are not always capable of being represented in the form or language of rights, it also reflects the fact that the Convention was drafted about, but not by children. In this way, its language is

---

29 U. KILKELLY et al, supra (note 8), 61–63.
30 Ibid., 75–79.
31 M. FREEMAN, 'The Future of Children's Rights', (2000) *Children and Society*, 277–293 at 287.
32 U. KILKELLY et al, supra (note 8), 37–39.
33 This issue was identified as a cross-cutting theme in the research. Ibid., xviii.

unfamiliar and unrepresentative of children and arguably contradicts its own standards. As FREEMAN highlights: "*[the] 1989 Convention was not formulated by children, nor did they have any real input into it. How different a convention in which the child's voice is heard would look is a matter of some controversy. There is, though, not a little irony in having a Convention, which emphasises participatory rights (Art. 12) whilst foreclosing the participation of children in the formulation of rights to be encoded. The next Convention cannot afford to ignore the rights of children.*"[34]

In terms of the NICCY research, however, this problem obstructed the process of auditing implementation of children's rights in very few areas because in most situations, reading CRC provisions together produced a meaningful standard. With respect to children's concerns regarding their right to spend time together, for example, this right can be drawn from the freedom of association in Article 15, the freedom of expression in Article 13 and the right to play and leisure in Article 31. Similarly, as is highlighted below, children's concerns could generally be related directly to the failure to implement their rights under the CRC. Thus, while children complained about aspects of school or home life – areas which may not always be given express protection in the Convention – their principal complaint was frequently one of inadequate consultation, and thereby fell neatly within the sphere of Article 12. The indivisibility of Convention rights strengthened this approach although it does not compensate entirely for its failure to present children's rights in their own terms.

13. While some of the Convention's standards are weak, fortunately, some of these weaknesses can be remedied with reference to standards found elsewhere. For example, in the area of family life and alternative care, particularly secure accommodation, the case-law of the European Court of Human Rights provides detailed and strong guidance as to the rights of children and the corresponding duties of domestic authorities in vindicating those rights.[35] The fact that the European Convention on Human Rights has been incorporated into domestic law of the UK via the Human Rights Act 1998 made the use of these standards even more pertinent. In other areas, reference to the General Comments of the CRC Committee augment the potential of the CRC by providing greater guidance on the obligations of states and the benchmarks to be applied from this perspective. This approach was particularly valuable with regard to measures taken to implement the CRC, particularly with regard to mechanisms to co-ordinate and implement children's rights, the need to develop a national children's strategy which takes a rights approach to children's affairs, to ensure that all those working with children receive training on children's rights and to collect and publish comprehensive, up-to-date and disaggregated data on children's

---

[34] M. FREEMAN, supra (note 23), 282.

[35] Ibid., 61–63.

lives in order to understand and plan more effectively.[36] The Committee's most recent General Comment on implementing children's rights in early childhood would have been invaluable had it been published at the time of the research.[37]

14. Overall, therefore, while the process of translating the CRC into measurable standards was difficult, it was not impossible. Indeed, many CRC provisions contained language that could be applied usefully and meaningfully throughout the auditing process. The contribution of Article 12, the general principle which recognises the child's right both to express him/herself and have these views taken into account in all matters concerning the child, as well as the right to be heard, directly or indirectly in administrative and legal proceedings, was particularly important in this respect. Its unequivocal language and strongly inferred equation with the right to participation made it an effective benchmark against which law, policy and practice could be measured. Moreover, its status as a guiding principle and a provision with which all other provisions must be read supplemented its value in the process meaning that it could usefully be applied in all areas including family life, education, health and welfare and youth justice and policing.

15. In a similar vein, the interrelated and interdependent nature of CRC rights meant that inadequacies in one area could be ameliorated by more positive or equivocal protection elsewhere by reading these provisions together. For example, while Article 31 can be criticised for making only vague provision for the right to play and leisure, when considered with Article 12, Article 2 (non-discrimination) and Article 19 (the right to protection from all forms of abuse, injury and ill-treatment), it allowed conclusions to be drawn about children's equal access to play, their involvement in planning and the availability of safe play spaces – all of which were serious concerns of both children and those working with and for them in Northern Ireland.[38] In this regard, it is apparent that even quite vague provisions can be meaningful when considered in the light of other CRC imperatives. The collective approach advocated and promoted by the CRC Committee helps to translate weak standards into more powerful auditing tools against which law, policy and practice can be measured effectively. For this reason also, the research contains a section on cross-cutting themes

---

36 CRC Committee, *General Comment No. 5: General Measures of Implementation of the Convention on the Rights of the Child* (UN Doc. CRC/GC/2003/5, 2003); U. Kilkelly et al, supra (note 8), 2–18. The Committee's guidance on the 'Aims of Education' in Art. 29 of the CRC was similarly useful. CRC Committee, *General Comment No. 1: The Aims of Education* (UN Doc. CRC/GC/2001/1, 2001).

37 CRC Committee: *General Comment No. 7: Implementing Child Rights in Early Childhood* (UN Doc. CRC/GC/7, 2006).

38 U. Kilkelly et al, supra (note 8), 145–148, 152.

identifying areas where multiple breaches of CRC rights are apparent or where a single situation is leading to the breach of a number of interdependent rights.[39]

4. APPLYING THE STANDARDS IN PRACTICE

16. Once the standards to be used were identified, the second challenge encountered during this research was their application in practice. This related principally to practical difficulties regarding the quality of available data against which to measure the standards, the time scale and scope of the research and the political context in which the conclusions were to be drawn. It is obvious but nonetheless important to state that the process of determining the extent to which children's rights are underplayed and ignored is dependent on the availability of data that is comprehensive, up-to-date and disaggregated in nature. This is recognised by the CRC itself, Article 44 of which requires that reports to the CRC Committee for the purposes of monitoring implementation of children's rights: "contain sufficient information to provide the Committee with a comprehensive understanding of the implementation of the Convention in the country concerned."[40]

The CRC Committee has also expressed support for this demand linking the availability of data to the effectiveness of the implementation process. For example, in its General Comment on Implementation it has noted that the: "*[c]ollection of sufficient and reliable data on children, disaggregated to enable identification of discrimination and/or disparities in the realisation of rights, is an essential part of implementation.*"[41]

Moreover, the quality of available data is also linked to the success of the process of monitoring implementation of the CRC. In this regard, the Committee's Guidelines on reporting request that the reports contain relevant legislative, judicial, administrative and other information, including statistical data, to give the Committee a good basis for its analysis. For example, with respect to the issue of Family Environment and Alternative Care, the Committee's Guidelines request: "*specific detailed statistical data on the number of children per year within the reporting period in each of the following groups, disaggregated by age group, sex, ethnic or national background and rural or urban environment: homeless children, abused or neglected children taken into protective custody, children placed in foster care, children placed in institutional care, children placed through domestic adoption, children entering the country through inter-*

[39] Ibid., xiv–xxi.
[40] Art. 44(2) CRC.
[41] CRC Committee, supra (note 36), para. 48.

country adoption procedures and children leaving the country through inter-country adoption procedures."[42]

Relevant statistical information and indicators are also expressly requested in areas of Education and Leisure,[43] and children in situations of conflict, children in conflict with the law and children in situations of exploitation.[44]

17. The quality of available data in the UK as a whole was criticised by the CRC Committee in 2002 when it recommended that the establishment of: "*a nationwide system whereby disaggregated data are collected on all persons under 18 years for all areas covered by the Convention, including the most vulnerable groups, and that these data are used to assess progress and design policies to implement the Convention.*"[45]

It is clear therefore that the Committee's process of monitoring implementation of the CRC is dependent on the quality of available data on children's lives. Auditing law, policy and practice at domestic level is equally so dependent and despite the Committee's 2002 recommendation, there is still a significant lack of data on many aspects of children and young people's lives in Northern Ireland. In particular, the statistics produced in relation to the state of children and children's rights in Northern Ireland are limited and those that are produced cross different parameters, time scales and ages. While the publication of the Key Indicators of Personal Social Services in Northern Ireland, compiled by the Northern Ireland Statistics and Research Agency and the Social Services Inspectorate, has brought an improvement, there are wide variations across Social Services Trusts. There is no in-built quality control mechanism in either the collection or interpretation of data and in general more needs to be done to mainstream the practice of producing and maintaining up-to-date and disaggregated data across government departments and agencies.

18. In certain areas the lack of both quantitative and qualitative data prevented the assessment of whether children's rights were being underplayed or ignored. In other areas, it limited that assessment. With regard to the former, it was apparent during the research that the lack of disaggregated data on ethnicity – such data are not collected routinely in Northern Ireland – presented a barrier to considering the state of children's rights among children from ethnic minority communities, such as Travellers and non-national children. For example, unlike the rest of the UK, there is no existing data in Northern Ireland on the prevalence of disability in Black and

[42] CRC Committee, supra, (note 16), para. 17.
[43] Ibid., para. 22.
[44] Ibid., para 24.
[45] CRC Committee, supra (note 28), para. 19.

Minority Ethnic communities; nor is there any regional data on the demand for services by members of ethnic minorities making it difficult to assess the implementation of the right to health and health care for these children.[46] The problems of certain groups, such as children from migrant-worker communities, are un-researched and largely unknown. There are also major problems sourcing statistics on child refugees and unaccompanied minors in Northern Ireland, primarily because no single agency compiles all of this information and the British Home Office, which does collect data, does not break the data down either by region or by children who enter the country with families or alone. Similarly, there is a lack of statistics on the number of children whose families are homeless and on the reasons for homelessness among young people. In addition, there is no available data on children who have been sexually exploited and consequently little understanding of the scope of the problem and the services required to address it.

19. The poor quality of data was a hindrance in other areas. For example, with regard to children as victims of crime, data focusing on children's experiences of being victims of crime or their fear of crime are not routinely recorded and the Northern Ireland Crime Survey, for example, categorises a "young person" as being aged 16 to 29.[47] Similarly, the data on the Irish Traveller community is inadequate: for example the Census counts caravans not individuals, leading to under-representation. Moreover, the lack of effective mechanisms for collecting and monitoring data on applications for admission and selection, school suspensions and exclusions, school attendance and educational achievement also frustrated the drawing of conclusions on the Traveller children's right to education.[48] In relation to poverty, there has been persistent failure to agree a methodology for measuring child poverty making it almost impossible to measure progress in this area, particularly with regard to children living in severe poverty. There is no definitive guide to the health of Northern Ireland's children and although a various surveys have been carried out by some Boards and Trusts, there is no child health survey covering young children in particular. Moreover, there is a severe lack of detailed information on the nature and extent of substance misuse among young people and a need for more research in this area to identify gaps in service provision.[49]

20. In many ways, the researchers could sympathise with the CRC Committee to the extent that the lack of data frustrates an accurate and transparent understanding and analysis of the state of children's rights at domestic level. Fortunately, the auditing

---

46 U. KILKELLY et al, supra (note 8), 85.
47 Ibid., 184.
48 Ibid., 126.
49 Ibid., 14–15.

process for this research relied heavily on the testimony of a wide range of children and young people and the people who work with and for them and in many areas this supplemented the information gap, particularly from a qualitative perspective. However, the limited time scale of the project mitigated against the direct involvement of a wide range of adults and children including those marginalised or 'hard to reach' children. Moreover, while the commitment to carry out the research in line with children's rights values – particularly non-discrimination and the child's right to express themselves using age-appropriate media, to be heard and to have their views taken into account – was of central importance, it nonetheless represented a challenge, which necessitated the design, pilot and employment of appropriate methods which allowed children to express their views in keeping with their age and ability. The pilot, for example, took place with 243 children and revealed that, while the children were able to express their views through the chosen methods, whole-class discussion on the central themes of the research was necessary before beginning the task. Ultimately, therefore, while the consultation with children and young people yielded substantial rewards in terms of its insights into the quality of life for Northern Ireland's children and the concerns that they face in vindicating their rights, the collection and analysis of this data was resource-intensive and took longer than anticipated.

5. IDENTIFYING PRIORITIES FOR ACTION

21. While a significant merit of the research was that it entailed the collation of a huge body of evidence across all aspects of children's lives, the sheer volume of material from both primary and secondary sources was a challenge to summarise. The scale of the research meant that it produced a long list of areas where children's rights were being ignored or underplayed in Northern Ireland – a far greater list of problems and issues than it would be reasonable to expect NICCY to tackle in a single strategy. Accordingly, the team's second task was to identify which of the hundreds of issues raised should become priorities for the Commissioner's office. The setting of priorities was one of the most problematic aspects of the research process. In our discussions, objections raised from the philosophical (that there is no hierarchy of human rights and any ranking of identified breaches would undermine this basic notion) to the practical (the lack of existing precedents for doing this). Overriding all of this was a compelling concern about the need to ensure a degree of consistency across the core themes of the research, a difficulty exacerbated by the fact that responsibility for identifying priorities within each of the six core themes was divided amongst individual team members, each with a different subject expertise and disciplinary background. Ultimately, there was consensus that the Commissioner was not in a position to tackle all of the issues that blight children's lives in Northern Ireland, and that prioritisation was thus a necessary "evil". Moreover, having conducted the research, and immersed ourselves in the data, it was clear that we were in a strong position to offer an informed opinion to the Commissioner on the issues that should be included in his first strategy for office.

22. The fact that our remit was to identify areas where children's rights were "ignored or underplayed", provided us with an initial filter. There were several areas where, although existing practice indicated a breach of children's rights, there was evidence that the problem was not being neglected insofar as there was an acceptable and ongoing government initiative aimed at addressing the problem. For example, the content of Northern Ireland's statutory curriculum received widespread criticism from children who thought it did not teach them many of the things which they needed to know.[50] Adults agreed and argued that there should be an explicit focus on specific issues such as children's rights, cultural diversity and sex education. However, at the time of the research, the statutory curriculum was in the course of a major revision, which most interviewees considered would address the existing problems. In instances such as this, we highlighted the proposed policy development, identified any ongoing issues which were yet to be resolved, and advised the Commissioner to retain a "watching brief" to ensure that the proposed policies and initiatives were implemented effectively.

23. In terms of prioritising the other issues, a wide variety of approaches was considered and rejected. For example, one possible approach was to select those areas where there it might be considered easy, quickly or otherwise likely that the Commissioner would enjoy success in remedying the problem identified. A further possible approach was to prioritise those issues which, if tackled by the Commissioner's office, could have added value, such as raising awareness about children's rights or facilitating the voices of children to be heard. It was clear that no particular approach was mandated either by the terms of reference of the research. What was apparent, however, was that guidance as to the setting of priorities could be gleaned from the CRC, in particular, its fundamental principles, the indivisibility of its rights and existing areas identified by its CRC Committee's reporting process. Further assistance was to be gained from adopting an approach to priority setting which, in itself, respected the rights of children, in particular, their right to be heard. With these factors in mind, and in order to ensure that the selection process was as objective and transparent as possible, the team adopted the criteria that are set out below.

---

50 U. KILKELLY et al, supra (note 8), 178–181. Children wanted more time spent on things they enjoyed, such as art and sport, and wanted more information on topics such as drugs and sex education.

5.1. THE ISSUES MOST COMMONLY IDENTIFIED BY CHILDREN AND YOUNG PEOPLE

24. The Commissioner is required by law to have regard to the ascertainable wishes of children and young people in the exercise of his functions in line with Article 12 of the CRC.[51] Consistent with this statutory remit, it was considered appropriate to place particular emphasis on the areas where children and young people felt strongly that their rights were being denied. The children and young people who participated in the research were asked what they considered to be most unfair about family life, school, play and leisure and the area where they lived. They were also asked what they thought about the police and crime. Most of this research took place in school classrooms. Pupils were divided into groups, with each group focusing on one of these core themes. One consequence of this was that we were not able to place the issues raised in an overall rank order across the research themes. We can, however, identify the most frequently raised issues within an individual theme. For example, within schools, the most commonly voiced concern was not having a say in school decisions, particularly in relation to school uniform, the length of the school day, choice in relation to the curriculum and extra-curricular activities. For example, one young person summarised his views this way: "*We need to be able to leave our books in school, have longer lunches and breaks and better sporting equipment. By applying some of the above points to school, it would make school more enjoyable and maybe would encourage kids to stay in school and not go on the beak*[52] *and they would get on better with the teachers*".[53]

The need to have a greater say in decision-making was also one of the most common issues raised by children in relation to their family lives.[54] Other most frequently mentioned issues in this context were: disputes with parents, lack of privacy in the home, and difficulties with siblings. A typical concern was as follows: "*I think parents shout too much and I think they give us too much pressure. I know they try to do their best and sometimes they look after us too much and do not give us too much freedom. They are always worrying. I think children should do what they want but learn from their mistakes in the future*".[55]

When asked about play and leisure, the most significant issue for children and young people was the lack of access to safe and appropriate play and leisure facilities. The

---

51 Commissioner for Children and Young People (NI) Order 2003, Art. 6.

52 The phrase "on the beak" is used in Northern Ireland as slang for truancy.

53 U. Kilkelly et al, supra (note 8), 191.

54 Ibid., 57.

55 Ibid., 57–58.

concerns expressed echoed wider concerns about the state of their area. The quotation which follows is typical of many of the responses we received: "*My area has no playing facilities or anything to do. There are no places where we can play football or just run about and play something else. It is just all roads and nowhere to play. It could be dangerous for young children who want to play and they would go onto the roads and get knocked down and get hurt or even killed! All the facilities are too far away from where we live*".[56]

25. The issues of concern to children in Northern Ireland are similar to those that have been raised by children in other jurisdictions when they are asked about their experience of their rights.[57] However, it is not surprising that many of the responses reflect the fact that children in Northern Ireland have grown up in a society that is characterised by religious divisions and violent conflict. For example, social space in Northern Ireland is religiously segregated to such an extent that young people wearing Celtic or Rangers football shirts can become targets for sectarian attack if they venture into the "wrong" area. Many children expressed a desire for the conflict in Northern Ireland to end, a finding which is significant, particularly as it was generated in response to a question which asked children and young people about unfairness in their lives, and images of the police. Many of these young people remarked that they wanted Catholics and Protestants "to get along" and to "stop fighting with one another".[58]

26. As highlighted above, not all of the issues that were raised by children and young people as examples of unfairness in their lives could be classified as a breach of their rights under the CRC. Two examples illustrate this: a major issue for younger children related to disputes with siblings or the fact that older brothers and sisters were allowed to go to bed at a later time; another complaint concerned the choice of food in school canteens. Although these concerns were not breaches of rights in themselves, were indicative of a breach of other Convention rights. In particular, the children's complaints suggested a possible breach of Article 12 of the CRC, in that their views may not have been given due weight in a matter affecting them. In most cases, therefore, the issues of key concern to children and young people in the NICCY research could be linked directly to a breach of one or more provisions of the CRC and, as a result, those issues that were most commonly identified by children and young people under each of the core themes were then translated into a priority for action. So, for example, in relation to the concerns above, the report recommends that

---

56 Ibid., 202.

57 See, for example, V. Morrow, "'We are people too': Children and Young People's Perspectives on Children's Rights and Decision-Making in England", (1999) 7 *International Journal of Children's Rights*, 149–170.

58 U. Kilkelly et al, supra (note 8), 244–245.

NICCY works to ensure that: children's views are given due weight in school, increased efforts are made to support positive parenting initiatives, the right to safe play is given a higher profile through the development of a Northern Ireland play strategy, and that there is a specific strategy to address issues of community segregation and to promote tolerance.

5.2. EGREGIOUS BREACHES OF CHILDREN'S RIGHTS

27. There are some issues that may affect very few children but which constitute a fundamental threat to children's lives, safety and physical and mental well-being. Even though these issues were unlikely to emerge in the research conducted with children in school, the team agreed to prioritise these egregious breaches of children's rights, placing a particular emphasis on instances where children were being exposed to physical and/or mental harm. The rationale for this derives from Article 6 of the CRC which requires states parties to ensure to the maximum extent possible the survival and development of the child. The Committee has identified this as one of the general principles of the Convention and has stated that it expects States to interpret "development" in its broadest sense as a holistic concept, embracing the child's physical, mental, spiritual, moral, psychological and social development.[59] Many of the key issues that were identified under this criterion are particular to the Northern Ireland context and are by-products of the legacy of the violent conflict and what continues to be an "uneasy" peace'.[60] These include the sectarian harassment of children travelling to school, the use of plastic baton rounds as a means of crowd control and paramilitary punishment beatings meted out to children and young people alleged to have engaged in anti-social behaviour.[61] Also prioritised under this criterion was the issue of bullying in school, a concern raised in 14% of the submissions in relation to their school lives.[62] Bullying by teachers also emerged as a key issue across a range of focus groups. In the words of one NGO worker, which reflect the views of a number of professionals: "*Some teachers' attitudes to some children are disadvantaging those children and I am putting that in polite terms. At the other end, they are abusive to children; they are putting them down, they are reducing their self esteem*".[63]

A small number of interviewees also queried whether the extent of bullying in school could in some way be related to the high incidence of violence and harassment which

---

59 CRC Committee, supra (note 36), para. 11.

60 B. Rowan, *The Armed Peace: Life and Death after the Ceasefires*, (Edinburgh: Mainstream Publishing, 2003).

61 U. Kilkelly et al, supra (note 8), 256.

62 Ibid., 182.

63 Ibid.,184.

pervades Northern Ireland society. While a causal connection of this kind would be difficult to establish with any degree of certainty, it is apparent that the Northern Ireland conflict has had a significant detrimental impact on children's physical and mental well-being in a myriad of ways and that addressing these should be a priority for the Commissioner.

5.3. INCOMPATIBILITY WITH ONE OF THE CRC'S FUNDAMENTAL GENERAL PRINCIPLES

28. Instances where law, policy or practice was incompatible with the CRC's three other cross-cutting provisions – Articles 2, 3 and 12 – were also prioritised.[64] This criterion was chosen in recognition of the core nature of the CRC's guiding principles and in particular the fact that their implementation is widely accepted to be fundamental to the realisation of all rights.[65] For the reasons described earlier, the utility of Article 3 in this process turned out to be questionable: it is just too broadly worded to be used to rank different issues all of which have been identified as potential breaches of rights (and are *per se* not in children's best interests). The principle of non-discrimination in Article 2 was, however, valuable across the research project and ultimately led us to the conclusion that there were two groups of children – children with disabilities and Irish Travellers – who were particularly underserved across the core themes of the research.[66] In practice, however, it was Article 12 which emerged as one of the most significant crosscutting themes of the research. The conclusion that Northern Ireland does not listen to its children or, worse, that it affords them only minimalist, tokenistic opportunities to participate and engage with adults was a theme which cut across all areas of the research. There was no other single issue that was so commonly and widely identified by children and young people and the adults who work with and for them. One interviewee, who worked with disaffected young people, described it like this: "*Some of the young people I have met are really disheartened by life, you know. Really broken. They feel that they live in a community that does not listen to them, in a family that does not listen to them, in a system that did not listen to them and now they come to us and they think, what would you listen to us for? I think that is a big issue, self esteem and just being valued as a citizen or a member of your community*".[67]

64 The fourth general principle, Art. 6 CRC, was the focus of the second criterion – egregious breaches of children's rights.
65 CRC Committee, supra (note 36), para. 12.
66 U. KILKELLY et al, supra (note 8), xix–xx.
67 Ibid., xxiii.

Interviewees identified a need for a fundamental attitudinal shift among adults who hold the balance of power in the relationship dynamic with young people. As one NGO representative put it: "*this is not just about raising awareness of rights*" but also "*about creating cultures of understanding*".[68] In the light of this, the report recommends that NICCY take a leading role in promoting the right of all children to be heard and have their views taken into account in individual decisions as well as law, policy and in the political system generally.[69]

5.4. INSTANCES WHERE THE BREACH HAD THE KNOCK-ON EFFECT OF UNDERMINING CHILDREN'S ENJOYMENT OF OTHER RIGHTS

29. While it is widely accepted that all human rights are indivisible, interrelated and interdependent, there are certain fundamental rights which, when denied, can have a significant negative impact on children's enjoyment of their other rights. In recognition of this, and the fact that efforts to secure compliance in these areas could reap rewards across children's lives, the team decided to prioritise issues of this nature. Thus, the justification for this criterion rests with the strategic potential of addressing the issues in question as much as the ripple effects of non-compliance. For example, the lack of adequate provision for children with special educational needs was prioritised under this criterion. Many interviewees expressed concern about the failure to identify and make adequate provision for children with learning difficulties and warned of the knock-on effects of this in terms of children's intellectual development, self-esteem and mental well-being, and the risk of disaffection and exclusion from school.[70] In a similar vein, the fact that many children in Northern Ireland were living in poverty was prioritised, not simply on the basis that it was indicative of a breach of children's right of access to social security benefits under Article 26 or an adequate standard of living under Article 27, but because of the significant knock-on effect of this on children's rights to health, education and safety. The relative impoverishment of Northern Ireland compared with its UK and European counterparts is well documented.[71] The research identifies some of the key consequences of economic deprivation and highlights the fact that the targeted attempts by the UK Government

---

68 Ibid., xx.

69 Ibid., 51.

70 Ibid., 166–170.

71 L. Adelman, S. Middleton and K. Ashworth, *Britain's Poorest Children: Severe and Persistent Poverty and Social Exclusion*, (London: Save the Children, 2003); P. Hillyard, G. Kelly, E. McLaughlin, D. Patsios and M. Tomlinson, *Bare Necessities – Poverty and Social Exclusion in Northern Ireland: key findings*, (Belfast: Democratic Dialogue, 2003).

to tackle child poverty via back-to-work schemes and provision of child care places, have not been extended to Northern Ireland.

5.5. CONCERNS RAISED BY THE CRC COMMITTEE IN ITS CONCLUDING OBSERVATIONS ON THE UK IN 2002, WHICH HAVE NOT YET BEEN REMEDIED ADEQUATELY

30. The report prioritises a range of concerns highlighted by the CRC Committee in its periodic reports on the UK where the situation remained unchanged at the time of the research. For example, in 1995 the CRC Committee's response to the UK's first report expressed grave concern about the failure to protect the rights of Irish Traveller children.[72] In 2002, the Committee again expressed concern about the unequal enjoyment of a range of rights by Traveller children and recommended that a comprehensive strategy be developed with specific and well-targeted actions aimed at eliminating all forms of discrimination including racism.[73] The NICCY research confirmed that the impact of racism, exclusion and discrimination against Traveller children cuts across all areas of their lives and there that their rights are still being violated in the areas of education, poverty, health care, housing and family support.[74] The recommendations of a government working group established to address these issues in 1999 had been greeted positively within the Irish Traveller sector.[75] However, very few of its recommendations had been realised at the time of the research. One NGO representative commented: "*When Irish Travellers were chosen as a priority group under the PSI Initiative, there was a lot of optimism... Five years on, the social and economic conditions faced by most Travellers have at best stood still, and for many have actually got worse – and the optimism about government's intentions has evaporated*".[76]

31. While the Committee identified a number of specific concerns in relation to Northern Ireland in 2002, only one of these – the need for a prohibition on the use of corporal punishment in schools – has since been addressed.[77] Other concerns highlighted by the Committee, which have not yet been resolved fully, include: the

---

72 CRC, supra (note 28).

73 Ibid., para. 23.

74 U. KILKELLY et al, supra (note 7), xix –xx.

75 Office of the First Minister and Deputy First Minister, *A Response to the Promoting Social Inclusion Group on Travellers,* (Belfast: OFMDFM, 1999).

76 U. KILKELLY et al, supra (note 8), xix.

77 The Education and Libraries (NI) Order 2003 introduced a prohibition on the use of corporal punishment in independent schools.

high levels of religious segregation and low levels of religious integration in school,[78] the continued use of plastic baton rounds as a means of riot control, and the need to review emergency legislation. While many of these issues might have been prioritised under the previous four criteria, it was considered important that the Commissioner should be seen to actively support the work of the CRC Committee as the CRC's chief mechanism for enforcement and implementation.

32. These five criteria were applied by the team to select the issues that would be translated into priorities and recommendations. While the criteria do not have any official status beyond the research, they played a valuable role by providing a workable and objective guide for approaching the difficult task in hand. In practice, many of the issues identified fell within more than one of the criteria. So, for example, the issue of bullying was identified as a key concern by many children, constitutes a threat to children's physical and mental health, is a particular issue for Traveller children, children with disabilities and young gay and lesbians, has potential knock-on effects on children's enjoyment of other rights, including their mental health, and was raised as a concern by the CRC Committee on a UK-wide basis in 2002. The fact that issues often fell within one or more of the criteria could be seen to be a testament to the underlying rationale of the framework and therefore its credibility. However, in the end, the best indicator of the value of the criteria lay in the fact that they enabled the team to produce a list of priorities, which were not only evidenced-based and rationally defensible, but were also sufficiently specific to be of practical use to the Commissioner in determining his priorities for office.[79]

6. CONCLUSION

33. The NICCY research provides a case study of the CRC in action. The experience of using the standards to critique law, policy and practice on the basis of the evidence available adds support to the view that the CRC is an important set of international standards which is comprehensive and detailed but not without flaw. Children deserve that the gaps in its protection be addressed, but in the meantime, as the NICCY research shows, the CRC, together with other instruments, can be honestly and imaginatively used to measure the enjoyment of children's rights in a variety of contexts. It is also clear from this research that the Convention will not be fully

78 Only 5% of children in Northern Ireland attend "integrated" schools which have a religious balance in their intake. The vast majority of children are educated in schools, which are predominantly Catholic or predominantly Protestant.

79 The Commissioner used the research as the key evidence base in setting his priorities for office. See, Northern Ireland Commissioner for Children and Young People, *Corporate Plan 2005–2009* (Belfast: NICCY, 2005).

effective until such time as there are reliable and systematic ways of establishing what is happening in children's lives. In many ways, the study undertaken by the NICCY team enjoyed similarities, positive and negative, with the reporting process administered by the CRC Committee. The inadequacy of available data and the relatively short time scale within which the work had to be completed combined to frustrate the drawing of conclusions at times. Like the Committee's process, however, the NICCY research has already been found to have benefits beyond its original remit and conception. In addition to its original material, which gives a unique and comprehensive insight into the lives of children in Northern Ireland, it also gathers together in the one place a wide variety of literature and other research on children and their rights. Moreover, the many conclusions and recommendations made in the NICCY research have publicised the need for government action in a variety of areas, including those beyond the Commissioner's control. In this way, the report offers NGOs and others material that can be used not just for lobbying purposes but also to inform the next periodic report to the CRC Committee.

34. Finally the research project provides a working example of the need for and benefits of consulting children and young people about their experience of their rights. In 2005, the CRC Committee encouraged states to invest in research into children's lives and "*to develop national and local capacities from a rights-based perspective*".[80] The NICCY research provides a working model for those wishing to use the CRC to undertake children's rights-focused research elsewhere. A key lesson, which might be drawn from this process is that those wishing to establish what is happening in children's lives must take the time and make the effort to talk to children and young people directly. Only children can provide a direct insight into the dissonance between law and policy and the way in which their rights are being implemented in practice. Children not only have a direct and authentic insight into the issues that affect their enjoyment of their rights, but they are forthcoming when given appropriate opportunities to set out their concerns. As one girl told the NICCY team: "*It is our world too and if we do not say anything about it, who will?*"

[80] CRC, supra (note 40).

STRENGTHENING THE PROMOTION, PROTECTION AND FULFILMENT OF CHILDREN'S RIGHTS IN THE AFRICAN CONTEXT

JULIA SLOTH-NIELSEN[1]

1. INTRODUCTION

1. As it will be illustrated below, there have arguably been significant advances in the legal framework underpinning the fulfilment of children's rights in the African context in recent times, not only at the regional level, but also domestically and via constitutional reforms. This paper, therefore, has three main objectives. First, it intends to introduce the African system of children's rights protection and give an overview of recent developments, successes and challenges.[2] Second, it will reflect on the constitutionalisation of children's rights principles in African constitutions, with a particular emphasis on recent developments. With the South African developments as a backdrop, the significance of the constitutional protection of children's rights will also be examined. The third section will reflect on ongoing endeavours to domesticate international and regional children's rights principles in African municipal legal systems, providing concrete examples of significant trends, advances and strengths in processes undertaken or completed thus far. A concluding section will reflect on the extent to which the initiatives described above take forward the rights of the African child.

2. THE AFRICAN SYSTEM OF HUMAN RIGHTS PROTECTION

2. Traditionally, the needs of children have variedly been recognised and responded to often within the realm of "charity". The history and the process that culminated

---

[1] This work builds on a report done for Save the Children Sweden, (Kenya Office) on the draft Constitution of Sudan in June 2005.

[2] As other papers address this area as well, the review provided here will necessarily be limited.

in the adoption of the United Nations Convention on the Rights of the Child (hereafter the CRC or the Convention) in 1989 produced a global consensus on the need to delineate a specific code of enforceable rights for children within the broader human rights system.

3. It was in order to give the CRC a specific application within the African context that the African Charter on the Rights and Welfare of the Child (hereafter the ACRWC or the Charter) – the first regional treaty on the human rights of the child – was adopted by the OAU (now the African Union or the AU) Heads of State and Government on 11 July 1990.[3] However, although the African countries were overall speedy in their accession to the International Children's Rights Treaty and the CRC, State Parties have been slow to ratify the ACRWC, and it was not until 1999 that the fifteenth country ratified the ACRWC, thereby allowing the treaty to enter into force.

Subsequent to the coming into force of the ACRWC, the monitoring body of the Charter, the African Committee, was established when its first 11 members were elected in July 2001 during the 37th Session of the Assembly of Heads of State and Government in Lusaka, Zambia. The African Committee had its inaugural meeting in May 2002.[4]

4. It is perhaps significant for those more versed in the powers and the procedures of the UN Committee on the Rights of the Child (hereafter the CRC Committee) that the African Committee is accorded a far wider range of powers than the international

---

[3] One of the reasons for a separate African Charter on the Rights and Welfare of the Child was that during the drafting process of the Convention on the Rights of the Child (CRC) Africa was underrepresented. Only Algeria, Morocco, Senegal and Egypt participated meaningfully. Furthermore specific provisions on aspects peculiar to Africa were not sufficiently addressed in the UN instrument. Some of the peculiarities of the African situation omitted from the CRC were identified as: the situation of children living under, the then prevailing apartheid regime in South Africa, practices and attitudes having a negative effect on the life of the girl child and widespread harmful cultural practices in African society such as female genital mutilation. Other issues not considered by the CRC were problems of displaced persons arising from internal conflicts, the African conception of the community's responsibilities and duties and most pertinently, the particularly difficult socio-economic conditions of the continent.

[4] See, in general, D. Olowu, 'Protecting Children's Rights in Africa: A Critique of the African Charter on the Rights and Welfare of the Child', (2002) 10 *The International Journal of Children's Rights*, 127; D. Chirwa, 'The merits and demerits of the African Charter on the Rights and Welfare of the Child', (2002) 10 *International Journal on Children's Rights*, 157; A. Lloyd, 'Evolution of the African Charter on the Rights and Welfare of the Child and the African Committee of Experts: Raising the Gauntlet', (2002) 10 *International Journal on Children's Rights*, 179; A. Lloyd, 'Recent Developments: The Second Ordinary Session of the African Committee of Experts', (2003) 3 *African Human Rights Journal*, 31; M. Gose, *The African Charter on the Rights and Welfare of the Child*, (Bellville, South Africa: Community Law Centre, University of the Western Cape, 2002).

body. Article 41 of the ACRWC provides that in order to promote and protect the rights enshrined in the Charter, the Committee has the powers, amongst others:

- to collect and document information;
- to commission inter-disciplinary assessments of situations of African problems in the field of the rights and welfare of the child;
- to organise meetings, to encourage national and local institutions concerned with the rights and welfare of the child and where necessary, to give its views and make recommendations to governments;
- to interpret the provisions of the ACRWC at the request of a State Party, the AU or any other person or institution recognised by the AU.

Article 43(1) provides for the receipt by the African Committee of State Reports on the measures they have adopted to give effect to the provisions of the Charter.[5] Article 45(1) allows for the possibility of communications being made to the African Committee of Experts by individuals, non-governmental organisations, State or other organisations investigating violations of the provisions of the Charter. As it has been mainly through individual complaints that the potential of the United Nations (UN) and regional human rights instruments has been realised, particularly in the African system of human rights development, it is arguable that the power of the Committee to receive communications can be an invaluable tool to deal with individual complaints in order to strengthen the protection of children's rights on the continent. Finally, the Committee has the power to issue General Comments and to undertake investigations and studies.[6]

5. As indicated above, the African Committee is relatively new as it was established only in July 2001 and had its inaugural meeting in May 2002. It should be noted, however, that, although the African Committee is still a nascent institution whose work has mainly been hampered by financial constraints,[7] it has registered some modest achievements in the first four years of its existence. It has since its establishment held seven meetings during which it has amongst other things:

---

5 These reports are due within two years of entry into force, and thereafter every three years. According to the Guidelines for Initial Reports of State Parties, States that have already submitted reports to the CROC may use elements of that report for the report that it submits to the African Committee. The report may then highlight the areas of progress made in implementing rights that are specific to the ACRWC.

6 Arts. 45(2) and (3).

7 Personal Communication, Prof V. Dankwa, retired chairperson of the African Commission on Human and People's rights and former Special Rapporteur on Prison in Africa, October 2005. See also, Chapter 6 'Children's Rights in the OAU', in R. Murray, *Human Rights in Africa*, (Cambridge University Press, 2004).

- Adopted its rules of procedure.
- Developed guidelines for preparation of initial reports by State Parties on the implementation of the Charter.
- Developed, together with the Commission of the African Union, a reporting schedule indicating the dates by which State Parties should have submitted their initial reports.
- Initiated partnerships with civil society organisations as well as other relevant institutions working in the area of Children's Rights.
- Held thematic discussions on key issues and problems adversely affecting the rights and welfare of children namely the question of children and armed conflict and the impact of HIV/AIDS, poliomyelitis and malaria on children.
- Selected and disseminated annual themes for the celebration of the Day of the African Child.

The Committee has also undertaken advocacy missions to selected State Parties of the AU to lobby for the ratification and implementation of the Charter. In addition, a fact-finding mission to Northern Uganda was conducted in August 2005 resulting in a report, which made clear recommendations for follow-up.

Since December 2005, six new Committee members have been sworn in. There are nevertheless indications that this Committee, as it now stands, will achieve more than it's predecessor, as the first two country reports have been received (from Egypt and Mauritius) and one communication from Uganda has been filed for consideration by the Committee. Additionally, the process of recruiting a Secretary for the Committee has been finalised, and funds from UNICEF have been approved for assisting the Secretariat with a Senior Legal Officer and an Administrative Secretary; in short, there appears to be renewed optimism for improving the Committee's outputs.

A further encouraging factor is the existence of the increasing support from children's rights NGOs[8] for the work of the Committee to be developed, and for Committee members to be capacitated to fulfil greater role in promoting and fulfilling their children's rights mandate. A handful of INGOs have also attended recent meetings, such as Amnesty International, Save the Children, UNICEF and the International Red Cross.[9]

---

8 Such as the Institute of Human Rights and Democratisation in Africa, the African Child Policy Forum, African Network for the Prevention and Protection Against Child Abuse and Neglect, and the Children's Rights Project of the Community Law Centre which will have sent a delegate to the present meeting.

9 R. Murray, supra (note 7), 173.

Certain developments within the AU structure further bolster the optimism regarding any future contribution the Committee could make in the promotion and protection of the African child. These developments include the emerging work of the Pan-African Parliament and NEPAD which are gaining momentum, and in which processes human rights issues are playing a central role.[10]

6. It is instructive to mention the Protocol to the African Charter on Human and Peoples' Rights on the Establishment of an African Court on Human and Peoples' Rights, which entered into force on 25 January 2004, and which will complement the protective mandate of the African Commission on Human and Peoples' Rights, the quasi-judicial implementation body of the African Charter on Human and Peoples' Rights (African Charter) of 1987. The African Committee of Experts on the Rights and Welfare of the Child has standing before this new Court. As a judicial organ, which will be able to pronounce binding judgments, the Court offers the Committee a unique opportunity to further its overall mandate relating to the promotion, protection and fulfilment of children's rights in Africa through the Court's channels.

7. Having noted this, it has been stated that in regard to the prior work relating to children's rights of the overarching parent body, the OAU/AU, the focus has mainly been concerned with health, and in particular the need for measures to reduce infant mortality as well as the impact of HIV/Aids on the continent.[11] Improved access to primary education has been advocated for, and States have been urged to ratify ILO Convention 182 (1999) concerning the Elimination of the Worst Forms of Child Labour. Unsurprisingly, much attention has been devoted to the recognition of the impact of conflicts on children. MURRAY points out though, "*while it cannot be said that the OAU/AU has ignored the position of children, its approach does not evidence a coherent philosophy...*",[12] and mentions a rather ad hoc approach to children's rights. However, she links this to what she discerns as a welfare approach towards the child within the context of the family: "*...The OAU appears to have focused on other matters around development and welfare, moving the focus away from the individual rights of the child*". From an Africanist perspective, however, we would argue that this orientation is entirely appropriate, and that an undue emphasis on individual and justiciable rights masks the developmental gains that can be achieved through a concerted focus on child well-being at the institutional level. Indeed, the child's role

10 Meanwhile, the Protocol to the African Charter on Human and Peoples' Rights on the Rights of Women in Africa (adopted on 11 July 2003, and which entered into on force 25 November 2005) is also worthy of note as a result of the special opportunity it creates for promoting the rights and protection of the girl child.

11 R. MURRAY, supra (note 7).

12 R. MURRAY, supra (note 7), 181.

within the family and community is central to emerging African concepts within the children's rights sphere, as will be further explained below.

8. Although the children's rights work of African institutions is hampered by both the enormity of the challenges to fulfilment of children's rights, and a shortage of resources – administrative and research support, funds for site visits and so forth – it is nevertheless apparent that a renewed energy and vision for African children's rights has begun to emerge. This is evident not only from the increased visibility of the African Committee, and the recent favourable developments within the AU, however it is also apparent from the recognition of children's rights in the constitutional and domestic context in many African countries, as will be shown next.

3. CHILDREN'S RIGHTS IN AFRICAN CONSTITUTIONS

9. Modern constitutions generally spell out the commitments that democratic governments make towards the establishment of good society. These might include values such as the promotion of human dignity, freedom and equality. The standards reflect the fundamental ideals and aspirations that animate the three branches of government (judicial, legislative and executive), inasmuch as they set about defining the division and exercise of power. Charters of human rights spelling out the limits of state power vis-à-vis ordinary citizens are regarded as essential adjuncts to constitutional democracy, in that they constrain the unbridled exercise of power by Parliaments (replacing the theory of absolute parliamentary sovereignty) and serve to regulate the exercise of power by public bodies. In addition, as Davis and Cheadle point out, modern constitutions also reflect values and principles, generally stating the commitments that democratic governments make towards the establishment of good society.[13] This dimension obviously holds significant potential for the furtherance of children's rights via constitutional incorporation. The issue of justiciability of rights via judicial action is also worthy of discussion and is touched upon later in this paper.

10. Given this as the backdrop, many African countries have enacted[14] new constitutions during the last decade of the twentieth century. In addition to enshrining most internationally recognised human rights, the bill of rights of these constitutions have a commonality in that the majority have singled out children for special

---

13 D. Davis and H. Cheadle, *South African Constitutional Law: The Bill of Rights*, (Cape Town: Juta and Co, 2004), 2nd ed., 1.

14 Or undertaken amendments to existing constitutions, as in the case of Tunisia and Morocco.

protection, in addition to the rights that children may enjoy otherwise in the bill of rights.

No fewer than 34 constitutions[15] have been identified, all either adopted or amended since 1990,[16] which contain a children's rights provision. Several are of very recent origin, such as the Constitution of the Democratic Republic of the Congo, which was enacted on 18 February 2006 and the Constitution of Sudan, which was enacted in late 2005, while two others – that of Zambia and Kenya – both of which were proposed in 2005, are still in draft form.

3.1. DEFINITION OF A CHILD

11. Starting with concrete substantive examples drawn from African experiences, an obvious point of departure is the definition of a child as a person aged under 18 years. Although many African constitutions do not define a child, and indeed refer variously to "minors", young persons, juvenile offenders, infants,[17] and in the case of the Constitution of Sudan, to youths,[18] these are indefinite concepts and raise the very question as to who exactly is affected by the particular rights. In particular, some constitutions refer to the different notions mentioned above within the same constitution[19] and sometimes, for instance, in the case of the Constitution of Sudan,[20] within the same provision, which further heightens the confusion as to who is entitled to the specific rights in question.

---

15 Algeria, Republic of Angola, Republic of Benin, Burkina Faso, Republic of Burundi (transitional), Republic of Cameroon, Republic of Cape Verde, Central African Republic, Republic of Chad, Comoros, Republic of Cote D'Ivoire, Democratic Republic of the Congo, The Arab Republic of Egypt, Equatorial Guinea, Eritrea, Federal Democratic Republic of Ethiopia, Gabonese Republic, Second Republic of the Gambia, Republic of Ghana, Second Republic of Guinea, Lesotho, Republic of Madagascar, Republic of Malawi, Republic of Namibia, Fifth Republic of Niger, Sao Tome and Principe, Republic of Senegal, Republic of Seychelles, Republic of South Africa, South Sudan, Republic of Sudan, Fourth Republic of Togo, Republic of Uganda, draft Constitution of the Republic of Zambia, and the draft Constitution of Kenya, which was the subject of a referendum in November 2005, which failed to adopt the draft, contained an elaborate children's rights clause.

16 I.e. following the adoption by the United Nations of the CRC in 1989. The Constitution of Senegal also explicitly affirms adherence to the CRC in its preamble, which legally speaking could serve as an interpretive guide to the relevant provisions of the constitution.

17 Constitution of Niger Art. 18 and the Constitution of Togo Art. 31.

18 Art. 14, entitled Children, Youth and Sport.

19 For example, see Constitution of Senegal, Arts. 20 and 21.

20 Art. 14 Constitution of Sudan.

However, the South African Constitution, that of Ghana and the recent Constitution of the Democratic Republic of the Congo[21] define children along the same lines as the CRC and the ACRWC, namely as persons under the age of 18 years. This is definitely the preferred option, as is the specific use of the word child, rather than other less precise terms.[22]

This approach is further notable when seen against the traditional African view of children as persons who are still maturing into responsible adulthood.[23] In many African customary laws, the end of childhood was linked to factors such as rites of passage, to marriage or the activities a person would undertake[24] than being predicated on the fact of specific numerical age.

12. An additional noticeable trend in some African constitutions is the establishment of various age thresholds at less than 18 years for specific issues. Four examples are: the transitional Constitution of the Republic of Burundi,[25] in which (Art. 41) the age at which children should be separated from adults whilst in detention is pegged at 16 years (rather than 18 as specified in the 1955 UN Standard Minimum Rules for the Treatment of Prisoners, the CRC and various other documents). Another is to be found in the Constitution of the second Republic of the Gambia (which entered into force in 1997), which specifies that "children under the age of 16 years shall be entitled to be protected from economic exploitation and shall not be employed in or required to perform work that is likely to be hazardous or to interfere with their education or be harmful to their development" (Art. 29(3)). The 1990 Constitution of Namibia, under Article 20(3), also provides that "children shall not be allowed to leave school until they have completed their primary education or have attained the age of 16 years, which ever is sooner…." Finally, the Constitution of Uganda defines the child as "persons under the age of sixteen years" (Arts. 34(4) and (5)) for protecting children from social or economic exploitation.

This approach is clearly in conflict with Article 2 of the ACRWC, which defines a child as any human being under the age of eighteen years and, unlike the CRC, contains

21 The wording of an unofficial translation of Art. 41 reads, "a child means every human being, without distinction between male and female, who has not yet reached the age of eighteen years". <http://hrw.org/reports/2005/drc0406/9.htm>.

22 In stark contrast from this approach, the Constitution of Malawi, under Art. 14 defines a child as "...persons under sixteen years of age".

23 G. Odongo, "The Domestication of International Law Standards on the Rights of the Child with Specific Reference to Juvenile Justice in the African Context" (unpublished LLD dissertation, University of the Western Cape, 2005), 151.

24 B. Rwezaura, 'Competing Images of Childhood in the Social and Legal Systems of Contemporary sub-Saharan Africa', (1998) 12(3) *International Journal of Law, Policy and the Family*, 253–278.

25 Adopted in 2001. See also, the Constitutions of Namibia and Uganda in this regard.

no proviso to the effect that the definition of a child may be adjusted to accommodate laws under which a child attains majority at an earlier age.[26] Under the ACRWC, there is no room for deviating from the principle that special protection must be offered to all persons less than eighteen years of age.

The above examples of ages set at lower than 18 are, however, in the minority, and it is clear that the overwhelming tendency is to extend the protection by children's rights to all children aged below 18 years.

3.2. CIVIL AND POLITICAL RIGHTS

13. Both the CRC and the ACRWC contain civil and political rights. These provisions are not only substantive, but also include numerous procedural issues. Accordingly, many African constitutions include an array of civil and political rights for children. Key amongst these are:

- the right to equality (Art. 2 of CRC and Art. 3 of ACRWC)[27]
- the right to life (Art. 6 of CRC and Art. 5 of ACRWC)[28]
- the right from birth to a name and nationality (Art. 7 of CRC and Art. 6 of ACRWC),[29] and the right to birth registration[30] (of particular concern in the African context)
- children's rights to know and be cared for by their parents (Art. 5 of CRC and Art. 19 of ACRWC)[31]

---

26 D. Olowu, 'Protecting Children's Rights in Africa: A Critique of the African Charter on the Rights and Welfare of the Child', (2002) 10 *The International Journal of Children's Rights*, 127 at 130.

27 Constitution of Burkina Faso (Art. 23) states, amongst other things, that children are equal in rights and duties within their familial relations and that their parents have the natural right and the duty to bring up and educate their children. Parents must give their children respect and assistance. See also, the Constitution of the Republic of Cameroon, which provides that "there shall be no discrimination towards children born out of wedlock, nor any discriminatory designation as to their parentage"; see also, the Constitution of Malawi, which states that "all children, regardless of the circumstances of their birth, are entitled to equal treatment before the law"; see also, the draft Constitution of Kenya, which did not survive a November 2005 referendum, which specifically also refers to equality of treatment of children born in or out of wedlock.

28 Constitution of the Federal Republic of Ethiopia.

29 Constitution of the Federal Republic of Ethiopia, Constitution of South Africa, Constitution of the Second Republic of the Gambia, Constitution of Malawi, Constitution of the DRC.

30 Art. 40(1) (6) of the draft Constitution of Zambia.

31 Constitution of South Africa, Constitution of Uganda, Constitution of Malawi and Constitution of Namibia, to cite but four examples. The draft Constitution of Kenya provided further, along similar lines, that a child's mother and father, whether married to each other or not, have an equal responsibility to protect and provide for the child (Art. 40). The Constitution of the DRC provides for children's right to enjoy the protection of their family, society, and of public authorities. (unofficial translation).

- children may be separated from their parents only by judicial decision and in accordance with the provisions of law, if they do not fulfil their fundamental duties towards their children (Art. 9(1) of CRC and Art. 19(2) of ACRWC)[32]
- the right to adoption only in accordance with law (Art. 21 of CRC and Art. 24 of ACRWC)[33]
- freedom from being subjected to corporal punishment or cruel and inhuman treatment in schools and other institutions responsible for the care of children (Art. 19 of CRC and Arts. 11(5) and 16 of ACRWC)[34]
- the right that no child may be detained except as a measure of last resort and the detention must be for the shortest period of time (on Art. 37(b) of the CRC)[35]
- children must be kept separately from adults whilst in custody (Art. 37(c) of CRC).[36]

14. There is a unique provision in the draft Zambian Constitution of 2005, probably aimed at giving effect to the provisions of Article 30 of the African Charter on the Rights and Welfare of the Child, which provides for the child's right not to be incarcerated on account of the mother's incarceration (clause 42 (j)). This is highly unusual, and most prisons systems in Africa and elsewhere recognise that whilst it is not optimal for children to be incarcerated along with their mothers, this it is outweighed by other considerations relating to early childhood development. Another

32 Constitution of the Republic of Cameroon, Art. 46 (4) and the Constitution of the Republic of Seychelles, Art. 31(d).

33 Constitution of the Republic of Cameroon.

34 Constitution of the Federal Republic of Ethiopia; see also, the Constitution of the Republic of Ghana, which includes a general protection for children against torture or other cruel, inhuman or degrading treatment or punishment. Clause 41(6)(g) of the draft Constitution of Zambia alludes to the right of children "to be free of corporal punishment or other forms of violence or cruel and inhumane treatment in schools and other institutions responsible for the care of children". Protection of children from corporal punishment in the home has begun to feature in Constitutional texts, *viz* in the Constitution of Sudan, and the Constitution of DRC (Art. 41 provides for the duty of parents to care for their children and to assure their protection against all acts of violence both inside and outside the home).

35 See the Constitutions of Burundi, Zambia and South Africa, where this provision has given rise to fairly extensive jurisprudence. See for a recent survey, J. SLOTH-NIELSEN, 'Chapter 23: Children', in D. DAVIS and H. CHEADLE, supra (note 13); M. GOSE, supra (note 4), points out that unfortunately the principle of minimal use of detention has no equivalent in the ACRWC.

36 Constitution of the Federal Republic of Ethiopia, Constitution of the Second Republic of the Gambia, Constitution of South Africa, Constitution of Uganda, to cite four examples. The Constitution of the Federal Republic of Ethiopia provides quite elaborately that juvenile offenders admitted to corrective or rehabilitative institutions, and juvenile who become wards of the State or who are placed in public or private orphanages, are to be kept separately from adults. Some constitutions require separation of children in custody from adults, but restrict this to children aged below 16 (Burundi), which does not fulfil the requirements of international law.

unique feature is to be found in the 2006 Constitution of the DRC, which prohibits accusation of witchcraft being brought against children.[37]

15. For the benefit of the girl child in particular, the majority of constitutions prohibit discrimination based on gender.[38] Actually, more often than not, the child is referred to not as he or it, but as "child" or "children". This highlights that African constitutions recognise the principle of non-discrimination, based *inter alia* on gender, as a fundamental principle and have adopted a gender-neutral language in providing for children's rights. In addition, some constitutions prohibit discrimination on the basis of age[39] and birth status[40] explicitly.

3.3. SOCIO-ECONOMIC AND CULTURAL RIGHTS

16. Children's access to socio-economic rights has been afforded mention in African constitutions, too. The following socio-economic and cultural rights contained in children's rights clauses derived from African constitutions can be given as examples:

- The living conditions of citizens under the age of working or those unable or never able to work are guaranteed.[41]
- The State, with the collaboration of family and society, shall [...] create conditions for the fulfilment of the economic, social and cultural rights of the youth, particularly in respect of education, vocational training and culture, access to a first job, labour, social security, physical education, sport and the use of leisure time.[42]
- Every child has the right to individual measures to ensure or improve the care that is necessary to his or her well-being, health and physical safety [...].[43]
- Every child has the right to basic nutrition, shelter, basic health care and social services.[44]

17. Another notable socio-economic right relatively frequently encountered in African constitutions is the right to education. However, the right to education is

---

37 In clause 41 Constitution of the DRC.
38 See, for example, Constitution of Sudan Art. 18, Constitution of Namibia Art. 10(2), Constitution of Niger Art. 8, and Constitution of Sierra Leone Art. 27(3).
39 See, for example, Constitution of the Republic of South Africa Art. 9(3).
40 See, for example, Constitution of Malawi Art. 20.
41 Constitution of the People's Democratic Republic of Algeria, Art. 59.
42 Constitution of the Republic of Angola , Art. 31.
43 Constitution of the Republic of Burundi , Art. 39.
44 Section 28(1)(c) of the Constitution of South Africa, Art. 40 (6)(f) of the draft Constitution of Kenya, and clause 42(5)(f) of the draft Constitution of Zambia.

usually dealt with separately from children's rights, as everyone may be affected by the implementation of this right and not just children; see as an example section 29 of the South African Constitution referring to everyone's right to basic education. A perusal of comparable provisions in African constitutions concerning education reveals that these provisions are not insufficient or inadequate.[45] One additional provision that is found from time to time concerns the purposes of education, for example to aim at the complete development of the person. Another issue is a provision enabling private schools to be recognised.

18. However, it is apparent from the above examples, drawn from over 30 constitutional texts, that providing for socio-economic rights for children in African constitutions is not common. Generally, African countries tend to include socio-economic "rights" under "directive principles of State policy", which are not justiciable but only serve as guiding principles.[46]

19. The most significant array of socio-economic rights are provided for in various clauses of the draft Zambian Constitution, including the general right to survival and development, the right to adequate nutrition, shelter, health, basic health care services, social security[47] and social services.[48] The Zambian provision is clearly modelled on the South African version, which appears to have inspired a similar provision in the draft Kenyan constitution of 2005. The inclusion of socio-economic rights for children in recent constitutions is obviously a welcome development in the context of child well-being indicators in the African context, and it is instructive that fulfilment of children's socio-economic rights are afforded heightened protection by comparison to those of adults, as the general socio-economic rights provisions are worded (as in the South African Constitution) as the right to have access to a particular rights (access to food, and access to adequate shelter and housing), whilst children's socio-economic rights are more strongly and directly stated.

20. However, there is a major caveat, namely the limited nature of the State obligation in relation to fulfilling these rights progressively and subject to available resources. Clause 33(2) of the draft Zambian Constitution, for instance, provides that "The government shall take reasonable measures, within its available resources, to

---

45 See, for instance, section 29 of the Constitution of the Republic of South Africa; Art. 44 of the Constitution of Sudan; the Constitution of the second Republic of the Gambia; and clause 42(5)(c) of the draft Constitution of Zambia, the latter three providing expressly for the right to free basic primary education.

46 See, for example, Constitution of Lesotho (chapter 3); Constitution of Ghana (chapter 6); Constitution of the Second Republic of Gambia (Arts. 215–218).

47 This is an addition to the equivalent text in the draft Constitution of Kenya, and the South African version.

48 Clause 42(5) (f) draft Zambian Constitution.

achieve the progressive realisation of the rights guaranteed in this part, including legislation that establishes or provides for standards for the achievement of those rights".

21. At an earlier comment on the (then) draft Constitution of Sudan, we suggested three reasons why socio-economic rights were not commonly found in African constitutions, which provide otherwise for children's rights, even those of very recent origin.[49] First, we argued that African governments have been reluctant to commit to delivering specific socio-economic rights to children because of the general conditions of poverty they face. Second, there is a widely understood premise that families are primarily responsible for raising and maintaining children and a constitutional clause shifting this burden to the State might give the message that families and communities can abdicate their responsibility.[50] Third, there has long been a complex jurisprudential dispute about the jusiticiability of socio-economic rights: to what extent can courts of law pronounce upon them, thereby possibly interfering with executive decisions concerning the allocation of resources in society, and what remedies might follow any court ruling?

22. The South African context has been instructive in this regard. The 1996 Constitution, which heralded the decisive break with its apartheid past, includes an extensive children's rights provision[51] protecting both civil and political and socio-economic rights of children.[52] The Courts, both at Constitutional level and otherwise,

---

49 J. SLOTH-NIELSEN, *Measures to Strengthen Children's Rights in the Constitution of Sudan*, (Save the Children Sweden, Kenya Office, 2005).

50 Many African constitutions recognise and protect the family (parents) in general as an umbrella and fundamental element of society (such as the Constitutions of Sao Tome and Principe (50–51), Senegal (Arts. 17–20), Eritrea (Art. 22), DRC (Art. 40) and Guinea (Art. 16). Art. 24 of the Constitution of Rwanda provides that "[p]arents shall have the right and duty to raise their children."

51 J. SLOTH-NIELSEN, 'The Contribution of Children's Rights to the Reconstruction of Society: Some Implications of the Constitutionalisation of Children's Rights in South Africa', (1996) 4 *The International Journal on Children's Rights*, 323; J. SLOTH-NIELSEN, 'Children's Rights in the South African Courts: An Overview since Ratification of the UN Convention on the Rights of the Child', (2002) 10 *The International Journal on Children's Rights*, 138.

52 Section 28 of Act 106 of 1996, the South African Constitution upon which some more recent endeavours appear to be based (draft constitution of Kenya, Zambia, Constitution of Sudan) provides as follows:

(1) Every child has the right –
  (a) to a name and a nationality from birth;
  (b) to family care or parental care, or to appropriate alternative care when removed from the family environment;
  (c) to basic nutrition, shelter, basic health care services and social services;
  (d) to be protected from maltreatment, neglect, abuse or degradation;
  (e) to be protected from exploitative labour practices;
  (f) not to be required or permitted to perform work or provide services that –
    (i) are inappropriate for a person of that child's age; or

have had numerous occasions on which to assess the constitutionality of laws and policies involving the children's rights, including in the arena of socio-economic rights. Furthermore, the South African Constitution was hailed as the first in the world in entrenching socio-economic rights to such a degree, because in addition to the children's socio-economic rights referred to above, there are other clauses, applicable to all citizens, dealing with the right to have access to social security, to health care, to housing and to sufficient food and water. During the constitutional drafting process, fierce debates raged about whether socio-economic rights should be included in the South African Constitution. However it was argued that implementation of civil and political rights also costs money (for example setting up systems for voting and the administration of elections), and that without redress for the poor after apartheid, the new constitutional era would deliver only the "hollow benefits" of civil and political rights. This argument held sway with the resultant inclusion of the mentioned socio-economic rights, confirmed by the agreement that they were indeed justiciable in the First Certification judgment of the Constitutional Court.

23. We mentioned earlier that we would return to the issue of justiciability of constitutional rights, and it's relevance to children's rights in African context.[53] The South African experience has shown that measurable gains for children can be achieved by rendering constitutional rights justiciable at law, and a wide array of cases can be cited to illustrate this point. Areas in which children have benefited from constitutional protection include the abolition of corporal punishment as a judicial sanction and in schools, extension of customary inheritance laws to girl children, expansive interpretation of the principle that detention should be a matter of last resort and used for the shortest appropriate period of time, and regular recourse to the best interests of the child principle to justify access to maintenance, sentencing decisions, mother tongue education and a host of other varied spheres.

(ii) place at risk the child's well-being, education, physical or mental health or spiritual, moral or social development;

(g) not to be detained except as a measure of last resort, in which case, in addition to the rights the child enjoys under sections 12 and 35, the child may be detained only for the shortest appropriate period of time, and has the right to be –
(i) kept separately from detained persons over the age of 18 years; and
(ii) treated in a manner and kept in conditions, that take account of the child's age;

(h) to have a legal practitioner assigned to the child by the State, and at State expense, in civil proceedings affecting the child, if substantial injustice would otherwise result; and

(i) not to be used directly in armed conflict, and to be protected in times of armed conflict.

(2) A child's best interest is of paramount importance in every matter concerning the child.

(3) In this section "child" means a person under the age of 18 years.

53 The Constitution of Sudan similarly provides for a Constitutional Court with an array of powers, which would include pronouncing on children's rights-related issues.

However, in relation to children's socio-economic rights, the progress expected has, legally speaking,[54] been less successful than expected. The first setback occurred in the Grootboom case, concerning the right to have access to housing.[55] The nub of the ultimate decision handed down in the Constitutional Court entailed that the right of everyone to have access to housing (section 26(1) of the Constitution), a right to be realised progressively within available resources, meant that the government's housing policy could be reviewed for reasonableness, and where there was no policy or plan in place to deal with those in desperate need (in this instance, homeless people who had been evicted from State land in a harsh winter, who had nowhere to go) the policy would not be reasonable. In essence, the nature of the State's obligation was to provide access to the relevant socio-economic rights protected in the Constitution "on a programmatic and co-ordinated basis, subject to available resources". In this case, the relevant policy was held to violate the constitutional imperative as it did not cater for those in desperate need. [It has been noted, further, that the Constitutional Court decision did not give the community the housing they sought: it gave them only the right to a plan, which plan towards long-term housing development must also include provision for those in desperate need. This community is still, five years later, without housing!].

However, the fact that children specifically were granted the right to shelter in the Constitution (in addition to everyone's right to have access to housing) led many earlier commentators to believe that children would have a basic claim to some form of shelter given them by the State – a "first call" as it were. This interpretation was roundly rejected by the Constitutional Court, which said that giving children a priority claim could derail a carefully constructed scheme for the progressive realisation of the right to housing for all. Also, in a now well-known statement, the Court said that children could then become stepping stones (used by adults) to benefits and resources, instead of being valued for who they are! The Court maintained that while children are in family care, it is their families who must provide for their socio-economic rights, such as food, shelter and health care.

24. There has been only one further major constitutional case dealing with socio-economic rights, namely the Treatment Action Campaign (TAC) case,[56] which was

---

54 There have been many improvements consonant with children's rights introduced by the South African government which are not linked to prior judicial action, such as the introduction and roll out of the child support grant, now reaching over seven million children, the introduction of free primary health care for children aged below six years, and various nutritional feeding schemes.

55 *Government of the Republic of South Africa and Others v Grootboom and Others*, (2000) (11) BCLR 1169 (CC).

56 *Minister of Health v. Treatment Action Campaign*, (2002) (10) BCLR 1033 (CC); the *Khosa and Others v Minister of Social Development and Others* (2004) (6) SA 505 (CC) which dealt with the claims to social grants by a community of Mozambican citizens who enjoyed permanent resident status in

an attempt to force the government to expand and roll out the provision of anti-retroviral to HIV positive pregnant mothers giving birth in State clinics to prevent mother-to-child transmission of the disease. The rights concerned were everyone's right to have access to health care (section 27 of the Constitution), and children's rights to basic health care (section 28 (1)(c)). In this case, the Court clarified the fact that children were not only entitled to be provided with socio-economic rights by the State when they were not in family care. The State's obligation would extend to those children born in public hospitals whose parents are too poor to pay for treatment themselves. Whilst this can be regarded as ameliorating some of the limiting effects of Grootboom on the scope and ambit of the constitutional socio-economic rights afforded children, the Court did not do so. However, concluding that children had a direct, individual entitlement to claim basic health care services (on demand, as it were), rather, it used the right in the Constitution to conclude that the government's rigid and restrictive policy on anti-retroviral was unreasonable because it excluded and harmed a particularly vulnerable group.[57]

25. As can be discerned, however, the jurisprudence on the enforceability of socio-economic rights is still developing, and the constitutional inclusion of socio-economic rights for children can at least be regarded as providing a suitable platform for further development.

3.4. PROTECTION RIGHTS

26. African constitutions include a considerable array of rights aimed at the protection of children. Due emphasis seems to be placed on protection rights for the simple reason that the situation in which the African child finds himself or herself requires extensive measures of protection. The protection rights provided for include both general provisions – such as the duty upon the State to protect children from abuse, neglect, maltreatment and degradation[58] – as well as a number of provisions

---

South Africa, and whose children were born here and were therefore nationals of South Africa and hence found to be entitled to be beneficiaries *ex lege*, did not augment the jurisprudence in relation to children's rights significantly.

57 *Minister of Health v. Treatment Action Campaign*, supra (note 56), para. 80.

58 Section 28(1)(d) of the Constitution of South Africa. See too, the Transitional Constitution of the Republic of Burundi for a further example (in Art. 39), which reads "every child has the right to individual measures to ensure or improve the care that is necessary to his or her well-being, health and physical safety, and to be protected against abuse, acts of violence or exploitation". A similar clause is found in the Constitution of Cape Verde, which provides that "all children shall have the right to protection by family, society and public authorities with a view to their integral development" (Art. 73).

targeting areas in which children are particularly vulnerable. Two notable areas are child labour and armed conflict. A sample of some of these provisions is provided next:

- No child may be used directly or indirectly in armed conflict. The protection of children is ensured in periods of armed conflict.[59]
- All children shall have the right to special protection in the case of illness, becoming orphans, abandoned and deprived of a family environment.[60]
- Child labour shall be prohibited;[61] every child has the right not to be subjected to exploitative practices, neither to be required nor permitted to perform work, which may be hazardous to his or her health.
- No young person shall be the subject of traffic in any form.[62]
- The law shall accord special protection to orphans and other vulnerable children.[63]

27. The Constitution of the DRC specifically refers to the obligation of public authorities to ensure the protection of children in difficult circumstances and to bring to justice the authors and accomplices of acts of violence against children,[64] and further requires that all the other forms of exploitation of minor children are severely punished by law. It also grants special protection of the State and society to specified groups of children with special needs. These children are girls, orphans, children either of whose parents is in prison, children with a disability, refugee children and homeless children.[65]

28. From a cultural point of view, the protection provision in the draft Constitution of Zambia is worthy of note for protecting children not just from harmful cultural rites and practices but referring directly to female circumcision, tattooing and forced early marriage before the age of 18 years.[66]

29. As regards armed conflict, section 28(i) of the South African Constitution, which provides that children under the age of eighteen years are "not to be used directly in armed conflict" and are "to be protected in times of armed conflict", extends the limit

59 Transitional Constitution of the Republic of Burundi, 2001, Art. 40.
60 Constitution of Cape Verde, 1992, as amended, Art. 73.
61 Constitution of Cape Verde, Art. 73.
62 Constitution of Zambia, Art. 24 (4), and it is further provided that young person means someone aged below 15 years.
63 Constitution of Uganda (1995), Art. 34.
64 Constitution of the DRC, Clause 41.
65 This is a commendable addition to the constitutional array of children's rights. However, consideration could also be given to other groups with special vulnerability, such as victims of abduction and trafficking, abandoned children, and victims of the worst forms of child labour as defined in ILO Convention 182, to cite a few examples.
66 The establishment of 18 as the minimum age for marriage is a singular feature of the ACRWC not found in the CRC.

for participation in armed conflict to eighteen years, and offers more protection of children's rights than the CRC.[67]

3.5. THE BEST INTERESTS STANDARD

30. The best interest standard is not only one of the cardinal principles of the CRC and the ACRWC, but has become a legal norm capable of a very wide application. Few countries have explicitly constitutionally accepted the "best interest of the child" as the desirable standard for all actions concerning children in Africa.[68] Two examples are the Constitutions of Ethiopia[69] and South Africa.[70] In South African jurisprudence, the best interest principle has swayed courts adjudicating on children's issues in a wide variety of fields, including using the principle to limit school expulsions, deciding on language policy at schools, in rulings on spousal maintenance, a recent judgment relating to inter-country adoption, and in the juvenile justice sphere. As the founding principle underpinning a children's rights approach, it seems regrettable that the best interest principle has not been constitutionally protected on a wider scale in African constitutions.

3.6. DUTIES OF CHILDREN

31. The concept that rights entail obligations and that children are not only beneficiaries but also subject to duties towards their families, communities and nations is an especially African value, and one that is enshrined in the ACRWC.[71] Some argue that a constitution that gives children rights without stating their obligations to their families undermines family autonomy.[72] However, the notion of children's role, not just as beneficiaries, but as participants in an extended kinship community accords with Gose's view that child in this sense does not substitute for adults, however that they support adults in the fulfilment of their duties towards the family and in coping

---

67 The South African position predates the 1999 Optional Protocol to the CRC on Children and Armed Conflict.

68 It is also part of the ACRWC, which provides that "[i]n all actions concerning the child undertaken by any person or authority the best interests of the child shall be the primary consideration".

69 The Federal Democratic Republic of Ethiopia Constitution, under Art. 36(2) provides that "[i]n all actions concerning children undertaken by public and private welfare institutions, courts of law, administrative authorities or legislative bodies, the primary consideration shall be the best interest of the child".

70 Art. 28(2) provides that "[a] child's best interest is of paramount importance in every matter concerning the child".

71 Art. 31(1)(a) ACRWC.

72 T. Mosikatsana, 'Children's Rights and Family Autonomy in the South African context: A Comment under the Final Constitution', (1998) 3 *Michigan Journal of Race and Law*, 341 at 370.

with their functions.[73] The ACRWC also provides for children's duties towards their national community, and contributes to the promotion of African unity.[74] Although these provisions may be criticised as being legally unenforceable and of abstract character only, they illustrate most clearly the difference between the individualised approach to children's rights referred to by MURRAY, and the African conception of communitarianism (in South African parlance, ubuntu).

32. References to "duty" as a constitutional issue were traced in a few instances, namely the Constitution of the DRC,[75] the Constitution of Eritrea,[76] the Constitution of Guinea and the Constitution of Cape Verde. The Constitution of Cape Verde provides that "[m]inor children have the duty to obey their parents and respect their authority …",[77] while the Constitution of Guinea provides that "[c]hildren owe care and assistance to their parents".[78] Moreover, the duties of children towards their communities may well find a place in domestic children's law, as has occurred recently in South Africa.[79] Be it as it may, the language of "duty" should not be invoked to justify acts that are to the detriment of the child's well-being, such as abuse or child labour.

33. On a different but related note, as a mechanism for the domestic implementation of the international human rights obligations of the State and to assist in strengthening child rights protection, the constitutional rights for children discussed above are supplemented with institutional machinery. In general, a little over 45 constitutions of African countries provide for an independent judiciary. No fewer than 20 countries have established national human rights commissions/institutions.[80] Some are provided

---

73 M. GOSE, supra (note 4), 41.

74 Art. 31 (b) and (f) ACRWC.

75 Clause 40 provides that "Children have a duty to assist their parents", which is carefully phrased – assuming that the unofficial translation correctly reflects the original text – so avoid unwarranted inferences that children's duties could provide a mask for child labour.

76 Art. 22 of the Constitution of Eritrea.

77 Art. 81(5) of the Constitution of Cape Verde.

78 Art. 16 of the Constitution of Guinea.

79 Clause 16 of the Children's Bill 70 of 2005, passed by the South African Parliament on 14 December 2005, which provides that "every child has responsibilities appropriate to the child's age and ability towards his or her family, community and the State"; see also, The Children's Act 2001 of Kenya (section 21) discussed by G. ODONGO, 'The domestication of international standards on the rights of the child: A critical and comparative evaluation of the Kenyan example', (2004) vol 12 *International Journal on Children's Rights*, 419.

80 CRC Committee, *General Comment No. 2: The Role of Independent National Human Rights Institutions in the Promotion and Protection of the Rights of the Child* provides, under Art. 1, that "[i]ndependent national human rights institutions (NHRIs) are an important mechanism to promote and ensure the implementation of the Convention, and the Committee on the Rights of the Child considers the establishment of such bodies to fall within the commitment made by State parties upon ratification to ensure the implementation of the Convention and advance the universal realisation of children's

for in the constitutions while others are enacted by statutes with no explicit mention in the constitutions. Over 10 ombudsmen/public protectors are also provided for in African constitutions. The degree of success of these institutions in achieving their objectives is dependent on the availability and strength of particular legal, financial, political and social factors and the debate as to whether these institutions have succeeded in executing their mandate or indeed whether they are viable institutions, falls outside the parameters of my discussion today. Suffice it to say that they are constitutional organs that play an important additional role in the promotion and protection of children's rights.

34. It would be incomplete to conclude this section without briefly highlighting some of the main advantages of constitutionalising children's rights. First, constitutionalising children's rights draws attention to their special needs and place in society. Second, a constitutional charter of children's rights gives a heightened status for those rights as a constitutional provision has a legal effect overriding that of ordinary legislation, thereby binding the State's power. Furthermore, organs of States can be held to account on the delivery of children's constitutional rights. An instructive recent example is the Zuba case in South Africa, in which a provincial education and welfare department was placed under a structural interdict to report to the court periodically on concrete progress made towards building an alternative facility for sentenced juveniles, who were being detained in prison due to the lack of such facility in the province. Moreover, according children specific constitutional rights provides not only political justification for establishing social programmes and institutions for the protection and enforcement of children's rights, but at the same time it may enable children to make claims against the State.[81] In addition, the relatively rigorous procedure required for amending or repealing constitutional provisions leaves children's rights in constitutions on a concrete footing.

35. In conclusion, the constitutionalisation of children's rights in African constitutions represents a meaningful attempt to implement and comply with the CRC and ACRWC. However, although constitutionalisation has its benefits, the ultimate test lies in the extent to which constitutional and international law guarantees are fleshed out at municipal level. It is to the process of domestication of children's rights in African contexts that we now turn.

---

rights. In this regard, the Committee has welcomed the establishment of NHRIs and children's ombudsmen/children's commissioners and similar independent bodies for the promotion and monitoring of the implementation of the Convention in a number of State Parties."

81 L. M. Spitz, 'Implementing the U.N. Convention on the Rights of the Child: Children's Rights Under the 1996 South African Constitution', (2005) 38 *Vanderbilt Journal of Transnational Law*, 853 at 877.

4. DOMESTICATION OF INTERNATIONAL LAW IN MUNICIPAL CONTEXTS

36. Providing for child specific legislation is not a new idea in Africa.[82] However, the last decade has seen a continent-wide revolution in child law and the revision of many colonially inherited laws. In General Comment No. 5, Article 18, the UN Committee has highlighted that a comprehensive review of all domestic legislation and related administrative guidance to ensure full compliance with the Convention is an obligation. Commencing with the Uganda Children Act of 1996,[83] followed by legislative reform in Ghana, Kenya[84] and Nigeria, there are additional reform proposals on the table in Namibia, Lesotho and South Africa. Various other countries, such as Mozambique,[85] South Sudan,[86] Swaziland,[87] Sierra Leone, Tanzania and Malawi, are considering new children's rights legislation. In The Gambia, a new juvenile justice statute was passed in 2005,[88] and the constitutional developments in Zambia tend to suggest that legislative reform might be in the offing there too.[89]

These various pieces of childcare and protection statutes embody safeguards that are designed to protect children from all forms of social and economic exploitation; in many instances, they also regulate parental responsibility, the provision to children of various social services by the State and society as well as catering for the needs of children under difficult circumstances.[90]

---

82 As early as 1926, for instance, Sierra Leone had a legislation specifically protecting children.

83 J. Parry-Williams, 'Legal Reform and Children's Rights in Uganda: Some Critical Issues', (1993) 1 *International Journal of Children's Rights*, 49.

84 See G. Odongo, 'The Domestication of International Standards on the Rights of the Child: A Critical and Comparative Evaluation of the Kenyan Example', (2004) 12(4) *International Journal on Children's Rights*, 419.

85 See J. Gallinetti and J. Sloth Nielsen, 'Final Report on Consultative Process Mozambique', (4 March 2004).

86 The author was invited to South Sudan to provide expert advice at a workshop on children law reform in May 2005.

87 J. Gallinetti, 'Summary of Report on Consultative Process in Swaziland', Prepared for Save the Children Sweden, (14 October 2004).

88 M. Saine, 'Protecting the Rights of Children in trouble with the Law: A case study of South Africa and The Gambia', (unpublished LLM dissertation, University of Pretoria, 2005).

89 There are probably other examples that could be adduced here, such as Nigeria, where a criminal justice review was underway and, which explicitly included the possibility of new juvenile justice legislation.

90 The Children Statute No. 6 of 1996 of Uganda provides for care, support and maintenance of children as well as for local authority support for children, establishment of a family and children's court and provisions for children charged with offences. The Statute defines a child as a person aged below 18 years (Sec 3) and incorporates several provisions contained in the CRC and ACRWC such as the best interests principle, care and protection of children, children with disabilities, etc.

37. Writing in 1997 at the commencement of the South Africa process of reviewing the Child Care Act,[91] common themes and trends that then prevailed in law reform processes in Africa were identified. The legislation that formed the backdrop to that survey was that of Uganda and Ghana, and then the draft legislation of Namibia and Kenya. They were:

- An expressed commitment to enshrining principles contained in CRC and ARCWC in legislation.
- The repeal or revisiting of a large and outdated body of inherited colonial law.
- A pragmatic approach, given socio-economic and other resource constraints.
- Substantial evidence of devolution of power or decision-making to grassroots levels (for example village-based decision-making bodies).
- Awareness that there would be an ongoing interplay between statutory law, customary law and religious law.
- An explicit awareness of the role of the family (and extended family) in African society.

38. The various enactments, however, have differed as to their scope – especially the issue as to whether to include childcare and protection matters and juvenile justice in one statute, or to split them into two – and the processes followed have differed according to local socio-political dynamics. It is beyond the scope of this paper to discuss the provisions of each Statute or process in any detail. Nevertheless, a few common themes will be addressed in conclusion.

39. The first notable feature in most processes has been the review of existing laws, frequently leading to the conclusion that child law is fragmented, outdated and inappropriate for the African context. In Kenya, more than 67 legislative enactments concerning children were on the statute book prior to the adoption of the 2001 Act.[92] In some instances, adequate legislation existed but was simply not implemented under colonial rule, the juvenile justice Act of 1971 of Mozambique being a case in point. South Africa's existing Child Care Act 74 of 1983 was drafted at the height of Apartheid when the Bantustan policy was in full swing, and when black children were for the greater part excluded from the social welfare system.

40. Second, there was explicit consideration and assessment of the impact of these laws on children (and their child-friendliness), in a participatory and consultative way. As depicted in the Swaziland exercise, for example, these reviews involved interviews,

---

[91] J. Sloth-Nielsen and B. Van Heerden, 'New Child Care and Protection Legislation for South Africa? Lessons from Africa', (1997) 3 *Stellenbosch Law Review*, 266.

[92] G. Odongo, supra (note 23).

questionnaires and discussions with stakeholders, such as NGOs, policy makers, thereby creating the platform for significant citizen participation than simply being a top-down imposition.[93] In Mozambique, the legal review included participative workshops in far flung provinces, to raise awareness of the children's rights agenda, and the need for statutory reform. In the context of juvenile justice law reform process in Ghana, Kenya and South Africa, it is has been highlighted that, in raising awareness through processes of public consultation, the law reform endeavours made considerable advances in increasing the visibility of child law.[94] In Lesotho, ordinary villagers in remote mountainous regions were briefed, and workshops facilitated with tribal elders and community based representatives.[95] These approaches are of particular significance on a continent dominated by patriarchy, and in customary law environments where children suffer significant lack of legal status.

41. Third, there was an express attempt to interact in an interdisciplinary and inclusive way. As ASMAL states, "law reform is too important to be left to lawyers".[96] In this regard, the law reform processes in South Africa and Kenya, for instance, are exemplary in that they involved social workers, probation officers, police, academics, parents and children themselves. The Lesotho Law reform commission under whose auspices the Children's Statute of 2005 was drafted was headed by a sociologist, and drew in team members from a number of other disciplines. Nor has consultation been only multidisciplinary, however cognisance has had to be taken of the multi-religious nature of many African countries, and religious communities drawn in too.

42. Sharing of best practices within the continent has also been a key trend. A team from Lesotho visited South African and Ghana during the drafting process, for instance. South Africans, including practitioners have undertaken field trips to Namibia, Mozambique and Swaziland. The South Sudan exercise towards a children's bill has identified useful examples of best practice learned from other child law reform processes, and the sharing of best practices for the South Sudan process has also involved a field trip to Lesotho and to South Africa. This phenomenon is especially marked in the juvenile justice sphere, where local diversion initiatives and restorative justice have made great gains in adopted legislation and draft laws. The Lesotho statute

---

93 J. GALLINETTI, supra (note 87).

94 G. ODONGO, supra (note 23), 123–125. The same holds true for the process in the Gambia.

95 Dr I. KIMANE, Chairperson of the Lesotho Law Reform Commission at the University of the Western Cape/Miller Du Toit conference on 'The internationalisation of Child and Family Law', Cape Town, 25–26 January 2006.

96 K. ASMAL, 'Human Rights and the Administration of Criminal Justice: Law reform in the Age of Globalism', (Speech to the International Society for the Reform of Criminal Law, Johannesburg Thursday, 7 December 2000).

is exemplary and innovative in this regard, creating a promising and indigenous framework for restorative justice at village level.

43. Next, a focus on vulnerability (for example on orphans and vulnerable children) is one of the commonalities of recent children's legislation in Africa. This is done without losing the focus on children's individual rights in the nuclear family context (e.g. relating to parental rights and responsibilities) but ensuring that those who are marginalised and most at risk are expressly singled out. In the South African Children's Bill 70D of 2003, passed on 15 December 2005, special attention is paid to child victims of trafficking, to harmful cultural practices, to children with disabilities, and to addressing the problems experienced by children in the context of the AIDS pandemic.[97] The Mozambican process explicitly identified five categories of vulnerable children to whom special legal attention had to be paid, including children involved in commercial sexual exploitation, children in prison, children involve in child labour and children affected by HIV/Aids.

44. Mention must be made in conclusion of the fact that a child consultation process has accompanied many of the law reform initiatives noted above.[98] This is of course not unique to Africa.

5. CONCLUSION

45. Finally, one may ask whether undertaking constitutional and domestic law reform on children's rights, especially in places where there are no suitable pre-conditions and structures for implementation, where poverty prevails and services are extremely limited or non-existent, is not an exercise in vain, the creation of a paper tiger? I would argue not.

In most countries, the law reform process has been accompanied by an implicit understanding that the law is a platform or tool for development – there would be no expectation for an instant realisation. As argued in a previous note, in the context of South Sudan, "*it seems that there is much benefit to be derived from starting with a clear policy concerning needs and priorities, captured in statutory form. For a start, establishing a birth registration system and introducing a compulsory registration drive may over time improve children's access to health care and education. Addressing parental responsibilities*

97 Such as lowering the age of consent to HIV/Testing and treatment, an important consideration in the light of the growing number of children without parental care.

98 See, for instance L. Ehlers, 'Child Participation in Law Reform in Southern Africa' (unpublished Mphil dissertation, Faculty of Law, University of Cape Town, 2005).

through the lens of equality may ultimately lead to enhanced women's rights – under customary law women have no rights to their children. The progressive introduction of a minimum age of marriage may slowly increase the exceptionally early age at which most girls experience their first pregnancy ...."[99]

I therefore submit that child law reform is not only an undertaking to domesticate the CRC and the ACRWC, but that is it in fact a key policy planning instrument which is a pre-condition to strengthening children's rights in African context. As MAGOT from the recently emancipated South Sudan (with amongst the worst child well-being indicators in the world) noted: "*The challenges to law reform in a country so vast with no proper communication systems are very real. However, as the Chinese wisely said: journey of a million miles begins with one step.*"[100]

---

99 J. SLOTH-NIELSEN, 'A children's law reform process in South Sudan', Art. 40, volume 7, no 1 (Bellville, South Africa: Community Law Centre, University of the Western Cape, 2005).

100 A. M. MAGOT, 'The child law reform process in South Sudan', (unpublished paper presented at the University of the Western Cape/Miller Du Toit conference on 'Internationalisation of child and family law'), Cape Town, 25–26 January 2006.

THE PROTECTION OF CHILDREN'S RIGHTS BY THE EUROPEAN COURT OF HUMAN RIGHTS*

Mieke Verheyde

1. INTRODUCTION

1. The present paper contains an analysis of some child-related judgments of the European Court of Human Rights from a child rights' perspective. The idea of doing research in this area stems from the conclusion that although children's rights have been recognised universally by the adoption of the 1989 UN Convention on the Rights of the Child, the realisation of these rights remains a significant problem. Enforcement is hard because the monitoring mechanism under the CRC is rather week. It lacks an individual complaints procedure as well as binding concluding observations. In addition, domestic judges have difficulties enforcing the CRC rights. These rights are yet only sporadically being recognised as having self-executing force nor have they entirely been translated into domestic legislation and policy. It is therefore important to know whether another "supra-national" monitoring system allows for the possibility for children to petition for direct remedies for violations of their fundamental rights. Within the Council of Europe, the European Court of Human Rights offers such a possibility, at least to a certain extent. This Court indeed has always operated successfully and could therefore be a more efficient monitoring system through which children – at least those living within the council of Europe – can enforce their rights than its UN counterpart, the CRC Committee. Above this, the ECHR is incorporated in the legal system of most of the forty-six Council of Europe States. Clarifying how children may enforce their rights through the European Convention is therefore also important for children and their lawyers who wish to use this instrument as an enforcement tool before the domestic judges.

The European Court can however not monitor State compliance with the CRC in a direct way. Its competence is limited to monitoring the implementation of the

* All cases referred to can be consulted (in English and in French) at <http://www.echr.coe.int>.

European Convention on Human Rights. Looking at the text of this convention, it should be admitted that its potential for the protection of children's rights is not immediately evident: it contains only a few specific references to children. The question remains therefore whether and to what extent the Strasbourg organs creatively interpreted the European Convention in the sense that it offers children a legal basis to enforce their fundamental rights, which are in the meanwhile more specifically formulated in the CRC. By analysing some more recent case law of the European Court, this paper will in what follows, try to give an idea of how the court is interpreting its own Convention in a way that it protects the rights of children. It does this either by referring explicitly to the CRC or implicitly. This paper will go through several fields where explicit and implicit acceptance of the CRC standards by the ECtHR is clear. However, as will become clear, these good practice cases will be accompanied by some critical notes and examples of cases where the Court can still learn something from the CRC.

2. FAMILY LAW

2. In some family law cases, the Court gave its jurisprudence a more child-oriented slant in the sense that, where it had to consider a complaint regarding the rights of the parents, which also concerned the rights or interests of the child, it started dealing with these cases not only from a parents' rights perspective but also from a children's rights' perspective and expressly used the CRC provisions in its argumentation. An example of this is a case regarding international adoption against Romania.[1] In this case, two Italian couples each wanted to adopt a Romanian child. The children were nine years old and were in the care of a private educational centre. The Romanian Court made the adoption orders and ordered the children's birth certificates to be amended. However, the educational centre refused to deliver up the children's birth certificates and to transfer custody to the Italian couples. In addition, the girls themselves did not want to leave Romania to go and live with strangers and thus issued proceedings to have the adoption orders revoked. One of the girls also succeeded in this. The Italians complained before the European Court that the Romanian authorities' failure to enforce final judicial decisions had deprived them of all contact with their adopted children and thus violated their right to respect for family life under Article 8 ECHR. When answering the question whether the Romanian authority had taken sufficient measures to ensure the possibility for the Italian couples of creating a family tie with their adoptive children, the European Court balanced the interests of the adoptive parents (creating a family) against the interests of the children (not being imposed with new emotional ties with strangers). In this balancing exercise, the

[1] *Pini and Bertani and Manera and Matripaldi v. Romania*, 22 June 2004.

Court gave a lot of weight to the interests of the children, which in this case coincided with the view of the children. It was clear that at this stage it would not have been in the interests of the girls to go and live in Italy. Therefore, the Court decided that Article 8 was not violated. The Court expressly stated that the European Convention should be interpreted in the light of the CRC's standards. Strangely enough, it only referred to Article 21 CRC, which does not explicitly require that the child should be heard (only if required, the informed consent should be given) and not to Article 12 CRC (the main participation article, requiring that the view of the child should be taken into account and that the child should be heard in all proceedings affecting him or her).

This judgment has been criticised because it is one thing to say that it was not in the best interests of the girls to go to Italy and another thing to say that the State did do enough to respect the right to family life of the adoptive parents. In other cases, Article 8 was indeed deemed violated when the government did not take appropriate measures to facilitate such a contact, or to prepare the children to be united with their parents. In addition, in this case it was obvious that the government did not do enough. They did for instance not punish the private institution for refusing to cooperate in the execution of the adoption order. Therefore, the Court concluded that Article 6 was violated. Should the Court then have concluded a violation of Article 8? In my opinion it should not have. This case is different from the other cases in the sense that it does concern the tie of children with their adoptive parents and not with their natural parents. Above this, it concerns *international* adoption. The mere lacking of taking measures to execute the adoption order cannot be considered separately from the main question under Article 8 being the balancing of the rights of the children and those of the adoptive parents. It is subsidiary to this balancing. Thus the main question is whether it would have been in the girls' best interests in the first place to go to Italy, when the adoption order was given and before the private institution where they resided did everything to impede contact between the girls and the adoptive parents. According to the Court, it would most probably have been in their best interests. In my view, this is doubtful. According to the CRC, international adoptions are only justifiable as a matter of last resort and cannot be allowed if "any suitable manner to be cared for is available in the child's country of origin". It seems that the girls have found this suitable manner, since they were quite happy where they were staying. Also this "last resort" provision is in line with Article 20(3) CRC requiring due regard to be paid to "the desirability of continuity in a child's upbringing and to the child's ethnic, religious, cultural and linguistic background" and with Article 8 CRC, the child's right to preserve identity. The girls were already 9.5 years old at the moment the adoption order was given, so it is not that they did not have any background to consider. In sum, I think the Court made the right decision by not concluding a violation of Article 8 ECHR but it should have been clearer in its arguments. The violation of Article 6 ECHR is correct since a State cannot first give an adoption order and then not do anything to execute it, even if the order was a mistake in the first place.

3. In some other cases regarding placement and guardianship over the children after the parents have separated, the Court accepted the CRC standards, especially Articles 3 and 9, in a more implicit way. Actually, the CRC Committee heavily relies on the ECtHR jurisprudence when interpreting Article 9 of the CRC. It would lead me too far to go in the separate cases but generally, the Court accepted the following when assessing whether the parental rights have been respected in these cases.

In line with Article 9 of the CRC, the European Court of Human Rights is of the opinion that separation from the parents and breach of contact with a parent can only be justified if it is necessary for the *best interests of the child.* A separation can be considered as necessary and in the best interest of the child if there is *no other measure available* for the child with the necessary protection of her or his health and development.[2] *Also in cases of emergency,* the State must carefully assess the possible alternatives to taking the child into public care. Moreover, emergency measures are not always justified in cases of placement. They are only justified if the imminent danger for the child is actually established.[3] On the other hand, the Court made it clear that the authorities should act fast when child abuse within the family has been established,[4] as required by Article 19 of the CRC. This means that in cases of conflict between the right of the child not to be separated from his or her parents on the one hand and his or her right to be protected against neglect or violence within the family on the other hand, the State should make sure that the family life of the parents and the child are respected and may thus not act too hastily. In the meantime the State should make sure that it acts quickly enough, once the abuse has clearly been established – a difficult balancing exercise indeed.

4. It can thus be concluded that the European Court has in family law cases often decided in line with the CRC and referred to it, and its jurisprudence could even often be seen as a good practice and a guideline as how to understand some provisions of the CRC.

However, from the critical side now, it should be mentioned that the Court also made "mistakes" in the field of family law. For instance, sometimes it does not examine the best interests of the child where it should have done so. So was the case in *Shofman*

---

2 *Johansen v. Norway*, 7 August 1996, §§ 64 and 78.

3 *Haase v. Germany*, 8 April 2004.

4 *Z. ea v. UK*, 10 May 2001.

v. Russia last year.[5] In this case, a man wanted to contest paternity of his two-year-old son who was born during his marriage. After his wife informed him that the marriage was over and that she would be applying for maintenance for the child, the man's relatives told him that he was not the boy's father. A DNA test confirmed this. The man immediately petitioned for divorce and brought an action contesting his paternity. This was impossible because Russian family law set a one-year limitation period for a paternity action and since the applicant only applied when the boy was already two years old; his action was held to be time-barred. His wife's claim for maintenance was thus accepted. The European Court was of the opinion that Russia had failed to secure to the applicant the respect for his private life because of such an inflexible time limit. In general, the Court does not have any problem with time limits in this context but in a case like this, where a man was prevented from disclaiming paternity because he did not discover that he might not be the father until after the time limit had expired, it considered the State did not find a fair balance between the rights of the man and the general interests of ensuring legal certainty in family relations *and the protection of the best interests of the child.* The Court did mention the best interests principle but without further reasoning. It did not ask itself the question whether it might be in the best interests of the child to keep the family tie with this man, be it for emotional or for financial reasons or for both. Maybe the result would have stayed the same, being that the man's rights were violated but in any case, the interests of the child should at least have been given considerable weight in the reasoning of the Court, which was not the case.

3. PROTECTION AGAINST EXPLOITATION

5. Exploitation of children has firmly been condemned by the European Court, with reference to some CRC provisions (Arts. 32, 36 and 19 CRC). This was for instance done in *Siliadin v. France.*[6] Siwa-Akofa Siliadin was a Togolese national who arrived in Paris when she was 15 years old. A friend of the family had undertaken to regularise the girl's immigration status and to arrange her education. In the meantime, the girl would do some household work. However, in fact, the girl became an unpaid servant for this family friend and later to a couple of complete strangers to whom the family member had lent her. She was a "maid of all work" and worked from 7.30am until 10.30pm every day with no days off. She did not receive any education, slept in the children's bedroom on a mattress on the floor, wore old clothes, and with the exception of taking the children of the family to school, she was not allowed to leave the house. Her passport was confiscated and in the meantime, she resided in France

5 *Shofman v. Russia* , 24 February 2005.
6 *Siliadin v. France*, 26 July 2005.

illegally. After four years, a neighbour informed the Committee against Modern Slavery, which reported the matter to the prosecuting authorities. Criminal proceedings were brought against the couple, which led to their conviction and sentencing at first instance to 12 months' imprisonment (seven of which were suspended) and a fine because they had not paid the girl for her services. But the judges did not consider the girl's working and living conditions to be incompatible with human dignity. In appeal, the couple was totally acquitted. The higher judges believed it proved that the couple was saving money for the girl, which would be handed over upon her departure. The French prosecutor did not go to the Court of Cassation and hence the couple could not be criminally prosecuted anymore. The only thing, which was left for the girl, was 15,245 Euros paid in damages.

The European Court decided unanimously that France had not fulfilled its positive obligations under Article 4 of the ECHR entailing the prohibition on slavery and servitude. States should not only themselves refrain from committing such actions, they should also take preventive and repressive measures in order to ensure that individuals refrain from holding people in slavery or servitude. More concretely, the government must criminalise such activities and effectively implement the criminal law. France had failed in this respect. The European Court accepted that the girl had been subjected to forced labour. Indeed, she did not live and work for the couple of her own free will. On the contrary, she had been lent by a family friend and she stayed there because she was afraid of being arrested by the police since she was no longer in the possession of valid papers. The couple misused this fear. The Court did however not qualify the facts as a situation of slavery because the couple had not exercised a genuine right of ownership over her, thus reducing her to the status of an object. The Court considered the situation as one of servitude, which is linked to slavery and is an obligation to provide one's services under coercion. Neither slavery nor servitude is explicitly prohibited by the French criminal code. The couple had been prosecuted based on provisions regarding exploitation of individuals at work and regarding working and living conditions that conflict with human dignity. According to the European Court, these provisions are far more restricted than by Article 4 of the ECHR and do not suffice to restrain the treatment of "house slaves". Moreover, these criminal provisions can be interpreted in very different ways, which became clear by the fact that the French Court of Appeal refused to qualify the situation of unpaid labour as exploitation. Because of this, the couple could not be held criminally responsible, which is unacceptable in the eyes of the European Court. Everybody – and especially children – have the right to be effectively protected against grave infringements on a person's integrity. Only clear criminal standards and effective prosecution can do this.

In coming to this conclusion, the Court referred to the CRC, and more specifically to Articles 19 (abuse and neglect by caregivers), 32 (child labour) and 36 (other forms of exploitation). It emphasised several times, that especially children should receive protection against exploitative practices. From now on, it is clear that a child, residing within the Council of Europe can enforce his or her rights under these CRC articles before the ECtHR. This is important, because, this form of house slavery is a large-scale problem in the CoE States. This judgment will thus have a great impact in many countries that do not yet have precise criminal provisions on the matter. France has changed its legislation in the meantime.

4. JUVENILE JUSTICE

6. Another area of Strasbourg case law in which the influence of the CRC is evident is juvenile justice. In the cases T. and V., better known as the Bulger case of 1999 against the UK, the European Court based its judgment (partly) on Article 40 of the CRC, which contains, together with Articles 37 and 39, some specific guarantees for children in conflict with the law (amongst other things, it requires States to seek to promote a distinctive system of juvenile justice for children with specific positive rather than punitive aims; it contains a minimum list of guarantees for child delinquents, and it requires States to set a minimum age of criminal responsibility). The case concerned the conviction and sentencing of two 11-year-old boys who had abducted a two-year-old toddler from a shopping centre, taken him on a journey of over two miles and then battered him to death and left him on a railway line to be run over. The boys were convicted of abduction and murder. To a certain extent, the proceedings were modified in view of the boys' ages. They were seated next to social workers in a specially raised dock. Their parents and lawyers were seated nearby. The hearing times were shortened to reflect the school day. During adjournments, the defendants were allowed to spend time with their parents and social workers in a play area, and so on. However, in general, the trial was conducted with the formality of an adult criminal trial. The judge and counsel wore wigs and gowns. Above this, the trial was preceded and accompanied by massive national and international publicity. Throughout the criminal proceedings, the arrival of the defendants was greeted by a hostile crowd. On occasion, attempts were made to attack the vehicles bringing them to court. In the courtroom, the press benches and public gallery were full. The boys went to the European Court of Human Rights and argued that they had not received a due process as guaranteed under Article 6, §1 ECHR. The European Court stated that one of the elements of a due process is that an individual should be able to participate effectively to his or her process. In the case of minors, the age, maturity, emotional and intellectual capacities should be taken into account in order to respect this right. This means that the government might have to take steps to promote the child's ability to

understand and participate in the proceedings. In the Bulger case, where young children were charged with a grave offence attracting high levels of media and public interest, it was necessary to conduct the hearing in such a way as to reduce as far as possible his or her feelings of intimidation and inhibition. The special measures that were taken by the British government were deemed insufficient; the government also had to try to temper the intimidating influence of the public and media, which it could for instance have done by allowing only selected members of the public in the courtroom. Thus, although the European Court does not require that juvenile delinquents should be treated in a separate juvenile justice system, the Court recognised that criminal proceedings against children should be adapted to the age and maturity of the child delinquents in order to respect the latter's right to due process. This view of the European Court is a/o based on Article 40(2)(b)(vii) of the CRC (to which it refers), which contains a list of minimum, special guarantees for child defendants, amongst which the right to have his or her privacy fully respected at all stages of the proceedings.

From the critical side it should be noted that the Court did not consider that criminal proceedings against children as such are incompatible with the right to due process. The Court does in other words not require that juvenile delinquents appear before a special youth court. It does not put a duty on States to "seek to promote" a separate child criminal justice system as Article 40 § 3 of the CRC is doing. Neither did the Court ever take a general stance on how such a system should be made compatible with some minimum human rights guarantees of suspects.[7]

Further, the Court also took a less child-friendly approach on the issue of minimum age of criminal responsibility. In the above-described Bulger case, the Court did not find that the British minimum age of criminal responsibility of 10 years violated the European Convention. It based this decision partly on the fact that the CRC itself does not establish a universal minimum age of criminal responsibility neither did its Committee. The European Court actually used the CRC against the protection of children's rights. However, it forgot the fact that the CRC has to be interpreted in the light of what other instruments say, such as the Beijing Minimum Rules for the Administration of Juvenile Justice, which warn that the age should not be fixed too low. In addition, the Court did not take into account the fact that the CRC Committee considered this low minimum age to be unlawful.

---

7 *Cf.* Nortier case: right to an impartial court, *Nortier v. the Netherlands*, 24 August 1993.

5. FAMILY REUNIFICATION

7. Another area in which the European Court often took a child-friendly position is the field of family reunification. Article 10 of the CRC states that cases of family reunification should be dealt with in a positive, humane and expeditious manner. The European Court deals with this question in the following way:

- The European Convention does not (under Art. 8) impose a general duty on States to allow for family reunification on its territory. This is compatible with Article 10 CRC.
- It recognises that the right of the Contracting States to regulate the entry and length of stay of aliens on their territory can be limited by reasons of family reunification. Actually, in questions of family reunification the right of the Contracting States to regulate the entry and length of stay of aliens in their territory should be balanced against the right to respect for family life of the people concerned.
- States are only obliged to accept family reunification when this is the only way in which the family life of the people concerned can be respected. The situation of the children is one of the aspects that should be taken into account. It hence depends on the circumstances of the case whether a government is obliged under the ECHR to accept family reunification.

The following criteria seem to count:

1. The child's *identity*: what nationality they have, what language they speak and if they have a tie with the country, to which they would be extradited. This became for instance clear in a case against the Netherlands concerning the expulsion of a Moroccan man who had been married to a Dutch woman with whom he had had a child.[8] After the divorce, the Dutch government refused to extend his residence permit. The European Court was of the opinion that the Dutch government had violated the men's right to respect for family life because he had strong ties with his daughter who was born in the Netherlands.
2. The child's *age and degree of dependency*: younger children are in greater need to stay with their parents than teenagers. In a recent case[9] for instance, the Netherlands refused a Brazilian mother to stay in the country after she had separated from the Dutch father of her three-year-old daughter. The European Court concluded that the Netherlands had violated Article 8 of the Convention. Teenagers, on the contrary, are often considered too independent and it is therefore not necessary to reunite them or keep them together with their family. In *Aoulmi v. France*,[10] a

8 *Berrehab v. the Netherlands*, 21 June 1988.

9 *Rodriguez da silva and Hoogkamer v. the Netherlands*, 31 January 2006.

10 *Aoulmi v. France*, 17 January 2006.

man with Algerian nationality was sent back to Algeria, after having committed several criminal offences. His daughter was 16 and he claimed to have "special ties" with her, without explaining what this meant. The Court concluded that his daughter was not a reason enough for the man to stay in France.

3. The child's *right to health and to be protected against traditional harmful practices.* In a recent case,[11] for instance, the Court was of the opinion that the refusal of the Dutch government to let a fifteen-year-old girl of Eritrea join her family who had stayed in the Netherlands for quite some time now constituted a violation of Article 8. As mentioned above, in some other cases regarding teenagers the Court had concluded that family reunification is not necessary since they have reached an age that makes them sufficiently independent of their relatives. In this case, however, the girl risked being the victim of early marriage and school drop-out if she stayed in Eritrea. Hence, the conclusion of the Court that the Dutch government should have let her in.
4. The child's *right to education*: if it is clear that the children would have huge difficulties in adapting to the school curriculum in a country to which they would be extradited, family reunification is obligatory. In *Keles v. Germany*[12] for instance, the children were aged 6 to 13, they went to school in Germany and it would have been very difficult for them to adapt to the Turkish school curriculum. Germany should therefore have allowed this family to live in its territory.

These elements can however not be considered separately. Whether the State should allow a family to live in its territory depends on *all circumstances* of the case. Therefore, sometimes a child of the same age may in one case have to leave the country and in another, it should stay if the government wants to respect his or her respect for family life. Last year for instance, the Court came to different conclusions in two cases where the government expulsed a father to Turkey. In each of these cases a child of six years old was involved, who had never lived in Turkey and did not have the Turkish nationality. In the first case,[13] the Court considered that Article 8 ECHR was violated. The other elements in that case were that the other children of that family were older and would even have greater difficulty to adapt in Turkey and the father had committed only minor offences. In the second case,[14] no violation was found. The difference with the former case was that the other child of the family was only one year old and the father had committed major crimes. In my opinion, it is quite frustrating that the Court does not consider the child's right independently but lets it depend on the degree of the offences his or her parents have committed or the age of his or her brothers and sisters.

---

11 *Tuquabo-Tekle v. the Netherlands*, 1 December 2005.

12 *Keles v. Germany*, 27 October 2005.

13 *Ibid.*

14 Üner v. The Netherlands, 5 July 2005.

6. OTHER FUTURE CHALLENGES

8. Apart from the critical notes made above, I want to add two other issues the European Court up till now has failed to approach in a child-friendly way: one is the right of the child to an identity, the other is the right of the child to have a view and to have this view taken into account in decisions affecting the child.

The first area concerns *the right of the child to an identity*, and more specifically the right to know his or her personal history. In a case against France regarding anonymous births,[15] the European Court gave in its balancing exercise between the right of the child to know his or her origins (Art. 7 CRC) and the right of the mother to remain anonymous absolute precedence to the privacy rights of the mother. At least seven of the seventeen judges dissented to this opinion arguing that the Court had not taken into account various relevant international instruments, among which was Article 7 of the CRC. They were of the opinion that France, which has an ancient tradition that enables newborn babies to be abandoned in accordance with a set of procedures, should at least also have taken into account the rights of the child. This was not the case as the French legislation in this area made the disclosure of information completely dependent on the consent of the mother. According to the dissenting judges the rights of the child could only be respected when an independent authority has the power to decide, based on all the factual and legal aspects of the case and following adversarial argument, whether or not to grant access to the information. I hope that, in the future, the dissenting judges' opinion will become the opinion of the Court.

Further, The European Court did not yet recognise a general *right of the child to be heard and have its view taken into account.* In some cases, the Court did accept the importance to take the child's view into account in decisions about for instance the need of his or her placement or about contact with one of the parents after he or she has been separated from (one of) them. However, a general right to be heard in these kind of proceedings has not been read in Article 8 ECHR whereas the Court is paying a lot of attention to the procedural guarantees of the parents in these kinds of proceedings. Moreover, when the Court does take into account the view of the child, it seems not always to be very consistent. Last year, for instance, there were two cases before the Court regarding the right of divorced fathers to have contact with their daughters. In the first case,[16] the Court was of the opinion that, although the girl was clear about the fact that she did not want to have contact with her father, the government had not done enough to re-establish the contact. Four months later, in

---

15 *Odièvre v. France*, 13 February 2003.

16 *Bove v. Italy*, 30 June 2005.

another case,[17] the Court decided that the refusal of the daughter to see her father was the key argument that justified the suspension of the contact rights of the father. The Court may have had its reasons for this inconsistent approach (for instance the fact that in the first case the girl was only 10 years old when she first refused to see her father and in the second one, the girl was 12), but it should be clear about this in its judgments. Thus, the Court may still benefit from the guidance Article 12 CRC is offering in this regard.

7. CONCLUDING REMARKS

9. The European Court can be an effective enforcement mechanism of children's rights in several areas, such as family law, protection against violence, family reunification, juvenile justice and other areas that were not dealt with in this short presentation. Either the CRC provisions were implicitly adopted or, they were explicitly used by the Court in its judgments.

Nevertheless, some less positive conclusions must be drawn also. The Court did not always invoke the CRC where it had the opportunity of doing so. On occasion it only concurred and dissenting judges invoked the CRC. If the Court would have a systematic referral policy, maybe it would not "forget" to regard the case from the child's perspective also, which it has done even in very recent cases. Occasionally, the Court also refused to accept the CRC standards although the applicant's lawyers explicitly invoked them. Finally, like in the Bulger case, the Court even used the CRC against the protection of children's rights.

The question is therefore whether we can continue to believe that the Strasbourg jurisprudence will evolve by itself in the direction of the CRC. The ECHR is indeed a living instrument that evolves to maintain relevance to current legal and social conditions and some dissenting judges have more progressive opinions, which are often based on the CRC.

Or, is it time for some legislative action, such as adopting a new and comprehensive children's rights convention at the regional level or adopting a protocol for the ECHR that would ensure the addition of the various rights contained in the CRC which are appropriate for inclusion in the ECHR, but are not yet adequately covered by it?

Considering that even in the last two years the Court sometimes tends to forget to regard a case from the children's rights perspective, it might be concluded that

[17] *Suss v. Germany*, 10 November 2005.

something should happen on paper and the more efficient way would be the adoption of a protocol by the European Court because this would ensure the monitoring power of the European Court. What exactly should be included in an optional protocol is still the object of further research.

THE IMPLEMENTATION OF THE INTERNATIONAL CONVENTION ON THE RIGHTS OF THE CHILD IN FLANDERS (BELGIUM)

JOOST VAN HAELST

1. INTRODUCTION

1. The adoption by the General Assembly of the United Nations on 20 November 1989 turned the United Nations Convention on the Rights of the Child (the CRC) into the legal frame of reference for the rights of minors. This contribution will paint a picture of the implementation of the CRC in Flanders (Belgium).[1]

Flanders is part of the federal state of Belgium. Therefore, the federal state structure of Belgium cannot be ignored. The first section will outline the distribution of competences for the implementation of the CRC. In the second section, this paper will discuss some initiatives to arrive at the required national cooperation for the implementation of the CRC. Next, this paper will explain how Flanders has implemented the CRC in the context of its own competences. In this respect, this paper will limit to everything which is concerned with the general monitoring of the CRC and leave out the very diverse applications in the various different sectors of society.[2]

---

1 For a discussion in Dutch about the implementation of the CRC at the Flemish and the other levels of Belgium see: J. VAN HAELST, 'Méér dan 15 jaar IVRK in Vlaanderen en België', in *Kinderrechtengids*, (Mechelen: Kluwer), Part I, 1.1; for a discussion in French about the implementation of the CRC in the French Community see: F. VAN HOUCKE, 'Quelles avancées législatives pour les droits de l'enfant en Communauté française depuis la ratification de la convention relative aux droits de l'enfant?', in *Kinderrechtengids*, (Mechelen: Kluwer), Part I, 1.1.

2 This contribution is based on the author's experiences with the coordination of the Flemish policy on children's rights within the Government of Flanders. Nevertheless, the views expressed in the contribution are the author's and do not necessarily represent those of the Government of Flanders.

2. THE COMPETENCE FOR THE CRC IN FEDERAL BELGIUM

2. In Belgium, the federated states are on an equal footing with the federal government. In Belgium, each government has clearly allocated areas of competence. Both the federated states, including Flanders and the federal government have their own government and parliament. This federal state structure however should not be any reason to restrict the application of the CRC.[3]

For example, the Belgian (federal) government cannot state that Belgium is unable to observe an obligation in the CRC because it is part of the areas of competence of the federated states, such as the right to education. Conversely, the CRC does not give the Belgian government carte blanche either to intervene in the education policy of the federated states. After all, the comprehensive character of the CRC requires that every policy level in Belgium takes responsibility, both individually and jointly.

3. The CRC is what is known to Foreign Affairs as a mixed convention. In Belgium, the federated states are also competent with regard to foreign policy, and to conclude and approve treaties. The CRC entered into effect only after both, the federal state and the federated states had approved it. The same applies for the amendment of Article 43 of the CRC on the establishment of the Committee on the Rights of the Child. Flanders approved the CRC in the Decree of 15 May 1991, followed by the French and German-speaking Communities and the federal Chamber and Senate. In January 1992, the CRC entered into force in Belgium.

4. The CRC was supplemented on 25 May 2000 with two optional protocols. Belgium signed both protocols on 6 September 2000. The first, the Optional Protocol to the Convention on the Rights of the Child on the involvement of children in armed conflicts, was approved in the Act of 29 April 2002. It was decided that only the federal government was competent. The second, the Optional Protocol to the Convention on the Rights of the Child on the sale of children, child prostitution and child pornography, like the CRC, has a mixed character. It was approved by the federated states and the federal government. Flanders approved it in the Decree of 7 February 2003.

5. The Committee is the first interpreter of the CRC. In the organisation of the supervision and the follow up of the observance of the CRC, Flanders and Belgium

[3] CRC Committee, *General Comment No. 5: General Measures of Implementation for the Convention on the Rights of the Child* (UN Doc CRC/GC/2003/5, 2003), paras. 40–41.

therefore take into account the concluding observations and recommendations of the Committee.

For the execution of Article 44 of the CRC, the contracting States undertook to report on a regular basis, "*to submit to the Committee (…) reports on the measures they have adopted which give effect to the rights recognised herein and on the progress made on the enjoyment of those rights*" and to do so "*within two years of the entry into force of the Convention for the State Party concerned, and thereafter every five years.*" In pursuance of Article 45 of the CRC, the Committee is competent to make suggestions and general recommendations based on the periodic country reports.

6. In response to the Belgian reports of 1994 and 1999, the Committee formulated its observations in 1995 and 2002. In fact, the second periodic report of 1999 was only considered on 23 May 2002 by the Committee. The concluding observations were adopted on 7 June 2002.[4] The recommendations of the Committee for Belgium clearly reveal the demand for national cooperation:

- To establish a national commission for the rights of the child and provide it with adequate human and financial services (already in 1995).[5]
- Prepare and implement a comprehensive national plan of action for the implementation of the Convention, paying special attention to children belonging to the most vulnerable groups (e.g. poor households, asylum-seekers), through an open, consultative and participatory process.[6]

Furthermore, the Committee recommends that Belgium continues and expands the use of child impact assessments in the formulation of budgets[7] and policies and establishes independent human rights institutions in the German-speaking Community and at the federal level to monitor and evaluate progress in the implementation of the Convention.[8]

7. In addition to the CRC, the Special Session of the UN General Assembly of the United Nations on Children (New York, 10 May 2002), at which the nations of the world committed themselves to a series of goals to improve the situation of children and young people, deserves a mention. The General Assembly adopted the document "*A world fit for children*", which contains a Plan of Action.[9] There is no direct

4 CRC Committee, *Concluding Observations: Belgium* (UN Doc. CRC/C/15/Add.178, 2002).
5 CRC Committee, *Concluding Observations: Belgium* (UN Doc. CRC /C/15/Add.38, 1995), para. 13.
6 CRC Committee, *Concluding Observations: Belgium* (UN Doc. CRC/C/15/Add.178, 2002), para. 11.
7 Ibid.
8 Ibid., paras. 12–13.
9 General Assembly, *A world fit for children* (A/Res/S-27/2); <http://www.unicef.org/specialsession>.

connection between the CRC and the world action plan. Nevertheless, this plan is not without significance for countries which ratified the CRC because they are expected to take responsibility for its execution in the context of the periodic reports to the Committee. Paragraph 61, a) of the document "*A world fit for children*" reads: "*We shall encourage the member states of the Convention on the Rights of the Child to consider providing information on the measures that have been taken and the results that have been achieved in connection with the application of the current action plan in their reports to the Committee for the Rights of the Child*". The States have to draw up if possible by the end of 2003 national and, where appropriate, regional action plans with a set of specific time-bound and measurable goals and targets.[10] As indicated above, the Committee also sent a recommendation to Belgium to draw up a comprehensive national action plan.

8. To conclude this first section it can also be said that Flanders is largely competent for the implementation of the CRC by Belgium. In the context of this competence, it can act autonomously at many different levels, but must also enter into cooperative ventures with the federal government and/or the other federated states. We will discuss these internal cooperative ventures in more detail in the next section under "National Cooperation".

3. NATIONAL COOPERATION

9. The federal state structure of Belgium, in which all the governments are competent for the implementation of the CRC requires consultation and coordination.

An Interministerial Conference for the protection of the rights of the child was established in 1996. This was succeeded in 1999 by an Interministerial Conference on Children and Youth. In the context of this last Interministerial Conference the second Belgian periodic report was prepared and the cooperation agreement on the National Commission for the Rights of the Child was drafted. However, the composition of these interministerial conferences is purely of a political nature. With the establishment of the National Commission for the Rights of the Child and the drafting of a National Action Plan for Children, the aim is to involve the whole of society in the implementation of the CRC.

---

10 Ibid., para. 59.

3.1. THE NATIONAL COMMISSION FOR THE RIGHTS OF THE CHILD

10. Since 1995, the Committee has asked Belgium to establish the National Commission for the Rights of the Child. This commission has still not become operational. However, after a laborious process, the cooperative agreement for the establishment of the National Commission was finally signed by all the Belgian governments concerned (9!) in September 2005. Currently the cooperative agreement is being presented to all the competent parliaments for approval. However, it is important that the political will really exists to achieve a genuine well-founded agreement for cooperation. Most governments, including Flanders in the Decree of 24 February 2006, but still not all have by now fully completed the approval procedure. The third Belgian periodic report is due on 15 July 2007. It is not clear at all if the commission will be able to play its role in the reporting process.

3.1.1. Tasks

11. In the first place, the National Commission should serve as a consultation platform with broad representation.

12. The coordination of the periodic country report of Belgium for the execution of Article 44 of the CRC will be its main task. The report will be presented to the Committee for the Rights of the Child by the National Commission. The National Commission will supervise the execution of the measures, which are necessary to comply with the recommendations of the Committee for the Rights of the Child, and can make non-binding recommendations to the competent authorities for this purpose. The National Commission will have advisory competence for drafting international conventions and protocols, which concern the rights of the child. In addition, it will contribute to drawing up documents related to the rights of the child for international agencies. In addition, the Commission will play an important role in the collection of data at the national level.

All these tasks must always be carried out taking into account the respective competences of the different governments involved, and with respect for their autonomy.

13. The cooperative agreement provides for the participation of children in the activities of the Commission and that children must be involved in an appropriate and permanent way in the work of the National Commission in accordance with Article 12 *et seq.* of the CRC. The periodic report should also provide a summary of the efforts made for this purpose. Children and young people are also represented in the Commission.

3.1.2. *Composition*

14. The Commission is composed, on the one hand, of members with the right to vote, and of members with an advisory voice on the other hand. In principle, all the members, whether they have the right to vote or act in an advisory capacity, are appointed on the basis of their knowledge and experience with regard to human rights and the rights of the child.

15. Because the final responsibility for the periodic report, the main task of the commission, lies with the governments, it was decided that they alone should be competent to approve it. The members with an advisory voice have the opportunity of having their possible deviating views recorded in the report for approval. Another prerogative of the members with a right to vote is to determine the budget of the National Commission annually.

16. The cooperation agreement determines exactly how many members with the right to vote can be appointed by each government. In addition to the representatives of the governments, the commission will be composed of members with an advisory voice from a broad range of governmental and non-governmental organisations. First and foremost, this concerns all the ministers of the various governments who do not have the right to vote. In addition, the list includes the juvenile magistrates, the municipal councils, cities and provinces, the Flemish Children's Rights Coalition and the French-speaking coordination of NGOs for the Rights of the Child, universities, the administrations and institutions which focus on the welfare of children, the Flemish Children's Rights Commissioner and the General Delegate for Children's Rights of the French Community, UNICEF Belgium, the Centre for Equal Opportunities and for Combating Racism, solicitors and so on. In addition, the parliaments can appoint observers and the commission can be assisted by external experts.

17. In concrete terms, the participation of children and young people is provided by the presence of five representatives of children and young people. This concerns one representative of the Flemish Youth Council,[11] one from the Flemish Organisation for Pupils,[12] two from the Youth Council of the French Community and one from the Youth Council of the German-speaking Community.

---

11 For more information in English about the Flemish Youth Council, see <http://www.vlaamsejeugdraad.be/english.php>.

12 See for more information about the Flemish Organisation for Pupils (in Dutch only): <http://www.vsknet.be>.

3.2. NATIONAL ACTION PLAN FOR CHILDREN

18. The National Action Plan for Children provides an answer to the request of the World Action Plan and of the Committee to develop a national action plan.

19. Flanders started drawing up a Flemish Action Plan for Children's Rights in March 2003, and the Government of Flanders approved this on 2 April 2004. The French Community also drew up a separate action plan. Both entities involved the social organisations in this. In the autumn of 2003, the federal minister of Justice took the initiative to bring together the various governments to draw up a national action plan.

20. The government included their priorities in a structure of ten strategic objectives and translated them into operational objectives and concrete actions. For the ten strategic objectives, they went back to the prior declaration contained in the world action plan:[13] Put children first; Eradicate poverty: invest in children; Leave no child behind; Care for every child; Educate every child; Protect children from harm and exploitation; Protect children from war; Combat HIV/AIDS; Listen to children and ensure their participation; Protect the Earth for children.

21. In May 2004 the Federal Government subsequently also submitted this draft National Action Plan to a "Round Table", including the various other governments, the non-governmental organisations, the Flemish Children's Rights Commissioner and the General Delegate for Children's Rights of the French Community. After discussing the contribution of the round table and after the new governments took office at the level of federated states, the governments concerned approved the National Action Plan in 2005.

4. THE CRC IN FLANDERS

22. In Flanders, the Flemish Parliament implemented the CRC in two Decrees of 15 July 1997. The first Decree concerns the establishment of a Children's Rights Commissioner's Office, hereafter referred to as the "CRCO Decree",[14] the second one

[13] General Assembly, *A world fit for children* (A/Res/S-27/2), para. 7.

[14] Decreet betreffende de oprichting van een Kinderrechtencommissariaat en instelling van het ambt van Kinderrechtencommissaris of 15 July 1997, *B.S.* 7 October 1997, as amended on 31 January 2003, *B.S.* 13 February 2003 and on 15 July 2005, *B.S.* 9 September 2005 [Decree regarding the establishment of a Children's Rights Commissioner's Office and the introduction of the position of the Children's Rights Commissioner]. More information on the operation and the activities of the Children's Rights Commissioner's Office, including the annual reports and recommendations, can be found in Dutch only on the website: <http://www.kinderrechten.be>.

is about the introduction of the child impact report and the assessment of government policy in terms of observing the rights of the child, hereafter called the "CIR Decree".[15] These Decrees will be described in two separate sections further on.

These Decrees can be seen as two aspects of the same picture. The two Decrees were established at the same time in the spirit of the CRC. They were the result of a joint initiative by five female Flemish members of parliament. In accordance with the parliamentary preparation, the government and the parliament committed themselves to a joint project in which each took its own responsibility. As a result, children received the political attention they deserved. In addition, the parliament gave a clear mandate to the government to work on children's rights.

23. There is also the Flemish Youth Policy Plan which was introduced by the Decree of 29 March 2002 on Flemish Youth Policy, hereafter called the "Youth Decree",[16] and which is an instrument for integrating children's rights and youth policy at the Flemish level in the period 2005–2009. That will be described in more detail in the section on Flemish government policy.

4.1. THE CHILDREN'S RIGHTS COMMISSIONER'S OFFICE

24. The establishment of the Children's Rights Commissioner's Office is undoubtedly the initiative with which Flanders has most resolutely followed the path of promoting the interests of children in light of the CRC.

The approval of the CRCO Decree was preceded by visits to existing children's ombudsmen and by consultation with relevant partners in the working field and the academic world. The Norwegian model[17] in particular served as an inspiration.

For the execution of the CRCO Decree, the first Children's Rights Commissioner, Mrs. VANDEKERCKHOVE, took up her post on 16 June 1998, following an external selection procedure. The first mandate of the Children's Rights Commissioner came to an end

---

15 Decreet betreffende de instelling van het kindeffectrapport en de toetsing van het regeringsbeleid aan de naleving van de rechten van het kind of 15 July 1997, *B.S.* 7 October 1997 [Decree regarding the introduction of the child impact report and the assessment of government policy in terms of observing the rights of the child].

16 Decreet inzake het Vlaamse jeugdbeleid of 29 March 2002, *B.S.* 14 June 2002, as amended on 8 July 2005, *B.S.* 2 August 2005. [Decree regarding the Flemish youth policy].

17 For more information on the Norwegian children's ombudsman see: <http://www.barneombudet.no/ /english/>.

in 2003. After an evaluation, the Flemish Parliament reappointed the Children's Rights Commissioner for a second (and last) mandate of five years.

In 2005, the Children's Rights Commissioner's Office expanded to become an institution with twelve employees for a total of 10.5 full-time jobs. It has a multidisciplinary composition. A budget of 1,453,500 Euros was approved for the operating year 2005.[18]

The legal basis of the institution, its concrete operation and its international image consecutively will be discussed below.

4.1.1. Legally guaranteed independence

25. Following the example of Norway, the independence the Children's Rights Commissioner's Office is guaranteed by its legal foundation, its establishment by decree. Furthermore, the CRCO Decree provides many guarantees to ensure this independence. This concerns the position in the Flemish Parliament, on the one hand, and the execution of the post of Children's Rights Commissioner as described in the CRCO Decree, on the other hand.

a. Position in the Flemish Parliament

26. The establishment by decree is a necessary, formal condition to ensure an independent institution, but is certainly not a sufficient condition. After all, public institutions, which were established by decree, must also take part in the policy outlined by government and the competent minister supervising this.

The position in parliament further ensures the independence of the institution. Therefore, it is not the government, as in the French Community, which appoints the Children's Rights Commissioner. In Flanders, the Commissioner is appointed by parliament. Furthermore, this position in the parliament is largely worked out.

27. With regard to both personnel and budget, the parliament has the last word. The personnel team and the status of the personnel of the Children's Rights Commissioner's Office are determined by the parliament at the proposal of the Commissioner.

The funds that are needed for the operation of the Children's Rights Commissioner's Office are determined every year by the parliament at the proposal of the Commissio-

18 Kinderrechtencommissariaat, *Jaarverslag 2004-2005*, 17 [Children's Rights Commissioner's Office, Annual Report 2004–2005].

ner. Without this explicit provision, the independence of the Commissioner's Office would be seriously undermined since it could still be the government that decided on the funds. In this context, the Children's Rights Commissioner points out in a contribution that the annual determination of the budget could be the weak point of the institution, although up to now it has not been the case. After all, she points out that it is not out of the question that the parliament could intervene in the activities by failing to approve the requested budget.[19]

28. As an institution in the parliament, the Commissioner is accountable only to the parliament. The Commissioner reports annually to the president of the Flemish Parliament on the way in which she defends children's rights and promotes their interests. Furthermore, the Commissioner's annual report is made public.

b. The Children's Rights Commissioner's Office

29. The CRCO Decree for the establishment describes the tasks and competences of the Children's Rights Commissioner as follows.

The office is assigned three main tasks, each related to defending the interests of the child. It monitors the observance of the International Convention on the Rights of the Child. Secondly, it is responsible for monitoring, analysing, following up, evaluating and publishing the living conditions of the child. Thirdly, it acts as an interpreter of the rights, interests and needs of the child.

In carrying out these tasks, the Commissioner must particularly bear in mind the following points, using the Convention as a guideline: the dialogue with the child and the organisations active in the working field, the participation of the child in society, the conformity between the CRC and the Flemish regulations and the dissemination of information on the content of the CRC, in particular, for the benefit of children.

In the execution of his or her tasks, the Commissioner is competent to carry out studies related to the observance of the Convention, examine complaints related to a failure to observe the Convention and if possible refer these on to the competent bodies, either on his or her own initiative or at the request of the Flemish Parliament. The Commissioner has a broad right of initiative so that he or she can collect information at any time on any subject that falls within his or her competence. The Commissioner and his or her personnel are bound by professional confidentiality.

---

[19] A. VANDEKERCKHOVE, 'A framework for Child Advocacy', in E. VERHELLEN and A. WEYTS (eds.), *Understanding Children's Rights*, (Ghent: Children's Right Centre, Ghent University, 2003), 161.

30. Furthermore, within his or her area of competence, the Commissioner may not receive instructions from any government. The Commissioner works completely independently in the execution of his or her office. The Commissioner cannot be removed from office for views expressed or acts performed in the execution of his or her office.

The Decree describes the possibilities of dismissing the Commissioner in a very restricted way, which is at the request or with the agreement of the person concerned, when the person concerned reaches the age of 65, in an irreconcilable case to which we will return below and for serious reasons, without prejudice to what was said above about his or her independence.

Finally, a number of irreconcilable factors with other mandates or functions guarantee the independence of the Children's Rights Commissioner, even if these are not salaried. Even stricter rules are applicable for public mandates granted by election. The Commissioner may not have carried out such a mandate for three years before his or her appointment. By the fact of his or her appointment, the Commissioner is prohibited from applying for such mandate for three years after exercising his or her office.

This independence means that the Children's Rights Commissioner's Office follows the concrete government policy with a large degree of commitment but also with the greatest circumspection. For example, the Commissioner has no formal competence to advise government. In these matters, the Children's Rights Commissioner's Office makes use of its competence to advise on its own initiative. It only does so if it considers that it can have a greater influence on the content than by waiting with advice until the initiative is presented to parliament, when it already requires a basis in a decree. When participating in the working groups in the administration, it always formulates the proviso that it is participating as an observer. Its expertise certainly means that it is much appreciated. With regard to the Children's Rights Commissioner it is a matter of following the middle line between independence and commitment.

4.1.2. Operation

31. Based on the tasks of the CRCO Decree indicated above, the Children's Rights Commissioner's Office formulated its mission as follows:

"*The Children's Rights Commissioner's Office would like to strengthen the social and legal position of minors in Flanders by:*

- *Defending the continued execution of the CRC and promoting it.*
- *Arguing for living conditions, which promote the welfare of children and young people*".

32. Based on the tasks and competences in the Decree outlined above, the operation of the Children's Rights Commissioner is based on four principles: Advisory work; Ombuds work; Research work; Communication work.

In the context of the ombuds work of the Children's Rights Commissioner's Office, anyone can go to the Children's Rights Commissioner's Office with complaints about the violation of children's rights, irrespective of age. The research work concerns the task of the Children's Rights Commissioner's Office to examine the living conditions of children and young people in Flanders. Communication work concerns both the publication of the CRC's own work and raising awareness with regard to the CRC itself.

In this respect, it is guided by the following working principles:

- The belief in the competence of minors as full partners in society;
- The balance between the three sorts of rights: rights to protection, provisions and participation;
- An emancipatory approach by the CRC;
- A focus on change and impact.[20]

4.1.3. International image

33. The World Action Plan calls on the contracting contracting states to designate children's ombuds persons.[21] In its second General Comment in 2002, the Committee for the Rights of the Child considers so-called independent national human rights institutions for children or children's ombuds persons/children's rights commissioners as an important mechanism to promote and protect the rights of children.[22] The Committee refers to Article 4 of the CRC, which asks the Contractual State Parties to "*undertake all appropriate legislative, administrative, and other measures for the implementation of the rights recognised in the present Convention*". The importance of a General Comment of the Committee cannot be underestimated. At most, the Flemish Children's Rights Commissioner's Office responds to the recommendations of the commentary. As recommended by the Committee, the CRCO Decree explicitly refers

---

[20] Kinderrechtencommissariaat, supra (note 18), 12 [Children's Rights Commissioner's Office].

[21] General Assembly, *A world fit for children* (A/Res/S-27/2), para 31, B.

[22] CRC Committee, *General Comment No. 2: The Role of Independent National Human Rights Institutions in the Protection and Promotion of the Rights of the Child* (UN Doc. CRC/GC/2002/2, 2002).

to the CRC. In this way it makes it clear that it did not wish to identify the Children's Rights Commissioner as a party promoting the interests of goodwill for children without any obligation.

In this respect, Flanders certainly plays a pioneering role. After all, the Decree for the establishment of the Children's Rights Commissioner's Office dates from 1997, before the international recommendations referred to it. Furthermore, through the work of the "European Network of Ombudspeople for Children" (ENOC)[23] it contributed itself to drawing up the above-mentioned General Comment of the Committee. It also gave advice with regard to the establishment of an ombudsman for children in the Netherlands, Greece and Switzerland.[24]

34. Thus, it could be stated that the Flemish Children's Rights Commissioner opted based on her independent position not to participate in the defence of the periodic report of Belgium to the Committee for the Rights of the Child on 23 May 2002. The Commissioner submitted an alternative report to the Committee. It participated in the Pre-Sessional Working Group of the Committee as well as the Flemish and French-speaking coalition for children's rights and young people, supervised in the context of the "What do you think?" project of UNICEF Belgium.

Prior to the Committee session at which the State Party's report is reviewed, the Pre-Sessional Working Group of the Committee convened a private meeting with UN agencies and bodies, NGOs and other competent bodies such as National Human Rights Institutions and youth organisations, which have submitted additional information to the Committee.[25]

35. In contrast with the Flemish Children's Rights Commissioner, the General Delegate for Children's Rights of the French Community participated based on his position with the government and as a member of the government delegation in defending the Belgian report on the application of the CRC for the Committee. In contrast with Flanders, the French Community very clearly opted for an ombudsman for children appointed by and under the authority of government.[26]

---

23 <www.ombudsnet.org>.

24 Kinderrechtencommissariaat, supra (note 18), 15 [Children's Rights Commissioner's Office, Annual Report 2004–05].

25 CRC Committee, *Overview of the reporting procedures* (UN Doc. CRC/C/33, 1994), paras. 7–12 and CRC Committee, *Report on the twenty-second session – Annex VIII Guidelines for the participation of partners (NGOs and individual experts) in the pre-sessional working group of the committee on the rights of the child* (UN Doc. CRC/C/90, 1999), 111.

26 Décret instituant un délégué général de la Communauté française aux droits de l'enfant of 20 June 2002, *B.S.* 19 juli 2002 [Decree regarding the establishment of a General Delegate for Children's Rights of the French Community].

Despite the above-mentioned recommendation of the Committee for the Rights of the Child, the Federal government and the German Community have not yet appointed an ombudsman for children.

4.2. ASSESSMENT OF THE FLEMISH GOVERNMENT POLICY IN TERMS OF OBSERVING THE RIGHTS OF THE CHILD

36. In 1997, the Flemish Parliament gave the Government of Flanders a very clear mandate to work on children's rights by assessing government policy in terms of observing the rights of the child, in a decree. This CIR Decree provided the legal basis for the role of Flemish governmental organisations for the supervision of observing the CRC. This Decree introduced the Child Impact Report (CIR) for draft Decree and the annual reports on the rights of the child. Furthermore, this paper will discuss the crucial role of the coordinating minister and the contact points for children's rights and youth and the Flemish Action Plan that was drawn up for the execution of the global action plan and as part of the National Action Plan.

37. In 2002, the Flemish Parliament also approved the Youth Decree, which expands the existing youth work policy. The ultimate instrument for this is the Flemish Youth Policy Plan. In view of the fact that the second Youth Policy Plan 2005–2009 of the Government of Flanders is aimed at the integration of children's rights and youth policy, this paper will start by discussing this before examining the existing instruments for children's rights that will therefore also be amended.

4.2.1. The second Flemish Youth Policy Plan 2005–2009

38. As indicated, the Decree of 29 March 2002 on Flemish youth policy introduced a Flemish Youth Policy Plan. At the latest, 18 months after the start of every period of government, the Government of Flanders submits a Flemish Youth Policy Plan to the Flemish Parliament. This Youth Policy Plan determines the integrated youth policy of the Government of Flanders and devotes special attention to youth work policy. In a comprehensive vision of youth and youth work policy, it sets out the objectives of the Government of Flanders in all its areas of competence and determines results indicators.

The Government of Flanders approved the Second Youth Policy Plan 2006–2009 on 16 December 2005. As in the first plan, children's rights, serve as the "legal and ethical frame of reference". In the first chapter, the plan clearly sets the tone by opting for the integration of Flemish youth policy and Flemish policy on children's rights. By means of an evaluation and the revision of the Decree on Flemish Youth Policy, the aim is to provide a legal basis for that integration in this Decree. This envisages, amongst other things, an Annual Report on Youth Policy and Children's Rights instead of the current two yearly reports of the Government of Flanders on the observance of the CRC. The Child Impact Report (CIR) would be extended to a Young people and Child Impact Report (YoCIR). In anticipation of the introduction of these amendments, this paper will consider the CIR and the annual reports, as they exist today.

4.2.2. The Child Impact Report

39. As indicated above, the Child Impact Report (CIR) was introduced in a decree. The CIR is a public document that describes the situation of the child in his immediate environment, as well as the expected consequences of a proposed decision and the alternatives to this. Therefore it has a proactive nature.

The scope of application of the CIR obligation covers all the competences of Flanders – youth protection, health care, culture, environment, town and country planning and so on – but is restricted to draft decrees insofar as the proposed decision clearly and directly affects the interests of the child. Each minister evaluates whether this is the case, when he or she submits a preliminary draft decree to the Government of Flanders for its approval in principle. Therefore, no CIR has to be drawn up when this concerns proposals for an Act of an individual member of parliament, draft decisions, regulations or a draft decree if the draft does not clearly and directly affect the interests of a child. Meanwhile decree about 30 CIRs have been drawn up.

40. The spread of the first methodology in April 2001 resulted in acceleration. After the evaluation, a new adapted methodology was introduced from August 2004. Much more than the first methodology, this new one places the emphasis on examining the impact on the concrete situation that children live in. An evaluation against the principles of the CRC is necessary but not sufficient. The official who draws up the CIR is also asked to collect information from children's rights and youth organisations.

It has been decided to have the CIRs drawn up by the administration that is competent in terms of the content for the draft decree concerned. In this way, the competent administration aims to raise awareness during the actual process of establishing regulations.

However, it should be noted that the CIR is not yet widely applied and even where it is used, it is too often dealt with as a formality. In my opinion there are three reasons for this: the limited scope of application itself combined with a limited degree of enforceability, the lack of specific expertise with regard to the report on the impact on children, but also the lack of transparency and the closed character of the creation of regulations.

The limited scope of application has already been outlined above. The enforceability of the CIR obligation is as follows. In the Government of Flanders, the coordinating minister for children's rights is responsible for the compliance with the report on the impact on children by fellow ministers (and himself). The ultimate decision is for the government as a whole. In the context of its formal-legal advisory capacity, the Council of State supervises the compliance with the CIR obligation by the government. In fact, the Council has already provided sanctions for the absence of a CIR by providing its advice subject to the drafting of the CIR. Ultimately the final control lies with the Flemish Parliament, which can be assisted by the Children's Rights Commissioner's Office, without prejudice to the competence of the latter to formulate advice on its own initiative.

41. Secondly, the CIR is a very recent phenomenon. There do not appear to be any examples elsewhere. Impact reports related to other target groups are also quite rare.

42. Thirdly, there is a lack of transparency, also for the officials concerned, with regard to the process of regulations, a problem that the Flemish Government is tackling in the context of drawing up legislation. Experience has shown that the process of moderating the law is not effective.[27] This also proves that the report on the impact on children is important not only for children, but for society as a whole.

43. The Government of Flanders recently introduced the Regulatory Impact Analysis, abbreviated as RIA, in the context of aiming for a moderation in legislation. RIA is a structured analysis of the aimed for objectives and of the expected positive and negative effects of a proposed regulation, in comparison with alternatives. The guidelines, which were disseminated for drawing up a RIA, refer to the CIR for the impact on children.[28] The Flemish Action Plan for Children's Rights (see below) provides for the integration of the CIR into the RIA. Thus, the scope of application of the CIR could be expanded and the CIR should be more widely applied.

Up to now the legal obligation to draw up a CIR has not been introduced by the other governments of Belgium. As far as I know, the CIR is not yet applied anywhere in other countries either.

---

27 P. Van Humbeeck, 'Betere Vlaamse regelgeving: voorstellen voor een slagvaardig beleid', (2004) *T.v.W.*, 225.

28 See in English: <http//www.wetsmatiging.be/general/en.cfm>.

4.2.3. *The annual report on the rights of the child*

44. In the context of the evaluation of its policy and in relation to observing the rights of the child, the Government of Flanders has to present a report to the Flemish Parliament and the Children's Rights Commissioner every year on the implementation of the CRC. This annual report gives the government and the parliament the possibility of entering into a debate on the application of the CRC. These annual reports can be viewed as an interim Flemish report in the context of the periodic reports regarding the Committee for the Rights of a Child.

Submitting a report to the Flemish Parliament also raises the awareness of the parliament. For several years, the parliament has opted to discuss the annual report of the government together with that of the Children's Rights Commissioner. With the contributions of almost all the administrations and institutions of the Government of Flanders, through the contact points for children's rights (see below), the annual report of the government relates to virtually all the Flemish competences.

Up to now, the structure of such a report looked as follows. The chapter on "Horizontal policy" examines the coordinated, inclusive policy of the coordinating minister for children's rights, which is discussed in further detail below. The second chapter, "Vertical policy", discusses the measures which are taken in the various policy areas. This is done on the basis of the four basic principles of the CRC: the interests of the child, non-discrimination, the right to life, survival and the development and the participation of the child. This streamlining should emphasis the comprehensive character of the CRC. Finally, the "Policy conclusions" have been formulated for several years in the third chapter. The first annual report concerned the year 1998.[29]

45. In addition, the CIR Decree provides for another yearly report, with regard to the respect for the rights as described in the Convention in those countries or regions with which Flanders has concluded an exclusive and general cooperation agreement approved by decree.

46. The second Flemish Youth Policy Plan 2005–2009 puts forward an "Annual report on youth policy and children's rights". This annual report could then monitor all of the children's rights and youth policy and in this way integrate these annual reports.

47. By way of comparison, it should be noted that other Belgian governments have also introduced a system of reports; the federal government has also introduced an

29 The annual reports are available in Dutch at <http://www.vlaanderen.be/kinderrechten/>.

annual report[30] and the French Community a three-yearly report[31] to be prepared by a permanent follow up group CRC in the Observatory for the Childhood, the Youth and the Assistance for the Youth.[32]

4.2.4 Coordination of Flemish policy on children's rights

48. Both, at the governmental and at administrational level, the Flemish Policy on children's rights is coordinated, respectively by the coordinating minister and a coordinator for Children's Rights, supported by contact points in the Government of Flanders, which ensure a connection with the various different competences. The Reflection group on Youth Policy and Children's Rights ensures the commitment of the children's rights and youth organisations.

a. Coordinating minister for children's rights and youths

49. Since February 1997, the Government of Flanders has had a so-called coordinating minister for children's rights. As far as I know, this is unique. I do not know of any other countries and/or regions where such a decision has been taken. Up to 2004, this task was allocated to the Flemish minister of welfare in an individual government decision.

50. In of 2004, the new Government of Flanders took another step by allocating the coordination of the policy on children's rights as a competence to a member of the Government of Flanders.[33] In this way the coordination of the policy on children's rights not only became a task, but also an explicit competence.

Another choice that the new Government of Flanders made was to allocate this competence to the Flemish Minister for Youth. Since 1999, the Government of Flanders has actually had a minister for Youth. In this new period of government, this minister has opted for the integration of children's rights and youth policy.

---

30 Wet tot instelling van een jaarlijkse rapportage over de toepassing van het Verdrag inzake de rechten van het kind of 4 September 2002, *B.S.* 17 October 2002 [Act on the introduction of an annual report on the application of the Convention on the Rights of the Child].

31 Décret instaurant la réalisation d'un rapport sur l'application des principes de la Convention internationale des droits de l'enfant of 28 January 2004, *B.S.* 17 februari 2004 [Decree regarding the realisation of a report on the application of the CRC].

32 Décret portant création de l'Observatoire de l'Enfance, de la Jeunesse et de l'Aide à la Jeunesse of 12 May 2004, *B.S.* 18 June 2004 [Decree regarding the creation of the Observatory for the Childhood, the Youth and the Assistance for the Youth].

33 Besluit van de Vlaamse Regering tot bepaling van de bevoegdheden van de leden van de Vlaamse Regering of 27 July 2004, *B.S.* 4 August 2004, err. 16 August 2004, as amended [Decree determining the competencies of the members of the Government of Flanders].

51. The presence of a coordinating minister for children's rights in the Government of Flanders is an important guarantee for the compliance with the rights of the child in every aspect of Flemish government policy. In the Flemish Parliament, the Children's Rights Commissioner has the ultimate supervision of the compliance with the CRC in Flanders. In relation to the Government of Flanders and the administration, the Children's Rights Commissioner is an external agency. It is clear that because of the approval of the CRC, the Government of Flanders has the obligation to ensure the compliance with the rights of the child itself, as an internal quality guarantee. The integration of children's rights in youth policy makes it possible to integrate the CRC even better in the policy for minors.

52. The coordinating minister for children's rights has a specific budget for "subsidies for children's rights". Without going into detail, this seems the place to describe some of the constant factors in the Flemish subsidy policy. After all, they fall within the task of the coordinating minister to monitor the policy on the implementation of the CRC.

The first constant factor concerns the subsidies of the Centre for the Rights of the Child at the University of Ghent with a view to the necessary creation of expertise at the level of the rights of the child. This was subsidised by the Government of Flanders for information and advice at the level of children's rights. The starting point is Article 42 of the CRC that reads: "*States Parties undertake to make the principle and provisions of the Convention widely known, by appropriate and active means, to adults and children alike*". The Centre for the Rights of the Child, which is currently engaged in a cooperative venture with the Centre for Human Rights at the same university, was established in 1978 by Professor VERHELLEN and is currently run by Professor DE BIE.[34]

The second constant factor is the Flemish Coalition of Children's Rights, the network of Flemish non governmental organisations established in 1996.[35] Currently this organisation encompasses 28 Flemish NGOs. It aims to monitor compliance with the CRC, make an active contribution to promoting the rights of the child, and an active and constructive contribution to the reporting process with regard to the observance of the CRC. The Coalition of Children's Rights does this by collecting information and expertise related to the application of the CRC, developing and strengthening the network of NGOs, which are active with regard to children's rights, promoting interests, lobbying, monitoring policy, and publicising the vision and recommendations of NGOs.

34 For more information, also in English, see: <http://www.centrumkinderrechten.org/>.

35 For more information, also in English, see: <http://www.kinderrechtencoalitie.be>.

With regard to other projects that are subsidised, reference can be made to the project, "What do you think?" that is coordinated by UNICEF Belgium and was established in 1999.[36] It aims to promote the participation of children and young people. In the first place, it aims to involve minors themselves in the reporting process to the Committee. For example, it was responsible for the contribution of the points of view of children and young people in the Pre-Sessional Working Group of the Committee.

b. Network of contact points for children's rights (and youth policy)

53. The policy support, the preparation and the execution of decisions taken by the coordinating minister for the policy on children's rights, lies with the coordinator of children's rights. Shortly after the appointment of the coordinating minister in 1997, the coordinator of children's rights was appointed. This official has now a position in the Flemish Ministry for Culture, Youth, Sport and the Media.

Since 1998, the coordinator has been responsible for the coordination of a network of approximately 25 contact points for children's rights spread throughout the Government of Flanders.[37] In execution of a decision of the Government of Flanders dated April 1998, contact points for children's rights were identified in the Government of Flanders with a view to provide the "*information required by the decree*" in the context of the annual reports to the Flemish Parliament and the Children's Rights Commissioner. Subsequently the contact points were also charged with acting as a coach in drawing up CIRs. In addition, they were also involved in editing the Flemish contribution to the reports of Belgium for the Committee for the rights of the child in execution of Article 44 of the CRC. The services of the Government of Flanders and the Flemish public institutions, which have connections with the rights of the child, 25, altogether, established each a contact point for children's rights, which ensures the connection with the competences of its own administration. Therefore, the contact points cover a broad range of competences that are not purely child-oriented. Harder sectors, such as town and country planning, the media, the environment and housing also cooperate with the implementation of the CRC.

54. The tasks of the contact points for children's rights should be distinguished from those of the Children's Rights Commissioner's Office. While the external recognisability of the Children's Rights Commissioner's Office is essential, the contact point for children's rights principally has the following twofold task:

---

36 For more information in Dutch and French, see: <http://www.whatdoyouthink.be>.

37 For the list of contact points for children's rights, see: <htttp://www.vlaanderen.be/kinderrechten>.

- To serve as a contact for policy (functionally/functionally competent minister/...) with regard to the rights of children;
- To raise the awareness of policy related to children's rights within the Flemish Government. This requires a proactive attitude.

It is important to mention that the contact points for children's rights can be viewed as a sort of "group of colleagues" within the Government of Flanders, who are jointly responsible for the internal awareness-raising of the Flemish administration with regard to the CRC. Through the coordinator for children's rights, under the responsibility of the coordinating minister for children's rights, they are involved, amongst other things, in the CIR, the annual reports, the youth policy plan, the Flemish Action Plan for Children's Rights and the Flemish contribution for the periodic Belgian report. The contact points can be seen as a governmental network in the Flemish administration.

55. As a result of a reorganisation of the Government of Flanders and for the execution of the second Flemish Youth Policy Plan, the intention is to identify "*contact points for children's rights and youth policy*" in the various new administrative entities in the autumn of 2006. These new contact points would also have a legal basis in the Youth Act.

4.2.5. Flemish Action Plan for Children's Rights and the establishment of a Reflection Group

56. The Government of Flanders approved the Flemish Action Plan for Children's Rights on 2 April 2004.[38] The Flemish Action Plan implements the World Action Plan and the recommendations of the Committee to Belgium as regards the competences of the Flemish Community. It is also intended to serve as the Flemish aspect of the National Action Plan for Children to be drawn up by Belgium. Therefore, it has the same structure as the National Action Plan. The Flemish plan was integrated into the National Action Plan.

In cooperation with a broad interdepartmental working group, the "Flemish Working Group on Children's Rights", the coordinating minister for children's rights prepared the Flemish Action Plan. The working group consisted of representatives of the ministers, the contact points for children's rights of the Government of Flanders, the NGOs united in and represented by the Flemish Coalition for Children's Rights, UNICEF Belgium, which is responsible for the coordination of the project "What do

---

[38] This can be consulted on the website in Dutch and in the future probably also in English: <http://www.vlaanderen.be/kinderrechten>.

you think?", the Flemish Youth Council, the University of Ghent – Centre for the Rights of the Child, the Flemish members of Parliament, and the Flemish Children's Rights Commissioner as an observer. To draw up this plan, Flanders has adopted a procedure, which closely complies with the Committee's request for an "*open, consultative and participatory process*".

57. Based on the consideration that a youth policy and a policy on children's rights can strengthen each other, the objectives and actions of the plan were given further concrete form in the second Flemish Youth Policy Plan 2005–2009. This will be followed up with the above-mentioned annual reports.

Meanwhile, the ad hoc working group charged with preparing this plan was converted first into a "Reflection group on children's rights", and in early 2006, into a "Reflection group for youth policy and children's rights".

At the Flemish level there is thus a consultation platform with broad representation for the youth and children's rights policy of the government of Flanders.

5. CONCLUSIONS

58. The implementation of the CRC in Flanders proves that international human rights treaties can be used in a proactive way. They imply more than merely submitting reports afterwards. This certainly also has to do with the role of the Committee for the Rights of the Child. Through its recommendations it encourages State Parties to actively pursue a policy on children's rights.

Flanders is part of federal Belgium. Due to the comprehensive nature of the CRC, children's rights can only be guaranteed in Flanders provided all competent authorities will do so, both individually and in mutual co-operation. The rights of children living in Flanders must be guaranteed vis-à-vis both the Flemish and federal authorities which each have competencies that are relevant to children. The federal state structure must not be used as a reason for not complying with the commitments made within the framework of the CRC. On the contrary, the federalisation of Belgium, which entails increased responsibility for the Regions, allows the federal authorities and federated states to develop their own mechanisms for guaranteeing compliance with the CRC. The fact that the National Commission has still not come into effect illustrates that co-operation is not self-evident, neither at the national nor at the international level. However, federalisation also creates new dynamics. It has naturally also fostered the implementation of the CRC in Flanders. Moreover, there is the position of the Children's Rights Commissioner's Office in the Flemish Parliament, which provides guarantees for the independence of the Children's Rights Commissioner, as recommended by the Committee. The Flemish Government is the first authority that has started to work on the introduction of a legal obligation to draw up child impact reports, which was also recommended by the Committee. Since 1998, the Flemish Government has submitted annual reports to the Flemish Parliament and the Children's Rights Commissioner about the implementation of the CRC. Since 1997, a co-coordinating minister, with the assistance of a co-coordinator and contact points for children's rights, has been responsible for co-coordinating the Flemish policy on children's rights. In 2004, Flanders drew up its own Flemish Action Plan for Children's Rights.

59. The Flemish authorities have now decided to integrate the children's rights and youth policies. This is the new challenge Flanders is currently facing with regard to the implementation of the CRC. Meanwhile, this policy choice may contribute to a further sustained harmonisation of all policy measures that are relevant to minors. The Flemish Action Plan for Children's Rights, for instance, will now also be monitored through the Flemish Youth Policy Plan.

III. IMPLEMENTATION OF THE CRC FROM AN NGO PERSPECTIVE

DEFENCE FOR CHILDREN INTERNATIONAL: OUR OBJECTIVES, OUR ACTIONS AND OUR PRIORITIES

A case study of DCI sections in the Africa region

LAURENCIO E. AKOHIN

1. INTRODUCTION

1. This presentation will mainly focus upon the creation of Defence for Children International, its areas of practice, and its priorities. We will also highlight the tri-yearly plan of action, and finally, we will describe the implementation of the convention in the region of Africa.

2. WHO ARE WE?

2. Defence for Children International (DCI), is a non-governmental organisation that was created by NIGEL CANTWELL and CANON MOERMAN in 1979, the International Year of the Child. The creation of DCI as a worldwide movement came at a time when children's rights had long been neglected by existing international organisations. The International Year of the Child created a window of opportunity to shed light upon the numerous children who were victims of human rights violations, such as torture, prostitution, economic exploitation, arbitrary detention, and even trafficking and trade.

3. Since its creation, DCI has mobilised the NGO community and became actively involved in the elaboration of the Convention on the Rights of the Child (CRC), by forming an ad hoc group of NGOs in 1983, which was then joined by UNICEF in 1987. This ad hoc group contributed much to the final text of the CRC, which was adopted by the United Nations General Assembly in 1989. After the adoption of the text, DCI then engaged in the process of promoting the CRC by seeking its endorsement by several States.

4. Since its establishment in 1979, DCI has developed into a worldwide network, with national sections and associated members active in 45 countries across the globe. DCI also is in consultative status with the United Nationals Economic and Social Council (ECOSOC), UNICEF, UNESCO and the Council of Europe. This allows DCI to work actively in a number of strategic spheres where questions related to the children's rights are discussed. Experience teaches us the importance of this type of lobbying.

3. WHAT ARE THE OBJECTIVES OF DCI?

5. The mission in DCI is to:

- Defend and protect children's rights, as a complete matter of right, in accordance with the United Nations' Convention on the Rights of the Child, its additional protocols and all other appropriate international standards related to the matter;
- Stimulate collective awareness and solidarity to situations involving children's rights;
- Research, promote and implement the most relevant means to ensure the protection of children's rights in real life situations, by preventing and resolving cases directly and by offering appropriate solutions.

6. To achieve this and in order to reach these objectives, DCI adopts the following approaches:

- To participate in different sessions of the United Nations and in international conferences, and to monitor the implementation of international standards on children's rights.
- To encourage cooperation and actions on the national, regional and international scales.
- To write and circulate ad hoc publications, for example the publication of the French speaking tribune, monthly newsletters of the International Executive Council (IEC), of the International Secretariat (IS), publications pertaining to programmes, and so on.
- To conduct investigations in direct response to cases of children's rights violations, whether individually or jointly.

4. WHAT ARE THE AREAS OF INTERVENTION AND PRIORITIES OF DCI?

4.1. AREAS OF INTERVENTION

7. DCI covers various areas of activity in regards to the CRC, as the CRC does not authorise any separation of its articles. Since the adoption of the CRC, DCI has continued to monitor those countries that have ratified the CRC, concentrating upon each country's methods of implementation of the CRC.

8. DCI has developed several mandates such as, juvenile justice, more specifically for children in conflict with the law (all DCI sections). Another main mandate of DCI is child labour and child trafficking (Ecuador, Paraguay, Togo, Cameron and Costa Rica).

In addition, education and participation of children (we are protagonists), sexual exploitation and child soldiers (in Uganda, Liberia, Sierra Leone, Angola, etc.) also are DCI mandates.

Additional to these main themes developed at the international level by DCI's International Secretariat, each of the member sections of the movement has its own areas of activity that suits its individual agenda according to local characteristics and national needs.

4.2. PRIORITIES

9. The juvenile justice mandate has been recognised as the movement's priority on the international scale since DCI's International General Assembly in 1997. This priority was also reaffirmed in July of 2005 during the International General Assembly in Bethlehem.

4.3. CONSIDERING THE JUVENILE JUSTICE MANDATE

10. Fifteen years after the adoption of the Convention on the Rights of the Child, the developments achieved worldwide vary in the area of juvenile justice. Some State Parties, who have ratified the CRC, have not made positive steps towards the creation of a system of juvenile justice as per their commitment taken with their endorsement of the CRC.

In regards to research, there are no studies, which assess the degree of advancement of juvenile justice systems on an international level. Therefore, there is currently no mechanism to shed light upon the current characteristics or tendencies of juvenile justice systems worldwide. Furthermore, there are no studies on the progress or achievements of individual countries in the area of juvenile justice.

On the other hand, no country could claim the possession of the perfect way to handle these questions. Whether it is in developed countries or in developing countries, a large number of young people and teenagers are dealt with through a judicial system that is of a purely penal essence.

11. In a large number of countries, many children are detained without any charge. They are simply arrested or placed in administrative custody. During these periods of administrative custody, their rights are seriously violated. Children "in conflict with the law" are arrested and detained in inhuman and debasing conditions.

In poor countries with a low Gross Domestic Product (GDP), the economic situation has drawn the focus away from the most vulnerable populations, commonly referred to as "pockets of poverty". Furthermore, high numbers of people under the age of eighteen tend to live in these pockets of poverty. In those conditions, young people and adolescents are often compelled to adopt a survival attitude which often results in a propensity to commit crime and violent acts. Unfortunately, the largest part of the youth and adolescents in conflict with the law come from those communities.

12. Despite these troubling issues, the issue of children in detention tends to be placed at the bottom of political and social agendas of governments. For us at DCI, we realise that a large number of governments adopt particularly repressive measures against juvenile delinquents. Moreover, in these countries, juvenile justice systems tend to be weak in structure or non-existent.

13. In response to these observations, we believe that it is urgent and of the highest importance to develop a global programme that promotes the implementation of international standards in such a way that detention, judgment, and sanctions faced by juveniles are in accordance with the law. Furthermore, DCI believes that deprivation of liberty should only be used as a last resort and that alternative measures should be explored.

Additionally, this global project aims to encourage States to develop preventive action and to strengthen social and educational responses in the area of juvenile justice.

4.3.1. Considering the objectives

14. The objectives set forth by this important theme unfold into two categories, in compliance with the structure and the hierarchy of the movement, and are displayed on the national level of the sections and the international level (the IEC and the IS).

15. First, at the national level, two regional programmes were set up in the South-America region and in the Africa region. These programmes bring together all sections participating in the activities of the programme; it involves 5 sections in Latin America and 12 in Africa.

The specific objectives of these programmes are mainly focused on the following aspects:

- To raise collective awareness of the international standards and norms regarding juvenile justice and children's rights in general;
- To strengthen the capabilities of the key players in the juvenile justice administration;
- To protect and assist juveniles in conflict with the law through legal and social assistance;
- To encourage alternative measures to detentions.

16. On the international scale, specific objectives include:

- Monitoring the implementation of the CRC, of its additional protocols and other appropriate international instruments related to it, particularly those dealing with juvenile justice in order to assess the extent of the achievements and the difficulties faced by State Parties in protecting, defending and guaranteeing children's rights. It will also put forward recommendations to improve the living conditions of the children and their families and enhance the mechanisms intended to protect children's rights at both the national and international levels;
- Promoting juvenile justice systems that respect children's rights and promote measures preventing the children from being in conflict with the law;
- Including of the theme of juvenile justice at all levels and in political agendas as a subject of high priority;
- Developing networks to build international alliances and promote the defence of children's rights, particularly the rights of those children in conflict with the law;
- Strengthening the capabilities of the different bodies of DCI and of other NGOs that are active in the field of juvenile justice in order to give them the means to defend children's rights in a global manner;

- Calling public attention to the situation of children's rights and juvenile justice so that the public mobilise, protect and defend children's rights generally and the rights of the children in conflict with the law.

4.3.2. Considering the implementation

17. The implementation of the theme of juvenile justice is supported by the worldwide campaign "NO KIDS BEHIND BARS", which was set up during the International Conference on Juvenile Justice.

The official announcement of the campaign is underway and will be launched by the Dutch section (DCI Netherlands is spearheading the campaign) in collaboration with the International Secretariat. The campaign will hold international conferences and mobilise campaigns in member countries.

18. The documentation centre of DCI is yet another source of pride for DCI. The documentation centre was created in order to raise collective awareness on children's rights at the international level. Since its creation in 1987, the collection has grown tremendously, and today it includes more than 17,000 articles. Access to the collection is open to the public and is often visited by researchers.

The documentation centre of DCI is unique in that it contains children's rights information published from all over the world. The subject areas also cover a vast array of topics such as children in conflict with the law, juvenile justice, child labour, child soldiers, street children and abused children. The collection is available in several languages and is composed of articles, case studies and reports from newspapers, newsletters, magazines, bulletins, press clippings, books and official government and United Nations' documents.

5. STRATEGIC PLAN OF ACTION

19. Since November 2005, the new members of DCI set up an international strategic action plan, which incorporates DCI's main mandate of juvenile justice. Included in this strategic action plan is a plan to draft an international report on children's rights, which stresses the theme of juvenile justice. This would be done annually and would include a detailed analysis of the juvenile justice system in a number of pre-selected countries. Due to its experience, DCI is a pivoting point in the field of juvenile justice. This dimension will be strengthened and will be used to develop the entire strategic plan of action.

DCI intends to elaborate and publicly announce its positions and recommendations regarding the issue of juvenile justice. DCI is also planning to begin the preparations for an international conference on juvenile justice that will take place in 2009, which is DCI's 20th anniversary.

The success of this action plan requires DCI to strengthen its capabilities at the national, regional and international levels.

20. DCI is aware of the existence of a large number of players that are involved in juvenile justice and recognises that it would be an illusion to think that it would be possible to work solo on such an ambitious project. Thus, DCI recognises the importance of creating and developing international alliances in order to maximise the impact of this project.

21. On the regional scale, our offices will be reinforced and better equipped in order to carry out the task of first responders as imparted to them by the new strategic plan of action. Within the sections, centres are set up for the assistance and the social and legal defence of children in conflict with the law; they serve as advisory bodies for the children and their families. Experts in the area of children's rights provide services in these centres. They are lawyers, psychologists, social workers and education specialists.

6. DIFFICULTIES FACING THE IMPLEMENTATION OF THE CRC IN THE AFRICA ZONE: WHAT ABOUT AFRICA'S SECTIONS?

22. The implementation of the CRC in Africa presents particularities that are worth mentioning. It is true that the endorsement of the international instruments and more particularly the 1989 CRC is the responsibility of the States; nevertheless, the progress achieved by its application is not the outcome of the public authorities in Africa. They are champions in endorsing the CRC but they are reluctant when it comes to the political decision to implement the CRC.

As far as the CRC is concerned, its implementation is often approached as a charity action and is strictly humanitarian. This is due to the lack of State administrative bodies that are necessary for its implementation. Thus, in our countries of the southern hemisphere, it is often the work of social partners, represented by NGOs and associations that visibly provide services to children and their families.

23. For example, in the field of juvenile justice, 95% of delinquency cases stem from poverty. The precarious living conditions of these children push them to come up with survival solutions that throw them into the streets. In order to survive these children then commit violent acts and petty theft and are then placed in detention centres.

During detention, children sometimes share the same cells as adult detainees. Furthermore, pre-trial detention periods have lengthened, as the state cannot assign pro bono attorneys to organise their defence. The government's only response is that they lack the financial and material means to change these situations due to the general economic situation regarding poverty.

24. On our side, in the DCI network of Africa, sections that have social and legal defence centres conduct outstanding actions that are praiseworthy. DCI staff conduct visits to the detention centres on a regular basis, provide legal assistance in court, monitor children's nutrition, health and general welfare in cases of detention, and when the resources are available, provide personalised assistance in reintegrating children into society.

Furthermore, sections in Togo and Uganda have successfully initiated actions on penal mediation and have thereby implemented alternative measures to detainment. This tremendous work is often done in collaboration with other organisations that share DCI's vision.

7. CONCLUSION

25. As the poet said: "*the child is the father of the man*". If children are the future of mankind, we need to make sure they are also its present.

TERRE DES HOMMES: THE APPLICATION OF THE CONVENTION ON THE RIGHTS OF THE CHILD FROM THE POINT OF VIEW OF THE NGOs

BERNARD BOËTON

1. INTRODUCTION

1. The Convention on the Rights of the Child, despite its imperfections, does however have an irrefutable advantage in that it provides *a universal language*, by its contents (with its two Optional Protocols), and also by the fact that almost all States in the world have ratified it.

Our working practice in 30 countries has shown us that the Convention is no bible of solutions, but a handbook, the reading of which, beyond the diversity of cultures and generations, provides us with a range of basic concepts, which are *services for*, *the protection* and *participation* of the child. It stipulates standards relating to civil law and criminal law, as well as all the collective rights, in terms of the objectives to be attained.

2. Beyond Article 1, which defines the child by age, the body of its text postulates a fuller definition that one could summarise as follows: "Children are human beings under 18 years of age, whose dignity is equal to that of any other human being, and who, according to their age and maturity, exercise a relative capacity *to distinguish*, *express* and *defend themselves*. They also have, from birth, *an inalienable right* to develop in a healthy and durable *environment*, within a natural, cultural and social *community*, which owes them priority attention in terms of *affection*, *protection*, *education* and *health*, since they also ensure the *future of mankind* and the promise of progress".

All individual, institutional, public and private players in any given society can agree on this definition.

2. WHAT IS THE SPECIFIC APPROACH OF THE NGOs AMONG THESE PLAYERS?

3. The abbreviation NGO is a generic term for organisations that perform primarily three functions: urgent humanitarian activities, long-term development programmes and the defence of human rights.

4. The NGOs, by their legal status as associations or foundations, form part of what is called *civil society*. They are the visible proof that a true democracy must be participative, in order that the NGO may act in a spirit of service (and not of power) and that an NGO may initiate projects, warn, propose and denounce if necessary, all existing forms of discrimination of which children may be the victims today, while promoting conditions for their future, in particular in terms of equal opportunity.

5. However, what the NGOs are asked to do is often paradoxical. NGOs are asked to be politically neutral, although they have to be run by committed militants. However, neutrality does not consist of keeping silent. For example, Terre des hommes was asked to analyse the Swiss teaching programme "*Objective to grow*" to identify the sectarian arguments at the origin of this method.

NGOs are asked to intervene in emergencies, but also to act on the causes of the misfortunes of mankind; to act in foreign orphanages, but also with clandestine children in European suburbs; to act on the ground, but at the same time they are reproached for not being elected (e.g. criticisms formulated by many participants at the Davos Forum).

Furthermore, they have to promote the right of interference, but they have to respect the sovereignty of States (e.g. should we leave an area of intervention if we cannot reach the victims; who deserves priority?); they have to denounce the persons responsible for unacceptable situations, but NGOs have to obtain their authorisation to reach the victims (e.g. emergency interventions in conflict situations); they have to denounce human rights violations by States, but to be the last bulwark of the State in combating "globalisation" (e.g. in the list of the 250 Davos Forum workshops, not a single mention was made of human rights).

They are asked to promote the universality of human rights, but to respect the diversity of cultures (e.g. domestic girls in Black Africa, female genital mutilations, etc.); to analyse the impact of macro-economic policies on the rights of the child, while reproaching them for their economic incompetence (e.g. the effects on public services of the structural adjustments imposed by the international financial institutions); to stick to assisting the victims, but not to be the "after-sales service" in armed conflicts.

In addition, they have to pursue torturers, but not to replace either the police force or the courts (e.g. the role of the NGO in legal procedures or in combating "sexual tourism" or child trafficking); to be managed like companies, but not to act according to economic criteria (e.g. specialised medical care in Switzerland for African children affected by congenital diseases inoperable in their countries); to have the ability to conduct military interventions; to function democratically and to find (all) the answers, but without asking too many questions, and so on and so forth.

3. WHAT ARE THE PRINCIPAL OBSTACLES WHEN NGOs IMPLEMENT THE RIGHTS OF THE CHILD?

6. Children are not a priority for many governmental authorities, whereas, in many countries, they represent nearly 45% of the population. Let us recall here that approximately 125 to 130 million children are born in the world each year (of which a third are not registered at birth). The rights of the child are thus not those of a minority, worthy of mere human compassion. They are the rights of about half of mankind. We militate so that State budgets cater for this dimension of the problem and so that the conditional nature of bilateral or multilateral assistance does not prejudice the operation of the basic public services but rather regards them as a priority.

7. The child is still all too often regarded as a commodity and a quasi-discretionary property belonging to the parents, the community, the institutions and sometimes even the State. Articles 12 to 16 of the Convention, concerning the participation of the child, its freedom of expression, religion or association, still pose problems, particularly amongst public opinion. Moreover, our experience on the ground has shown that on certain problems, public opinion appears even more resistant than the authorities do. For example, in the area of juvenile justice, the alternatives to detention for juvenile delinquents are poorly understood and accepted by public opinion, which is more sensitive to child victims than to child delinquents, without realising that these delinquents are *also* victims whereas the ministries concerned, certain judges, prosecutors and police officers understand the cause. Another example, even in our countries, is that the rights of the child are still sometimes seen as being in opposition to the rights of the family or society.

8. Nowadays, we are witnessing the development of the most serious forms of organised transnational criminality towards children, and precisely because they are children. The Terre des hommes programmes to combat child trafficking in Central Europe, Africa and Asia have revealed the scope and gravity of this phenomenon, which is not always perceived as such. In the children's home communities, migration is a right, whereas there is obviously child exploitation or even a "contemporary form of slavery".

9. The lack of statistical data in many countries is frightening. It is obviously difficult to have statistics on the clandestine forms of child exploitation; however, outside the capital of the country it is even impossible to obtain from the juvenile courts information on the number of cases of delinquency and even the number of children in prison.

10. Access to the most dangerous and most extreme situations is limited, and indeed is being increasingly restricted. For example, how is the situation of the rights of the child in Chechnya, in Somalia, in North Korea, etc.?

11. There is increasing quasi-ideological resistance to multilateralism in human rights. It is not rare to hear that "*human rights are the business of the NGOs*", which could be interpreted as "*human rights are not the business of the State or of the private sector*". At the World Social Forums as at the Davos Open Forum, we do not cease, each year, to say that the role of the NGO is to require that all the players, public and private, respect the rights of the child, under the control of the State in its regulating role.

12. However, the obstacles also come from the operation of the NGOs themselves. The need to plan, evaluate, give account, professionalise or even co-ordinate, is not always obvious, sometimes for a simple question of "flag", so vital for fund-raising both among the general public and from institutional donors.

Certain NGOs have problems concentrating on a precise area of competence. Even if the area of the rights of the child can be regarded as less sensitive – or more easily consensual – than others, it is often difficult to be operational while at the same time denounce the persons responsible for situations. More especially it is often the very authorities that are responsible which have to be asked for authorisation to work. In emergencies – as currently in Darfur (Sudan), we can collect testimony from minors who have been the victims of serious violations of their rights, however any disclosure or denunciation on our part would immediately result in our being prohibited from working with the refugees.

4. WHAT ARE THE LEVERS ON WHICH THE NGOs CAN RELY ON IN THEIR WORK?

13. Many public, national, regional and international institutions and organisations give the NGOs credit for working professionally in their analyses, observations and information, and involve them, albeit still largely insufficiently, in an official or abstract capacity, in their policies – the Committee on the Rights of the Child, the UN High Commissioner for Human Rights in general, the Council of Europe and the European Union (except for financial contributions). In addition, UNICEF, by virtue of its status, has a very useful ability to collect and synthesise information worldwide. As with many other NGOs, Terre des hommes is constantly requested to take part, for example, in consultative groups of the Swiss Federal Police on human trafficking, or to contribute to the working groups of the bodies of the European Union or the Council of Europe.

14. We live in a world where it has been largely proven, by a number of coalitions of NGOs on given themes, that significant results can be obtained by joining forces at the national, regional or international level. It suffices to recall the role of the NGOs in the pressure exerted for the drafting, adoption and ratification of the Convention on the Rights of the Child. One could also take the examples of the Coalitions against anti-personnel mines, for the International Criminal Court. At the Rome Conference in 1998 on the creation of the International Criminal Court, we led a delegation of associations of parents of child victims of organised crime from 5 countries (China, Argentina, Belgium, Algeria, and France) in order to ensure that the victims be heard and for them to submit their demands. In 1995, we also called on several NGOs, in Belgium, to publicise the "Spartacus affair", from which we learned that although working together to collectively publicise a matter does not necessarily influence a legal judgment, there is no doubt that the Court followed the procedure in minute detail.

15. The development of networking, starting from skills, which can henceforth be found in all countries – technical, medical, educational, legal or other – we must continue to capitalise on the experience gained, which presupposes that the internatio-nal organisations of the "countries of the North" – as we say – lend a far more open ear to the players of the future in the countries of intervention, not only with respect to their needs, but also to their concepts of development, which can be different. A true partnership cannot be simply budgetary, but also conceptual and strategic. Terre des homes supports national NGOs, which implement the right to education in other forms and with fewer means, such as by informal or functional education methods. Indeed, can we continue to promote a concept of development throughout the world, based on a mode of growth, which is being ever more contested here at home? Since the concept of the Third World is no longer geographical now and crosses all countries, the initiatives taken in certain so-called "poor" countries can be applied and tested in the "rich" countries. For example, the system of micro-credits, initiated in Bangladesh, is widely used in Western Europe. Functional education methods are also used for the elimination of illiteracy among migrant populations.

16. The increasing importance of rights in reading situations and as a lever for action is decisive given the consequences of globalisation. For example, in the light of the prospects for privatising public education and health services, the NGOs have a fundamental role in demanding that the State, which is at the same time source and guarantor of human rights, meets its obligations. In Switzerland, for example, we are militating against a new "Asylum Act", which causes considerable prejudice to unaccompanied minors, as they will be forced to survive clandestine because their cases will not even be considered.

That does not mean that the State is to be expected to assume the entire burden because the private sector, of which the NGOs form a part, has its role to play, too. However, to demand that the State, by exercising its supervisory and regulatory role, ensures equal opportunity with respect to the basic rights of the child, which it has adopted and ratified. Moreover, it could be, in years to come, one of those "quirks of history", in that the NGOs become the last bulwark of the State.

5. CONCLUSION

17. A rights-of-the-child implementation strategy would imply working simultaneously in three strategic directions:

- to improve the laws (and procedures);
- to manage concrete projects;
- to make the authorities aware of public opinion.

This is not just a simple list since none of these three elements can progress without the other two. Let us take the example of juvenile justice:

- one cannot manage a programme of alternatives to detention for juvenile delinquents if these alternatives do not appear in the law;
- lobbying the legislator is credible only if one can prove by action which of these alternatives will work, albeit for only some of the delinquents;
- one will be able neither to improve the laws, nor convince the judges and prosecutors, nor yet meet the objectives of the projects, without convincing all

the players of the need for complying with international standards, or without working on public opinion to convince them of the need for educational measures and punishments for these minors.

However, that does not mean that each NGO working on the rights of the child must necessarily be simultaneously involved. Networking by complementing each other, and in the form of a coalition of players specialised in each of these fields, is the condition for effectiveness.

Then there is the co-operation between international NGOs and national NGOs. There are by now competent national workers in all countries, which do not necessarily have any money, however there is especially an international network for capitalising on experience and better practices.

Finally, let us not forget the principal lever of the NGO, which is the ability to stir the conscience and will of each individual. The "international community" is each one of us.

18. We will conclude with a few quotations:

From Michel FOUCAULT ("Said and written"): "*The misfortune of men should never be a mute residue of politics. It creates an absolute right to rise up and to address those who hold power. We must refuse the task sharing that is very often proposed to us. It is up to individuals to be indignant and speak out, and up to governments to reflect and act. It is true that good governments like the pious indignation of their subjects provided that it remains lyrical. (...) We should realise that very often it is the governments that speak, and that wish and are capable of doing nothing but speak (...). We can and must refuse the theatrical role of pure and simple indignation that is proposed to us" (...).*
The NGOs "are the initiatives which created this new right – that of private individuals to intervene effectively in matters of politics and international strategies."

From Edmond KAISER, founder of "Terre des hommes": "*Dreams are the prerogative of those whom a vigilant heart prevents from sleeping.*"

Especially from Judge H. SIMON (of Breslau in 1848), and this is, in my opinion, the best possible definition of an NGO: "*Only he who resists can offer support.*"

IV. HUMAN RIGHTS EDUCATION

ARE WE EDUCATING CHILDREN AS PEOPLE WITH RIGHTS OR JUST TALKING ABOUT IT?

KATARINA TOMAŠEVSKI

1. INTRODUCTION

1. It is a habit of lawyers to answer yes-or-no questions by saying "it depends". Although this habit is not well liked and for good reason, answers to the question, which is posed in the title of this contribution, vary a great deal depending on who is answering. People who are carrying out numerous programmes in human rights education are likely to claim to have transformed human rights education from theory into practice. The beneficiaries of their programmes may or may not agree. Both sides – the teachers and the learners – may be right. The reason is that teaching and learning are two separate processes. Children do not necessarily learn what they have been taught; they learn both less and more. Proverbially, they learn as much, if not more, outside the classroom than inside it.

In the worst-case scenario, an adult version of human rights which is imposed upon the young conflicts with their own visions. The same words – human rights – often have a different meaning for the generation that carries out the teaching and for the generation that is learning, especially because of what the young are *not* taught. Three recent European examples of youth protests against governmental policies denying their rights illustrate how many of these children would state that they are *not* educated as people with rights. The choice of European exporters of human rights education highlights questions, which should be, but are not posed. They are discussed in sequence, starting from the immense growth of human rights education programmes and their invisible effects, and leading to the parallel growth of programmes labelled as rights-based development.

2. WRONGING CHILDREN'S RIGHTS IN (ADULTS') SILENCE

2. Three recent European examples illustrate the depth and the breadth of this intergenerational conflict about the meaning of human rights:

- One example was the schoolchildren's political protest against the Second Iraq War in the winter and spring of 2003 in the United Kingdom. They formed a part of the two million voices against the war.[1] Their right to a voice was denied and many were punished as truants.[2] The message was that they should sit at school, listen to what they are taught, repeat all of it accurately, but whatever they might have been told about human rights applied neither to them nor to Iraqi children.
- Another example was the mobilisation of three million people in France at the beginning of 2006, in solidarity with the youth who were offered an entry into employment with considerably lesser rights than adults had given themselves. An editorial in Le Monde has lamented "*irresponsible policies which have not prepared the youth for the future, but have rather loaded a €100 billion public debt onto their shoulders*".[3] The price of this sin of omission is widespread youth unemployment. The sin of commission is age-based discrimination, which forces the young to work to pay the cost of old-age pensions and health care which adults have granted them as their rights.
- On 2 May 2006, more than 10,000 schoolchildren protested in front of Danish parliament government's plan to abolish group exams. Another 42,000 signed a petition to keep the group exam.[4] It enables pupils and students to work together and learn together but clashes against competitiveness, which today informs evaluations of learning performance. It is impossible to teach children to cooperate and to compete at the same time. As they compete against each other for better

---

1 A. MURRAY and L. GERMAN, *Stop the War. The Story of Britain's Biggest Mass Movement*, (London: Bookmarks Publications, 2005).

2 In a widely publicised case, 15-year-old ELENA GRICE was suspended from school. She had organised "a walkout in protest against the war" on 20 March 2003, in which 500 children were joined by parents and teachers. She was suspended for organising the protest and for getting into verbal duels with some of the teachers during the build-up of the walkout. Her argument was that children had a right to join the protest if they wished to do so; the teachers' instructions were that children were legally required to stay in school, even with their parents' written permission to join the protest. She was un-suspended by a judicial order, with the judge saying that "she is a very silly girl, but even silly girls are entitled" to complete their education, see C. DYER, 'Banned pupil is 'silly girl' says judge', (3 May 2003) *Guardian*.

3 "Une jeunesse qui ne supporte pas, ou mal, cette France bloquée et commence à prendre conscience de l'irresponsabilité des politiques passées à ne pas prépaper l'avenir, sauf à avoir accumulé 100 milliards d'euros de dette publique sur ses épaules.", see 'Jeunesse en colère', (9 March 2006) Edito du Monde, *Le Monde*.

4 See, 'Disgruntled students take to the streets', (5–11 May 2006) *Copenhagen Post*.

test results, as do their schools and their countries, cooperation remains an abstract term. Children learn by example, not by exhortation. Although it is difficult to find teachers who enjoy teaching-to-test, and most learners intensely dislike it, measuring learning outcomes and ranking guides' education. The pressure of standardised testing converts children into "cookie-cutter test takers".[5]

These three countries, the United Kingdom, France and Denmark, claim a long human rights tradition and export their definitions of human rights through their foreign policies and the vast network of actors, governmental and non-governmental, who carry the message into the regions and countries that are called "developing" or, closer to home, "transitioning".

3. WHY SO MUCH HUMAN RIGHTS EDUCATION AND SO LITTLE TO SHOW FOR IT?

3. The huge number of programmes in human rights education reaches into millions, precisely 395,000,000.[6] This creates a perception that human rights education is broadly, if not universally, accepted and supported. The United Nations have added to this an assertion that "*all human rights are universal, indivisible, interrelated, interdependent and mutually reinforcing*".[7] If such assertions reflected reality, human rights work would be redundant. The need for human rights education stems precisely from widespread resistance to human rights. Two questions should, but routinely do *not* inform programmes in human rights education:

- The first one is how to tackle the abyss between *should* and *is*, between the apparently generous human rights guarantees in international human rights instruments and many national constitutions and the ground-level reality, where these are conspicuous by their absence;
- The second question is how to accommodate the gap between educational interventions being, by nature, *micro-level* interventions while human rights protection necessitates changing *macro-level* policies.

Where human rights education is confined to micro-level interventions, it is slanted towards everyday ethics and children are taught to be nice to other children. The limits

---

5 S.-K. YOON, 'South Korea: Lessons in learning', (28 February 2002) *Far Eastern Economic Review*.

6 This number was shown by using the Google search engine for "human rights education" on 16 May 2006.

7 General Assembly – Human Rights Council, *Draft resolution submitted by the President of the General Assembly* (UN Doc. A/60/L.48, 2006), preamble.

stemming from macro-level policies loom large. The examples in the introductory part of this text show that children are taught *not* to help other children with exams or to protest when other children are targets of their governments' warfare in the name of national security or war against terror(ism). Their tendency to focus on what they are *not* taught leads them to question, "to talk about principles that cannot be found in practice",[8] to challenge the gap between *should* and *is*, between micro-level human rights protections and their absence on the macro-level.

Moreover, obstacles to human rights education for children and young people also include resistance to the very assertion that children are people with rights. A parents' statement that children "are uncontrollable because they know that they have rights"[9] illustrates the heritage of centuries of the treatment of children as the property of their parents. Where formal commitments have been made to human rights education, such views are seldom voiced. Consequently, they remain unchallenged and unchanged, are driven underground, and impede human rights education. Children are then taught *about* human rights but *not* educated as people with rights.

4. In practice, human rights education may amount to no more than a recital of abstract terms culled from the international human rights documents created through diplomatic negotiations. Usually these are poorly translated, or not at all, from American English, which has become the language of globalisation. A recital of abstract human rights norms comes dangerously close to a secular religion, a set of universal truths that pretend to be self-evident, which it might be in an ideal world, but surely is not in ours. The distance from the lives of learners and their teachers is enormous. The majority cannot understand terms such as "empowerment" or "mainstreaming" or even "gender", which are taken for granted in many human rights education programmes.

Also, textbooks on human rights education often need to be challenged and changed. Too many include messages that are contrary to both intent and content of human rights education. In Turkey, cherishing "the glorious Turkish history" and honouring "the great Turks whose services have made the great Turkish nation" forms part of the curriculum.[10] A textbook for human rights education ends its first chapter by homework: pupils should go to the nearest military garrison to study *in situ* the army's

---

8 B. FERNANDO, 'A flowed approach to national implementation of human rights', (2006) vol. 5, No. 1 *Article 2 of the International Covenant on Civil and Political Rights*, 34.

9 G. KHUMALO, 'Corporal punishment lives on', (20 March 2003) *Natal Witness*, (Pietermaritzburg, South Africa).

10 A.M. KAZAMIAS, *Education and the Quest for Modernity in Turkey*, (Chicago: University of Chicago Press, 1966), 148.

love for the country.[11] There is no mention of any past or ongoing human rights violations, despite many ongoing legal reforms to halt them. A textbook for civics in India goes one step further and misdescribes rights, emphasising that the individual "must have sense of loyalty and love for the State. In return the government of the State gives him some social and political rights – such as the right to vote".[12]

5. With so much information at the fingertips of all who can afford modern technology, children have vast possibilities for teaching themselves whatever they may be keen to know. Teachers then become "mediators between the students and varied sources of information".[13] It is teachers who translate abstractly defined aims of education into messages, which children can recognise and internalise. With the advent of human rights education, teachers are required to help children learn about human rights. Yet, *their* rights are often denied or violated.[14] Results often confirm what Bishop WALSH has said about prisoners: "*The way we treat people forms the kind of people they become.*"[15]

4. WHY SCHOOLING DOES NOT NECESSARILY LEAD TO LEARNING?

6. It is a sobering indictment of education that too many children and young people find it boring. We have deprived them of political rights until they become adults, but made education compulsory for them. European pupils spend on average 7,000 hours at school while compulsory education may extend it to 14,000 hours.[16] Their questions about the rights which we have given ourselves to mould their lives, form the essence of human rights education. Therein lies a paradox. Bringing human rights to life through education can be impossibly difficult or extremely easy. Difficulties appear insurmountable where self-censorship impedes questioning of the choices – and the errors – which have been made. Everything becomes easier when the processes of

---

11 E. YAMANLAR, *Vatandaslik ve insan haklari egitimi (Education in Citizenship and Human Rights)*, (Istanbul: Ders Kitaplari Anonim Sirketi, 2000), 62.

12 A.C. SHARMA, *Learning Civics*, (New Delhi: Pitmar Publishing Company, 1997), vol. 1, Fifth Revised Edition, 58.

13 J. SAVOVA, *Education and Teachers in Central and Eastern European Countries, 1991–1995*, (Geneva: International Bureau of Education (IBE/UNESCO), 1996), 21.

14 Particularly high casualties amongst teachers and institutionalised denial of their rights have been noted in Ethiopia, while in Colombia three teachers are still killed every month. Commission on Human Rights, *Report of the Special Rapporteur on the right to education*, KATARINA TOMAŠEVSKI, (UN Doc. E/CN.4/2003/9, para. 37), and *Report on mission to Colombia* (UN Doc. E/CN.4/2004/45/Add.2/UN Doc.Corr.1), paras. 39–42).

15 *Newsletter for Irish Prisoners Overseas*, Issue No. 28, January 1999, 4.

16 EURYDICE – *Key Data on Education in Europe*, 5th edition, Office for Official Publications of the European Communities (EUR-OP), January 2003, <www.eurydice.org>.

teaching and learning no longer divide people into active depositaries of wisdom and passive recipients of knowledge. This triggers the process of learning, together, our mutual bonds of rights and duties, freedoms and responsibilities.

To bridge the gap between formal human rights commitments and the real-life environment in which teaching and learning take place, a learning process of its own is necessary. More than anything, it requires courage. The courage to acknowledge that human rights are denied and violated everywhere, that human rights are not "what foreigners lack",[17] but, rather, that human rights are protection against abuse of power that has not yet been attained, anywhere, hence we need to learn how to recognise and oppose it, so as to be able to prevent it in our own environment.

Whether the two parallel processes, teaching and learning, translate human rights objectives for education into reality depends on the congruence between these objectives and the operative guidance for teaching and learning as well as the concordance – or discord – between in-school and out-of-school learning.

5. WHY EDUCATION IN EUROPE LEADS TO INCREASING RACISM?

7. Children learn through observation and imitation. They are likely to start perpetuating discriminatory practices much before they learn the word *discrimination.* By the time their curriculum includes the term *discrimination,* they are likely to have internalised the underlying prejudice. Prejudice is formed in late childhood and adolescence and sustained from one generation to another through social usage. When it favours individual and group self-interest, it is easy to rationalise. Discriminatory practices can be countered by changing the rules of behaviour; their underlying rationale usually remains unexplored. It is customary to label this underlying rationale as irrational and believe that its cause is ignorance, to be eliminated through education. However, this rationale often includes preservation of an assumed superiority, keeping privileges, or fear of competition. As early as 1957, the first United Nations study into discrimination in education highlighted the underlying rationale thus: "*A policy based on fear of losing a privileged position necessarily entails measures to deny education to an entire population group, or to allow it access only to education at a lower level.*"[18]

---

[17] Speech by Francesca Klug on the promotion of human rights, Human Rights in Education Conference, 26 September 2001, Department of Education and Northern Ireland Human Rights Commission, January 2002, 49.

[18] C.D. Ammon, *Study of Discrimination in Education*, (New York: United Nations, 1957), No. 1957.XIV.3, 10.

The inevitable effect of exclusion from education is the lack of formal educational accomplishments and the consequent inter-generational transmission of deprivation. Nevertheless, the previous denial of human rights of the victims of educational exclusion is easily converted into factual evidence of their inferiority, feeding the perpetuation of exclusion.

Four decades later, the European Union exemplifies how much this rationale permeates what young Europeans learn. Formally, "all European education systems aim to be inclusive" and combating exclusion is prioritised.[19] The Euro-barometer surveys in the past decades have shown an increase in the proportion of Europeans self-declared as "quite racist" or "very racist".[20] The fact that this proportion has increased in the past decades and reached one-third of Europeans highlights the necessity to ask why the abyss between the formal commitment to inclusiveness and/or combating exclusion and the self-assessments by the "products" of the national education systems a third of whom have learned exactly the opposite of what they were taught.

In 1947, the first United Nations report on discrimination emphasised that "*the whole field of action to prevent discrimination requires a vast programme of education*". Law cannot be effective, and may be counterproductive, unless it enjoys support by those whom it addresses. Hence, the emphasis on education to engender such support. Looking back at the year 1947, it is worthwhile recalling that education is a capacious term and its outcomes can be both positive and negative: "*Forcing a prejudiced person to read or hear exhortations on tolerance may only increase his prejudice. Overenthusiastic appraisals of the contributions of a minority may create a reaction of distaste for members of that minority; and programmes improperly presented, even with the best intentions, may create an awareness of group difference that did not previously exist.*"[21]

Although often introduced as the functional equivalent of human rights education, citizenship education undermines human rights as properties of *all* members of humanity and substitutes "involvement in public affairs by those who have the rights of citizens".[22] Citizenship education may underpin xenophobia because it inevitably has to address lesser rights for non-citizens. Although often introduced as the

19 European Commission, *European Report on Quality of School Education*, Brussels, May 2000, 6.

20 European Monitoring Centre on Racism and Xenophobia, *Attitudes Towards Minority Groups in the European Union. A Special Analysis of the Eurobarometer 2000 Survey*, Vienna, March 2001.

21 Sub-Commission on the Prevention of Discrimination and the Protection of Minorities, *Report on the prevention of discrimination (Prepared by the Secretary-General)* (UN Doc. E/CN.4/Sub.2/40, 1949), paras. 17 (c) and 177.

22 Qualifications and Curriculum Authority, *Education for Citizenship and the Teaching of Democracy in Schools. Final Report of the Advisory Group on Citizenship*, London. 22 September 1998, 9.

functional equivalent of human rights education, citizenship education undermines human rights as properties of *all* members of humanity by substituting only "those who have the rights of citizens".[23] Moreover, citizenship education can focus on responsibilities[24] rather than rights.

6. WHY IS TOLERANCE AN UGLY WORD?

8. In 1978, UNESCO forged the concept of a right to be different, positing that "*all individuals and groups have the right to be different, to consider themselves as different and to be regarded as such*".[25] SACHS revisited this concept in 2000. Delivering a judgment in the name of South Africa's Constitutional Court, he took that line of argument one step further, affirming "*the right of people to be who they are without being forced to subordinate themselves to the cultural and religious norms of others*".[26] In an ideal world, education would adapt to each child. In our imperfect world, the right of each child to be regarded as different remains a distant dream.

Children are, in practice, reduced to the few denominators that are monitored and thereby inform education laws and policies. These are often only sex and age, rarely disability, only sometimes the child's mother tongue, religion or race. Because education encompasses huge numbers of learners and teachers, the emphasis is on numbers and, thus, statistical averages. Diverse children are reduced to the minimum common denominator, the individual child forced "to sink or swim within the mainstream".[27]

9. The objective towards which education should be moulded is defined as *tolerance* in many international human rights instruments.[28] Setting the limits of the intolerable is the first necessary step towards creating space for teaching and learning tolerance. *Tolerance* implies acceptance, albeit passive, of "the other", and "the other" is constantly created and re-created. Asked what they may want, none of "the other" has ever said "to be tolerated". *Tolerance* routinely fails to guide effectively education

---

23 Ibid.

24 Citizenship education in England comprises "social and moral responsibility, community involvement and political literacy." See *Citizenship education and human rights education: an overview of recent developments in the UK*, (Manchester: British Council, 2003), 8.

25 Art. 1 (2) *Declaration on race and racial prejudice*, adopted by the General Conference of UNESCO on 27 November 1978.

26 Constitutional Court of South Africa – *Christian Education South Africa v. Minister of Education*, Case CCT 4/00, (18 August 2000), para. 24.

27 Supreme Court of Canada – *Eaton v. Brant County Board of Education*, (1997) 1 *S.C.R.*, 241, para. 67.

28 The aims of education have been defined as promoting *tolerance* in Art. 26 (2) of the Universal Declaration of Human Rights or Art. 29 (1) (d) of the Convention on the Rights of the Child.

in the desired direction because choice of the aim is inadequate to the task in hand,[29] demonstrating that human rights guidance should be altered. This could be an easy task if international human rights instruments were treated for what they are, outcomes of intergovernmental negotiations. Calling them *instruments* indicates their purpose. They are tools for improving human rights protection, to be used when they are adequate to this task and discarded when this is not the case. A phenomenon, which could easily be called *human rights fundamentalism*, impedes progress in this direction. The original text of each human rights instrument is treated as if it were sacrosanct even if it was negotiated long ago, by governments that exist no longer, for a world that has changed beyond recognition.

10. The changing pattern of discrimination points to the need for changing human rights safeguards against it. The internationally prohibited division of humanity by race, sex or colour has been expunged from educational curricula. An emphasis on provenance, however, defines "the other" as immigrants. Race and religion are routinely the principal denominators of exclusion. Paradoxically, many European countries have banned collecting data on race or religion. This makes discrimination statistically invisible. As we have learned in human rights work, making problems invisible allows human rights violations to thrive. Opposing them necessitates exposing their existence and their causes.

In most countries, however, domestic law protects individuals against being publicly insulted but prohibitions of group defamation are rare. Maligning "foreigners" can be deemed an expression of patriotism and is often a vote-winner. This has often been emphasised by the ECRI (European Commission against Racism and Intolerance) which has, in the case of Denmark, pointed out those negative stereotypes and prejudices "*are promoted by public opinion leaders, including political elites from across the political spectrum*".[30] Their inevitable influence on children and young people undermines human rights messages in school-based education. In addition, COULBY has pointed out that schools and universities "*are being involved in the encouragement of xenophobia as a mode of state-building*".[31]

---

29 An illustration of divergent interpretations of "tolerance", singled out in the international human rights instruments as a key value education should promote, was provided by teachers in South Africa: 46% defined its meaning as "putting up with" or "having patience" with different opinions and attitudes, routinely adding the importance of "keeping your differences of opinion to yourself". See: *Values, Education and Democracy: School-based Research Report*, (Pretoria: Department of Education, 2002), 2.

30 European Commission against Racism and Intolerance, *Second Report on Denmark*, adopted on 16 June 2000, Doc. CRI (2001) 4, 3 April 2001, para. 28.

31 D.COULBY, 'Education in times of transition: Eastern Europe with particular reference to the Baltic States', in D. COULBY et al. (eds.), *Education in Times of Transition. World Yearbook of Education 2000*, (London: Kogan Page, 2000), 17.

The language we use still embodies the hierarchy of rights-holders and the rights-less, with former colonisers freely moving around the world with the full range of self-granted rights as "expatriates" while the colonised are denied rights as "migrants". Similarly, the speakers of international languages, especially English, provide expensive services for their mastery, internationally examined, graded and certified, while those speaking a "vernacular" are denied even a right to call their language by its proper name.

11. Also, the general principle whereby education should adapt to each child, the much-quoted "best interests of each child" principle, raises unanswered questions regarding children with disabilities. Statistics place their number between 1% and 41% and this huge difference reflects the absence of an underlying agreement on what disability is.[32] There is even more disagreement on how education should respond to disability. The ongoing process of drafting a convention on the rights of people with disabilities within the United Nations has revealed discord. Preferences for all-inclusive education, with particular educational remedies provided to children with disabilities in mainstream schools, clash against desires for separate schools.[33] Fears that segregation might lead to the institutionalisation of disadvantage and "educational ghettos" underpin opposition to segregation. Advocates of segregation posit the preservation of their culture as the key value that education should respect. Reconciling the two divergent approaches is difficult even in theory. It becomes easier with the advent of equal rights of all and the best interests of each child as guiding principles, forcing a change of paradigm in designing education.

---

[32] K. Tomaševski, *Education Denied: Costs and Remedies*, (London: Zed Books, 2003), 151–154.

[33] Drafting takes place through periodic meetings of the Ad Hoc Committee on a Comprehensive and Integral International Convention on the Protection and Promotion of the Rights and Dignity of Persons with Disabilities. The first draft of the first, substantive, part of a future convention has been developed in the form of "Chair's Draft Elements", which affirms as one of the underlying principles "diversity and the right to be different" as well as "the right of all children with disabilities to inclusive education in their own community". In its Position and Opinion concerning the Working Group Draft from January 2004, the World Blind Union has suggested that the future convention provide for choice between inclusive or special education, noting that "full inclusion is often wrongly interpreted to mean full-scale mainstreaming of all students with disabilities in the same classroom, no matter the disability and no matter the possibility to utilise the lessons. Students who are Deaf, Blind and Deafblind gain more benefit in schools or classes of their own, with teachers and support staff who are qualified and skilled in sign language, Braille and tactile communication skills." All documents are available at <www.un.org/esa/socdev/enable/rights>.

7. TEACHING ABOUT PRIVATE VIOLENCE, AND SILENCE IN THE FACE OF PUBLIC ABUSES OF POWER

12. At the intersection between school and society, conflicting messages may cause confusion. Formal schooling is only one message carrier since education is, in the broadest sense of this term, the sum total of what children learn from their parents and peers, from the mass media as well as from the hugely developed advertising and entertainment industry, much of which is specifically targeted at children. Studies into violence have revealed that "youths who observe adults accepting violence as a solution to problems are apt to emulate that violence".[34] BONNET has argued that violence against children was a taboo until the 1960s because it reveals the shameful behaviour of adults.[35] Children victimised by violence are likely to become violent adults, however, this early link in the causation of violence is seldom explored. School-based programmes for the prevention of violence, where they exist, tend to be an optional add-on to the compulsory curriculum.

It is as difficult as it is necessary to expose schoolchildren to abuses of power that have led to the development of human rights protections. Individuals as well as countries tend to remember the pain they have suffered, not the pain they have inflicted on others. Victimhood is one-sided in history textbooks, epitomising what TYACK has called calls "*the pedagogy of patriotism*".[36] School textbooks rarely describe abuses committed by one's own government against populations of other countries or the people in one's own country, although history abounds with such examples.

8. QUESTIONING CONFLICTING VALUES

13. Since education is compulsory, it bestows upon governments a right to force new generations into school to be taught whatever the government has decided they should be taught. A US/USSR 1977–1989 textbook study entitled its final report "*School Textbooks: Weapons for the Cold War*".[37] Education as a duty recalls its definition as the main pillar of social control alongside law enforcement. Because school reaches

---

34 D.K. CRAWFORD and R.J. BODINE, 'Conflict resolution education: Preparing youth for the future', (2001) 8 (1) *Juvenile Justice*, 21.

35 C. BONNET, *L'Enfant Cassé*, (Paris: Albin Michel, 1999).

36 S. MONDALE and S.B. PATTON (eds.), *School: The Story of American Public Education*, (Boston: Beacon Press, 2001), 5.

37 F. PINGEL, *UNESCO Guidebook on Textbook Research and Textbook Revision*, (Paris: George Eckert Institute for International Textbook Research and UNESCO, 1999), 11.

the largest number of children and young people at their most impressionable age, the purpose of schooling is more often to instruct children in what they should think rather than teaching them how to think.

Attacks on schools because they epitomise an alien, imposed ideology and culture has demonstrated, in a frightening manner, why compulsory schooling may be rejected, sometimes even violently.[38] The law prohibits and punishes attacks on schools. Enforcing such law does not facilitate understanding what led to attacks on schools in the first place. Understanding does not mean justifying, least of all condoning, however, being better able to prevent not only attacks on schools but also the underlying rejection of education.

Conflicting demands upon education distort commitments to human rights by prioritising competition and income-earning skills. Uniform criteria for assessing learning accomplishments cloak in silence barriers to learning. International ranks of language proficiency, which constantly show superior performance of learners in the North, reflect the fact that "the language of instruction is the same as the language spoken at home by a dominant proportion of the pupils".[39] Moreover, excellent performance in multiple-choice tests reflects good memory and skills, not necessarily knowledge, least of all creativity. It underpins the values, which children and young people internalise through learning to compete rather than cooperate. The message is that performance is valued, while effort is not.

14. It is those who cannot compete in today's world that should benefit from human rights education to help those challenge and change macro-policies, which have excluded them from enjoying their human rights. They are portrayed as statistics, in terms of the millions denied health care, water and sanitation, nutrition, housing or education. Statistics are proverbially numbing, and the millions of the excluded are treated as an in-built feature of today's globalising world. Lively academic debates

---

[38] In its passive form, rejection of education has become known in West Africa as *déscolarisation*, the abandonment of formal education based on the former colonial language and designed for (now non-existent) public sector employment. See: M.F. LANGE, *L'école au Togo: Processus de scolarisation et institution de l'école en Afrique*, (Paris: Karthala, 1998), 237–295. In its violent form, as armed attacks on schools and teachers, rejection of education seen as an imposition of an alien ideology, language or religion by the government has been reported from numerous parts of the world, including Indonesia. See: Commission on Human Rights, *Report of the Special Rapporteur on the right to education*, KATARINA TOMAŠEVSKI: *Mission to Indonesia* (UN Doc. E/CN.4/2003/9/Add.1), paras. 38 and 49.

[39] J. NAUMANN, 'Curriculum and languages: teaching in African languages and learning strategies', in *Curriculum Development and Education for Living Together: Conceptual and Managerial Challenges in Africa, Final Report of the Seminar held in Nairobi, Kenya, 25–29 June 2001*, (Geneva: International Bureau of Education and Kenya National Commission for UNESCO, 2003), 35.

persist on the fate of economic and social rights; however, they do not inform governmental policies.

Globally, children's rights to education or health care have been subsumed under *development* rather than human rights. The OHCHR (Office of the High Commissioner for Human Rights) has stated that governments should strengthen the people's ability to meet their own needs by "*creating conditions in which the market can supply the services that they demand*".[40] Of course, the market does not supply services; they are sold at a price. The message to children excluded from school because it has been priced out of its reach is that they are rights-less.[41] The proliferation of rights-based approaches demonstrates that human rights are in danger of becoming a weasel word.[42]

15. A common language to merge human rights and *development* has yet to be developed. To begin with, assumptions are different. Development requires optimism, a belief that governments and intergovernmental organisations are committed to development. Human rights work institutionalises professional pessimism because it inquires into abuses of power. Human rights are safeguards against abuses of power; these abuses ought to be exposed and opposed. Exposing them ruptures the silence in which they thrive. Opposing them dispels a myth that human rights commitments are universal and merely need to be tapped. The objective of human rights work is to prevent abuses of power and effective safeguards can only be developed by examining past and ongoing abuses.

It is as difficult as it is important to tackle ongoing abuses of power, which have deprived millions of children of their birthright to education or health care. This denial has been institutionalised globally and is evidenced in a changed vocabulary. The previous *right* has become *access* to education or health.[43] It is therefore easy for the

---

40 OHCHR, *Frequently Asked Questions on a Human Rights-Based Approach to Development Cooperation*, OHCHR (Doc. HR/PUB/06/8), United Nations, New York and Geneva, 2006, 2.

41 An exercise in stocktaking has revealed that not even primary education is free in half of the countries in the world, with the denial of free and compulsory education as each child's right most prevalent in Sub-Saharan Africa and Eastern Europe and Central Asia. See: K. TOMAŠEVSKI, *The State of the Right to Education Worldwide. 2006 Global Report: Free or Fee?*, (Nijmegen: Wolf Legal Publishers, June 2006).

42 On 6 May 2006, K. TOMAŠEVSKI carried out a Google search using 'rights-based development' as keyword. The result was 1,170,000 entries, illustrative of profound differences in defining a link between human rights and development. The first dozen entries presented widely differing definitions. Each advocated 'a' human rights approach to development, distinct and presumably unique. Some argued for improved quality of life, others for judicial enforcement of inalienable rights, yet others for helping duty-bearers (including NGOs) perform better.

43 The author's critique on the subsequently abolished United Nations Commission on Human Rights for its lack of effort to articulate and defend economic and social rights, especially the right to education, can be found in: K. TOMAŠEVSKI, 'Has the right to education a future within the United Nations? A behind-the-scenes account by the Special Rapporteur on the right to education

OHCHR to claim that the market rather than a government can supply a service. This conforms to the definition of access. That it also conforms to the definition of the denial of rights through their transformation into traded services is probably the most important and the least discussed facet of human rights education.

9. LEARNING BY DOING

16. We all learn about human rights living in a world where human rights protection is much closer to utopia than reality. Yet, universal human rights necessitate globalisation of human rights education as their corollary. So, one can ask oneself, how do we teach human rights without living them? It becomes easier when we acknowledge that moral principle is something that puts one at variance with accepted practice, that daring to insist that society should actually embody its professed human rights principles is often labelled utopian, or worse. It becomes even easier when we define human rights as a process. Indeed, wherever there is abuse, there are always people who will expose it and try to right the wrong. Human rights protection was built on their courage to speak truth to power. It was institutionalised through nudging, often shaming governments into substituting the rule of law for the law of the ruler. Human rights education built on that success, legitimising demands that all human rights be protected, always and everywhere, and facilitating progress towards a situation "in which no one – neither those who give orders, nor those who carry them out, nor those who let the abuses happen – can say: 'I did not know'."[44]

17. Governmental policy, from the global to the local level, should be informed by human rights law. This requirement implies its knowledge and acceptance by all key actors of decision-making. Law cannot be effective, and may be counterproductive, unless it enjoys support by those whom it addresses. The role of human rights education is to engender support for human rights law as a part of the political project to ensure its application, following the juridical task of developing human rights law. However, human rights have been introduced in formal education merely a decade ago in most countries. Previously, we had to unlearn what we had been taught at school so as to create space for human rights. The obvious starting point was to challenge education, which was designed and delivered without a mention of human rights. Worse, it was often overflowing with anti-human-rights messages. Pre-military education served (and still does) to point out who the enemies are and prepare young

---

1998–2004', (2005) 5 (2) *Human Rights Law Review*, 205–237, available at <www.right-to-education.org>.

[44] International Committee of the Red Cross, *Special report: stemming the tide of violence. ICRC activities in relation to the international community's prevention strategies*, ICRC, Geneva, 1998, 5.

people to kill following orders. Exposing gross abuses of education inevitably led to dismantling a myth that education is inherently good. Such abuses included instrumentalising education in the preparation of genocide. Although the Convention against Genocide is one day older than the Universal Declaration of Human Rights,[45] neither its prohibitions nor its anticipated sanctions were brought to bear upon abuses of education until the turn of the millennium. More than five decades elapsed between setting a human rights norm and bringing it to bear upon unruly reality.

18. Human rights activism has developed around its initial mobilising slogan, whereby exposing human rights violations is the first necessary step towards opposing them. Oftentimes, it is depicted as a criticise-and-complain syndrome. Indeed, the retroactive mode of exposing past abuses of power in order to remedy them and compensate their victims fails to address prevention. Human rights work is no exception to the rule that prevention is always better than cure. Translating this into practice requires overcoming the eternal obstacle of hindsight being much more prevalent than foresight. Retrospective detection of who, when, where, how and why in human rights violations forms the basis for prevention. Because education is seen as the cause and cure for all ills, human rights education emerged as a recipe to preventing violations, through teaching and learning the values, knowledge and skills necessary for righting wrongs and for preventing abuses of power. This places human rights at the boundary between science and art. Knowledge of what happens without their protection combines with skills needed for an effective mobilisation of shame to alter government policies and practices. Amplifying and reinforcing commitments to human rights through education necessitates additional skills to detect and alter the values motivating the conduct of those acting in the name of government as well as those challenging that conduct. These skills are in shortest supply.

---

[45] The Convention on the Prevention and Punishment of the Crime of Genocide was adopted by the General Assembly of the United Nations on 9 December 1948 and entered into force on 12 January 1951. The prohibited acts listed therein include forcible transfer of children from one group to another as well as "direct and public incitement to commit genocide". The instrumentalisation of education in Rwanda in the preparation of genocide was detected in 1997 as a major factor in the 1994 genocide. Commission on Human Rights, *Report on the situation of human rights in Rwanda submitted by René Degni-Ségui, Special Rapporteur* (UN Doc. E/CN.4/1997/61), para. 25.

TOWARDS A TRANSDISCIPLINARY MODEL WITHIN CHILD AND YOUTH RIGHTS EDUCATION

RICHARD C. MITCHELL

1. TRANSDISCIPLINARY THINKING WITHIN CHILD RIGHTS EDUCATION

1. Within the literature of the social and traditional sciences there are growing epistemological and methodological trends towards transdisciplinarity. This chapter considers this evolution in the context of human rights education and stems from the notion that multi- and even interdisciplinary methods are no longer adequate to conceptualise the proliferation of new knowledge in this field. Its purpose is two-fold: firstly, to build the case for transdisciplinary thinking within the field of child and youth rights education, and secondly to offer one such heuristic model derived from a secondary analysis of the author's doctoral study of Canadian and Scottish approaches.[1] As philosophers DELEUZE and GUATTARI suggest, the rhizome is a more appropriate metaphor to understand the immense number of possible interconnections and assemblages making up temporal reality. In principal, the rhizome is anti-hegemonic,[2] is more concerned with space than of time, disables the formation of power centres and thus, will be drawn upon to reframe child rights teaching and learning.

Inspired by educators such as Brazilian FREIRE, African-American women's scholar bell hooks, and US critical theorist GIROUX, this author discusses transdisciplinarity and human rights teaching as a transformative pedagogy concerning the kinds of knowledge which are at once between the disciplines, across the different disciplines

---

1. R.C. MITCHELL, 'Postmodern reflections on the UNCRC: Towards utilising Art. 42 as an international compliance indicator', (2005) 13 *International Journal of Children's Rights*, 315–331.
2. G. DELEUZE and F. GUATTARI, *A Thousand Plateaus*, (Minneapolis: University of Minnesota Press, 1987), also R. LORT, 'Incorporeal Part III: Rhizomatic Ontologies', (2003) *Retort Magazine*, ISSN 1445- 7164.

and beyond all discipline such as NICOLESCU contends.[3] NICOLESCU's definition calls us to reconsider our perceptions of reality based upon what quantum physics has shown about the nature of the universe, and is one of the most widely referenced in this emergent discourse. He observes that multidisciplinary research concerns a topic, which may not be limited by one disciplinary perspective but whose goal nonetheless remains anchored within one disciplinary framework. While still concerned with one disciplinary framework, interdisciplinarity concerns the transfer of methods from one discipline to another. Its three defining degrees are concerned with levels of application, epistemology or the potential for generating completely new disciplines such as in the case of mathematical physics or computer art. Transdisciplinary research generally creates its own criteria and standards because of its unique, emergent qualities.[4]

Sociologists BECK and SZNAIDER have also observed the social sciences being reshaped by a "trans-disciplinary cosmopolitanism" and a resultant movement away from "methodological nationalism".[5] In the same journal TURNER, who has previously argued for a distinct theory of human rights,[6] links transdisciplinary cosmopolitanism with the theoretical tension between local and global expressions of citizenship. The latter, he claims, simply does not exist. "*Citizenship contrasts sharply with human rights*", TURNER argues, due to implicit obligations by the state upon "*the individual to carry out various civic duties such as military service, or at the very least, gainful employment*". He contends the emerging notion that physically and mentally disabled people share similar social and political benefits as other citizens creates a "*lack of fit between duties and rights, for example in the case of children's rights.... This lack of fit in the case of disabled persons accounts for the fact that they are discriminated against and are so often treated as second-class citizens*", he observes.[7] It is apparent, however, that such Enlightenment-era conservative notions of active citizenship being premised upon a dualism of "rights and responsibilities" are being challenged by the UN Convention on the Rights of the Child (or the CRC).

---

3 While developmental psychologist J. PIAGET is widely credited with coining the term in 1970, the definition underpinning this chapter builds upon B. NICOLESCU's definition found within the International Center for Transdisciplinary Research and Studies in Paris, and his *Manifesto of Transdisciplinarity*, (New York: State University of New York Press, 2002).

4 W. RUSSELL, 'Forging new paths: Transdisciplinarity in Universities', (2000) 53 *Wisenet Journal – Australia's Women in Science Inquiry Network*, 1–4, < http://www.wisenet-australia.org/>.

5 U. BECK and N. SZNAIDER, 'Unpacking cosmopolitanism for the social sciences: a research agenda', (2006) 57 *The British Journal of Sociology*, 1–23.

6 B. TURNER, 'Outline of a theory of human rights', (1993) 27 *Sociology*, 489–512.

7 B. TURNER, 'Classical sociology and cosmopolitanism: a critical defence of the social', (2006), (147) 57 *The British Journal of Sociology*, 133–151.

As TURNER suggests, the debate over emerging expressions of local and global citizenship is frequently being premised upon human rights pedagogies stemming from the cosmopolitan expression of children's rights. In a similar vein, Malawian legal scholar KAMCHEDZERA maintains that the African Charter on the Rights of the Child was not an expression of cultural relativity, neither was it designed to infringe upon the principle of universality of human rights. Instead, he argues, it was meant to be complimentary to the CRC, which is solely a set of "*minimum standards*".[8] However, to mitigate early concerns for infantilising[9] children within Southern nations through the CRC implementation, UK women's scholar BURMAN encourages theorists and practitioners alike to engage in "disciplinary tourism" and experiment with ideas from outside western psychology. As feminists and child-rights activists have rightly pointed out, BURMAN argues it would be "*ironic*" to dispense with the notion of individual citizens precisely when women and children were beginning to acquire hard-won rights there-by.[10]

Canadian sociologist STASIULIS argues that in contrast to the "*bankruptcy*" of domestic approaches to child citizenship and "*empowerment rights*", the larger children's rights movement offers an alternative image due to its synergy between central concepts of participation and protection.[11] Once again, the strictly juridical and legalistic constraints upon emerging forms of citizenship are seen as shifting as the CRC becomes more fully applied in the cultural milieu and lived experiences of young people. Building upon these introductory theorists, the focus of the chapter moves now to consider more closely how transdisciplinary thinking might aid adults and young people within human rights educational contexts.

It is also built upon an explicit assumption that accurate knowledge of the CRC is a prerequisite to exercising its rights, understanding violations and monitoring its outcomes. Since these terms have been committed to by 192 nations[12] the chapter is framed by CRC Article 42, arguably its least ambiguous text. The CRC states in Article

---

8 G. KAMCHEDZRA, 'The African Child Charter: finally in force amidst enhanced justification', in E. VERHELLEN (ed.), *Understanding Children's Rights – Collected Papers presented at the 5th International Interdisciplinary Course on Children's Rights*, (Belgium: University of Ghent, 2000), 362–383.

9 See E. BURMAN, 'Local, global or globalised: Child development and international child rights legislation', (1996) 3 *Childhood*, 45–66, and V. PUPAVAC, 'The infantilisation of the South and the UN Convention on the Rights of the Child', (1998), in H. J. STEINER and P. ALSTON (eds.), *International Human Rights in Context – Law, Politics, Morals*, (New York: Oxford University Press, 2000), 517–518.

10 E. BURMAN, 'Beyond the baby and the bathwater: Postdualistic developmental psychologies for diverse childhoods', (2001) 9 *European Early Childhood Education Research Journal*, 5–22.

11 D. STASIULIS, 'The active child citizen: Lessons from Canadian policy and the children's movement', (2002, p. 532) 6 *Citizenship Studies*, 507–538.

12 Office Of The High Commissioner For Human Rights, 'Status of Ratification', (2006), retrieved 25 May 2006 from <http://www.ohchr.org/english/bodies/crc/discussion.htm>.

42 that, "States Parties undertake to make the principles and provisions of the Convention widely known, by appropriate and active means, to adults and children alike".

The argument for adopting a transdisciplinary approach within child and youth rights pedagogy and for considering CRC Article 42 as one such cross-cutting framework are considered again in the following four sections. The first begins with a comparative overview of salient issues confounding Canadian child rights legislative, policy and research agendas through a rhizomatic, transdisciplinary lens. Secondly, a theoretical discussion relocating children's rights education in the larger discourse of human rights occurs. Thirdly, empirical support is offered from a selection of texts obtained through secondary analysis of existing qualitative data from the author's doctoral study. Finally, a key finding from this study suggesting that the CRC's drafters had conceived of Article 42 as a compliance indicator has shaped development of a heuristic model[13] reprinted here as a contribution towards transdisciplinarity within human rights education. The model is posited as the type of "transdisciplinary tool" and new "model of analysis" called for by educators GIROUX and SEARLS GIROUX to promote active citizenship in democratic societies.[14]

2. COMPETING AND COMPARING CANADIAN CITIZENSHIP DISCOURSES

2. Rather than utilising a conceptual framework from the 1948 Declaration of Human Rights as many have done,[15] this author views new opportunities for human rights education through the transdisciplinary implementation of the CRC. As many authors have noted, the CRC represents the most widespread expression of human rights in history spreading in the rapid, unpredictable fashion of the horticultural rhizome. For better and for worse, the CRC moved throughout the world in the 1990s similar to the rhizome which grows at or just below the soil surface and is distinguishable from more common root systems by the presence of innumerable nodes such as those visible in the bamboo, iris, or spider plants.

---

13 R.C. MITCHELL, supra (note 1), 325.

14 H. GIROUX and S. SEARLS GIROUX, *Take Back Higher Education – Race, Youth and the Crisis of Democracy in the Post-Civil Rights Era*, (New York: Palgrave Macmillan, 2004, 102).

15 See for example C. LOHRENSCHEIT, 'International approaches to human rights education', (2002) 48 *International Review of Education*, 173–185, and J. A. LINDGREN ALVES, 'The Declaration of human rights in postmodernity', (2000) 22 *Human Rights Quarterly*, 478–500.

Diverse theorists within philosophy,[16] psychiatry,[17] nursing,[18] and children's rights educa tion[19] have drawn upon this metaphor of the rhizome to discuss transdisciplinary theoretical developments in their respective fields. While beginning from the Canadian legal and educational contexts, the author observes that nations in both the developed (or minority) world and the developing (or majority) world will encounter similar concerns when teaching children's human rights. Building on a variety of disciplinary approaches in this way also permits the foundation of the growing Canadian controversy surrounding children's rights education to be made more explicit. Within this context, it is worth re-emphasising that many dozens of nations have signed and ratified the CRC, and notwithstanding the unprecedented cultural diversity, because of common texts many will encounter similar challenges within their own legal, educational and political systems. Nevertheless, due to an overall dearth of applied research in human rights education, misunderstandings frequently prevail and the fullest significance of the civil rights of young people is still at a fragile phase.[20]

3. Up to this historical juncture, Canadians have been proud of their international reputation for human rights promotion at home and abroad. Indeed, it is part of the national identity that former Prime Minister Brian MULRONEY co-hosted the 1990 UN World Summit for Children, and similar to dozens of UN-member states at that time, ratified the CRC within the following year. However, as the UN Decade for Human Rights Education (1995–2004) passed by, frequent invitations from UN sources to develop and implement rights-based curricula were largely ignored across the country. As one consequence, in 2004 the Canadian Senate Standing Committee on Human Rights began to investigate the growing lack of domestic compliance with the treaty's core principles and provisions.

Committee chair Senator Raynell ANDREYCHUK observes that the original intent was to examine how Canada could maximise the impact and application of the CRC. However, "in the course of the study the Committee became increasingly convinced that, *in both theory and in practice*, children's rights in this country are not understood, or indeed provided" notwithstanding the increasing rhetoric that "children are citizens

---

16 G. DELEUZE and F. GUATTARI, supra (note 2).

17 C. JUNG, *1953–1979: The Collected Works of C.G. JUNG - 20 Vols. Symbols of Transformation, Bollingen Series XX*, translated by R.F.C. HULL and edited by H. READ, M. FORDHAM, G. ADLER, and WM. MCGUIRE, (Princeton: Princeton University Press, 1956).

18 D. HOLMES and D. GASTALDO, 'Rhizomatic thought in nursing: an alternative path for the development of the discipline', (2004) 5 *Nursing Philosophy*, 258–267.

19 J. ALLAN and J. I'ANSON, 'Children's rights in school: Power, assemblies and assemblages', (2004) 12 *International Journal of Children's Rights*, 123–138.

20 P. DAVID, 'Implementing the rights of the child: Six reasons why the human rights of children remain a constant challenge', (2002) 48 *International Review of Education*, 259–263.

with rights" (emphasis added).[21] The Senators also found it is not well understood in Canada that the UN Committee on the Rights of the Child has repeatedly recommended "nationwide education" to be undertaken in the framework of CRC Article 42.[22] As is the case for most nations, the CRC Committee requested that the treaty be integrated into the "*training curricula for professional groups dealing with children*".[23] Surprisingly, neither recommendation has occurred in any systematic or meaningful way to date.

Much of this lack of understanding may be clearly attributed to various forms of disciplinary myopia springing from the myriad definitions of childhood within psychology, psychiatry, medicine and nursing, anthropology and sociology, legal studies, political science, social work, education and so on – each one struggling to come to terms with a single textual version of human rights not yet widely applied in any field of practice.[24] British human rights sociologist O'BYRNE notes that the central problem with the very idea of children's rights lies within these definitions of childhood, which differ vastly across time and space. Nonetheless, he argues that when one pays attention to violations of human rights targeted towards children "*specifics of age are irrelevant*", and we thereby avoid the "*quicksand of defining childhood*".[25] His analysis is also salient when considering the fundamentals of human rights education found within the CRC.

Although unsubstantiated by the available research, the promotion of young peoples' rights is still frequently misconstrued in Canada as a conflict with the rights of others – particularly families and adults providing services.[26] Meanwhile, the very notion of rights for children engenders the type of "*unproductive*" and "*hysterical debate*" noted by DAVID[27] – a debate often characterised by adult fears of losing control that are fed by a profound lack of information. This would explain why the 2004 National Child Day poll found that Canadians know very little about children's issues, and scored 33% overall on a 10-question survey. Indeed, 14% knew nothing at all about contemporary

---

21 Canadian Standing Senate Committee On Human Rights, *Chair's Forward – Who's in Charge Here? – Interim Report on Effective Implementation of Canada's International Obligations with Respect to the Rights of Children* (3 November 2005), Retrieved 26 May 2006 from <http:// www.parl.gc.ca/common/Committee_SenRep.asp?Language=E&Parl=38&Ses=1&comm_id=77>.

22 I. COTLER, 'Federal Justice Minister's Testimony to the Senate of Canada Standing Committee on Human Rights' (11 April 2005), Retrieved 25 May 2006 from <http:// /www.parl.gc.ca/common/Committee_SenProceed.asp?Language=E&Parl=38&Ses=1&comm_id=77>.

23 CRC Committee, *Concluding Observations: Canada* (UN Doc. CRC/C/15/Add.37, 1995), para. 19.

24 B. SAUNDERS and C. GODDARD, 'The textual abuse of childhood in the English-speaking world – the contribution of language to the denial of children's rights', (2001) 8 *Childhood*, 443–462.

25 D. O'BYRNE, *Human Rights – An Introduction*, (Essex: Pearson Education Limited, 2002), 374–375.

26 R. B. HOWE and K. COVELL, *Empowering Children – Children's Rights Education as a Pathway to Citizenship*, (Toronto: University of Toronto Press, 2005).

27 P. DAVID supra (note 20), 261–262.

children's rights concerns.[28] While Canada consistently rates as one of the best places to live in the world for most adults, the UN's findings for Canadian efforts to improve Aboriginal children's lives are alarming.[29] These latter findings stand in contrast to various commitments to the UN such as those found within "A Canada Fit for Children", which once again invites educators to participate in disseminating greater awareness of the CRC.[30] Increasingly, researchers and non-governmental civil society actors are commenting upon the unfinished business from both the 1995 and 2003 Concluding Observations on Canada – de facto national report cards on human rights education.

Confusion over the CRC's basic tenets is widespread amongst institutional stakeholders and policy-makers alike in Canada. In a participatory action healthcare study, researchers noted that neither educators nor pupils within a large urban high school had ever heard of the CRC – a state that continues at the time of this writing. A co-participant discussed the distinct lack of accurate human rights knowledge: "*Use of the CRC is something that affects every single aspect of my life... I've never taken a course; I've never had anyone sit down and teach me about the Convention. It is one of the things I would like to see happen within our education system over the next few years hopefully. But I have been involved in courses where I have informed various teachers that I have about the Convention and been able to dedicate a class or two towards learning about it.*"[31]

In a 2005 submission to Senate Human Rights Committee noted previously, CRC researcher WILLIAMS opines that due to jurisdictional ambiguities, and "*the culturally blind, adversarial nature of human rights discussions*", the CRC is still relatively unknown across Canada and remains "*a text without a context*". She observes the profound lack of human rights knowledge in general while acknowledging the treaty has also met with a "*lukewarm response*" by Aboriginal peoples "*many of whom have seen the CRC as yet another instrument of dominant culture oppression*".[32] Some

---

28 IPSOS-REID/Save The Children Canada, 'Making the Grade on International Children's Day', (2004), Retrieved 12 January 2005 from <http://www.ipsosna.com/news/>.

29 C. BLACKSTOCK, 'First Nations Child and Family Caring Society testimony to the Canadian Senate Standing Committee on Human Rights' (2005), Retrieved 25 May 2006 from <http://www.canadiancrc.com/Senate_hearings_child_rights_38th/Senate_hr_child_rights_38th.htm>.

30 Government Of Cananda, *A Canada Fit for Children – Canada's Plan of Action in Response to the May 2002 United Nations Special Session on Children*, (2004, 14), Retrieved 26 May 2006 from <http://www11.sdc.gc.ca/en/cs/sp/sdc/socpol/publications/2002–002483/page02.shtml>.

31 R. C. MITCHELL, 'Implementing children's rights in British Columbia using the population health framework', (2000, p. 342) 8 *International Journal of Children's Rights*, 333–349.

32 S. WILLIAMS, 'Meeting Canada's Obligations under the UN Convention on the Rights of the Child: From Paper Concepts to Living Benefits for Children – Testimony to the Senate of Canada Standing Committee on Human Rights Hearings' (2005), Retrieved 25 May 2006 from <http://web.uvic.ca/iicrd/graphics/IICRDBrieftoSenateCommittee(final).pdf>.

domestic legislation contains provisions consistent with the CRC and the courts have considered the CRC in over 100 cases.[33] Nevertheless, serious questions are being raised about whether the document has made any impact on the individual lives of young people.

In comparison, Scottish educators ALLAN and I'ANSON contend that rights-based relationships within schools are better understood as a "rhizome" with its form "*which sends out new connections upon the same plane with no discernable centre*". In contrast to fixed, "*arborescent structures*" within educational systems "*a rhizome never ceases to connect*".[34] Also drawing upon philosophers DELEUZE and GUATTARI[35] for their analysis, these theorists describe new rights-based approaches within the local context of power relations between teachers and students. In a similar analysis of their own field, Canadian nursing scholars HOLMES and GASTALDO argue for "*transdisciplinarity, diversity and plurality*" to transcend traditional disciplinary structures within their respective field. They, too, observe that in contrast to the "*arborescent tradition and the resulting Cartesian binaries it frequently generates, DELEUZE and GUATTARI purport that 'the multiple must be made'. The multiple, according to these philosophers, is the rhizome*".[36] As previously noted, this concept in philosophical thought may be traced historically to numerous sources including the writings of Swiss psychoanalyst, psychologist, and contemporary of FREUD, Professor JUNG.[37]

In the Canadian child rights discourse to date, the dominant arborescent tradition is a medicalised approach to children's development that has also underpinned the (mis)understanding and dissemination of the CRC since its ratification as well as various research agendas into its impact.[38] In one expression of this dominance, well-known educational researchers COVELL and HOWE found their hypothesis for "*the contagion effect of children's rights education...generally was supported*" in a Nova Scotia study.[39] Furthermore, HOWE and COVELL declare, "*it is only in adolescence that children's cognitive capacity, identity development, and interests in social issues converge to allow both the motivation to learn about and the ability to fully understand the*

---

33 Society For Children And Youth Of British Columbia, *Canadian Judicial Consideration of the United Nations Convention on the Rights of the Child*, (Victoria: Prepared by Robin M. Junger Law Corporation, 2003).

34 J. ALLAN and J. I'ANSON, supra (note 19), 126.

35 G. DELEUZE and F. GUATTARI, supra (note 2).

36 D. HOLMES and D. GASTALDO, supra (note 18), 259, 261.

37 C. JUNG, supra (note 17), xxiv.

38 See R.C. MITCHELL, 'Ideological reflections on the DSM-IV-R (or Pay no attention to that man behind the curtain, Dorothy!)', (2003a) 32 *Child and Youth Care Forum*, 281–298 and R.C. MITCHELL, 'Canadian health care and child rights – what are the links?', (2003b) 94 *Canadian Journal of Public Health/Revue Canadienne de Santé Publique*, 414–416.

39 K. COVELL and R.B. HOWE, 'The impact of children's rights education: A Canadian study', (1999, p. 179) 7 *International Journal of Children's Rights*, 171–183.

implications of rights education".[40] As we have noted, educators in many parts of the world are arriving at a different set of conclusions[41] and such theoretical and ontological views have been completely deconstructed within the sociology of childhood discourse.[42] Perhaps because of this over-medicalised approach to childhood and youth studies in Canada, one youth-led policy analysis found that both policy makers and researchers overlook important, ongoing contributions made by young people. While those under 18 years of age are allowed to drive a vehicle and required to pay income taxes when they work… "despite their active participation in both the critical dialogue and community solutions focused on important societal issues, youth influence is restricted to the popular sphere. Marginalised youth have even less voice, often lacking the access to opportunity, education, and necessary supports for their basic wellness. Youth under the age of 18 cannot vote in any level of government elections, thus eliminating the one official avenue by which to give their input. Real opportunities for youth to be involved in decision-making are few, even in policy areas which directly concern youth".[43]

For researchers from the Canadian Policy Research Networks, it is quite clear that voting in civic or federal elections along with the ability to sign legally contracts are prerequisites for citizenship – in tandem with the ability to leave home. These investigators have begun to consider the ambivalent nature of various constructions of "youth" and "citizenship" found in the literature and through the binary "rights and responsibilities" as well as access and sense of identity. However, they note that Canadian "*citizenship is a status traditionally reserved for adults, and while many people might accept that youth are citizens, at the same time they might be skeptical of the notion that youth, even those over 18, are full citizens. Somehow, it seems that they cannot be more than citizens-in-becoming.*" With the slightest nod to post-modern relativism they "*admit that this vision of citizenship is derived from a western notion of 'the good life' [and]…does not take into account cultural differences such as societies in which adult*

---

40 R.B. Howe and K. Covell, supra (note 26), 121.

41 See for example C. Carter and A. Osler, 'Human rights, identities and conflict management: a study of school culture as experienced through classroom relationships', (2000) 30 *Cambridge Journal of Education*, 335–356, and D. Devine, 'Children's citizenship and the structuring of adult-child relations in the primary school', (2002) 9 *Childhood*, 303–320.

42 See for example L. Alanen and B. Mayall (eds.), *Conceptualizing Child-Adult Relations*, (London: Routledge/Falmer, 2001); P. Alderson, *Young Children's Rights – Exploring Beliefs, Principles, Practice*, (London: Jessica Kingsley Publishers Ltd, 2000); P. Christensen and A. James (eds.), *Research with Children: Perspectives and Practices*, (London: Falmer Press, 2000); A. James and A. Prout (eds.), *Constructing and Reconstructing Childhood: Contemporary Issues in the Sociological Study of Childhood – 2nd Edition*, (Hampshire: Routledge/Falmer Press, 1997); and B. Mayall, 'The new sociology of childhood and children's rights', 8 *International Journal of Children's Rights*, 243–249.

43 J. Lui, *To Engage or not Engage… What is our Policy?*, (Vancouver: EnvironmentalYouth Alliance, 2000).

children remain in the family home even while they are founding their own families".[44] Indeed – nor does their version account for the fact that most citizens with physical or intellectual challenges are excluded from this vision of the "good life". As we have also seen, such age- and stage-based linear trajectories utilised to support their analysis portray child and youth development mechanistically, and often pathologically, as patients, as family members alone, as unfinished adults, or as future tax-payers and investments who are "not yet" competent or worthy.

While Canadian citizenship has overcome many of its most overt expressions of discrimination during the past century to include voting rights for women beginning in 1915, and for Aboriginal adults living on reserves in 1960, the emancipatory thrust of this rights and citizenship discourse is currently stalled for under-18-year-olds. Sociologist STASIULIS observes the truncated efforts to re-configure Canadian citizenship for under-18's, and note the failure of government and the manner in which state policy, the courts and children's politics have responded to the "*imaginary of the active child citizen*".[45] Furthermore, the sole focus upon and promotion of adult human rights within Canada's Citizenship and Immigration website[46] provides additional evidence of this theoretical and legal disjuncture abrogating core principles from the CRC. In fact, children and young people play a central role in Canadian societies, as they do in all societies whether in the minority or majority worlds. Their participation in human rights education could allow many young people to play an even larger role beyond the often tokenistic, paternalistic public displays.

However, to take up transdisciplinary thinking as an epistemological approach epidemiologists ALBRECHT, FREEMAN and HIGGINBOTHAM argue it must be understood as "*an emerging philosophy underpinning health and social science... [and while such ideas] appeal to academics prepared to work beyond the constraints of a traditional university, transdisciplinary research and publications have been scarce*".[47] They argue that traditional social scientists as well as social constructionists, poststructuralists and postmodernists have each begun to consider the value in transdisciplinary thinking in order to neutralise the effects of various ideologies embedded within and across all disciplines. Through this overarching approach, conceptual blind spots in the citizenship and rights discourse may be ameliorated in Canada and many other states in the throes of an epochal transformation in adult-child relations.

---

44 C. BEAUVAIS, L. MCKAY, and A. SEDDON, *A Literature Review on Youth and Citizenship*, (Ottawa: Canadian Policy Research Networks, 2001), vi, 10.

45 D. STASIULIS, supra (note 11) 507.

46 Citizenship And Immigration Canada, (2006), *The Canadian Refugee System – What Does it Mean to be a Canadian Citizen?*, Retrieved 26 May 2006 from <http://www.cic.gc.ca/english/pub/citizenship.html>.

47 G. ALBRECHT, S. FREEMAN, and N. HIGGINBOTHAM, 'Complexity and human health: The case for a transdisciplinary paradigm', (1998, pp. 55–56) 22 *Culture, Medicine and Psychiatry*, 55–92.

In a review of the UK government's struggle with the rights and responsibilities agenda, for example, SUCH and WALKER[48] found that younger children well understood both the moral and relational components of responsibility in very complex ways. Moreover, by questioning dominant constructions of young people's roles in the family and larger society, 19-year-old University of Sussex student BURKE cogently observes that unequal power relations with adults prevents the vast majority of institutions from fulfilling any notion of fuller citizenship. He contends: "*I am not a citizen in the making. I am a citizen today... Citizenship is something which every young person is automatically entitled to and not something which needs to be earned or taken away. Citizenship is a right not a charitable act*".[49]

To sum up, one way forward in Canada and perhaps within other states grappling with inconsistencies in educating young people about their human rights appears to lie through a simple recognition that disciplinary myopia is obscuring the emergence of an inclusive pedagogy of citizenship. As authors in various fields are also arguing, new theoretical development appears better understood as a rhizomatic expression of transdisciplinarity. Taking this approach a step further, the following section reconsiders the cross-cutting nature of child rights pedagogy not as an expression of childhood or youth theorising but from a solely human rights perspective.

3. RE-THEORISING CHILDREN'S RIGHTS AS HUMAN RIGHTS

4. Adopting post-modern, social constructionist perspectives British educators MOSS and PETRIE insist that researchers, policy actors and practitioners "*have no choice between 'theory' and 'no theory', or indeed, between 'theory' and 'practice'* ". In fact, they observe, newer ethnographic research accounts of the experiences of children simply cannot be neutrally produced or interpreted. "*Theories – whether in the form of academic, political or professional ideas, or offered in the guise of 'common sense' – shape our understandings and govern our actions, whether we recognise this or not*".[50] As noted previously, within much of the current child rights education literature hegemonic theories within developmental psychology are being counter-balanced by the sociology of childhood and these offer the two dominant disciplinary lenses through which much participatory and applied research on the CRC has been focused.

48 E. SUCH and R. WALKER, 'Young citizens or policy objects? Children in the 'rights and responsibilities' debate', (2005, p. 39) 34 *Journal of Social Policy*, 39–57.

49 M. BARRY (ed.), *Youth Policy and Social Inclusion – Critical Debates with Young People*, (Oxfordshire: Routledge, 2005), 53.

50 P. MOSS and P. PETRIE, *From Children's Services to Children's Spaces –Public Policy, Children and Childhood*, (London: Routledge/Falmer, 2002), 17-20.

Sociological approaches to research and practice start with vastly different beliefs about the nature of development of young people, and both FREEMAN[51] and MAYALL[52] note the intersection of this "not-quite-so new sociology of childhood" with the child and youth rights discourse. Sociologist JENKS maintains such tenets have opened up new approaches for investigating children's social realities. "*What is it we want from children and childhood? My answer is to say: go back to the phenomenon and show how it is built up*".[53] However, few ethnographic accounts have returned to UN policy sites for an analysis of how new children's rights educational statutes are being generated under international law.[54]

Australians, SAUNDERS and GODDARD express deep reservations regarding the views of many authors within the new sociological studies of childhood. Their policy study suggests that "*the insight and language development of those who wrote the United Nations Convention on the Rights of the Child has either been ignored or is yet to be discovered by authors, even those purportedly concerned about 'childhoods' and children's rights*".[55] Adopting a similar position, British human rights sociologist O'BYRNE contends that more attention has been paid to "welfare rights" than "liberty rights" of children while he also rejects dualistic extremes represented by universalist versus cultural relativism in human rights thinking. In his shift towards "interdisciplinarity" within human rights pedagogy, O'BYRNE draws deeply upon US philosopher RORTY who bridges the tired modernist/post-modern divide by inviting social scientists to "*move beyond epistemological perspectives which claim that we can, somehow through critique or reason, know the world*". Such extremist points-of-view are "flawed", and O'BYRNE contends that disciplinarity within academic circles results in the trend to discuss children's rights as distinct from human rights. This is because "*paradoxically, teaching and research on children's rights often adopt a broader approach... a key problem with the idea of children's rights lies in the definition of childhood which of course differs across time and space*".[56]

Also similar to SAUNDERS and GODDARD, in the Northern European debate regarding child citizenship ROCHE contends there is a need to rethink the value of the language

---

51 M. FREEMAN, 'The sociology of childhood and children's rights', (1998) 6 *International Journal of Children's Rights*, 433–444.

52 B. MAYALL, 'The new sociology of childhood and children's rights', (2000) 8 *International Journal of Children's Rights*, 243–249.

53 C. JENKS, 'Zeitgeist research on childhood', in P. CHRISTENSEN and A. JAMES (eds.), *Research* with *Children – Perspectives and Practices*, (London: Falmer Press, 2000), 62–76.

54 C. PRICE COHEN and S. KILBOURNE, 'Jurisprudence of the Committee on the Rights of the Child: A Guide for Research and Analysis', (1998) 19 *Michigan Journal of International Law*, 633–728.

55 B. SAUNDERS and C. GODDARD, 'The textual abuse of childhood in the English-speaking world – the contribution of language to the denial of children's rights', (2001) 8 *Childhood*, 443–462.

56 D. O'BYRNE, supra (note 25), 374.

of rights as well as the social significance of this language. Rights are not just about state-citizen relations but "*how civil society should imagine itself*".[57] Once again, in contrast to this approach, from the US context GIROUX notes children are being offered *increasingly less* standing as citizens in the public sphere, "*and thus are denied any sense of entitlement or agency*". Their voices are being drowned out of public debate while "policies and legislative practices are constructed in terms of their needs" the majority of which "are framed within the realm of the private sphere of the family".[58] This conceptualisation of children's "needs" dominates the psychological literature and places policy discussions primarily within the context of the family. LOWDEN recounts a decade of dispute regarding interpretations of children's rights within nursing as a result.[59]

As O'BYRNE and others have observed, nursing theorist LOWDEN argues that diagnostic and clinical concerns within this human rights discussion are heavily weighted by contemporary evolution in the meanings of childhood, which are always culturally, historically and politically constructed. Sociologist MITCHELL contends that similar to the "Wizard of Oz", the vast majority of Canadian and American theoretical frameworks have obscured children's rights through an ideologically constructed curtain,[60] and in line with this view, COPPOCK declares bluntly that "*child psychiatry can undermine or overtly breach the core principles of... the rights of children*".[61] Indeed, this stance is congruent with the "*disciplinary tourism*" argued for by BURMAN,[62] and both ethnographic and participatory researchers have begun to uncover how young people impact upon their own development, the development of their siblings, peers, and even that of their caregivers and therapists.

5. Authors from across disciplines are recognising that interpersonal and institutional exchanges of power are, in fact, central to making new meaning of children's rights in applied settings. Similar to Scots researchers ALLAN and I'ANSON,[63] drawing upon a diverse theoretical literature DEVINE argues that a "*theory of power is central*" to any new understanding of human rights within the educational contexts. She contends that contemporary pedagogues *must* take the structural dynamics of adult/child relations into account through "citizenship models" that emphasise connectedness,

---

57 J. ROCHE, 'Children: rights, participation and citizenship', (1999) 6 *Childhood*, 475–493.

58 H. GIROUX, *The Abandoned Generation – Democracy Beyond the Culture of Fear*, (New York: Palgrave Macmillan, 2003), xiv.

59 J. LOWDEN, 'Children's rights: A decade of dispute', (2002) 37 *Journal of Advanced Nursing*, 100–107.

60 R.C. MITCHELL, supra (note 38).

61 V. COPPOCK, ' Medicalising children's behaviour', in R. Franklin (ed.), *New Handbook of Children's Rights*, (London: Routledge, 2002), 139–154.

62 E. BURMAN, supra (note 9), 14–15.

63 J. ALLAN and J. I'ANSON, supra (note 19).

interdependence and the broader community.[64] Echoing these analyses, US sociologist LENZER points towards the broader, systemic analysis as she maintains that "*it is important to discuss the UNCRC within the larger framework of human rights*".[65]

As noted in previous sections, transdisciplinary thinking assumes that "knowledge about the nature of the system, as a whole inexorably demands a transdisciplinary mode of thinking".[66] Former US educators GIROUX and SEARLS GIROUX point out that while many teachers may feel "*forced to work within academic disciplines, they can develop transdisciplinary tools*" that challenge the existing limits of established fields, and "*contest the broader economic, political, and cultural conditions that produce unequal relations of power*".[67] Rather than viewing adults and children as two fixed developmental categories, a rights-based approach facilitates the kind of adult/child engagement that makes sense of the interconnected nature of all societal and institutional relationships. White considers the development of children and young people in this context declaring, "*the key issue here is recognition that children should not simply be regarded as scale model adults, but taken on their own terms, as a set of development subjects requiring a distinctive and particular approach*".[68]

Against a backdrop of European "risk society" for young people, JANS also observes, "*Due to changing social conditions active citizenship becomes a dynamic process rather than a standard, clear-cut set of rights and responsibilities. Furthermore, childhood presents itself more and more as an ambivalent social phenomenon. On the one hand, children are seen as autonomous individuals, on the other hand, as objects of protection. Nevertheless, today children can be seen as active citizens. Their ability to learn and play allows them to give active meaning to their environment. Accepting playful and ambivalent forms of citizenship, child participation presents itself no longer as an utopia, but as a fact.*"[69]

6. To conclude, this section of the chapter has argued for the continued re-conceptualisation of "children's rights" as "human rights", and the debate about "universalised" ontological arguments regarding the nature of "childhood" and its

---

64 D. DEVINE, 'Children's citizenship and the structuring of adult-child relations in the primary school', (2002) 9 *Childhood*, 303–320.

65 G. LENZER, 'Children's studies and the human rights of children: toward a unified approach', in K. ALAIMO and B. KLUG (eds.), *Children as Equals – Exploring the Rights of the Child*, (Maryland: University Press of America, 2002), 207–225.

66 G. ALBRECHT, S. FREEMAN and N. HIGGINBOTHAM, supra (note 47), 71.

67 H. GIROUX and S. SEARLS-GIROUX, supra (note 14), 102.

68 B. WHITE, 'A World Fit for Children? – Children and youth in development studies and policy', *Paper presented on the occasion of the 51st anniversary of the Institute of Social Studies*, (The Hague/ISS, 9 October 2003).

69 M. JANS, 'Children as citizens – Towards a contemporary notion of child participation', (2004) 11 *Childhood*, 27–44.

dominant theories has been bracketed. Consequently, how to obtain new human rights knowledge has been foreground through the ongoing international dissemination of CRC principles and provisions in global and local classrooms. In fact, new epistemological and methodological approaches supporting human rights research are emerging quite unpredictably in the non-linear, rhizomatic ways described previously by diverse theorists.

4. NEW LESSONS FROM EMPIRICAL RESEARCH

7. This final section of the chapter draws empirically upon a small number of interview texts from one such qualitative, comparative policy study in support of this paper's thesis.[70] This section highlights three dominant themes that emerged during an exploratory, grounded theory policy study of the CRC in Scottish and Canadian educational systems: the role of educators, the roles of governmental and non-governmental actors, and the role of the UN Committee on the Rights of the Child. While comparing child rights education in both policy and practice settings, the author built upon previous research investigating CRC Article 42 in a Canadian healthcare setting.[71] The following texts describe key themes derived from informant interviews obtained from participants during United Nations sites in Geneva and New York, Canadian and Scottish governmental and non-governmental settings, and educators and pupils from classrooms in both nations.

4.1. ROLE OF EDUCATORS

8. A Canadian CRC curriculum developer discussed her research: "*I heard children were far too young in primary grades, and that these ideas were too abstract. Of course they were thinking from an adult perspective*". In support of this view, a senior student from British Columbia reported how she had learned about the CRC from her mother, but then found it necessary to deploy this knowledge to her own instructors. She did not learn about the CRC's principles at any level of her education. "*Not in any of my classes. No and not by any of my teachers. I took the initiative to do a workshop on human rights in my high school in Career and Personal Planning so I could get credit for it. That is all the child rights education I ever received*". A second senior high school student from the same Canadian city concurred with his counterpart: "*I learned 'zero'. We never even covered the Canadian Charter or the Universal Declaration. It is hard to say why it is not in schools. It is as if the joy of learning is beat out of you in your school years*

[70] R.C. Mitchell, supra (note 1).
[71] R.C. Mitchell, supra (note 31).

rather than encouraged. I think the whole area of empowerment in schools needs to be changed."

In contrast, a Scottish educator and CRC researcher looking into rights-based participation of pupils within a local school argued: "*It is not just a neutral experience – it changes the very nature of professional practice such that what it is to be an adult, and a child, are being re-negotiated!*" Furthermore, the Department Head from the University of Edinburgh's School of Education acknowledged: "*I am interested in how children's rights are translated into actual practice Period 1 on Monday. The Education for Citizenship framework is proposing schools introduce the CRC into that curriculum*".

4.2. ROLES OF GOVERNMENTAL AND NON-GOVERNMENTAL ACTORS

9. The Child and Youth Advocate from the province of Alberta offered the following insight into the denial of participation rights for young people from foster care during drafting of that province's new protection legislation in 2002: "*That is an interesting question [re: Art. 42]… From a policy perspective, I don't think that it shows up in very many places at all… interesting. Right now the Child Welfare act is undergoing a review. And I am aware there are some discussions about specifically mentioning 'child rights' and perhaps even articulating what this means in legislation. Now between you and me do I think that will happen? No… There is not anything that the government has done or children's services has done to identify something called 'children's rights' because that isn't a very popular thing to do in this province.*"

In a similar account, the former British Columbia Deputy Child and Youth Advocate echoed his colleague's viewpoint: "*I don't think the Convention lives very well here in British Columbia… as far as government officials, there's really no focus on the CRC here… I say this carefully and with good intentions not wanting to slam the NGOs but I think there's been a real failure both in the government and with the non-governmental organisations in BC to make this thing live… The views of children and youth? Other than the Advocate's Office, there hasn't been a coordinated champion for the CRC here.*"

A Canadian Senator offered her reflections on the participation of young people within Canada's educational and political systems. "*The issue… is jurisdiction in the Canadian context and the provinces have absolute jurisdiction over education. The only role the federal government can play is to provide supporting materials… Article 42 can't be implemented directly… from a federal point of view there's nothing we can do. You know about the [1999] UNICEF and Elections Canada decision to have an election on children's rights. The Reform Party went back to their ridings and addressed all local School Boards that said they would have the election and put pressure on them. Many didn't because of their inaccurate arguments.*"

In sharp contrast to Canada once again, a researcher and director for the non-governmental organisation *Save the Children* in Scotland discussed how history and culture have each intersected in the rights debate to impact new forms of citizenship teaching for children and young people. "*I think it's a culture that inhibits rights... We don't really have rights... it's not really nice, it's a little bit pushy, it's a little bit demanding. It's rights and responsibilities. But what babies have responsibilities? Tell me. Dirty babies have the same rights as clean babies! Bad kids have the same rights as good kids! If you start making conditions and say that you only have rights if you're a nice kid... Our stance would be children have rights. That's it! They may learn about them better if you put them into a context that appreciates others' rights. Like all adults, the reality is that you still have your rights anyway.*"

4.3. ROLE OF CRC REPORTING AND UN TREATY MONITORING

10. The current Chair of the Committee on the Rights of the Child Professor DOEK spoke of innovative approaches towards rights-based teaching and power sharing that the Committee has encountered during their evaluation of hundreds of domestic reports under Article 44 to date. "*In terms of the best kinds of schools, there are many good examples but one that stands out is those early learning centres in the north of Italy [Reggio Emilia]. They have innovative and very democratic styles of teaching, and of simply being with even very young learners... part of this new kind of rights culture also has to do with sharing power or perhaps losing a certain level of control, at least some of the control, you were used to as a teacher.*"

Finally, during participant observations at the 2002 UN Special Session for Children, the author interviewed the director of a US-based NGO and a key participant in the Ad-Hoc Group during the CRC drafting. This authoritative key informant provided archival documents that supported her recollections of the lengthy negotiations leading to the exact wording for CRC Article 42.[72]

"*It was 1987 and the NGO Ad Hoc Group suggested we have a proposal about the implementation of the CRC... Article 42 did not have the word 'appropriate' in the First Reading and the word appears something like 45 times in the Convention... It*

---

[72] C. PRICE COHEN and S. KILBOURNE, 'Jurisprudence of the Committee on the Rights of the Child: A Guide for Research and Analysis', (1998) 19 *Michigan Journal of International Law*, 633–728.

seemed that would be something you could measure if you were measuring the extent to which a country were living up to its obligations... if you are making the 'principles and provisions' known. The opposite to that is Article 44 and making the reports widely available to the public... between the two it's like a see-saw."[73]

These observations from a participant during the treaty's drafting in New York were deemed authoritative due to her role during a ten-year process of negotiation leading to adoption of the CRC at the UN in 1989. Her recollections and supporting archival materials became significant findings from the study. Recalling the relationship between basic human rights educational knowledge obliged within Article 42, and the periodic domestic reports required under Article 44, such a "minimal approach" to compliance to the treaty was deemed by CRC drafters to be capable of measurement by individuals, organisations and States Parties alike. Her argument that this approach to treaty compliance – simply letting educators, adults and young people have basic knowledge of the treaty's existence – was envisioned as the starting point necessary for "adults and children alike" to understand the CRC's core principles.

11. After a rigorous coding of 50 interview transcripts obtained during the study and a thorough analysis of research themes that each pointed towards institutional power relations, the following theoretical model was developed taking into account the monitoring and reporting "balance" described by PRICE COHEN.[74]

Figure 1. Transdisciplinary CRC Model

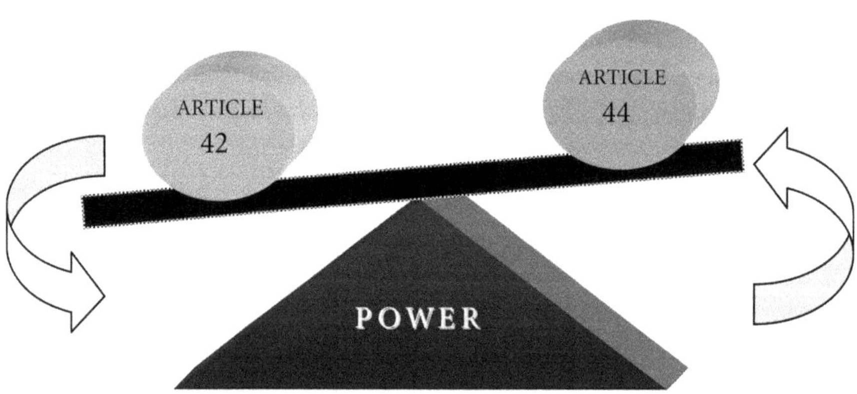

[73] For further analysis see: R.C. MITCHELL, supra (note 1), 324-325.

[74] This *transdisciplinary* child rights implementation model is herewith represented for wider application with permission of the publishers.

Based upon an additional thematic analysis of fieldwork and data, the transdisciplinarity of the CRC is highlighted within the accompanying model, and is presented in support of introducing basic human rights knowledge within educational settings across disciplines, between disciplines and beyond all discipline. The dynamic process illustrated in the model also implies a type of rhizomatic balance for human rights educators accounting for Article 42's core "principles and provisions"– one that allows for both non-linearity and local contingency. In addition, recommendations contained within domestic child rights reports under Article 44 are highlighted. These systemic events may be represented within local educational contexts as illustrated by resting upon the fulcrum of interpersonal, national and international power relations. Such an approach to the macro- and micro-systemic features embedded within the CRC also takes into account the inherent agency of young people within such exchanges of power.

5. CONCLUSION

12. Inadequate Canadian efforts to educate children, young people and adults about the CRC are currently being reviewed by the Canadian Senate Standing Committee on Human Rights, and offer a critical context for this discussion. While numerous UK and European nations are considering the CRC within the pedagogy of citizenship, in Canada, the debate has stagnated and consequently few children or adults are receiving any basic education concerning the treaty.

13. The author has presented both theoretical and empirical arguments that children's rights are better understood as a transdisciplinary, rhizomatic expression of international human rights law rather than any essentialised expression of "childhood". Such a contention contrasts the more traditional arborescent expressions of childhood and youth theorising within an emergent, discrete yet transdisciplinary rights discourse transcending most contemporary legal, educational, philosophical, political and sociological debates about the nature of young peoples' human rights. To support this stance, salient literature and selected findings from a secondary analysis of the author's doctoral study comparing CRC educational policies within Canada and Scotland were presented. As NICOLESCU suggests: "*For the moment, the term transdisciplinarity retains a certain pristine charm, mostly because it has not yet been corrupted by time. It has begun spreading around the globe, popping up in unexpected places, giving voice to a lively new concept that is not yet widely understood… It was coined to give expression to a need that was perceived – especially in the area of education*

– to celebrate the transgression of disciplinary boundaries, an act that far surpassed the multidisciplinary and the interdisciplinary approaches."[75]

This is a remarkably similar description of how the UN Convention on the Rights of the Child continues to move throughout the increasingly globalised community of nation states.

[75] B. NICOLESCU, supra (note 3), 1.

THE RIGHT TO EQUAL ACCESS TO EDUCATION OF INTERNAL MIGRANT WORKERS' CHILDREN IN CHINA

HAINA LU

1. INTRODUCTION

1. Lack of equal access to education for migrant children in China is a serious issue, which has been criticised and discussed by academia,[1] the media and policy-makers in China, as well as by human rights NGOs[2] and international organisations,[3] since the problem emerged in the 1980s, when China's economic reform began. The problem reached its peak in the middle of the 1990s and drew extensive public attention, which led to the promulgation of a series of regulations to address the issue.[4] However, the problem persists and many factors continue to contribute to it.

This article intends to first present the latest picture of migrant children's education, including government measures to address the problem; second, to point out the gap between China's performance and its obligations under international human rights law; third, to analyse the factors behind this gap; and finally, to suggest some realistic approaches to improve the situation – in other words, what can be done under the existing political, social and economic circumstances of China.

---

1 See, for example, D. SOLINGER, *Contesting Citizenship in Urban China,* (Berkerley: University of California Press, 1999), 266–269.

2 See, for instance, Human Rights in China, *Shutting Out the Poorest: Discrimination Against the Most Disadvantaged Migrant Children in City Schools,* 8 May 2002; see also Human Rights Watch, *China: Right to Education and the Rights of Education by Children Affected by AIDS,* submission from Human Rights Watch to the Committee on the Rights of the Child, June 2005.

3 K. TOMAŠEVSKI, *Report submitted by the Special Rapporteur on the right to education,* (UN Doc. E/CN.4/2004/45/Add.1, 2003).

4 C. FROISSART, 'Les Aleas du Droit à L'Education en Chine: Enquete sur la Scolarisation des Enfants de Travailleurs Migrants à Chengdu', (2003) 77 *Perspectives Chinoises,* 10.

2. GENERAL SITUATION OF MIGRANT CHILDREN'S EDUCATION IN CHINA

2. Since the early 1980s, when China started its economic reform and loosened the control of movement of its population, millions of rural labourers have flooded into cities to seek employment and a better life. Many of these internal migrant workers bring their children with them. However, these migrant children are often denied access to city public schools, or are charged prohibitive additional fees. Consequently, a large number of migrant children do not receive the compulsory education that China's Constitution provides for.

This problem is rooted in China's *hukou* system (household registration system), which was created in the 1950s and is aimed at restricting freedom of movement by a strict control of residence, especially by preventing rural populations from moving to cities.[5] The obtainment of a *hukou* is based on registration at birth and is extremely difficult to change afterwards, and especially to change from a rural *hukou* to an urban one. Lack of a local *hukou* means lack of entitlement to local public services, such as education and health care. As a result, migrant children do not have a *right* to attend local public schools, which means that they *may* be enrolled by meeting various requirements but the school has the discretion to refuse them.

3. Migrant children actually face four possibilities. First, relatively wealthier migrant parents may try to have their children enrolled in local public schools. Those migrant children who are allowed into public school are required to pay a "temporary schooling fee" (借读费) which may amount to 20,000 yuan (around 2000 Euros) in Beijing,[6] which is beyond the financial capacity of most migrant parents. Moreover, many schools levy "donation fees" (赞助费), or "school-choosing fees" (择校费) and other types of charges on migrant students although such practices were made illegal in 1997.[7] Second, some migrant children may enter private schools especially established for them, which charge less than public schools but are often of poor quality. The problem with these private schools will be explained later. Third, when migrant parents are unable to enrol their children in either public or private schools, they may send their children back to their village for education, or leave them there in the first place.

5 For more detail on China's *hukou* system and migrant workers, see D. SOLINGER, supra (note 1); T. ZHANG, (ed.), 'Migrant Population in China', (2001) 34, *Chinese Law and Government*; A. CHAN, *China's Workers under Assault: The Exploitation of Labor in a Globalizing Economy*, (Armonk, New York: M.E. Sharpe, 2001); J. KNIGHT and L. SONG, *Towards a Labor Market in China*, (New York: Oxford University Press, 2005), 86–114.

6 K. TOMAŠEVSKI, supra (note 3), para. 27.

7 The 1997 Provisional Measures on the Management of Fees Charged by Schools Offering Compulsory Education provide that public schools should not charge students anything other than "miscellaneous fees" (杂费) and a "temporary schooling fee", without approval from competent authorities.

According to media reports and academic surveys, these so-called "left-behind children" (留守儿童) are of significant number,[8] and some are reported to have various social and psychological problems.[9] Last, and worst, migrant children who cannot be enrolled in city schools and who cannot stay in their village (because there is no one to take care of them) are left to play on the streets of the city, or enter child labour.

4. Among migrant children, there is also an issue of gender discrimination in access to education. Some surveys conducted by academics show that girls are more likely than boys to be left at home; boys are more likely to be enrolled in public schools (which may mean that parents are more willing to pay for boys' education than for girls').[10] The choice of migrant parents is strongly influenced by the traditional prejudice against women in Chinese society, which can be particularly strong in the rural areas from where many migrant parents come.

5. It is impossible to estimate accurately how many migrant children have missed the opportunity to receive compulsory education. The official statistics available are based on the registration of migrant workers at the local administration of the city where they work, but many migrant workers are not registered, for various reasons.[11] Estimates of the number of internal migrants currently vary between 120 and 200 million,[12] but no one really knows the exact number. A survey in 2003, conducted by the Chinese Centre of Children, shows that nationwide there are around 20 million floating children of school age; 9.3% of them are out of school; 6.85% of them have never been enrolled in school. Disaggregated data by age shows that among children aged eight to fourteen the drop-out rate increases from 0.8% to 15.4%.[13] Child labour becomes a serious problem among migrant children. Among floating children between ages twelve to fourteen, approximately 60% of them have started working,[14] while the minimum age to work, according to China's labour law, is sixteen.

---

8 See, for instance, 'Special Seats for Rural Left-behind Children', (6 April 2006) *Chinanews*, <www.china.org.cn/english/China/164704.htm>, accessed 27 April 2006. It was estimated that the number "left-behind children" may reach 10 million, see <www.china.org.cn/chinese/zhuanti/nmg/951117.htm>, accessed 27 April 2006.

9 Y. Zhou, 'Survey Report on Public's Attitude toward the Status of Children's Life and Mentality Who Stay at Countryside Alone', <www.chinasurvey.com.cn/ >, accessed 27 April 2006.

10 J. Du & W. Ye, 'Education Status of Floating Children and its Influencing Factors' (流动儿童的教育状况及其影响因素), (2003) 9 *Journal of Fujian Party School*, 54–59.

11 Ibid.

12 'Answering Questions of Journalists by the Responsible Person of Research Department of the State Council'. <http://news.xinhuanet.com/politics/2006-03/28/content_4354231.htm>, accessed 9 April 2006.

13 P. Li, 'Survey on the compulsory education of peasant workers' children in Shanghai' (上海外来民工子女义务教育调研),(2004) 6 *Questions of Historical Education* (历史教学问题).

14 Ibid.

3. AN OVERVIEW OF NATIONAL LEGISLATION AND POLICIES ON THIS ISSUE

6. Legislation and policies are among the first steps that a State can undertake towards the full realisation of the right to education.[15] An overview of relevant Chinese legislation and policies allows us to evaluate the efforts that China has made to tackle the problem.

3.1. CONSTITUTION AND ACTS

7. Article 46 of the 1982 Constitution stipulates that "Citizens have the right and duty to receive education". The 2004 Amendment to the Constitution adds a prominent human rights provision, which states that "Citizens are equal before the law. The State respects and protects human rights". Thus, it can be derived from the two provisions that the right to equal access to education is protected in China's Constitution.

The 1986 Compulsory Education Act stipulates that all children aged six to fifteen must receive education for nine years. The Act also requires that students receiving compulsory education should not be charged a tuition fee and that the State shall provide scholarships to help poor students. However, compulsory education is not free in China and students are charged "miscellaneous fees" and other fees under various titles.[16]

In the 1995 Education Act, the right to equal access to education is expressly granted and gender discrimination is prohibited. In Article 37, the State is required to provide various forms of subsidies to children in financial difficulty in order that they receive education.

These Acts do not touch upon the education problem of migrant children but provide general principles in education policy. However, these Acts do not indicate how to guarantee that these principles are carried out.

---

15 CESCR Committee, *General Comment No. 3: The nature of State parties obligations (Art.2, para.1 of the Covenant)*(UN Doc.E/C.12/1990/23, 1990), paras. 2–3.

16 For more detail about miscellaneous fees for education in China, see Human Rights Watch, supra (note 2).

3.2. RELEVANT ADMINISTRATIVE REGULATIONS AND LEGAL DOCUMENTS

8. The 1992 Executive Regulation of Compulsory Education Act has provisions directly relevant to migrant children's education. Accordingly, the local government of the area in which a child's *hukou* is registered is responsible for providing her/him with nine years of compulsory education. Article 14 stipulates that children who go to school in an area other than their *hukou* should obtain approval from the authorities of their *hukou* and apply for temporary schooling to the authorities of the receiving area. Such a provision makes education of migrant children in cities officially possible but it does not grant migrant children a *right* to receive education in city schools.

The 1998 Provisional Measures for the Schooling of Floating Children, issued by the State Education Commission and Ministry of Public Security, tends to address the problem by holding the authorities of the receiving areas principally responsible for the compulsory education of migrant children. Nevertheless, this regulation remains negative towards migration since it requires the authorities of the sending areas to strictly control the migration of children.[17] Moreover, the regulation provides complicated and costly administrative procedures, and explicitly allows the charging of "temporary schooling fees". In order to enrol their children in urban schools, migrant parents have to obtain all types of permits from the authorities both of their home and receiving areas. The "permits" requirement has two major impacts: first, urban schools are not open to "undocumented" migrant children whose parents are "undocumented" (without a temporary residence, a work permit or an identity card), nor to migrant children born out of wedlock or in breach of China's "one child" policy; second, these burdensome procedures constitute practical obstacles for migrant children to be enrolled in urban schools.

In 2001, the Decision of the State Council on the Reform and Development of Compulsory Education requires attention be given to the compulsory education of "floating children" and established the "Two Principles" (两为主), which have been guiding policy on the education of migrant children since then: the government of the receiving area is the main responsible party and it is in principle for public schools to receive migrant children (以流入地政府为主，以公立学校为主).[18]

---

17 See Art. 3 of the 1998 Provisional Measures (流动儿童少年就学暂行办法).

18 See Para. 12 of the Decision (国务院关于基础教育改革与发展的决定 (2001 年 5 月 29 日, 国发[2001]21 号)).

9. The year 2003 can be seen as the turning point of the official position towards peasant migrant workers although the education problem of migrant children did not see substantial changes. In January of that year, the Secretariat of the State Council issued the Notice on the Management and Service of Peasants Entering Cities for Employment.[19] In September, the Decision of the State Council on Further Strengthening Education in Rural Areas was issued.[20] On the same day, the Secretariat of the State Council issued the Notice on Conducting Good Work on Education of Children of Peasant Workers Who Move to the City for Employment.[21] All three legal documents reiterate the "Two Principles" for addressing the education problem of migrant children and require that migrant children should be treated equally in terms of admission conditions including fee charging. They also indicate various measures to tackle the problem. However, national regulations did not receive a positive response at the local level. The national authorities admitted in 2006 the failure of many local authorities to implement the "Two Principles".[22]

In March 2006, the State Council issued Certain Opinions on Resolution of Problems Concerning Peasant Workers ("Certain Opinions", hereafter), which clearly require the local authorities of receiving areas to effectively incorporate peasant workers into the local public services system. Compared to the regulations in 2003, the 2006 Certain Opinions made progress by requiring the local authorities to finance public schools according to the actual number of students enrolled at schools and expressly banned "temporary schooling fees" and any other additional charges on migrant children.

However, none of these regulations eliminates "permits" requirements for enrolling migrant children, which means that "undocumented" migrant children are still excluded from urban public schools.[23]

---

19 国务院办公厅关于做好农民进城务工就业管理和服务工作的通知 (2003 年 1 月 5 日, 国办发[2003]1 号).

20 国务院关于进一步加强农村教育工作的决定 (2003 年 9 月 17 日 , 国发[2003]19 号).

21 国务院办公厅转发教育部等部门关于进一步做好进城务工就业农民子女义务教育工作意见的通知 (2003 年 9 月 17 日 ,国办发 [2003]78 号)

22 See supra (note 12).

23 For instance, according to the Education Committee of Beijing, migrant children can be enrolled at Beijing's public schools and exempted from "temporary schooling fees", but their parents have to obtain temporary residence, an employment certificate in Beijing, and a certificate by the home area saying that no guardian is available in the home area before submitting an application to the local administration in Beijing, see <www.china.org.cn/chinese/EDU-c/1163857.htm>, accessed 16 April 2006.

3.3. NEW PROMISES OF THE CHINESE GOVERNMENT

10. In the Report on the Government Work delivered by Premier WEN JIABAO at the Fourth Session of the Tenth National People's Congress (NPC) on 5 March 2006, the Premier promised to make nine-year compulsory education universal and to eliminate tuition and miscellaneous fees for all rural children by the end of 2007. He also indicated the need to solve the problem with regard to the education of children from low-income urban families and rural migrant families in order to ensure that all children receive compulsory education.[24]

In the Eleventh Five-Year Plan (2006–2010) for national economic and social development approved by the same session of the NPC, Chapter 28 is devoted to "Developing Education as a Priority", which emphasises equal access to education of rural migrant children and sets the target to increase the education budget to the share of 4% of the national gross domestic product (GDP).[25]

The Draft of the Amendment to the 1986 Compulsory Education Act was submitted to the Standing Committee of the NPC on 25 February 2006 for the first examination, and on 27 April 2006 for the second examination, which provides completely free compulsory education. More importantly, the Draft holds provincial governments instead of those at the county or township level responsible for ensuring the equal right to receive compulsory education of migrant children and for financing compulsory education.[26]

4. THE GAP BETWEEN CHINA AND INTERNATIONAL STANDARDS

11. Among major international human rights treaties, China has ratified the Convention on the Rights of the Child (CRC), the Convention on the Elimination of All Forms of Discrimination against Women (CEDAW), the Convention on the Elimination of All Forms of Racial Discrimination (CERD), and the International Covenant on Economic, Social and Cultural Rights (CESCR). China has signed but not ratified the International Covenant on Civil and Political Rights (ICCPR). However, as regards the right to education of migrant children China is still far from fulfilling its international obligations. The gap between China's implementation and

---

24 <http://english.gov.cn/official/2006-03/14/content_227248.htm>, accessed 17 April 2006.

25 <www.china.com.cn/chinese/news/1156674.htm>, accessed 17 April 2006.

26 See "Compulsory Education Will Enter a New Phase: Guarantee by Government Budget (义务教育将进入新阶段：政府预算来保障), (18 January 2006) *People's Daily*.

its international obligations exists mainly in the following aspects of domestic legislation, policies and practices.

4.1. THE PRINCIPLE OF NON-DISCRIMINATION IN ACCESS TO EDUCATION

12. The right to equal access to education is a fundamental human right granted by all major international and regional human rights instruments.[27] Compulsory primary education should be available and free to all. Any fees imposed, whether direct or indirect, "constitute disincentives to the enjoyment of the right to education and may jeopardise its realisation".[28] While free compulsory education may be implemented progressively, the State obligation to non-discrimination is to be implemented "fully and immediately".[29] The CESCR Committee confirms that it is "a minimum core obligation" to ensure the right to access to public educational institutions and programmes on a non-discriminatory basis.[30]

13. According to the definition given by CERD on racial discrimination and that given by CEDAW on gender discrimination, discrimination means "any distinction, exclusion, restriction or preference based on a number of grounds which has the purpose or effect of nullifying or impairing the recognition, enjoyment or exercise, on an equal footing, of human rights and fundamental freedoms".[31] While not every differentiation constitutes discrimination, the case law of the European Court of Human Rights (ECtHR) and UN monitoring bodies developed four criteria to determine whether a differential treatment constitutes discrimination: (1) whether there is a differential treatment; (2) whether the situations are comparable; (3) whether an objective and reasonable justification exists; and (4) whether the means is proportionate to its aim.[32]

14. According to these criteria, there appear to be three types of discrimination in access to education of migrant children, respectively on the grounds of social status, legal status and the gender of migrant children.

---

27 Such a protection can be found in Art. 26 of UDHR, Art. 13 of CESCR, Arts. 2 and 28 of CRC, Art. 10 of CEDAW, Art. 5(v) of CERD, Art. 30 of CMW, Art. 2 of Protocol No. 1 to ECHR combined with Art. 14 of ECHR, and Art. 13 of the Protocol of San Salvador.

28 CESCR Committee, *General Comment No. 11: Plans of action for primary education (Art. 14)* (UN Doc.E/C.12/1999/4, 1999), para.7.

29 CESCR Committee, *General Comment No. 11*, para.10.

30 CESCR Committee, *General Comment No. 13: The right to education (Art. 13)* (UN Doc.E/C.12/1999/10, 1999), para.57.

31 W. Vandenhole, *Non-Discrimination and Equality in the View of the UN Human Rights Treaty Bodies*, (Antwerpen: Intersentia, 2005), 33.

32 Ibid., 33–34.

First, additional fees charged on migrant children constitute discrimination on the ground of the social status. Such a differential treatment based on the type of *hukou* has the effect of impairing the enjoyment of the right to education by migrant children on an equal footing with non-migrant children. While this differential treatment is a result of the existence of the *hukou* system which constitutes a violation of freedom of movement in the first place, lack of a local *hukou* cannot serve as an objective and reasonable justification for charging additional fees on migrant children, nor can it justify denying their access to education. Although objective difficulties do exist such as lack of resources of the local education system due to the massive scale of internal migration, these difficulties should be immediately tackled by the State rather than be used for decades as the excuse to avoid implementing its international human rights obligation. Even if such a differential treatment might have a justification (which the author doubts), the amount of additional fees which are prohibitive for many migrant parents and the lack of any access for many migrant children to primary education are by no means compatible with the principle of proportionality.

Second, requiring migrant parents to provide legal documents as a pre-condition for enrolling their children in local public schools constitutes direct discrimination against "undocumented" migrant children on the ground of their legal status. In international law, legal status of children is a prohibited ground for differential treatment in education. The CRC Committee has expressed its concern at discrimination against illegal or undocumented children,[33] children of migrant families or migrant children.[34] The CERD Committee expressly required the State to ensure that public educational institutions are open to children of undocumented immigrants.[35] The CESCR Committee confirms that "the principle of non-discrimination extends to all persons of school age residing in the territory of a State Party ... irrespective of their *legal status*" (emphasis added).[36] Article 30 of CMW also provides equal access to public schools for each child of a migrant worker irrespective of the irregular situation of either the parents or child. The "illegal" status of a migrant child is thus not a justification for denying her/his access to education not to mention the fact that such illegal status of internal migrant children in China is created by its *hukou* system in breach of international human rights law. Compared to documented rural migrants, undocumented migrants are more disadvantaged because they often have employment

33 See, for instance, CRC Committee, (UN Doc. CRC/C/15/Add.265), para. 18 (Costa Rica); (UN Doc. CRC/C/15/Add.230), para. 55 (Slovenia); (UN Doc. CRC/C/15/Add.212), para. 49 (Syrian Arab Republic).

34 See, for instance, CRC Committee, (UN Doc. CRC/C/15/Add.227), para. 30 (Netherlands Antilles); (UN Doc. CRC/C/15/Add.150), paras. 22 and 41 (Dominican Republic).

35 CERD Committee, *General Recommendation No. 30: Discrimination Against Non Citizen* (UN Doc.01/10/2004), para.30.

36 CESCR Committee, *General Comment No. 13*, para. 34.

that is more unstable and receive lower payment and thus have less capacity to afford the education of their children.

Third, female migrant children in China particularly suffer from discrimination in access to education. The principle of non-discrimination may have a horizontal effect on third parties and the State has an obligation to protect individuals from discrimination by non-State actors.[37] Article 2 of the CEDAW obliges State Parties to take all appropriate measures to eliminate discrimination against women by any person, organisation or enterprise. While discrimination against female migrant children in access to education is mainly exercised by their own parents, China has the obligation to outlaw such practice and to promote the idea of gender equality to migrant parents. However, there is no evidence that China has made significant efforts in this regard.

15. Lack of equal access to education places migrant children in a constantly disadvantaged situation, and affects their right to enjoy other human rights, in particular the right to work, social security and an adequate standard of living. This will continue to affect their future generations and thus has a long-term impact on Chinese society. The right to education of migrant children is also related to the right to work of their migrant parents because without the right to have their children equally educated in the city where they work, migrant workers cannot enjoy the right to work on an equal footing with their urban counterparts.

4.2. AVAILABILITY, ACCESSIBILITY AND QUALITY OF EDUCATION FOR MIGRANT CHILDREN

16. According to the CESCR Committee, compulsory education shall include the elements of availability, accessibility, acceptability and adaptability.[38] Functional education institutions and programmes have to be available in sufficient quantity, have safe buildings, sanitation facilities, qualified teachers, teaching materials and so on.[39] Education has to be physically reachable and economically accessible.[40] The latter means not only free education for all but may also imply the State's obligation to provide financial assistance to children who cannot afford education-related expenses such as textbooks, uniforms and transportation. Acceptability of education requires the form and substance of education to be acceptable and of good quality.[41] Education also has to be flexible so that it can adapt to the needs of students within their diverse

---

37 W. VANDENHOLE, supra (note 31), 18.

38 CESCR Committee, *General Comment No. 13*, para. 6.

39 Ibid., para. 6(a).

40 Ibid., para. 6(b).

41 Ibid., para. 6(c).

social and cultural settings.[42] China has obligations to respect, protect and fulfil each of the above-mentioned "essential features" of the right to education.[43]

Migrant children are often denied access to local public schools because the latter do not have additional resources for these "outside" children. China thus failed to provide availability of education by not actively developing an adequate system of schools to enrol migrant children. By closing private schools for migrant children but not enrolling them in public schools, China also failed to respect the availability of education.[44]

Children of rural migrant workers often live on the outskirts of the city, while public education resources are more likely to be concentrated in the centre of a city.[45] Even if migrant children can be enrolled in public schools, many of them need to travel a long way to reach the school. Unlike their city counterparts, migrant children cannot enjoy subsidies for public transportation.[46] This reality is inconsistent with the requirement that education be physically accessible. Additional charges on migrant children, burdensome school-related costs, and China's failure to ensure an educational fellowship system to assist migrant children also deter the economic accessibility of education.

The quality of education in public schools varies from one school to another. There has been a long-time practice in China of distinguishing between "important schools" 重点学校 and "normal schools" 非重点学校. The former obtain the best teachers and more financing. This distinction has been recently prohibited officially but still exists in reality. Migrant children are more likely to be enrolled in "normal schools" because "important schools" often charge high "donation fees" and are very competitive even for urban children. Moreover, rural migrant children often suffer from attitudes of discrimination from teachers and urban classmates.[47] While migrant children often have language difficulties and an unfavourable studying environment, special programmes targeting them for help with these difficulties do not exist. Instead, migrant children are often blamed by the school for their lower academic performance in school. In this sense, China has failed to meet the requirement of adaptability of education.

---

42 Ibid., para. 6(d).

43 CESCR Committee, *General Comment No. 13*, para. 50.

44 Ibid.

45 D. Liao, 'Research Report on the Education Problem of Peasant Workers' Children in Shanghai Area' (上海地区民工子女教育问题研究报告), (2004) 12 *Shanghai Education Research* (上海教育科研), 4–8.

46 Human Rights in China, supra (note 2), 28.

47 For more on this topic, see Human Rights In China, supra (note 2), 27–29.

Private schools for migrant children normally charge less than public schools, but they have various problems.[48] First, many of these schools cannot qualify as "functional education institutions" due to poor budgets, lack of qualified teachers, and lack of government supervision of quality.[49] Second, local administrations often fail to license qualified private schools of migrant children in addition to summarily closing down the least qualified.[50] The unstable situation of unlicensed schools has resulted in frequent movements of the school and reluctance for further investment.[51] Although national regulations require the local administration to license qualified private schools and provide financial support and training to teachers,[52] these regulations do not provide for necessary financial support by the national government of local authorities for the implementation of these regulations. In fact, these regulations did not receive a positive response at the local level.[53] Third, the illegal status of unlicensed schools for migrant children may prevent them from issuing diplomas recognised by educational authorities and consequently obstructs students when they seek to enter secondary and higher education.

4.3. THE RIGHT TO FUNDAMENTAL EDUCATION

17. As Article 13(2)(d) of the CESCR provides for the right to fundamental education, China has the obligation to provide fundamental education opportunities to individuals who have not received or completed the entire period of their primary education. For those migrant children who missed their opportunity to receive complete primary education and have grown up, fundamental education or adult education should be available, accessible, acceptable and adaptable for them.[54] Unfortunately, this type of education does not seem to be available to most grown-up

---

48 J. Chen, 'Study on the Problem of Education of Floating Children in Beijing' (北京市流动儿童教育问题初探), (Additional Edition of 2004) (海淀走读大学学报), *Academic Journal of Haidian Zoudu University*, 108–113.

49 Y. Ren, 'Report on the Teaching Resources in 13 Schools for Migrant Workers' Children in Beijing' (北京 13 所打工子弟学校师资情况报告), (2003) 8 *China Reform* (中国改革), 58–60; X. Shen, 'Sociological Analysis of Education Model of Migrant Populations' Children in Guangzhou' (广州市外来人口子女教育模式的社会学分析), (2004) 11 *Youth Studies* (青年研究).

50 For instance, in Beijing, it was estimated in 2004 that there were about 400 underground schools for migrant children. See: Xinhua News Agency, *Illegal Schools for Migrant Workers' Kid Await Government Approval*, 20 February 2004. <www.china.org.cn/english/culture/87841.htm>, accessed 27 April 2006.

51 Human Rights In China, supra (note 2), 30–31.

52 See, for example, the 1997 Regulations on the Running of Schools by Social Forces (社会力量办学条例).

53 C. Froissart, supra (note 4), 10.

54 CESCR Committee, *General Comment No. 13*, paras. 21–27.

migrant children. Although adult education exists in China, it is mostly for urban citizens or offered by fee-charging private schools.

4.4. THE RIGHT TO EFFECTIVE REMEDIES

18. The right to education cannot be effectively protected if victims cannot address the violation and obtain reparation. Article 8 of the Universal Declaration of Human Rights (UDHR) provides that "everyone has the right to an effective remedy... for acts violating the fundamental rights granted him by the constitution or by law". Article 13 of the European Convention on Human Rights (ECHR), combined with Article 2 of Protocol No.1 to ECHR, provides for a right to an effective remedy to violations of the right to education. Article 6 of CERD guarantees effective protection and remedies against racial discrimination, which violates an individual's human rights as well as the right to seek reparation or satisfaction for damage resulting from such discrimination. The CERD Committee goes further in its General Comment No. 26 to clarify that the right to an effective remedy "is not necessarily secured solely by the punishment of the perpetrator of the discrimination" and financial compensation for material or moral damage suffered by a victim may be considered.[55] The CESCR Committee pointed out in its General Comments that the right to non-discrimination and the right to primary education free for all are "justiciable" and any person suffering from violations of these rights shall have an effective remedy.[56] A State seeking to justify its failure to provide any domestic legal remedies for violations of economic, social and cultural rights needs to show either that such remedies are not "appropriate means" or that they are unnecessary.[57]

19. China has the obligation to provide effective remedies to migrant children whose right to education is denied or restricted because of discrimination. However, the Constitution cannot be applied directly by the courts in China.[58] Therefore, violation of a constitutional right cannot be addressed in the courts unless there is a concrete provision in a specific law. However, China's Compulsory Education Act and Education Act contain merely principles and do not provide for any judicial or administrative remedies to individuals. Moreover, there is not a general anti-discrimination law in China. As a result, legal remedies are not available for migrant

[55] CERD Committee, *General Comment No.26: Art. 6 of the Convention*, 24/03/2000.

[56] CESCR Committee, *General Comment No.3*, para. 5.

[57] CESCR Committee, *General Comment No.9: The domestic application of the Covenant* (UN Doc.E/C.12/1998/24, 1998), para. 3.

[58] Z. Li, 'The role of domestic courts in the adjudication of international human rights: a survey of the practice and problems in China', in B. Conforti and F. Francioni (eds.), *Enforcing International Human Rights in Domestic Courts*, (The Hague: Martinus Nijhoff Publishers, 1997), 329–352.

children and their parents to address the violation of the right to education because of discrimination.

5. FACTORS BEHIND THE GAP

5.1. HIGHLY DISCRIMINATIVE APPROACHES IN EDUCATION

20. The education problem of migrant children has to be viewed in the broader context of China's discriminative education system.[59] The *hukou* system created a highly dualistic urban/rural society. While urban citizens are provided with all public services, rural residents are left on their own. Financial and human resources are disproportionately allocated to "important schools" rather than "normal schools", to higher education than to basic and middle education, and to elite universities than to normal universities.

5.2. FINANCING OF EDUCATION: LOW INPUT AND DECENTRALISED EDUCATION FINANCING

21. General poor budget and localised financing for education make city schools unwilling to enrol migrant children without charging additional fees. First, low input of the national budget in education in general reduces the ability of city schools to absorb migrant children. While education is "recognised as one of the best financial investments States can make" according to the CESCR Committee,[60] China's education budget constituted only 2.5% of its GDP throughout the 1990s and 3.4% of GDP in 2004.[61] Although there are no legally binding criteria for education spending as a share of GDP, the world average in 2003 was 5.1% and UNESCO recommends a minimum of 6%. China's education budget, even reaching its 4% target, is still behind most developing countries.[62] Second, financing of compulsory education is mainly the responsibility of local governments at the district level in cities and at the township

---

59 Z. YUAN, 'Narrowing the gap: an important question of China's education policy' (缩小差距：中国教育政策的重大命题), (2005) 3 *Academic Journal of Beijing Normal University: social science edition* (北京师范大学学报：社科版).

60 CESCR Committee, *General Comment No. 13*, para. 1.

61 The data is from ZHOU JI, Minister of the Education Ministry, at the press conference on 24 March 2004. <http://news.xinhuanet.com/video/2004-03/24/content_1381752.htm>, accessed 24 May 2006.

62 The Special Rapporteur on the right to education recommended in her report about China that "the budgetary allocation for education be increased to the internationally recommended minimum of 6% of GDP". See: K. TOMAŠEVSKI, supra (note 3), para. 16.

level in rural areas (before 1996, it was at the county level).[63] While cities are normally wealthy enough to finance public schools, many rural counties and towns have even failed to pay teachers' salaries and had to impose a range of charges on peasants to fund education. Consequently, the quality of city schools is much better than that of rural schools. It explains why some urban authorities are concerned that relaxing control will lead to an "influx" of migrants because of education benefits.

5.3. LACK OF A HUMAN RIGHTS-BASED APPROACH IN LEGISLATION AND POLICY-MAKING

22. China's legislation and policies to solve the educational problems of migrant children are seriously lagging behind the problem, which resulted in unaccountable numbers of children growing up without basic education. Moreover, legislation and policies are often vague, simply claiming principles and doing little in guiding practice, and thus do not result in much progress in reality. Policy-making in China is based on utilitarian concerns such as social stability, economic development rather than human rights values, justice and the principle of equality. The problem of migrant children has finally attracted attention because of massive media reports and academic research on this issue. The government considers this issue a threat to social stability and damaging to the image of cities.[64]

There is a worrisome tendency in policy-making that education is likely to be regarded as a tradable commodity rather than a basic human right. For instance, in March 2006 when the National People's Congress (China's parliament) held its annual conference in Beijing, certain representatives raised the question why poor students cannot afford university education nowadays as they could in the 1950s. The spokesperson of the Ministry of Education answered that parents should change their way of thinking because China now has a market economy. He compared China's top public universities such as Beijing University with expensive clothes and said that those who do not have the money should just buy cheaper ones. He criticised parents as "irrational" if they expect their children to enter top universities without considering their financial capacity.[65]

---

63 According to new legislation, the national government will increase its contribution to education in rural areas but it will not directly benefit migrant children. See: The Notice of the State Council on Strengthening the Reform of Budget Guarantee Mechanism for Rural Compulsory Education, 24 December 2005, (国务院关于深化农村义务教育经费保障机制改革的通知, 国发[2005]43 号).

64 Human Right In China, supra (note 2), 10–11.

65 See 'Ministry of Education: Illegal fee-charging for education is due to insufficient education funding' (教育部：乱收费屡禁不止是因为教育投入不足), 6 March 2006, <www.bj.xinhuanet.com/bjpd_sdzx/2006-03/06/content_6393844.htm>, accessed 25 April 2006.

5.4. PROTECTION OF LOCAL INTERESTS

23. Although for a decade, the central government issued policies requiring local governments to make efforts to provide compulsory education to migrant children, local authorities are not enthusiastic about implementing them for various reasons. First, rural migrants are considered outsiders with inferior status compared to their city compatriots, and the city does not have the responsibility to share resources with them.[66] Negative perceptions of rural migrants contributed to the unwillingness of cities to accept them. Local authorities and even local people often see migrants as causing many social problems: contamination of the city's image, crime and so on.[67] Second, the evaluation of political achievement of local officers is based on economic indicators such as local GDP growth. Education is a soft indicator and does not draw much attention especially when it concerns disadvantaged groups such as rural migrants. Local authorities do not have strong incentives to solve the problem even if the central government requires them to do so. Third, there are also practical difficulties even if a strong political will exists for solving the problem. For instance, many local authorities have a fear – not completely ungrounded – that more rural migrants will flood into cities if free access to education is provided and cause an unbearable burden on the local education system. In Shanghai, for instance, the Pudong district tried to enrol migrant children in public schools without charging "donation fees". Suddenly, a huge number of migrant workers brought their children to this district and caused a crisis of local education resources.[68]

6. SOME RECOMMENDATIONS

24. First, China needs to adequately evaluate the situation of migrant children. The inefficiency of policies is closely linked to the lack of adequate and correct information. More research and surveys must be done to discover the real situation of migrant children in receiving areas. Authorities which collect statistics, national or local, need to collect disaggregated data about migrant children by age, gender, place of origin and so on.

25. Second, China needs a general anti-discrimination law to address pervasive discrimination in legislation, policies, and public and private practices. This law should allow discrimination in legislation and policies to be reviewed and abolished

66 D. Solinger, supra (note 1), 103–107.

67 Ibid.

68 C. Zhang, 'Compulsory Education of Peasant Workers' Children: who will fill the financial vacuum?' (民工子女义务教育：财政真空 谁来补?), (1 July 2004) *Nan Fen Chuang* (南风窗), 58–60.

immediately. It should place sanctions on discriminative practices and allow victims such as migrant children to address discrimination they suffer and obtain reparation.

26. Third, the above-mentioned example of the Pudong district in Shanghai illustrates that an individual action by certain localities may create new problems rather than solve the existing ones. It means that an integral approach at least at the city level is necessary in order to avoid this phenomenon.

27. Fourth, China needs to increase its *national* budget for compulsory education and to equally distribute resources. According to the new policy, the responsibility for financing compulsory education will be shifted to the governments at the provincial level from those at the district and county level. If implemented, this policy will be able to redress the poor educational funding in rural areas. Nevertheless, regional disparity in terms of education funding will remain. Children in wealthier coastal regions will receive education of better quality compared to those in the hinterlands, as it has always been. Equal distribution of education funding by the *national* government is the key to equal access to education.

28. Fifth, China should disconnect access to education from the legal status of migrant children and their parents. The CESCR Committee recommends that China dismantle the *hukou* system to ensure that internal migrants enjoy the same education benefits enjoyed by those in the urban areas.[69] While dismantling the *hukou* system as a whole probably will not happen in the near future, less fundamental reform is foreseeable such as eliminating the "permits" requirement for enrolling children in schools.

29. Sixth, education should become a "hard" indicator for evaluating local officials' political performance. One important method of the central government to control local officials is their promotion. Only when compulsory education of migrant children becomes a hard criterion for promotion will local authorities of receiving cities take this issue seriously and implement national policies.

30. Seventh, the quality of private schools for migrant children should be carefully supervised. China is obliged to maintain a transparent and effective system to monitor minimum educational standards for these private schools.[70] For those who have met the qualifications, China should license these schools and recognise the diplomas they issue. The local government should assume clear responsibility for providing financial

---

69 CESCR Committee, *Concluding Observation People's Republic of China*, (UN Doc. E/C.12/1/Add.107, 2005), paras. 37, 46, and 66.

70 CESCR Committee, *General Comment No.13*, para. 54.

and material support to private schools for migrant children and training to their teachers.

31. Finally, China needs to build up a rights-based mentality of policy-making, which is also conducive to what the government is promoting: social stability and economic growth.

7. CONCLUSION

32. Although the education problem of migrant children is unlikely to be solved in the short term, there are some positive signs for the future. Some substantive progress can already be seen on the ground. Local authorities of some cities and provinces such as Beijing, Suzhou in the Jiangsu Province, Sichuan Province, and Chong Qin have promised to provide free compulsory education to all from September 2006. In some other places, fees are reduced to the same level as those for local residents. The draft Amendment of Compulsory Education Law, if adopted by the legislature, will provide a more solid legal ground for guaranteeing this basic human right.

Nevertheless, questions remain in terms of access to education of "undocumented" migrant children. It is not clear either whether by the end of 2007 migrant children will enjoy free compulsory education in city schools as other rural children are supposed to enjoy since the national government has not yet promised free education for urban children.

A final point is to emphasise that children grow up fast and cannot wait. The approach of "develop first, distribute next" should by no means apply to the education of children.

THE RIGHT TO EDUCATION IN THE REPUBLIC OF IRELAND: TEACHING THE CELTIC TIGER

AOIFE DALY

1. INTRODUCTION

1. Ireland has undergone a significant boom economically, referred to as the "Celtic Tiger", in the past decade. In the years from 1996 to 2005, Ireland outperformed the rest of the EU in relation to income, employment and public finances.[1] This means that Ireland has resources available to provide for the right to education (a right which is enshrined under Art. 42 of the Irish Constitution) to a very high standard. The right to education is considered so vital that both the International Covenant on Civil and Political Rights and the International Covenant Economic, Social and Cultural Rights regard it as being non-derogable.[2]

Indeed Ireland does enjoy a relatively high standard of education, as acknowledged by the Committee on the Rights of the Child.[3] Every child resident in the State is entitled to free primary education. This right has been enshrined in the 1937 Constitution, Bunreacht na hÉireann.[4] However, it is clear that education is not receiving the resources it is due in accordance with the principle of progressive realisation of economic, social and cultural rights.

"Progressive realisation" refers to the obligation of a state to realise rights within the maximum resources available. States Parties to the Convention on the Rights of the

---

1 Central Statistics Office, *Measuring Ireland's Progress*, (Dublin: Central Statistics Office, 2005).

2 This means that the right cannot be suspended.

3 Children's Rights Alliance, *Children's Rights, Our Responsibilities, concluding observations of the Committee on the Rights of the Child following the examination of the First National Report of Ireland on the implementation of the Convention of the Rights of the Child,* (The Children's Rights Alliance: Republic of Ireland, 1998). It was stated that, "The Committee also appreciates the high level of education and advanced health system established in the State Party", (p. 6).

4 Constitution of Ireland, Bunreacht na hÉireann, adopted on 1 July 1937 and entered into force on 29 December 1937.

Child and other international human rights treaties are obligated to improve the conditions of the right to education to the maximum of their available resources.[5] Clearly, the Irish state has huge resources at its disposal due to the current economic boom. However, research of the Organisation for Economic Co-operation and Development (OECD) shows that Ireland currently ranks 21st out of 27 OECD countries for education spending.[6] Spending on primary and post primary level education in Ireland increased at only half the rate of economic growth in the Celtic Tiger era (1995–2002).

As well as the fact that Ireland is lagging behind in spending on education, there are many instances where investment in education has achieved little. This has occurred because either it was targeted inappropriately, or it was not properly administered on the ground.[7]

There are many anomalies regarding the implementation of educational rights in Ireland. On the one hand, education standards are relatively high (as the Committee on the Rights of the Child has acknowledged). On the other hand, education in Ireland still lags behind in many areas, particularly for disadvantaged groups. This chapter will outline the successes and failures regarding the child's right to education in one of the world's most successful economies.

2. RECENT IMPROVEMENTS FOR CHILDREN'S RIGHTS IN IRELAND

2. It is useful to look at the right to education in Ireland in the context of children's rights in Ireland generally. There have been significant developments for children's rights in Ireland in recent years. The National Children's Strategy was published in 2000. The strategy is rooted in the UN Convention on the Rights of the Child, and is aimed at improving children's lives. Ireland is one of the few countries in the world with such a strategy.

The purpose of the National Children's Strategy is to provide a framework for improving the lives of all children, especially those who experience disadvantage or have particular needs. The strategy offers a vision of: "*An Ireland where children are*

---

5 Art. 4 of the Convention on the Rights of the Child outlines that "States Parties shall undertake such measures to the maximum extent of their available resources".

6 Organisation for Economic Co-operation and Development, *Education at a Glance*, (Dublin: OECD Publishing, 2005).

7 Children's Rights Alliance, *From Rhetoric to Rights: Children's Rights Alliance Second Shadow Report to the UN Committee on the Rights of the Child*, (Dublin: Children's Rights Alliance, 2006).

respected as young citizens with a valued contribution to make and a voice of their own; where all children are cherished and supported by family and the wider society; where they enjoy a fulfilling childhood and realise their potential."

The National Children's Office was set up to lead and oversee the implementation of the National Children's Strategy. This office supports the Minister for Children in implementing the National Children's Strategy.

The Strategy also provided for the appointment of an Ombudsman for Children in 2004. The Ombudsman for Children is an independent office, accountable to the Irish parliament. The primary aim of the Office of the Ombudsman for Children is to provide an independent mechanism to support the rights of children.

3. RESISTANCE TO RIGHTS-BASED APPROACH

3. Despite these achievements, the Irish government continues to resist adopting a human rights-based approach in policy, legislation and service provision, including that relating to children. Amnesty International outlines that human rights based approaches seek to ensure that human rights are a central frame of reference in policymaking, by ensuring that people have the means to demand their human rights and to participate in decision-making processes.[8]

It is widely held in Ireland that the government believes that adopting a rights-based approach would lead to unsustainable funding obligations.[9] The Children's Rights Alliance in Ireland points out that this is despite the fact that human rights are not merely achieved through increased funding, but also through good management of existing funds.[10] Because commitments of the Irish government to children are not rights-based, there is no fundamental obligation to fulfil the commitments made when the Convention on the Rights of the Child was ratified in 1992. The only obligation is that imposed through public accountability.

Furthermore, although the state has confirmed to the international community that it is dedicated to children's rights by ratifying the Convention on the Rights of the Child, it has not incorporated the Convention into domestic law. This is in spite of

---

8 Amnesty International Irish Section and the International Human Rights Network, *Our Rights, Our Future, human Rights Based Approaches in Ireland: Principles, Policies and Practice*, (Dublin: Amnesty International, 2005).

9 See, e.g. Children's Rights Alliance, supra, (note 7) and Amnesty International Irish Section and the International Human Rights Network, supra, (note 8).

10 Children's Rights Alliance, supra, (note 7).

the fact that the Convention explicitly states in Article 4 that, "States Parties shall undertake all appropriate legislative, administrative, and other measures for the implementation of the rights recognised in the present Convention".

Under Ireland's dualist system, domestic law takes legal precedence over international instruments. Unless the Convention is incorporated into the Irish constitution, it is not binding on domestic law, the courts or the Government. Amending the constitution will require a referendum. Numerous children's organisations in Ireland have emphasised that the incorporation of the Convention at constitutional level is necessary for the full realisation of the rights of the child,[11] including the right to education.

K. TOMAŠEVSKI (former UN Special Rapporteur on the Right to education) calls for human rights mainstreaming within education around the world.[12] To "mainstream" human rights in education policy-making and practice means to emphasise, "the centrality of human rights in all activities"[13] around education. Unfortunately educational rights have not yet been "mainstreamed" in Ireland, nor is the rights-based approach the norm.

4. EARLY CHILDHOOD CARE AND EDUCATION

4.1. OBLIGATIONS REGARDING EARLY CHILDHOOD CARE AND EDUCATION

4. "Early childhood care and education" (ECCE) is a term covering both pre-schools and day care, because it is widely accepted that the two should be (and are) closely linked.[14] ECCE is often the first introduction of the child to a formal education system. There is no right to early childhood care and education under international law. It is not, for example, a stipulation of the Convention on the Rights of the Child that a state provide ECCE. Drafting states resisted including a reference to pre-school education in the Convention because of the funding implications of doing so.[15] However, there are many reasons why the provision of ECCE (and pre-school

---

11 Children's Rights Alliance, supra, (note 7) and K. HOLLAND, 'Rights of children must be recognised, says ISPCC', (Wednesday June 28,2006) *Irish Times*.

12 K. TOMAŠEVSKI, *Manual on Rights-Based Education: Global Human Rights Requirements Made Simple*, (UNESCO Bangkok: Asia and Pacific Regional Bureau for Education, 2004), 1.

13 UN General Assembly, *Road map towards the implementation of the United Nations Millennium Declaration: Report of the Secretary-General* (UN Doc. A/56/326, 2001), para. 201.

14 Department of Education and Science, *Ready to Learn: The White Paper on Early Childhood Education*, (Dublin: The Stationery Office, 1999).

15 G. VAN BEUREN, *The International Law on the Rights of the Child*, (The Hague – Boston – London: Martinus Nijhoff Publishers, 1998).

education in particular) is highly desirable (and possibly an obligation) for such a wealthy country.

As regards early childhood care and education in the international legal context, there are a variety of non-binding recommendations and declarations, which can be viewed as a moral standard for the fulfilment of pre-school education. Pre-school education is acknowledged as a natural entry point for the provision of 'Education for All'. This provision, supported by UNESCO,[16] emphasises that "learning begins at birth".[17]

Provision of early childhood care and education is also desirable for a state on a very practical level. It has been repeatedly highlighted through research that pre-school has significant benefits for children, their families and society. Children who have received pre-school education, for example, perform significantly better academically.[18] Children who receive pre-school education are also more likely to finish school, hold a job, have higher earnings, and commit fewer and crimes throughout their lives.[19] Undoubtedly, pre-school education is of huge benefit to children and society.

4.2. INADEQUACIES IN THE IRISH SYSTEM

5. Despite these statistics, Ireland spends less than 0.2% of gross domestic product (GDP) on early childhood care and education. This is significantly below the 0.4% average across OECD countries.[20] As well as this lack of prioritisation of early childhood care and education for funding, there is a significant failing around co-ordination in the ECCE system.[21] Responsibility for ECCE is currently split between

16 UNESCO, *Policy Brief on Early Childhood No. 31 – Pre-Primary Education: The Valid Investment Option for EFA*, (Education for All, March April 2006), "pre-primary education deserves prioritisation on the condition that it promotes the child's holistic development, that it is delivered in an environment meeting some minimum pedagogical standards, and that there is a phased plan for the inclusion of younger age groups".

17 Jomtien World Declaration on Education for All, see: <http://www2.unesco.org/wef/en-conf/Jomtien%20Declaration%20eng.shtm>.

18 F. Campbell et al., 'Early Childhood Education: Young adult outcomes from the Abecedarian Project', (2002) 6 *Applied Developmental Science*, 66–87; S. Daniels, 'Can Pre-School Education Affect Children's Education in Primary School?', (November 1995) 21 (2) *Oxford Review of Education*, 163–79.

19 L.J. Schweinhart et al., *Lifetime Effects: The High/Scope Perry Preschool Study Through Age 40*, (Ypsilanti MI: High/Scope Press, 2005).

20 National Economic and Social Forum, *Early Childhood Care and Education, NESF Report No. 31*, (Dublin: NESF, 2005).

21 Ibid., 24.

seven government departments.[22] Centralisation is intended through the planned Early Childhood Development Office at the Department of Education and Science; however, this office has yet to be established.

School in Ireland is not compulsory until age six;[23] however, children can start infant classes in the formal school system after their fourth birthday. The coverage rate of education for the age group three to six years is just 56%, which is amongst the lowest in Europe.[24] In any case, the formal school system is widely held not to be the most appropriate setting for pre-school age children to receive ECCE, because the teaching methods and curriculum are unsuited to this age group, amongst other reasons.[25]

There have been significant steps taken by the Irish government to increase funding for early childhood care and education. However, this has not happened in the context of recognition that it is in the best interest of child to receive pre-school education. It has primarily been part of an effort to facilitate working mothers, and to tackle disadvantage.

4.3. ACHIEVEMENTS OF THE IRISH SYSTEM

6. It must be noted that there have been achievements in the area of early childhood care and education in recent years. The Centre for Early Childhood Development and Education (CECDE) was established in September 2001. One of its agreed key functions is to coordinate and enhance early education provision, including parental involvement, with particular focus on disadvantaged and special needs groups. Funding (€499.3m) became available to the childcare sector under the Equal Opportunities Childcare Programme (EOCP) 2000–2006.

Childcare has remained high on the political agenda this year. A five-year National Childcare Programme 2006–2011 has been put in place. The placement of responsibility for this programme and for early childhood policy under the new Office of Minister for Children has been seen as a positive step. However, these programmes are intended to increase childcare places for working parents. The direct aim of these programmes

[22] C. Corrigan, *OECD Thematic Review of Early Childhood Education and Care, Background Report*, (Department of Education and Science 2004). The Departments are Education and Science; Justice, Equality and Law Reform; Health and Children; Heritage and Local Government and Community, Rural and Gaeltacht Affairs; Social, Community and Family Affairs; Environment, Trade and Enterprise.

[23] Educational (Welfare) Act, 2000.

[24] Organisation for Economic Co-operation and Development *Early Childhood Education and Care Policy Country Note for Ireland*, (OECD Directorate for Education 2004) 6.

[25] Ibid, 6.

is not to facilitate early education (although this may be achieved indirectly in childcare facilities). Many pre-schools obtain funding through the EOCP; however, this is on a very ad-hoc basis, and only on the premise that the pre-schools facilitate childcare. This is despite the fact pre-schools only last 3 to 4 hours (therefore not facilitating a mother to work at all). This policy makes little sense, and confuses pre-school workers trying to apply for funding to run their pre-schools.[26]

It is indeed an achievement that the Department of Education and Science operates a number of pre-school programmes for disadvantaged children. These aim to expose young children to an educational programme that will enhance their development and counter the effects of social disadvantage. These programmes include the Early Start Pre-School Pilot Project, which caters for pupils aged 3 to 4 who are most at risk in areas of social disadvantage. Each Early Start class attracts special capitation funding, a qualified primary teacher and a childcare assistant, a start-up grant for materials and equipment, and an additional grant to foster parental involvement. In total, the Early Start Project caters for a total of 1,680 places. It is still a pilot project and has not been mainstreamed to date.

4.4. THE FUTURE FOR EARLY CHILDHOOD CARE AND EDUCATION IN IRELAND

7. Clearly, there have been significant steps taken by the Irish government in the area of early childhood care and education. However, despite the planning that has occurred (and the funds that have been made available), serious failings persist. The way in which the funding is being distributed does not acknowledge the value of pre-school education for all children. Instead, there is a narrow focus on pre-school for disadvantaged children and childcare for working mothers.

There are currently plans for a new National Childcare Programme. This is to be welcomed as a step towards facilitating early childhood care and education. However, the Children's Rights Alliance state that the Government should develop an integrated, universal, high- quality early childhood care and education system. This should be achieved through investing in the development of quality services and through placing the best interest of the child at the centre of the Programme.[27] Such a system would ensure that young children are adequately prepared to start primary school and the rest of their educational experience.

---

[26] J. WHYTE, A. DALY, P. BUJIA and N. SMITH, *Reconceptualising Preschool Playgroups*, (Dublin: Children's Research Centre, draft report, to be published 2006).

[27] Children's Rights Alliance, supra, (note 7).

5. PRIMARY SCHOOLS- PHYSICAL ASPECTS

5.1. CLASS SIZE

8. Class size has a significant effect on the quality of education. Class sizes in Irish primary (and second level) schools are significantly higher than in many other EU countries. The Irish government have measures to reduce class size over the next two years. However, despite Government commitments to reduce primary class sizes, the average primary class size in 2002 in Ireland was 24. This was one of the highest among EU countries.[28] More than one in four of the State's primary school students are in classes of 30 or more, according to the latest Government statistics.[29] This is an increase of 5,000 children in the past two years.

Furthermore, the number of teachers is an issue for primary schools in Ireland. Ireland had the fifth highest reported student-to-teacher ratio in the EU at primary education level in 2002/2003.[30] This seriously detracts from the quality of education for children in Irish primary schools.

5.2. INFRASTRUCTURE

9. Sub-standard school building conditions persist in Ireland. Approximately 4,000 primary schools in Ireland are dilapidated, some with poor sanitary conditions and dangerous electrical wiring.[31]

However, progress has been made in improving the infrastructure of many schools. The Irish Minister for Education recently acknowledged that there is a necessity to improve school facilities in a system where some schools are over 150 years old.[32] The government has announced a five-year school modernisation programme. €491 million will be spent building and modernising primary and secondary schools in 2007.

However, the difficulties in securing school buildings for new residential areas in Ireland have been widely documented by the media.[33] The government requires a €63,500 local contribution for new State-owned school buildings to be built. This

---

[28] Central Statistics Office, *Measuring Ireland's Progress*, (Dublin: Central Statistics Office, 2005).

[29] J. Downes, 'Primary school pupils in classes of 30 or more up by 5,000', (Saturday July 15, 2006) *Irish Times*.

[30] Central Statistics Office, supra (note 28).

[31] S. Flynn, 'INTO will step up campaign to upgrade schools', (Monday May 23, 2005) *Irish Times*.

[32] A. Kerr, 'Hanafin challenged on lack of new school buildings', (Mon May 29, 2006) *Irish Times*.

[33] Ibid.

makes it difficult to establish new schools, despite rising numbers of children due to start school in many areas. The multi-denominational school movement has been particularly vocal on this issue.

6. MULTI-DENOMINATIONAL EDUCATION IN IRELAND

10. The Irish primary school system is denominational in nature. An incredible 99% of Irish primary schools are under the management of a religious body. Almost all of these schools are publicly funded by the state but privately owned by religious bodies. This system of education is unique to Ireland and leads to a significant lack of educational choice. The Irish constitution states that, "The State shall not oblige parents in violation of their conscience and lawful preference to send their children to schools established by the State, or to any particular type of school designated by the State." (Art. 42.1.3)

Yet in practice many families have no choice but to send their children to schools where the religious education, as well as the entire ethos of the school, is focused on one denomination. This has been found to run contrary to educational rights. In March 2005, the UN Committee on the Elimination of Racial Discrimination recommended that the Irish state actively promote the establishment of multi-denominational and nondenominational schools. The Committee emphasised the link between religious and racial discrimination, and stated that the current system violates the rights of children of minority religious backgrounds.

State support for the development of new multi-denominational schools is needed for this recommendation to be implemented. At present, there is little government support for this. The €63,500 local contribution required for new State-owned school buildings makes it particularly difficult to establish multi-denominational schools (who do not have the support of the local church as denominational schools do). The state already provides extensive supports for other school bodies such as the Gaelscoil (Irish-speaking school) movement (€400,000 per annum). Yet in 2004, the Chief Executive of Educate Together (the Irish multi-denominational school organisation) stated that Government support for the work of Educate Together constitutes less than 7% of the organisation's basic needs.[34]

The religious curriculum in Ireland is also a concern from a human rights perspective. It is the preserve of the religious bodies that manage the schools and is not regulated

[34] P. Rowe, 'Inclusive Schools Need More Support', (Monday October 4, 2004) *Irish Times*.

by the state. All State schools teach religious classes. Parents may request for their children to be exempt from these classes, however the children themselves may not. This is despite the fact that a motion was passed by Dáil na nÓg (the Youth Parliament) that "religion" as a school subject should be replaced with a subject focusing on morals, ethics and other cultures.[35]

The Department of Education and Science has issued guidelines for schools, *Guidelines for Schools Intercultural Education for Primary Schools.* The Children's Rights Alliance in Ireland emphasise that a major weakness of the guidelines is that they do not cover the religious education curriculum.[36] This is because the religious bodies that manage the schools control the religious curriculum. In a country experiencing such high levels of immigration, such religious restriction is an increasing concern.

7. INEQUALITY IN THE IRISH EDUCATION SYSTEM

11. Article 28 of the Convention on the Rights of the Child places a duty on States Parties to recognise the educational rights of children "on the basis of equal opportunity". The Committee on the rights of the Child made its concluding observations on Ireland's first report in 1998.[37] The Committee was concerned about the difficulties faced by children from vulnerable and disadvantaged groups, regarding the enjoyment of their fundamental rights. These groups included children belonging to the Traveller community (a nomadic minority group indigenous to Ireland), children from poor families and migrant children. The concerns of the Committee extended to the right to education.

7.1. THE RIGHT TO EDUCATION OF DISADVANTAGED CHILDREN IN IRELAND

12. Tomaševski states that "*there is a close correlation between low levels of education and poverty*".[38] This is certainly the case regarding education in Ireland. Economic growth and public investment in Ireland have often been irregular in their geographic

---

[35] Office of the Minister for Children, *Delegate Report: Dáil na nÓg*, (Dublin: Office of the Minister for Children, 2006) and A. Kerr, 'Replacement of religion as school subject urged', (Monday March 27, 2006) *Irish Times*.

[36] Children's Rights Alliance, supra, (note 7).

[37] Children's Rights Alliance, supra, (note 3).

[38] K. Tomaševski, supra, (note 12), 3.

distribution. This has created areas of inequalities where children are exposed to fewer educational opportunities in practice.[39]

There have been legislative and policy developments aimed at combating this disadvantage in the education sector. The enactment of the Education Act, 1998 and the Education (Welfare) Act, 2000 are particularly relevant. They involve attempts to ensure that those children who are in need of support to stay in the school system are identified early and receive the necessary support.

The Irish government is to be commended on the fact that there has been much funding and planning designed to counter educational disadvantage in recent years. The Educational Disadvantage Committee (EDC) was set up as a statutory body under the Education Act, 1998 to advise the Department of Education and Science on the policies and strategies to be adopted to identify and correct educational disadvantage. The expenditure on targeting children from disadvantaged backgrounds in 2006 is in excess of €640m.[40]

However, unfortunately, equal access to education continues to be problematic for many children in practice. One in ten Irish children leaves primary school with serious literacy problems. For children in disadvantaged communities, this figure rises to one in three.[41] Furthermore, there has been no improvement in national reading standards between 1998 and 2004, despite the increase in resources.[42] The capacity of a child to read and write affects his/her possibilities of staying in school, going to university, and gaining employment.

Both the International Covenant on Economic Social and Cultural Rights (Art. 13) and the Convention on the Rights of the Child (Art. 28) place a duty on states to make primary education compulsory. The Convention on the Rights of the Child also obliges the state to "Take measures to encourage regular attendance at schools and the reduction of drop-out rates" (Art. 28). Despite this, Ireland has a high level of absenteeism at both primary and secondary level. This problem is particularly serious in areas of disadvantage, where almost one in five students miss more than 20 days of school per year.[43] Another problem is that 1,000 children annually do not transfer from primary to secondary level school.[44]

---

39 Children's Rights Alliance, supra, (note 7).
40 Barnardos, *Make the Grade*, (Dublin: Barnardos, 2006).
41 Department of Education and Science, National Assessment of English Reading in 2004, (Dublin: Education Research Centre, 2006).
42 Barnardos, supra, (note 39).
43 National Education Welfare Board, *Pre-Budget Submission*, (Dublin: National Education Welfare Board, 2005).
44 K. Holland, 'The most difficult transition year', (Saturday August 20, 2005) *Irish Times*.

Early school leaving is also a significant problem in Ireland; 18% of young people do not sit their Leaving Certificate.[45] The link between early school-leaving and poverty is explicitly recognised in the Government's National Anti- Poverty Strategy. The most recent statistics show that students in disadvantaged areas are much more likely to leave school earlier than students from affluent areas.[46]

Disadvantaged children are also less likely to receive third-level education. There have been efforts to encourage children from disadvantaged areas to go on to university level, such as the introduction of free fees for all Irish students.[47] However, there is a stark disparity between young people from disadvantaged backgrounds who are attending college compared to those attending from wealthier backgrounds; 89% of young people with a "professional worker" father were going to college in 2003, compared to 28% of those whole father was "unskilled".[48]

There is much work yet to be done to ensure that disadvantaged children have equal access to education in practice, despite the many initiatives already attempted.

7.2. THE RIGHT TO EDUCATION OF IRISH TRAVELLERS

13. The Traveller community is a nomadic minority group indigenous to Ireland. They are often a much marginalised group in Irish society,[49] including in the area of education. There are numerous education initiatives specific to Traveller children being run by the Department of Education and Science to attempt to provide for the educational needs of Traveller children. Schools receive a capitation grant for each Traveller child pupil. Resource Teachers for Travellers (RTT) are allocated to schools, which have 14 Traveller children with identified need. Furthermore, a Traveller Education Strategy is currently being prepared. The Strategy is intended to help improve the educational achievement of Traveller children.

However, despite these accomplishments and supports, clear differences exist between Travellers and the rest of the population in terms of educational outcomes. A recent

45 Economic and Social Research Institute, *Annual School Leavers Survey 2004*, (Dublin: ESRI, 2006).

46 Department of Education and Science, *School Retention Rates for 1994 Cohort*, (Dublin: Government Publications, 2005).

47 However an increasingly large 'registration fee' is proving a further obstacle for students. For the 2005/2006 year it was €775, and it is increasing every year. There is, however a grant available for students of low-earning parents.

48 Higher Education Authority, *A Review of Higher Education Participation in 2003*, (Dublin: Fitzpatrick Associates and Phillip O'Connell, 2005).

49 For details of the types of exclusion faced by Traveller community in Ireland, see the website of the Irish Traveller Movement at <http://www.itmtrav.com>.

Department of Education and Science report showed that the levels of achievement of Traveller pupils were not on a par with their non-Traveller peers.[50] The transfer rate for Travellers to secondary level education was 85% in 2003.[51] This is a much lower than that of the "settled" population, which is almost 100%. Another major problem regarding Traveller students and education is the high drop out rate from secondary school. The majority leave prior to completing the Junior Cycle. Small numbers of Travellers receive qualifications such as the Junior or Leaving Certificate.[52]

The Irish Travellers Movement attributes this partly to the low level of attainment of Traveller children in primary education.[53] They express concern about the quality of RTT practice. It is claimed that Traveller children are often assigned "low level tasks" (drawing and colouring) when they are withdrawn from class (and core subjects) to the RTT.[54]

TOMAŠEVSKI states that "*acceptable standards of education are necessary for achieving...an environment within which every child can achieve his or her fullest potential*".[55] Evidently the system of educational support for Traveller children needs to be examined, because if primary school children *are* being given low-level tasks (when they are capable of more), they will not achieve their fullest potential. This will then affect secondary level outcomes. It is hoped that the Traveller Education Strategy will facilitate this examination.

7.3. THE RIGHT TO EDUCATION OF MIGRANT CHILDREN IN IRELAND

14. There are an increasing number of non-Irish-national pupils attending schools in Ireland. Since 2002, 170,600 migrants are estimated to have arrived in Ireland; 10% of these migrants were under 14 years of age.[56] Education has been found to play a vital part in the support and integration of refugee and asylum-seeking children in Ireland.[57]

50 Department of Education and Science, *Chief Inspectors Report 2001–2004*, (Dublin: Department of Education and Science, 2005).

51 See the website of the Irish Traveller Movement at <http://www.itmtrav.com>.

52 Ibid.

53 Ibid.

54 See the website of the Irish Traveller Movement at <http://www.itmtrav.com>.

55 See K. TOMAŠEVSKI, *Manual on Rights-Based Education: Global Human Rights Requirements Made Simple*, (UNESCO Bangkok: Asia and Pacific Regional Bureau for Education, 2004).

56 P. CULLEN, 'Classroom revolution: The changing ethnic mix in our schools', (Tuesday April 12, 2005), *Irish Times*.

57 A.F. KEOGH and J. WHYTE, *Getting On: The experiences and aspirations of immigrant students in second-level schools linked with the Trinity Access Programmes*, (Dublin: The Children's Research Centre, 2003).

Legally, all children (irrespective of their or their parents' citizenship or residency status) are entitled to access the Irish education system. However, provision of additional funding and teaching resources to schools to assist migrant pupils often falls short of what is required. Many migrant pupils are in need of English language support. The level of provision for them is grossly inadequate, according to the Irish National Teacher's Organisation. The organisation has expressed that only a maximum of 28 pupils can receive language support in a school, even though often many more children are seeking it.[58]

However, it is positive that one research study[59] outlines that all the children in the study were enrolled in schools within weeks of arriving in Ireland. It also outlines that all the children in the study were doing very well in school. However, this study did highlight that the Irish policy that asylum seekers cannot enter third-level education causes problems for young people. It is particularly problematic for those who have sat their Irish Leaving Certificate and are then left with nowhere to go from there.

It is apparent that the Irish government has yet to heed the recommendations of the Committee on the Rights of the Child and ensure that disadvantaged, Traveller and migrant children are not at a disadvantage in the education system, despite some gains that have been made.

8. EDUCATION FOR CHILDREN WITH DISABILITIES IN IRELAND

15. Children with disabilities are another group who are at a disadvantage within the education system in Ireland. Article 23 of the Convention on the Rights of the Child places a duty on the state to ensure that the child with disability has "effective access to and receives education". According to UNESCO, the education of children with disabilities should be suited to the individual needs of the children, regardless of the extent of disability or need.[60]

However, according to experts in disability discrimination law, Ireland lags far behind the United States in terms of access for people with disabilities to education.[61]

---

58 S. Fynn, 'Inadequate provision for schoolgoing immigrants', (Thursday April 20, 2006) *Irish Times*.

59 K. Smyth and J. Whyte, *Making a New Life in Ireland: Lone Refugee and Asylum –Seeking Mothers and their Children*, (Dublin: Children's Research Centre/Vincentian Refugee Centre, 2005).

60 UNESCO, *Review of the Present Situation of Special Education*, UNESCO, Geneva, 1988.

61 M. McDonagh, 'EU lags behind US in provision of access for disabled, seminar told', (Wednesday June 07, 2006) *Irish Times*,.

BASSER[62] claims that education for children with disabilities in Ireland is problematic for "extra-legal" reasons. She states that these reasons include a historic approach that involved people with disabilities being viewed as "uneducable", together with a narrow understanding of the meaning of "education", as limited to the acquisition of academic skills and knowledge.

There has been a large amount of policy and legislation relating to people with disabilities enacted in Ireland in recent years, which has gone some way towards dealing with these problems. This legislation, however, also has many downsides for people with disabilities.

8.1. RECENT LEGISLATION

16. The Disability Bill, 2004, gives people with disabilities the right to a needs assessment. The Education for Persons with Special Educational Needs Act, 2004, acknowledges that persons with special educational needs have the same right to education as their peers without those needs. The Act aims to ensure that children with special educational needs will be able to leave school with the skills necessary to participate to the level of their ability in society. Education is to be "inclusive" unless there is a specific reason why a specialised placement is necessary for a child.

The Irish government claims that these initiatives form a National Disability Strategy built on an equality framework. However, the Children's Rights Alliance makes the point that neither the Bill nor the Act is rights-based.[63] The 2004 Act is extremely problematic regarding resources. The Act makes the provision of many services for children with disabilities resource-contingent. There is no obligation on the state to provide additional resources to implement the Act.

8.2. ISSUES AROUND EDUCATIONAL PROVISION FOR CHILDREN WITH DISABILITIES

8.2.1. Co-ordination in the Sector

17. Traditionally, there has been a lack of co-ordination within the disability sector. The lack of co-ordination exists within and between both non-governmental

---

[62] L.A. BASSER, 'Justice for All? The Challenge of Realizing the Right to Education for Children with Disabilities', (2005) 8, *The Journal of Gender, Race & Justice*, 531–549.

[63] Children's Rights Alliance, supra, (note 7).

organisations and statutory bodies.[64] The Education for Persons with Special Educational Needs Act, 2004, provides for coordination between the Health Service Executive and the Department of Education and Science. However, it is claimed by the Children's Rights Alliance that in practice, coordination is deeply flawed.[65]

Section 16 of the Act provides for Liaison Officers between the Department and the HSE to be appointed. Unfortunately, this section of the Act has not yet been commenced and the lack of co-ordination regarding education for children with disabilities persists.

8.2.2. Information Deficit on Children with Disabilities

18. There are important gaps in our information and data systems on children's rights to education. These gaps affect whether and how Ireland provides support and services for children pursuant to their rights under the Convention on the Rights of the Child.[66] We do not know, for example, how many children suffer from specific learning disabilities such as dyslexia and ADHD. Nor do we know how many children have special needs, or if they are having those needs addressed.

8.2.3. Preschool Education for Children with Disabilities

19. It is clear that in Ireland, early intervention for children with disabilities of pre-school age is seriously lacking. There is no national protocol regarding services for these children. As with later stages of education, criteria for receiving support for pre-school education relate to eligibility for funding rather than to the needs of the individual children.[67]

Problems in accessing early childhood care and education abound, for example the staff of mainstream pre-schools have reported being seriously unprepared to deal with pre-schoolers with disabilities.[68] These failures are extremely detrimental for a child with disabilities, as early interventional is so vital for future educational outcomes.

---

64 K. HOLLAND, 'Minister warns of duplication by disability groups', (Monday May 01, 2006), *Irish Times.*

65 Children's Rights Alliance, supra, (note 7).

66 E. FITZGERALD, *Counting Our Children: An analysis of Official Data Sources on Children and Childhood in Ireland,* (Dublin: Children's research Centre, 2004).

67 Centre for Early Childhood Development and Education (CECDE), *On Target? An Audit of Provision of Services Targeting Disadvantage and Need from Birth to Six Years in Ireland,* (Dublin: CECDE, 2004).

68 J. WHYTE, F. DALY and A. DALY, *A Study of the Needs and Experiences of Preschoolers with Special Educational Needs Attending Mainstream Childcare and Education in Co. Roscommon,* (Dublin: Children's Research Centre, draft report, to be published 2006).

8.2.4. *Early School Leaving and Children with Disabilities*

20. Early school leaving is a significant issue regarding the education of children with disabilities. More than 21% of 15 year olds with a physical disability have left school, compared to 6% of non-disabled young people.[69] The amount of people 25 to 36 years old without any educational qualifications in Ireland is 6%; however, the amount of people who have disability/illness without qualifications is four times this number.[70] Those with disability/illness since birth have "strikingly low levels of education".[71]

The Children's Research Centre has been commissioned by the Government to research why early school leaving is so prevalent amongst young people with physical disability and how the problem can be tackled. This is a very positive move towards better facilitating young people with disabilities to finish school.

8.2.5. *Educational Supports for Children with Disabilities*

21. It is positive that the level of supports available to students with special educational needs increased significantly in the past decade. The overall numbers of pupils with recognised assessed special educational needs went up by 41% in the five years to 2003.[72]

The Education for Persons with Special Educational Needs Act, 2004, covers the need to identify children who have special educational needs and to address those needs. Assessment processes are outlined in the Act. Where a need is identified, the Act stipulates that an educational plan needs to be drawn-up for the child, and schools are entitled to resources to implement the plan. However, this provision to the school is subject to available resources.

There has been a large increase in the numbers of children with special educational needs enrolling in mainstream schools, and fewer children attending special schools. However, decisions about the provision of services and equipment for children with disabilities are often made in the interests of the school rather than the interests of the child. A part of this problem is that special needs equipment belongs to the school,

---

69 E. FITZGERALD, *How far towards equality?* (Dublin: National Disability Authority, 2005).

70 Economic and Social Research Institute, *Disability and Social Inclusion in Ireland*, (Dublin: Economic and Social Research Institute, 2003).

71 ESRI, supra, (note 45), 36.

72 National Disability Association, *Disability Agenda*, (Dublin: National Disability Association, August 2005). See the National Disability Association Website at <http://www.nda.ie>.

not the child.[73] As a result, children moving from primary to post primary school need to re-apply for their supports.

Additional problems stem from the fact that teachers need further training in the area of disability. One study reported a lack of knowledge amongst teachers regarding types of disabilities and the needs associated with them.[74] The same study identified serious difficulties in gaining access to mainstream primary schools.

8.2.6. *Education for People with Severe Disability in Ireland*

22. There are particularly serious problems around providing for the right to education for children with severe disability in Ireland. BASSER[75] claims that the availability of recourse to the courts to enforce the right to education of those with severe disabilities has in some ways redressed the disadvantage they experience in education.

The 1996 case O'Donoghue v. Minister for Health[76] concerned an eight-year-old boy with severe disabilities who had been denied access to school education in any form. It was held in the High Court of Ireland that all children are educable and that all children, regardless of "ability", have a constitutional right to a free primary education. It was also held that for children with disabilities it is desirable that education begin as early as possible given the benefits of early intervention.

Another high-profile case (the Sinnott Case)[77] concerned a young person who had severe disability since birth and had only received two years of state-funded primary education in his life. He was over 18 at the time the case was taken. The High Court found that the constitutional right to free primary education continued as long as the need for that education continued. On appeal by the state, the Supreme Court rejected this finding. It held that the constitutional right terminated at the age of majority, that is, at eighteen years of age.

This disappointing finding is compounded by the case of a 14-year-old autistic boy (Lewis O' Carolan). His parents failed in a High Court battle to have the state fund a placement for their son at an autism-specific centre in Wales. Experts had said this

---

73 C. HEARY, D. HOGAN and C. SMYTH, *Living with an Acquired Brain Injury During Childhood and Adolescence: An Irish Perspective,* (Dublin: Children's Research Centre, 2003).

74 National Disability Authority, *Special Education Provision for Children with Disabilities in Irish Primary Schools – the Views of Stakeholders,* (Dublin: NDA, 2005).

75 L.A. BASSER, supra (note 62).

76 *O'Donoghue v. Minister for Health,* [1996] 2 I.R. 20

77 *Sinnott v. Minister for Education,* [2001] 2 I.R. 545.

placement would help him reach his full potential. Instead, the Health Service Executive offered him a place in psychiatric unit in Ireland. This unit was criticised in a report in 2005 by the Inspector of Mental Health Services for its use of straitjackets and protocols over the use of psychotropic medication. The Irish Autism Action support group estimates that the cost of the placement in Ireland is much more expensive than that in Wales.[78]

The Sinnott and O' Carolan cases display a lack of engagement with the rights-based approach regarding education for children with disabilities by both the government and the courts. Clearly, the best interest of the child has not been the priority in these cases. They are just a few examples of the continuing failure on the part of the state to provide properly for the educational needs of children and young people with disabilities.

While attempts are being made to improve the educational lives of children with disabilities in Ireland, they are still at a huge educational disadvantage, as the figures on early school leaving and educational attainment show. TOMAŠEVSKI (2004) states that, "*if a school syllabus and infrastructure in place are to really allow for every child's greatest development, any potential barrier to this must be identified at the earliest opportunity*".[79] There are clearly barriers for children with disabilities regarding education in Ireland. Many of these are not being identified or dealt with by the Irish government.

9. PARTICIPATION RIGHTS IN THE IRISH EDUCATION SYSTEM

23. Article 12 of the Convention on the Rights of the Child directs that states must assure to the child who is able to form his or her own views the right to express those views freely in all matters affecting them. The Convention was the first international human rights treaty to enshrine such a right for children. It remains the most controversial of children's rights, as traditionally children have been seen as being in need of protection, not of empowerment.

Like other states, improvements to children's rights in Ireland have mostly involved protecting their interests, rather than facilitating them to be active decision-makers in their own lives. Regarding the implementation of Article 12 of the Convention, in 1998 the Committee on the Rights of the Child stated its concern that the views of the child are not generally taken into account in Ireland, including within schools.

---

78 C. O'BRIEN, 'Parents reject care offer for son', (Saturday August 06, 2005) *Irish Times*.
79 K. TOMAŠEVSKI, supra (note 12).

However, the establishment of the National Children's Office represented a significant step in the right direction regarding this right. The Office is committed to ensuring children in Ireland have a say on matters that affect them. It has been behind some significant initiatives to further the participation rights of children. Many of these initiatives have been within the education system.

9.1. POSITIVE INITIATIVES

24. Most schools in Ireland now have a student council. Student councils are representative structures for students, whereby they become involved in the affairs of the school. Children's Research Centre research[80] indicates that in some cases student councils in Irish secondary schools can create a more positive school environment. They can have a real impact on issues such as bullying and staff-student relations. However, it was found that generally, students did not have a very good opinion of their council. Many students felt that the attitudes of staff were a serious barrier to the student council.

The research suggests that for the successful operation of a student council in Irish schools, the student council must be given a clearer role and a higher profile in the school. It was also advised that clear lines of communication between students and staff are necessary.

Despite the barriers to the participation of students in decision-making in school matters, there are significant steps being taken on participation rights outside the school environment in Ireland. Comhairle na nÓg (youth councils) provide young people with an opportunity to have a voice in local and national issues of relevance to them. Dáil na nÓg (the national youth parliament) provides young people with this opportunity at a national level one day per year. A recent evaluation[81] concluded that 78% of the young people involved felt that Dáil na nÓg would result in things being better for young people. This is indeed a very positive result. The evaluation also advised that Dáil na nÓg should happen over two days instead of one.

---

80 A.F. Keogh and J. Whythe, *Second Level Student Councils in Ireland: A Study of Enablers, Barriers and Supports*, (Dublin: The Children's Research Centre/The National Children's Office, 2005).

81 Office of the Minister for Children, *Delegate Report: Dáil na nÓg*, (Dublin: Office of the Minister for Children, 2006).

9.2. ACCESS TO INFORMATION ON SEXUAL HEALTH

25. Participation rights are often considered to include civil and political rights such as the right to information. Young people in Ireland generally do not have adequate access to information on sexual health. This is despite the fact that the Convention on the Rights of the Child, Article 24, obliges states, "to develop preventive health care… and family planning education".

Ostensibly, the policy in Ireland is that sex education is taught through the curriculum in Irish secondary schools. However, schools have discretion as to what kind of sex and sexual health education they provide, if any. It is also possible for parents to ask that their children be exempt from sex education in school. This is despite the fact that the European Court of Human Rights has established that it is permissible for states to have a compulsory sex education programme in State schools.[82]

Recent research conducted with a sample of early school leavers aged 13 to 18 years found that a large number of the young people had only a superficial understanding of sexually transmitted infections (with the exception of HIV/AIDS). The young people also perceived themselves as invulnerable to sexually transmitted infections.[83] The same study suggested that young people have few social supports when it came to accessing information and advice on sexual health issues.[84]

There have been calls for sex education provision to be standardised.[85] There have also been recommendations that school based relationship and sexuality education urgently needs to be extended to all primary and secondary schools. Research highlights that programmes on sex education should be part of wider community interventions. Youth friendly sexual health services have also been recommended.[86]

9.3. HUMAN RIGHTS EDUCATION

26. Children need to be aware of their rights to participate effectively in society. In 1998, the Committee on the Rights of the Child recommended that the Irish

---

82 *Kjeldson, Busk Madsen and Pederson v. Denmark*, Judgement of 7 December 1976, Series A No.23, 1 EHRR, 711.

83 P. Mayock and T. Byrne, *A Study of Sexual Health issues, Attitudes and Behaviour; The Views of early School Leaver,* (Dublin: Crisis Pregnancy Agency, 2005).

84 Ibid.

85 Issue raised at Children's Research Centre Conference, *Adolescent Sexual Behaviour and Sexual Health,* Trinity College Dublin, (22 September 2005).

86 P. Mayock and T. Byrne, supra, (note 83).

government promote human rights education in the country.[87] There are some efforts to this end already in place. At primary level, the Social, Personal and Health Education (SPHE) curriculum is intended to foster in children respect for their own dignity and that of others, and to promote a healthy lifestyle and a commitment to the democratic process. However, as SPHE has a moral and spiritual dimension, it is always developed within the context of the ethos or characteristic spirit of the school. As mentioned earlier, most schools in Ireland are church-run, resulting in a prevalence of a religious-oriented SPHE curriculum.

At secondary level, Civic, Social and Political Education (CSPE) aims to prepare students for participatory citizenship. The syllabus is based around the concept of citizenship, and includes much teaching on democracy, rights and responsibilities, human dignity and law. However, within these curriculae, the human rights elements are optional. Furthermore, teachers are not trained or supported to teach human rights.[88]

Publicising of the Convention on the Rights of the Child is also issue in Ireland. Article 42 of the Convention outlines that, "States Parties undertake to make the principles and provisions of the Convention widely known, by appropriate and active means, to adults and children alike". The Government claims that the National Children's Strategy mirrors the Convention, and that the strategy was widely distributed throughout the State. The NCO has been active in promoting this strategy. Nevertheless the publicising of the Convention in Ireland has been minimal.

The Department of Education and Science have stated that they will consider introducing for all schools an ethics curriculum that explores ethical issues, as well as different religious and cultural practices. A movement towards such a curriculum is to be encouraged. Young people at Dáil na nÓg (Youth Parliament) this year voted in favour of motions that an intercultural studies programme should be introduced in all schools at all levels, and that the subject of religion in schools should be changed to a subject on morals, ethics and other cultures.[89]

The Committee on the Rights of the Child has encouraged Ireland to develop a systematic information campaign on children's rights for children and adults alike. The Children's Rights Alliance recommends the undertaking of a human rights audit

87 Children's Rights Alliance, supra (note 3).
88 Children's Rights Alliance, supra, (note 7).
89 Office of the Minister for Children, supra, (note 81).

of the education system, which would include the Department of Education and Science, the curriculum and schools themselves.[90]

It is hoped that the improvements in the area of participation rights for children and young people in Ireland will be built upon in the future in accordance with these recommendations.

10. CONCLUSION

27. It is clear that there have been many steps taken to further the right to education in the Republic of Ireland. Legislation has been put into place (particularly the National Children's Strategy) that benefits children's rights as regards education. Much funding has been put into place.

However, serious failings still persist. All of these failings are closely related to two general issues. Firstly, spending on education has not increased in line with the rate of economic growth in the Celtic Tiger era. Secondly, the Irish Government continues to resist adopting a rights-based approach in policy, legislation and service provision.

There are many actions which the Irish government can take to further the right to education in Ireland. An integrated, universal, high-quality early childhood care and education system is needed. Such a system should have as its focus the provision of ECCE for all children, as opposed to solely for disadvantaged children or for the benefit of working parents.

More effort needs to be put into accommodating children from disadvantaged groups, (including children belonging to the Traveller community, children from poor families and migrant children) who face educational inequality. Children with disabilities also face strong resistance from the government to a rights-based approach to their education. The efforts of the government in court battles would be much better used if channelled into accommodating the needs of these children in accordance with the principle of the best interest of the child. Furthermore, the voices of children and young people need to be heeded as regards their needs around participation rights and their right to information.

The right to education in Ireland can and will be furthered by the enshrining of the Convention on the Rights of the Child in domestic law and the embracing of the rights-based approach. This will require a significant change in mindset and approach

---

[90] Children's Rights Alliance, supra, (note 7).

by the Irish government. It is hoped that the government will make this change so that we have an education system fit for the Celtic Tiger.

EDUCATIONAL IMPLICATIONS OF THE CONVENTION ON THE RIGHTS OF THE CHILD AND ITS IMPLEMENTATION IN EUROPE

PAULÍ DÁVILA BALSERA and LUIS MARÍA NAYA GARMENDIA

1. INTRODUCTION[1]

1. Amongst the general bibliography devoted to the study of the Convention on the Rights of the Child (CRC), dealing with its contents, its fundamental principles and, above all, its application can be – and in fact is – undertaken from many different perspectives. Amongst all these, this contribution focuses on the principles underlying the Convention. These principles form one of the main pillars of the very meaning, which the Convention has acquired, and which guide many policies deriving from the acceptation of the Convention by the majority of State Parties. The reason for this is that the Convention is in the tradition with that kind of international treaty and that its educational value is unquestionable. This paper presents, primarily, an analysis of the educational implications of the CRC, based on those articles directly related to education (Arts. 17, 19, 23, 28, 29, 30, 31, 32, 37, 39 and 40) and wherein, in an explicit manner, we can perceive obligations or proposals of an educational nature.

In the second part of the paper, we analyse the implementation of the said articles in the majority of European countries, given the conviction that there are differences in this context. In order to carry out the task, we have used the final reports of the Committee on the Rights of the Child, as primary sources, which facilitate comparative studies with their increasing homogenisation.

[1] This Article falls within the remit of research funded by the Ministerio de Educacion y Ciencia of Spain, project reference number: SEJ2004-01690/EDUC.

2. EDUCATIONAL IMPLICATIONS OF THE CONVENTION

2. If we examine the three international treaties on children's rights from 1924 to 1989, we observe that education appears in all of these as a core element; like, in international treaties on human rights, education is incorporated as a fundamental right. There are two perspectives to this: as a goal to be achieved for the whole population, (i.e. as a right in itself), and as an objective in achieving an education in harmony with human rights. Thus, the rights of the child are based not only on the aim, but also on the means, of achieving a content-orientated education regarding human rights. Consequently, they provide guidelines on the obligations of the State and the family with regard to the availability, accessibility but also with regard to the acceptability and adaptability, by mean of the content of the curriculum, that undoubtedly guides many educational policies.[2]

In this sense, we can see that all the educational policies undertaken in the West, and under which various educational systems from the nineteenth century,[3] have generally been aimed at the training of citizens, apart from vocational training. Thus, we have a twin concept involving, on the one hand, compulsory schooling and, on the other, the setting up of a national curriculum. This double perspective is present, in a more wide-ranging manner and in defence of human rights, in all the legal instruments and provisions since the Declaration of Human Rights in 1948 and up to the Convention in 1989. Consequently, whether through the recognition of human rights or recognition of the rights of the child, education has had an explicit recognition, given that, without the right to education, the other recognised human rights can only be understood with difficulty.[4] In implementing this right, we can perceive that the responsibilities of governments with regard to the exercise of this right to education require an educational system where primary schooling is compulsory and free. This regards economic, social and cultural rights since these rights set the goals for education, provide guidelines on the content of the curriculum and, finally, recognise the right to choose for the parents and private initiative. This needs to be situated

[2] K. TOMAŠEVSKI, *Education Denied: Costs and Remedies*, (London: Zed Books, 2003); K. TOMAŠEVSKI, 'El derecho a la Educación, panorama internacional de un derecho irrenunciable', in L.M. NAYA. (ed.), *La educación y los derechos Humanos*, (Donostia: Erein, 2005), 63–90; or more recently K. TOMAŠEVSKI, *Human Rights Obligations in Education. The 4-As Scheme*, (Nijmegen: Wolf Legal Publishers, 2006).

[3] The majority of European Constitutions incorporates "Right to Education" in different ways. To this end, one can consult: "Legal status of the right to education" in the Right to Education project, <http://www.right-to-education.org>.

[4] K. TOMAŠEVSKI, supra (note 2); P. DÁVILA and L.M. NAYA, 'Infancia y Educación en el marco de los DD.HH.', in L.M. NAYA (ed.), *La educación y los derechos Humanos*, (Donostia: Erein, 2005), 91–135.

under the framework of the repeated principle of "the development of the human personality", and the creation of schools – (here civil rights and freedoms are also involved).[5]

Interpreting this right,[6] the Convention goes a bit further, as it not only takes on board this legacy, but since we can also find many educational elements in the articles therein, both explicitly and implicitly. These articles can be classified into two main pillars of rights underpinning the Convention; firstly, civil, economic, social and cultural rights and, secondly, those involving protection and aid. As we will see further on, many of these rights can be analysed, both in their effectiveness and in their violation, in the schools themselves. In this way, the schools or, to use a more general term, educational centres are a good reference for analysing the various situations involving childhood and for setting out guidelines for good educational practice. For example, educators talk or should talk about diversity, multiculturalism, the inclusive school and other similar concepts, as a principle of non-discrimination, protected by human and children's rights legislation, and not only as a pedagogical invention without a framework of rights. However, there is a quite noticeable lacuna in the training of many educators, as was shown in a study about the training of teachers and other educators at Spanish universities.[7]

3. The relations between institutions and agents that are involved in the right to education can be divided into three planes. Firstly, at a micro level underlining the role of the school as an observatory of children's and educational rights; secondly, observing at a macro level the presence of Convention rights related to education and their correspondence with an educational system and finally, at a legislative and educational level, outlining government obligations and educational implications of those articles of the Convention directly related to education. The illustration below shows the articles that uphold the rights of the child and their educational implications within the educational centre (school), either totally or partially. This can also be analysed in schools since a school is a register and, at the same time a good on-site observatory that helps to find out about these rights and enable educational action, as far as possible.

---

5 K.D. Beiter, *The Protection of the Right to Education by International Law*, (Leiden – Boston: Martinus Nijhoff Publishers, 2006), 37.

6 Until December 1999 the *Committee on Economic and Cultural Rights*, the body guaranteeing compliance with the Pact, did not provide any interpretation of this right, basing itself on the contributions of K. Tomaševski.

7 Spanish Section of Amnesty International, *Educación en Derechos Humanos: asignatura suspensa. Informe sobre la formación en las Escuelas de Magisterio y Facultades de Pedagogía y Ciencias de la Educación para la Educación en materia de Derechos Humanos*, (Madrid: Amnistía Internacional, 2003) or P. López, 'Educación en Derechos Humanos: suspenso', in L.M. Naya (ed.), *La educación y los derechos Humanos*, (Donostia: Erein, 2005), 155–173.

Illustration 1: The school as an on-site observatory and a centre for educational action

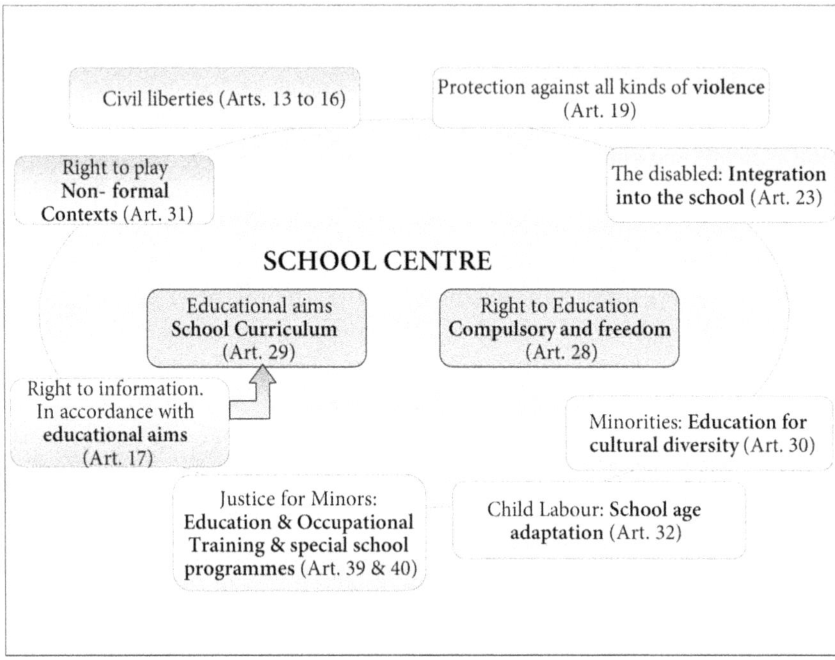

This concept is relevant to those who, from the perspective of education, are focused on the study, analysis and even educational intervention in schools. It enables both researchers and professionals, who carry out research in schools, to detect the situation of the rights of the child in a space where educational action is feasible. Thus, when considering the monitoring of the rights of the child in schools, we should take into account both the stages of childhood and adolescence in terms of the educational processes and in terms of development of the personality as well as the characteristics that distinguish persons who have rights themselves and the elements that have to be considered in order that education fulfil the basic principles of the Convention.

This approach also helps to detect the need of education professionals to have access to educational initiatives, in those spheres where the need for some kind of trained professional in the educational field is evident. For example, in the mass media, a sphere that has scant professional training value for educators, their presence is evident in Article 17, which expressly mentions educational objectives; the same happens with social integration processes in cases of children in conflict with the judicial system.

4. The structure of the educational system and its levels of teaching should be considered in tandem with the right to education, the basic principles and the rights of protection. We wish to show the necessary correspondence between the educational system and the rights in childhood. This vision, without doubt, widens our view about the school and educational space in such a way that children are not just pupils in the teaching-learning process, but are persons who have legal rights and, in many cases, need attention and protection.

Once the educational implications have been outlined on both levels – the school and educational system – we can refer to those articles of the Convention wherein some explicit mention of education appears and that indicate the government obligations in accordance with the governing principles of the Convention. For example, Article 17 contains an explicit reference to Article 29 on the aims of education. Although we cannot observe this article in practice in a school, it is clear that aspects like "*encourage the dissemination of information and material that is of social and cultural benefit to the child*" could well have repercussions in school texts and material. The same may occur with play and cultural activities – Article 31, for example, implies that education is not exclusively the role of the school. Other articles dealing more with protection and aid, such as Articles 19, 23, 30, 32, 39 and 40, are precisely those that are more subject to certain discriminatory practices, both social and school-based. In these cases, the school takes action, or should take action, favouring school integration behaviour and respect for diversity in education regarding human rights. Thereby, we deem it pertinent to carry out a comprehensive, integrated educational plan with respect to the rights of the child. In this way, we can underline the true educational character underlying the whole Convention.

3. THE IMPLEMENTATION OF THE CRC IN EUROPE

5. The research into the implementation of the Convention also requires other frameworks of understanding that bear directly on education. For example, we should not forget that one of the key themes to be considered with respect to the exercise of recognised rights is that related to age – the Convention places the limit at 18 years.[8] Nevertheless, if we analyse this question as a function of various indicators, we will see considerable variability. For example, in the majority of cases, the minimum age for working is 15; or for marriage in some places in Europe it is less than 18; or more seriously, the age of legal responsibility (in Switzerland it is 7, although

8 An exhaustive work detailing this data can be found in A. MELCHIORE, *At What Age?* (UNESCO, IBE, Right to Education, 2004).

generally it is about 14 years). This may impede the enjoyment of the right to education.[9]

Moreover, regarding questions, which are more directly related to education, there exists another series of indicators that we should keep in mind, such as the starting and finishing ages of compulsory education. In the majority of European countries, it starts at the age of 6 and ends at 15 to 18 so that obligatory school attendance lasts for ten years. However, the "school life expectancy" for a four-year-old child (including infant, primary and secondary level schooling as well as higher education) is usually longer, even as much as 19 years (*Belgium*) or 18 years (*Finland*). The percentage for registrations at primary level is normally between 90 and 100 per cent of the school population. The teacher-pupil ratio is also an indicator of the quality of education; most cases register a ratio of less than 20 pupils per teacher. Regarding funding for education, crucial indicators are: a free education system – recognised in the majority of European countries (in some cases texts books, school material, extramural activities, school canteen or school transport have to be paid for); and also the percentage of gross domestic product (GDP) earmarked for education fluctuates between 3 and 7 per cent. This whole set of statistical indicators is the backdrop onto which we have to pin the right to education, as is recognised by the majority of reports from international bodies.[10]

Using this data, we can conclude that there are different groups of countries that have certain homogeneity. However, in many cases, the economic, social and political situation of the various countries would be the most suitable criterion as this is a clearly dividing factor when analysing the situation of childhood, especially taking into account the processes of economic transformation that many European countries are undergoing. Below we will deal with each one of the aforementioned educational ambits and their implementation in Europe based on the documentation that we have studied.[11]

---

9 See for an interesting study on this question P. Trinidad, *El niño en el derecho internacional de los derechos humanos*, (Cáceres: Universidad de Extremadura, 2002).

10 See for example UNESCO: *Global Education Digest 2005*, UNESCO Institute for Statistics, Montreal, 2005, <http://www.uis.unesco.org>; as well as the UNITED NATIONS, *Millennium Development Goals Report 2005*, UNITED NATIONS, New York, 2005, <http://millenniumindicators.un.org/unsd/mi/pdf/MDG%20BOOK_SP_new.pdf>; UNICEF, *Study on the impact of the implementation of the Convention on the Right of the child*, (Florence: Innocenti Research Centre, 2004).

11 To this end, the recommendations of the Committee to all European countries and incorporated into the reports (CRC/C/15/) with their respective addenda, have been analysed. One can also consult P. Dávila and L.M. Naya, 'La infancia en Europa: una aproximación a partir de la Convención de los Derechos del Niño', (2003) 9 *Revista Española de Educación Comparada*, 83–134.

3.1. ACCESS TO INFORMATION

6. Access to information (Art. 17) is one of the rights considered civil and political, but which, nevertheless, incorporates a recommendation directly related to education. In clause (a), it states, "*Encourage the mass media to disseminate information and material of social and cultural benefit to the child and in accordance with the spirit of article 29*".[12] So, reference is being made to educational objectives that should also impregnate the news information content to which children have access. However, a multitude of research on audiovisual media content showed us that there are very real attacks in this field on the mental integrity of children. The content of the audiovisual programmes, in general, and according to Article 29, can be revised and made suitable when dealing with programmes specifically for children or broadcast at times when children are listening or watching. However, this suitability is not considered when children are exposed to broadcasts at other times and which lack these educational aims. As has been brought to light by POSTMAN,[13] one can even talk about the loss of childhood, given that children share the same audiovisual culture as adults. The same can be perceived with videogames that have a violent content and with the internet, particularly regarding its pornographic content.[14]

Nevertheless, despite the existing of a series of recommendations since 1996 on "the Child and Mass Media" affecting schools, parents, the media and journalists themselves, the fact is that educational aims, insofar as Article 29 is concerned, do not appear to have priority when considering their recommendations, which concentrate on promoting positive images about the equality of the sexes, on disabled persons or on the prevention of juvenile delinquency rather than on complying with the said educational aims.

In this sense, the Committee has made clear its concern about the scant measures of protection for children in *Serbia & Montenegro*, *Croatia*, *Luxembourg* and *Lithuania*, where hostile feelings or the absence of pluralism can be propagated. Protection measures are also limited, with respect to the circulation of pornographic material in

---

12 CRC Committee, *General Observation No. 1* (CRC/GC/2001/1, 2001), para. 21, insist in a similar vein in their recommendation to governments to take appropriate measures to this end; R. HODGKIN and P. NEWELL, *Manual de Aplicación de la Convención sobre Derechos del Niño*, UNICEF ,Geneva, 2004, First edition 2001, 251 [Original title: *Implementation Handbook for the Convention on the Rights of the Child*].

13 N. POSTMAN, *La desaparición de la Niñez*, (Barcelona: Círculo de Lectores, 1982).

14 The General Assembly approved the "Protocol to the Convention on the Rights of the Child on the sale of children, child prostitution and child pornography", through Resolution A/RES/54/263 of 25 May 2000, and entered into force on 18 January 2002. To date, 67 State Parties have signed or ratified this Protocol.

the *Czech Republic, Luxembourg, Austria, the Netherlands* or *Monaco.*[15] Only *Germany* and *Finland* receive praise from the Committee for measures adopted in order to educate the media and for penalising the trade in sexual services. In this vein, the case of *Sweden*, where a Council against violence-fiction has been created, is notable.[16]

We cannot overlook, likewise, the existence of a number of NGOs, including UNICEF itself, which organises information-programmes where the educational aims incorporated into the Convention are present. It is necessary to know the impact of these programmes in order to be able to evaluate whether they are sufficient measures to mitigate the successes achieved through the commercialisation of programmes aimed at children.

One series of indicators can help us to eliminate content, which is out of line with this right, for example, when monitoring xenophobia, racism or sexism and also in the positive sense: positive images of disabled persons, health promotion, the publishing of children's books, the linguistic needs of minorities or information and material prejudicial to their well-being.

3.2. PROTECTION AGAINST ALL FORMS OF VIOLENCE

7. Although the content of Article 19 is more wide-ranging, given that it states, "*to protect the child from all forms of physical or mental violence, injury or abuse, neglect or negligent treatment, maltreatment or exploitation, including sexual abuse*", it is of interest to us to emphasise that this has a direct relation to Article 28(2) on school discipline without violence: "*States Parties shall take all appropriate measures to ensure that school discipline is administered in a manner consistent with the child's human dignity*". This refers to the State Parties' responsibility for the prevention of all kinds of violence against children, whether by state-officials or by parents, by teachers or by others charged with their care. In addition, the Committee has emphasised that corporal punishment in the family, in schools, in other institutions, or within the penal system, no matter how light it might be, is incompatible with the Convention.[17]

The Committee has pointed out that both legal and educational measures are needed in order to change attitudes, customs and practices. In this way we can differentiate these countries where legislation prohibits all kinds of violence or ill-treatment of children – in different spheres and, in some cases, with caveats – (*Germany, Andorra,*

---

15 P. DÁVILA and L.M. NAYA, supra (note 11).

16 CRC Committee, *Concluding Observations: Sweden* (UN Doc. CRC/C/65/Add.3), para. 99.

17 R. HODGKIN and P. NEWELL, supra (note 12), 278 and 285.

Austria, Denmark, Estonia, Spain, Finland, Greece, Iceland, Latvia, Malta, Monaco, the Netherlands, the United Kingdom [except Northern Ireland], Switzerland, Sweden and Turkey). In this sense, *Sweden* has been the first country in the world to prohibit corporal punishment, by means of a Paternity/Maternity and Guardianship Code, whereby children cannot be subjected to corporal punishment or any other offensive treatment.

In contrast with the above-mentioned countries, the Committee criticises certain other countries for allowing a certain "permissiveness" in discipline at home (*Finland, Switzerland, France, Spain and the UK*); while clearer criticism is aimed at countries where there is no clear prohibition of corporal punishment in the family, within other forms of child-care, in schools and in the penal system, and where there is a request by the Committee to expressly prohibit all corporal punishment (*France, Poland, Belgium, Italy, Croatia, the Ukraine, Portugal, Luxembourg, the Czech Republic, Bulgaria, Malta, Slovenia, Slovakia, Macedonia, Lithuania and Serbia & Montenegro*). The *Russian Federation* and *Belarus* are singled out for the heaviest criticism. So, the map of school discipline should take into account these observations, in which practically no country escapes criticism or is not subject to recommendations to definitely eliminate this type of discipline with violence. In any case, legislation appears not to be sufficient to change the long traditions of social and school behaviour.

Indicators analysing this right can be observed in the legislation on the protection against all forms of corporal punishment, both at home and in public sector and private schools and public sector and private care institutions. A special phenomenon is *bullying* which is becoming more visible.

8. Besides, and within the framework of protection against all forms of violence, we can include Article 32 of the Convention, relating to economic exploitation and child labour, and wherein it concretely specifies that "*State Parties recognise the right of the child to be protected from economic exploitation and from performing any work that is likely to be hazardous or to interfere with the child's education.*[18] Thus, this right is related to another series of articles, apart from the optional protocols; above all, it has been the subject of special attention by the International Labour Organisation (ILO), in its 1973 Agreement nº 138, on the minimum working age, (signed by 135 States up to 2004), and in its 1999 Agreement nº 182, on the prohibition of the worst forms of child labour, (signed by 151 States up to 2005).[19] Moreover, there is another series of

[18] Ibid., 528.

[19] According to the latest ILO report, May 2006, child labour in the world is on the decline for the first time; the real number of child workers having dropped by 11 per cent between 2000 and 2004, dropping from 246 to 218 million. Moreover, the number of children and young people between the ages of 5 and 17 trapped in dangerous employment fell by 26 per cent – to 126 million in 2004

Agreements from the ILO.[20] It should be pointed out that there are not many reservations about this article of the Convention.

The recommendations of the Committee are aimed at, in the majority of cases, the suitability of fixing ages "taking into account the pertinent provisions within other international instruments". The question that interests us is if the non-fixing of these ages can hinder the schooling of children and their education. In this sense, the Committee, on presenting its reports, always praises those countries that have ratified the two above-mentioned Agreements (*Romania, France, Spain, the UK, Belgium, Italy, the Ukraine, Germany, Portugal, Slovenia, the Czech Republic, Hungary, Slovakia, Turkey, Greece, Moldova* and *Estonia*) and recommends the State Parties that have not ratified the Agreements, to do so (*Denmark, Iceland* and *Austria*). Despite this, in some cases there exist situations for concern, such as the following: the ever-increasing number of children who live or work in the street (*the Russian Federation, Bulgaria, Belarus* and *Romania*); the illicit use of children as a workforce (*Italy*); the employment of children who have not completed the compulsory cycle of schooling or immigrant children who are victims of forced labour (*France*); insufficient protection in labour legislation for minors between 15 to 18 years (*Finland*); the legal permission for undertaking light work by children over 12 (*Austria*) or the employment of children in family-run businesses, on the land, in the tourist industry and which interfere with the right to education (*Malta, Andorra, Turkey, Monaco* and *Moldova*).

3.3. NON-DISCRIMINATION: DISABLED CHILDREN, CHILDREN OF MINORITIES AND INDIGENOUS PEOPLES

9. Non-discrimination, being one of the basic principles of the Convention, runs through the whole document. Consequently, it is also present in educational practices and policies regarding the protection of children. Also, and with respect to disabled children, our starting point is that disability cannot and should not be an obstacle to enjoy the benefits of human rights, as has been pointed out in a number of international treaties on the subject.[21] Therefore, following this point of view, the Convention

from 171 million the previous year. According to the report, this drop was even more pronounced amongst the younger age group (5 to 14). ILO, *The end of child labour: within reach*, ILO, Geneva, 2006, <http://www.ilo.org/dyn/declaris/DECLARATIONWEB.DOWNLOAD_BLOB?Var_DocumentID=6176>.

[20] R. Hodgkin and P. Newell, supra (note 12), 523.

[21] With reference to the European case, see: Commission of the European Communities, 2003, Equality of opportunities for disabled persons, Ref. COM (2003) 650 final. One can also consult the UN document: <http://www.un.org/spanish/esa/social/disabled/dis50y00.htm>.

incorporates these rights into two cases that have educational repercussions. We refer, on the one hand, to the right of disabled children (Art. 23), incorporating the right to enjoy a full and decent life, apart from ensuring that the child has "effective access to and receives education, training … preparation for employment". So, in defence of this right, both non-discrimination and the right to education are involved, given that there exists interdependence between disability and human rights.[22] Moreover, there also exists another set of rights within the sphere of non-discrimination against children of minority groups or of indigenous peoples; it is embodied in Article 30 which recognises their right to "*enjoy their own culture, to profess and practise their own religion, or to use their own language*".

With respect to disabled children, as the Committee indicates, "*States should actively combat attitudes and practices that discriminate against children with disabilities and who are denied equality of opportunities to enjoy their rights guaranteed by the Convention*"[23] and also "*systematically recommends that they adopt all the means necessary to integrate children with disabilities into the general educational system*".[24] This recommendation, affirms that the educational system should include the integration of children with disabilities and, consequently this involves, as TOMAŠEVSKI has pointed out, taking accessibility into consideration, i.e. making the school accessible to all those children who in some way may be subject to discrimination.

On analysing this question, we could almost come up with a discrimination map of *disabled children* in Europe, as a function of the recommendations of the Committee. We can consider certain countries as carrying out a positive effort in terms of their national legislation, where the principle of non-discrimination prevails, recognising school integration in cases such as *Austria, Belarus, Spain, Slovenia, Finland, France, Iceland, Italy, Latvia, Lithuania, Luxembourg, Norway, Portugal, the UK, the Czech Republic, San Marino* and *Sweden*). These are countries where one should believe that non-discrimination is generally recognised. Nevertheless, the Committee has pointed out that this legal recognition is either not sufficiently applied to disabled persons or, in reality, there exists patent discrimination, either in the access to schools or in non-integration into normal schools. This was the case in the European Union up to 2004

22 "Human rights are applied to disabled persons" although there is no reference to them in the International Covenant on Civil and Political Rights nor in the International Covenant on Economic, Social and Cultural Rights. R. HODGKIN and P. NEWELL, supra (note 12), 278.

23 Report on the 16th period of sessions, September/October 1997, CRC/C/69, paragraph 338 e) R. HODGKIN and P. NEWELL, supra (note 12), 350.

24 The 1996 Report from the Special Investigator on the supervision of the application of Uniform Norms observed that in 10 of the 80 countries that provided information on their legislation, there was no guarantee that the disabled child had a right to education, R. HODGKIN and P. NEWELL, supra (note 12), 357.

in[25] *Germany* (2), *Belgium* (2), *Greece* (1), *Ireland* (1), *Luxembourg* (1) and *the United Kingdom* (2). New members of the EU (from 2004): *Cyprus* (2), *Slovenia* (2), *Estonia* (1), *Lithuania* (1), *Latvia* (1), *Malta* (1) and *Poland* (2). Candidate countries: *Romania* (2) and *Turkey* (1). Other European countries: *the Russian Federation* (2), *Macedonia* (1), *Moldova* (1), *Norway* (2) and *the Ukraine* (2).

10. With regard to *minorities and indigenous peoples*, the Committee points out, "the proposals in Article 30 may appear superfluous. However, the overwhelming evidence of serious and persistent discrimination that minorities and indigenous peoples suffer justifies the affirmation of their rights in an article to itself".[26] The application alone of the principle of non-discrimination would avoid the need for this specification and which, in fact, is necessary to avoid situations involving the violation of recognised rights.[27] This article, as the Committee points out, is more concerned about cultural, religious and linguistic rights than economic or political rights. The motives behind discrimination, in the majority of the cases, are ethnic or linguistic – those involving minority groups that exist in the State Parties.[28] One of the ethnic groups discriminated against, if not the most discriminated against in Europe, is without doubt the Roma minority, as is stated in reports such as that of the final observations of Committee. Thus, in the majority of countries, we find similar recommendations. With regard to the European Union up to 2004: *Austria* (1), *Spain* (2), *Finland* (2), *France* (2), *Greece*, (1), *Italy* (1, 2), *Portugal* (2) and *the United Kingdom* (2). New members of the UE (from 2004): *Slovakia* (1), *Slovenia* (2), *Hungary* (1), *Lithuania* (1), *Poland* (1,2) and *the Czech Republic* (1,2). Candidate countries: *Romania* (2). Other European countries: *Belarus* (2), *Macedonia* (1), *Moldova* (1), *Norway* (2) *Serbia and Montenegro* (1), *Switzerland* (1) and *the Ukraine* (2).

A good example of what the Committee has indicated is encapsulated in the recommendation to *Slovakia*: "*the Committee takes note with concern that most Roma children attend special schools as a result of real or perceived differences of language or culture between the Roma and the majority of the population; the fact that the Law does not provide for education in the Roma language, together with the stereotyped and negative description of the Roma people and their children in general (...) behoves us to*

---

25 The numbers within brackets signify that these recommendations were made to the first report by the State Party (1), or to the second report (2). We have maintained the separation of EU countries up to 2004, as the majority of reports are prior to that date. Thus, it is necessary to know the dates of these reports. To this end, one can consult P. DÁVILA and L.M. NAYA, supra (note 11).

26 Ibid., 489.

27 We can find almost literal antecedents in Art. 27 of the International Pact on Civil and Political Rights.

28 France, as with Turkey, expressed reservations with this Article, being applied to principles of equality and non-discrimination, the existence of minorities in France not being recognised in the sense that they have specific legal rights. R. HODGKIN and P. NEWELL, supra (note 12), 493.

recommend that the State Party draw up new measures aimed at guaranteeing that these children enjoy equality of access and opportunities regarding attendance at normal schools, with support classes if necessary".[29] Here it is clear that the Committee defends, as a step prior to adaptability, that the right to education be complied with, and with regard to availability and acceptability.

However, together with this clear discriminatory practice, we also have to consider the recommendations involving other ethnic minorities and *xenophobic and racist* expressions dealt with by the Committee, with exceptions such as *Germany*, which receives praise for its campaigns to prevent racism.[30] The general tone of recommendations reflects the difficulties these minorities have in accessing those rights. The European Union up to 2004: *Belgium* (2), *Denmark* (2), *Greece* (1), *the Netherlands* (1) *the United Kingdom* (2), and *Sweden* (2). New members of the EU (from 2004): *Cyprus* (2). Candidate countries: *Croatia* (1) and *Romania* (1). Other European countries: *Andorra* (1), *the Russian Federation* (2), *Iceland* (2), *Liechtenstein* (1) and *Switzerland* (1).

11. Another motive for discrimination is language, to such an extent that those States that do not have this right recognised or that, in fact, violate the right, also receive recommendations from the Committee, suggesting the teaching in the minority language.[31] In this vein, we can point out the following cases: The European Union up to 2004: *the United Kingdom* (1). New members of the EU (from 2004): *Estonia* (1) and *Latvia* (1). Candidate countries: *Turkey* (1). Other European countries: *Belarus*: (2) and *Serbia & Montenegro* (1).

Elaborating on these linguistic aspects, the Committee insists on the training of teachers in order to attend to these minority languages, as well as the drawing up of teaching material in these languages. We should also consider discrimination for religious reasons, with some recommendations from the Committee regarding cases related to the Muslim minorities or to religious education. This is the case in *France* and *Germany* where the Committee have expressed its concern about the legislation being debated in certain Landers (in Germany) on the prohibition on female schoolteachers wearing a veil, given that this does not contribute to the child's understanding of freedom of religion. Nevertheless, the most notable case is that of *Norway* where parents who do not wish their children to receive religious instruction must present an official document indicating the beliefs of the child, a situation that may constitute a violation of his/her private life.

---

29 CRC Committee, *Concluding Observations: Slovakia* (UN Doc. CRC/C/15/Add.140), paras. 47–48.

30 CRC Committee, *Concluding Observations: Germany* (UN Doc. CRC/C/15/Add.43), para. 6.

31 R. HODGKIN and P. NEWELL, supra (note 12), 496.

Likewise, and despite the fact that one of the discriminations in general in the world is that of impediments to access to education for *girls and in some cases boys*, the fact is that, the recommendations concerning this – in Europe – are not so evident. The following cases are referred to: The European Union up to 2004: *Italy* (2) and *Portugal* (2). New members of the EU (from 2004): *Cyprus* (2). Candidate countries: *Turkey* (1), *Romania* (2). Other European countries: *the Russian Federation* (1), *Macedonia* (1), *the Holy See* (1) and *Serbia & Montenegro* (1).

3.4. ILL-TREATMENT, CHILD VICTIMS AND JUSTICE FOR MINORS

12. One of the ambits that have required great attention, both by international treaties and by the recommendations of the Committee itself, is the situation of children in conflict with the law, of torture, degrading treatment and the recovery of child victims from any kind of exploitation. In such a way, the Committee itself has frequently grouped together the three related articles, which are Articles 37, 39 and 40. Clearly, this set of rights is related to respect for the legal norms that should prevail. Nevertheless, our reading of the situation is directed at highlighting those elements that have a more direct relation to "physical and psychological recovery and to social reintegration" (Art. 39), or pointed out in Article 40.4 on various measures and "education and vocational training programmes and other alternatives to institutional care shall be available to ensure that children are dealt with in a manner appropriate to their well-being and proportionate both to their circumstances and the offence". Likewise, paragraph 1 of Article 40 emphasises the positive objectives of reintegration that a juvenile courts system should have. Here there are also echoes of the aims of education set out in Article 29, amongst which are the inculcation of respect for human rights and the preparation of the child for a responsible life in a free society.[32] That is to say, the question is to what extent the State provides educational means for recovery and social reintegration; we understand these to be fundamental and that they should prevail according to the principles of the Convention. Following the practice of the Committee, we also have brought together these three articles, although it is true that the observations made about educational aspects are rare, focusing more on aspects of legal provisions or on the measures to be taken to harmonise the age of criminal responsibility with the spirit of the Convention.

Regarding this last point, the Committee insists that imprisonment should be the last recourse and that what should prevail is "*the adoption of a system aimed at children and that recognises the child as having legal rights and fundamental liberties and*

[32] Ibid., 642.

emphasising the need that, in all measures relating to children, the primordial consideration is the greater interest of the child".[33] To this end, at all times and in all circumstances, any form of ill-treatment or punishment mentioned in this article, including in family life or within the school system, has to be impeded and combated. Around this central core of concerns, we can hang respect for these rights, given that Article 40 envisages no mercy for offenders, from accusation to sentencing, passing through the investigation process, the arrest of and charging of the offender, custodial prison sentences and trial. Nevertheless, as the Committee points out, in all regions of the world and in all the legal provisions of the Convention relating to the administration of justice of minors, in many cases this is not reflected in national legislation or practice, which is a reason for great concern.[34] Also recommended to the large majority of State Parties is that all persons working in any way with children in conflict with juvenile courts should receive training in the basic principles and provisions of the Convention on the Rights of the Child and on the pertinent regulations and directions of the United Nations.[35]

With respect to recovery and social reinsertion, they should be undertaken within an atmosphere that foments the health, the self-respect and the dignity of the child. Moreover, the opinion of the child has to be taken into account, for example, in the planning and application of programmes, including individual cases. In general, the Committee frequently deplores the lack of suitable measures for the recovery of child victims, as is demonstrated by the cases of *Poland, Denmark, the United Kingdom, the Ukraine* and *Bulgaria*. But more cause for scandal is the fact that there are many European countries without a system of justice for young people (*Belarus, Iceland, the Czech Republic, Moldova* or *Estonia*); or those where the system is not compatible with the Convention (*France, the United Kingdom, the Ukraine, Bulgaria, Hungary, Luxembourg, Austria, Latvia, Lithuania* and *Greece*); or where there is abuse of internment measures (*the Russian Federation, Romania* and *Macedonia*); or where there are cases of long preventive detentions (*France, Lithuania, Bulgaria* and *Turkey*). Another cause for great concern is where the age of legal responsibility is less than 18 (*Poland, Denmark, the United Kingdom, Belgium, Portugal, Cyprus, Slovenia, Ireland, the Netherlands, Malta, Turkey, Switzerland* and *Estonia*). In this sense, it should be recalled that no discrimination should take place because of age.

Nevertheless, what causes most concern for the Committee is not just these aspects of social reintegration set out in the measures incorporated in Article 40(4), but that

---

33 CRC Committee, *Report on the ninth period of sessions, May/June 1995* (UN Doc. CRC/C/43 Annexe VIII, 1995), 585.
34 Ibid., 639.
35 Ibid., 598.

in many cases we are unaware if suitable measures of rehabilitation are really being undertaken. In this sense, the following cases have been gathered: The European Union up to 2004: *Luxembourg* (1) and *the United Kingdom* (1). New members of the EU (from 2004): *Latvia* (1), *Lithuania* (1) and *Poland* (2). Other European countries: *Moldova* (1) and *the Ukraine* (2). From our perspective, this is one of the weakest points when gathering information from the various State Parties and which possibly has repercussions for the few recommendations that the Committee has made in this highly important aspect of social reintegration, not only for children in conflict with the law, but also for those who have been deprived of freedom or were the victims of any type of exploitation. Other causes for worry are the policies being carried out regarding internment, which should be a last recourse.[36]

3.5. THE RIGHT TO EDUCATION, EDUCATIONAL AIMS AND PLAY

13. From the perspective in which we are analysing the Convention and its implementation in Europe, the key articles for studying the educational perspective are undoubtedly Articles 28 and 29, as in these we find an amalgam of questions relating to education, above all, those related to government obligations in education. The Convention has correctly maintained the legacy of the right to education within the ambit of international instruments.[37] Nevertheless, we deem it pertinent to highlight the contribution, both theoretical and methodological, of TOMAŠEVSKI, a contribution of such wealth, providing us with valid analysis tools for gaining knowledge of the right to education and its situation in the world.[38] More explicitly we refer to the analysis of the right to education which she has referred to as "the 4 As" – Attainability, Accessibility, Acceptability and Adaptability – in order to explain the complexity of the obligations of governments and parents in relation to the right to education. The following graphic outlines aspects related to the right to education, just as how it is interpreted by Article 13 of the International Covenant on Economic, Social and Cultural Rights and subsequent interpretations and observations made by the Committee on Economic, Social and Cultural Rights itself and other principles that guide the Right to Education in international treaties, such as the Convention itself. This graphic synthesises the contributions of TOMAŠEVSKI in many aspects and we point out the educational and schooling consequences that, in our view, each one

36 M. FERRARI, J. COUSO, M. CILLERO, and N. CANTWELL, *Internación de niños: El comienzo del fin?*, (Florence: Centro de Investigaciones Innocenti, 2002).

37 K.D. BEITER, supra (note 5).

38 Our analysis is more limited, as we are merely trying to focus on the observations and recommendations of the CRC Committee in this highly important aspect, in the knowledge that an in-depth study of this right requires the presence of the interdependence of many other rights linked with education.

of the indicated categories has, in accordance with the focus explained earlier in this article:

Illustration 2: The 4 As and their school and educational consequences

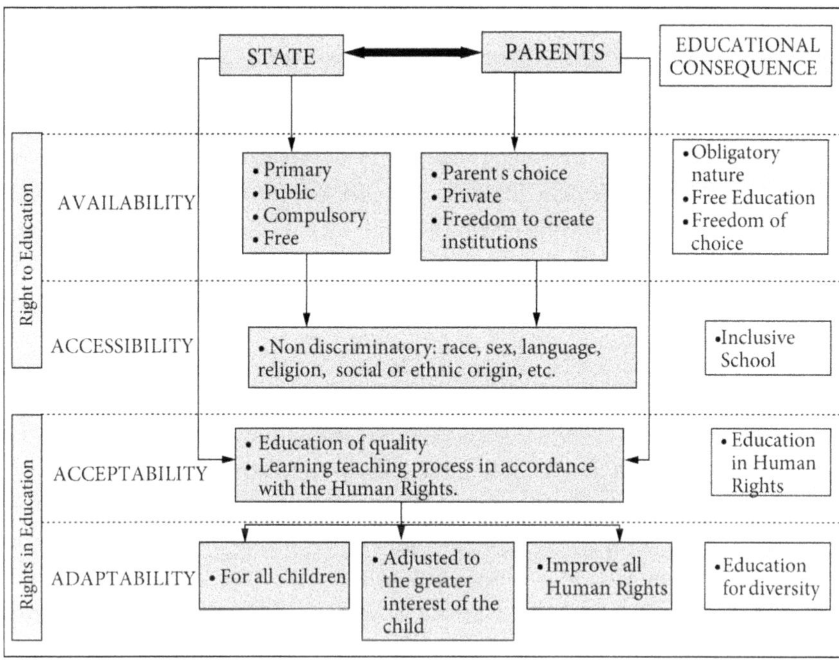

With this graphic, we wish to illustrate the governmental obligations of the States, in the sense that they have to invest in education, in infrastructure and maintenance; assuring non-discrimination, particularly against girls and other groups discriminated against and enabling their access to school centres. In the same way, the State has to establish and apply norms in education that permit acceptable education rights that adapt to cultural diversity. This means the search for and the establishment of indicators, which enable us to confirm not only the recognition of the right to education but also of rights in education.[39] The quest for these indicators is the biggest challenge for those with regard to a correct application of the rights of children.

14. The core concerns of the Committee are: abandonment, desertion, school absenteeism and deprivation of the right to an education; discrimination, maternal

---

[39] Apart from the works of K. TOMAŠEVSKI one can consult: J. HENAIRE and V. TRUCHOT, 'Les indicateurs du droit à l'éducation : le défi d'une mise en œuvre', (2002) (CIFEDHOP : Défis éducatifs et droits de l'homme, Geneva), 57–80.

schools; schools in rural areas, discipline; schooling age and access to secondary education. As regards Article 29, most recommendations refer to the inclusion of human rights in school programmes. Thus, as regards *abandonment, desertion and school absenteeism*, the Committee referred to the following cases: The European Union up to 2004: *Spain* (2), *Finland* (1), *Greece* (1), *Italy* (1) and *Portugal* (2). New members of the EU (from 2004): *Slovenia* (1), *Estonia* (1), *Latvia* (1), *Lithuania* (1) and *Malta* (1). Candidate countries: *Bulgaria* (1). Other European countries: *the Russian Federation* (1), *Macedonia* (1), *Moldova* (1), *Serbia & Montenegro* (1) and *the Ukraine* (2). The European Union up to 2004: *Luxembourg* (1) and *the United Kingdom* (1). New members of the EU (from 2004): *Latvia* (1), *Lithuania* (1) and *Poland* (2). Other European countries: *Moldova* (1) and (2). Also here there are clear examples of discrimination – in various spheres which have to do with disabled persons and Roma or linguistic minorities. As such, when considering this aspect we should link it with what has been outlined above and express the limits of the right to education and access to the same.

Other aspects considered are related to difficulties to access secondary education in cases in *Belarus, Slovenia* and *Macedonia,* amongst others. Another cause for concern is the situation of maternal schools in the cases of *Iceland* and *Lithuania*, where the local attendant is scarce; which does not mean that there exist sufficient maternal schools in the rest of the European countries. The fact that populations in rural areas have difficulties in accessing compulsory schooling is also discriminatory, as is observed in cases in *the Russian Federation, Romania, Poland* and *Greece.* Another aspect already considered is that of school discipline. The situation in Ireland in this regard is of concern, given that "*The Committee is concerned at the situation of children expelled from the school arising from the sanctions imposed by teachers, as well as by the negative consequences these expulsions have and their possible repercussion in the rates of abandonment and school attendance*".[40] Finally, a number of State Parties have received eulogies from the Committee for their favourable procedures in the educational field. Such cases are: *Germany* (1), *Denmark* (1), *Finland* (1, 2), *Italy* (2), *Portugal* (2), *Slovakia* (1), *Turkey* (1) and *Norway* (1).

With respect to free education, the references by the Committee are less numerous and, in the majority of cases, what is pointed out is the extra cost to the family budget due to extramural activities, the purchase of school materials or of school texts (*Andorra, Serbia & Montenegro, the Ukraine*) or the increase in budgetary assignations for education (*Portugal*) or, on the contrary, budget cuts (*Sweden*). Apart from these, TOMAŠEVSKI's observations on the cost of education are pertinent with reference to the payment of taxes.

[40] CRC Committee, *Concluding Observations: Ireland* (UN Doc.CRC/C/15/Add. 85), para. 22.

15. The educational aims set out in Article 29(1) continue a legacy in this type of convention, be it with regard to the development of the personality and a responsible life, or respect for parents, for other national or cultural identities or, with a more modern theme, respect for the natural environment.[41] Therefore, we can affirm that "there exists an international consensus about the aims of education capable of overcoming the barriers of religion, the nation and culture in numerous regions throughout the world".[42] Moreover, many of these aspects impregnate programmes and curricula in schools, although not always in the direction according to the guidelines of the Convention.

What appears to worry the Committee more is the scant presence of human rights in the education of children and amongst the professionals in education. In this sense, the map of the presence of human rights and the Convention in the educational system provide almost a black and white panorama but, above all, peppered with recommendations for the State Parties to incorporate the rights announced in the Convention into their school curricula. We have a block of countries where this recognition is observed or measures have been taken: *Belarus, Italy, Cyprus, Slovenia, Austria, Monaco* and *Estonia.*

There is another group of States that is a cause for concern because the countries therein do not sufficiently reflect the content of Article 29: *Romania* and *Croatia* and, finally, the majority of States receive similar recommendations, more or else expressed in the following manner: "The government should study the possibility of incorporating the Convention into the school curricula" at any of the educational levels. We find the following countries in this situation: *the Russian Federation, France, Norway, Poland, Denmark, the United Kingdom, Belgium, the Ukraine, Germany, Portugal, the Holy See, Serbia & Montenegro, Iceland, Finland, Bulgaria, Ireland, Luxembourg, the Netherlands, Slovakia, Latvia, Lithuania, Turkey* and *Switzerland.* However, the inclusion of the Convention provisions in school curricula should not remain the sole response to Article 42, but should also mean that awareness about rights is an ongoing process, which includes and affects future generations of children.[43] There are also other relevant aspects – those referring to other kinds of respect for minorities, dealt with above.

---

41 A detailed analysis of this right is found in the CRC Committee, *General Observation No. 1*, (CRC/GC/2001/1, 2001), on the aims of education; R. HODGKIN and P. NEWELL, supra (note 12), 470–473. Moreover, we have to consider the interpretation of the Committee on Economic, Social & Cultural Rights and, above all, the interpretations of K. TOMAŠEVSKI.

42 R. HODGKIN and P. NEWELL, supra (note 12), p. 474.

43 Ibid., 477.

Finally, another Article – Article 31 – bears a relationship with educational content, mentioning rest time, play and cultural activities and about which we could almost venture to say it is the only right differentiating adults from children. Its antecedents are found in the Declaration of the Rights of the Child of 1959. In this vein, special attention is paid to children working in domestic service and those who undertake non-dangerous tasks in the family home and, thus, may not be covered by these Agreements (*Andorra*). In general, countries have interpreted the number of hours that should be given over to compulsory schooling in a very varied manner and have very different practices regarding the school timetable. There are countries wherein the school day is interrupted with frequent periods of rest. All in all, it should not be forgotten that compulsory school education obliges children to a full-time occupation, if one includes the actual class times, homework and "outside school" activities. If, apart from all this, the child has some kind of remunerated work, it is possible that he or she has no free time for months on end.[44]

Some cases are worthy of mention such as the case of *Norway*, where the Norwegian Cultural Fund has launched an experimental programme called "Go for it!", where children can initiate and organise their own cultural activities with a subsidy from the central government,[45] or in *Germany* for example, where measures have been taken to enhance the access of the poorest children to extramural activities, including rest time activities.[46]

4. CONCLUSIONS

16. From all the above it is possible to draw some conclusions, always limited by whatever documentation is available and at hand, and by the need to interpret these conclusions within the European framework and its multifaceted characteristics and economic social, political, cultural, religious and educational conditions, all of which bear on the implementation of the rights of the child. There also exists the temptation to reduce things to a map of behaviour models with respect to the compliance and/or violation of these rights, but we do not believe this to be our remit. We also wish it to be said that, with this analysis, we are not criticising the Committee's activities, but merely demonstrating what kind of recommendations they have given in each case, taking into account that much of the information requested in the control list is not provided by the State Parties and are not, therefore, reflected in the Committee's

44 Ibid., 506.

45 CRC Committee, *State Report: Norway* (UN Doc. CRC/C/8/Add.), 7 para. 407.

46 CRC Committee, *Concluding Observations: Germany* (UN Doc. CRC/C/15/Add. 43), para.31.

recommendations – all of which diminishes the quality of the data to which one can potentially gain access.

What is notable with regard to *access to information* is the scant interest in demonstrating the educational character that the mass media, according to the Convention, can and should have. Certain ambivalence is also observed with respect to the use of *corporal punishment:* on the one hand, there exists legislation prohibiting it; on the other, there are certain "permissive" policies. The recommendations are aimed at eliminating this type of corporal discipline. Finding the balance between the end of the period of education and working age is the main reason for ratifying the ILO Agreements on *child labour*. In the cases of children in *conflict with the law*, there is little attention given to re-educational measures to favour social reintegration.

Non-discrimination throughout the whole of Europe is one of the greatest causes for concern, above all given the *clear discrimination against disabled persons and the Roma minority,* despite the fact that many European countries have incorporated the principle of non-discrimination into their national legislative corpora. Other cases, growing forms of xenophobia and racism in various countries of the EU can be observed. Finally, concerning the right to education, its compulsory and free nature does not appear to be the most worrying problem – although there is growing abandonment and school absenteeism, apart from the discriminations referred to above, all of which shows us that in Europe there is still a long road to go to achieve, not only school integration, but also an education in harmony with human rights.

V. WORKING CHILDREN

THE STRUGGLE AGAINST CHILD LABOUR: A WINNABLE FIGHT

JOOST KOOIJMANS[1]

I. INTRODUCTION

1. The last decade has seen an upsurge in international attention to the scourge of child labour. Today, the economic exploitation of children is undeniably an issue that all countries, both in the industrialised and developing world, need to address in their national legislative and policy frameworks. The release on 4 May 2006 by the International Labour Organisation (ILO)[2] of its second Global Report on Child Labour[3], entitled "*The end of child labour: Within reach*",[4] demonstrates that the heightened attention to child labour since the 1990s has also resulted in progress in global efforts to eliminate child labour. The report provides new global estimates on the extent of child labour and gives examples of effective national action in combating child labour. The report further explores strategic frameworks and policy initiatives that are contributing to the elimination of child labour.

2. This paper will paint a picture of the current state of affairs in the struggle against child labour, and will explore linkages between national and international action, the normative framework, as well as provide some pointers towards future priorities in fighting child labour. The first section will clarify some basic concepts and take stock of the findings of the Global Report. The second section will describe the international standards relevant to child labour. Next, the linkages between ILO standards on child

---

[1] The views expressed in the article are the author's and do not necessarily represent those of the International Labour Organisation.

[2] All ILO publications mentioned in this article can be accessed at <www.ilo.org/childlabour>.

[3] The first Global Report was published in 2002; ILO, '*A Future Without Child Labour*', the Global Report under the Follow-up to the ILO Declaration on Fundamental Principles and Rights at Work, Report to the International Labour Conference, 90th session 2002, Report I (B).

[4] ILO, '*The end of child labour*' – *Within reach*, Global Report under the follow up to the ILO Declaration on Fundamental Principles and Rights at Work, Report to the International Labour Conference, 95th Session, Geneva, 2006, Report I (B).

labour and international action be will explored briefly. The paper will conclude by discussing some successful approaches against child labour and a look ahead.

2. CHILD LABOUR TODAY

2.1. SOME BASIC CONCEPTS: WHAT IS CHILD LABOUR?

3. No one denies that there are forms of work that children – boys and girls below the age of 18 – can legitimately do, and that such work may even be beneficial to children in preparing them for a productive life as adults. Thus, not all work done by children should be qualified as "child labour", which should be targeted for elimination. Unacceptable work for children, that is, child labour, concerns work for which the child is either too young (i.e. work done below the required minimum age) or work which because of its detrimental nature is altogether considered unacceptable for children.

4. ILO Conventions therefore specify a system of minimum age levels for admission to work or employment, and identify a number of activities to which no child should be subjected. The Minimum Age Convention, 1973 (No. 138), which consolidates a series of minimum age Conventions adopted by the ILO since 1919, obligates ratifying State Parties to set minimum age levels for admission to light work and regular work and qualifies hazardous work as work that should normally be barred to anyone below the age of 18 years. The Worst Forms of Child Labour Convention, 1999 (No. 182) requires countries to "take immediate and effective measures to secure the prohibition and elimination of the worst forms of child labour as a matter of urgency".[5] The Convention defines these worst forms, to be prohibited for all persons less than 18 years, as:

(a) all forms of slavery or practices similar to slavery, such as the sale and trafficking of children, debt bondage and serfdom and forced compulsory labour, including forced compulsory recruitment of children for use in armed conflict;
(b) the use, procuring or offering of a child for prostitution, for the production of pornography or pornographic performances;
(c) the use, procuring or offering of a child for illicit activities, in particular for the production and trafficking of drugs as defined in the relevant international treaties;

[5] Art.1, Convention No. 182 of the International Labour Organization concerning the Prohibition and Immediate Action for the Elimination of the Worst Forms of Child Labour, adopted on 17 June 1999 and which entered into force on 10 November 2000.

(d) work which, by its nature or the circumstances in which it is carried out, is likely to harm the health, safety or morals of children.[6]

As will be described below in more detail, Convention No. 182 complements Convention No. 138, which in its turn provides the basic framework for national and international action for the elimination of child labour. As such, Convention No. 182 focuses on the worst forms as a priority target, while Convention No. 138 sets forth the ultimate objective of the effective abolition of child labour, and also clarifies what should be targeted as child labour by providing for the minimum age standards.[7] The Conventions will be described in more detail in the next chapter.

2.2. THE EXTENT OF CHILD LABOUR TODAY

5. The ILO's above-mentioned new Global Report indicates that the number of child labourers globally has fallen by 11 per cent over the last four years, or 28 million fewer than 2002. This translates into a decline in child labour worldwide from 246 million children (the ILO's previous estimates in 2002) to 218 million children. The sharpest decrease is in the area of hazardous work by children, where there has been a 26 per cent reduction overall. There is an even steeper decrease of 33 per cent in respect of children between the ages of 5 and 14 at risk in hazardous work.[8] Almost 7 out of 10 working children are in the agricultural sector; whereas 22 per cent work in services and 9 per cent in industry, including mining, construction and manufacturing.

These new global estimates were produced using the exact same methodology as for those released in 2002. They are based on over 60 surveys carried out in more than 40 countries by various international agencies, including the ILO, UNICEF and the World Bank.[9]

6. The remarkable decline in child labour is not evenly spread among the continents. Latin America and the Caribbean stand out in terms of a rapid decline of child labour. The number of children at work in the region has fallen by two-thirds over the last four years, with just 5 per cent of children aged 5–14 now engaged in work. With 26

---

6 Ibid., Art. 3.

7 For a fuller description of the historical events since 1919 leading up the adoption of the Conventions, see: J. Kooijmans, 'The ILO Conventions on Child Labour: Selected issues', in A. Weyts (ed.), *Understanding Children's Rights*, (Ghent: Ghent University, Belgium, 2004), 315–331.

8 ILO, supra (note 4), 5–9.

9 For more detailed information regarding the methodology used, see: ILO, *Global child labour trends 2000 to 2004*, ILO, Geneva, 2006 (forthcoming in print), available at: <http://www.ilo.org/dyn/declaris/declarationweb.indexpage>.

per cent, or close to 50 million child workers, the proportion of children engaged in economic activities in sub-Saharan Africa is currently the highest of any region in the world. In the Asian-Pacific region, 122 million children aged 5–14 are engaged in work, 5 million fewer than four years ago. Less than 20 per cent of Asian children in that age group are now at work. In industrialised countries, about 2.5 million children under the age of 15 were at work in 2000. The reasons for the marked decline in Latin America (notably Brazil and Mexico) will be explored further on.

2.3. PRIORITIES IN THE STRUGGLE AGAINST CHILD LABOUR

7. Despite progress, the scale of the problem of child labour is still enormous. While the end goal remains the total elimination of child labour – as stated by the international community in numerous treaties and statements – there is consensus that those forms of child labour that are considered highly detrimental to children require priority action as a matter of urgency. This notion gave rise in 1999 to the adoption of Convention No. 182, and underlies the goal as proposed in the Global Report that the ILO and its State Parties commit themselves to eradicating the worst forms of child labour by 2016. To do this, all countries are requested to design and put in place appropriate time-bound measures[10] by 2008.

3. INTERNATIONAL STANDARDS ON CHILD LABOUR

3.1. THE ILO CONVENTIONS ON CHILD LABOUR

8. In comparing the two ILO Conventions No. 138 and No. 182, a remarkable difference is the approach towards policy and action against child labour. Convention No. 138 requires measures mainly in the legislative field and makes only very general demands on policy against child labour by governments. In contrast, Convention No. 182 makes, in addition to legislative requirements, quite detailed demands in the way that governments should shape policy and action to fight the worst forms of child labour. In other words, Convention No. 182 is in many respects a standard for policy, programmes and technical cooperation.

[10] The concept of time-bound measures will be discussed below in more detail.

Today, with 145 ratifications,[11] over 80 per cent of the ILO member states, Convention No. 138 remains the basic framework for both legislative and policy measures to combat child labour. Convention No. 182, which entered into force on 19 November 2000, has enjoyed an unprecedented rate of ratification. Today, it has been ratified by 161 member states,[12] some 90 per cent of the ILO membership. The Global Report points out that the two Conventions have had a significant impact on the way countries act against child labour, and have helped shape technical cooperation.[13]

3.1.1. The Minimum Age Convention No. 138

9. Convention No. 138, supplemented by Recommendation No. 146, sets forth in Article 1 that principal commitments of a ratifying State are:

1. to *pursue a national policy* to ensure the effective abolition of child labour; and
2. to *raise progressively the minimum age* for employment or work

The framework as to the minimum age is follows:

	General	**For developing countries ("where economy and education facilities are insufficiently developed")[14]**
General minimum age (Article 2)	Not less than the end of compulsory schooling, 15 years or more	14 years
Light work (Article 7)	13 years	12 years
Dangerous work (Article 3)	18 years (16 years under certain conditions)	18 years (16 years under certain conditions)

The above rules can be visualised in the following figure[15] as a function of the age of the child and the rough type of work or activities.

---

11 As at 15 June 2006. For up-to-date information regarding the ratification of ILO Conventions, see the ILOLEX database at <www.ilo.org>.

12 As at 15 June 2006.

13 ILO, supra (note 4), 5–9.

14 The flexibility foreseen for developing countries regarding the level of the minimum age is optional and needs to be used at the time of ratification. Article 2(4), Convention No. 138 of the International Labour Organisation concerning Minimum Age for Admission to Employment, adopted on 26 June 1973 and which entered into force on 19 June 1976.

15 Adapted from figure 2, ILO, supra (note 3).

Children between the minimum age and 18				
Children between 12/13 and the minimum age				
Children below 12/13 years of age				
	Work[16] excluded from minimum age legislation	Light work	Non-hazardous, non-light work	Hazardous work (and also other worst forms of child labour)

Shaded areas = child labour for abolition

10. As stated before, Convention No. 138 covers all sectors of economic activity, and employment as well as work. Because it may not always be easy for countries to initially meet the Convention's requirements for all sectors and forms of work or employment, the Convention features several clauses[17] allowing flexibility: countries may for example initially exclude limited categories such as family undertakings. Work carried out within the framework of education and vocational training is under certain conditions excluded from the application of the Convention. Work done for artistic performances may, under individual permit, even be permitted below the minimum age prescribed by the Convention.

11. With the objective of the effective abolition of child labour, the Convention recognises that the fixing of minimum ages is of course by itself not sufficient. As noted, the Convention requires the pursuit of "a national policy" as well. The Convention does not make any specific demands on the shape and content of such a policy, leaving it essentially to the countries themselves to determine this taking into account national and local circumstances. However, the non-binding Minimum Age Recommendation No. 146 (supplementing Convention No. 138) suggests that policy measures may include:

- adequate facilities for education and vocational orientation and training;
- promotion of employment-oriented development in rural and urban areas;

[16] For example, household chores done by children in their own home, and work carried out in the context of education and training under protective conditions.

[17] Arts. 4 and 5, Convention No. 138 of the International Labour Organisation concerning Minimum Age for Admission to Employment, adopted on 26 June 1973 and which entered into force on 19 June 1976.

- extension of economic and social measures to alleviate poverty, and also to ensure family living standards and income which are such as to make it unnecessary to have recourse to the economic activity of children;
- social security and family welfare measures aimed at ensuring child maintenance;
- facilities for the protection and welfare of children and young persons.

3.1.2. The Worst Forms of Child Labour Convention No. 182

12. Convention No. 182, accompanied by Recommendation No. 190, reflects widespread recognition over the past years and a global consensus that there should be an immediate end to the worst forms of child labour. Convention No. 182 covers all girls and boys under the age of 18[18] in line with the definition of the child under the Convention on the Rights of the Child. It calls for "immediate and effective measures to secure the prohibition and elimination of the worst forms of child labour as a matter of urgency".[19]

13. The Convention, as noted above, defines the worst forms of child labour as follows: (a) slavery and forced labour, including child trafficking and forced recruitment for armed conflict; (b) the use of children in prostitution and the production of pornography; (c) the use of children in illicit activities such as the production and trafficking of drugs; and (d) work likely to harm the health, safety or morals of children.

As to the exact types of work to be prohibited as hazardous work under item (d) above, the Convention leaves the matter to national determination after consultation with employers' and workers' organisations and taking into consideration relevant international standards.[20] This determination in each country is extremely important as a first step to clarify what is to be eliminated and to take concrete actions accordingly. Hazardous work is a category closely related to how the conditions of work are regulated and safety and health of workers are protected in general and especially for young workers. For children who have already reached the general working age, the removal of the hazards or increased protection of their occupational safety and health could be a solution in this category of worst forms of child labour.

---

18 Art. 2, Convention No. 182, supra (note 5).
19 Ibid, Art. 1.
20 Ibid., Arts. 3 and 4.

The other three categories under (a) to (c) are as we noted before, "unconditional" worst forms[21] because improving working conditions in no way make these forms more acceptable.[22]

14. In contrast to Convention No. 138, the Convention provides significant detail concerning the policy and operational aspects of the fight against child labour. It requires ratifying States to design and implement programmes of action[23] to eliminate the worst forms of child labour as a priority and establish or designate appropriate mechanisms for monitoring[24] implementation of the Convention. It also calls for time-bound measures[25] for prevention; to provide support for the removal of children form the worst forms of child labour and their rehabilitation; to ensure access to free basic education or vocational training for all children removed from the worst forms of child labour; to identify children at special risk; and to take account of the special situation of girls.

15. The Convention also calls for international cooperation or assistance in efforts to ensure the effective implantation of its provisions, including support for social and economic development, poverty eradication and education.[26] International cooperation is of particular significance to worst forms of child labour of a transnational nature, such as the trafficking of children for the purpose of exploitation.

16. In keeping with the tripartite principles of the Organisation, the Convention also provides for broad consultation among governments, workers and employers – the "social partners" in the ILO's tripartite structure. However, the Convention also requires that programmes of action should be designed and implemented, taking also "into consideration the views of other concerned groups".[27] Thus, the Convention recognises the importance of the contributions of other actors, such as non-governmental organisations, community-based groups, and importantly, of children and their parents.

---

21 ILO, supra (note 3), para. 31.

22 The term "worst forms of child labour" encompasses both hazardous work and the "unconditional" forms mentioned above. The difference is that while hazardous work, through changes in the work environment and the work itself can sometimes be modified to remove the hazardous aspects, the unconditional forms can under no circumstance be considered acceptable.

23 Art. 6, Convention No. 182, supra (note 5).

24 Ibid., Art. 5.

25 Ibid., Art. 7.

26 Ibid., Art. 8.

27 Ibid., Art. 6(2).

3.1.3. Supervision of the implementation of the Conventions

17. How is the application by countries of Conventions No. 138 and No. 182 monitored? All ILO Conventions are subject to the ILO's supervisory mechanism. Since the system is based on the provisions of the ILO Constitution, separate Conventions like Convention No. 182 do not contain their own provisions on reporting and monitoring. Supervision is based on Governments' regular reports to be submitted to the ILO in accordance with Article 22 of the Constitution on the implementation of ratified Conventions (to be submitted periodically every two years for both Convention No. 138 and No. 182). These reports together with other information such as the country's legislation, employers' and workers' comments are examined by the independent Committee of Experts on the Application of Conventions and Recommendations.[28] Its report is submitted to the International Labour Conference, where it is discussed by a tripartite committee, including discussion of selected individual cases. These discussions have highlighted certain situations in countries with respect to child labour.

18. An important feature of the ILO's system is the involvement of the social partners – employers and workers – in the supervisory system. Workers' and employers' organisations are encouraged to submit their comments and observations on governments' reports, in this way helping to assess the degree of application of a Convention in question in practice. Child labour is one of the topics that tend to encounter a wide disparity between the legal norm and the actual practice in many countries. While non-governmental organisations as such are not given the role of supplying information officially to the ILO's system, increasingly formal constituents such as workers' organisations submit comments based on detailed information accumulated by concerned NGOs.

19. The unique supervisory system of the ILO standards is in practice linked to the UN system of monitoring the Convention on the Rights of the Child (CRC) and other human rights instruments. Information flows between the two systems both ways: outstanding comments of the ILO supervisory organs, as well as ILO activities on child labour in the country and other practical information help the UN Committee on the Rights of the Child examine the issues of child labour in detail when examining a country report. Likewise, information supplied by governments under the CRC in their reports has been highly useful for the ILO, especially concerning the practice of child

---

[28] The comments on the application of a particular Convention by a particular country made by the Committee of Experts can be found at <www.ilo.org> through 'International Labour Standards' by using either the APPLIS or ILOLEX databases.

labour or economic exploitation, but also as regards other aspects such as the definition of the child, education, sexual or other types of child exploitation and abuse.

20. This exchange of information has also found its way into the comments issued by the UN Committee on the Rights of the Child and the ILO Committee of Experts. Both the CRC and the ILO Committee of Experts now frequently refer to each other's comments. In other words, the commonalities between the two systems – for example ILO standards and CRC children's rights – in terms of substantive content have naturally lead to close linkages in international monitoring.

3.2. RELATIONSHIP WITH THE UN CONVENTION ON THE RIGHTS OF THE CHILD AND ITS PROTOCOLS

21. The Conventions clearly complement the CRC and its Protocols. A number of common features deserve mention here.[29]

3.2.1. A common framework

22. Article 32 of the CRC, which provides for the child's right to be protected against economic exploitation, refers to "the relevant provisions of other international instruments" in its second paragraph. Any work carried out by children in conditions below those established by UN Conventions or by the ILO should be considered as economic exploitation. This has indeed been the position of the Committee on the Rights of the Child in examining reports from countries on the CRC's implementation. The Committee has frequently referred to Conventions No. 138 and No.182 as the framework in assessing the national situation of child labour, and has been systematic in recommending State Parties to the CRC, if not yet, to ratify them.

3.2.2. The definition of the child

23. Convention No. 182 covers all persons under the age of 18, according to its Article 2, in line with the definition of the child under the Convention on the Rights of the Child. The manner in which a "child" is defined in national law varies per country. From the perspective of the Convention, it does not matter whether someone under the age of 18 is called baby, child, adolescent or young person under national laws, as long as all such persons are covered by the measures of protection against the

---

29 See also: Y. Noguchi, 'ILO Convention No. 182 on the worst forms of child labour and the Convention on the Rights of the Child', (2002) 10 *International Journal of Children's Rights*, 355–369.

worst forms of child labour. In fact, even if the law defines a "child" as a person under 18, if protection against the worst forms of child labour in a particular situation is available only up to a lower age, this will have to be extended to cover all girls and boys under 18.

It is worth noting that Convention No. 182 does not even allow the exception where "under the law applicable to the child, the age of majority is attained earlier (latter part of Article 1 of the CRC)". In some cases, marriage is allowed from an age lower than 18 and that gives the persons majority before reaching 18 years of age. However, for the purpose of the Convention, any girl or boy under 18 must be protected from the worst forms of child labour, even if she or he has been married and thus attained the age of majority.

However, this does not mean that the Convention requires a complete prohibition of all work for all persons under 18. As mentioned earlier under Convention No. 138, children who are under 18 but have attained the general minimum age for work, usually lower than 18, can legitimately work, as long as it does not fall within any of the criteria of the worst forms of child labour.[30]

3.2.3. More than just economic exploitation

24. Many of the issues raised by the Conventions have a direct relationship with the CRC. Of course, Convention No. 138, dealing mostly with "traditional" forms of child labour, is directly linked to the CRC through its Article 32. The worst forms addressed by Convention No. 182 to an important extent are also expressly linked to the CRC: children in illicit production and trafficking of drugs (Art. 33), sexual exploitation (Art. 34), trafficking in children (Art. 35) and children in armed conflict (Art. 38). It can therefore never be overemphasised that the ILO's relationship is not only with Article 32 of the CRC, but also touches on several other areas of the rights of the child. In a departure from "classic" ILO labour standards, almost exclusively dealing with labour issues[31], many of the issues covered by Convention No. 182 are not at all normal types of employment or even "labour" – they are criminal offences in practically all countries.

25. Does the ILO recognise prostitution as work, by including it among the worst forms of child "labour"? The answer is clearly in the negative. Convention No. 182

---

30 See, for instance, ILO/IPU, *Eliminating the worst forms of child labour – A practical guide to ILO Convention No.182*, in Handbook for Parliamentarians No.3, ILO/IPU, Geneva, 2002.

31 With the notable exception of Convention No. 29 of the International Labour Organisation concerning Forced Labour, adopted on 28 June 1930 and which entered into force on 1 May 1932.

calls for immediate and effective measures to secure the prohibition and elimination of, amongst other things, the use, procuring or offering of a child (i.e. under 18, as explained above) for prostitution, for the production of pornography or for pornographic performances. An ILO report to the International Labour Conference in 1998 – one of the preparatory documents for the drafting of Convention No. 182 – indicated: "Child prostitution, child pornography and the sale and trafficking of children are crimes of violence against children. They must be treated as crimes... Yet while they are crimes they are also forms of economic exploitation akin to forced labour and slavery."[32]

3.2.4. Linkage with the Optional Protocols

26. The two areas of issues covered by the Optional Protocols to the CRC[33] – that is, the sale of children and sexual exploitation, and armed conflict – are both explicitly covered by Convention No. 182. In fact, the period of negotiation and elaboration of these international instruments overlap. Thus, the Optional Protocols both refer to Convention No. 182 in their preambles. While they cover topics common to Convention No. 182, as separate international legal instruments they each have their own scope of application and requirements. The Optional Protocol on armed conflict, for instance, goes further than Convention No. 182 since it prohibits the *participation* of children under the age of 18 in armed conflict, and governs both voluntary and forced recruitment of minors, while Convention No. 182 targets the forced recruitment for armed conflict as part of forced labour of children.

27. All the same, the two optional Protocols and Convention No. 182 complement each other in addressing the involvement of children in armed conflict, and sale and sexual exploitation of children, two important issues of the worst forms of child labour. For example, because the Optional Protocols concentrate on one issue each, they offer more precise definitions of certain concepts and describe in more detail the measures to be taken by ratifying countries. Beyond doubt, the Protocols therefore will be useful guidelines for understanding and implementing Convention No. 182. The system of reporting on the implementation of the Optional Protocols further adds to the possibilities of international supervision over these worst forms of child labour.

---

32 ILO, '*Child labour – Targeting the intolerable*', Report to the International Labour Conference, 86th Session, Geneva, 1998, Report VI (1), 66.

33 The *Optional Protocol to the Convention on the Rights of the Child on the involvement of children in armed conflicts*, adopted on 25 May 2000 and which entered into force on 13 February 2002 and the *Optional Protocol to the Convention on the Rights of the Child on the sale of children, child prostitution and child pornography*, adopted on 25 May 2000 and which entered into force on 18 January 2002.

3.3. OTHER INTERNATIONAL INSTRUMENTS RELEVANT TO CHILD LABOUR

28. Apart from the ILO Conventions and the CRC, other international instruments are relevant to aspects of child labour, in particular its worst forms. ILO bodies supervising the application of international labour standards have already been dealing with the issue of the commercial sexual exploitation, trafficking and forced labour of children in several countries under the Forced Labour Convention, 1930 (No. 29). The United Nations Convention against Transnational Organised Crime and in particular its additional Protocol to Prevent, Suppress and Punish trafficking in persons, especially women and children (known as the "Palermo Protocol", adopted in 2000),[34] are important instruments for shaping legislative and policy action against the trafficking of adults and children, and are having their impact on both national legislation and international instruments against human trafficking. Notable international instruments related to the use of children in armed conflict are the Rome Statute of the International Criminal Court, adopted in 1998, which qualifies the recruitment of children below fifteen years for use in armed conflict as a war crime,[35] and the 1977 Additional Protocol to the Geneva Convention of 12 August 1949, and Relating to the Protection of Victims of Non-International Armed Conflicts (Protocol II).[36]

4. LINKING STANDARDS TO ACTION

29. This section will first examine how Convention No. 182 can help to shape national and international action against child labour. Second, it will present some important findings by the 2006 Global Report on Child Labour regarding the manner in which Conventions No. 138 and No.182 have influenced national legislative and policy action.

---

34 UN General Assembly Resolution of 15 November 2000: *United Nations Convention against Transnational Organised Crime* (UN Doc. A/RES/55/25, 2000).

35 Art. 8(2)(e)(vii), Statute of the International Criminal Court.

36 The Additional Protocol, adopted on 8 June 1977 and which entered into force on 7 December 1978, provides in Article 4(3)(c): 'Children who have not attained the age of fifteen years shall neither be recruited in the armed forces or groups nor allowed to take part in hostilities'.

4.1. CONVENTION NO. 182 AND RECOMMENDATION NO. 190 AS A GUIDE FOR ACTION

30. As was noted above, Convention No. 182 is very much an action-oriented instrument. Generally, all ILO standards require that provisions of a Convention have to be applied in both law and practice. For example, where Convention No. 138 only sets forth a minimum age, ratifying States must take measures both to fix such a minimum age in law and to make such national legislation effectively applied in practice.

In the case of Convention No. 182, such requirements for action are spelt out as substantive provisions. Not only does this provide more guidance for governments in taking action, it also makes it easier to point to the inaction of governments, and place pressure on them through the supervisory machinery of the ILO. But importantly, the specific requirements also shape the nature of policy action by governments and the international agencies that support them. In addition to the Convention, its accompanying – not legally binding – Worst Forms of Child Labour Recommendation No.190 offers a wide range of guidelines for action, from international efforts in gathering and exchanging information, extraterritorial pursuit of related offences by nationals even when the offences are committed in another country, to a wide social mobilisation. Even though not binding, Recommendation No. 190 is a unanimously adopted international instrument – reflecting a global consensus on its contents – and should be referred to as a guideline for action in any country, irrespective of the ratification of Convention No. 182, and also for action at local or international level.

Thus, the principles of the Convention and the Recommendation go much beyond a simple prohibition of the worst forms of child labour. Child labour is a complex issue, and demands a comprehensive and integrated approach, so as to break the vicious cycle of poverty, social inequality and child labour. Measures needed to eliminate child labour including its worst forms, effectively and in a sustainable manner, encompass a wide range of economic and social support to the children and their families. This comprehensive approach must guide countries in how the protection of children's rights is to be integrated into social and economic development strategies.[37]

---

37 ILO contribution to the UN Secretary General's Report to the United Nations General Assembly Special Session on Children, a document submitted to the preparatory committee at its second substantive session, (UN Doc. A/AC.256/CRP.8, 22 January 2001), 55.

31. One illustrative example of how Convention No. 182 has helped shape technical cooperation activities by the ILO is the development of Time-Bound Programmes (TBPs). A TBP is essentially a set of tightly integrated and coordinated policies and programmes to prevent and eliminate a country's worst forms of child labour within a defined period of time. It is a comprehensive approach that operates at many levels, including international, national, provincial, community and individual or family. TBPs emphasise the need to address the root causes of child labour, linking action against child labour to the national development effort, with particular emphasis on economic and social policies to combat poverty and to promote universal basic education and social mobilisation.[38] Today, some twenty countries are implementing ILO/supported TBPs, while a number of others are also setting time-bound goals by themselves to achieve the elimination of one or more worst forms of child labour.

4.2. THE 2006 GLOBAL REPORT: HOW STANDARDS CONTRIBUTE TO NATIONAL ACTION AGAINST CHILD LABOUR

32. To what extent have the Conventions contributed to concrete action against child labour? The ILO's 2006 Global Report on Child Labour notes that it is inherently difficult to obtain a complete picture of all actions and measures that countries have taken to combat child labour.[39] Yet, it suggests that a reliable way of measuring the impact of the Conventions on action since 1999 can be found through the supervisory work of the ILO's Committee on the Application of Conventions and Recommendations (CEACR). The comments adopted by the Committee in respect of the application by countries of the Conventions reflect the steps that ratifying countries have taken to implement these instruments and eliminate child labour. Taking 1999 as a starting point, the cases of action registered by the Committee provide a reasonably accurate picture of the extent to which countries' commitments under the Conventions have given rise to positive measures. The picture emerging from the Committee's work since 1999 provides an interesting overview regarding areas of high activity and areas where more action is required.

---

38 For more information on TBPs, see <http://www.ilo.org/public/english/standards/ipec/timebound/tbp.htm>.

39 ILO, supra (note 4), 17.

Figure 1.5. Action reported under Convention Nos. 138 and 182 since 1999 (percentage of reports submitted)

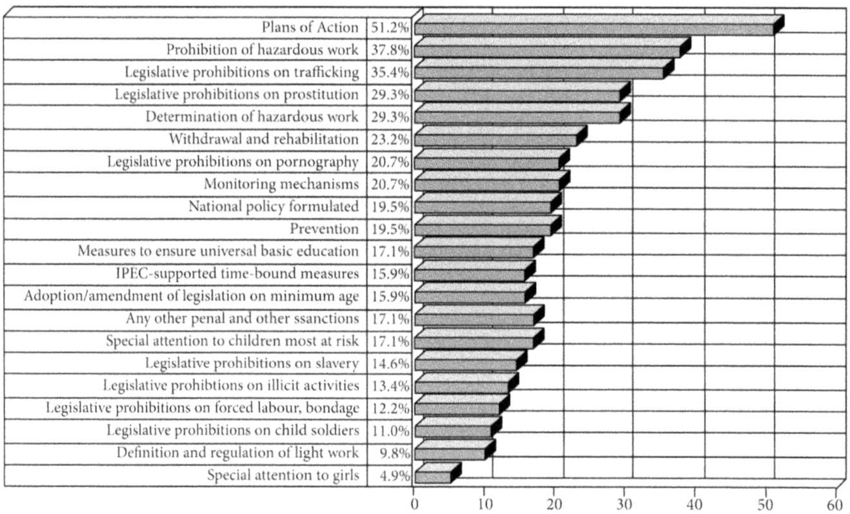

Source: 2006 Global Report on Child Labour[40]

33. The picture presented here is of course by no means complete but it provides valuable pointers for setting the future agenda for the fight against child labour. Many countries have taken steps towards formulating partial or comprehensive policies towards fighting child labour, a central requirement under both Conventions No. 138 and No. 182. Coupled with this high activity in policy formulation, a significant development can be seen in the adoption of Plans of Action to tackle one or more categories of child labour and its worst forms. Other areas where high levels of activity can be distinguished are the adoption of legislation against the trafficking of human beings, particularly children, the involvement of children in prostitution and the production of pornography, and the prohibition of hazardous work for all children under 18 years. While this high activity in policy formulation and the adoption of plans of actions is encouraging, it must be noted that within those policies and plans of action there is only limited attention to the most vulnerable children, and even more modest attention for the special situation of girls. Having adequate consideration for the special position of these groups is a critical factor for success in fighting child labour, and particularly its worst forms.

34. The global picture also indicates that governments have reported only modest attention to measures to combat the forced labour of children, including bonded child

40 Ibid.

labour. This is disappointing, since last year's Global Report on forced labour estimated that children represented between 40 and 50 per cent of all victims of forced labour, or 5.7 million children in forced and bonded labour.[41] Likewise, very little action has been reported on improving legislation against the use, procuring or offering of a child for illicit activities, in particular for the production and trafficking of drugs. This is of particular concern, because practice has shown that very few countries have adequate legislation in place in this field to begin with, so that the lack of legislative activity leaves important gaps in national legislation and in the overall application of Convention No. 182.

35. In all, while there are many encouraging signs that allow for the conclusion that the Conventions have had a positive impact on national frameworks for combating child labour, there are also areas where increased emphasis is necessary. This should provide guidance not only for countries, but also for the ILO's technical cooperation activities and for the activities of other international agencies, workers' and employers' organisations, and non-governmental organisations.

5. THE FIGHT AGAINST CHILD LABOUR CAN BE WON

5.1. WHAT IS CONTRIBUTING TO THE DECLINE IN CHILD LABOUR?

36. The ILO's new Global Report is careful not to draw any premature conclusion as to which factors have contributed to the significant decline in child labour worldwide. Insufficient analysis and research is currently available to assess the new data. However, based on knowledge available within the ILO and its partner organisations such as UNESCO, UNICEF and the World Bank, the Report suggests a number of factors of which it can safely be said that they are contributing to reductions in child labour.

37. To begin with, the Report notes that international awareness of the problem of child labour and increased political commitment – as expressed through increased ratification of international standards on child labour and growing policy in the areas of poverty reduction, basic education and human rights – has increased significantly since the 1990s. The importance of this is not to be underestimated, and the Report

---

41 ILO, '*A global alliance against forced labour*', Global Report under the follow-up to the ILO Declaration on Fundamental Principles and Rights at Work, Report to the International Labour Conference, 93rd Session, Geneva, 2005, Report I(B), para. 61.

cites this as a central element in the progress made.[42] This achievement is clearly thanks to the many actors at the national and international levels – NGOs, international organisations, trade unions and employers – who have raised child labour to the top of their agendas.

38. A second, and perhaps the most important, finding in the Report is that there is a direct correlation between policy choices and reduction in child labour. The report notes: "*Economic growth alone will not eliminate child labour, though clearly it is important. Policy choices matter, and those which open gateways of opportunity for poor people, are central to efforts aimed at eliminating child labour.*"[43] The Report discusses a number of examples from East Asia, including China, and from Brazil to illustrate that in addition to poverty reduction, the decision to focus on mass education in particular is an important prerequisite for moving countries to the transition point in tackling child labour. Concerning Brazil, for example, the Report argues that the combination of engaged civic society, including the establishment of a quadripartite National Forum for the Prevention and Eradication of Child Labour, coupled with the introduction of nine years of compulsory education and proactive programmes (including conditional cash transfers) to enable the poorest families to keep their children in school, resulted in a net enrolment rate of children aged 7–14 years of more than 97 per cent. The Brazil case, and similar evidence from other countries, illustrate that where countries make the right policy choices in terms of poverty reduction and investment in mass education, spectacular inroads can be made towards the elimination of child labour.[44] Indeed, there is a clear link between child labour developments and trends in children's education, but the extent varies between countries and regions. Experience shows, for instance, that appropriate investment in primary and lower secondary education significantly decreases children's work participation rates. In Latin America and the Caribbean, 95 per cent of all primary school-age children are now in school. The region has also made great strides towards increasing secondary schooling in the last few years. In contrast, Sub-Saharan Africa has the highest prevalence of primary school-age children out of school. In Eastern and Southern Africa every third child misses out on primary school. In West and Central Africa this is true for almost half the children.[45]

39. Of course, the work done by international organisations, including the ILO through its International Programme on the Elimination of Child Labour (IPEC), have also contributed to reductions in child labour. Both through projects – designed to

---

42 ILO, supra (note 4), 9.
43 Ibid., xi.
44 Ibid., 10–15.
45 Source of the figures: UNESCO, *Children Out of School. Measuring Exclusion from Primary Education*, UNESCO Institute for Statistics, Montreal, 2005.

develop practical and affordable policy approaches to child labour – and through upstream policy work, their activities have contributed to a more conducive environment in which countries are better able to make the policy choices that can effectively fight child labour. Evidence from independent evaluations suggests that countries where IPEC has been a long-standing partner are now among those where the most significant reductions in child labour have been made.

40. Another important factor for progress is the emergence of a worldwide movement against child labour over the last decade. This movement consists of a loose constellation of individuals, groups, organisations and governments committed to the abolition of child labour.[46] In terms of the Global Report, this concept refers to international action that promotes an enabling environment for national and local action. As such, it consists of the ILO and its social partners (workers and employers), other international agencies such as UNICEF, UNESCO, WHO and the World Bank, the international donor community, NGOs, the media and research community, and to some extent children and their families. While the movement is stronger today than ever before, the Global Report notes that it is still fragmented, and hampered by a multiplicity of actors and views. The Report argues that the movement could be a much more effective facilitator for allowing countries to make the right policy choices if it were to work in a more coherent manner. From a practical point of view, for example, this would require a more systematic focus on children and child labour in international development and poverty reduction efforts, such as the Millennium Development Goals and Poverty Reduction Strategy Papers. It is for this reason that one of the future priorities of the ILO will be to act as a galvanising force to strengthen the worldwide movement.

5.2. THE CHALLENGES AHEAD

41. Despite the decline in child labour, and the fact that a growing amount of experience is now leading to a better understanding of what works in the fight against the scourge, more than two hundred million children are still trapped in unacceptable exploitation. The Global Report identifies a number of challenges that must be met to further reduce and eventually eliminate child labour. The basic premise of all these challenges is that the fight against child labour can ultimately only be won at the national level. Any action, whether national or international, must in the end serve to strengthen national responses and be designed to help countries make the –

[46] ILO, *The worldwide movement against child labour: progress made and future action* (forthcoming).

sometimes painful – policy choices necessary. Broadly said, the challenges listed by the Report are as follows:[47]

- There is a need for greater national ownership, supported by employers' and workers' organisations, and backed up by a more vibrant worldwide movement to create the environment in which technical tools and frameworks are put to optimum use.
- The elimination of child labour needs to be mainstreamed into key development and human rights frameworks, such as the Millennium Development Goals (MDGs), and Poverty Reduction Strategies (PRSs).
- At national level many countries are ready to deal with child labour, but international financial support for that commitment is lacking. It should be more widely accepted that it makes economic sense for the international community to support national efforts to combat child labour.
- The elimination of child labour has to be placed on the international development agenda for Sub-Saharan Africa in particular.
- Other challenges include HIV/AIDS, links with youth employment, and the growth of the informal economy where much of the world's child labour, particularly its worst forms, is found.

42. These challenges imply at the international level a more coherent approach to child labour by all involved, including international agencies and NGOs. At the national level, governments need to be encouraged to make more profound responses. In order to reinvigorate the struggle, the Global Report suggests an ambitious target: that all worst forms of child labour be eliminated by 2016, and that to achieve this all countries design and put in place appropriate time-bound measures by 2008.[48] This is as much a practical goal as a political one. It is practical in the sense that given the right responses, the current trends suggest that this can indeed be achieved around the year 2016. It is also practical in the sense that it sets a clear agenda for action by the international community. It is also a political goal, because it challenges countries and international actors to adopt the right approaches, because today we know in broad lines what those responses should be.

43. For itself, the ILO also sets out a number of tasks. In line with the comments made above concerning the remaining challenges, the ILO over the next four years will strengthen its efforts to develop coherent and comprehensive approaches to abolishing child labour.[49] The action plan presented in the Report rests on three pillars:

---

47 ILO, supra (note 4), 53–66.
48 Ibid., 85.
49 Ibid., 86–89.

- Supporting national responses to child labour, in particular, through effective mainstreaming in national development and policy frameworks;
- Deepening and strengthening the worldwide movement against child labour; and
- Promoting further integration of child labour concerns within overall ILO priorities, which make Decent Work a global goal.

In its conclusion, the Report notes "*The challenge of the next four years will be for the ILO to work in a more focused and strategic way to act as the catalyst of a re-energised global alliance in support of national action to abolish child labour. This transformation in approach to global leadership will ensure that the ILO will contribute more effectively to consigning child labour to history*".[50]

6. CONCLUSION

44. Given the present understanding about child labour, it does not sound overly ambitious or idealistic to say that, yes, child labour can be eliminated within a reasonable period. It requires concerted action, wise governance, some economic growth and real political commitment. It must be recognised that the persistence of child labour stands in the way of success on many other fronts, such as the Education of All initiative, the MDGs and poverty reduction strategies. If this is properly understood, then mankind will succeed in making child labour history.

[50] Ibid., 90.

WORKING CHILDREN'S EXPERIENCES AND CHILDREN'S RIGHTS

ANTONELLA INVERNIZZI

1. INTRODUCTION

1. This text draws on two qualitative studies on children's work. The first was carried out in Lima (Peru) with a group of working children and their families who mainly sold sweets in the city centre. The second also included children, parents and other young adults living in different areas of the Algarve (Portugal) and working in many different settings.[1] The focus of the research was on children and adults' views and practices, their work, how they worked and what they intended to do.

2. The first question is to establish whether practices these two studies examine are to be considered "child labour" or "worst forms of child labour". As a matter of fact, most of the work observed in Portugal was illegal, as any work performed by young people under the age of 16, including light and part-time work alongside school, is against the law. However, some children's work did not entirely conform to definitions of light work. Although light work by children is considered by Peruvian legislation, some aspects of street trade by children involved some kind of risks or hazards, exploitation, long hours and/or problems with education. Nonetheless, as will be discussed later, there are many conflicting ways of defining child labour and these different discourses impact on the way working children's experiences are studied.

3. In point of fact, there are two main lessons to be learned from the two qualitative studies. The first one is that children's experiences and views of work are wide-ranging.

[1] For the study in Lima (Peru) see: A. INVERNIZZI, *Enfants travailleurs dans les rues de Lima: entre stratégies de survie et socialisation*, Unpublished PhD thesis, (Switzerland: Université de Fribourg, 1999); A. INVERNIZZI, *La vie quotidienne des enfants travailleurs. Stratégies de survie et socialisation dans les rues de Lima,* (Paris: L'Harmattan, 2001); A. INVERNIZZI, 'Street-working children and adolescents in Lima: work as an agent of socialization', (2003) 10(4) *Childhood*, 319–341. For the study in the Algarve (Portugal) see: A. INVERNIZZI, 'Perspectives on children's work in the Algarve (Portugal) and their implication for social policy', (2005) 25(2) *Critical Social Policy,* 198–222 and A. INVERNIZZI, 'Children's work in Portugal. An exploration of children's motivations, family organisation and views on socialisation.' (2006) *International Journal of Children's Rights.*

Even when the study focuses on a restricted number of children who all worked or had worked as sweet sellers in the same street in central Lima, an unlimited multiplicity of experience was perhaps the main trait. It is necessary to fully consider that diversity rather than attempt to construct a single profile, which would prompt policies and practices that would be at best inefficient and at worst oppressive for a number of working children.

4. Diversity of children's experience appears even more important in the study in southern Portugal when dealing with a variety of tasks from employment in civil and public construction, restaurants and hotels, work in family businesses (again including restaurants and hotels, construction, carpentry, etc.) or farms. Furthermore, it included domestic tasks and the care of young children, the elderly or sick and disabled parents. The degree of input varied from a few hours a week to full time. As in the Peruvian study, children regularly expressed positive views on their work and most of them thought about positive and negative aspects with the overall evaluation being a balance of both. This indicates the significance of HOBBS and MCKECHNIE's[2] conceptualisation of work in terms of a balance of advantages and disadvantages rather than simplistic approaches considering "good" or "bad" work. However, a number of children did not express positive opinions of work and, despite economic needs and input, did not believe this should be part of their lives. A framework capable of dealing with this range of experience and opinions somehow needs to include a complex set of questions about how the child relates to his or her work and the nature of advantages and disadvantages according to his or her specific circumstances.

5. When looking at the entire research data, differentiation appears to relate to external aspects, such as economic situation and socio-cultural context as well as the significance of those factors and, undoubtedly no less important, the child's person and identity.

6. The second lesson learned from these works is that when research is about their experience it must focus on children rather than on standard categories or concepts such as "work", "domestic tasks", "exploitation", "education", "leisure", "poverty", and so on. They apportion lives in a way that might threaten any possibility of understanding experience as subjects and thus deny them somehow the same status of subjects that the UN Convention on the Rights of the Child (the UNCRC) intends to promote.

---

[2] IWGCL, '*Working Children: reconsidering the debates*', Report of the International Working Group on Child Labour, Amsterdam, 1998.

7. The first part of this text presents ethnographic data, which is set out under four categories: "survival" and improvement of living standards, "socialisation" and identity construction, participation and exploitation.

8. The second part identifies some of the implications of the analysis for the promotion of working children's rights, underlying existing contradictions between different Articles of the UNCRC as well as different policies and discourses on child labour.

2. FACETS OF CHILDREN'S WORK: SURVIVAL, SOCIALISATION, PARTICPATION AND EXPLOITATION[3]

9. The main hypothesis of the study is that economic practice related to children's work can be interpreted simultaneously as forms of survival, exploitation, socialisation and participation. These dimensions are very much interdependent and understanding of any of them requires consideration of the others. This text intends to point out some of these interdependent relationships and, in illustration, will particularly focus on features related to "socialisation" and construction of identity.

2.1. CHILDREN'S WORK AS A STRATEGY FOR SURVIVAL AND IMPROVEMENT OF ECONOMIC CONDITIONS

10. Research in Portugal and Peru focused mainly, and deliberately, on work carried out by children in family settings or any instance related to family life. Thus, a major restraint on the research is that working children living on their own or living where they work are not included. There is indeed a degree of interest in looking at family organisation of work since it is recognised that this form of child work predominates worldwide[4] as much as in Portugal.[5] Understanding of children's experiences of work therefore needs to include examination of family organisations in the economic, social and cultural context where they exist.

---

3 The first version of paragraph 1 was published in German: A. INVERNIZZI. 'Die Arbeit von Kindern: Gedanken zu den vielfältigen Überlebens-, Sozialisations-, Partizipations- und Ausbeutungserfahrungen', in B. OVERWIEN (ed.), *Von sozialen Subjecte. Kinder und Jugendliche in vershiedenen Welten*, (Frankfurt – London: IKO, 2005).

4 ILO, '*A future without child labour*', Report of the Director-General, International Labour Conference, International Labour Organization, 90th session, Geneva, 2002.

5 SIETE, '*Caracterização social dos agregados familares portugueses con menores em idade escolar*', Lisbon, ILO/SIETI/DETEFP, 2001.

11. Peruvian reality includes very harsh economic conditions for a large part of the population and children's work remains essential in many cases. In extreme poverty, their work is clearly required as a means of covering the basic need for food. Although Portugal also shows high rates of poverty compared to other European countries, poverty levels are not comparable. Generally speaking, family dependency on children's work is thus lesser in the Portuguese situation. Children's contribution remains, however, essential for the survival of families from the most economically disadvantaged groups and particularly those who live off agriculture and animal keeping or those families affected by such hardships as accidents, illness or unemployment.

12. Children's work is nonetheless not simply driven by economic constraints. Complicated and sophisticated processes involving children in family activities are related to social and cultural aspects as well as economic ones. To give an example; working children in Lima often explained their work as a way to "*help their mother*" or to "*help their brothers or sisters*". Such forms of mutual support in the family essentially include intricate practices whereby, for instance, one child takes responsibility for the cost of a sibling attending school or a family devises a shared project to improve the quality of their housing. The contribution of each member of the family is worked out and gradually the money required is saved. It would be easy to dismiss such acquisitions if considering only aspects related to poverty. In fact, some mothers in Lima use the expression "*working for the stomach*" to describe work that provides very little income. However, when looked at in detail, the expression does not only describe economic qualities but is characteristic of daily efforts that do not leave space for any other project and thus is the source of a feeling of impotence. An identical activity can be "*working for the stomach*" in one case but conversely be part of a plan leading to improvement in family living standards in another.

By way of example, if the plan is to purchase the door of the family house it is part of a more developed plan. Having a door will create the basis for entirely new organisation of the family. A house without a door requires a constant presence in order to protect belongings against potential thieves. This is often the task of children. The new door leaves time for other activities, including work or school and new projects can be planned. Children's contributions might be outstanding in such minute and detailed projects that allow some families to overcome or keep out of worst forms of poverty and thus ensure education and more viable economic conditions.

13. As observed by MORROW, interdependence in family relationships[6] is a key element in understanding working children's experiences. However, cultural and social dimensions give specific content to these forms of interdependence where work might be positively valued in some cases and not in others. Paradoxically, the hypothesis here is that those images of childhood that are more favourable to children's work (and generally seen as main causes of child labour) are also those that often promote more progressive involvement of the working child. They more often allow time for the child to learn and are based on relatively precise criteria for assessing danger and risks. They also tend to provide higher degrees of autonomy and participation in family decision-making. The Peruvian study instead shows that some of the families who are not keen to see their children involved in work have been forced to send them out to generate some kind of income at a point in their lives when economic conditions become impossible. Some children thus went out into the streets unprepared, without adult support or knowledge that would have helped them to have a more protected and positive experience. Not only did they have to learn alone but their efforts were also dismissed by parents. Confronted with poverty and uncertain living standards, more positive views of children's work appeared often more capable of creating flexible working conditions for children as well as small but realistic plans for successive improvement of very difficult living standards.

2.2. CHILDREN'S WORK AS SOCIALISATION AND IDENTITY CONSTRUCTION

14. The idea that work might be a form of socialisation may seem very naïve;[7] it is however, the notion that best summarises young people and adults' thoughts on many occasions.

15. In the Peruvian study, observation of routines and informants' views often identified positive outcomes of children's work as a learning process. Clearly, one cannot dismiss harsh living conditions and their impact on what children are expected to learn. An eloquent statement in this respect was that of a grandmother who, when explaining why she had her very young grandchildren working with her in the streets, mentioned that in fact "*life is not bought*" ("*la vida no es comprada*"). She meant that life does not belong to us, adults might die and children be left alone. For a child who

---

6 V. MORROW, 'Responsible Children? Aspects of children's work and employment outside school in contemporary UK', in B. MAYALL (ed.), *Children's Childhoods: observed and experienced*, (London: Falmer Press, 1994), 114–127.

7 For critique of the concept of socialisation, see A. INVERNIZZI, 'Children's work in Portugal. An exploration of children's motivations, family organisation and views on socialisation', (2006) *International Journal of Children's Rights.*

does not have any adult support the ability to work in the street might become the only means of survival.

16. However, the consistent presence of poverty and an uncertain living standard should not obscure the fact that children's work might be positively valued for its general educational potential. Learning relates to the ways in which children and adults might have an impact on their environment as well as in their own life generally and departs from "*work for the stomach*" lacking an outlook.

17. Factors related to education clearly appeared also in southern Portugal. From 101 questionnaires distributed in three different schools in the Algarve, 93 pupils answered an optional open question: "*What do you think about children who work and/or help at home? It is good or bad? Why*?" What is interesting about the data is shown in the advantages and disadvantages of work openly revealed by pupils. Socialisation problems were mentioned by 11 adolescents with regard to formal education that work would make problematic. Advantages of working as part of socialisation were expressed by 24 pupils in terms of education.[8]

18. Literature on children's work in European countries also accentuates facets of socialisation; MORROW underlines for instance "*the possibility to gain useful experience for the future*" and gaining a "*source of reference for future job applications*".[9] In Portugal, young people mention them, however young adults and parents, mainly in rural areas, mostly emphasise dimensions of work related to socialisation.

19. Informants' views on "socialisation through work" suggest at least four key questions: What are the reasons given for work being an appropriate experience for children or, conversely, a negative one and to what kind of work does it refer? What about the acquisition of skills and competence, and the construction of the child's identity, which is self-image and social representations? What can we learn about the relationship between work and school? Which activities are considered appropriate for learning and preparing the young person's future?

20. Let's start with the first question. In many adult and child informants' views, work can be a suitable experience for the child but this can only be understood in relation to the precise context in which he or she lives and in relation to specific work or tasks. Children themselves tell of positive and negative aspects of work and only some of

---

8 An almost identical proportion (25 questionnaires) mentioned economic reasons or advantages whereas 46 questionnaires described aspects of cooperation or solidarity within the family. A particular number took more than one factor into account within the same answer.

9 V. MORROW, supra (note 6), 141.

them simply consider this experience wholly positive or negative. A challenging finding in this respect is that work might be appropriate for ensuring the child a kind of "protected" environment. In a number of families in both Lima and the Algarve, adults said that they needed to organise activities that allow them to keep children under their supervision. Mothers working in the streets of Lima said that leaving children at home alone all day long whilst they were working was a very unsuitable and risky alternative. In Portugal as well, the question of supervision was seen as essential by a number of parents. They said that they needed to organise activities with children, especially where leisure activities were scarce and they also wanted them to learn a few skills and have work experience. For young people in rural areas work was a pursuit for avoiding boredom, especially during summer holidays. According to that logic young people helped in restaurants, shops or other small family businesses because that way they spent most days with relatives. Some working parents took children to work with them during school holidays for similar reasons.

Behind the idea of work as a supervised activity there is clearly a concept of "good" and "bad". Many parents see young people's employment as a source of exploitation and would not favour it. Working with family, relatives or family friends instead is positively valued because it is assumed that it offers some kind of adult supervision.

Clearly, the idea that work is a source of protection and supervision is relatively challenging in a context where we normally merely assume children must be protected from work. Findings far from indicate that children do not suffer abuse and exploitation in these contexts. What needs to be examined, however, are precise mechanisms that respectively create ample protection, supervision, training, exploitation or abuse.

21. A second question more specifically concerns what children learn through work. It is actually a very broad question that includes social, economic, cultural, emotional and even aesthetic traits.

Some skills and information children acquire are strictly related to precise activities. Street working children in Lima knew about places to buy cheap sweets, learned how to deal with heavy traffic on certain streets and where cars stopped and drivers would have had time to buy goods. Similarly, a Portuguese child responsible for a number of goats learned precise skills for tending them daily. Other skills and competence might have a more general relevance, for instance ways of interacting with middle-class clients in Lima was valued a useful skill for any work requiring direct contact with wealthier sectors of the population. In rural areas of the Algarve where a number of families live off subsistence agriculture, some adolescents expressed an interest in working in a restaurant or a shop in order to see "*how it is when one works with money*". Such interests are very dependent on the context but also the young person and his or her preferences. Some informants also stressed the idea that choice is not about specific work that would be good in itself, rather more than the fact that the child likes it and he or she might be able to discover interests and talents that may become meaningful for generation of income later in life. This was the case for the child who learned to tend goats and developed a great passion for animals.

This correlates with the idea expressed by adults and children assuming a child might learn a lot by tackling different activities. Another thought about learning through work is, in fact, more general. Through work, children learn about control of their environment. This may be very limited in harsh economic conditions but is also an important requirement. Control over use and management of money was frequently mentioned by both Peruvian and Portuguese informants.

Self-esteem and confidence are other key aspects described as important positive outcomes of work experience. Some young people describe a positive role of work in the construction of identity and particularly in terms of self-esteem and confidence. Not all children share this view but a number of them consider positive outcomes thus.

22. A further key question is about the relationship between work and school. The assumption of an automatic link between children's work and poor school performance or non-attendance has been criticised as simplistic and it has been suggested that attention should be paid to problems within the school system.[10] In Latin America where enrolment rates appear very satisfactory when compared to other continents, questions arise about, for instance, the outcome of years of education for most economically deprived children. They most frequently face failure and repetition and, paradoxically, school attendance does not necessarily make them literate and numerate as one would expect.[11]

The Portuguese portrait of education is also problematic. In fact, professional qualifications apparently remain a relatively difficult objective: one in two young adults (18–24 years) is an early school-leaver; that is, he or she did not complete secondary school or obtain professional qualifications and is not in training. The Portuguese situation is very far from the European Union level, where "only" one in five is an early school-leaver.[12] Furthermore, one Portuguese young adult in four did not complete nine years compulsory school.[13] Among the questions that need to be addressed in

---

10 See for instance J. BOYDEN, B. LING and W. MYERS, *What Works for Working Children*, (Stockholm: Rädda Barnen/UNICEF, 1998).

11 Ibid.

12 A. FRANCO and S. JOUHETTE, 'Labour Force Survey. Principal results 2001. EU and EFTA countries', (2002) N. 19 *Statistics in focus. Population and Social conditions.*

13 Ministerio da Educação, Cartografia do abandono e insuceso escolares, Lisboa, 2003, <www.min-edu.pt>.

both Peru and Portugal are access to school, efficiency of the school system, educational content and distance from children's own culture as well as distance from the working world.

In such relatively problematic educational contexts, one might better understand why even in a European country a small number of adults and young people say that full-time work is proper experience for the young person to learn and adequately prepare for his or her future. Such statements are not frequent and especially focus on young people with repeated failure in school or who have been delayed in studies for different reasons. Generally, adults in Portugal said that education is the main means of giving children a decent future and make genuine efforts to guarantee attendance and professional training. However, some of them similarly say, "*not all children have a head for school*" or "*not all children can achieve at school*". What children and adults observe in their communities is that if school, professional training or academic studies might bring better incomes and more stability for young people, work experience at a young age might guarantee that they avoid the worst form of poverty and marginality.

23. Work is however more generally positively valued as a part-time activity besides school. Contact with the working world appears to offer complementary knowledge and skills, allows contact with different occupations and young persons to learn about possible work they might like to do in the future. Noteworthy statements here are about what the child likes, his or her talents and inclinations. It might be tending goats or sheep, driving a tractor or selling in the market and it is good that the child shows interest and pleasure. A further suggestion made by informants in that respect, however, is that part-time work besides school may also provide alternative skills and aptitude if educational projects should fail or the economic situation become problematic. Flexible ideas about socialisation seem more sensible than predetermined and idealised paths in these contexts.

2.3. CHILDREN'S WORK AS PARTICIPATION: AUTONOMY AND SELF-DETERMINATION

24. Article 12 of the UNCRC is the usual reference for defining children's participation, stating that the child has the right to express his or her views freely and should be given opportunity to be heard in any proceeding affecting his or her life. Those views should be given due weight in accordance with the age and maturity of the child. There are good arguments for believing that a too narrow view of participation, however, is a good enough basis for the objective of this text. When only referring to Article 12 of the UNCRC, the matter of working children's participation actually appears to be extremely broad. It encompasses many different and contrasting definitions and objectives as well as arenas or contexts (from local to international) in which it takes place.

25. This text specifically focuses on children's individual decisions, which appear to give them increased self-determination or, at least, self-preservation. These are decisions taken in "natural" settings and thus have no connection with any adult specific and formal attempt to promote their rights.

Participation is a rather abstract concept and it is certainly not part of the informants' vocabulary in either Lima or the Algarve. When analysing ethnographic data, it is nonetheless possible to identify a significant number of decisions children take because they work. Young people decide to work or not to work, in what to work, take decisions about how to use income for leisure time, clothes and other purchases, and some of them decide how to manage and organise their work. There are more "controversial" decisions whereby young people sometimes decide to economically support the family instead of going to school or learn to work rather than go to school. In Peru some children were able to decide where to live, with whom and thus move out of the family home.

The three last decisions are "controversial" because they are generally seen as against the "child's best interest". It could be argued that they cannot be treated as "decisions" because they are parental decisions by children or because the child is "just reacting" to a bad situation instead of making a decision. In the Peruvian study[14] a principle was developed in the analysis that challenged that assumption. It was argued that each time:

1. a child decides something;
2. that goes against parental views of his or her best interest;
3. and/or there is conflict with the familial "best" organisation for economic survival;
4. but is nonetheless authorised or, at least, gains reluctant consent of an adult or parent; the overall event indicates that the child was somehow entitled to take that decision.

26. An example drawn from research in Lima is the child's decision to create his or her own business in the street instead of helping the mother at her sales pitch. Some children maintain a distinction between "help" and "work". "Help" is generally an unpaid task where the child conforms to the organisation and direction of an adult or another young person. "Work" in this context is an independent task whereby the

[14] A. INVERNIZZI, *La vie quotidienne des enfants travailleurs. Stratégies de survie et socialisation dans les rues de Lima,* (Paris : L'Harmattan, 2001).

child autonomously organises tasks and manages income. In some cases allowing the child to start an independent business is economically less viable than collective organisation within the mother's business. However, some mothers clearly accept the young person's independence, the reason simply being that he or she "wants it". That entitlement to independent activity appears to relate to cultural views of childhood, wherein economic independence of the child through his or her work is promoted at an early age.[15]

That situation proves that children take key decisions. However, the fact they conflict with adult views is not a main characteristic of children's decisions but more so a rather inflexible means of proving they are able to be independent and not under adult influence.

27. Proving children's ability to take independent decisions has actually long been a key feature of formalised experiences of participation. Fear of manipulation is probably what has provoked the idea that children and young people have to be put in decision-making situations without adult influence. It is actually a position that has been challenged, showing that participation is often a matter of shared decisions with adults[16] based on interdependent relationships rather than absolute independence of the child. From this perspective, one has to acknowledge that many children take important decisions with their parents and other adults and this equally has to be recognised as a form of participation.

28. On this basis another supposition may be understood in terms of participation. For example, we can consider the gist of a group discussion held in a Portuguese class where the majority of pupils had repeated experiences of failure and school desertion. The debate became slightly heated when we asked pupils to discuss the idea that work jeopardises education. One girl agreed with the idea: "*If we people want to get a good job, we need to know languages ... there is no future in construction*". A firm reply came from two boys: "*If farmers do not work, what shall those who speak English eat?*", "*What will doctors eat if we all go to university?*", "*Who will build their houses?*", and so on. The discussion then focused on professional opportunity in relation to professional training: being qualified does not mean having a job. Some young people expressed

---

15 In the Algarve, many parents in rural areas consider young people's employment is too frequently hazardous and involves high levels of economic exploitation. However they sometimes have to compromise, accepting the young person's stubborn decision to work. A few of them say they finished contacting the employer and checking working conditions, which means that they ultimately agreed with the child's decision.

16 See for instance P. ALDERSON, 'Understanding, Wisdom and Rights: Assessing Children's Competence', in D. K. BEHERA (ed.), *Children and Childhood in our Contemporary Societies*, (Dehli: Kamla- Raj Entreprises, 1998).

a view that if children do not want to study they must be allowed to work and even at younger ages. Indeed, some children leave school and some of them clearly in order to work.

One might argue that those young people do not have knowledge and competence required to properly examine employment opportunities related to access to professional training and the labour market. One might also suggest that they are perhaps simply reporting parents' views which were put forward to justify the fact that some of them have been withdrawn from school in order to work on the family farm. However, one might also consider some of the arguments employed earlier regarding young people's socialisation under very difficult circumstances. When struggling for family survival as well as keeping the family farm going, helping ill or disabled parents, faced with difficult access to school and professional training or experiencing repeated failure at school, some young people might consider spending as many as 12 or 13 years in compulsory education is not necessarily "in their best interest". This is especially likely, if later in their lives, they will be unable to afford professional training, to complete it or find a job in the profession they learned. Such situations are frequent enough in their communities to suggest that their position does not entirely lack rationale.

29. When accepting such decisions as legitimate examples of children's involvement in decision-making we must consider other arguments. Firstly, and even when considering one specific issue, one cannot identify any single "right" decision that might be applied to all working children. The majority of children seen in southern Portugal wanted to go to school and complete professional training. However, this does not invalidate the decision a few of them in a particularly difficult situation made. In other words, children's opinions need to be measured against their normal lives as well as their experience. Secondly, we also have to admit that the framework in which these decisions are normally examined is precisely the one that invalidates the significance of their actions and denies them the status of subjects. Generally, they would be understood as lacking of protection, parental abuse or even lacking of discipline when it comes to school attendance rules. However, even though many of the tasks they are involved in are forbidden in both Portuguese and Peruvian contexts, many decisions may not differ in their nature from others recognised as "genuine" participation.

2.4. CHILDREN'S WORK AND EXPLOITATION

30. Over the last 20 years, literature about exploitation of working children has moved from definitions encompassing economic exploitation and hazardous activities toward a multiplicity of factors including indirect exploitation, inequality, poverty and structural adjustment as well as a variety of concerns about the child's physical, psychological, social and moral development. Thus indicators of exploitation have, for instance, included characteristics such as physical and verbal abuse by parents and the child's emotional dependence on adult employers. Extension of the notion of exploitation is certainly important in order to take account of different contexts and children's working conditions. However, when applying criteria drawn from literature on working children's everyday experiences in Lima, one has to conclude that no single activity could be considered non-exploitative and that such criteria locate the responsibility for exploitation in parents or adult conduct. An explanation of that systematic condemnation of working children's everyday activities is found in the idealised western image of childhood, influencing how we understand child development. Practices not conforming to that image are often understood as undermining child development, thus as abuse or exploitation.[17]

31. This kind of conceptual vicious circle must be broken. Firstly, it is especially important because, in the most simplistic discourse on working children the general assumption is that any exploitative work requires elimination of work rather than elimination of exploitation. Secondly because, as described earlier, it does not recognise efforts that children and adults take on in order to protect children. Paradoxically, as seen above, one specific kind of work might precisely be a form of protection from what are seen as more hazardous, exploitative or neglected conditions. Thirdly, because as a result of expansion and confusion about definition, the very essential notion of exploitation has become so diluted that one might argue it has lost any potential for analysis of children's work. Indeed, situations of exploitation and abuse of working children should instead be analysed in detail and action taken in order to protect them in a similar way to how we attempt to protect adult workers. Working children's views might be exactly the vital starting point for identification of conditions and situations that exploit them. However, when research focuses on children's everyday routines, views as well as those of parents', exploitative aspects of their work are the most difficult to define.

32. In informants' terms in Lima, negative relationships at work are most often classified as "abuse". In the Algarve a few parents also used the term "oppression". Occasionally informants described cases of children's "bad" work and related them to a relationship wherein other social actors took advantage of the situation, but in many cases this kind of explanation was entirely absent. Rather than exploitation or abuse, thus, analysis borrowed the concept "overburden". This term describes not only

[17] A. Invernizzi, *Enfants travailleurs dans les rues de Lima: entre stratégies de survie et socialisation*, Unpublished PhD thesis, (Switzerland: Université de Fribourg, 1999).

an excessive amount of work but also specific situations involving some kind of physical or symbolic "overload". Overburdened children expressed, even sometimes confusedly, interests opposed to work carried out. In ethnographic data, that situation sometimes appeared the outcome of a very low standard of protection (for instance when children feel unable to achieve what is required by adults or express fears and insecurity in accomplishing work in the streets). Instead, overburdening sometimes had to be explained by the child's low level of independence (in completing work, deciding about conditions and use of income). In some cases, it related to lack of recognition which could be either or both symbolic and financial.

Thus, children's views of "bad" work include more diverse facets than what we usually consider "exploitation" or "abuse". Both in Peru and in Portugal, children sometimes left more protected work in order to become independent, test competence, and learn or gain autonomy. That is not necessarily about financial recognition but about, for instance, self-confidence. It is in this context that one needs to replace forms of emancipation where the child is entitled to have his or her own (less viable) business despite the family driven economic need. For young people whose ambition is to gain independence, "bad" work is one not allowing learning and exercising forms of self-determination, relating concurrently to the above dimensions of socialisation and participation.

In the Algarve, the most evident aspects of exploitation revealed by informants are economic and there was general agreement about the fact that young people are very often not paid as much as adult workers even when carrying out the same amount of work. In some cases, exploitation was a matter of not being paid at all at the end of a contract. Young people in this situation do not have formal support, as an adolescent repeatedly exploited said: "*because we are young, we cannot put them (the employers) in a tribunal*".

33. The second criteria generally mentioned by adults and mainly parents relates to hazard and the weight of certain activities and the fact that employers do not allow young people to rest when they need to. This is considered a main difference when compared to work performed within the family or for relatives and friends. Here, working conditions are assumed to retain some qualities of family life and the workload is adapted to the child's capabilities. Because it is seen as a form of "mutual help" rather than employment, family work is generally not paid and so is part of work for relatives and family friends.

Such situations are very challenging when trying to apply the notion of exploitation. Not only is the evaluation of the justness of the transaction difficult, it is also risk involved. A child might find a particular activity strenuous whereas another who is accustomed considers it acceptable. Similarly, street work in Lima may be dangerous for an inexperienced child whereby others have learned how to move in traffic. Furthermore, some dangers relate to the living environment rather than working conditions.

34. Even more challenging is setting limits of abuse that relate to aspects of socialisation. It has been argued that classical stances on children's work in terms of socialisation disregard economic exploitation.[18] Indeed, systems of economic exploitation often find justification in the notion of the young person learning and thus being less productive. However, to entirely accept that approach leads to dismissal of young people's activities and views that justly relate work to socialisation and learning processes.

35. For instance, Nicolai, a 16 year old living in the Algarve constantly helping on his family farm provided three criteria of work as exploitation. Beside saying that exploitation was about not being paid and not being paid as an adult he added that it was about not being trained properly, also including being made fun of by adults because of lack of skills.

In the view of young people like Nicolai, for instance, work is good when it is also a means of learning. What Nicolai learns, clearly, has to have a positive value and whereas other young people do not have high regard for farming, Nicolai does like this work and considers it could become a viable alternative if his education should fail or he should not be able to find a job later. Conversely, working conditions whereby the young person is intentionally left without training is precisely what he identifies as exploitation.[19]

Another interesting set of comments about abuse related to the fact that children's work does not have to be a form of punishment. Nicolai's parents said that, for instance, employment is generally exploitative for young people but also accepted that unpaid work in the family should provide him or her with some other form of recompense. Free time and leisure expenses are thus the balance for Nicolai's work. His mother pointed out: "*people cannot oppress their children... as they deserve it [they must have their freedom]*". Nicolai's father also said that his contribution had to be compensated with autonomy in part of the farm's management. In his mother's terms:

---

18 O. NIEUWENHUYS, 'The Paradox of Child Labor and Anthropology', (1996) 25 *Annual Review of Anthropology*, 237–251.

19 A group discussion gave information of a similar vein. Some adolescents condemned parents' habit of withdrawing girls from school to take care of siblings. They said that children and not parents should decide this. However, they suggested that the alternative choice was not to go back to school but to be allowed to work outside the family.

"*children shouldn't be punished with work*". She means that there has to be some kind of gratification for the young person's work but also points out the rule saying that the hardest and most unpleasant work must be carried out by adults. Interestingly, this is exactly what other young people in the Algarve described as abusive work, for instance where the share of labour was unjustifiably unequal and some children were constantly overloaded or when punishment did excuse the fact they were not paid what they had been promised.

36. What informants seem to show are informal rules about the way children's work needs to be organised around learning processes without denying recognition of that work and respect for the worker. Ridicule of the person who is learning, using punishment as a means by which adults avoid unpleasant tasks or distribute them in an unfair manner, or as justification for not giving the financial reward promised, are all denial of the value of the work as well as the worker's effort.

37. The fact that children's work includes aspects of socialisation may provide a positive self-image or greater self-determination but does not exclude, even in family contexts, aspects of abuse or oppression. Rather than applying abstract concepts of exploitation, the way adults and young people experience these different facets might provide more detailed criteria for promoting children's interests. It is, however, a task that is still pending.

3. WORKING CHILDREN'S RIGHTS

3.1. CHILDREN AS SUBJECTS: A CHILD RIGHTS APPROACH

38. The subdivision of children's lives according to different activities and objectives is an option generally adopted in order to make sense of our complex world and increase effectiveness of action to attempt to promote their rights. However, it also has dangerous implications. It might shatter their experiences, make some of the sense children and adults attach to their activities meaningless and thus deny the effort and rationale of their actions. Furthermore, that rationality is embedded in the place where they live and it must be accepted that they are influenced by not only socio-economic conditions but also by different cultures and particularly views on issues such as being a child, growing up, bringing up children or being and becoming a "good" member of their community.

39. Child focused studies faithfully provide a picture of working children's everyday lives that includes these diverse facets and provides a sense of their actions. It is an important task that recognises children as subjects. In this sense, the approach adopted here seems to conform to what has been identified as a "child-rights oriented discourse" on child labour. ENNEW, MYERS and PLATEAU define that discourse as a child centred approach that sees child labour as "*work that is detrimental for children involved*".[20] Scrutiny of work therefore needs to include analysis of situations and should, ideally, take into account views and experiences of children in order to assess "*conditions that impair children's growth and well-being and violate their rights*"[21] with reference to the UN Convention on the Rights of the Child.

40. However, the foregoing analysis reveals that this is not an easy task. Firstly, because if the child-rights approach suggests the importance of considering the indivisibility of rights in practices that promote the best interests of the child, national and international policies in fact appear to give priority to one or another right and secondly, because a child-rights approach is only one of a number of conflicting discourses on child labour adopted by policy-makers.

3.2. THE INDIVISIBILITY OF CHILDREN'S RIGHTS: WHICH RIGHT HAS THE PRIORITY?

41. A holistic approach on working children's lives inevitably suggests that several UNCRC articles are highly relevant for policy and practice. This also relates to the significance of the advantages children gain through work that has been emphasised by experts.[22] Some of them have been presented above around notions of learning and identity construction (socialisation), self-determination and autonomy (participation), survival and improvement of living conditions and protection from/exposure to hazards and exploitation. Clearly, an exclusive focus on exposure to exploitative and hazardous features of children's work somehow conflicts with the principle that children have to be seen as subjects. Children might intend to improve their living conditions and this might theoretically be linked to other articles of the UNCRC. However, when prioritising Article 32 and exclusively aiming for reduction of harm, risks or economic exploitation, whatever children do will be automatically seen as

---

20 J. ENNEW, W. MYERS and D. PLATEAU, '*The Meaning, Nature and Scope of Child Labor*', Draft for the Colloquium on Combating Abusive Child Labor, Iowa, July 2003, 5.

21 Ibid.

22 See for instance IWGL, supra (note 2); M.F.C. BOURDILLON, 'Child Labour and Education: A Case Study from South-Eastern Zimbabwe', (2000) 15 *Journal of Social Development in Africa*, 5–32,; M. WOODHEAD, *Children's Perspectives on their Working Lives: A Participatory Study in Bangladesh, Ethiopia, The Philippines, Guatemala, El Salvador and Nicaragua*, (Stockholm: Rädda Barnen, 1998).

"wrong". As BOURDILLON states,[23] the issue of the priority given to any Article of the UNCRC is central in the reflection on child labour.

42. Besides focus on the best interest of the child (Art. 3) protection of children against work that is harmful, exploitative or detrimental for the child's development (Art. 32) and inclusion of children in decision-making processes (Art. 12), there is the need to pay proper attention to other issues. Even in a European context, more focus deserves to be placed on examination of the impact of poverty and standards of living on child development (Art. 6) as well as complex relationships between, school, work and professional training (Arts. 28 and 29). Certainly more articles should be included in this list but, in a particular way, identification of exact rights should belong to communities. Maybe, in conclusion, it is exactly the value of specific child-rearing practices and socialisation in difficult economic and social conditions that has to be acknowledged. Reference to Article 5 of the UNCRC (i.e. the respect for the responsibilities, rights and duties of parents, relatives and communities who provide direction and guidance in the exercise of the child's rights) should be made. This might appear controversial but also essential to promote actions in partnership with children, parents and communities.

3.3. CONFLICTING DISCOURSES ON CHILD LABOUR: WHICH CONFORMS TO THE UNCRC SPIRIT?

43. A further dilemma in thinking about policies and practices promoting working children's rights is located in the multiple and conflicting discourses on child labour that underpin them. Besides a "child-rights" discourse, ENNEW, MYERS and PLATEAU[24] identify three other discourses. First, child labour is simply considered children's involvement in the labour market that takes the form of exploitation. This is the oldest "*labour market discourse*", which defines child labour "*primarily as the participation of children in what 'should be' exclusively adult labour markets*". It thus seeks elimination of child labour "*by enlisting the power of the State through child labour legislation such as minimum age laws, through workplace inspection by government agents, through prosecution of law violations and through providing compulsory public education*". ILO Convention 138 sets a minimum age for employment, and is thus based on this approach. A second, more recent discourse called "*human capital discourse*" conceptualises child labour as "*a result of underdevelopment*" and understands it as "*activities and working conditions that undermine the development of health, knowledge and skills, which*

---

[23] M.F.C. BOURDILLON, 'Translating Standards into Practice: Confronting local barriers', in B.H. WESTON (ed.), *Child Labour and Human Rights*, (Boulder – London: Lynne Rienner, 2005), 143.

[24] J.ENNEW, W. MYERS and D. PLATEAU, supra (note 20).

children require to contribute later as adults to national economic development and their own prosperity". Children are primarily seen as human potential and great importance is lent to formal education. This discourse is held by international organisations involved with development issues as well as in many education systems. A third notion, embedded in "*social responsibility discourse*", sees child labour as "*a problem of 'social exclusion' leading to work that exploits, alienates and oppresses children and separates them from society's normal protections and opportunities [...]*". Exploitation results in isolation and what is therefore required is mobilisation and inclusion rather than prohibition of work. This discourse has been assumed by non-governmental organisations, particularly in developing countries. Working children's organisations which defend the right of children to work and be protected against exploitation and abuse have adopted this kind of discourse.[25]

44. The first and second discourse seem, for instance, to dominate public discourse by government and the media in Portugal and explain the fact that any work under the age of 16 is forbidden despite the different functions it fulfils for young people. However, one could argue that these two discourses have important limitations. On the one hand, age-related legislation might precisely be seen as a denial of children's status as subjects. On the other hand, human capital discourse tends to focus on economic development of the nation and equates it with positive development of the child as well as with his or her prosperity as an adult. That equation seems rather simplistic as many other factors related to poverty such as inequality, oppression and discrimination are entirely overlooked. Economic development of a nation might not go hand in hand with economic prosperity of some sectors of the population.

45. Although it might be suggested that the spirit of the UNCRC promotes a holistic approach with children as the subjects of rights, it also refers (Art. 32) to international standards that adopt an entirely different approach to child labour. One has, therefore, to conclude that conflicting discourses on child labour present a real dilemma when approaching working children's rights.

4. CONCLUSION

46. When researching working children's experiences, work appears to present a set of advantages and disadvantages specific to their living environments that they evaluate differently. Bad work, for children and parents, is often the outcome of this balance of advantages and disadvantages rather than simply exploitative or the hazardous

[25] M. Liebel, *A will of their own. Cross-cultural Perspectives on Working Children*, (London: Zed, 2004).

features of a specific activity. A simple focus on Article 32 of the UNCRC therefore generates a very partial and fragmented picture of their experience.

47. It is a problem precisely addressed by LIEBEL who suggests that working children's organisations' primary goal is the defence of the subject against that fragmentation of their lives.[26] What is suggested in this text is that research aimed at promoting children's rights should also aim at focusing on defending children as subjects. Many of the young people who participated in either research did not help the family at any point in time, look for money with another and learn or play with others. They somehow combine some of these as too do the adults around them. Fragmentation of their lives denies consistency of their actions. However, it is not just a holistic approach that needs to be adopted but also healthy scepticism toward any implicit and supposedly naturally justified prioritisation of specific rights over others. However, a more important dilemma facing the promotion of working children's rights is that the child-rights approach is only one among other discourses on child labour. Other discourses appear to fail to address the best interest of the child from a holistic perspective and consider children as subjects. Research findings show that there is considerable potential for partnership with them to generate policies and practices that decrease abuse and exploitation whilst promoting their other rights and well-being in general.

---

[26] M. LIEBEL, supra (note 25).

CURRENT CHALLENGES IN ANALYSING CHILD LABOUR IN ROMANIA

MARIA-CARMEN PANTEA[1]

1. INTRODUCTION

1. While it is estimated that 90% of child labour is to be found in Africa and Asia,[2] there is still a limited consideration given to the escalading phenomenon of child labour in Eastern Europe. Most of the time when child labour issues are addressed, the high incidence of child labour in South Asia and Africa is a legitimate matter for concern. While acknowledging the especially critical situation of child labour in the above regions, the present paper is an attempt to explore the phenomenon of child labour in the Eastern European context, particularly in Romania.

Moreover, child labour in Romania is far from resembling the industrial forms more often associated with Victorian England or today's textile industry of South Asia. Unlike the regions of South Asia, there are no industrial units based mostly on the use of child labour. Mainly, child labour refers to children who are combining a (limited) school attendance with work in small family farms. For the majority of the population, it is not school attendance, but school performance that is affected by work.

2. The very concept of child labour tends to be associated with industrial settings due to either historical approach in developed countries, or to a more recent corporatist need for a cheap labour force in less developed ones. However, while dominated by the concept of employment, many classifications of children's work may risk overlooking the various situations children work in. The present paper offers information on child labour in Eastern European countries, with a special focus on Romania. It does not cover issues of child trafficking.

---

1 Supported by the open society institute – with the contribution of the international policy fellowship of Osi-Budapest.

2 F. SIDDIQI and H. PATRINOS, *Child Labour: Issues, Causes and Interventions*, Human Resources and Operations, Policy Working Paper 56, (Washington DC: World Bank, 1995).

3. Statistically, one of the specificities of child labour in Eastern Europe is represented by children working in non-industrial settings, mostly in households and agriculture. This paper especially explores the work performed by children, work that does not fully meet the criteria to be considered child labour, but still, is jeopardising their education. As both "childhood" and "labour" are socially constructed, being defined differently by different societies at different times, for the purpose of this paper, there will be relied on ILO and UNICEF categories: *light work*, *child labour* and *worst forms of child labour*. The concern is to explore what the existing conceptual tools and legislative standards can tell about the situation of children performing the border between housework and child labour in the particular context of transitional economies based on family farms.

4. The main questions to be addressed are: Which are the main legislative and institutional limitations that prevent the recognition and elimination of child labour in today Romania? Is child labour an ethnic issue, a cultural practice of the Roma minority not to be addressed, or rather a severe social problem? What can be said about the relation between poverty, education and child labour in Romania? More broadly, what can the situation of working children from Romania tell about the Romanian society as a whole, about its values and priorities? As the research is at the beginning, the following paper has a descriptive character and is based on empirical evidence extracted from recent studies, on limited statistical data available and on the analysis of international and Romanian legal documents.

2. INTERNATIONAL REGULATIONS ON CHILDREN'S WORK

5. The international regulations apply to economic activities (work) only. There are mainly three important international legislative documents regulating children's work, namely: ILO Convention No. 138 from 1973 (which states the minimum age for legal employment and work), ILO Convention No. 182 from 1999 (which refers to the worst forms of child labour) and the UN Convention on the Rights of the Child (UN CRC). Unlike ILO Conventions, the UN CRC does not settle specific age limits, but recognises the right of the child "to be protected from economic exploitation and from performing any work that is likely to be hazardous or to interfere with the child's education, or to be harmful to the child's health or physical, mental, spiritual, moral or social development".[3]

[3] Art. 32, CRC.

6. UNICEF generated a tendency to consider child labour issues in the terms established by ILO Convention No.138. According to the UN CRC, a child is "every human being below the age of eighteen years unless under the law applicable to the child, majority is attained earlier".[4] UNICEF operates distinctions among three important categories, namely: "*children's work*" (light work), "*child labour*" and "*worst forms of child labour*".

The first category is "*child work*", which is considered "children's participation in economic activity - that does not negatively affect their health and development or interfere with education, and which can be positive".[5] Work that does not interfere with education (light work) is permitted from the age of 13 years under ILO Convention No. 138. This category acknowledges that not all work is detrimental to children, and that, to a certain extent, work can be regarded as a right not to be denied to children.

The second category used by UNICEF is "*child labour*", which is more narrowly defined and refers to "children working in contravention of the above standards, which means all children below 12 years of age working in any economic activities, those aged 12 to 14 years engaged in harmful work, and all children engaged in the worst forms of child labour".[6]

The third category is "*worst forms of child labour*", which refers to children being enslaved, forcibly recruited, prostituted, trafficked, forced into illegal activities and exposed to hazardous work. Some institutions[7] make a distinction inside this third category, between "*hazardous work*" (i.e. any activity or occupation which, by its nature or type has, or leads to, adverse effects on the child's safety, health and moral development) and "*unconditional worst forms of child labour*" (i.e. forms of slavery, trafficking, debt bondage, serfdom and forced or compulsory labour, including recruitment of children for use in armed conflict, in prostitution, pornography and for illicit activities)

4 Art. 1 CRC.

5 UNICEF, *Cf.* Convention No. 138 of the International Labour Organisation concerning Minimum Age for Admission to Employment, adopted on 26 June 1973 and which entered into force on 19 June 1976.

6 ILO Convention No. 138 refers to the ages of 13 and 15. However, Article 2(4) Convention No. 138, state that under specific conditions, a State Party may substitute the ages of 12 and 14 for the ages of 13 and 15 with reference to the age of employment or work.

7 See, for example IPEC and the Statistical Information and Monitoring Programme on Child Labour.

3. ROMANIAN LEGISLATION ON CHILD LABOUR

7. Romania ratified the UN Convention on the Rights of the Child (1989) in 1990, ILO Convention No. 182 on the Worst Forms of Child Labour (1999) in 2000 and ILO Minimum Age Convention (1973) in 1975. In spite of the fact that Romania was among the first countries to ratify the UN Convention on the Rights of the Child, until 2004, when the new child rights legislation[8] was adopted, the existing laws were focused on children's protective rights only, while overlooking the participation rights. Until 2004, for example, children did not have the right to advance an official complaint by themselves.

8. Officially, child labour is illegal in Romania. The Romanian Constitution and the Labour Code, the main legislative documents with regard to children's work, are not in total agreement with regard to the minimum age for employment. On the one hand, according to the Constitution, the general and minimum age of admission to employment is 15. On the other hand, the Labour Code provides that the general age of admission to work and employment is 16. Under specific situations, the Labour Code permits children to work with parental agreement at age 15, although only "according to their physical development, aptitude, and knowledge".[9]

However, it is important to note that during communism, the minimum age for employment was 16. Moreover, there is no minimum age for admission to unpaid employment, which usually takes place in rural areas and within the family. Even if ILO Convention No. 138 (which Romania has ratified) refers to all forms of employment or work (with or without payment and contract of employment), the Romanian Labour Code excluded the category of unpaid work.[10]

The ILO Convention provides the commitment of ratifying States to increase the minimum age for admission to employment and work, which "shall not be less than the age of completion of compulsory schooling and, in any case, shall not be less than 15 years".[11] In Romania, the age at which compulsory education ends is 16, but the Constitution and (under specific circumstances) the Labour Code, permit the employment of children at age 15. Still, the Constitution (Art. 20) stipulates that in the case of inconsistencies between the covenants and treaties on fundamental human rights Romania ratified, and internal law, the international regulations shall have

---

8 Law 272/2004.

9 Art. 7, Labour Code, Romanian Parliament, 2003.

10 According to the International Confederation of Free Trade Unions [2005], in 2004 the ILO Committee of Experts on the Application of Conventions and Recommendations criticised the exclusion of such work from the Romanian Labour Code.

11 Art. 2, para. 3, ILO Convention No. 138.

priority. Under these circumstances, there is a need to reconsider the internal laws referring to the minimum age of employment.[12]

9. The International Programme on the Elimination of Child Labour (IPEC) has been active in Romania since March 2000. Child labourers were recognised as a specific category for the first time in Romanian legislation in 2001. The majority of governmental programmes on the elimination of child labour and the subsequent documents, were initiated following Romania's legal obligations after ratifying the international conventions. As the elimination of child labour is an EU priority with regard to child protection, new institutions and new links among the existing ones were established in order to develop national programmes for the elimination of child labour.

10. However, for the moment, one cannot speak about a consistent national dialogue on child labour among the State institutions responsible (Ministry of Work, Social Solidarity and Family and its territorial offices). Most of the national reports have a limited distribution inside the country. Many others are edited in English, which has the advantage of launching the issue of child labour into a potentially international debate, but also the disadvantage of a limited in-country circulation. For the moment, this research cannot include any reliable evidence on the efficiency of the National Programmes. Still, if relying on international evaluations, reviews are controversial.

11. On the one hand, according to the ILO-IPEC Coordinator for Europe and the Middle East,[13] Romania's progress "*was the basis for the country's nomination as the focal point for all ILO-IPEC programs carried out in Eastern Europe during 2004–2007*". On the other hand, in November 2005, the International Confederation of Free Trade Unions[14] considered that "*enforcement of child labour legislation tends to be lax except for extreme cases*". According to the U.S. Department of State, "*the roles and responsibilities of the agencies that enforce child labour laws remain ill defined, and these laws are often only enforced when a particularly grave case becomes public*". Moreover, despite the high rates of child labour, in 2004 there were no reports of anyone being charged or convicted under any of the child labour laws (according to the Romanian Labour Inspection and to the International Confederation of Free Trade Unions, 2005).

---

12 M. Dutu, *Study on the current Romanian legislation regarding child labour and international regulations*, (Bucharest: ILO, Ministry of Work and Social Solidarity, IPEC, 2002).

13 Romanian Ministry of Labour, Social Solidarity and Family, The Press Office, 'Enforcing of the International Programme for Combating Child Labour in Romania [...]', 18 February 2004, <www.mmssbf.ro>.

14 International Confederation of Free Trade Unions (ICFTU), '*Internationally-Recognised Core Labour Standards in Romania*', Report for the WTO General Council Review of the Trade Policies of Romania, Geneva, 28 and 30 November 2005.

4. ROMANIA – GENERAL CONTEXT AND THE INCIDENCE OF CHILD LABOUR

12. Romania has a total population of 21.7 million,[15] with children accounting for 17.29% of the total population and 65% of the children live in urban areas.[16] The average number of family members was 2.9 in 2002, while families with three or more children accounted for only 13%.[17] Due mainly to a slow economic development, a late start of the reform, as compared to other former communist countries, Romania accumulated delays. The amazing growth of the informal sector (the gross added economic value of the informal sector represented 28.0% of the GDP in 2000)[18] is due to legislative inefficiency, high levels of corruption and massive lay-offs from State-owned companies. Young people aged 15 to 24 represent over 40% of the total unemployed.

13. According to a 2003 census, 47% of the Romanian population lives in rural areas, often with very limited opportunities for education, legal employment and transportation. The higher poverty rate is among Roma ethnic groups that account for 2.5% of the whole population.[19] The groups most vulnerable to poverty are the Roma minority, children, young people, families with more than 3 children and single-parent families. According to the governmental sources,[20] 80% of the children from the Roma population live in poverty, out of which 43.3% live in severe poverty. Eighty-eight per cent of the Roma in Romania, as compared to 84% in Bulgaria and 91% in Hungary, live below the national poverty line.[21]

14. As stated in an ILO/IPEC country Report,[22] increase of the poverty in Romania is "*not only the result of economic polarisation, but also the consequence of deficient state financial support and limited access to services*". The monthly child allowance (conditional on school attendance) is approximately 7 Euros, representing 7.5% of the minimum salary in 2006. Still, in May 2006 a law, which conditioned the child

---

15 Census of Households in 2002.

16 ILO, IPEC, PROTECTCEE, Romania, Country Situation at <www.ilo.org/public/english/standards/ipec/protectcee/countryprofiles.htm>.

17 Ibid., 1.

18 The data on labour force for Romania comes from the Research on Labour Force in Households (AMIGO) 2004, ILO, IPEC, PROTECT CEE, Romania, Country Situation, 2004 at <www.ilo.org/public/english/standards/ipec/protectcee/countryprofiles.htm>.

19 Ibid., 1. However, accurate data referring to the Roma minority is hard to be obtained.

20 CASPIS (National Anti-Poverty and Social Inclusion Commission) cited by ILO/IPEC.

21 UNICEF, *The State of the Worlds Children 2006. Excluded and Invisible*, UNICEF, New York, 2006.

22 International Programme on the Elimination of Child Labour, ILO, PROTECT CEE, Romania Country Situation at <www.ilo.org/public/english/standards/ipec/protectcee/countryprofiles.htm>.

allowance on school attendance was declared unconstitutional and another law is expected to follow.

15. According to the survey of the National Institute of Statistics, over 90% of the economically active children (EAC) live in rural areas. Sixty per cent of them live in the South, South-West and Northeast of the country. As almost half of Romanian cities are medium and small size, with a population maintaining close contacts with agriculture,[23] both children from urban and rural areas are engaged in agricultural activities: over 90% of children from rural areas and about 40% of children from urban areas. More than two-thirds of the children working in industry and construction live in rural areas.

16. However, far from being an apolitical issue, in Romania and in many other East European countries, child labour is rarely addressed. Often political agendas are attached to the topic and its existence is often underestimated, concealed or manipulated. In spite of a relative lack of official concern, child labour is an emerging phenomenon in Eastern Europe today and particularly, in Romania.

17. Currently, apart from a small number of pilot qualitative studies on child labour,[24] there is controversial monitoring of the phenomenon. Statistical data to document the phenomenon of child labour and children's work in Romania is difficult to obtain due also to the fact that the largest proportion of children work in family farms. Moreover, as children's work in agriculture does not have the same intensity all year long, the statistics relating only to a "reference week" might generate distorted data. Apart for the individual estimates of GHINARARU based on economic indicators,[25] there is only the survey of the National Institute of Statistics,[26] the categories of which can offer only a limited base for international comparison.

18. In the following this paper will present briefly the main data provided by the two studies mentioned above. Both agree upon the fact that the greatest majority of children (89%) work in agriculture related activities and only a small category is working in industrial settings such as constructions, in retail and other services. However, the incidence of child labour is significantly different in the two studies.

---

23 C. GHINARARU, *Child Labour in Romania*, (Bucharest: Ro Media Publishing House, 2004).

24 See S. CACE et all, *Copiii rromi care muncesc. Studiu de caz in localitatea Calvini, Județul Buzău*, 2001, available at <www.iccv.ro/romana/revista> and E. STATIVA, *Baseline Survey on rural child labour in five selected counties in Romania*, (Bucharest: ILO, Romanian Government, 2001).

25 C. GHINARARU, supra (note 23).

26 National Institute of Statistics, *Ancheta asupra activitatii copiilor*, Raport National, (Bucharest: ILO and INS, 2003).

On the one hand, the individual estimates of GHINARARU, issued with the support of the ILO and the Romanian Government,[27] show that out of Romania's 5 million children, 900,000 are involved in "economic activities". More than 60% of the 900,000 are performing activities in rural households other than their own. Approximately 300,000 children are working with a certain frequency in exchange for payment and most of the time without legal form. The above-mentioned statistics exclude the services provided by children in their own households. The report considers this last category as being "child labourers", according to international regulations. Moreover, 60,000 to 70,000 children are involved in the worst forms of labour. They are the children who are begging, stealing, are victims of human trafficking or are involved in prostitution and drug dealing. The survey makes known the (even if isolated) cases of bonded child labour in Romania.

On the other hand, according to the survey of the National institute of Statistics, there are 40,620 child labourers according to parents' declarations and 70,690 according to children's declarations. The number of economically active children is, according to the same sources 82,884 (based on parents' declarations) and 141,905 (based on children's declarations). No specific reference to the category of "worst forms of child labour" is made, although the study includes children who, according to the ILO standards, do enter this category.

One possible explanation for the difference between the two studies may comes from the difficulty of setting the boundary between "economic activity" and "household activity". This is particularly difficult in the context of a subsistence type of agriculture based on family farms, like the Romanian one. The next section will explore the problematic categorisation of children performing the border between domestic work and child labour.

5. WORK AS "ECONOMIC ACTIVITY" OR "IS CHILDREN'S HOUSEWORK, WORK?"

19. The International Programme on the Elimination of Child Labour (IPEC) defines work in terms of "economic activity". According to the IPEC,[28] "*Economic activity covers all market production (paid work) and certain types of non-market production*

[27] The statistical survey '*Children's Work in Romania*' was made by the Romanian Ministry of Work, Social Solidarity and Family, the US Department of Labour and by UNICEF Romania in 2004.

[28] ILO, IPEC and SIMPOC, *Every Child Counts. New Global Estimates on Child Labour*, ILO, Geneva, 2002.

(unpaid work), including production of goods for own use".[29] The area of work, according to this definition, is not restricted to paid and formal activities. It can also include unpaid activities carried out in the informal sector. The IPEC considers as working, "*the children engaged in unpaid activities in a market-oriented establishment operated by a relative living in the same household*", but also "*children working as maids or domestic workers in someone else's household*".[30]

However, it is important to highlight a distinction, which will become highly relevant when considering the particularities of child labour in Eastern European countries, particularly in Romania: according to the above-mentioned definition, "children engaged in domestic chores within their own households are not considered as economically active".[31] Programmes designed towards the elimination of child labour do not target this category. It is inside this last group of economically active children, where one may find the distinction between "*light work*", "*child labour*" and "*worst forms of child labour*".

While considering the fact that Romania has mainly subsistence-type agriculture, based on family farms, the classification of services performed in one's own household as "non-economic" may be problematic. Most Romanian working children live in rural areas and work without payment (or are paid in kind) in agriculture or agriculture-related activities. They come from large and poor families and from the poorest regions of the country. Due to a short industrial tradition in Romania, a great part of the urban population maintains close connections to the countryside. For this reason, urban children, also, are declared to be working in agriculture.[32]

20. The distinction between "housework" and "economic activity" is based on the underlying assumption that children's involvement in home-based activities is less severe and displays a lower level of risk. On the one hand, this assumption might seem reasonable. Children were always involved in different types of work around the household. Moreover, it is generally admitted that far from being detrimental, such activities might have positive effects on children's long-term development. The same work, if performed for other households than their own, might expose children to a higher level of abuse.

However, one may also acknowledge that often, children are involved in home activities that might hinder their development. These activities might be time and

[29] Ibid., 29.
[30] Ibid., 29.
[31] For statistical reasons, IPEC considers one hour of work during the reference week as sufficient for considering a person as economically active during that week.
[32] C. GHINARARU, supra (note 23).

energy consuming. They might also interfere with school performance, if not, even with school attendance. As everywhere in the world, girls' domestic work, less socially visible, tends not to be recognised as such. Even if for Eastern Europe and particularly, Romania, there are no reliable data on children's involvement in "domestic activities" in their own household, the existing research[33] displays a high number of children involved in so-called "non-economic activities" that do affect their school performance.

21. Once again, it is very difficult to set the boundary between detrimental and non-detrimental housework. Still, we argue that when considering the specific case of transitional economies, like the one of Romania, certain divisions operated inside the comprehensive category of "non-economic activity" might be regarded as appropriate. In the situation in which often, children's work in their own household is not considered economic activity and the law respects the right to privacy, it becomes practically impossible to impose legal limitations on children's domestic activities. However, certain possibilities for controlling these abuses inside households should be made operational.

6. "CHILDREN'S WORK" VS. "CHILD LABOUR" DURING COMMUNISM

22. The history of recognising child labour as a social problem is very recent in Romania. Before communism, work in the household and agriculture was considered a moral obligation of children and successful stories recall the hard balance between school assignments and other work obligations. During communism, new perspectives towards work were meant to promote the image of physical work as not less valuable than the intellectual one. The "brotherhood between the workers, peasants and intellectuals" (not by chance in this order), demanded schools to contribute to the seasonal agricultural work. According to GHINARARU, the involvement of children and students in agricultural work came out more as a practical need in order to counteract a shortage of the workforce in rural areas after forced industrialisation.

Organised sometimes in micro-cooperatives (following the collectivist model), children from the age of 11 (and sometimes, in rural areas, the primary school pupils), worked on a field for at least two weeks annually. However, in rural areas mostly, this period was usually extended. Most of the time, children did not receive the unsurprisingly, extremely small pay themselves.[34] As schools had to fulfil a certain "economic

[33] Ibid.

[34] Ibid.

plan" annually, out of children's monetary contributions, and due to the scarcity of cash in the countryside, the schools retained the amount to be delivered as "economic planning". The official discourse constructed children as valuable economic agents, capable of combining work with education. The formative value of work was a strong argument for an increased involvement of children in agriculture and later on in industrial training.

Children's attitudes towards agricultural work were controversial. Enjoyed as a short-term alternative to the formal demands of schooling, work in agriculture was also tiresome and unrewarding. Accompanied by teachers, children received precise work assignments that were to be fulfilled manually. The use of basic mechanical tools was most of the time restricted due to the high number of children and in order to avoid the risk of accidents. Children worked in the field for at least 8 hours daily. Often secure transportation means were not provided. For high school pupils, working camps were arranged in order to make the work more efficient.

23. While work was considered in Marxist terms a source of fulfilment and satisfaction, there was still a highly politicised discourse on "child labour" as pertaining to third world countries and even to the highly industrial capitalist societies. The implied meaning was that societies that are not built on communist principles risk having a large category of persons excluded from the welfare system. On the contrary, what a communist system like the Romanian one proposed, was an egalitarian society in which work came out as a need for prosperity and not for mere survival. Under these circumstances, it became a legitimate social expectation for the children also to contribute to the common welfare. Their work was idealised in an attempt to defy a capitalist social order, presented in terms of social polarisation and child labour in the most excluded communities. It is not by chance that the focus was on the worst forms of child labour (associated with chronic poverty and homelessness) and not on the forms of labour exploitation that could have been easily associated with the situation of children from Romania.

24. During communism, large State orphanages were established in order to cope with a high number of children left without parental care. The phenomenon, concealed from public scrutiny until the 1990s, became a highly debated issue soon after. Besides the large category of children from the former State institutions, the new phenomenon of street children became and remained a matter of concern. Since the 1990s, different debates were issued, from their victimisation to criminalisation. However, what is particularly relevant for this particular paper, is the relation of street children with labour, which is going to be explored below.

7. 'CHILD LABOURERS' AND/ OR 'STREET CHILDREN'?

25. In various East European countries, often when issues of child labour are approached, the problem of street children comes into the open. In Romania, like in other accessing countries, the problem of street children is highly politicised as one required condition for EU integration. Under these circumstances, there is a strong political and social concern for the situation of street children. Where is the category of "street children" situated in the debate on "child labour" and what are the potential consequences of one classification or another?

There is a large international debate on the definition of street children. The very appellation came under severe criticism.[35] The concept "street children" is accused of being problematic as it overlooks the different actual circumstances children live in. Who is a "street child"? Does a child who spends his/her nights together with the family and works on the streets during the day, enter this category? Where can one draw the line between street children and child workers as long as many children work and live on the streets?

26. In Romania, street children are officially considered the major group of children involved in the worst forms of child labour.[36] There are four distinctions made inside the heterogeneous category of street children. Recent Romanian policies[37] distinguish between: a) street children (those who live on streets permanently and do not maintain any relation with their family); b) children in the street (those who are coincidentally in the street and who maintain occasional relations with the family); c) children on the street (those being permanently on the street, sent by family to earn money through different work, begging and stealing); d) families with children in the street.

However, even if stated, the above-mentioned distinctions are rarely applied. Instead, the more generic appellation "street children" is given place. What we find problematic is that even if many street children work, the connection between their category and child labour is rarely made. Most of the time when addressed, the issue of "street children" is associated with the lack of parental and State support, vagrancy, the use of hallucinogenic substances and delinquency. It generates mainly concerned attitudes that do not address the practical needs of children in these situations.

---

35 C. PANTER-BRICK, 'Street Children, Human Rights, and Public Health: A Critique and Future Directions', (2003) 13 *Children, Youth and Environments,* 147–171.

36 C. GHINARARU, supra (note 23).

37 Proiect Strategie Naþionalã n domeniul protecþiei ºi promovãrii drepturilor copilului 2006–2010 [Project of National Strategy in the field of children's rights' protection and promotion 2006–2010].

27. Street children occupy a very small fraction of the child labour phenomenon as a whole. The exact number of street children from Romania is very hard to establish, but most estimates are around 2000, which represent less than 1% of the total population of children. As an extremely visible category, street children can be seen begging, washing cars, selling goods, collecting waste products, loading and unloading products in local markets, stealing and practising prostitution. According to GHINARARU, "*they are the only economically active children who can be considered [...] as engaging in the worst forms of child labour*".

Consequently, one could easily comment on the disproportionate interest in this category. This is by no means to say that street children are not a severe social problem that needs to be addressed immediately. What we do consider problematic is that the issue of "street children" might risk taking over the whole problem of child poverty and social exclusion. Programmes designed to meet the needs of "street children" rarely address the situation of those living in poverty or in other situations that might lead to different ways of living on the streets.

Under the pressure to fulfil EU integration requirements, there is only a limited concern for the less visible issue of child labour, child poverty, school dropouts and social exclusion. The large majority of children live and work in remote villages or in the privacy of their households, less evident to public scrutiny. However, there is almost silence on the less visible forms of children's work. Even official documents[38] gradually move the focus from child labour towards its worst forms. The major risk is to overlook a large category of child labourers and economically active children.

28. The fact that the great majority of street children are Roma[39] and that most of the Roma children are working, might generate the idea that street children and child labour are an ethnic problem. However, the statistical demonstration of GHINERARU[40] shows that the higher incidence of child labour is not to be found in the regions with a higher proportion of Roma. Consequently, we argue that there is a great risk of misunderstanding severe social problems like child labour and street children as "ethnic" ones.

As the next section tries to demonstrate, there are deep structural dysfunctions of the economy characterised by minimum consumption and household production for subsistence, which in turn generate poverty. In such a larger context, child labour

38 See for example, the National Plan of Action for the Elimination of Child Labour 2006–2010.

39 IPEC, *Roma Working Children and their Families Socio-Cultural Characteristics and Living Conditions*, (Bucharest: Ro Media Publishing House, 2002).

40 C. GHINARARU, supra (note 23).

appears as a family need and economic demand. Due to its economic and social exclusion, the Roma population has the highest risk of being in situations that involve child labour. It is definitely not because this particular ethnic group has a cultural propensity towards child labour.

8. POVERTY AND CHILD LABOUR IN ROMANIA

29. Poverty is considered most of the time the cause of child labour. Statistically, the highest incidence of child labour is to be found in less developed countries. However, for the case of East European Countries, economic research has demonstrated that the link between poverty and child labour is more complex than it might seem at first sight.[41] Even if the high rates of poverty in Romania today might be easily employed as good reasons for the phenomenon of child labour, the link between poverty and child labour cannot be established without great caution.

The fact that there is no significant variance in the extent of child labour in country regions with different poverty rates, is a proof that there could be other factors than poverty as such, that might have a higher influence. The following arguments are taken from a recent and reliable economic study conducted by GHINARARU. This paper will present some of its findings, as they are highly relevant for the particular economic situation of transitional Romania.

To start with, the above-mentioned study demonstrates that poverty is only an aspect and not a direct cause of child labour. In reality, "at the origin of child labour and child economic activity lie distorted economic realities, which usually prevent nations and, therefore individuals, to achieve their full potential".[42] More precisely, according to the author, it is not poverty *per se* which causes child labour, but a specific type of economic organisation that can accommodate child labourers, characterised by low productivity, lack of economic openness and a high level of informal economic activities.

In particular, children's entry into work is encouraged in economic systems that have the household as production units rather than as consumption units. Under these circumstances, households are producing for their own use, with the contribution of

---

41 Also for developing countries, the relation between poverty and child labour is not always linear. Different cultural practices and caste systems (India) that generate child labour are, in fact, maintained because of the poverty. For a detailed discussion of the role of poverty in shaping cultural patterns that favour child labour, see M. WEINER and M. MURSHED, 'Unraveling Child Labor and Labor Legislation', (2001) *Journal of International Affairs.*

42 C. GHINARARU, supra (note 23).

(frequently) all its members who become "part of the Non-Observed Economy".[43] Post communist Romania fits perfectly into such a pattern. Unlike other post communist countries, in Romania, the economic growth was not sustained by consistent reforms. Consequently, the demand for cheap, irregular labour, as the one provided by children could not be easily discouraged. GHINARARU concludes that linear progress in transition is the main factor that influences the phenomenon of child labour, for the case of transitional economies.

The land retrocession after 1989 led to the re-establishment of private farms. Due to a scarcity of resources and investment in agriculture, in certain regions, people rely mainly on physical work. Under these circumstances, children became involved in the agricultural activities of their own family. A great part of such a contribution still is legally considered "domestic work" and consequently a "non-economic activity". Children's work in rural households becomes a social expectation, a matter of family solidarity.

30. As stated above, the link between poverty of the region and the incidence of child labour is problematic, since the highest incidence of child labour is not to be found in the regions with the highest poverty rate. However, the link between poverty and child labour should not be handed over without careful consideration. First, if the "poverty argument" is not fully able to explain the extent of child labour, it might still, be valuable for explaining its forms. This allows one to consider the more recent phenomenon of "children's unemployment".[44] It refers to children who do not attend school, but who do not work either. In such situations, families need children's work for their survival, but the households/communities are so poor that there are not many opportunities for children's work. As previous research has demonstrated, children's work depends on the household capacity and its resources.[45]

Under these circumstances, there is a relatively low incidence of child labour in the poorest households/ communities, but a high number of children have become involved in the worst forms of child labour. This phenomenon might explain why the highest incidence of child labour is not to be found in the regions with the highest poverty rate, both nationally (East of Romania) and in the region (Ukraine).[46] It might also establish the link between poverty and the worst forms of child labour such as child trafficking, child labour migration and prostitution.

---

43 Ibid., 28.

44 ILO, *Child Labour*, a textbook for university students, ILO, Geneva, 2004.

45 S. BHALOTRA and C. HEADY, 'Is child labour in rural economies caused by poverty?' (12 January 2004) 21 *Research Highlight* at <www.id21.org/society/s1csb1g1.html>.

46 For detailed statistics, see C. GHINARARU, supra (note 23).

31. Finally, it might be relevant to revise the methodology of data gathering with regard to child labour in Romania. Apart from an implicit tendency to minimise its incidence,[47] it might also be possible to have important distortions in data gathering. Even if statistically,[48] the highest incidence of child labour is not to be found in the poorest regions, there are other factors that might interfere with the very process of data gathering. As for the moment, many intersectorial teams involved in monitoring child labour in Romania are based in municipalities; it might be possible for some remote rural areas to remain unrepresented in the final data. Moreover, the processes of data collection might be influenced by the limited capacity of municipalities from less developed regions. Under these circumstances, distorted data could be produced: due to its greater monitoring capacity, it may become possible for a developed region to identify a higher incidence of child labour, than identified in less developed ones.

9. EDUCATION AND CHILD LABOUR

32. The poverty argument comes into the open once again when examining the link between children's work and education. According to this argument, due to the high poverty rate and to other factors of social exclusion, children have to work instead of going to school. However, for the moment, there is no demonstrated link between school dropouts and child labour in Romania. Most of the time, children do attend school and try to combine school with work. It is not school attendance, but school performance that diminishes due to the work they perform. Obviously, sooner or later, the low school performances do lead to school dropouts (in 2005, 6 out of 10 children of 14 years old did pass the national examination tests required for high school attendance).[49] Moreover, the average duration of school attendance in Romania (excluding pre-school) is one of the lowest in Europe (13.5 years in 2004).[50] However, once again, in the absence of reliable statistics, the link between child labour and schooling cannot be examined.

In Romania, school attendance is mandatory until the age of 16. However, only 70% of children of 14 did attend school in 2004/ 2005.[51] Even if there are laws that stipulate parents' responsibility for sending their children to school and penalties for refusing

---

47 See for example the omission of the category of "worst forms of child labour" in the National Report of National Institute of Statistics, Bucharest, 2003.

48 National Institute of Statistics and ILO, '*Ancheta asupra activitatii copiilor*', National Report, Bucharest, 2003.

49 M. Miclea, Romanian Ministry of Education and Research, Raport asupra starii sistemului Naþional de învãþãmânt, 2005, at <www.edu.ro>.

50 Ibid., 56 .

51 Ibid., 57 .

it, these regulations are almost never applied. The rate of school dropout decreased because child allowance is conditioned by school attendance (even if its amount is extremely low – less than 8 Euros). Under these circumstances, rather than being associated with a future professional achievement, school attendance tends to become an "administrative issue"[52] for many children who combine school attendance with work.

However, not all poor parents fail to send their children to school and not all parents who do not send their children to school are so poor they cannot afford it. According to the National Institute of Statistics, for example, children's work is essential for survival for only 3% of the families, while decrease in the household standard of living accounts for 55% of responses.

When analysing deprived parents' attitude towards education, the international literature is divided in mainly two directions. The first direction claims its roots from a "culture of poverty" argument. It states that undereducated parents are not able to understand the advantages of schooling. The second direction affirms the opposite: poor parents, also, want the best for their children and are willing to make sacrifices for their schooling.

With regard to Romania, it is difficult to decide which the parents' attitude towards education is. STATIVA's survey[53] demonstrates that parents' attitude towards the value of education and work is rather contradictory. On the one hand, in many counties, children are working five hours a day. However, at the discursive level, parents do consider education as being valuable and that if educated, children would have a better chance to obtain a job.[54] At the same time, in spite of the hard workload of children, parents surveyed had surprisingly high professional desires for them. Under these circumstances, the author of the research is quite sceptical about parents' declarations that "should be looked upon with reserve".

In the North East, work prevents children sometimes from attending school fully. However, with reference to the situation of children from south rural areas, existing research explains that due to associative and mechanical work of land, there is less demand for child labour. Still, it is surprising that even under these circumstances; children are not attending school consistently. The author's explanation, based on interviews with children, their parents and teachers, is that a certain degree of

---

52 C. GHINARARU, supra (note 23).

53 E. STATIVA, *Baseline Survey on rural child labour in five selected counties in România*, (Bucharest: ILO, Romanian Government, 2001).

54 Ibid., 46.

ignorance from the parents towards formal education might lead children from the South not to attend school regularly.

What might be the causes that generate such an attitude? The remoteness of rural areas has the disadvantage of keeping people far from society in which education is a marketable good. The traditional way of production these families are exposed to prevent them from understanding the value of formal education in a market economy. Still, according to GHINARARU, poor parents do value formal education. What prevents them from investing in children's schooling is their lack of confidence in the current education system, which is "still unable to cope with the demands of the market".

33. It is considered that (depending on the level of proximity from a developed city), parents are aware of the current economical dysfunctions. The current lack of demand for different occupations in industry makes them more sceptical about the use of education. The lack of "stories of success" by means of education might be another reason for considering schooling not a profitable investment. The cost/benefits rate of investment in education from the socially and economically disadvantaged groups might also influence their view on education. Still, it would not be considered that parents from areas where child labour is a large phenomenon, do have the "perception that education itself (is) just as an accumulation of theoretical knowledge (that) does not lead you much further in society based on competition".[55]

It would rather be considered that the reduction in the number of vocational and high schools in rural areas, combined with parents' limited resources in covering the costs of transportation and housing for the children above 14, might prevent them from going to school. Under these circumstances, parents tend to invest in children who do well at school and withdraw their support for those who are not successful, while associating school with the idea of literacy. Under these circumstances, child labour is maintained due to traditionally rooted attitudes that construct work (and less education) as the most suitable preparation for life.

Moreover, children's own motivation for work, as an alternative to school, might be an important indicator for a certain level of school dropout. It does make a difference if children are pushed towards work from their families, or if they are attracted to work by their siblings. Different programmes are needed to assist these two categories. Unquestionably, further analysis of children's own views on the value of education and the value of work, would be able to give new insights into the issue of child labour in Romania today.

[55] C. GHINARARU, supra (note 23), 66.

10. FINAL CONSIDERATIONS

34. When approaching child labour, a large body of literature from developed countries relates mainly to two phenomena. The first is child labour as a historical issue for Western countries and the second, child labour as it pertains today in Asia and South Africa. With reference to the present state, child labour is most of the time "exotised" by becoming symbolically, a racial issue.[56] Even if the incidence of child labour in Eastern Europe does not have the gravity it has in other parts of the world, the analysis of the way child labour takes place in Eastern Europe might be able to challenge its racial character, which was discussed by KITZINGER.

Moreover, child labour in Romania is far from resembling the industrial forms more often associated with Victorian England or today's textile industry of South Asia. Unlike the regions of South Asia, there are no industrial units based mostly on the use of child labour. Mainly, child labour refers to children who combine (limited) school attendance with work in small family farms. For the majority of the population, it is not school attendance, but school performance that is affected by work.

35. Societies that, during communist regimes, considered children as "the future of nations", are discovering that before being "the future", children are "the present". Too often, their present situation does not fit the idealistic image. The research on child labour in Eastern Europe is particularly significant as it speaks about the values of the particular societies in which it takes place. It speaks about how these societies respect and protect the rights of one of the largest minority groups. Light might also be shed on how issues of power and control are handled with reference to children as a social category in a former totalitarian society.

Eastern Europe faces a high incidence of children working in agricultural households and not necessarily for an industrial employer (as it used to be the case for other industrialised countries or for present textile industries from the countries of the South). The qualitative study of their work is able to give new insights into the domestic division of labour, which has mainly been studied from gender perspectives.

36. IPEC defines work in terms of "economic activity". Children engaged in domestic chores within their own households are not considered as economically active. Under these circumstances, programmes designed towards the elimination of child labour do not target this category. It is inside this last group of economically active children

---

[56] S. KITZINGER, 'Who are you kidding? Children, Power and the Struggle against Sexual Abuse', in J. JAMES and A. PROUT (eds.), *Constructing and Reconstructing Childhood*, (Philadelphia: Fulmer Press, 1990).

that one may find the distinction between "*light work*", "*child labour*" and "*worst forms of child labour*". As argued that when considering the specific case of transitional economies, where many children are involved in agricultural household cores, certain divisions that operated inside the comprehensive category of "non-economic activity" might be regarded as appropriate. As most children work not for financial independence, but mainly out of solidarity for the family needs, the research of child labour in Eastern Europe might be able to touch on the recognition of their roles.

37. According to the principles of cultural relativism, both "childhood" and "work" are social constructions, defined differently by different cultures, societies and States. What may be "abusive" (work) in a culture may be "tolerable" (work) in another.[57] In this respect, one of the most controversial aspects of the legislation on child labour is that States are given the competences to decide which type of work is abusive or harmful.[58] This paper cited the particular case of Romanian legislation that refers exclusively to employment and permits it (with a few legal discordances) from the age of 15 while the age at which compulsory education ends is 16. We argued that even if child labour is an alarming phenomenon, there is slow enforcement of child labour legislation and seemingly a high degree of official ignorance towards law violations with regard to child labour.

38. It is argued, following GHINARARU'S arguments, that children's work is not an effect of poverty *per se,* but of a particular type of economic structure, that encourages subsistence production at the level of households. More precisely, children's entry into work is encouraged in economic systems that have the household as production units rather than as consumption units. Under these circumstances, households are producing for their own use, with the contribution of (frequently) all its members who become "part of the Non-Observed Economy". Post communist Romania fits perfectly into such a pattern.

39. The history of recognising child labour as a social problem is very recent in Romania. It has taken place after a few decades of communism that constructed children's work as highly valuable. At present, child labour tends to be a politicised issue, whose approach hardly goes beyond the discussion of the worst forms of labour, represented by street children. In this paper it is suggested that the fact that the great majority of street children are Roma,[59] does not make the phenomenon an ethnic issue,

---

57 B. WHITE, 'Defining the Intolerable. Child work, global standards and cultural relativism', (1999) 6 *Childhood*, 133–144.

58 Ibid., 141.

59 Save the Children Romania, *Raport al Salvaþi Copiii România către Comitetul Naþiunilor Unite pentru Drepturile Copilului – Geneva referitor la al Doilea Raport Periodic al Guvernului României pentru intervalul 1995 – 2002*, 2002, at<http://www.salvaticopiii.ro>.

but a social problem. There are deep structural dysfunctions of the economy that push the Roma children to the margins of social concern and it is because of it, that the Roma population has the highest risk of being in situations that involve child labour.

40. With reference to the relation between education and child labour in Romania, this paper highlighted that it is not school dropout (except for the worst forms of child labour), but rather school performance that is jeopardised by work. As parents, most of the time, introduce their children to work, their view on education is highly relevant. However, the empirical evidence is controversial. At the discursive level, parents do consider education to be valuable, but still, accept and consider that it is good for their children to work from an early age. The household duties children perform, prevents them sometimes from fully complying with school assignments, which leads to school dropouts mainly at the age of 14.

41. On the whole, we consider that the study of child labour for Eastern European countries is able to increase the visibility of children as active members of their households. New insights into the discussion of domestic division of labour are more likely to follow when children's work is not as much a matter of financial independence, but of family solidarity, as it seems to be the case in Eastern Europe. At the same time, the topic is particularly significant as it speaks about the current values of Eastern European societies. It speaks about how they respect and protect the rights of one of the largest minority groups. It might also shed light on how issues of power and control are handled with reference to children in post totalitarian societies.

VI. ECONOMIC, SOCIAL AND CULTURAL RIGHTS

A ROLE FOR THE COURTS IN ENSURING THE ENFORCEMENT OF THE SOCIO-ECONOMIC RIGHTS OF THE CHILD: OVERCOMING THE 'COUNTER-MAJORITARIAN OBJECTION'[1]

AOIFE NOLAN

1. INTRODUCTION

1. Never before has there been such a level of acceptance that children are socio-economic rights-bearers. However, this has generally failed to translate into concrete change for children in terms of effective executive and legislative action aimed at ensuring the vindication or realisation of their rights. Despite the widespread support for children's rights demonstrated by the near-universal ratification of the United Nations Convention on the Rights of the Child (CRC),[2] the high levels of deprivation experienced by children worldwide demonstrate that these rights have often not been effectively vindicated by law- and policy-makers at a domestic level. The failure to give effect to children's socio-economic rights is most often the product of legislative or executive indifference and inertia in relation to child socio-economic rights issues. In light of the apparent unresponsiveness of the elected branches of government, advocates are increasingly focussing their efforts to secure the vindication of children's socio-economic rights on the judiciary.

This paper defends a role for the courts in ensuring the vindication of children's socio-economic rights where the elected branches of government have not done so. In it, I argue that it is legitimate for the courts to act assertively in order to ensure that children's socio-economic rights are implemented. Such judicial activity may extend

---

1 This paper is taken from A. Nolan, *Children's Socio-economic Rights and the Courts – Evaluating an Activist Approach*, unpublished PhD thesis, (Florence: European University Institute), Chapter 2.

2 Nov. 20, 1989, 1577 UNTS 3.

to the courts prescribing steps that the state must take in order to fulfil the positive obligations imposed by children's socio-economic rights. In doing so, the courts exercise control over the discretion of the other organs of government with regard to law- or policy-making. This paper will focus on the positivistic legal legitimacy within a constitutional liberal democracy of the courts acting assertively in order to guarantee children's socio-economic rights. In particular, I will argue that the courts may behave in this way even where such judicial behaviour appears *prima facie* to be undemocratic or counter-majoritarian.[3]

The claims made in this paper may undoubtedly have implications for judicial treatment of children's civil and political rights. However, I have chosen to focus on socio-economic rights as, in my view, these are the rights that are of the greatest importance to children. While civil and political rights become increasingly relevant as children advance in age, economic and social rights are of critical importance from birth.[4] This is due to their direct link with the child's physical and mental development. Although there is no question that some civil and political rights are fundamental to ensuring that a child's current welfare and future development are not impaired,[5] others are not.[6]

2. A FEW DEFINITIONS

2. This paper begins by setting out a number of definitions of terms that will be employed frequently in this paper.

3. In this paper, "socio-economic rights" refers to legal, constitutional socio-economic rights that are expressly enumerated in, or implied from, provisions of national constitutions. For my purposes, "socio-economic rights" include health rights,

3 Clearly, there are other "legal legitimacy"-related critiques of the courts' behaving in the way contemplated in this paper. One that is of particular importance is the question of the compliance of such activity with the separation of powers doctrine. Due to space constraints, this issue will not be dealt with at length in this paper. For a discussion of whether the separation of powers doctrine acts as a bar on the adoption of an assertive approach to children's socio-economic rights by the courts, see A. NOLAN, *Children's Socio-Economic Rights and the Courts: Evaluating an Activist Approach*, unpublished PhD thesis, (Florence: European University Institute, 2005), Chapter 3 (available from author). For the same reason, the paper will not seek to evaluate the 'efficacy' of such behaviour in terms of the ability of such activity to bring about the desired result of enforcing children's rights.

4 V. LEARY, 'The Social and Economic Rights of the Child', (1995) *Law & Policy* 353, 353.

5 For instance, those rights relating to the protection of life and bodily integrity.

6 E.g., the right to peacefully assemble, the right to freedom of movement and other "self-determination" or other "freedom" rights, the exercise of which might arguably actually be damaging to children's welfare and development.

the rights to a minimum standard of living, housing, food, water, education, as well as social security rights.[7] The paper will focus on those socio-economic rights that are operational against the state, rather than those assertible against non-state actors.

Although the rights at issue in this paper are constitutional socio-economic rights (which, depending on the legal system in question, may be more binding on states than rights provided under international human rights conventions), the arguments made in it are relevant to a consideration of how courts may ensure that CRC rights are vindicated at a national level. This is because many of the arguments made against the judicial enforcement of children's socio-economic rights are likely to be similar regardless of whether the rights at issue are enshrined in the domestic law or the CRC.

4. I will take "childhood" to begin at the time of birth.[8] The arguments presented in this paper are largely concerned with the inability of children to exert effective influence on political decision-making processes and the appropriate role to be adopted by the judiciary in relation to their rights and interests in light of this. The key reason for children's incapacity to exercise influence on democratic processes is their unenfranchisement. Therefore, I define a "child" as any person who has not yet reached adulthood in terms of being of an age to participate directly in democratic decision-making processes by exercising their right to vote.[9]

5. It is also important to clarify what I mean when I say "democracy". Democracy is both an ideal and a method.[10] "No explicit definition of democracy is settled among

---

7 We note that some rights may be classified as either civil and political or socio-economic in nature. For instance, the rights to life, equality, trade union/labour rights and property rights. For the purposes of this paper, however, these rights will not be considered as "socio economic" rights.

8 That is not necessarily to conclude that unborn children may not have certain socio-economic rights that can or should be vindicated by appealing to the courts. However, we wish to avoid the complications inherent in dealing with the rights of the unborn, including the potential conflict between the socio-economic rights of the mother and those of the unborn child.

9 This linkage of the end of "childhood" to enfranchisement becomes somewhat complicated when applied to jurisdictions where children become enfranchised for different elections at different ages. For instance, in various *Lander* in Germany and Austria, the voting age in local elections is 16 rather than 18. The question arises whether children become adult when they are enfranchised for *any* or for *all* public elections. The simplest answer seems to be "any" as this is the age at which children are able to exert some influence on democratic decision-making processes. However, it must be borne in mind that where a person is enfranchised for some elections and not for others they may not participate on equal terms with other "fully enfranchised" members of society and some of the arguments that may be made in this paper may apply to them to varying degrees (as, indeed, they may to any politically disadvantaged or excluded minority). In the vast majority of countries, children become enfranchised for the purpose of all elections at the same age. Therefore, the arguments made in this paper will proceed on the basis that children become entitled to vote in all elections at the same age before which they have no opportunity to participate directly in democratic decision-making procedures.

10 W. Riker, *Liberalism Against Populism*, (San Francisco: W.H. Freeman and Company, 1982), 6.

political theorists or in the dictionary. On the contrary, it is a matter of deep controversy what democracy really is. People disagree about which techniques of representation, which allocation of power among local, state and national governments, which schedule and pattern of elections, and which other institutional arrangements provide the best available version of democracy."[11]

For the purpose of this paper, a democracy will be defined as rule by the people where "the people" includes all *adult* citizens not excluded by some disqualifying factor, such as confinement to prison or to an asylum for the mentally ill, or some procedural requirement, such as residency within a particular electoral district for a reasonable length of time before the election in question. "Rule" means that laws or public policies are determined either directly by vote of the electorate or indirectly by officials freely elected at specified intervals and by a process in which the vote of each voter who chooses to vote counts equally and in which a majority-decision is determinative.[12]

This definition of "democracy" is not dependent on controversial substantive values, but instead is an objective description of how legislatures are established and how law is enacted within most constitutional democratic systems. While it makes clear that rule by the people is the central tenet of a democratic system, it does not specify if, or how, this rule may be limited by other procedures such as judicial review or policymaking.

3. A BRIEF COMMENT ON CHILDREN'S POSITION IN SOCIETY

6. Children are now formally recognised as a minority rights group through the provision of their own UN Convention, and share many experiences of oppression with other minority groups in society.[13] In general, children have limited access to money, no right to vote, no right either to express an opinion or be taken seriously, little access to the courts and no formal voice in society at all.[14] They wield no significant political or economic power and are utterly excluded from the vast majority of important societal institutions such as, elected bodies, banks, trade unions, and so

[11] R. DWORKIN, *Freedom's Law – The Moral Reading of the American Constitution*, (Cambridge, Mass.: Harvard University Press, 1996), 15.

[12] This definition is largely based on that set out by J. R. PENNOCK in *Democratic Political Theory*, (Princeton: Princeton University Press, 1979), 7.

[13] M. JOHN, *Children's Rights and Powers: Charging Up for a New Century*, (London: Jessica Kingsley Productions, 2003), 196.

[14] Adapted from G. LANSDOWN, 'Children's Rights', in B. MAYALL (ed.), *Children's Childhoods: Observed and Experienced*, (London: Falmer Press, 1994), 33, 35.

on. Moreover, they are excluded from those decision- policy- or law-making bodies, which are of the greatest importance to them, such as school boards, government committees on education, juvenile justice and child health services, etc. On the rare occasions when societies have considered children as a discrete group, it has generally been in order to dismiss them as irrational, legally incompetent beings, who are inferior to adults and whose enjoyment of rights is subject to the views of their parents or the state or both.

Children occupy a different position in society from that of other socially disadvantaged groups. MASLOW COHEN points out that, in comparison to the elderly, the disabled and the incarcerated (three other groups of public dependents), children's dependency is the more complete and profound due to the absence of a suitable engine to forward their claims to public resources.[15] They have no way either to alter or improve their dependent status, but only to outlive it if they can, and so they are at the fullest mercy of public policy and law.[16] Unlike other socially disadvantaged groups who have benefited from the use of litigation to achieve social reform, children suffer from a primarily natural rather than an artificially produced dependence, based as it is on factors such as their relative physical weakness, inexperience and immaturity.[17] Thus, such dependence cannot be ended merely by social or political changes.

4. CHILDREN AS SOCIO-ECONOMIC RIGHTS BEARERS

7. The position of children in relation to economic, social and cultural rights differs from that of other groups for several reasons. The most obvious of these is the fact that children may be more vulnerable to violations of their rights and less able to protect themselves or capable of taking advantage of protections that are available. Due to their nature and condition, children have a reduced capacity to meet their socio-economic needs either by obtaining or creating sustenance from the resources of their environment.[18] Furthermore, they are less likely to have the skills necessary

---

15 Examples of engines to forward disadvantaged groups claims to public resources would be the vote in the case of the elderly; the equality principle in the case of the disabled; and the public's apprehensions of urgency and necessity in the case of the incarcerated. See: J. MASLOW COHEN, 'Competitive and Cooperative Dependencies: the Case for Children', (1995) 81 *Va L. Rev.* (*Virginia Law Review*), 2217 at 2227.

16 Ibid.,2226–7.

17 Ibid. See, e.g., D. ARCHARD, *Children: Rights and Childhood*, (New York: Routledge, 1993); G. LANSDOWN, supra (note 14) at 35.

18 C. WRINGE, *Children's Rights: A Philosophical Study*, (London – Boston: Routledge and Kegan Paul, 1981), 135–6.

to gain a stake in the resources of the community by negotiating special rights (i.e. rights that arise from transactions or relationships) for themselves.[19]

In addition, children are often affected in a different way from adults by violations of a similar nature.[20] The physical and psychological effects that children suffer because of violations of their socio-economic rights will nearly always be greater than those experienced by adults due to their age and lower level of physical and mental development.[21] This is true both in relation to (a) the immediate impact that socio-economic rights violations may have on a child's physical and psychological state, and (b) the long-term detrimental effects on the child's development and future prospects resulting from such violations.

A final point is that the rights granted to children may be different from those accorded to others[22] and those rights that are shared may need to be implemented and enforced in a different way than they would be in the case of other, adult members of society.

5. THE 'COUNTER-MAJORITARIAN OBJECTION' – AN INTRODUCTION

8. The "counter-majoritarian difficulty"[23] arises where the courts act in a way that results in the substitution by the judiciary of its will for that of "the people", as represented by the actions and policies of their democratically elected representatives. The counter-majoritarian objection to judicial review is that when a court invalidates a legislative act or the action of an elected executive, "it thwarts the will of representatives of the actual people of the here and now; it exercises control, not in (sic.) behalf of the prevailing majority but against it".[24]

In constitutional democracies, "nothing can finally depreciate the central function that is assigned in democratic theory and practice to the electoral process; nor can it

19 Ibid., 137.

20 'Children's Rights' in OFFICE OF THE HIGH COMMISSIONER FOR HUMAN RIGHTS, *Training Manual on Human Rights Monitoring*, (Geneva: Office of the High Commissioner for Human Rights, 2001).

21 While we are aware that there are groups of adults within society that are at least as vulnerable as children (due to disability, pregnancy age, or disadvantages/disabilities such as being illiterate in a developed country, etc.) we wish to compare the relative situations of an adult of reasonable good health and education by the standards of the society of which she forms part with that of an average child in the same society.

22 See OFFICE OF THE HIGH COMMISSIONER FOR HUMAN RIGHTS, supra (note 20).

23 A. BICKEL, *The Least Dangerous Branch – The Supreme Court at the Bar of Politics*, (1962), 16.

24 Ibid., 17.

be denied that the policy-making power of representative institutions, born of the electoral process, is the distinguishing characteristic of the system. Judicial review works counter to this characteristic".[25] The counter-majoritarian objection to all or certain forms of judicial activity is founded on the identification of democracy with majoritarianism. The majoritarian premise "insists that political procedures should be designed so that … the decision that is reached is the decision that a majority or plurality of citizens favours or would favour if it had adequate information and enough time for reflection".[26] The principle is based on the notion of self-determination or self-governance: decisions affecting the people should be made by the people: that is, by a majority of the electorate or their elected representatives.

9. There is much debate as to whether judicial review or other forms of judicial activity are, in fact, counter-majoritarian. Some commentators argue that courts do not act in a counter-majoritarian way due to, amongst other things, their tendency to make decisions that accord with the views of the elected branches of government and public opinion,[27] while others make claims about the imperfectly majoritarian nature of law-making practices and the results produced by political processes.[28] It has been asserted that judicial review is not a long-term counter-majoritarian force due to the possibility of courts being persuaded to reverse their decisions or public opinion changing to agree with that of the court, by convincing those in control of judicial appointments to fill vacancies with nominees that disagree with a particular decision.[29] Alternatively, a court's decision may also be reversed by constitutional amendment. However, merely because judicial review is not counter-majoritarian in the sense of being final or irreversibly contrary to the will of the majority does not mean that such activity is not objectionable for being counter-majoritarian at the time a decision is taken or for the period that that decision stands unreversed.

In representative democracies, effective representation of the will of the majority by their representatives is guaranteed by political accountability.[30] The presumption is that representatives who are electorally accountable are dependent upon public

---

[25] Ibid., 18–19.

[26] R. Dworkin, supra (note 11), 15–6.

[27] See, e.g., B. Friedman, 'Dialogue and Judicial Review', (1993) 91 *Mich. L. Rev. (Michigan Law Review)* 577, 587–614; R. Dahl, 'Decision-Making in a Democracy: The Supreme Court as a National Policy-Maker', (1957) 6 *J. PUB. L. (Journal of Public Law)* 279, 285.

[28] See, e.g., M. J. Klarman, 'Majoritarian Judicial Review: The Entrenchment Problem', (1997) 85 *Geo. LJ (Georgetown Law Journal)* 491, in which Klarman details some of the different theories that dispute the majoritarian character of the lawmaking process and the results of political processes.

[29] C. Eisgruber, *Constitutional Self-Government*, (London: Harvard University Press, 2001), 97.

[30] R. Brown defines political accountability as "broadly, the requirement that public officials stand periodically for election". See: R. Brown, 'Accountability, Liberty and the Constitution', (1998) 98 *Colum. L Rev.(Columbia Law Review)* 531, 533.

approval in order to ensure their re-election. Therefore, it is claimed that the policies and laws they produce are more likely to be a reflection of the will of the majority than those made by unelected policy- or law-makers, such as judges.[31]

10. The issue of the relative accountability of elected policymakers and unelected members of the judiciary has been dealt with at length by commentators, some of whom dispute the view that, while elected policy-makers are entirely accountable, judicial policy-makers are the opposite.[32] This is an extremely important debate. However, the focus of this paper is children and, like courts, legislatures are unaccountable to children due to the latter's unenfranchisement. Therefore, while it is necessary to mention the issue of accountability in order to give a full picture of the arguments arising around the counter-majoritarian objection, I do not wish to become embroiled in a lengthy discussion about a principle that is of limited relevance to children due to their position in democracy.

6. THE ALLEGED PROBLEMS WITH THE COURTS' ACTING ASSERTIVELY TO ENSURE THAT CHILDREN'S SOCIO-ECONOMIC RIGHTS ARE GUARANTEED IN TERMS OF THE COUNTER-MAJORITARIAN OBJECTION

11. The judicial behaviour defended in this paper undoubtedly may involve the judiciary acting in a way that is counter-majoritarian. Where the judiciary acts in such a way as to control the discretion of the other (elected) branches of government with regard to making policy or law (which can be viewed as the law or policy-making discretion of the prevailing majority) its behaviour is counter-majoritarian.

---

31 Some commentators dispute the possibility of representation of the views of other by elected representatives. E.g., postmodernist theorists on representation claim that any representation inevitably distorts its subject's grounded and unique actuality, embodying assumptions that restrict the subject to its orthodox, readily recognizable meanings. They argue that political representation is just such a distortion, spawned by the unfounded assertion that one person represents the views of others and sustained by the manipulation of political symbols through mass media and bureaucratic systems. (M. FEELEY and E. RUBIN, *Judicial Policy Making and the Modern State- How the Courts Reformed American's Prisons*, (Cambridge: CUP, 1999), 331). However, for the purposes of this paper we shall work on the basis that representation of voters by elected representatives is, in fact, possible.

32 In our comments here we refer to unelected judges – not judges such as those in state courts in the US who have to run for office and are, therefore, accountable to the electorate in much the same way as other elected officials.

The activity defended in this paper is arguably "more" counter-majoritarian than simple judicial review (which has traditionally been regarded as limited to the invalidation or striking down of unconstitutional legislation). This due to the fact that, amongst other things, it involves the courts outlining a positive obligation on the state and setting out steps that the state must take in order to fulfil that obligation. However, if we regard counter-majoritarianism as the "legitimacy benchmark" for judicial behaviour, then any behaviour that exceeds that benchmark will be illegitimate – regardless of the form that activity ultimately takes.

12. Another claim that might be made in relation to the prescription of steps by the courts is that, while a failure on the part of the legislature to act to ensure children's rights may justify the courts' placing children's socio-economic rights issues "on the legislative agenda", as it were, it does not legitimise the courts' going further and stating how these rights should be implemented.[33] Another way of presenting this is: while the courts do not act in an unacceptably counter-majoritarian way in telling the legislature to act in relation to rights, they do so when they go further and tell the legislature how they *should* act in relation to detailed applications of such rights.

This claim is easily countered. The distinction between the courts placing issues on the legislative/governmental agenda and dictating how they should be dealt with is far from watertight. Take a situation where a court finds that a government's failure to act violates a socio-economic right. Even if the court does not expressly dictate how the government should proceed to vindicate this right, the granting of a declaratory order stating that a particular government failure constitutes a rights violation together with the implicit or express understanding that the government is to remedy this, may be regarded as telling the legislature how they should act in relation to these rights – at least to a certain extent. The difference between the two outcomes is in the degree of discretion that they leave the elected organs of government in relation to detailed applications of a right.

---

[33] For instance, FABRE argues that in cases where the government is not doing anything or is not doing enough to respect people's constitutional rights to resources, the courts can either ask the government to do more, or tell them what they should do in order to respect the constitution. They should do this by simply reminding the government of what its duties are, should tell them how to fulfil these duties by a certain date as deemed reasonable, but should forbear from spelling out in any detail how the government should fulfil them. (C. FABRE, *Social Rights Under the Constitution – Government and the Decent Life*, (Oxford: OUP, 2000), 150). FABRE offers two justifications for this approach. First, there is some value to democratic decision-making and, being committed to protecting rights from the attack by the democratic majority does not entail that one should seek to prevent the majority from having any say whatsoever in the way constitutional rights are to be respected. Second, allowing for some democratic decision-making on constitutional rights is one way of avoiding the backlashes against right-holders that might be facilitated by putting too stringent a control on the majority. (Ibid., 150).

13. The courts' dealing with *socio-economic rights* raises further issues with regard to the counter-majoritarian objection. It is arguable that the budgetary implications involved in vindicating socio-economic rights make it particularly undesirable that an unelected judiciary should effectively overrule the elected branches of government on such issues. However, this claim is unsustainable in light of the fact that many civil and political rights also have implications for governmental spending and public resources and, therefore, similar objections should be made against court interference with legislative or executive action in relation to these rights.

7. FORWARDING CHILDREN'S SOCIO-ECONOMIC RIGHTS-RELATED INTERESTS THROUGH DEMOCRACY – THE ISSUE OF REPRESENTATION

14. The next part of this paper will focus on the representation of children and their interests in democracy. Providing a comprehensive picture of the representation of children in democracy is crucial because of its implications for the notion of governance representative of the will of the people. This idea is central to majoritarian conceptions of democracy and hence goes to the heart of the counter-majoritarian objection.

Clearly, the claims made may not be fully true of all modern representative democracies. Rather, my aim is to present a series of general observations that may be contribute to an understanding of the representation of children's socio-economic rights-related interests in democratic decision-making processes. Examples from Ireland, South Africa and the United states will be used to support my assertions.

7.1. DIRECT REPRESENTATION OF CHILDREN'S SOCIO-ECONOMIC RIGHTS-RELATED INTERESTS IN THE DEMOCRATIC SYSTEM

15. Children are unenfranchised and have no opportunity to exert direct influence on the policymaking process through exercising their right to vote. They do not, and cannot, constitute a political constituency able to gain ground through political action.[34] The executive and the legislature are not electorally accountable to them and

[34] J. SLOTH-NIELSEN, 'Chicken Soup or Chainsaws: Some Implications of the Constitutionalisation of Children's Rights in South Africa', (1996) 6 *Acta Juridica*, 7.

are, therefore, not immediately dependent on their goodwill in order to ensure re-election. As result, children's interests are unlikely to occupy a large space on the agenda of elected law and policy-makers.

It is arguable that children's exclusion from democratic processes leaves them particularly vulnerable to violations of their *socio-economic rights*. This is due to the fact that, being unable to participate in democracy, they cannot successfully compete with other, enfranchised groups in order to bring about the resource allocation that is often required to give effect to socio-economic rights.[35] The finite resources at the government's disposal as well as the existence of numerous competing claims for those resources from different groups does not bode well for the guarantee of children socio-economic rights through democratic processes where the cost of giving effect to their rights is perceived as threatening the rights claims of other, enfranchised groups or governmental priorities.

7.2. INDIRECT REPRESENTATION OF CHILDREN'S SOCIO-ECONOMIC RIGHTS-RELATED INTERESTS IN THE DEMOCRATIC SYSTEM

16. Although children do not vote, it might be argued that others who are enfranchised will protect their socio-economic rights within democracy through representation of their interests in the political system. There are numerous mechanisms by which children's socio-economic rights-related interests may be represented in democratic decision-making processes; for example, through the activities of ombudsmen, youth wings of political parties, etc. Here, however, the paper will focus principally on the effective representation of children's interests by particular societal groups participating directly in democratic processes through voting.

The first step here will be to consider the theory of virtual representation and children.[36] The theory of virtual representation is most closely associated with BURKE.[37]

---

35 While both civil and political rights and socio-economic ones are resource-dependent to some extent, it is accepted that the former will generally entail greater governmental expenditure than their civil and political counterparts. This is due to the more directly resource-dependent nature of socio-economic rights, as well as the fact that the mechanisms necessary to ensure civil and political rights are more likely to already be in place.

36 J. ELY is one commentator who has dealt with the issue of 'virtual representation' of marginalised groups within the legislative and other democratic decision-making processes. (See, in particular: *Democracy and Distrust*, (Cambridge, Mass.: Harvard University Press, 1980)). He argues for a particular participation-oriented, representation-reinforcing approach to judicial review in which judicial review is deployed against systemic biases in legislative decision-making. (KLARMAN, supra (note 28), 747.) He deals with children only briefly and does not appear to view them as a group that

Burke held that "*virtual representation is that in which there is a communion of interests and a sympathy in feelings and desires between those who act in the name of any description of people and the people in whose name they act, though the trustees are not actually chosen by them*".[38] Thus, constituencies could legitimately be represented by legislators possessing "a communion of interests and a sympathy in feelings and desires" with their constituents even if the representatives were not actually elected by the people said to be represented.[39]

Virtual representation could arise for children in three ways:

1. There could be a communion of interests between children and elected representatives such as to guarantee virtual representation for children.
2. There could be a communion of interests between children and those members of society who vote such as to guarantee virtual representation for children.
3. There could be feelings of empathy with or sympathy for children on the part of legislators or adults generally such as to guarantee virtual representation for children.

7.2.1. Representation of children by elected representatives

17. The notion of interest representation is incorporated within a proceduralist theory of democracy. Interest representation operates because the representative's interests are the same as the interests of a majority of her constituents.[40] Thus, representation of citizens by their elected representatives occurs through interest congruity. I will argue briefly here that children cannot rely on elected representatives to represent them on the basis of their shared interests.

---

would qualify for judicial intervention under his theory (See *Democracy and Distrust* at 160). My aim in this section is *not* to make a case that the courts acting assertively is justified on the basis that such activity will ensure the effective representation of children in the democratic process. Rather, our intention here is to demonstrate that the non-representation of children in democracy means that their socio-economic rights are unlikely to be guaranteed by democratic means. For a discussion of Ely's work and other "representation-reinforcing" theories of judicial review in the context of children and their socio-economic rights, see: A. Nolan, supra (note 3), chapter 2.

37 C. Peters, 'Adjudication as Representation', (1997) 97 *Colum. L Rev.(Columbia Law Review)* 312, 343.

38 "Letter from Edmund Burke to Sir Hercules Langrishe, M.P. (Jan. 3, 1792), Source: <http://www.ourcivilisation.com/smartboard/shop/burkee/extracts/chap18.htm>.

39 C.Peters, supra (note 37), 343–4. For an in-depth consideration of Burke's concept of virtual representation, see: H. Pitkin, *The Concept of Representation*, (Berkeley: University of California Press, 1967), 172–180.

40 C.Peters, supra (note 37), 343.

Viewing politics from a cynical point of view, the main concern of most elected policymakers is incumbency and, even where they may be regarded as having "a communion of interests and sympathy in feelings and desires" with children, these shared interests will generally be subordinated to their desire to ensure re-election. Hence, where children's interests may prove a political liability or their vindication may require an elected representative to go against popular opinion or alienate other enfranchised groups competing for the same resources, the legislator's primary interest in incumbency will override those interests that they share with children and virtual representation will not occur.

One can think of numerous scenarios in which political representatives might choose to ignore or subordinate common interests with children in favour of forwarding their own political interest. An instance involving children's socio-economic rights might arise where an elected representative is faced with the option of choosing between allocating public monies to primary education facilities or, alternatively, to increasing health care benefits for the elderly. In such a case, a representative may well decide to ignore her/his shared long-term interest with children in ensuring that there will be an educated workforce in the future (which will, in turn, be in a position to contribute to the social welfare system when the representative reaches retirement age, thereby ensuring her pension). Instead, she/he may go for the option, which will benefit her/his short-term incumbency interest by attracting support from enfranchised elderly voters.

Furthermore, with regard to shared interests, one might argue that there are instances where the "incumbency" interest of elected representatives is best served when they ignore their shared interests with certain children and actively work against such children. For instance, where such children are members of unpopular minorities; where they occupy a sphere regarded as outside the normative socialising control of adult society;[41] where they cannot or will not fulfil their expected roles in the transmission of "traditional values";[42] or where they are the subject of societal hostility.

18. BURNS and CRAWFORD provide a US example of where it has served politicians to work against children. They discuss the vested interest of politicians in promoting tougher legislation surrounding juveniles in the aftermath of school shootings in the United States. They observe that "*[i]n juveniles and more specifically juvenile delinquents, politicians have an ideal target for action. Increasing the penalties directed towards juvenile delinquents is a no-lose situation for politicians, mainly because such*

41 S. STEPHENS, 'Introduction', in S. STEPHENS (ed.), *Children and the Politics of Culture*, (Princeton: Princeton University Press, 1995) 1, 11. STEPHENS provides the example of street children.

42 Ibid.

an approach has become popular with the general public. Juveniles are not permitted to vote in popular elections, and they are not likely to develop lobby –, or special interest groups. Thus, politicians do not fear losing juveniles' votes upon election day nor any threat of opposition."[43]

19. However, the primary reason why virtual representation of children in the political process by elected representatives may not work is the fact that often there is no real communion of interests between the two groups. For instance, research commissioned by the Constitution Review Group in Ireland revealed that lower socio-economic groups are significantly underrepresented in the Irish houses of parliament.[44] As most of the Irish children who suffer violations of their socio-economic rights are from social and economically disadvantaged backgrounds, it is clear that they have a very different socio-economic status from that of elected politicians. Due to the difference in their respective socio-economic statuses, the interests of Irish elected representatives will not generally coincide with those of such children and will not be affected by a measure impacting negatively upon them.

20. In short, the lack of mutual interests and the willingness of the members elected branches of government to jettison those interests that they do share with children mean that political representatives cannot be presumed to ensure the representation of children in the democratic process.

7.2.2. Representation of children by parents

21. At first glance, it seems only logical that parents will ensure that the interests of children are represented effectively in the democratic process. Children's interests (both socio-economic and other) often overlap and are entwined with those of their parents. We may presume that parents want what is best for their children and will hence vote for candidates and policies that will benefit their own children's interests. This belief in the concern of parents for their own children may be expanded into a

---

[43] R. BURNS and C. CRAWFORD, 'School Shootings, the Media, and Public Fear: Ingredients for a Moral Panic', (1999) 32 *Crime, Law & Social Change* 147, 157.

[44] While 32% of the population between the ages of 21 and 70 belong to the skilled manual, semi-skilled manual and unskilled manual categories, only 2% of the membership of the 27th Dáil in 1992 belonged to the skilled manual category and no member of that Dáil came from either of the other two categories (cited in G. WHYTE, *Social Inclusion and the Legal System – Public Interest Law in Ireland* (Dublin: Institute of Public Administration, 2002), 32). Of those deputies elected to the 29th Dáil in 2002, almost half were professionals and very few were manual workers of any skill level (i.e. skilled manual, semi-skilled manual and unskilled manual). (Source: M. GALLAGHER, 'Stability and Turmoil: Analysis of the Results', in M. GALLAGHER, M. MARSH and P. MITCHELL (eds.), *How Ireland Voted* (Palgrave: MacMillan, 2003) at 114).

broader presumption that adults who are parents will vote in favour of measures that benefit children's interests generally.

a. Parents representing their own children's interests

22. It is probably safe enough to presume that parents will act so as to ensure that their children's interests are represented in the political process – at least to the extent that they share these interests or that such interests do not interfere with other interests of their own. One example might be the parent of a child with learning disabilities who is likely to vote for a candidate promising to establish appropriate educational programmes for such children. Such a vote may be viewed as forwarding the interest of the parent in not having to foot the bill for the child's education. At the same time, it may be construed as a vote for the shared interest of the child and parent in ensuring that the child receives a proper education which will, in turn, promote the child's autonomy and independence from the parent. Another instance might be of parents who vote in favour of candidates promising to provide social housing to families with children. In this case the parent (as well as the child) will benefit directly from such a policy as he or she will share the housing provided.

While most parents will ensure the effective representation of their children out of love and concern, even the most selfish and indifferent of parents may seek to ensure their children's socio-economic interests through the political system by supporting candidates espousing policies that will reduce their obligation to materially provide for their children.

However, parents' interests often diverge from those of the child[45] and this is when virtual representation of children's interests by parents may be lacking. For instance, a parent may not vote for a measure that aims to introduce compulsory health check-ups for children conducted in schools. Although the parent may have an interest in the child remaining healthy (based both on love and self-interest) and is aware that such check-ups would mean that the child would receive better medical attention than she/he would otherwise, the parent may feel that his interest in family privacy[46] and

[45] W. FITZGERALD, 'Maturity, Difference, and Mystery: Children's Perspectives and the Law', (1994) 36 *Ariz. L. Rev.(Arizona Law Review)* 11, 65. FITZGERALD is writing about children's interests in "their own care, support, control, custody and familial relationship". However, her point is also true of children's socio-economic interests.

[46] That is, the protected absence of official supervision of family life. (D. ARCHARD, *Children, Family and the State*, (Aldershot: Ashgate, 2003), 147).

parental autonomy[47] should take precedence over the child's interest in benefiting from superior health services.

The above example is illustrative of one of the major obstacles to the effective representation of children's interests by parents through the political system. Many parents might argue that their own children do not need strong protection or provision from the legislature as they, the parents, will provide it. This view is premised on the idea of parental autonomy and a (sometimes misguided) belief that a parent will always be able to identify objectively what is best for her child. Notions of family privacy and parental autonomy may result in a reluctance on the part of parents to permit significant state interference with family autonomy – to the extent that they will not forward or "turn over" children's interests to the democratic process. This will amount to a lack of representation of children by their parents.

23. A less benign reason for parental failure to virtually represent children is where parental interests are served through the disadvantaging of those of their children. A historical example of this is the opposition of many parents to the introduction of compulsory education and labour laws in the United States in the 1920s arising from, amongst other things, the benefit to the socio-economic conditions of the parent brought about by the income provided by their children's labour.[48]

24. Even if it were always true that children's interests were adequately represented by their own parents, in the absence of virtual representation by non-parents this would prove insufficient to protect the interests of all children in society for a number of reasons. First, children who live in poor socio-economic conditions often come from families where parents do not vote.[49] Alternatively, socio-economically

47 D. ARCHARD defines "parental autonomy" as "the freedom of parents to rear their children as they see fit". (*Ibid.*).

48 For more on this, see: B. BENNETT WOODHOUSE, "Who Owns the Child?": MEYER and PIERCE and the Child as Property', (1992) 33 *Wm. and Mary L. Rev.(William and Mary Law Review)* 995.

49 For instance, in an Irish context, MARSH and GALLAGHER have stated that there is evidence of a negative relationship between turn-out in a constituency with semi-skilled or unskilled manual occupations (See: 'Voter Turnout in 2002 and Beyond', in M. GALLAGHER, M. MARSH and P. MITCHELL (eds.), supra (note 44), 148). HARDIMAN cites studies which found "strong correlations at the aggregate level between low electoral participation and social deprivation in the Dublin area" and which suggest that long-term non-voters are far more likely to be socially disadvantaged and to lack knowledge of and interest in political institutions than regular voter, and "accidental", and short-term non-voters. (See: N. HARDIMAN, 'Inequality and the Representation of Interests', in W. CROTTY and D. SCHMITT, *Ireland and the Politics of* Change (1998), 122, 135). These findings would appear to indicate that socio-economically disadvantaged parents are less likely to vote than their more affluent counterparts, thereby resulting in a loss in representation of their children's interests.

disadvantaged children may have parents who *cannot* vote .[50] An American example of this would be children whose parents have been convicted of a felony, living in states where the law provides that once a person has been convicted of a felony, they lose their right to vote. As there is often a much higher level of felony convictions per capita in disadvantaged communities than in relatively well-off ones, children living in such conditions will suffer from a disproportionate lack of representation due to their parents' disenfranchisement. Third, children may not have parents or guardians to vote on their behalf at all. This is a growing issue in societies such as South Africa where AIDS has led to a huge number of child-headed households.[51] Such children have no parent or guardian to represent their interests at the polls. Therefore, they must rely on groups other than their own parents in order to ensure that their interests are represented in the democratic process. Finally, when, due to parental neglect or abuse, children have been taken from their parents and put in state care, not only do they arguably have no parent to vote on their behalf,[52] but also their legal guardian (the state) is not empowered to vote on their behalf. Indeed, the state may have serious conflicts of interest with efforts to vindicate children's socio-economic interests, in light of, amongst other things, the costs that giving effect to such interests may entail for the state.

b. Parents representing children's interests generally

25. The paper will now turn to the issue of parents ensuring representation for the interests of children in general and not just the particular interests of their own children. MNOOKIN states that, "*Parents are the obvious potential spokesmen for*

---

[50] For instance, a recent report by the Mexican American Legal Defense Fund (MALDEF) found that Latinos are more likely to be banned from voting compared to their percentage of the voting population as a result of these laws. (See: MALDEF. *Diminished Voting Power in the Latino Community: The Impact of Felony Disenfranchisement Laws in Ten Targeted States* (2003). This will clearly have a significant impact on the representation of children from Latino communities by their parents.

[51] It is estimated that by 2010 more than two million children in South Africa under the age of five will have lost their mothers to AIDS. (Budget vote speech to the national assembly, Minister of Social Development 3 April 2001: <http://www.info.gov.za/speeches/index.htm> (accessed 1 September 2005)). However, children may also be orphaned or left without adult care-givers for a range of reasons, not just because of the HIV/Aids pandemic. For example, parents may die from other causes, such as motor vehicle accidents. Alternatively, they may migrate and otherwise abandon their child. (See: J. SLOTH-NIELSEN, *Realising the Rights of Children Growing up in Child-headed Households – A Guide to Laws, Policies and Social Advocacy*, (Bellville: Community Law Centre, 2004), 6: <http://www.communitylawcentre.org.za/ser/docs_2004/Child-headed-households_1.pdf>, (accessed 13 October 2006).

[52] We say "arguably" because in some developed, countries children are removed from low-income families on the grounds that parents have failed to provide their children with necessities or because of homelessness. The removal of such children is not due to their parents being 'bad' and unloving. Thus, such parents may vote to represent their children's interests.

children.... [However, the] more diffuse the payoff to one's own child; the less likely an individual parent is to pursue it. Parents may not feel their own children are sufficiently affected by broad policies to warrant the effort of participating. Moreover, since most parents look first to their own children's interests, parent groups tend to split into self-protective factions instead of focussing on the needs of children in general."[53]

Furthermore, it must be borne in mind that while parents may be prepared to represent the interests of a particular group of children in the political process, this will not necessarily mean they will represent *all* children. This can be linked to the notion of "other people's children". Other people's children may be "shiftless or dangerous influences on one's own children; they may be potential competitors to one's own children in schools or in entry into limited occupations; they may impose social costs that detract from one's own children's opportunities".[54] These concerns mean that 'other people's children' may not necessarily be a group whose interests parents are interested in representing and forwarding in the democratic process.

The concept of family autonomy may also play a part in explaining the unwillingness of parents to represent the interests of other people's children. Children are regarded as part of a family that bears primary responsibility for assuring their needs. This is reflected in both national[55] and international law[56] and results in a sense among parents that they merely have a duty to ensure that the socio-economic needs of their own children are met. This reduces children's issues to matters of private rather than public concern and may well translate into a reluctance on the part of parents to represent the interests of children generally in the law and policy making processes.

Finally, even where parents are prepared to vote to forward children's interests while their children are still young, once their own offspring reach majority this "parental solicitude" may disappear. On a related note, there is evidence that as people (parents

53 R. MNOOKIN, *In the Interest of Children – Advocacy, Law Reform, and Public Policy*, (New York: W.H. Freeman & Co., 1985), 39.

54 W. N. GRUBB and M. LAZERSON, *Broken Promises: How Americans Fail Their Children*, (Chicago: University of Chicago Press, 1982), 78. For more on this issue, see ibid. at 78–85. While the authors write in an American context, much of what they write is applicable to other societies in which there are sharp social and economic inequalities. See also B. BENNETT WOODHOUSE, 'The Constitutionalisation of Children's Rights: Incorporating Emerging Human Rights in Constitutional Doctrine', (1999) 2 *U. Pa. J. Const. L. (University of Philadelphia Journal of Constitutional Law)* 1, 2–3.

55 E.g., in the case of *Grootboom* v *Oostenberg Municipality and Ors* 2000 (3) BCLR 277 (C), para. 77, the South African Constitutional Court held that the obligation to provide for children's socio-economic needs (in this case, shelter) is imposed primarily on the parents or the family of the children and only alternatively on the state.

56 E.g., Art. 18 of the CRC states that parents or, as the case may be, legal guardians, have the primary responsibility for the upbringing and development of the child.

or otherwise) age, their willingness to vote in favour of measures that would forward children's socio-economic interests may decrease.[57]

We should note also that if parents do vote in such a way as to ensure that children in general are represented in the democratic process, this does not necessarily mean that children's representation by parents will be effective. Even if we assume that those parents who reside with children vote in their interest, children may still be substantially underrepresented overall where the number of voters who can be presumed to vote to forward children's socio-economic interests (i.e. generally parents) is smaller than or similar to the number of voters not doing so.[58]

7.2.3. Representation of children by adults generally

26. It has been asserted that, "*Every rights movement has had powerful help from the outside in addition to the heroes who have arisen from within the oppressed groups. The children's rights movement differs only in that, thus far, rights are claimed, fought for and administered primarily by those outside of that group, by adults. But all adults were once members of that group and can legitimately claim representation.*"[59]

WRINGE has pointed out that, when it comes to meeting the needs of others, there will always be other, more pressing priorities in a free society of rational individuals until the provision for need brings some tangible advantage to the provider. This might be some crude material advantage like economic return, political influence or social approval, or some more subtle benefit such as the easing of a tender conscience.[60]

---

57 Evidence of this is a poll conducted by the Gallup organisation in 1983, asking whether people would vote to raise taxes for their local schools if the school board were to make a request. Those polled who were younger than fifty were evenly split in their response; those older than fifty were opposed, sixty-two to twenty-eight percent. Cited in J. MASLOW COHEN, supra (note 15), 2245.

58 In a US context, J. RUTHERFORD has pointed out that in an average United States congressional district in 1997, parents and the children who live with them comprised over two-thirds of the people but controlled only just over half the votes. See: J. RUTHERFORD, 'One Child, One Vote: Proxies for Parents', (1998) 82 *Minn. L. Rev. (Minnesota Law Review)* 1463, 1465–6. In contrast, adults not living with children comprised less than one-third of the people but controlled nearly half the votes. As a result, when the pie is divided, children were dramatically underrepresented in the political process. (*Ibid.* at 1466)

59 A. MCGILLIVRAY, 'Why Children Do Have Equal Rights: In Reply to Laura Purdy', (1994) 2 *International Journal of Children's Rights*, 243, 253–4.

60 C. WRINGE, 'Liberal Individualism, Welfare Rights and the Right to Education', in M. FREEMAN and P. VEERMAN (eds.), *The Ideologies of Children's Rights*, (Dordrecht: Martinus Nijhoff Publishers, 1991), 191,194. Children cannot form part of this "society of rational individuals" as their lack of autonomy renders them neither free nor equal, both of which are prerequisites for membership of this entity.

This comment may be extended to include the catering for children's socio-economic rights needs through representation of children's interests by adults in majority-decision making processes. In her critique of the treatment of children under American law, FITZGERALD points out that adults "*retrieve children's issues from the private realm of family life when responding to children's needs also serves our own purposes as adults*".[61] The same is true in relation to children's socio-economic rights. Unless adults gain from the vindication of children's interests, they may not ensure that such interests are represented in the legislative or policymaking process.

27. There is an additional problem with adults representing children. While we may argue that adults share the same socio-economic interests as children (e.g. in health, shelter, social security), some of these shared interests may be of different importance to the two groups. We have already argued that children are less capable of supporting themselves than adults are. Therefore, a child would arguably be most concerned that adults represent their interest in ensuring that the state provides the goods and services necessary for their survival. However, adults may regard other child-interests related issues as more pressing as they have greater implications for the interests of adults (for instance, the reproductive health rights of minors). In addition, some adults may prefer to advocate for some rights of children, while ignoring others. Thus, even well-intentioned adults may jeopardise some of their children's socio-economic rights-related interests by failing to vote to forward all of them. Thus, even where adults do represent children's interests, they may not represent *all* of these interests or accord the relative priority to different interests that children themselves would.

28. Voting on child-related issues is not the only way by which adults in general may ensure that children's socio-economic rights are forwarded through majoritarian decision-making processes. There are many groups of (enfranchised) adults who campaign on issues that will positively impact on the enjoyment of socio-economic rights by children. Such groups include women's groups, trade unions, and other organisations of professionals.

It is important to note, however, that with many policy issues that affect directly on children, it is agendas and interests other than children's needs and rights that fuel and define the campaign.[62] However, beneficial adult self-interested goals are to children, they are by no means identical to children's own individual interests.

61 W. FITZGERALD, supra (note 45), 14–5.

62 N. HAYES, *Children's Rights – Whose Right? A Review of Child Policy Development in Ireland*, (Dublin: The Policy Institute, 2002), 30.

Lobby or interest groups for adults may only address children's issues or purport to represent children where the needs of children provide support to the ends of the group.[63] Therefore, where children's interests diverge from or threaten those of adults, they will not be effectively represented. Furthermore, in campaigns run by adults, which aim to forward the interests of both children and adults, children's interests are likely be subordinated to those of adults because the adults running the campaigns may be expected to accord greater priority to their own interests.

Another issue is that many groups who claim to "speak for" children lack the same claim to representativeness that other groups campaigning in the policy-making process (for instance, trade unions) would have.[64] There is no formal criteria for determining the representativeness of such groups and they may have little claim to authority over their alleged "support base" of children. This should be borne in mind when considering whether such groups should be considered as representing children's interests.

Finally, in the absence of a particular concern for children (which most adults may not share) there is little incentive for adults to form lobby groups to ensure representation of children. If the individuals to be served wield few votes (in children's case, none), those who might organise on the individuals' behalf have limited incentive and capacity to serve them.[65]

7.2.4. Ensuring virtual representation through sympathy or empathy

29. Virtual representation may not occur only when there is a "communion of interests and sympathy in feelings and desires". It is arguable that where there is a sufficient sense of empathy with, or sympathy for, children, enfranchised adults will vote to ensure children's interests are effectively represented. At first glance, this would seem to be particularly true in relation to parents. The fact all adults once were children would appear to suggest that they will have a greater insight into the position of, and empathy with, children than they would in relation to socially disadvantaged groups of which not all adults will have been members (i.e., women or non-nationals). However, virtual representation based on "empathy" or "sympathy" is likely to be limited in much the same way that virtual representation based on a "communion of interests" is, that is, to situations in which children are perceived as non-threatening and where those who empathise do not have a competing interest in the social goods

[63] R. MNOOKIN, supra (note 53), 40.

[64] This and the following sentence are adapted from HARDIMAN's comments in relation to organisations claiming to speak for disadvantaged groups. N. HARDIMAN, supra (note 49), 136–7.

[65] J. RUTHERFORD, supra (note 58), 1495.

necessary to vindicate children's rights. Such empathy is likely to be overridden in situations in which those who are empathising have interests that would not be served by acting on that empathy. In addition, the fact that all adults have been children does not mean that they have all been socio-economically deprived children, thus it cannot be presumed that they will have any particular empathy with such children, or any insight in relation to those of their socio-economic interests that need to be represented in democratic processes.[66]

Any effective system of representation of children cannot be dependent exclusively on "sympathy" or "empathy" as this would only lead to representation of children in limited circumstances and would not provide for those groups of children who are unlikely to generate the widespread sympathy or empathy amongst voting adults required to ensure that their interests are represented in democratic processes.[67] If "sympathy" were sufficient to ensure that children's material needs were met, there would arguably be no call for children to have socio-economic rights at all. Such rights would not be necessary as parental and adult sympathy, empathy or affection would ensure that children's socio-economic needs were met.[68] Claims about the lack of necessity for children's rights have been criticised for being premised on a false, golden view of the life-experiences of children and for idealising adult-child relations by emphasising that adults (and parents in particular) have the best interests of children at heart.[69] The same critiques may be levelled at the notion that the presumptions underlying the claim that sympathy or empathy will ensure effective virtual representation of children.

7.2.5. Bringing children's interests/rights to bear through their exercising indirect influence on democratic decision-making processes themselves

30. It is often argued that children are incapable of organising themselves into an effective lobby[70] due to their lack of resources and, depending on their age, lack of

[66] Obviously this argument is weaker in relation to developing countries such as South Africa where many voting adults can indeed empathise with poor children due to having experienced similar conditions during their childhood.

[67] For instance, adolescent rapists living in appalling prison conditions.

[68] Obviously, there are numerous other justifications for and advantages in having rights (e.g. the close relationship between rights, dignity and respect and the importance of the status of "rights-bearer"). For more on this, see M. FREEMAN, 'Taking Children's Rights More Seriously', in P. ALSTON, S. PARKER and J. SEYMOUR (eds.), *Children, Rights and the Law*, (Oxford: Clarendon Press, 1992); M. FREEMAN, 'The Limits of Children's Rights', in M. FREEMAN (ed.), *The Moral Status of Children – Essays on the Rights of the Child*, (Dordrecht: Martinus Nijhoff Publishers, 1997), 83, 84–87; A. MCGILLIVRAY, supra (note 59).

[69] M. FREEMAN, 'Taking Children's Rights More Seriously', supra (note 68), 55–6.

[70] J. RUTHERFORD, supra (note 58), 1474.

organising abilities.[71] Furthermore, since the ranks of childhood are continuously depleted by entry into adult life, no "children's movement" on the model of the women's movement or civil rights movement can be envisaged.[72] There are groups of children (generally older adolescents) to whom some of these claims may not apply. However, the issue of the transience of childhood will apply to all.

Ultimately, the major obstacle to children ensuring indirect representation of their interests by the activities of a "child lobby" is not simply the limited capacity of children to form such a group but the fact that where children's aims collide with those of other more influential groups in society, they will lose. In other words, the parameters of the effectiveness of a children's lobby will be defined by the extent to which the aims of that lobby group do not threaten the interests of other societal groups.

There are many numerically insignificant groups that exert a far greater influence on political policymaking and lawmakers than can be accounted for in terms of the number of votes they wield. Often this can be attributed to the economic influence of such groups. An important contributory factor to the lack of indirect representation of children in democracy is their economic powerlessness.

Children generally have far fewer financial resources than adults have and are unlikely to be able to acquire more due to, amongst other things, legal limitations upon their ability to earn money.[73] Furthermore, children often do not have the same degree of control or freedom of choice regarding their assets as adults do. In addition, the resources available to children will vary greatly with a great disparity between those of children from different socio-economic backgrounds. Thus, those children who are most at risk of socio-economic rights violations are likely to have far fewer resources available to them than their wealthier counterparts. Finally, and perhaps most importantly, while they are consumers and form a market at which marketing and advertising campaigns are increasingly being aimed, children (and particularly younger ones) may lack the knowledge, experience and judgment that is required in order to use the money they have in a strategic way. This developmental deficit is as strong a contributor to children's economic powerlessness as is their fiscal deficit. It

---

71 Ibid., 1494.

72 O. O'NEILL, *Constructions of Reason – Explorations of Kant's Practical Philosophy*, (Cambridge: Cambridge University Press, 1989), 203.

73 There are several such limitations – not all of which are state-condoned. The first restriction of children's ability to earn money are regulations on child labour, which aim to remove children from the workforce in order to enable them to benefit from education and to protect them from economic exploitation. A less benevolent limitation on children's earning power is the fact that their minority is often used as an excuse to pay children less than adults are for work of equivalent value.

results in their failing to use the (generally limited) economic resources available to them to exert indirect influence on the political process in such a way as to turn themselves into a political or social force to be reckoned with.

Another reason for children's limited ability to ensure their own indirect representation in the democratic process is their lack of control over the media. Children are effectively excluded from participating in media activities apart from serving as the subject of news stories and, therefore, the media rarely presents children's issues from children's perspectives. Children are often portrayed by the media as problematic victims[74] or dangerous delinquents.[75] The media is a key tool for any group seeking to exercise indirect influence on public opinion and the political process. Children's incapacity to employ it poses a critical obstacle to their ensuring that they benefit from indirect representation in political processes.

8. THE EXCLUSION OF CHILDREN FROM DEMOCRATIC PROCESSES – A BLOW AGAINST THE COUNTER-MAJORITARIAN OBJECTION TO JUDICIAL INTERVENTION TO GUARANTEE CHILDREN'S SOCIO-ECONOMIC RIGHTS?

31. At the most fundamental level, the counter-majoritarian objection is premised on the notion that "the people" governed should correspond to "the people" governing. The actions of elected representatives are taken to be the expression of the will of the prevailing majority in the society governed and hence should not be overruled by judges who, as unelected officials, cannot presume to speak for a constituency. Arguably, for the actions of the elected branches of government to be legitimately regarded as the will of the majority of a society, each member of society must have had an opportunity to participate and have their views taken into account

[74] For instance, there has been much sympathetic media coverage in South Africa of the plight children who are living with HIV/AIDS. However, referring to children affected by HIV/AIDS as "victims" may lead to further stigmatisation and is disempowering, especially when considering that many of these children survive in adverse conditions and continue to live full lives. (C. DESMOND, 'Children challenge victim stereotype', (2005) 55 *ChildrenFIRST*: <http://www.childrenfirst.org.za/shownews?mode=content&id=21153&refto=4019> (accessed: 13 October 2006).

[75] For more on this, see, e.g., comments of the Committee on the Rights of the Child made during the CRC Committee, *Day of General Discussion on The Child and the Media*, (UN Doc. CRC/C/50, 1996), para. 245, where the committee encouraged the media to contribute to improving the image of the child through their reporting. Reference was made to the most common stereotypes in media reporting about children, such as the "violent teen-ager" or the misrepresentation of children from specific groups.

– either directly through voting or indirectly through representation of their views by others.

Although children are undoubtedly affected by the decisions of "the majority" (that is, the majority of the electorate), their unenfranchisement means that they cannot have direct input into the democratic system by voting and are expressly precluded from forming part of that majority. Furthermore, we have argued above that children's views are not taken into account in democracy due both to their exclusion from direct participation in majority-decision making processes and the frequent failure of those who do directly participate to effectively represent children's views and interests. Thus, children do not have either a direct or an indirect input into majority-decision making processes and, while forming part of the *governed* people, do not form part of the *governing* people. Therefore, the principle of self-government ensured by political accountability that underlines (and, arguably, justifies) the counter-majoritarian objection would appear not to apply to children.

32. In conclusion, children have socio-economic rights that must be assured by the societies to which they belong. An absolute application of the counter-majoritarian objection to the courts acting in an assertive way to ensure the enforcement of children's rights may result in children's claims to provision and protection by society being rendered meaningless. This is due to children's extremely limited ability to exert influence on the elected branches of government and the ineffective representation of their rights and interests by others. In the absence of judicial intervention, children's rights risk being unvindicated, with children simultaneously failing to enjoy political equality and the other benefits and protections that theorists claim are accorded to citizens under a majoritarian conception of democracy. This greatly weakens the counter-majoritarian objection to the courts acting assertively in order to ensure that children's socio-economic rights are guaranteed.

THE CHILD'S RIGHT TO PLAY: THE RIGHT TO BE A CHILD

JAN VAN GILS

1. INTRODUCTION

1. In the Convention on the Rights of the Child (CRC) there is very little attention for the child's right to play. This is remarkable because everyone knows that to play is the most typical behaviour of children and at the same time, everyone agrees that children should have more opportunities to play. Nevertheless, starting from both this scarce attention and the basic philosophy of the CRC, it is possible to develop some strong arguments to pay more attention to children's play, because taking into account children's viewpoints on play proves that the right to play means the right to be a child.

This paper is based on the assumption that the CRC continuously requires discussions and interpretations. In discussing such interpretations in order to apply them on a concrete domain, we have to place every article within the global convention on the one hand and we have to listen to children to learn about their approach on the other.

2. HOW TO UNDERSTAND THE CRC?

2. When evaluating the progress and the achievements of the CRC, the analyser will be in confrontation with some rights that are very difficult to determine. And when they are hard to define, they are also hard to be evaluated. Some illustrations: it will ask a lot of discussion to give a clear definition of the right to freedom of association, or the right to privacy and the right to access to information. The problems to define these rights are largely related to the difficulty to realise a good balance of participation on the one hand and protection on the other. As far as it concerns the freedom of association, children have – apart from this right – also the right to be protected against some of its (legal) consequences, which they can hardly oversee. And what about the right to privacy in their own room if parents assume their children are using drugs? Is not it the duty of parents to take care of their children? What is, in both cases, the right balance between the right to protection and the right to participation?

The discussions on such questions are very important for the application of the CRC. They will make the CRC a living document that is much more than an icon, a symbol, a bible containing the final knowledge and wisdom concerning children. Teachers and parents and other educators too often see the CRC as the end of the discussion. These educators were always surprised when confronted with the idea that one of their tasks is the interpretation of the CRC: they have to be partners in the discussions with the authorities on how to read and interpret the CRC.

While having such discussions, people should be aware that the convention is written by adults and for adults, and in a very specific historical context.[1] Children were not involved in the process. So the conceptual frames were born in adult brains. In addition, it might be possible and it is even probable that children give different meaning to some concepts than adults do. However, we should not be concerned about such different approaches; it should not cause a problem because the CRC solves this problem stating that the State Parties assure the child to have the right to express his/her views freely in all matters affecting the child. Thus, applied to itself, the CRC stimulates the discussion with children, listening also to their views.

For that reason, there should be more discussion on the content of the CRC, while involving children. During the last decade several ways of organising children's participation have been developed; now is the moment to apply this expertise to involve children in the discussion on the interpretation of the Convention. This is not a plea to make a "childish" translation of the CRC, or to elaborate a new CRC. The worldwide accepted document is a very basis if everyone accepts it has to be interpreted repeatedly because every interpretation has its historical, social and cultural roots. So within every period, within every social and cultural context those discussions should be organised and should lead to appropriate steps.

3.HOW TO UNDERSTAND ARTICLE 31 OF THE CRC?

3.1. THE COMPREHENSIVE APPROACH OF THE CRC

3. Before illustrating children's approach to the right to play, it is important to stress that for a correct interpretation we have to take into account the comprehensive

---

1 As a historical document, the CRC has the characteristics of the period in which it was written, telling us a lot about that period, especially about the attitude to children at that time. It is quite relevant to be aware that the CRC was written at the end of the 20th century, called – by Ellen Key – the century of the child, but what we prefer to call the century of the protection of the child.

approach of the Convention.[2] The Convention should not be seen as an enumeration of articles, but as a coherent whole, since all articles interact with all articles; they are interwoven, adding meaning to each other.

4. Talking about play, we have to take into consideration the broad context offered by several articles of the Convention. The first group of articles, which is directly related to play:

- Article 12: The child has the right to express her/his own views freely in all matters affecting the child.
- Article 13: The child has the right to freedom of expression.
- Article 14: States Parties shall respect the right of the child to freedom of thought, conscience and religion.
- Article 15: States Parties recognise the rights of the child to freedom of association and the freedom of peaceful assembly.
- Article 31: States Parties recognise the right of the child to rest and leisure, to engage in play and recreational activities appropriate to the age of the child and to participate freely in cultural life and the arts.

All of these articles have a strong interrelation; they all are related to "participation" of the child, to the very own way children participate in social life. All of these articles stress the idea that children live in a social context, that they belong to society and that they can contribute to social life by expressing their feelings, their ideas and their opinions.[3]

Another characteristic that these articles have in common is the word "freely" or "freedom". While playing, children need a lot of freedom to organise their life, and to dispose of their time, of the use of space and of their contact with other people: they need self-determination.

Within this context, playing is more than engaging in playful activities. The right to play is more than the right to have some time for childish activities. Within the context of the whole Convention, the right to play is the right to belong to society which respects the approach of children as a very typical contribution to social life and to children's own development, even if this has characteristics (playfulness) that are unusual to adults.

---

2 M.S. Pais, 'Monitoring Children's Rights. A view from Within', in E.Verhellen (ed.), *Monitoring Children's rights*, (The Hague – Boston – London: Martinus Nijhoff Publishers, 1996).

3 E.Verhellen, 'Ombudswork for childeren. A strategy for a fully-fledged position of children in our society', in E.Verhellen (ed.), *Ombudswork for childeren*, (Leuven – Amersfoort: Acco, 1989).

However, there are a lot more articles that can be related to play:

- Article 3: "In all actions concerning children .... the best interest of the child shall be a primary consideration." This is a very important and strong Article calling for action but it has to be interpreted. We have to participate in the discussion on this interpretation by stressing the idea that the best interest of the child definitely has to be related to play and playing should be taken into account in all actions concerning children.
- Article 17: "The States Parties shall encourage the mass media to disseminate information and material of social and cultural benefit to the child ..." Information about how to play is of great social and cultural benefit to the child and such information should be disseminated by the mass media. This idea can introduce a more interactive approach of the media, which is the way children like it.[4]
- Article 24: "States Parties shall take appropriate measures to develop preventive health care." Talking about health care, we also have to include mental health care. This is a very typical Greek approach;[5] anyway, maybe playing is the most powerful preventive activity to mental health.
- Article 27: "States Parties recognise the right of every child to a standard of living adequate for the child's physical, mental, spiritual, moral and social development." When children are playing, they are developing themselves in several respects. This is at least one good criterion to judge if the standard of living is adequate for children: does it permit children to play? It is remarkable that during the last few years, the actions of UNICEF in disaster areas have paid more and more attention to children's play.
- Article 29: "States Parties agree that the education of the child shall be directed to the development of the child's personality, talents and mental and physical abilities to their fullest potential." In stimulating the development of the child to its fullest potential, education should create more space and time for play directed by children themselves.

In trying to consider the Convention as a whole and to situate children's play into this context, playing should not be seen as an activity children are doing on a safe island far away from social life. To play is very strongly related to all the aspects of the development of the child, to the health of the child and to the social position of the child. To play continuously is a characteristic of children's lives. To plea for play is to plea for the rights of the child, and to plea for the rights of the child is to plea for play.

---

4 J. Van Gils and M. Bosscher, *Kinderen en televisie: tegengestelde belangen*, (Leuven – Apeldoorn: Garant, 1997).

5 H. Agathonos, *Children as citizens of Europe. From rhetoric's to reality*, (Belfast – paper, 1998).

3.2. ARTICLE 31

5. If one reads Article 31 of the CRC without accounting for the context of the whole CRC, one must be disillusioned. Article 31 states:

"1. States Parties recognise the right of the child to rest and leisure, to engage in play and recreational activities appropriate to the age of the child and to participate freely in cultural life and the arts.

2. States Parties shall respect and promote the right of the child to participate fully in cultural and artistic life and shall encourage the provision of appropriate and equal opportunities for cultural, artistic, recreational and leisure activity."

In this article, play seems to be reduced to recreational activities, to joyful activities offering children some rest after a period of hard working, for example in the classroom. It seems to be a compensatory approach to play: during work stress and tensions are built up, and from time to time children need the opportunity to release them in order to be able to function normally (read: like adults), and to work during another period of time. Play is the valve that allows children to release superfluous energy. In fact, this interpretation refers to an old approach of children's play being a useless activity that one has to allow in order to avoid bigger problems. It is also related to prevention of criminality, while children are playing, they do not do anything worse – the devil finds work in idle hands.

However, studying the whole article, we recognise that play being integrated into an article talking about participation in cultural life and in the arts, cannot be coincidental. The whole article makes us suppose that the term "recreation" is not used in the original and out-of-date sense of the word: re-create, create once again, restore. Play, recreation, cultural and artistic activities all belong to the same category and to culture in the broad sense of the word. All these activities have in common the fact that they refer to the universal human capacity to classify, codify and communicate their experiences symbolically.[6] This approach opens a totally different dimension of children's play and fits more with the conclusions of the CRC's comprehensive approach.

6. Without trying to write an all-inclusive definition of play, the analysis we have made offers a few characteristics:

- the word freely refers to the possibility of children organising their own lives;
- this because self-determination contributes to the development of social life, to the health and to the overall development of the child;

[6] Definition retrieved from <http://en.wikipedia.org/>.

- to play refers to children's contribution to cultural life, not just as a passive consumer but also as an actor.

4. AN OVERVIEW OF 18 RESEARCH PROJECTS IN A SECONDARY ANALYSIS

7. Nevertheless, even if there are wise words starting from the Convention, the floor has to be passed to the children, since they have not yet been involved in the discussion/interpretation.

For this analysis, we refer to 18 research projects finalised during the last decennium. None of them are focused on play as such, but all of them are qualitative research projects with children in the age group of 8 to 13, and they all relate to children at play. We made a secondary analysis of the research, looking for the way children talked about play. Can we retrieve the meaning of play in all the data? The data we used was not collected for our purpose. However, it was very useful because it was based on children's experience of play rather than their opinions on play, and because they are offering different approaches to the same behaviour. We figured out what children mean while talking about play in different contexts and we did not reduce children's play to what we as adults and as researchers define as "playing".

We refer to research on the perception of time and the passing of time among 8 and 11 year olds,[7] but also to general research into the social environment of children;[8] to research into the perception of sports by 11 year olds[9]; to international research about what children think about their family;[10] to research into the perception of television by children;[11] and to research on the way they perceive nurseries.[12] We also

7 J.VAN GILS, *De tijdsbesteding, de tijdsbeleving en de opvoeding op woensdag*, senior dissertation, (Leuven: K.U.L., 1992), ["The passing of time, the perception of time and education on Wednesday"].

8 J.VAN GILS, *Wie niet weg is, is gezien. Hoe beleven kinderen het gezin, de school en de vrije tijd*, (Brussel: KBS, 1992), ["If you're not gone, you're caught. How do children perceive family, school and leisure time"].

9 In co-operation with the University of Antwerp; see: H. VAN PELT et al., *Sportbeleving bij kinderen*, (Antwerpen: UIA, 1995), ["The perception of sports by children"].

10 J. VAN GILS, *Kinderen over het gezin. Vergelijkende kwalitatieve studie betreffende de beleving van het gezin bij kinderen van 7–12 jaar in België, Frankrijk, Nederland, Portugal en Spanje*, (Meise: Kind en Samenleving, 1995), (also published in French and Spanish), [Children about the family. Comparative qualitative study on the perception of the family by children at the age of 7 to 12 in Belgium, France, the Netherlands, Portugal and Spain"].

11 In co-operation with the KUL, Catholic University of Leuven; see: J.VAN GILS and M. BOSSCHER, supra (note 4).

12 M. BOSSCHER, *Kwali-tijd in de buitenschoolse kinderopvang*, (Meise: Kind en Samenleving, 1997), ["Quali-time in the nurseries outside school"].

refer to two investigations, performed in East Flemish boroughs (Hamme and Wachtebeke) into the leisure time of children and to research into the way young people formulate their need for care.[13]

We also used the piles of letters concerning very different themes, which we received through some very renowned children's magazines and which are an endless source of inspiration.[14] Recently, there have been a lot of research projects focusing on children's approaches in different parks.[15] An analysis of children's perspectives on the city of Brussels was also conducted,[16] and there was an important project on children's autonomous mobility.[17]

The table below gives a quick view of the target groups of the above-mentioned investigations:

	Age
Sports (1)	10 years old
Leisure (2)	11–14 years old
Nurseries (1)	5, 8, 11 years old
School (1)	6–11 years old
Family (1)	8–11 years old
Care (1)	10–11 years old
Perception of time (1)	8, 11 years old

13 Established in co-operation with the University of Ghent; see: G. VERSCHELDEN, M. BOUVERNE-DE BIE and J. VAN GILS, *Belevingsonderzoek bij kinderen en jongeren. Kinderen en jongeren over hun behoeften aan zorg.* (Gent: Universiteit Gent, 2000), [Children and their needs for care].

14 We organise the discussion columns in the following magazines, *Zonneland* ["Land of the sun"] and *Zonnestraal* ["Ray of sunshine"]. In these columns, children between the age group of 8 to 11 bring forward topics for discussions, which they would want to present to their peers.

15 Projects on how children experience green spaces, see: M. JANS, *Kinderen in het Vrijbroekpark*, (Meise: Kind en Samenleving, 2003); M. JANS, *Kinderen en jongeren in het provinciaal domein d'Ursel*, (Meise: Kind en Samenleving, 2003); W. VANDERSTEDE, *Kinderen in de Provinciale Groendomeinen. Regio Antwerpen: het Rivierenhof*, (Meise: Kind en Samenleving, 2004); W. VANDERSTEDE, *Kinderen in de Provinciale Groendomeinen. Regio Antwerpen: het Hof van Leysen*, (Meise: Kind en Samenleving, 2004); W.VANDERSTEDE, *Kinderen in de Provinciale Groendomeinen. Regio Antwerpen: Vrieselhof*, (Meise: Kind en Samenleving, 2004); W.VANDERSTEDE, P. DEKEYSER and B.VAN DER WEE, *Kinderen in de Provinciale Groendomeinen. Regio Kempen, Provinciaal Domein Prinsenhof*, (Meise: Kind en Samenleving, 2004); W.VANDERSTEDE P. DEKEYSER and B. VAN DER WEE , *Kinderen in de Provinciale Groendomeinen. Regio Kempen, De Avergten*, (Meise: Kind en Samenleving, 2004).

16 J.VAN GILS, *Kinderen filosoferen over de stad. Een belevingsonderzoek op basis van filosofische gesprekken van Brusselse kinderen van 10 à 12 jaar*, (Meise: Kind en Samenleving, 2000), [Children philosophise about the city].

17 Vervoersafhankelijkheid en vervoersautonomie van kinderen (10–13 jaar), Onderzoeksrapporten, [Research project 2004–2005, of Belgian Federal Public Planning Service, Science Policy, Transportation dependency and transportation autonomy of children – report in English soon available on the website <http://www.k-s.be>].

Perception of TV (1)	10 years old
Magazines (many)	8–9 years old, 10–11 years old
City of Brussels (1)	10–11 years old
Green areas (7)	8–14 years old
Autonomous mobility (1)	10–13 years old

4.1. PLAYING: AN OPEN CONCEPT

8. A first impression of children's ideas about play can directly be developed from the research into the perception of time. It strongly seems that children very often use the word playing to define a certain occupation that cannot be described by a more concrete name.[18] Children talk about playing in the garden or playing in the streets as activities that cannot be described in more detail. Therefore, children describe circumstances, but very often, we do not receive a more detailed description of the activity itself: "What have you been doing? I have been playing. And what were you doing while playing? I played with my dolls in the garden."

There is a difference between the description of concrete activities and the description of playing. When children are discussing concrete activities, they talk about going for a ride on their bikes, about going roller-skating, about having a talk with the neighbours. However, the description of playing is rather vague; they talk about playing outdoors, playing indoors, playing hairdresser, playing with the dog and so on. The word "playing" is used for a wider scope of activities, a more open category and a less sharply outlined category. It is a name for activities, which still need to be interpreted.

Children talk about fighting with water and playing with water; they talk about practising judo and playing judo, and there is a distinction between the two. Playing refers to a quality of an activity which implies that its objective still has to be interpreted by the children. The real purpose of it is various, and not yet clearly defined.

Another illustration is children asking, "Can I go and play?". This is a fairly fundamental question. They are not asking for something very definite, they are asking for a very general permission. By asking, "Can I go and play?" children request to have a say in the passing of their time. "Can I go and play?" is a request for the right to self-determination. By saying, "Yes", parents give their children a kind of carte blanche, a free hand. Parents do not know what their children will do, because the children

[18] H. AGATHONOS, supra (note 5).

themselves do not know it (yet). If they want to go outside to play in the streets, it is because there is mostly something interesting to do, or because they have arranged to meet a friend, or whatever. What they are planning to do is not yet defined. They are going to play.

Perhaps, development psychologists will claim that the above-mentioned linguistic usage is simply linked up with the development of concepts. As long as they do not have a better word at their disposal, children use the word "play". In that case, "play" is just a primitive word. This kind of interpretation is a typical example of adult-centrism; the adult considers himself the standard and proceeding from this approach children are not yet fully-grown people. The only purpose of being a child is to become an adult; being a child is a temporary phase, unavoidable, a waiting room for the real life. What they will be when they grow up is of major importance – that is what it is all about; that is the only aim.

The interpretation that the linguistic usage involved with playing is merely an early phase in the development of people, does not respect the child's perspective or the play of the child. Someone who really tries to understand what playing means to children will not lose oneself in such educationalism, psychology or sociology, which start from the adult frame of reference; he or she will listen to the child and try to understand its personal interpretation.

Consequently, from the children's viewpoint, to play is an open concept. It offers the child the possibility not yet to know what to do, or to hide the real objective of the activity.

4.2. PLAYING OUTDOORS

9. The second conspicuous phenomenon, which has been perceived is, if children are talking about playing, about really playing, they are talking about playing outdoors. If one asks children "tell us about your playing", children start immediately talking about playing outdoors such as playing in the streets, in the garden, in the playground, in the woods, on the beach, etc. Only when asking questions that are more specific on indoor activities, we obtain information about playthings, a playroom, a computer and so on. Inside their home children play with dolls, or on the computer, but that does not seem to be the "full" playing, the playing in the real sense of the word. Playing indoors is a kind of substitute for real playing because the activities children want to do outdoors, are impossible. For example, if children are jumping and running, they are causing noise nuisance for the neighbours.

This is also conspicuous in the context of school: if children are talking about "playing" in this context, then they are talking about playing outdoors. Party games, knocking things together are considered fun; however, if children are talking about really playing, they have to be able to get outside.

A strong illustration of this statement can be found in the audience survey of children. During summer, children watch television only half as much as in winter. This conclusion is reached repeatedly in many studies. In summer, children go and play outdoors, and in this context, playing can counter watching television. Playing in winter cannot beat the television offer, but summery playing can.

4.3. PLAYING AND SPORTS

10. Looking at the way children perceive sports, we see that practising sports has to do with control, competition, teamwork and spectators. These four elements keep popping up when children are talking about sports! Even informal sport is characterised by them. In this way, the trainer is neither an entertainer, nor animator. She/he needs to know this particular branch of sport and she/he has to teach the sport. And before and after the training session, children will play: in the changing rooms, in the shower, on their way to and from the sport grounds, etc.

The difference between play and sports is not about a certain gradation. Playing is no underdeveloped form of sport, or sport is no derivation of playing; they are fundamentally two different things. Among other things this illustrates the complexity of children: children do not just want to play, they want to practise a sport as well; children do not just want to explore the world at their own pace, they also want to be taught all sorts of things: they want both.

4.4. PLAY AND FIGHTING

11. In a nutshell, starting from the above-mentioned data we have concluded that playing is a quality of activities that still can be defined by the children, that it is preferably done outdoors, and that it is fundamentally different from practising a sport.

12. KUIK[19] conducted an ethnographic study at the school playground among children of the age of 10 and older. She spent a long time with the children in order

[19] S.KUIK, *Mag ik op je rug? Van de kinderen en hun dagen in vriendschap en ruzie*, (Amsterdam: Het Spinhuis, 1996), ["Can I have a piggyback ? About children and their friendship and fights."]

to discover their personal interpretation of their activities. She hoped to write a nice story about playing; instead, it turned out to be a story about fighting. The activities of the teenagers could not be characterised as playing in the sense of playing games. The word "fighting" was more appropriate. This fighting was not about changed moral categories, big conflicts, less tolerance or great mutual discrepancies. It turned out that children were constantly arguing, about what was beautiful and what was not (earrings or piercings for instance), about which clothes were in vogue and what music was up to date, what drinks and what sweets were tasty. They compared the ways someone talked back at someone, whether that person was overdoing it or not, and they had arguments about what they were going to do. The children were constantly arguing. In fact, KUIK concluded the children were always looking for standards and rules; they were constantly having a row with standards. Obviously, as this fighting is a way of interpretation, it seems to be an extremely important activity since the search for values, for standards is to a considerable extent, taking place by fighting. This study is especially important because it allows looking at these children's rows from a different point of view; they contribute to the human process of sense giving. This study supports the plea to give children more space for self-development and to suppress the adult impulse to react with "classic educational intentions". This is why it is advisable to be rather careful with all kinds of preventative campaigns against bullying: they may restrict – proceeding from a typically adult way of perceiving fights – children's field of experience.

However, in this context it is important to determine that this fighting happens in the context of playing. And we recognise a similar fight, when children are organising their games; the fight about the rules often takes more time than the game itself. Perhaps, every way of playing is a form of fighting: "fighting with yourself, fighting with your environment, fighting with others and while fighting finding your own place". Children are busy exploring and exploring contains a lot of conflict material. Material for conflicts with yourself (playing is often accompanied by crying), material for conflicts with the material environment (children are very strongly concentrated on getting a grip on that environment), material for conflicts with others (rows). Perhaps many educational ideas about a harmonious development are very naïve, and maybe playing should rather be considered dealing with conflicts.

4.5. SOCIAL CHARACTERISTIC OF PLAYING

13. In the study on the family, playing was brought up in two different contexts: playing with parents and playing with a brother or sister.

It was conspicuous that children of the age group of 7 to 8 talked about playing with their parents with more enthusiasm than about playing with their brothers and sisters. This playing very strongly reflects the "being together". In this context, playing means getting attention, having fun, being occupied with something very intensely, larking about, teasing and tickling; the feeling of solidarity, of belonging together is at the centre stage. In this context, playing is acting communicatively and dialogically.

The older children (9 to 10 years) have similar feelings of belonging together but they prefer chatting with their parents to playing. Playing figured prominently when they talked about their brothers or sisters, and about pet animals: being occupied in an exploring way, looking for meaning, interpreting, exploring, looking for a place of their own, etc. gain the upper hand and in that way partners are more than welcome (as we explained in relation to the fighting).

Philosophising with children on the city, the neighbourhood and the street, children explain that they really like to hang around with other children, to chat with neighbours (young and old) and finally to play with peers. Thus, other people are very important for a good and inspiring play-environment. Applying BRONFENBRENNER's ecological circles[20] and the research on children's range of action,[21] we can understand that the partners are changing with the age of the children; however of more importance is the general statement that playing has very strong social characteristics.

The same phenomenon was perceived both, in pre and after school childcare and at home. Children of 9 years old were very clear about it: when there are no peers in the nursery, it is unpleasant to be there. They also often complain about not being allowed to go and play with a friend. Consequently, the presence of other children can be considered as the most important quality of a good play-environment. The next quality is to have a private place for themselves and their friends. That is the reason why rhododendrons are so popular in parks. They offer the best opportunities to find a place to stay, chat and be together. A last illustration of this statement is that children are characterising their important activities in the parks by being together, being contemplative[22] and being explorative; however, the first thing they mention is being together.

---

20 U.BRONFENBRENNER, *The Ecology of Human Development: Experiments by Nature and Design*, (Cambridge, MA: Harvard University Press, 1979).

21 J.VAN ANDEL , *Woonomgeving en kinderen. Een onderzoek naar de invloed van ruimtelijke kenmerken en veranderingen van de woonomgeving op kinderen van 6 tot 12 jaar*, (Eindhoven: Technische Universiteit, 1985).

22 "being contemplative" should be understood as enjoying, being open to impressions coming from outside.

4.6. PLAYING AS A PRIVILEGED DOMAIN FOR AUTONOMOUS TIME MANAGEMENT

14. The nursery study as well as the study on the perception of time, shows that children from the age group of 8 to 9 onwards talk about having control over their own agenda, programme and organisation of their day. It explains the number of very strong reactions against homework. What seems very unjustified to children is that their so-called leisure time is taken up by homework and lessons. For example, when the teacher goes on with the lesson after the sign to stop, they become very angry about it – the teacher should not take up any break-time. The ability to control their own time is of major importance to children; that is why they spend so much time discussing what they are going to play. This fight for autonomy is also a fight for space for self-development, for learning what they want to learn: sports, computers, knocking things together, working with clay, acting and so on. This way of learning does not exclude adult support but it offers the children the possibility to make an appeal to guidance, to be taught all kinds of interesting skills.

These observations teach us more about human nature than about children's play. Nevertheless, they inform us about the symbolic value of children's play. The right to play seems to be evident to children; to play is their privilege. Pleading for autonomy, they use playing as the lever.

The price they have to pay for it is called "boredom". When children themselves decide about their activities, sometimes they do not know what to do. Adults understand this as a very negative moment and they are afraid of it, because to them this kind of boredom is at the origin of undesirable behaviour. However, children explained to us that they developed several strategies to fill up these empty moments by watching television, sitting on a swing or talking to their mother. These are moments in which they are going to decide what they are going to do. They have to make a decision. Indeed this is the price they have to pay for autonomous time management.

4.7. POLYCHRONIC LIFE

15. While conducting our research on children and television, we ran into the concept "polychronic life".[23] Children watch television polychronically, while adults proceed from the idea that children watch television monochronically.

[23] L. BARRIOS , *Familia y televisión*, (Caracas : Monte Avila Latinoamaricana, 1992).

Being polychronically occupied with something refers to "being occupied with a number of activities at the same time". It refers to fluently switching from one occupation to another. Being monochronically occupied with something means "being concentrated on one occupation and exclusively being occupied with it".

Adults teach children to work monochronically: "when you watch TV, you do not read and *vice versa*; when you are doing your homework, you make sure you won't get distracted. If you want to play with something else, you first have to tidy up and so on."

That is not how a child's perception works. Children live polychronically – they are very open to all what is happening in their environment; they play along with it; they react to it. Educators then tend to say that children are easily distracted, but play experts stipulate that these children react in an extremely alert way; they have spotted everything; they are all eyes and ears.

Children watch television polychronically: they are watching a programme, but at the same time they are playing or reading. They zap very easily from one programme to another and they switch just as easily between television and playing, and at that moment, the television is switched on needlessly. For children, this polychronic way of life has many advantages. Children learn to deal with the television while zapping: they learn how to quickly assimilate information, they learn how to deal with images in an incredibly skilful way, they quickly spot connections, and they quickly link up the connection between two things. Children are able to think circularly, while adults tend to think linearly.

Playing too is pre-eminently such a polychronic way of being occupied, since it is characterised by similar fast changes in rhythm and activity, by a tangle of connections, constantly linked up by children. They start to play with a ball, suddenly they spot a skateboard and the next moment, they start to skate. This is how the playing evolves, how it develops. This is a very open lifestyle, a very creative one as well.

5. CONCLUSION

16. In itself, this analysis offers no spectacular novelties. However, it puts the emphasis on a number of dimensions, which to children probably sum up the essence of playing. But these are often the same dimensions adults sometimes have problems with. For instance, quickly changing activities are often interpreted as a lack of concentration; hanging around looking for what they will do, is often seen as boredom and thus to be avoided; playing outdoors is easily related to social danger and exploring while fighting is often seen as disrespectful to each other. For the sake of convenience, adults tend to forget some dimensions of playing, or in every way, they find them less important than all kinds of educational occupations, since adults state that the value of the education comes before the value of playing. However, the objective is to combine children's concerns about play with the approaches of the CRC.

17. Where the CRC uses a few times the word "freely", it refers to the children's needs to organise their own life. Children make it more concrete; they need "permission to play"; they need the possibility to organise some activities (need for space and for time) without always knowing what they will end in. They ask for chances to have friends to play with. Their play includes discussions, fights, conflicts which they have to deal with themselves.

Self-determination means that children want to explore their world themselves; they want to define their world. They do not want to be guided all the time: they want to look for their own way, their own experiences, and their own development.

However, there are aspects children do not mention. They do not worry about their social development or their health. Nevertheless, it is good that these protection rights are described in the CRC: children need people that are concerned about those rights. The concerns about play safety expressed by the European Play Safety Forum[24] and the initiatives of Speelom[25] are concrete illustrations of the balance between participation rights and protection rights.

18. Considering all these reflections, especially from the viewpoint of the child, the right to play is not an additional right, limited to a very small part of CRC Article 31. It reflects fully the right to be a child, here and now. In the whole CRC there is no article that stresses as explicitly the right to be a child in the present, without delaying his 'raison d'être' to the future.[26] So while stressing the importance of the right to play, people are supporting the right to be a child.

---

24 See Manifesto of the European Play Safety Forum on <http://www.fepi-play.org/>.

25 Speelom vzw, p.o. Vijverlaan 53, 2610 Wilrijk, Belgium.

26 Starting from these conclusions, a model can be developed to obtain data from both children and adults to evaluate the child's right to play. It can be very useful while writing the reports State Parties have to submit to the Committee on the Rights of the Child. And of course NGO's can use it to write their reports, (see: Annex).

ANNEX 1

Suggestions for the evaluation of the Child's Right to Play
To be used for the national or NGO report on the Rights of the Child.

Produced by the Research Centre Childhood and Society, Belgium, May 2006

1. COLLECTION OF DATA

1.1. What kind of data?

Data about the play opportunities in everyday situations of the child: in schools, child care, living environment and hospitals.

Data about the situation in every setting: the spatial situation, the time available for play, the tolerance of adults, the presence of other children and the possibilities for the children to define for themselves the play circumstances (or are they totally offered / defined by adults?).

1.2. Where and how to collect the data?

Offer the possibility to children of several ages and to other experts (play leaders, teachers, parents, youth workers, etc.) to give their opinion.

To know about children's opinions, you can have an informal or a formal talk with them on the themes mentioned above.

To question older children (+11) or adults, you can ask for an evaluation of every item on a scale from 1 to 5. Collect those forms and make tables of them.

2. INTERPRETATION OF THE DATA

While interpreting the data, you make an evaluation of the play situation. This evaluation will describe the real problems but should at the same time offer the authorities suggestions about how to optimise the situation.

The data should offer information to identify and describe the worst situations and the causes of it:

- is there a lack of legal guidelines? (on urban planning, on safety guidelines, on the school curriculum, etc.)
- is there a lack of training possibilities? (for volunteers, for professionals, for teachers, etc.)

- is there a dominance of adult centred objectives in educational initiatives?
- are play problems related to the poverty of the children, their housing situation, their illegal situation, a disability, etc.?

Add comments on how those situations can be changed, for example by working on infrastructure, on better timetables, by campaigns to influence the public opinion, by organising training courses for play leaders, etc.

Describe the responsibility of the authorities.

	Time available	Space	Tolerance	Friends	Self-determination
School					
Childcare					
Living environment					
Hospitals					

A RIGHT TO TREATMENT FOR CHILDREN WITH A PSYCHIATRIC DISABILITY

A legal analysis of international human rights law

FIONA ANG

1. INTRODUCTION

1. In this presentation, it is examined if a right to mental health or even psychiatric treatment exists for children under public international law, and in particular international human rights law. The question whether children[1] with a psychiatric disability[2] have such a right to treatment[3] is analysed from a legal point of view.

Therefore, it is essential to consult the legal sources of public international law, both at the universal and the regional – in this case European – level. The universal binding sources most relevant for this paper are the Convention on the Rights of the Child (CRC), the International Covenant on Economic, Social and Cultural Rights (CESCR), the International Covenant on Civil and Political Rights (CCPR), the Convention Against Torture (CAT), and the draft International Convention on the Rights of Persons with Disabilities (draft DAC). In case the text of these treaties is not unambiguously clear, it needs to be interpreted in line with the rules of public international law.[4] This presentation takes into account non-binding universal sources

---

1. A "child" is any human being below the age of eighteen years (*cf.* Art. 1 CRC).
2. This terminology was chosen to comply with human rights discourse (*cf.* the draft International Convention on the Rights of Persons with Disabilities). "Disability" is a generic term encompassing problems at all three levels of functioning, as explained in the International Classification of Functioning, Disability and Health, created by the World Health Organization, see: <http://www.who.int/classifications/icf/>.
3. "Treatment" is used in the broadest possible sense, including all types of care administered by a health professional aimed at the diagnosis, conservation, restoration or improvement of someone's health.
4. *Cf.* the Vienna Convention on the Law of Treaties.

such as the drafting history (*travaux préparatoires*), the documents issued by the UN monitoring bodies (General Comments, Concluding Observations, Individual Communications), and other UN instruments such as the Declaration on the Rights of Disabled Persons (Disability Declaration),[5] Principles for the Protection of Persons with Mental Illness and the improvement of mental health care (MI Principles),[6] and the Standard Rules on the Equalisation of Opportunities for Persons with Disabilities (Standard Rules).[7]

At the regional European level, the binding sources include the European Convention for the Protection of Human Rights and Fundamental Freedoms (ECHR) and the European Social Charter (ESC). Non-binding yet however quite strong with regard to their legal value,[8] are the judgments rendered by the European Court of Human Rights. Also at the European level, a body of experts monitors states' compliance with a treaty: the European Social Committee issues observations regarding the ESC. A number of non-binding regional instruments exists which may be relevant to children with a psychiatric disability.[9]

As is the case with most patients' rights, a right to treatment is only recognised in several non-binding instruments. According to the MI Principles, there is a right to "appropriate" treatment,[10] while the Standard Rules acknowledge a right to "regular" treatment.[11] Even in the relatively old Disability Declaration, a reference is made to a right to "medical, functional and psychological treatment".[12] However, since these instruments are clearly non-binding, thus not legally obliging States to realise this right to treatment, it becomes necessary to examine whether a right to treatment could be derived from the binding treaties. These treaties contain provisions that can easily be associated with a right to treatment: the right to health (1), the prohibition of cruel, inhuman or degrading treatment (2), the right to privacy (3), and the right to recovery and reintegration (4).

5 Adopted by the UN General Assembly by resolution 3447 (XXX) of 9 December 1975.
6 Adopted by the UN General Assembly by resolution 46/119 of 17 December 1991.
7 Adopted by the UN General Assembly by resolution 48/96 of 4 March 1994.
8 This case law is in theory merely binding upon the States involved. However, in practice, it is generally complied with and followed, including domestic courts.
9 Quite significantly is the Council of Europe Recommendation Rec(2004)10 *concerning the protection of the human rights and dignity of persons with mental disorder* (adopted by the Committee of Ministers on 22 September 2004).
10 MI Principles 8(1) and 9.
11 Standard Rule 2(6).
12 Disability Declaration, para. 6.

2. A RIGHT TO TREATMENT FOR CHILDREN WITH A PSYCHIATRIC DISABILITY UNDER BINDING HUMAN RIGHTS LAW

2.1. HEALTH

2. The right to health is laid down in Article 24 CRC, Article 12 CESCR and Article 11 ESC. If combined, two elements may indicate the existence of a right to treatment for children with a psychiatric disability: whether the right to health encompasses a right to *mental* health, and whether it implies a right to *treatment*.

2.1.1. CRC

3. Neither of those two elements is present in Article 24 CRC.[13] A right to *facilities* for treatment is recognised, as is the right to *access health care services*. A right to mental health is totally absent in the text of this provision. The *travaux préparatoires* are silent on these omissions. The CRC Committee, however, has made it very clear in its General Comment 4 on Adolescent Health that Article 24 CRC is applicable to mental health.[14]

Noteworthy in this regard is that the CRC Committee has declared that primary health care should give special attention to mental health.[15] Bearing in mind the fact that the state obligation to provide primary health care is a "minimum core obligation", this means that this particular obligation should be implemented immediately and presumably regardless of the resources available to a State.[16]

---

13 Art. 24 CRC:
"*1. State Parties recognise the right of the child to the enjoyment of the highest attainable standard of health and to facilities for the treatment of illness and rehabilitation of health. State Parties shall strive to ensure that no child is deprived of his or her right of access to such health care services.*
2. State Parties shall pursue full implementation of this right and, in particular, shall take appropriate measures: [...]
(b) To ensure the provision of necessary medical assistance and health care to all children with an emphasis on the development of primary health care; [...]".

14 E.g. CRC Committee, *General Comment No 4: Adolescent Health and Development in the context of the Convention on the Rights of the Child* (UN Doc. CRC/GC/2003/4, 2003), paras. 22, 29, 39 and 41.

15 Ibid., para. 41(a).

16 CRC Committee, *General Comment No 5: General Measures of Implementation* (UN Doc. CRC/GC/2003/5), para. 5.

Another relevant provision in the CRC is Article 23,[17] to date the only existing binding provision specifically dealing with the rights of children with a disability. In Article 23, assistance given to children with a psychiatric disability must be designed to ensure effective access by the child to health care. The drafting history of this provision reveals that the drafters of the CRC have chosen the phrase "effective access" to make sure that a child with a disability is "*not only guaranteed access* to services but [that he or she is] placed in a position to *receive them effectively*".[18] This phrasing points to an obligation for States to ensure children with a disability, including a psychiatric one, a right to treatment.

2.1.2. CESCR

4. Still at the universal level, the right to health is also recognised in Article 12 CESCR,[19] which is undoubtedly applicable to children. The text explicitly mentions the right to mental health and obliges States to take steps to achieve the full realisation of this right, including those steps necessary to create conditions "which would assure to all medical service and medical attention in the event of sickness". According to the *travaux préparatoires*, this phrase was added because the drafters were concerned that "quite apart from the importance of an accurate diagnosis, assistance in the form of drugs, hospitalisation, etc. was often necessary".[20] This clearly indicates the existence of an obligation for States to create conditions necessary for realising a right to treatment for all.

---

17 Art. 23 CRC: "*3. Recognising the special needs of a disabled child, assistance extended in accordance with paragraph 2 of the present Article shall be provided free of charge, whenever possible, taking into account the financial resources of the parents or others caring for the child, and shall be designed to ensure that the disabled child has effective access to and receives education, training, health care services, rehabilitation services, preparation for employment and recreation opportunities in a manner conducive to the child's achieving the fullest possible social integration and individual development, including his or her cultural and spiritual development [...]*".

18 UN Doc. E/CN.4/1983/62, para. 65.

19 Art. 12 CESCR:
"*1. The State Parties to [the CESCR] recognise the right of everyone to the enjoyment of the highest attainable standard of physical and mental health.*
2. The steps to be taken by the State Parties [...] to achieve the full realisation of this right shall include those necessary for:
(a) The provision for the reduction of the stillbirth-rate and of infant mortality and for the healthy development of the child;
(b) The improvement of all aspects of environmental and industrial hygiene;
(c) The prevention, treatment and control of epidemic, endemic, occupational and other diseases;
(d) The creation of conditions which would assure to all medical service and medical attention in the event of sickness."

20 Cited by B. Toebes, *The Right to Health as a Human Right in International Law*, (Antwerp – Groningen – Oxford: Intersentia/Hart, 1999), 44.

Likewise, the CESCR Committee has strengthened the case for the existence of such a right in its General Comment No. 14 on the Right to Health. In this elaborate document, it specifies that the medical services mentioned in Article 12 CESCR include "appropriate mental health treatment and care".[21]

2.1.3. ESC

5. Article 11 ESC[22] gives the impression that the ESC is merely concerned with the prevention of health problems and the general promotion of health, being silent on both a right to treatment and a mental dimension of the right to health. Nevertheless, the European Social Committee has made numerous statements on States' implementation of mental health issues.[23] From the Committee's observations, it furthermore becomes clear that the right to health also in the European context encompasses not only preventive or promotional aspects, but also curative – treatment-related – aspects.[24]

2.2. CRUEL, INHUMAN AND DEGRADING TREATMENT

6. The second right that can be associated with the treatment of children with a psychiatric disability, is the right not to be tortured or treated in a cruel, inhuman or degrading way. In the particular context of non-refoulement, the bodies monitoring or enforcing this right consider that the absence of psychiatric treatment can be a violation of the prohibition of torture or cruel, inhuman and degrading treatment. The principle of non-refoulement is laid down in the 1951 Geneva Refugees Convention, forbidding States to deport an individual to a country where there is a risk that he or she will be tortured. In this context, it seems that the lack of medical, including psychiatric, treatment, is taken into account to determine this risk.

---

21 CESCR Committee, *General Comment No 14: The Right to the Highest Attainable Standard of Health (Article 12 CESCR)* (UN Doc. E/C.12/2000/4, 2000), para. 17.

22 Art. 11 ESC: "*With a view to ensuring the effective exercise of the right to protection of health, the Parties undertake, either directly or in co-operation with public or private organisations, to take appropriate measures designed inter alia:*
1. to remove as far as possible the causes of ill-health;
2. to provide advisory and educational facilities for the promotion of health and the encouragement of individual responsibility in matters of health;
3. to prevent as far as possible epidemic, endemic and other diseases, as well as accidents."

23 *E.g.* European Social Committee, *Conclusions: Norway* (ESC, 1996), 121–122.

24 L. Samuel, *Fundamental Social Rights: Case Law of the European Social Charter*, (Strasbourg: Council of Europe Publishing, 2002), 269.

2.2.1. CCPR

7. At the universal level, the Human Rights Committee used this line of reasoning in an Individual Communication, which dealt with a national from Iran suffering from a psychiatric disability: "8.5 [...] *the Committee considers that deportation of the author to a country where it is unlikely that he would receive the treatment necessary for the illness caused, in whole or in part, because of the State party's violation of the author's rights would amount to a violation of Article 7 of the Covenant.*"[25]

However, it would be difficult to deduct from this mere sentence a legal right to treatment. Firstly, it concerns only an Individual Communication, not a General Comment interpreting the CCPR. Secondly, there is only one of them. Finally, the Human Rights Committee took various factors apart from the absence of psychiatric treatment into account, while a right to treatment could only be derived if this absence of treatment were decisive to determine a violation.

2.2.2. ECHR

8. In addition, the European Court of Human Rights has considered this issue with regard to Article 3 ECHR in the context of non-refoulement. From *D. v. UK*, it appears that the lack of medical treatment may contravene Article 3:[26] "*Against this background the Court will determine whether there is a real risk that the applicant's removal would be contrary to the standards of Article 3 (Art. 3) in view of his present medical condition. In so doing the Court will assess the risk in the light of the material before it at the time of its consideration of the case, including the most recent information on his state of health [...]*

The abrupt withdrawal of these facilities will entail the most dramatic consequences for him. It is not disputed that his removal will hasten his death. There is a serious danger that the conditions of adversity, which await him in St Kitts, will further reduce his already limited life expectancy and subject him to acute mental and physical suffering. Any medical treatment which he might hope to receive there could not contend with the infections which he may possibly contract on account of his lack of shelter and of a proper diet as well as exposure to the health and sanitation problems which beset the population of St Kitts. [...] There is no evidence of any other form of moral or social support. Nor has it been shown whether the applicant would be guaranteed a bed in either of the hospitals on the island which, according to the Government, care for AIDS patients [...]."

---

[25] Human Rights Committee, *C. v. Australia*, individual communication (UN Doc. CCPR/C/76/900/1999).

[26] ECtHR, *D. v. UK*, 2 May 1997, paras. 50 and 52.

However, it should be noted that this case did not concern psychiatric treatment: it dealt with a person who was terminally ill.

Bensaïd v. UK did relate to psychiatric treatment. The Court stated the following:[27] "*The difficulties in obtaining medication and the stress inherent in returning to that part of Algeria, where there is violence and active terrorism, would, according to the applicant, seriously endanger his health. Deterioration in his already existing mental illness could involve relapse into hallucinations and psychotic delusions involving self-harm and harm to others, as well as restrictions in social functioning (such as withdrawal and lack of motivation). The Court considers that the suffering associated with such a relapse could, in principle, fall within the scope of Article 3.*"

Nevertheless, given the high threshold to be reached for the application of Article 3 ECHR, the Court would not easily judge that there has been a violation of this provision.

2.3. PRIVACY

9. In the same judgment, *Bensaïd v. UK*, the Court also considered whether the deportation of Mr Bensaïd would violate Article 8 ECHR. Remarkably, it noted:[28] "*'Private life' is a broad term not susceptible to exhaustive definition. [...] Mental health must also be regarded as a crucial part of private life associated with the aspect of moral integrity. Article 8 protects a right to identity and personal development, and the right to establish and develop relationships with other human beings and the outside world [...] The preservation of mental stability is in that context an indispensable precondition to effective enjoyment of the right to respect for private life.*"

Stating that mental health is in fact part of "moral integrity" as included in the right to privacy, the Court however did not find that there had been a violation of Article 8 in this particular case. Too many factors were too speculative and hypothetical to determine that the lack of psychiatric treatment violated Mr Bensaïd's right to privacy.[29]

---

[27] ECtHR, *Bensaïd v. UK*, 6 February 2001, para. 37.

[28] Ibid., para. 47.

[29] Ibid., para. 48.

2.4. RECOVERY AND REINTEGRATION

10. Finally, Article 39 CRC[30] should be taken a closer look at when examining the possible existence of a right to treatment for children with a psychiatric disability. Not much research has been done regarding this particular provision,[31] which is rather unfortunate given the latter's unique status in international human rights law. It can be noted that – in spite of the phrasing in terms of an obligation – it is generally accepted that this provision does indeed contain a *right* to physical and psychological recovery and social reintegration.[32]

The text of Article 39 CRC reveals that this provision is applicable to children who are victim of certain situations: neglect, exploitation or abuse; torture or cruel, inhuman or degrading treatment; armed conflicts. However, the CRC Committee has expanded the applicability *ratione personae* considerably. In its General Guidelines on Reporting and its Concluding Observations, it has judged that the right to recovery and reintegration should also be realised for children in conflict with the law,[33] victims of drug abuse,[34] children in institutional care,[35] victims of natural disasters,[36] and internally displaced children.[37] Therefore, the CRC Committee has clearly made Article 39 applicable to a 'wide range of potential child victims'.[38]

Ratione materiae, Article 39 CRC deals with, *inter alia*, the psychological recovery of child victims. Although, as stated above, not much research has been conducted regarding the exact extent of the notion of "psychological recovery", it can be pointed

---

30 Art. 39 CRC: "*State Parties shall take all appropriate measures to promote physical and psychological recovery and social reintegration of a child victim of: any form of neglect, exploitation or abuse; torture or any other form of cruel, inhuman or degrading treatment or punishment; or armed conflicts. Such recovery and reintegration shall take place in an environment which fosters the health, self-respect and dignity of the child.*"

31 L. N. Robinson, 'The Globalization of Female Child Prostitution: a Call for Reintegration and Recovery Measures via Article 39 of the United Nations Convention on the Rights of the Child', (1997) *Indiana Journal of Global Legal Studies*, 239 at 256.

32 *E.g.* CRC Committee, *Concluding Observations: Austria* (UN Doc. A/55/41, 2000), para. 451. See also S. Detrick, *A Commentary on the Convention on the Rights of the Child*, (The Hague: Kluwer Law International, 1999), 668.

33 CRC Committee, *Reporting Guidelines for Initial Reports* (UN Doc. CRC/C/5, 1991), para. 23(b)(iv).

34 Ibid., para. 23(c)(ii).

35 *E.g.* CRC Committee, *Concluding Observations: Uruguay* (UN Doc. A/53/41, 1998), para. 341.

36 *E.g.* CRC Committee, *Concluding Observations: Nicaragua* (UN Doc. A/55/41, 2000), para. 769.

37 *E.g.* CRC Committee, *Concluding Observations: Russian Federation* (UN Doc. A/55/41, 2000), para. 901.

38 R. Hodgkin and P. Newell, Implementation Handbook for the Convention on the Rights of the Child, (New York: UNICEF, 2002), 580.

out that according to Jaap DOEK, current Chair of the CRC Committee, it certainly includes psychiatric treatment.[39]

3. CONCLUSION

11. In conclusion, the question whether a right to treatment exists for children with a psychiatric disability under public international law can be answered in a qualified positive way. No absolute or firm confirmation can be given, since to date there is no single binding treaty text providing for such a right. Notwithstanding this silence in binding human rights law, nevertheless, it should not be ignored that there are many factors pointing to an existence of such a right.

39 J. DOEK, 'The Protection of Children's Rights and the United Nations Convention on the Rights of the Child: Achievements and Challenges', (2003) *Saint Louis University Public Law Review*, 235 at 242.

VII. CHILDREN'S RIGHTS AND THE FAMILY

CHILDREN'S RIGHTS IN RELATION TO THEIR FAMILY

NIGEL CANTWELL

1. INTRODUCTION

1. The Convention on the Rights of the Child (CRC) "*is a parent's nightmare. It usurps the right of parents to determine the moral and spiritual development of their children. It wipes out parental rights, and gives children nearly unlimited freedoms to determine their own destinies without parental interference. The upcoming [...] summit will prove to be yet another effort of the United Nations to destroy the traditional family and to place all authority for parental decisions in the hands of a totalitarian UN agency.*"[1]

These words are come from the chairperson of an organisation that claims to represent 43,000 churches and who appears to have been inexplicably preoccupied about the likelihood that UNICEF would be put in charge of arbitrarily splitting up families following the UN General Assembly's Special Session on Children in 2002.

2. It is of course always useful to look at what "the opposition" is saying, including in its most extreme ideological forms such as the citation above. Over the period since the CRC was first officially mooted, in the late 1970s, varying degrees of fear or fury have indeed been expressed about the effects that "children's rights" could have on the sanctity and stability of the family and on parental "authority". These have sometimes come from rather surprising quarters – including certain government delegates, during the drafting itself, who were often quite adamant that their country would never agree to the inclusion of certain formulations. Interestingly, all the proposed provisions that they contested – essentially concerning civil rights – were nonetheless accepted in the end.

3. Problems have also arisen in this regard at grass-roots level in the more traditional societies, where many of the thrusts of the CRC may be viewed as Western-inspired

1 L.P. SHELDON, *United Nations Children's Fund Seeks to Usurp Parental Rights*, Traditional Values Coalition, 2 January 2001 at<http://www.traditionalvalues.org>.

and dangerous. Refugees in a camp in Jordan, for example, reportedly look on the CRC as a Western initiative to break up the family unit, and which can allow and promote public intervention into the privacy of the family unit.[2]

4. Against a conflictual background such as this, it is even more necessary to look at the reality of how – taking inspiration from the title of this Conference – the theory (and interpretation) of the CRC meets practice on the fundamental issue of children's rights and the family.

2. "THE FAMILY": WHOSE ROLES AND RESPONSIBILITIES?

5. It would be helpful to have a neat definition of "family" in order to examine its relationship with children's rights. However, attempts to find a universally acceptable and sufficiently comprehensive definition have understandably always proved hazardous; in the end, rather like the concept of "the best interests of the child", it is surely best left to interpretation according to the circumstances and the society involved. The problem is nonetheless compounded in the framework of the CRC in that the latter's provisions refer variously to "parents" and "family", as well as to a range of other related terms. While parents are obviously subsumed under "family", it is rather less evident to argue for systematically equating "parents" with "family" where only the former term is used.

6. Some commentators[3] have sought to take the widest definition in the CRC to be the basic reference point for interpretation throughout the treaty: "parents [...], the members of the extended family or community as provided for by local custom, legal guardians or other persons legally responsible for the child" (Art. 5). While this may be an attractive proposition, in particular, for defending the notion of the CRC's universality, it may not stand up to a number of challenges:

- it is not the first – which would make it potentially the baseline – mention of "parents and others" in the operative provisions of the Convention, and previous Article 3 indeed takes a more restrictive view, talking only of "parents, legal guardians or other individuals legally responsible for [the child]", which would

---

[2] L. HAMMAD, *Cultural interpretation of the CRC*, workshop presentation, International Interdisciplinary Conference on Children's Rights, Ghent, 18–19 May 2006.

[3] See for example: E. BREMS, *Human rights: universality and diversity*, plenary presentation, International Interdisciplinary Conference on Children's Rights, Ghent, 18–19 May 2006.

therefore only include "members of the extended family or community as provided for by local custom" if they are also legally recognised;

- the mention under Article 5 concerns only very specific duties – "to provide [...] appropriate direction and guidance in the exercise by the child of the rights recognised" in the CRC – to which the broader definition seems particularly well-suited;
- in the context of subsequent articles, there would often seem to be good reason for specifying a more limited list of duty-bearers; blanket application of the broader definition would therefore be inappropriate, and an attempt at its selective application would clearly be fraught with dangers.

7. Although the term "family" appears throughout the CRC, only four times does the treaty explicitly mention the wider family as such: "family members" (Art. 2.2), "members of the extended family" (Art. 5), "another member of the family" (Art. 9.4) and "other members of the family" (Art. 22), although it also refers rather ambiguously to "members of [the applicants'] family" (Art. 10.1), as well as to "relatives" in the very specific context of Article 21 on adoption.

At various points, however, it uses a range of terms to describe those who might be acting *in loco parentis*, and whose number could well include extended family members. Sometimes these references are made in addition to parents, as with "legal guardians" (Art. 14, Art.18, etc.), "other individuals legally responsible for [the child]" (Art. 3), "others responsible for the child" (Art. 27), or "others caring for the child" (Art. 23.2, Art. 23.3). In other cases, parents and, potentially, the wider family and many others are quite simply included implicitly in the term used, for example: "those responsible for his or her care" (Art. 23.3) and "persons having responsibility for the maintenance of the child" (Art. 26).

In sum, the rights and duties of the "family" as regards the child – and consequently the latter's rights in their respect – are not always distinguishable from those of alternative caregivers, and in some instances are limited to parents alone or at best to wider family members on condition that they have *legal* responsibility for the child.

Finally, it can be noted in passing that the CRC's only reference – albeit an oblique one – to the child's responsibilities in this sphere states that the child's education "shall be directed to [...] the development of respect for the child's parents" (Art. 29), not the family. Indeed, we have to look to the African Charter on the Rights and Welfare of the Child (Art. 31) to find that "[e]very child shall have responsibilities towards his family...".

3. NO RIGHT TO A FAMILY

8. Whatever children's rights in relation to the family may be, it is important to emphasise that those rights concern *their* family. As such, they notably do not include "the right to *a* family", despite the surprisingly frequent slogans and affirmations proclaiming this to be the case.

The CRC sets out, *inter alia*, conditions (e.g. in Art. 9) under which children's ties with their parents may justifiably be partially or wholly suspended, or definitively annulled. In parallel, it strongly emphasises the desirability of the child's growing up in a family environment (Preamble) and implicitly suggests (Art. 20) that, where the child cannot live with the biological family, a family-based alternative solution should be considered first. Nowhere does it stipulate, however, the child's *right* to live in a family environment.

To preserve the full potential of the CRC as a common basis for understanding and action, it is vital to avoid qualifying recommended policy objectives and desirable aims such as these – and, even worse, what are nothing more than "claims" from certain quarters – as "rights". Not only would the denomination "right" be inaccurate in itself, however accepting it could set precedents for other such transformations. This would risk undermining the whole *raison d'être* of a treaty that, precisely, sets out to clarify the nature of children's human rights.

4. PROTECTION OF THE FAMILY AND ITS ROLE; PROTECTION OF THE CHILD IN (OR FROM) THE FAMILY; PROTECTION OF THE CHILD WITHOUT PARENTAL CARE

9. The present review of the letter and spirit of the CRC and assessment of its impact in the light of experience to date focuses on three main inter-linked areas:

- Protection of the family and its role
- Protection of the child in (or from) the family
- Protection of the child without parental care

4.1. PROTECTION OF THE FAMILY AND ITS ROLE

10. Undeniably, a main thrust of the CRC is to promote the role of the parents – and in some cases the wider family – as the child's primary caregivers. This involves both respecting their responsibility for nurturing, protecting and guiding the child, and assisting them to do so whenever necessary and possible. The State's obligation to support parents in providing the child with "an adequate standard of living" (Art. 28) and its recognition of their responsibilities for providing "appropriate direction and guidance" (Art. 5) are just two of many possible examples of how this fundamental principle is enshrined in the treaty.

11. Probably, the principal global concern in this regard is the frequency of lack of compliance with these obligations, and how easily this is allowed to lead to family breakdown. The material poverty of parents remains a significant factor in the "voluntary" relinquishment of a child to an institution, not only in Africa and Asia but also in certain Eastern European and Central Asian countries. In many industrialised countries, as ATD Fourth World has shown,[4] lack of financial means may be the immediate or underlying justification for removing children from parental care, since it is viewed as constituting neglect. Yet, it is generally true that material support to the family, wherever, would be far less costly than providing alternative care, even when accompanied by other forms of supervision and guidance.

12. Discrimination – including marginalisation and stigmatisation – on various grounds is another key factor militating against family preservation in many instances. Here, the State's obligation towards the child is crystal clear: his or her protection is to be ensured against discrimination on the basis of "the status, activities, expressed opinions or beliefs of the child's parents [...] or family members" (Art. 2.2). Undoubtedly, such discrimination would include, for example, not providing adequate support of all kinds to single mothers, and allowing or mandating deprivation of parental care on the grounds of the parents' economic status. Of special concern in this regard is the situation of children of indigenous peoples, as well as those from a minority background such as Roma, who still regularly make up an often unconscionably large proportion of those whose parents are deemed incapable of providing adequate care, often as a result of passive or active discrimination.

---

[4] ATD Fourth World, *How Poverty Separates Parents and Children: a Challenge to Human Rights*, (Méry-sur-Oise: Fourth World Publications, 2004).

4.2. PROTECTION OF THE CHILD IN (OR FROM) THE FAMILY

13. Here, we confront the supposedly thorny issue of parental responsibility and "authority" in the face of "children's rights". In reality, this is not an issue at all as far as the CRC is concerned, and it can consequently be dealt with very briefly.

14. Most of the preoccupations raised in this regard have revolved around children's civil rights, and more especially in Articles 13–16 of the CRC on the rights to freedom of expression, of thought, conscience and religion, and of peaceful assembly, as well as protection of privacy. These rights are almost identical to those contained in the 1976 International Covenant on Civil and Political Rights (ICCPR), applying to all human beings. They are essentially designed to prevent arbitrary interventions by the State in those spheres, and were reaffirmed in the CRC simply in order to demonstrate, without a shadow of doubt, that they apply also to children – they did already, by virtue of the ICCPR, however this fact was barely acknowledged. The rights come with all the usual safeguards (e.g. subject to public safety and public order conditions) and in no way, of course, constitute a *carte blanche* for children's behaviour and activity, any more than they do for that of adults.

15. Often linked with this is the concern over the implications of "the child's right to be heard", a term that is often intriguingly (or deliberately?) misinterpreted as a "right to decide". While the overall tenor of Article 12.1 is a basis for promoting children's greater participation in all aspects of their lives by being able to express their views and have them taken properly into account, in no way does it imply some kind of overriding voice on decisions made. What it requires is that children be consulted on matters affecting them, and that their opinions be taken seriously. The biggest problem in this respect does not lie in the text itself, therefore, but/however in the need for its purpose and scope to be understood and imparted convincingly in the face of such "concerns".

16. Of a far more important and complex nature, however, is the question of protection from maltreatment in the home.

There are obviously recognised limits to allowing a child to remain in parental care: indeed, the CRC does not promote the simplistic idea that children should grow up in "a family environment" as such , however explicitly in one where there is "an atmosphere of happiness, love and understanding" (Preamble).

Removal of a child from parental care to ensure his or her protection is one of the most critical decisions to be made from a children's rights perspective. Necessarily, therefore, it is an option subject to a number of safeguards, including the possibility of judicial review (Art. 9) and, in principle, due consultation with the child concerned (Art. 12). In Article 19, which is specifically devoted to the problem of intra-familial child abuse and neglect, the emphasis is more on prevention and support than on extracting the child from the family home, with judicial involvement foreseen only "as appropriate" at the very end of the provision.

Balancing the child's right, "as far as possible, to know and be cared for by his or her parents" (Art. 7) and that to protection from maltreatment (Art. 19) is constantly shown to be extraordinarily difficult in practice. The prediction of violent behaviour can never be more than a question of risk assessment, not one of "yes" or "no". If assessment shows a 50, 60 or even 70 per cent risk, what action would be deemed appropriate? Social workers responsible for initial decision-making in this regard have been sanctioned as much for leaving children in family situations that have later proved fatal as for erring on the side of caution and "unjustifiably" securing the child's removal. The judiciary and the medical profession too have been severely criticised for authorising or instigating removal on grounds subsequently shown to be baseless.

Social workers and other professionals therefore frequently feel themselves "in a bind", and one that is exacerbated in some countries where they report having to leave children in high-risk situations quite simply because no alternative care (in foster homes) is available.

17. Two trends in responses to these CRC obligations are discernible. One promotes family preservation. This may involve, in the more serious cases, intensive support and supervision by a specially trained social worker who stays with the family in its home for part or all of the day over a given period, or the temporary transfer of the entire family to a special unit where support and supervision is again provided. The other favours increased authority to remove children from any situation determined to be potentially dangerous, alongside the rapid expansion of alternative care solutions.

4.3. PROTECTION OF CHILDREN WITHOUT PARENTAL CARE (DEPRIVED OF THEIR FAMILY ENVIRONMENT)

18. In the context of this discussion on children's rights and the family, it is interesting to note that the CRC strongly protects the right of the child to be cared for by his or her *parents* (as in Arts. 7 and 9). However, the CRC requires that the State take over the protective role when the child is "temporarily or permanently deprived of his or her *family* environment" (Art. 20).

19. On the basis of the drafting process, there is no reason to read too much into this distinction in terms of the intentions of the legislator. At the same time, the non-exhaustive list of measures to be taken by the State in such circumstances indeed focuses firmly on placements outside the *family* as opposed to outside the parental home: foster care, *kafala*, adoption or residential care. Thus, although in many countries more and more formal foster care placements are being made with kin, recognition of this as an option on any significant scale did not come about until after the CRC was adopted. "Foster care" in the context of Article 20 could therefore be interpreted essentially as being provided by persons unrelated to the child following a formal decision by the competent authorities. Equally, while *kafala* may indeed be ensured by members of the child's extended family, it takes on many forms and the role of kin is in no way a necessary characteristic of the arrangement. As for intra-familial adoptions, they constitute a small minority of the total.

In other words, there would be grounds for arguing that State intervention is not required under the CRC if a child without *parental* care is in *kinship* care, that is looked after informally within the extended family. If so, this would nonetheless give rise to questions regarding the protection of the child in kinship care, and notably the role of the State in that respect.

This and the other issues surrounding out-of-home care are particularly topical in that efforts are now under way to draw up what could become United Nations Guidelines for the Protection and Alternative Care of Children without Parental Care – or, in the end, maybe other wording to that effect. At present, the goal is to secure adoption of such Guidelines by the UN General Assembly by the end of 2007.

20. As it stands today (many more consultations are foreseen), the draft of the potential Guidelines first places major emphasis on ensuring that children are not needlessly or arbitrarily separated from their parents and families. However, it then looks, in the light of international standards and experience to date, at the whole range of alternative care options and what is required to ensure that children's rights are respected and protected in those situations. During the review and consultations for drawing up the draft, wide ranges of concerns were identified, such as:

- Informal care arrangements, usually in the form of kinship care, are by far the most common worldwide, but bring with them a number of risks in terms of child protection and other rights violations. Although they are "family", kinship carers may nonetheless need material and other support to fulfil their role appropriately, and this may not be available in regard to such informal placements. Furthermore, it is not rare that instances of child abuse, neglect and exploitation are reported in these situations. On both counts, the role of the State needs to be examined, even when kinship arrangements are made precisely to avoid intervention on the part of official services;

- Where de-institutionalisation is envisaged or under way, much faith is put into the development of foster care programmes, however these cannot be seen as a panacea. Many industrialised countries are finding that the "ceiling" has been reached in terms of foster parent recruitment. In countries – the majority – where formal foster placement has so far not been a known or widespread practice, the development, and particularly the creation from scratch, of foster care systems is too often poorly conceived and resourced (financially and professionally), in part because so much emphasis has been placed to date on their comparative cheapness vis-à-vis residential care.

21. Three further problems deserve special mention in our discussion here:

1) Too many children in alternative care do not really understand why they are there – that is why they are not with their parents – and even if they do, they may disagree with the reasons given or the form of care provided. Undoubtedly, this jeopardises the likely success of the placement. It also evokes the wider problem of how little attention may be paid to consulting with the children concerned, at all stages and not just once they are in alternative care, when their right to *their* family has to be questioned or when, in the absence of their parents, other solutions have to be proposed.
2) It is very frequent to find that, once a child enters the care system, he or she will remain there until reaching the age of majority (and may then, moreover, be unceremoniously ejected and left to his or her own devices). This is especially true of residential care. In many countries, virtually the only way out is adoption, be it domestic or intercountry. This means that, in reality, little or no effort is being made in such cases to reintegrate the child in the parental home, or at least with the wider family, while the child is in care. In some cases, indeed, contact with family is passively or actively discouraged by the facility concerned, clearly indicating the intention to sever the child's relations with them. Similarly, in emergency situations, facilities may refuse to co-operate in family tracing efforts.
3) The other particularly preoccupying issue is that of child-headed households. From some angles, these may constitute the only realistic means whereby siblings can remain together, conserving what remains of their family, and they usually seem to correspond to the children's wishes when faced with the other possible options available. At the same time, of course, there is full awareness of the special vulnerability of children – and the high risk of violation of their rights – in these households. There is clearly a dilemma: should the *de facto* existence of child-headed households and the obvious protection needs of the children concerned (including especially the household "head") lead to their legal recognition because

that is a precondition to their receiving the level of systematic support and protection required? Or would such recognition in fact have the counter-productive effect of elevating them to an "over-acceptable" form of alternative care that might discourage efforts to seek out more secure and stable responses to these children's plight?

22. Finally, in this section it is worth mentioning the debate over whether residential care (*aka* institutionalisation) or intercountry adoption should be looked on as the "last resort" in terms of alternative childcare, once it has proved impossible to find a domestic family-based and permanent solution. This is not a constructive approach to the problem, however. While few would argue that long-term institutional placements constitute an optimal care option for the vast majority of children, it would be equally difficult to maintain that intercountry adoption constitutes a feasible and logical response to overuse of institutions.

What is required, on the contrary, is to seek out the "first resort" response that corresponds best to the needs, circumstances and wishes of each individual child at a given moment. Under certain conditions, that "first resort" might be intercountry adoption or residential care, as well, of course, as any of the other types of alternative care settings.

5. INTERNATIONAL CO-OPERATION

23. One aspect of the CRC that seems to have aroused little debate or response is the implication of the last line of Article 4 which foresees recourse to international co-operation "where needed" to promote and enable compliance with the CRC provisions regarding economic, social and cultural rights in particular. International co-operation is further specifically reaffirmed as necessary in regard to children with disabilities (Art. 23), health (Art. 24) and education (Art 28).

Of course, many multilateral and bilateral assistance programmes in these and other fields exist with this goal in mind. However, co-operation, or development assistance in its various forms, is usually looked on almost entirely from the point of view of its being a moral obligation of the international community or the economically privileged nations. In addition, all too often it is they who set the agenda.

However, Article 4 suggests that both the responsibility and the discretion for determining the "need" for international co-operation should lie with the State Party within whose jurisdiction the children concerned are living. It also implicitly suggests that such co-operation be essentially oriented (save in extreme circumstances where intervention rather than co-operation seems to be required) towards helping those States Parties in their efforts to implement the CRC's provisions, rather than in the form of direct assistance.

24. When it comes to children's rights in regard to their family, therefore, States that are unable to furnish the necessary support (financial and other) that optimal family preservation and alternative care programmes require should be identifying that "need" and actively seeking appropriate co-operation, rather than accepting responses that do not always correspond to improved implementation of the fundamental thrust of the CRC. In this respect, one might question, for example, the logic behind the attempts of governments of certain "receiving countries" to secure increases in the number of "adoptable children" from elsewhere who could be entrusted to their citizens. From a CRC point of view, while the role of intercountry adoption is certainly recognised, it would seem that international co-operation should focus on enabling the child to remain with his or her family with the consequence that there would be fewer, not more, children requiring a new family abroad.

6. CONCLUSION

25. Consideration of the child's position vis-à-vis his or her family, as reflected in the letter and spirit of the CRC and the obligations it places on States, involves in particular taking account of two potentially conflicting requirements: protecting the child's family and protecting the child in the family. Inevitably, therefore, it also means addressing the question of the use, quality and purpose of alternative care, as constituting or mirroring the moment at which the child-parent relationship is substantially modified, temporarily or definitively, or even annulled. Consequently, the issue is somewhat more complex than it may seem at first sight.

26. While close analysis of the CRC brings to light certain "technical" uncertainties regarding the rights relationship between children and their family, the treaty incontestably espouses an approach that fully supports the primary role of the parents and the family in nurturing, protecting and guiding the child, and sets out States' obligations to this end. At the same time, it necessarily provides for the State to ensure the protection and welfare of the child when parents – and in some cases wider family – are unwilling and/or unable to fulfil that role, for whatever reason. The issue of "State intervention in family affairs" has often been magnified out of all proportion, however, giving rise to some of the most virulent but also the least justified criticisms of "children's rights".

27. The CRC does not and could not – quite simply for practical reasons – require States to grant the child an absolute right to live with his or her family, or indeed to live in a family environment. While the child therefore has no "right to a family" as such, the CRC unequivocally calls for policies that promote family preservation as well as family-based alternative care wherever necessary and appropriate.

28. Ensuring that, in line with the CRC, priority is effectively given to family preservation efforts is proving to be neither a clear-cut exercise nor an easy task in practice, however, whether at national level or in terms of international co-operation. Lack of appropriate material and other support to parents still accounts for many cases of "spontaneous" child abandonment or relinquishment, as well as of removal of children from parental care by the authorities. The easier and higher-profile – though generally also far more costly – "alternative care" response to children at risk of being separated from their parents in such ways remains common. States experiencing "family preservation" problems are frequently neglecting to request assistance from the international community in overcoming them. At the same time, when the international community does become involved, on request or spontaneously, in tackling the problem of children without parental care, its responses may diverge significantly from the CRC-based goal of supporting parents in accomplishing their roles and responsibilities towards the child.

CHILDREN'S RIGHTS IN FAMILY COURT PROCEEDINGS

RUTH FARRUGIA

1. INTRODUCTION

1. Children's rights have for many years been assumed to be best served by their family. Parents and extended family members are consistently expected to defend the rights of children who are dependent on them. In reality, where Family Court proceedings involve contested custody issues, children's rights take on a completely different nature. They notionally become an additional party within the suit, with special stakes in the outcome, which may be diverse from the requests made by adults and even other minor siblings.

2. Malta has recently established a Family Court with improved services for children's participation. This paper will examine the position of children in the context of this Family Court and in particular in the scenario of family breakdown. It will look into the rights of children in relation to the rights of other family members and attempt to analyse the extent to which children's rights are protected, promoted and enforced through participation.

3. Although at law there would seem to be greater interest in according children their rights within the family, the practical implications of this are slower to come. For instance, the institution of a Child Advocate to represent children in a lawyer-client relationship is being confused with the general notions of promoting the best interests of the child. A number of jurisdictions make provision for the appointment of a Guardian *ad litem* to promote the best interests of the child and a child advocate to represent the child's wishes. Where one person is called upon to undertake both objectives, there have been serious conflicts of interest casting doubt on the rights of children to exercise those rights.

4. The paper will attempt to define those factors, which promote and support the enforcement of children's rights in relation to their family and will identify them within the local, European and international context. It is undisputed that there should

never be competition between children's rights and other family rights, however during litigation things change. The implications of rights monitoring and effectiveness are most felt where put to the test in court and this paper will maintain this leitmotif throughout. To better illustrate the position, this paper will share the results of research into the functioning of the first year of the Family Court, which are currently under way.

2. CHILDREN'S RIGHTS WITHIN THE FAMILY – SOURCE OF RIGHTS

5. Children's rights are invariably deemed to be best protected by their families and in the majority of cases, this is so. The opening sections of the Maltese Civil Code clearly state:

"Marriage imposes on both spouses the obligation to look after, maintain, instruct and educate the children of the marriage taking into account the abilities, natural inclinations and aspirations of the children."[1]

Furthermore, "in default of the parents, or where the parents do not possess sufficient means, the liability for the maintenance and education of the children devolves on the other ascendants."[2] The law still speaks of the authority of parents over their children, rather than responsibility towards them so much that Sections 131(1) and 132(1) state, "a child shall be subject to the authority of his parents for all effects as by law established" and "a child shall obey his parents in all that is permitted by law".

This is a notion lagging behind the United Nations Convention on the Rights of the Child where "State Parties shall use their best efforts to ensure recognition of the principle that both parents have common responsibilities for the upbringing and development of the child. Parents or, as the case may be legal guardians, have the primary responsibility for the upbringing and development of the child. The best interests of the child will be their basic concern."[3]

---

1 Laws of Malta, Chapter 16, Article 3B, < http://www2.justice.gov.mt/lom/home.asp?lng=ENG>.
2 Laws of Malta, supra (note 1), Section 7.
3 Art. 18(1), UN Convention on the Rights of the Child, adopted on 20 November 1989 and entered into force on 2 September 1990.

6. Parental authority may end *ipso jure*, by operation of law,[4] or following a judicial process. It is the latter, which is of interest in this context and is based primarily on five main reasons:[5]

1. the parent "exceeding the bounds of reasonable chastisement, ill-treating the child or neglecting his education",
2. "if the conduct of the parent is such as to endanger the education of the child",
3. "if the parent is interdicted or under a disability as to certain acts",
4. "if the parent mismanages the property of the child",
5. "if the parent fails to perform any of the obligations set out in Article 3B[6] in favour of the child".

In such eventuality, the child would be placed under the care of the non-offending parent, under the care of third parties so authorised by the court such as a tutor or under the care of the Minister responsible for Family and Social Solidarity by means of a care order where the child is deemed to be "in need of care, protection or control".[7]

Whoever is assigned responsibility for the child, there is a duty incumbent on that person to ensure that the child receives due care and protection and that the best interests of the child motivate any decision taken in matters relating to the present and future well-being of the child. However, precisely what the concept of best interest means is in itself another point for deliberation.

3. "BEST INTERESTS" IN COURT PROCEEDINGS

7. In circumstances where the family is living ostensibly with no problems, the interests of each separate family member are catered for and balanced. Where the family faces conflict and in particular where the family unit breaks down and court proceedings are initiated, these interests no longer retain their balance and it becomes ever more important to provide clear definitions. Practice shows that when the interests of component family members come into direct competition with the

[4] Laws of Malta, Chapter 16, Section 150 cites the following reasons: death of both parents of the child, when the child attains the age of eighteen years, on the marriage of the child (which may take place at the age of sixteen), if the child with the consent of the parents, has left the parental home and set up a separate domestic establishment, and where registrations required at law following the death of one parent or remarriage are not made.

[5] Laws of Malta, supra (note 1), Section 154(1).

[6] Ibid.

[7] Laws of Malta, Chapter 285, Children and Young Persons (Care Orders) Act.

interests of the child, the perceived obligation of protection may be weakened or may in practice be subsumed into the interests of the same adult responsible for such protection.

8. Notions of best interests of the child, the welfare principle and the paramountcy principle have all contributed towards enhancing the status of the protection deemed attributable to the child. Most modern legislation takes the concept of best interest of the child to heart and stipulates that where interests may be competing, it is the interests of the child that should be given due importance. In those countries who do not openly proclaim the paramountcy principle, it is however not always clear whether the best interests of the child are always to be deemed supreme vis-à-vis those of other parties or whether such weighting remains the discretion of the court.

9. In Maltese law, Section 149 is a blanket provision, which empowers the court to act in the child's best interests: "Notwithstanding any other provision of this Code, the court may upon good cause being shown, give such directions as regards the person or the property of a minor as it may deem appropriate in the best interests of the child".[8]

However, there are a number of other provisions within the same Civil Code (addressing the child within separation proceedings), which refer to this notion. The terms used vary between "interests", "best interests", "welfare" or "paramount consideration".

Section 47
"During the pendency of the action the court shall give such direction concerning the custody of the children as it may deem appropriate, and in so doing the paramount consideration shall be the welfare of the children."

Section 56(1) and (4)
"On separation being pronounced the court shall also direct to which of the spouses custody of the children shall be entrusted, the paramount consideration being the welfare of the children."
"The court may, at any time, revoke or vary such directions respecting the children where the interests of the children so require."

Section 57(3)
"It shall be lawful for the court at any time to revoke or vary such directions, for the better welfare of the children."

---

8 Chapter 16, supra (note 1).

Section 58(1)
"The court may, where it shall deem it expedient so to do in the interest of the spouses and the children, order the suspension of the action for separation from such time as it may deem proper, and shall give such interim directions as circumstances so require."

Section 60(2)
"It shall be lawful for the court at any time to revoke or vary such directions, for the better welfare of the children."

Section 61(1)
"Any agreement between the spouses respecting the custody of the children may at any time, on the demand of either of the spouses, or of any relative of the spouses, be annulled by the competent court, where the interests of the children so require."

Section 131(4)
"The court, after hearing the parents and the child if the latter has reached the age of fourteen years, shall make those suggestions, which it deems best in the interest of the child and the unity of the family. If the disagreement between the parents persists, the court shall authorise the parent whom it considers more suitable to protect the interest of the child in the particular case, to decide upon the issue, saving the provisions of section 149."

This use of different terms does little to enhance the operation of the principle and the final section cited is even more confusing as it juxtaposes the interest of the child with the unity of the family.

4. THE FAMILY COURT

10. In the last decade or so there have been a number of legislative and judicial innovations that have helped in minimising the ordeal of separation proceedings. One principle improvement has been the introduction of the unitary system of family matters whereby criminal and civil jurisdictions come together to address issues united by family concerns. Furthermore, previously, separation proceedings were put on the same footing as matters dealing with commercial litigation, for instance promoting a very impersonal atmosphere and causing unnecessary lengthy proceedings for separation suits. Today the family court provides a more focused humane environment and speedier proceedings, minimising as much as possible the traumatic effects of a marital breakdown.

The remaining shortfall rests in the fact that the family division system fails to have its own court of appeal, which means that matters reach a bottleneck once they are treated in the first instance. The setting up of a court of appeal, which would deal exclusively with appeals regarding family-related matters, would further enhance the procedure aimed at providing an effective solution within a reasonable time. Experience in foreign jurisdictions has shown that where a specialist appellate court has not been established the period that elapses until the appeal is heard causes irremediable prejudice, especially where minors are involved. When such appeals are to be heard according to the ordinary roster with all the other cases, the benefits gained from having a specialist family division would be lost as such cases would be treated the same as the others.[9]

11. Another consideration worth noting that is found in New Zealand and Australia is that judges that are appointed to handle family matters are specialists in this field. The judges in the family court must be qualified to sit in Family Court if they are "by reason of training, experience and personality, suitable to deal with matters of family law". In these and most other jurisdictions, children are legally represented in contested cases representing the children's best interests independently of the parties. Furthermore free counselling services, resolution of family disputes by conciliation, and psychologists are all catered for.

12. In Malta, there were a total of three White Papers leading up to the introduction of the Family Court, all united in the stress laid on the fact that the "role of trained social workers and other professionals is as crucial as that of a member of the Judiciary". However, it did not address the means whereby different professions could agree to determine similar criteria in fulfilling their roles. Where the notion of best interests of the child in separation proceedings requires such deliberation, recent work has highlighted the discrepancies between the way lawyers and social workers operate in relation to children.

A contemporary finding in this field has shown how lawyers use the concept of "reasonableness" to justify their decisions on how to balance these diverse obligations, and highlights the comparison of these understandings with the social work perspectives. The research brings into sharp distinction the multiple tensions between the different approaches, between reason and emotion, and between the interests of the child, the social worker, the lawyer and the local authority. It analyses the challenges for lawyers and social workers in child care proceedings and highlights the various interests of the child, the social worker, the lawyer and the local authority

---

[9] Commission for setting up of the Family Division.

concluding the sad observation that good lawyers defending children are not so common since it is a very low-key job and is not well paid.[10]

5. THE CHILD'S RIGHT TO BE HEARD

13. Within the conflicting scenario of defining and enforcing the best interests principle, probably the most important right when dealing with the rights of children in marital breakdown relates to listening to what children have to say. This right to be heard frequently raises numerous concerns among all the actors involved in the separation proceedings.

The parents may feel that a child will end up taking sides against them and may reveal circumstances, which they wish to keep confidential. The judges and lawyers although ostensibly welcoming of the child's right to express an opinion, may feel that this is an additional hurdle to be faced in a battle always lamented as being too long anyway. This is compounded with the sceptical stance of many that children cannot possibly have a grounded opinion and will be swayed by whichever adult appeals to their grasping inclination. Others feel that encouraging children into the litigation arena will do untold damage to their psyche and even worse, a number of professionals have the opinion that what children say cannot be trusted, so why bother listening.

14. The European Convention on the Exercise of Children's Rights in its Preamble states: "Children should be given the opportunity to exercise their rights, in particular in family proceedings affecting them, that the best interest of children should be promoted."

The UN Convention on the Rights of the Child Article 12 holds: "State Parties shall assure to the child who is capable of forming his or her views the right to express those views freely in all matters affecting the child, the views of the child being given due weight in accordance with the age and maturity of the child.

For this purpose, the child shall in particular be provided the opportunity to be heard in any judicial and administrative proceedings affecting the child, either directly or through a representative or an appropriate body, in any manner consistent with the procedural rules of national law."

Furthermore, CRC Article 9(2) refers specifically to the child's right to be heard in relation to separation proceedings of his/her parents, during which "all interested

10 J. Dickens, 'Being 'The Epitome of Reason': The Challenges for Lawyers and Social Workers', in Child Care Proceedings, (2005) 19 *International Journal of Law Policy and the Family*, 73–101.

parties shall be given an opportunity to participate in the proceedings and make their views known".

15. Article 12 of the CRC does not set an age limit upon which a child is granted this right to express his or her views freely. However, a number of countries do set such limits, especially in custody laws. Section 131(4) of the Maltese Civil Code obliges the court to hear both the parents and the child if the latter has reached the age of fourteen years, before making those suggestions, which it deems best in the interest of the child and the unity of the family. On the other hand, Section 6A (1) of the said Code grants a discretionary right to the judge to hear children above the age of fourteen.

In practice, the Maltese Courts seem to be reluctant to hear children who are below that age of fourteen years. The courts justify this by citing the argument that children below that age are unable to form an opinion and to decide what is best for them without being influenced by external factors. In a recent child abduction case,[11] the court went so far as to pronounce that a minor of a tender age is incapable of deciding for himself and furthermore to know what is deemed best for him.

16. Although it is true that children below a certain age could be too young to form an opinion, they do have the competence of thought and capability of decision-making. It is true that their decision may not have been the right one, however to completely ignore what they have to say is also unreasonable, in that children should be given the opportunity to be heard and express their desires.

6. LEGISLATION AFFECTING THE CHILD'S RIGHT TO REPRESENTATION

17. Malta does not have a comprehensive Children Act nor does there seem to be any political commitment to introduce such legislation notwithstanding considerable public support from professionals and lay persons claiming to have the best interest of children at heart. Representation of children within the court setting relies on the fragmented legislation already cited and on the very recent introduction of two very important Offices: the Commissioner for Children and the Child Advocate. On paper, this would seem ideal as a response to the promotion and protection of children's rights to representation; however, practical shortcomings threaten to stultify the offices themselves and render them impotent in their mission to empower children. At the least, until a Children Act is introduced, it would benefit children for the courts in

11 *Satchell v. Camilleri*, First Hall Civil Court, 28 June 1998.

separation proceedings to be guided by a checklist of relevant factors, such as are found in the English Children Act.[12]

6.1. COMMISSIONER FOR CHILDREN

18. The Commissioner for Children Act[13] was introduced in keeping with a commitment made following Malta's first (and to date, only) report before the United Nations Committee on the Convention on the Rights of the Child. Although the most basic premise underlying the appointment of the Commissioner for Children is the focus on children's rights, the legislator insisted on inserting an additional function relating to family into the list drawn up for the working of the Commissioner:

Article 9: The Commissioner shall have the following functions:

(a) to promote and advocate the rights and interests of children;
(b) to ensure that children are given the opportunity to express their opinions and that these are in fact considered;
(c) to promote the protection of family unity;

Again at Article 10:
The Commissioner shall be guided by the following general principles:
(a) that the best interests of children and the family are paramount;

19. There was no mistake in this introduction. Although the implication of placing the Child Commissioner in a potentially conflicting situation was raised in numerous quarters, the legislator insisted on the inclusion of family unity as a concept alongside the rights of children. This has culminated in the proclamation that the paramountcy principle applies to children and family contemporaneously! Of course in an ideal setting this would be perfectly feasible but to place the Commissioner for Children in a position whereby both interests must be gauged as paramount is tantamount to a mockery of the entire raison d'être of such a law. Conflicting issues have already been

12 English Children Act, Section 1 (3) a) the ascertainable wishes and feelings of the child concerned (considered in the light of his/her age and understanding); b) his/her physical, emotional and educational needs; c) the likely effect on the child of any change in his/her circumstances; d) the child's age, sex, background and any characteristics which the court considers relevant; e) any harm which the child has suffered or is at risk of suffering; f) how capable each of his/her parents, and any other person in relation to whom the court considers the question to be relevant, is of meeting the child's needs; g) the range of powers available to the court under this Act in the proceedings in question.

13 Laws of Malta, Chapter 462, Commissioner for Children Act.

raised in the two years since the inception of the Office and nowhere as glaringly as within the context of separation cases before the court.

This is only one shortcoming of the Office, although the clear lack of practical and logistical support from the authorities begs to question the true motivation for setting up the Commissioner's role at all. If the honest reason behind its constitution was the promotion and protection of children's rights, the laundry list of inadequacies would have been addressed or at least started to be tackled within the past two years.

6.2. CHILD ADVOCATE

20. The Family Court was set up following a Legal Notice[14] and since December 2003, Malta has hosted the Office of the Child Advocate.

Article 7(2) of the said Legal Notice holds that the court: "shall proceed to appoint a children's advocate where in its opinion this is required in the interests of any minor children of the spouses, and shall thereupon proceed with the pre-trial stage of the case in which the court shall fix time limits within which the parties shall produce all documentary evidence in support of their case and produce such witnesses whose evidence cannot be introduced by affidavit."

21. In practice, such appointment may be made *ex officio* by the court, at the request of the mediator hearing the case or at the request of one of the parties. As the child is not a party to the proceedings, it is not possible for a child to request the appointment of a child advocate. Furthermore, no practical efforts have been made to enable effective access to representation for the child *per se*. Even when appointed, the child advocate is expected by the court to submit a report relating to the wishes of the child but also in relation to the best interests of the child. This conflict of roles has led to the production of reports where the child advocate lists the wishes of the child but then makes an opposing conclusion on the grounds of best interests. Additional concerns such as lack of confidentiality of the child's contribution have also been raised as once the report is filed it becomes part of the court proceedings and may be viewed liberally by both parties.

22. The introduction of the role of the child advocate as a representative of children who must defend and promote the best interest of the child has been endorsed by authorities as another step forward in helping the child to be heard and as another progression in bringing Maltese law more in line with CRC Article 12. The child

[14] LN 397 of 2003.

advocate may be present both in the mediation stage and in litigation before the family division however, it has already been pointed out that a child is only represented by a child advocate where the judge deems it proper. This is inconsonant with Article 12 (2) of the CRC: "For this purpose, the child shall in particular be provided the opportunity to be heard in any judicial and administrative proceedings affecting the child, either directly, or through a representative or an appropriate body, in a manner consistent with the procedural rules of national law."

In the past two years, the number of child advocates has dwindled from the original three part-time appointees to two equally part-time advocates with similar lack of practical and institutional support. Their selection has been arbitrary and no training has been provided to enable them to address their role. In the circumstances, they have managed to give life to an institute crucial to the representation of the child but one wonders how much longer this tenuous hold will continue and at what cost.

In looking at comparative jurisdictions, the dissonance is glaring. The United Kingdom has a statutory Children's Panel and the American Bar Association within the Conference on the Ethical Issues in the Legal Representation of Children,[15] provides amongst a number of guidelines, that a child lawyer is to be certified by the State. Furthermore, s/he should be in possession of a certificate that includes training in counselling, negotiations, child development and psychology, and professional team approach, amongst other requirements. According to the US Supreme Court, "the right to representation by counsel is not a formality…it is of the essence of justice".[16]

6.3. GUARDIAN AD LITEM

23. In order, for the Office of the Child Advocate to work effectively a number of jurisdictions have set up the Office of the Guardian *ad litem* or children's guardian. In this way, the child advocate can fulfil the role of representation and faithfully represent the child's wishes to the court, as would be the case with any adult able client, while the guardian's responsibility is to ensure that the best interests of the child are also relayed to the court. Although this recommendation was made to the authorities prior to the introduction of the child advocate and indeed during the workings of the first committee appointed to draft a document for the setting up of the family court, the issue seems to have been shelved permanently.

15 Fordham Law Review, Volume LXIV, Number 4, 1996.

16 Haw. Rev. Stat. S. 587 – 34c.

The repercussions of such a decision on the adequate representation of children within the separation setting are easily identifiable. The reports of the present child advocates try to fulfil both roles simultaneously, principally because these are the instructions that have been issued to the child advocates. From a child rights viewpoint the guardian *ad litem*'s most significant relationship during the court proceedings while working closely with the child's lawyer is the best way of ensuring that the child is truly heard.

This provision is vital to represent, safeguard and promote the welfare of children involved in family court proceedings. The guardian *ad litem* performs at the heart of a debate about the constituents of good child care. The most important characteristic identified by children and young people is the guardian *ad litem*'s ability to listen to them and to explain things to them. A guardian *ad litem* offers the means by which obligations under Article 12 of the UN Convention on the Rights of the Child can be fulfilled in the court system. One can only hope that the Maltese authorities will remedy this state of affairs as soon as possible.

6.4. MEDIATION

24. Legal Notice 397/2003 introduced the notion of compulsory mediation within the family court. Reactions to this were varied in that although the concept of mediation was greeted as a step in the right direction, the notion of compulsory mediation was viewed as completely divergent to the very notion underlying mediation, which holds that it should be approached by persons who choose it. This said, the next concern was the position of children within this enforced mediation process.

Regulation 4(4) of the Legal Notice states that:

"the mediator shall in the first place attempt to reconcile the parties. During this stage, the mediator shall hear the parties".[17]

Furthermore regulation 4(6) of the Legal Notice states that:

"The mediator may in camera hear the parties separately or together, in the presence of their advocates or legal procurators, and he may also hear any minor children of the spouses, the children's advocate, if any, and the advocates or legal procurators of the parties."

[17] LN 397 of 2003, Regulation 4 (4).

25. It is important to read this within the context of the Parliamentary debates leading up to the introduction of mediation in the Family Court since if one merely examines the Legal Notice enacting the role of the mediator one would fail to see the real intention of the legislator. "Having a mediation process of a maximum of 2 months is right. The State is not telling spouses that they should reconcile. Mediation is aimed at ensuring that the spouses know what they are going into....The mediation process would also protect the rights of the children, often forgotten in separation proceedings."[18]

It is comforting to note that in the Parliamentary debates, the rights of the child are acknowledged and referred to directly. However, these rights do not feature in the legislation *per se.* In practice, mediators do their best to keep children out of the mediation process and request the appointment of a child advocate where it becomes apparent that the information given by the parties is so conflicting as to warrant the child's viewpoint. Perhaps it is beneficial that mediators do not perceive themselves as fit to carry out such investigation by inviting the child to participate in the mediation session(s) and refer to a person better suited to the job. The greatest concern is that there are no set criteria for mediators in making such a decision so that the views of children may be disregarded when mediation is taking place to determine issues directly affecting their present and future well-being.

7. EFFECT OF FAMILY BREAKDOWN ON CHILDREN'S RIGHTS

7.1. RESIDENCE

26. The legal repercussions of family breakdown affect children in a number of ways. The child's residence is a primary concern and must be determined with regard to the needs of the child and the position of the parent(s). As Maltese law still has no legislation relating to cohabitation and frowns upon extramarital relationships (still calling them by their Roman law term: concubinage) there have been a number of judgments where a cohabiting parent has been prevented access to a child on the grounds that the immorality of such relationship would adversely impact on the child. Consensual separation agreements countersigned by the court also frequently refer to the obligation of the primary carer not to expose the child to the presence of a third party, that is, a cohabitee.

---

[18] Parliamentary debates 2004, intervention by Parliamentary Secretary C. Mifsud Bonnici.

Where such behaviour is deemed detrimental to the child the court may order that access be permitted only subject to supervision. The effects of supervised access visits on the parent and more importantly, with all respect, on the child have been shown to be questionable. There may be limited cases where there are serious reasons for the imposition of such supervision, as in the event of sexual abuse, physical abuse, substance dependency and mental health problems, which may pose a threat to the safety of the child. However, in these circumstances, it would be better to question whether the access is permitted in the best interest of the child or rather in the best interest of the parent who insists on contact as a parental right rather than with any real benefit to the child subjected to it. Most children interviewed on this topic have lamented that supervised access has no positive aspects whatsoever from their point of view.

Having said this, the courts recently decided a case concerning custody rights of a mother who had left her husband to have a lesbian relationship.[19] The first court awarded custody to the father on the premise that bringing up the child in a lesbian home was not in the best interests of the child but this was overturned by the Court of Appeal, which held that the relationship did not render the mother an unfit parent and in the particular circumstances of the case it was in the best interests of the child to live with the mother as primary caregiver.

7.2. MAINTENANCE

27. The maintenance accorded to the child is also an issue, which directly affects the child. Although it not suggested that the child should enter into the discussion relating to quantum of maintenance payable, considerations as to this amount should stem from the needs of the child to be maintained. Separating families frequently experience a negative impact on their financial position for obvious reasons. The chilling reality that most single parent families headed by mothers constitute the new poor should serve as a grave cause for concern.[20] To date there are no set criteria operated by the court in adjudicating how much maintenance is to be paid both during the proceedings and following judgment.

28. Under Maltese law, maintenance includes food, clothing, health, habitation and education in relation to children so the parent(s) responsible for the payment of maintenance must make good for all these components. However, there are no clear guidelines as to the quality and quantity of the items determined by law so that the

---

19 Re A, Court of Appeal, 7 March 2006.

20 National Statistics Office Malta, Statistical report for 2004.

definitions rely on case law and a good lawyer convincing the court of the particular needs of the child. The fact that the child's requirements differ with age is also crucial in the allocation of maintenance as it is evident that a four year old and a fifteen year old need different amounts of maintenance according to varying stages in their development.

7.3. CONTACT

29. Parents may use custody rights to their advantage rather than addressing what the child really needs or using the best interest principle. The concept of "weekend fathers" is a harsh reality that children today are facing. In Australia, for instance, a recent trigger for change was a political concern for the position of non-custodial fathers. In 2003, a parliamentary inquiry into the law governing "custody arrangements", cited concern that "far too many boys are growing up without proper role models". On the other hand the committee expressed a hope that dual residence arrangements would become the new post separation norm "wherever practicable" and that 50/50 shared residence should be considered as a starting point for discussion and negotiation – this obviously does not count for the situations of entrenched conflict, family violence, abuse and the like.[21] Under Maltese law shared custody was suggested when the amendments to the family law were introduced in 1993,[22] but sadly never received any backing. In practice although the court does not make any provision for this form of custody arrangement, a number of parents choose to attempt it although they remain a very small minority.

8. FEEDBACK FROM CHILDREN

30. These practical issues mentioned with the legal context do not address the psychological impact of separation on the child. A small survey of children who have written to the Maltese Child Commissioner has opened the way to a research project addressing this issue more extensively and its results are due to be published in October 2006.

The children wrote to protest about the duration of separation proceedings asking for them to be concluded more expeditiously, particularly as their concept of time varies from that of an adult. They shared their distress at living with a parent who is

21 H. RHOADES and S. BOYD, 'Reforming Custody Laws: A Comparative Study', (2004) 18 *International Journal of Law, Policy and the Family*, 119–146.

22 Act XX1, 1993.

traumatised by the effects of separation, claiming that they are worried and hurt by the way their primary carer has been treated in court or by lawyers and at the impact repeated court appearances have on the atmosphere at home.

The children explained that they are aware of their reduced financial position and the additional worry caused to the primary carer now trying to make ends meet. They respond in different ways but a number have simply stopped asking for money to participate in school activities rather than burden their parent with additional financial stress. Their relationship with their parents had changed tremendously with many taking on the role of carer at a time in their life when they are too young and too immature to bear the load, aside from their vulnerability in response to the breakdown itself.

Another issue they raised refers to the way their family composition had changed. A good number feel that they now have to take sides and this is not limited to the relationship between the parents but also to the extended family. In a small country such as Malta where grandparents, cousins, aunts and uncles play an important role in the relational network of most children, it is disturbing for them to suddenly lose access to one side of the family following separation.

The loss of the family home, which is frequently sold on separation, also results in children losing their friends and neighbours with whom they may have deep and meaningful relationships built up over a number of years. The children invariably attend community and social activities in the same neighbourhood and must start afresh at a time when friendships are even more important than usual.

A general comment was their frustration at being excluded form the court process altogether. A small number wanted to institute court cases to make the judicial system listen to their views. They expressed disbelief at decisions affecting directly their present and future well-being taken without any consultation whatsoever. One teenager went so far as to say that she had lost all faith in justice and judges and although her dream had been to study to become a lawyer she wanted to have nothing to do with a system which so flagrantly abused children's rights.

31. A good number vociferously complained about access or contact and its modality. They feel that they are made to give up activities they would rather be doing such as playing a sport, attending a birthday party, camping, and so on, in order to spend two or three enforced hours in the presence of a parent with whom they have little or nothing in common. Although they are too immature to understand the impact that loss of even this tenuous relationship would have on them long term, they are right in feeling irked at the lack of consultation and the lack of flexibility in setting up meetings. The primary caregiver may be faced with imprisonment for failing to honour a contact agreement[23] so the child is pressured into being there, notwithstanding any other effects the sessions may have.

Statistics in the UK[24] illustrate that numerous times children are unhappy with the manner in which their time is split up with each parent and further show that the children often feel that their voice is not heard in court proceedings.

32. All the children wanted someone to talk to who would listen. Some tried to share their feelings with the school counsellor or a friend although many had turned to the Commissioner as a last resort. Although the child welfare agency does run a helpline,[25] the director has shared information that children never use this helpline to voice their trauma post separation.[26]

APPOGG seem to place more emphasis on physical abuse, violence and other related matters, but child response seems to indicate differently. This is reflected in the reality shared in the UK where 5,396 young people talked to Child Line in 2004 about concerns surrounding the separation or divorce of their parents. A large proportion of counselling conversations around these issues were spent discussing how to approach parents, what to say and how to appreciate the difficulties that parents may have in changing their view.

9. CONCLUSIONS AND RECOMMENDATIONS

33. The right of the child to be actively involved in court proceedings where decisions are taken which impact directly on him/her should be the starting point for any future amendments in this field. Strengthening structures already in place such as the office of the Child Advocate and the Child Commissioner should be given the priority they deserve. Additional investment should be made to get the office of the Guardian *ad litem* up and running. After separation, support should be made freely available to all children in the least intrusive and most effective way possible.

34. On pronouncing judgment, the Family Court Judge could strongly encourage the family as a whole to go to family therapy sessions. The role of the court stops at the time when the separation is legalised but the relationship continues long after.

23 Amendments to the Criminal Code, Chapter 12 Laws of Malta.

24 Children's Society, <http://www.childline.org.uk>.

25 APPOGG has a 24 hour service phone line 179, <http://www.appogg.gov.mt/>.

26 Interview with CHARMAINE SANT on 28 March 2006.

Parents may stop their spousal relationship but where they have children in common they will invariably continue to meet and share interaction at least until the children attain the age of majority and more probably until the children leave home to set up a family unit of their own and even after that. Parents and children desperately need to find a medium whereby they can find or continue a civilised exchange that certainly contributes towards minimising the trauma family breakdown brings with it.

35. The law does not and cannot directly remedy many of these issues. However, it does have a responsibility to promote an amicable solution for all if only because of the vested interest in not treating the same case later down the line. The least it can do is to listen to the child's concerns and affirm their importance. It should ensure that the little issues which may seem trivial to adults are covered by separation agreements and this can only be done effectively where children are professionally represented within the process at all stages both by an advocate as well as by a guardian who together ensure that the wishes of the child and the best interests reach the court before making its reasoned decision. This is the grundnorm of the Convention on the Rights of the Child.

AUTONOMY RIGHTS VERSUS PARENTAL AUTONOMY

MEDA COUZENS

1. INTRODUCTION

1. The 1989 United Nations Convention on the Rights of the Child (the CRC) has confirmed that children are regarded as subjects of human rights and not just subjects of protection. This position creates a direct link between the State and children, without parents or other adults playing a role as intermediaries. This innovation led to concerns that children would misuse their rights and that conferring rights upon children would lead to increasing tensions in the family. Some went as far as to suggest that the CRC abandons children to their rights and autonomy.[1] This paper argues that there is no inherent opposition between parental rights and children's rights within the CRC framework, mainly because parental rights are recognised, and must be used for the benefit of their children; or, in order to benefit children any parental action must respect children's rights. Although in some circumstances, the conflict between parental rights and children's rights is inevitable, in many circumstances this conflict is created by the lack of communication between parents and children. The paper illustrates the ambivalent attitude towards child autonomy prevailing around the world, and the failure to recognise formally children's autonomy even when this is exercised *de facto*.[2] The paper emphasises also that child autonomy is not just a legal issue, but has strong connections with the family environment, or socio economic and cultural context.

---

1 B.C. HAFEN and J.O. HAFEN, 'Abandoning Children to their Rights', (1995) 55 *First Things*, 18–24 <http://www.firstthings.com/ftissues/ft9508/hafen.html>.

2 For example, admitting that children can become criminally responsible at the age of 7, denying their ability to enter legally binding contracts until they reach majority, or not consulting with children when decisions regarding them are made contrasts starkly with children being recognised as having the right to enter into marriages before attaining majority, ascribing them the right to abortion regardless of age, or with the reality of children financially supporting their families through their work. It will probably take more time to create a coherent approach to child autonomy under the influence of the CRC.

2. THE CRC AND CHILD AUTONOMY

2. To start a discussion on child autonomy, it is first necessary to define the term "autonomy". In law, autonomy refers to the right to assert one's own personal and physical integrity, to express one's views freely, to take responsibility for one's life and to have decisions regarding one's own choices respected.[3] However, the recognition of autonomy is conditioned by the competence of the individuals to make informed and wise choices. Because such a competence is not presumed in children, parents are entrusted with the power of making decisions for their children until children reach a certain age, or until parents decide that children are mature enough to take over the responsibility for their own decisions.[4] This depicts indeed the principles promoted by the CRC, which is detailed below.

3. The CRC's position on child autonomy is mainly found in Articles 5 and 12–16, the core provisions being contained in Articles 5 and 12. These rights, often referred to as participatory rights, are the means that children can use to exercise their capacity for autonomy, in public life as well as within the family. In a very condensed interpretation of these provisions, a child who is able to form his/her own views has the right to express those views freely in all the matters concerning the child; those views should be given due weight in accordance with the age and maturity of the child. In exercising his/her rights, the child receives from parents or caregivers guidance or direction, which should be appropriate for the evolving capacities of the child. Very briefly, this is the essence of the CRC's position on child autonomy. The CRC does not recognise children as having a right to self-determination, however acknowledges children's ability to acquire autonomy gradually, under the protective guidance of their parents.[5]

---

3 G. LANSDOWN, *The evolving capacities of the child,* (Save the Children and UNICEF, 2005), 4.

4 Ibid.

5 As a brief historical reminder, it is worth mentioning that the term "autonomy" was first used in relation to children by children's liberationists in the USA during the 1960s–1970s. Advocating child self-determination, children's liberationists argued that children should be granted the same rights and responsibilities as adults. Although beneficial for the development of children's rights movement by introducing child autonomy into legal debate, children's liberationists' views are not widely embraced today, mainly because they failed to give due consideration to differences in development between adults and children. For more on children's liberationists and theoretical aspects regarding child autonomy see J. FORTIN, *Children's Rights and the Developing Law,* (London-Edinburgh: LexisNexis Butterworths, 2003), 2nd ed., 4 and onwards. Currently, although there is support for the idea of child capacity for developing autonomy, there is also a wide agreement on the necessity to protect children against decisions that could be dangerous for their well-being. See J. EEKELAAR, 'The Emergence of Children's Rights', (1986) 6 *Oxford Journal of Legal Studies*, 161; J. FORTIN, (this note) Chapters 1, 3, 4, 5, 9 and 10; M. FREEMAN, 'The Limits of Children's Rights', in M. FREEMAN and P. VEERMAN (eds.), *The Ideologies of Children's Rights,* (The Hague – London – Boston: Martinus Nijhoff Publishers, 1992).

4. There are two key elements for a correct understanding of the CRC's position regarding child autonomy, namely the difference between autonomy and capacity for future autonomy,[6] and the distinction between decision-making and consultation.[7] FREEMAN argues that the CRC does not grant the child autonomy, but protects the capacity for future autonomy. This formula allows a limited paternalistic intervention when a child's decision endangers his/her development.[8] The distinction between autonomy and capacity for future autonomy can be read in Articles 5 and 12 of the CRC. In family and public life, children have been recognised as having the right to be consulted and not the right to have their decisions followed. This distinction is supported by the condition that parental guidance and direction in children's exercise of their rights has to be exercised in accordance with children's evolving capacities,[9] and that the weight of decisions made by children is determined according to the age and maturity of the child.[10]

It follows that the CRC does not delegate to children the decision-making process and does not oblige children to express views;[11] it merely acknowledges that children can make valuable contribution to decisions that concern them and that decisions taken with children's participation have more chances to be child-centred decisions. The right to participate in decision-making regarding them protects children's capacity for future autonomy. Various studies in child development have shown that children achieve or grow in competence when they practice decision-making skills,[12] and the best results are obtained when the exercise of decision-making takes place under the protective supervision of adults,[13] most commonly parents.

The conditionality on evolving capacities, age and maturity leads to the conclusion that limitations of children's choices are legitimate, and they can be justified by the need to protect children. As the discussion below shows, a great deal of discussion regarding child participation takes place around the issue of competence or capacity of the child. Before discussing a few theoretical aspects regarding overriding children's wishes, it is worth mentioning that competence is not a condition for participation.[14]

---

6 M. FREEMAN, supra (note 5), 37–39.
7 J. FORTIN, supra (note 5), 19.
8 M. FREEMAN, supra (note 5), 37–39.
9 Art. 5 of the CRC.
10 Art. 12 para. 1 of the CRC.
11 G. VAN BUEREN, *International Law on the Rights of the Child*, (The Hague – London – Boston: Martin Nijhoff Publishers, 1998), 137.
12 G. LANSDOWN, supra (note 3), 16.
13 Ibid., 34.
14 For a discussion on the procedural character of Art. 12 of the CRC see generally A. BARRATT, '"The best interest of the child"– Where is the child's voice?', in S. BURMAN (ed.), *The Fate of the Child: Legal Decisions on Children in the New South Africa*, (Lansdowne: Juta Law 2003), 145.

There is no such condition required by the CRC and consequently, even incompetent children have the right to be heard. However, the competence is the decisive factor when assessing the weight to be given to children's views. The competence of children depends on moral, social, cognitive, physical and emotional qualities, and whose development does not follow a predetermined pattern. The level of competence depends on the nature of the matter that requires decision, children's personal experiences, expectations placed on them, social context and individual abilities.[15] A higher level of expectation, for example, placed even on young children enables them to prove a considerable level of capacity; however, when demands are too high, this might be detrimental for a child's development. If children are required to take responsibility for themselves or others without adult protective care and support, this might be rather detrimental for children.[16]

Although the wishes of a child may be overridden, participating in decision-making has a positive contribution to child development and implicitly safeguards a child's best interests. Consultation increases a child's confidence[17] and educates the child for a responsible adult life, stimulates the child to see him/herself as part of society,[18] and may have a therapeutic effect.[19] Children feel supported and important, and when their views are challenged, they learn to listen, to negotiate, to defend views and to accept challenges, all necessary skills for a future autonomous life.

5. As emphasised by LANSDOWN, the principle of the evolving capacities of the child is central to the balance sought by the CRC between the recognition of the increasing autonomy of the child and the protection to which children are entitled in accordance to their immaturity and youth.[20] Evolving capacities is a new principle of interpretation that recognises that as children acquire enhanced competencies, the need for direction diminishes, and the child gains increased responsibility for decisions affecting his/her life.[21] Therefore, the evolving capacities of the child and child's best interests mediate between child participation and child capacity for future autonomy in family or public matters.

---

15 G. LANSDOWN, supra (note 3), 23.

16 Ibid., 34.

17 A. FABER, *How to Talk so Kids Can Learn – at Home and in School,* (New York: Rawson Associates, 1988) cited in S. HART, 'Making sure the child's voice is heard', (2002) 48 (3–4) *International Review of Education*, 253, 255.

18 K. MCAULEY and B. BRATTMAN, *Hearing Young Voices* (Children's Rights Alliance – Republic of Ireland Limited and National Youth Council of Ireland, 2002), Chapter 4 para 4.3.2., <http://www.youth.ie>.

19 I. WAITE and H. STEAD, 'Reporting the Wishes and Feelings of Children', (1998) 44 *Family Law*, 45.

20 G. LANSDOWN, supra (note 3), 3.

21 G.VAN BUEREN, supra (note 11), 50.

The principle of evolving capacities of the child is intrinsically related to child development. When giving relevance to child development in judicial decisions, courts refer to "competence", "maturity" or "understanding", but these are vague terms that need to be clarified by referring to research on children's developmental processes.[22] Research shows that before early adolescence the majority of children lack the cognitive abilities to make important decisions for themselves, while the majority of the older adolescents are equipped with developmental capacity for making relatively sophisticated decisions.[23] Capacity or competence depends on moral, social cognitive, physical and emotional qualities that do not develop in a consistent pattern; children do not acquire a consistent and overall level of competence, which varies according to the nature of the task involved, children's personal experiences, expectations placed on them, social context and individual abilities.[24]

LANSDOWN made an investigation of the factors that affect the evolving capacities of the child, stressing the relationship between factors that influenced the development of the child, like adequate food, intellectual stimuli, time and space to play, education, socio-economic environment and the development of a child's competence. This author stresses also the different aims of the development of the child worldwide; while Western societies generally expect a child to become independent, highly educated and competitive, many other societies expect from children inter-dependence and integration.[25] However, on the other hand, in the Western world the dependence on parents is increased by the extended period of education, while in the developing world, children assume responsibilities earlier by engaging in domestic or paid work.[26]

6. Returning to the balance between participation and protection, it should be mentioned that by recognising children as having rights that they can use in order to build their future autonomy, the CRC does not exempt adults from their obligation of protecting children, competent or not. However, by recognising these rights the CRC requires that an adult decision aiming at overriding children's wishes should take into account children's rights. Children's rights could be classified into protective rights and autonomy or self-assertive rights.[27] Sometimes even the rights of the same child might conflict, so for example a protective right might conflict with a self-assertive right. The wishes of the child regarding a matter that concerns him/her could

---

22 J. FORTIN, supra (note 5), 72–74.

23 For a review of the literature regarding the children's developmental capacities for decision-making see J. FORTIN, supra (note 5), 72–74.

24 G. LANSDOWN, supra (note 3), 23.

25 Ibid., 10.

26 Ibid., 10.

27 H. BEVAN, *Child Law*, (London-Edinburgh: LexisNexis Butterworths, 1989), 11, cited in J. FORTIN, supra (note 5), 17. For more approaches on children's rights classification see J. FORTIN, supra (note 5), 17–18.

be overridden if this aims at protecting some other rights of the child.[28] When by exercising an assertive right the child endangers his/her future opportunities to make choices in the future, overriding a child's choice can take place in order to protect other rights of the child, as for example the right to life, right to education and right to protection against harm. In these situations children's choices may be overridden in order to fulfil their protective rights.[29]

This attempt of phrasing the justifications for overriding the views of the child within a rights framework comes as a reaction to the intrusive and overprotective approach of the relationships between children and adults promoted by welfare legislation, especially in Western countries. Most of these interventions were justified by the intention of safeguarding the welfare of the child, but the decision was made from an exclusively adult perspective, without listening to the children's opinions. Even currently, the balance between child participation and child protection is heavily dependent on the assessment of what constitutes the best interests of the child,[30] despite the above suggested rights framework which could be used for the same purposes.[31] However, it is important to note that although the idea of protection is still present in the "best interests" principle, Article 3 of the CRC departs from the welfarist approach to what constitutes the best interest of the child. By including the best interests of the child in the human rights treaty, States have recognised that this principle has now a legal component and the best interest of the child depends on the respect of the rights enshrined in the CRC.[32] Indeed, it is noticeable that courts[33] and legislature[34] are more open to the idea that children's best interests include the rights of the child, including their participatory rights.

7. As the subject of this paper is to investigate the relationship between child autonomy and family, the discussion will continue with investigating the participatory rights within the family, although occasionally, if required by the argument, reference might be made to participatory rights in the public sphere. The author considers it

---

28 J. EEKLAAR, supra (note 5), 170–171. EEKLAAR does not make a classification of rights as such, but a classification of children's interests in basic, developmental and autonomy interests.

29 J. FORTIN, supra (note 5), 18.

30 See for example two English cases, *Re R (A Minor) (Wardship: Consent to Treatment)* [1991] 4 All ER 177; *Re W (A Minor) (Medical Treatment: Court's Jurisdiction)* [1992] 3 WLR 758.

31 A rights framework was used, for example, in *Re Roddy (a child) (identification: restriction on publication)* [2004] 2 FLR 949.

32 G. VAN BUEREN, supra (note 11), 46–47; J. WOLF, 'The Concept of the 'Best Interest' in Terms of the UN Convention on the Rights of the Child', in M. FREEMAN and P. VEERMAN (eds.), supra (note 5), 125.

33 See, for example, *McCall v McCall* 1994 (3) SA 201 (C) or *Christian Lawyer's Association v National Minister of Health* 2004 (10) 1086 BCLR (T).

34 The English Children Act 1989; Children (Scotland) Act 1995.

important to give a brief discussion on parental responsibility, which is the new concept, which describes the relationship between the guiding parent and the child.

3. PARENTAL RESPONSIBILITY

8. The entire construction regarding the recognition and the use of participatory rights by children applies to children within their family environment, according to CRC Article 12 paragraph 1.[35] This has been interpreted by some authors as to suggest that the CRC erodes the family, by creating a legal conflict between parents and children, and weakens the commitment of the parents to their children.[36] As LANSDOWN suggested, these concerns fail to take into consideration that children's wishes need to be balanced against the rights of others, including the members of the family, and that even when the child is deemed capable, his/her capacity would not be the only criterion taken into account when making a decision within the family.[37]

The CRC's approach to the relationship between a child and his/her family is that the family is "the fundamental group of society and the natural environment for the growth and well-being of its members and particularly children"; it recognises that "for the full and harmonious development of his/her personality, (the child) should grow up in a family environment, in an atmosphere of happiness, love and understanding". The child develops and exercises his/her rights under the guidance and direction of parents, members of the extended family, guardians or other persons, legally responsible for the child.[38] The family is the normal environment of the child, and separation of the child from his/her family can take place just in exceptional circumstances.[39] The CRC underlines also that the primary responsibility for a child's upbringing and development belongs to the family, and just secondarily to the State.[40]

35 Art. 12 para. 1 of the CRC specifies that a child has the right to express views in 'all matters affecting the child'. Interpreting Art. 12 para. 2 together with Art. 12 para. 1, it becomes clear that Art. 12 para. 1 is *lex generalis* while para 2 refers to particular aspects of the right to participation.

36 B.C. HAFEN and J. O. HAFEN, supra (note 1).

37 G. LANSDOWN, supra (note 3), 58.

38 Art. 5 of the CRC.

39 Art. 9 of the CRC.

40 Art. 18 of the CRC. The same trend can be identified in legislation drafted under the influence of the CRC. For example, Art. 28 (1) (b) Constitution of South Africa Act 108 of 1996 and especially the interpretation given to this section by the Constitutional Court in *Government of the Republic of South Africa v Grootboom and Others* 2000 (11) BCLR 1169 (CC); the primary responsibility of the parents for their children is also implied in the Family Law Reform Act 1995 Australia, which encourages parents to settle their disputes regarding children privately, before accessing the courts.

To define the relationship between the child and the parent, the CRC uses *inter alia* the concept of parental responsibility. Different from parental authority or rights, parental responsibility reflects a more child-centred approach to the relationship between parents and children. First used in a policy document by the Committee of Ministers of the Council of Europe in 1984, parental responsibility is a modern concept according to which parents, in consultation with children, "*exercise powers to carry out duties in the interests of the child and not because of an authority this is conferred on them in their own interest*".[41] Parental responsibility marks a democratisation in the parent-child relationship, accommodating child participation by limiting parental powers and specifying the aim of parental rights.

The CRC fully reflects this position, implying that parental rights exist in order to enable parents to fulfil their responsibilities toward their children. The CRC has been influential in determining a change in national laws, which have abandoned the old terminology of parental authority, and replaced it with the term "parental responsibility".[42] These legislative changes have come in a context of wide judicial support for the idea that parental responsibility and rights should be exercised for the child's benefit. For example, in an English case, GILLICK, it was held that parental rights are derived from parental duties and they exist only as long as they are needed for the protection of the child; it was also stated that such rights exist for the benefit of the child and not for the benefit of the parent.[43] The European Court of Human Rights (ECtHR) decided that parental rights, protected by the European Convention on Human rights and Fundamental Freedoms (ECHR) within the ambit of the right to family life, are not unlimited,[44] and a parent is not entitled to use his/her right to family life in ways that could harm a child's development.[45] It can be argued therefore, that because participation in decision-making contributes to a child's development, parents must respect children's rights to express views within the family and public sphere.

Parental responsibility and rights are however limited by the evolving capacities of the child. Therefore, parental guidance and direction should diminish with the child gaining maturity to make independent decisions. As stated in GILLICK case "*[i]n practice most wise parents relax their control gradually as the child develops and encourage him or her to become increasingly independent*".[46] This is an optimistic view on the

---

41 Recommendation No. R (84) 4 cited in South African Law Commission (December 2001), *Review of the Child Care Ac, Discussion Paper 103: Project 110*, 197.

42 The notion of parental responsibility is now present, for example, in the Family Reform Act 1995 (Australia), Children (Scotland) Act 1995, Ugandan Children Statute 1996, Ghanaian Children Act (1998), and is proposed by the South African Children's Bill 70 of 2003.

43 *Gillick v West Norfolk and Wisbech Area Health Authority* [1986] AC 112.

44 *Nielsen v Denmark* [1988] ECHR 23 paras. 61 and 72.

45 *Johansen v Norway* [1996] ECHR 31 para. 78.

46 *Gillick* case, supra (note 43), 171.

relationship between parents and children, and relies on good parental practices. LORD FRASER was expressing a very optimistic view of the way in which the relationships between parents and children develop, relying very much on the good parental practices. However, sometimes, there is a need for a State's intervention to secure children's participatory rights within the family, an aspect that is dealt with in the next section.

4. SCOPE FOR STATE INTERVENTION TO SECURE CHILD CAPACITY FOR AUTONOMY WITHIN THE FAMILY

9. Traditionally, the family has been considered a sacrosanct institution, protected against the interference of the State; within the family, the right of the parents to decide what is in the best interest of the child went unchallenged by the State or the child. This background makes the role of the State in securing child participation within the family quite difficult, because an adult-centred interpretation of the right to family life or right to privacy might challenge the legitimacy of the State's intervention in support of the child.[47] It is true that child participation does not face challenges only within the family; child participation within the public sphere is confronted with reluctance in listening to children or with lack of adequate institutions to facilitate child expression. However, in the public sphere the facilitation of child participation has become a professional obligation developed under the influence of the CRC. Indeed, in many cases the value of child participation is recognised and internalised by professionals working with children. Moreover, the State can regulate the activity of institutions concerned with children's rights and welfare in a way that satisfies the right of the child to be heard.

10. However, to safeguard children's participatory rights within the family is a more difficult task. As an international treaty, the CRC does not create obligations for individuals, and the legal obligations that can be read in the CRC belong to the State. Therefore, some parents might argue that the obligation to listen to children's views is not opposable to them.[48] As far as the State is concerned, Article 12 paragraph (1) of the CRC does not make any distinction between private and public sphere;

[47] However, it is now increasingly accepted that the child him/herself has his/her own right to privacy or family life, a right that can be balanced against the rights of the parents. See, for example, *Yousef v the Netherlands* [2002] ECHR 716 (05 November 2002); *Gorgulu v Germany* [2004] ECHR 89 (26 February 2004); *Sylvester v Austria* [2003] ECHR 196 (24 April 2003); *Hansen v Turkey* [2003] ECHR 451 (23 September 2003).

[48] However, if the parents should have their children's best interest as their basic concern (Art. 18 para 1 of the CRC) and the best interests of the child can only be safeguarded by respecting children's rights, then there is at least a moral obligation on behalf of the parents to respect their children's rights, as a condition for their full development.

consequently, the State is equally bound to provide adequate mechanisms to ensure the respect for a child's right to be heard within the family. Some States have tried to secure that by enacting legislation that requires parents to consult their children when taking decisions concerning them. For example, the Children (Scotland) Act 1995 requires parents to take into consideration so far as practicable the views of the child when reaching "any major decision" involving a child's upbringing.[49] The Norwegian Children and Parents Act 1981 provides that parents should listen to a child's opinion before taking any decision concerning the child.[50] The proposed legislation in South Africa contains similar provisions with the Scottish legislation, requiring the holders of parental responsibility to consult with children, taking into consideration their age and maturity, over issues that would affect, *inter alia* a child's living conditions, education, health, personal relations with a parent or family member or, generally, the child's well-being.[51]

While these provisions recognise the right of a child to be consulted within the family, the enforcement of these provisions raises difficulties because of the private nature of the decision-making process within the family. The Scottish Law Commission acknowledged the fragility of Article 6(1) of the Children (Scotland) Act 1995, as being a "vague and unenforceable" provision. However, the importance of these developments should not be minimised. For example, the Swedish reform regarding the abolition of corporal punishment at home showed that the law carries an educational value, and has the ability of influencing a positive change in social attitudes.[52] The presence in the law of a requirement to consult with children associated, ideally, with a practice of State-supported consultation with children in public spheres could be useful in persuading parents that children deserve to be heard. Undoubtedly, such a legal provision supports children who wish to assert their participatory rights within the family, and strengthens their belief in the legitimacy of their request. Although a provision requiring parents to consult with children when taking decisions is unenforceable in the sense that the consultation of children cannot be secured by the State at the moment of decision, it could offer grounds for a judicial review of the decision at the child's request if the child is not consulted.

---

49 Section 6(1) of Children (Scotland) Act 1995. See generally L. Edwards, 'Hearing the Voice of the Child: Notes from the Scottish Experience', in C.J. Davel (ed.), *Children's Rights in a Transitional Society*, (Menlopark: Protea Book House, 1999), 37.

50 Section 31 ('The child's right of co-determination') of Act No. 7 of 1981,<http://odin.dep.no/bld/english/doc/legislation/acts/004071-200003/dok-bn.html>.

51 Clause 31 (2) (a) Children's Bill 70 of 2003.

52 J.E. Durrant, 'The Swedish Ban on Corporal Punishment: Its History and Effects', in *Family Violence Against Children: A Challenge for Society*, (Berlin – New York: Walter de Gruyter & Co., 1996), 19–25, <http://www.nospank.net/durrant.htm >.

11. Many parents are perhaps ill equipped to deal with dissenting views of the child and this could make them reluctant to allow the child to speak at all. When the conflict between parental views and child wishes is brought within the public domain, the bodies entrusted with the decision, usually the courts, use a set of predetermined criteria like competence, maturity, understanding or child's best interests, in deciding whose views are to be preferred. It is however, difficult to ensure that such criteria are applied within the family. VAN BUEREN suggested that given the novelty of evolving capacities of the child principle and its impact on the exercise of the participatory rights of the child, parents should be provided with guidance on how to assess the evolving capacities of their children.[53] When extending this idea, it can be argued that parents' education could be a useful tool in promoting parenting practices that take into consideration a child's right to be heard. This suggestion will be dealt with more extensively in the conclusion of this paper.

12. If generally the intervention of the State in the management of parent-child relationships is regarded with reluctance, there are circumstances when the abuse of parental rights causes harm to children. In these circumstances, the privacy rights of the parents cannot be used to perpetuate the harm created to children, and the intervention of the State is not just legitimate but constitutes an obligation.[54] Still debated is the issue of corporal punishment, but this issue is dealt with in the following section, which looks closer at some potential areas of conflict between parental and children's rights.

5. AREAS OF POTENTIAL CONFLICT BETWEEN PARENTAL VIEWS AND CHILDREN'S VIEWS

13. This section looks at the conflict between parental and children's views from the perspective of both developed and developing countries, stressing the specific factors that influence the value of children's capacity for autonomy in both types of societies. Very briefly, it can be observed that while the Western world is quite concerned with legal debates on child autonomy, and attempts to formulate legal or judicial guarantees for the exercise of children's capacity for autonomy, the developing world is less preoccupied with theoretical aspects, but supports child autonomy in the form of taking up social and economic responsibilities.

---

53 G. VAN BUEREN, supra (note 11),138.

54 See for example *A v United Kingdom* [1999] 27 EHRR 611; *E and others v United Kingdom*, Applicationno.33218/96,Judgement26 November 2002, <http://www.coe.int/T/E/Legal_affairs/>.

14. The most common areas that appear to involve a conflict between children's views and parental views in the Western societies are contact, custody, medical decisions and corporal punishment at home.[55] When children are not mature enough to make their own decision, parents have a right and a duty to decide. This situation has not been changed by provisions regarding the participatory rights from the CRC.[56] However, when decision-making abilities of older or more mature children are concerned, the right of the parents to make decisions needs to be balanced against the evolving capacities of the child in order to determine the extent of parental decision-making powers. In making this balance, LANSDOWN has suggested taking into consideration *inter alia* the following factors: failure to create consistent boundaries and explanations for the existence of these boundaries can create insecurity for children, who have no guidelines for what is expected of them; over-protecting children denies them the opportunity to gain confidence and ability to make choices; children that have no practice in making choices or opposing adult authority may be more vulnerable to abuse or exploitation; over-protection may lead to resentment and lack of communication with parents and a weak ability to advise, support or influence children.[57]

15. Within the complex reality of family relationships, conflicts can occur between a child's decision and his/her best interests, and a child's decision and parental views. In both sets of circumstances the best interests principle should play a mediating role, whether the decisions are taken by the judiciary or within the family. It seems that currently it is widely accepted that if the decision of a child, mature or not, runs against his/hers best interests, a child's views can be overridden by parents or courts.[58] However, if a child's decision conflicts only with the views of the parent, without being contrary to the child's best interests, there seems to be no reason to override the child's wishes. On the contrary, arguments can be brought to support the idea that letting the child make the decision according to his/her wishes contributes to the development of the child, a value that should be protected by parents.[59]

Sharing of the decision-making between parents and mature children refers back to the participatory form of parenting promoted by the concept of parental responsibility. The repartition of decision-making powers between parents and children has been subject of judicial attention, but the case law suggests a rather fragmented image of what children can or cannot decide for themselves. In 1985, the English House of Lords

---

55 The matter of corporal punishment within the family is equally problematic in developed and developing countries.

56 G. LANSDOWN, supra (note 3), 4.

57 Ibid., 34.

58 See generally J. FORTIN, supra (note 5), Chapters 1, 3, 4, 5, 9 and 10.

59 See generally G. LANSDOWN, supra (note 3).

decided that when children gain the ability to make decisions for themselves, the authority of the parents ceases.[60] Although this decision was progressive, and acknowledged the ability of children to make autonomous decisions before reaching an age established by law, it provides no guidance for situations in which children make dangerous decisions. One risk posed by this position is that in order to accommodate protection, courts have established very high standards for assessing competence, an aspect that led to declaring some teenagers GILLICK incompetents, and deny them the possibility to have an input in decision-making.[61] The same unqualified decision led to a distinction between consent to treatment and refusal of treatment. When a refusal of treatment is concerned, the courts have decided that a refusal of treatment of a competent or incompetent child can be overridden by parents or courts, if they believe that treatment is in the best interests of the child.[62] The reasoning employed by courts in refusal of treatment cases has diminished considerably the value of a child's consent, qualifying a child's position as only concurrent with parental consent. By arguing that a child's consent is only a procedural request necessary to protect the medical practitioner from criminal liability in the case of a medical intervention, the courts implied that a child's position had little weight when deciding on a medical intervention in the case of refusal of treatment. The danger of these decisions is that even in delicate matters, although the wishes of children may conflict with the views of their parents, the consent to treatment from parents entitles doctors to apply the treatment without it being necessary to seek a court's approval. Such a position shows indeed little respect for the views of the child, especially when the child is competent. While protective intervention is legitimate in life-threatening conditions, it would be desirable for courts to justify the overruling of the refusal of treatment by children through a balancing exercise between the protective rights and autonomy rights of the child.[63]

More recently, by applying the Human Rights Act 1998, which incorporates into English legislation the ECHR, the courts have shown more attention to children's self-assertive rights. When a girl of 16 intended to make public her experiences in the care system, the court found that it was a court's responsibility and duty to defend the right of a child who had a sufficient understanding to make an informed decision, to make his or her own choice.[64] Although in this case the parents did not oppose the child's decision to make public her story, the court stated that this factor was not determina-

60 *Gillick* case, supra (note 43).

61 *Re E (a minor)(consent to medical treatment)* [1993] FLR 386; *Re L (Medical treatment: Gillick competency)* [1999] 2 FCR 524. See also J. FORTIN, supra (note 5), 134.

62 *Re R (A Minor)(Wardship: Consent to Treatment)* [1991] 4 All ER 177; *Re W (A Minor)(Medical Treatment: Court's Jurisdiction)* [1992] 3 WLR 758.

63 J. FORTIN, supra (note 5), 84.

64 *Re Roddy (a child)(identification: restriction on publication)* [2004] 2 FLR 949.

tive in deciding the exercise of a competent child's right to privacy and freedom of expression, and even in case of parental opposition, the child's view would have been determinative of the case.

16. In matters regarding sex life, both legislation and case law seem quite permissive by comparison with the precautions taken in medical decisions. In a number of countries, a girl, regardless of age, can access abortion services without parental consent.[65] For example, according to South African legislation "any female person of any age" has the right to terminate her pregnancy within a certain period,[66] if the woman is able to give her informed consent.[67] Although, in the case of a pregnant minor the medical practitioner shall advise the woman to consult with her parents, extended family or friends, the absence of consultation does not lead to the woman being denied access to termination of pregnancy.[68] The above legislation has been challenged in court for failing to comply with the best interest of the child because it allows termination of pregnancy without parental consent or previous counselling.[69] The court rejected the claim, and it found that the best interest of the child is secured by the flexibility of the law, which gives relevance to the individual characteristics of a girl-child based on her intellectual, psychological and emotional development, and actual maturity.[70] The court rejected an age-based approach in the exercise of an autonomous decision, the presence of informed consent, which requires intellectual and emotional maturity being considered sufficient to protect the best interests of the child.[71]

17. The same concern for accommodating children's interests and views in a decision-making process is reflected in the jurisprudence of the ECtHR, with reference mainly to custody and contact. The right to personal autonomy is approached by the ECtHR in the context of the right to private life guaranteed by Article 8 of the ECHR. The court has moved from the position adopted in the Nielsen case,[72] where the rights of the child under Article 8 were not even considered, to accept that in family conflicts, both parents' and children's rights under Article 8 are engaged and need to be balanced

---

65 South Africa (see infra note 66); Netherlands, Sweden and the US (Connecticut and Maine) according to K. Scheiwe, 'Between autonomy and dependency: minors' rights to decide on matters of sexuality, reproduction, marriage, and parenthood. Problems and the state of debate – an introduction', (2004) 18 (262) *International Journal of Law, Policy and the Family*, 270.

66 Sections 1 and 2(1) (a) of the South African Choice on Termination on Pregnancy Act 92 of 1996.

67 Ibid., Section 5(1).

68 Ibid., Section 5(3).

69 *Christian Lawyer's Association v National Minister of Health* 2004 (10) 1086 BCLR (T).

70 Ibid., 1094A-C.

71 Ibid., 093H.

72 *Nielsen v Denmark*, supra (note 44).

against each other.[73] Although the court seems to consider the views of the child important in a parental dispute,[74] it attaches importance to the social circumstances in which those views were formed.[75]

18. By contrast, with the complicated reasoning employed to support or override children's capacity for autonomy, corporal punishment remains a matter in which not many courts venture into a balancing exercise between the rights of the parents to discipline their children and the rights of the child. With some exceptions,[76] courts have avoided discussing corporal punishment in the context of child dignity. Hopefully, with the recent firm position of anti-corporal punishment within the family expressed by the Committee on the Rights of the Child (CRC Committee), courts and legislature will re-evaluate their position regarding corporal punishment.[77]

19. The acknowledgement that children may have distinctive interests from their parents is reflected also in the procedural rules providing for separate representation for children in court. For example, the South African Constitution provides that the child has the right to have appointed in civil cases a legal representative at the State's expense if "substantial injustice would otherwise result".[78] In England, the Family Proceedings Rule 9.2A sets the conditions for a child bringing procedures in court or instructing a solicitor without the involvement of a next friend or guardian *ad litem*.

20. The developments presented above show a willingness to consider a child's potential to make independent decisions. Although the practice might sometimes be confused, there are attempts by courts and the law to balance parental intervention and children's participatory rights. However, the situation presented above reflects mainly the legal developments regarding child autonomy in developed countries, where the debate on child autonomy has reached the courts and is debated publicly.[79]

---

73 See cases indicated at supra (note 47).

74 *Sahin v Germany* [2003] ECHR 340 (08 July 2003).

75 *Hansen v Turkey*, supra (note 47).

76 See for example *Cambria, Cass, Sez. VI, 18 Marzo 1996 [Supreme Court of Cassation, 6th Penal section, March 18 1996], Foro It II 1996, 407 (Italy)* and *Israel Supreme Court, Criminal appeal 4596/98 Plonit v A.G. 54(1) P.D. p 145* (summaries of the cases are available on <http://www.endcorporal-punishment.org/pages/frame.html>.

77 CRC Committee, *General Comment No. 8: The right of the child to protection from corporal punishment and other cruel or degrading forms of punishment (arts. 19, 28(2) and 37, inter alia),* (UN Doc. CRC/C/GC8, 2006).

78 Section 28(5) Constitution of South Africa Act 108 of 1996.

79 The author would like to acknowledge as a limitation of this paper the fact that the discussion is based mainly on literature and case law from English speaking countries, and even in that case, mainly on sources from developed countries. This is mainly due to lack of accessible materials from other countries.

More research is needed to offer a complete picture of how child autonomy is valued by courts and families in developing countries.

There seems to be a low level of formal awareness and formal recognition of a child's capacity for autonomy in developing countries. In an African context, for example, the traditionalist and communitarian organisation of many African communities leave little scope for children to practise their capacity for autonomy in the form of expressing views within the family or wider community.[80] Here, one of the essential elements of children's upbringing is the obedience to adults. In many African societies decisions are made for the child without his/her participation,[81] the relationship between adults and children being characterised by "enormous filial respect, and in turn, is reinforced by the ethic of dominance".[82] The socialisation of the child within these values leads to perpetuation of a reduced participation of children in family and social life.[83] However, within the same societies a large proportion of children are forced by socio-economic and political conditions to assume a premature *de facto* autonomy. Paradoxically, these countries do not hesitate to state, even in international human rights documents, that children have responsibilities in social and political life,[84] or rely on children as breadwinners or soldiers, although they do not recognise them formally the right to be heard within the family or community.[85] For example, a project in Uganda and Sudan involving children affected by war revealed their experiences as heads of households and victims of sexual violence. The children resented the fact that despite their social contribution there had been little recognition for their changing role in society. The children also resented the fact that they had little

80 See, for example, CRC Committee, *Concluding Observations: Uganda* (UN Doc. CRC/C/Uga/CO/2, 2005), para. 35. But the low level of child participation within the family is not exclusively an African problem. For example, the CRC Committee made similar observations in analysing the country reports of Costa Rica, *Concluding Observations: Costa Rica* (UN Doc. CRC/C/15/Add.266, 2005), paras.21,22,<http://www.unhchr.ch/tbs/doc.nsf/(Symbol)/CRC.C.15.Add.266.En?Opendocument>; CRC Committee, *Concluding Observations: Hungary* (UN Doc. CRC/C/HUN/CO2, 2006), paras. 24, 25, <http://www.unhchr.ch/tbs/doc.nsf/(Symbol)/CRC.C.HUN.CO.2.En?OpenDocument>; CRC Committee, *Concluding Observations: Saudi Arabia* (UN Doc.CRC/C/SAU/CO/2, 2006) paras. 36, 37, <http://www.unhchr.ch/tbs/doc.nsf/(Symbol)/CRC.C.SAU.CO.2.En?OpenDocument>.

81 D.M. Chirwa, 'Participation rights: Challenging African legislation', (Dec 2001/Jan 2002) 40 *ChildrenFirst*, <http://www.childrenfirst.org.za/shownews?mode=content&id=17350&refto=2634>.

82 B. Rwezaura, 'The duty to hear a child: A view from Tanzania', in W. Ncube (ed.), *Law, culture, tradition and the children's rights in Eastern and Southern Africa*, 1998, 59 cited in T. Kaime, 'The Convention on the Rights of the Child and the legitimacy of children's rights in Africa: Some reflections', (2005) 5 *African Human Rights Law Journal*, 221, 231.

83 T. Kaime, supra (note 82), 231.

84 Ibid.

85 A comparison between Art. 12 para. 1 of the CRC and Art. 4 para. 2 of the African Charter on the Rights and Welfare of the Child (AC) reveals that although the CRC guarantees the right of the child to be heard in "all the matters", phrasing that includes family issues, the African Charter limits the guarantees of the right to be heard to judicial and administrative proceedings, with no reference to family or community matters.

control over their lives, and complained that traditional authorities require unquestioned respect from young people and do not acknowledge children's essential socio-economic contributions.[86]

It is regrettable that there is little jurisprudence on child autonomy available from developing countries, and this could be an indication of a low judicial development of children's autonomy rights. Unfortunately, although the CRC Committee requires States to provide information on how children's views are taken into consideration in judicial decisions,[87] there is little information on the orientation of the courts in considering children's autonomy rights. Consequently, the concluding observations of the Committee do not discuss judicial developments in child autonomy. It is important to acknowledge that a low level of judicial development of autonomy rights of children is not just an indication of a current state of affairs, but has effects for the future, to the extent that it deprives society of the potential educative role played by courts' decisions in encouraging the exercise of children's participatory rights.

Is this situation connected to the communitarian approach to human rights? Is this a result of a lack of knowledge of children's participatory rights, or lack of social interest in child autonomy? Is this a result of a hierarchy between the rights of the child: do autonomy rights become a concern only after the survival and development of the child are ensured? LANSDOWN has observed that "*in the legislation of many developing countries, there is an absence of recognition of children as needing special protection*".[88] It could be argued that this legislative situation is more child-autonomy-friendly because it does not put children through all the hurdles of proving that they are mature and competent. However, whether this orientation is the result of a conscious choice from legislature or whether the absence of protective legislation has indeed positive effects for children's capacity for autonomy remains to be clarified by further research.

21. The discussion referring to different approaches to child autonomy in developed and developing countries brings into discussion the criticisms of the CRC as being a Western-oriented convention that disregards the particularities of other cultures.[89] This criticism fails to take into account that culture is in a continuous change under

86 Women's Commission for Refugee Women and Children, *Against all the odds, surviving the war on adolescents: Promoting the protection and capacity of Ugandan and Sudanese adolescents in Northern Uganda*, (New York, 2001) in G. LANSDOWN, supra (note 3), 33.

87 CRC Committee, *General Guidelines for periodic reports* (UN Doc. CRC/C/58, 1996), para. 47 <http://www.unhchr.ch/tbs/doc.nsf/(Symbol)/CRC.C.58.En?Opendocument>.

88 G. LANSDOWN, supra (note 3), 32.

89 F. VILJOEN, 'Supra-national human rights instruments for the protection of children in Africa: the Convention on the Rights of the Child and the African Charter on the Rights and Welfare of the Child', (1998) 31 *CILSA*, 199 and 205.

the influence of social, economic and political factors, and that traditional cultural practices are open to challenge and substitution by universal human rights norms.[90] This cultural dynamic is illustrated by Africa, a continent in which social and cultural practices prevent sometimes the exercise by children of their participatory rights. African countries have made an international commitment to eliminate all those harmful social and cultural practices that affect the child's dignity, welfare, normal growth and development,[91] proving that the culture of human rights could have an impact in changing the values within society.

However, while the impact of cultural specificity in human rights protection cannot be ignored, the conflict between some cultural practices and human rights of the child is inherent.[92] This creates a real tension in children's lives, because although they have the right to be protected against harmful cultural practices, children have also the interest of being accepted as part of their cultures.[93] Of course, a mere international law commitment, as illustrated in the previous paragraph, does not suffice for an effective protection of children's participatory rights. There is a need for change in attitudes within society where participatory rights of children are obstructed by traditional practices. However, if a meaningful and sustainable change is to be achieved, the design and implementation of methods enhancing child participation must be constructed in a non-elitist manner, using language and symbols relevant for each community that requires reform.[94]

22. As implied above, child autonomy or capacity for autonomy is not just a matter of law, but has a complex relationship with education, socio-economic or political, and cultural context. A factor that will be briefly discussed below is the relation between the type of family relationships established between children and their parents, and a child's capacity for autonomy. It has been emphasised that parenting does not involve just providing care or making decisions for children, but involves also preparing children to make decisions for themselves.[95] A significant way to develop children's decision-making abilities is to encourage them to build and practice these

---

90 T. Kaime, supra (note 82), 233.

91 Art. 21 para. 1 AC.

92 For example FGM, forced feeding of women, nutritional taboos, son preference, female infanticide and dowry price. See the UN Office of the High Commissioner for Human Rights, *Fact sheet no. 23, Harmful Traditional Practices Affecting the Health of Women and Children* (not dated), <http://www.unhchr.ch/html/menu6/2/fs23.htm.

93 N.Thomas and C. O'Kane, 'When children's wishes and feelings clash with their 'best interests', (1998) 6 *The International Journals of Children's Rights*, 137 and 139.

94 T. Kaime, supra (note 82), 235.

95 B. Clark, 'From rights to responsibilities? An overview of recent developments relating to the parent/child relationship in South African common law', (2002) *CILSA*, 216, 225–226.

abilities within the protective family environment, under the guidance of their parents or carers.

However, some types of family settings are more open to child autonomy than others. For example, in a Turkish study analysing the value of children for their families, it was underlined that in the traditional, rural, low socio-economic status families the dependence of the parents at their older ages on the support provided by their children, influences parental practices in the sense that child autonomy is not encouraged since an autonomous child develops aims independent of the aims of the family.[96] Child rearing practices are also connected with the socio-economic status and level of education of parents, a higher socio-economic status and higher level of education being associated with parenting methods that encourage more child autonomy.[97]

However, like any social phenomenon, the structure of the family and the way the relationships between the family members are structured are in a continuous state of change. The Turkish study cited above made a comparison between the qualities desired by parents from their children in 1975 and 2003. While in 1975, the quality preferred by parents was obedience, the independence of the child not even being mentioned by respondents,[98] in 2003 parents desired to an equal extent, obedience and independence, parents with higher socio-economic status and education having more support for independence.[99] These changes in parental attitudes due to the process of modernisation, industrialisation and urbanisation, do not come without tensions. A study on parent-child relationships in Hong Kong revealed that children are subjects of conflicting messages on what constitutes a good relationship with their parents. While generally teachers and professionals dealing with children transmit Western views, more supportive for child autonomy, parents at home employ more traditional methods, emphasising the importance of obedience to parents.[100] But it is not just children that feel this tension; under the mixed influence of Western and traditional ideas on child rearing, parents are concerned that they do not know how to build a relationship encouraging independence, which at the same time would allow them to discipline their children.[101]

---

96 C. Kagitcibasi and B. Ataca, 'Value of Children and Family Change: A Three Decade Portrait from Turkey', (2005) 54(3) *Applied Psychology: An International Review*, 317, 319–320.

97 Ibid., 332.

98 Ibid., 335.

99 Ibid., 332.

100 L. Fong, Y. Yee, Pattie, 'A search for new ways of describing parent-child relationships: Voices from principals, teachers, guidance professionals, parents and pupils', (2005) 12(1), *Childhood* 111–137, 125.

101 Ibid., 129.

Literature has also emphasised that another factor in increasing the conflict between adults and children is the lack of awareness of their reciprocal expectancies. For example, THOMAS and O'KANE found that children valued more the possibility of offering their views than having their wishes complied with; by contrast, adults' belief was that children wanted mainly to have the decision taken according to their sole view.[102] In the Hong Kong study cited above, it was found that children were not aware of the filial respect expected by their parents, and this had the potential of creating disputes between parents and children.[103]

The last few paragraphs have shown that the quality of the relationship between children and parents can influence the way in which a child's capacity for autonomy is supported within the family. However, this should not detract attention from other issues that have also impact on the development of a child's capacity for autonomy within the family environment, like macro-economic and social factors such as, poverty, lack of education of both parents and children, and lack of opportunities for development.

6. CONCLUSION

23. As mentioned throughout the paper, the exercise by children of their participatory rights within the family remains a challenge because of the inherent parental discretion in allowing the exercise of the right to be heard and in evaluating the weight of a child's wishes. The limited scope of a State's intervention within the family leaves the State with few means to ensure that children's participatory rights are respected within the family. Enacting legislation that requires parents to consult with their children, as we have seen in the cases of Scotland and Norway, remains open to challenges regarding implementation. However, the State can indirectly stimulate a change in parental practices through court decisions that discuss a child's capacity for autonomy, and which send a message about what constitutes good parental practice.

24. Rather than approaching child participation as a cause of conflict within the family, it should be acknowledged that an enhanced participation of children improves reciprocal knowledge between parents and children, and has the ability of increasing the respect between parents and children.[104] Perhaps a more genuine adherence to the idea that children's capacity for autonomy needs to be exercised within the family can be obtained through education. The CRC Committee requires States to provide

102 N. THOMAS and C. O'KANE, supra (note 93), 147.

103 L. FONG, Y. YEE, PATTIE, supra (note 100), 128.

104 G. LANSDOWN, supra (note 3), 58.

information on "*what measures have been taken to raise the awareness of families and the public in general of the need to encourage children to exercise their right to express their views*".[105] In this undertaking, it would be appropriate to inform parents or carers of the reasons for taking children's views seriously. A part of this process should consist of informing parents that children's views have an intrinsic value, and children are capable of expressing critical views and balancing alternatives.[106] Studies that have proved the abilities of children to make critical judgements, in either the family or the public sphere, should be used as a tool to raise awareness among parents about children's ability to express valuable views. By doing so, it is more likely that States will gain social acceptance of the idea that children's capacity for autonomy is a value that needs to be protected within the family.

25. The ways in which these methods are promoted should be carefully balanced. Aggressive methods of influencing parenting methods might generate reluctance from parents, and a plain rejection of practices that could, if accepted, have benefited the family in the long run. Although the obligation to implement the CRC belongs to the State, NGOs could be successfully involved in promoting a more sensitive attitude to children's views within the family and society at large.

---

105 CRC Committee, *General Guidelines for periodic reports* (UN Doc. CRC/C/58, 1996), para. 46, <http://www.unhchr.ch/tbs/doc.nsf/(Symbol)/CRC.C.58.En?Opendocument>.

106 A study commissioned by UNICEF to investigate child participation in South Asia showed that despite an initial reluctance from parents regarding their children's participation in various community projects, for reasons like losing respect for parents, distraction from school or housework, the success of children's involvement diminished parental fear, which was replaced by a growing pride of their children. G. LANSDOWN, supra (note 3), 28, citing UNICEF, *Wheel of Change: Children and young people's participation in South Asia*, (UNICEF, Kathmandu, 2004).

THE RIGHTS OF THE ADOPTED CHILD AND THE PUBLIC FAMILY POLICIES IN INTERCOUNTRY ADOPTION

SALOMÉ ADROHER BIOSCA

1. INTRODUCTION

1. The main legal research on intercountry adoption (IA) is focused on the process of constitution of adoption and the child's best interests during it, such as legal research into the prevention of trafficking of children, assuring that adoption is a way of searching for the best family for a child who does not have one...and so on. The studies and the regulations attend mainly to the *pre-adoption* period or the adoption process. This is the matter regulated in Article 21 of the CRC and in the 1993 Hague Convention on Protection of Children and Co-operation in respect of IA.

2. Nevertheless, many "disrupted" adoptions have regularly been constituted, but do not work after some time. The social and psychological studies on this matter have usually found the cause to be adaptation problems in relation to some characteristic of the child: age, health or psychological problems, etc. However, the most recent studies conclude that the adaptation of the family and the child depends also on the capacity of the adoptive environment to compensate the risks associated with the history of the child and to facilitate the adaptation.[1] This social psychology approach is coincident with social policy studies that propose models, which consider the family as the subject (more than an object) of family policies because of its strength to cope

[1] A. BERÁSTEGUI PEDRO-VIEJO, *La adaptación familiar en adopción internacional. Una muestra de adoptados mayores de tres años en la Comunidad de Madrid*, (Madrid: Consejo Económico y Social de la Comunidad de Madrid, 2005), 357. The author of this recent study concludes: "Los patrones de adaptación del menor están explicados en una proporción muy relevante por el proceso de adaptación de la familia a la adopción internacional. En este sentido, unas bajas tasas de estrés, una percepción positiva de la situación (en términos de control, conformación de las expectativas y reestructuración positiva) una mayor adaptación familiar así como unos bajos niveles de sobrerreactividad en las intervenciones educativas de los padres, interactúan para mejorar los niveles de adaptación del niño" (...) Los adoptantes serán los principales aliados del sistema de protección de menores en su tarea de proporcionar a los niños un entorno seguro y estable de desarrollo".

with different situations and problems. Therefore, the duty of the market, the state, the third sector and society is to help the family to fulfil its functions trusting in its capacity instead of substituting it.[2] From this point of view, family adaptation after adoption is a longer, and perhaps most important time to be taken into account also by the law and regulations on IA.[3] The main objection to this proposal is that "*the adoptive family becomes a family like any other*, in the sense that it must benefit from the same protection and the same offers of assistance as any other family, without being suspected more than another of dysfunctions. Nonetheless, it remains different since it must reconcile itself with the fact that the adoptee comes from somewhere else, bearing a path of earlier disruptions and abandonment before his/her entry into the adoptive family".[4]

3. Of the matters to be regulated by the law during the whole life of the adoptive family (the post-adoption period), some questions need to be underlined: family friendly policies or regulations that facilitate reconciliatory work and family life; economic support for IA families; public facilities to support post-adoption services to help the family and the child facing the difficulties of the matching process, and finally helping the child to search for his/her origins ("back to the roots" policies).

4. The present contribution will face this matter studying especially the family policies implemented in Spain, which is nowadays one of the main receiving States for IA in the world.

2. APPROACH TO THE PHENOMENON AND THE REGULATION OF INTERCOUNTRY ADOPTION

2.1. THE CASE: SPANISH COUNCIL OF STATE ADVICE NUMBER 2548/2002[5]

5. To illustrate the approach of this paper, it will start with a real case that took place recently in Spain. A Spanish married couple resident in Madrid, wishing to adopt a

---

2 G. Rossi, 'Le politiche sociale per la famiglia', in G. ROSSI (ed.), *Interventi a favore dellga coniugalità e della genitorialità*, (Milano: Vita e pensiero 2005), 41–58.

3 In relation to IA, a very recent seminar held at Innocenti Istitute has attended particularly to this period: European Network on National Observatories on Childhood, *ChildONEurope 2003–5 Activities European seminar on post-adoption. Which Approaches, Models and Support Services to Adoptive Families Relations*, (Florence: The Institut degli Innocenti, 2006), (CD Rom).

4 SSI. EDITORIAL "Post adoption: the usefulness of professional support for the adoptee and his adoptive family", Monthly Review nº 2/2006, February 2006.

5 <http://www.consejo-estado.es/>.

Russian child, applied on 7/12/1996 to the Spanish central authority in IA in the "autonomous community" of Madrid ("Instituto madrileño del menor y la familia"-IMMF). This authority, after being satisfied that the applicants were eligible and suitable to adopt, prepared a report including the characteristics of the child the parents would be qualified to care for. They would prefer a four-year-old boy, who is physically and psychologically healthy. The IMMF had accredited an intermediate private institution (these intermediate bodies in Spain are called "Entidades colaboradoras de adopción internacional" – ECAIs), which worked with Russia and had informed the applicants they could supervise the adoption process with them. The couple signed a contract with this ECAI and the process started.

Eight months later (22/10/96) the Russian authorities informed the ECAI that a child had been preassigned: a six-year-old girl with some ophthalmic problems (strabismus) and mild mental retardation due to institutional care. The Spanish central authority had ensured that the prospective parents had agreed (nevertheless they affirmed two years later that they had been forced to by the ECAI, even though the child did not have the characteristics they had asked for) and approved such decision. The adoption was constituted in Russia (2/6/98) and a girl called Eugenia arrived in Madrid with her new parents.

When Eugenia was integrated into her new family, they observed the following medical and psychological problems: myopia and light astigmatism in both eyes requiring the girl to wear glasses; malformations in palate and gums, and several caries in the teeth; behaviour disorders, attention-deficit and hyperactivity disorder, cognitive distortion, mental retardation; and early sexual activity that affected her sister's development. The IMMF had various meetings with the family after the adoption in which the adoptive parents expressed all these problems.

On 23/3/2000, the parents sued for damages against the IMMF asking for €600,000 because of the dentist expenses, special education expenses and contemptuous damages and finally decided to "break" the adoption: on 6/4/2000, the IMMF declared the girl "abandoned" and placed her in a Spanish institution for the care of children.

The IMMF demanded from the Council of State an Advice about its civil liability in this case of disrupted adoption. The Advice number 2548/2002 (on 7/11/2002) concluded that the IMMF had performed adequately in the pre-adoption period and in the post-adoption period.

2.2. THE CONCEPT OF IA AND IA AS A SOCIAL PHENOMENON

6. An adoption is *international* if one or several of its elements (residence or nationality of the child or of the foster parents, authority who constitutes the adoption…) are connected with more than one country. Nevertheless, this paper will refer to intercountry adoption as the adoption in which the child resides in one State, the foster parent or parents in another and the child moves and leaves his/her country of origin to live far away with his/her new family because of the adoption.[6]

IA is a "peculiar and quiet migration",[7] a phenomenon characteristic of the 1950s, which started after the Second World War,[8] increased with the Korean and Vietnamese wars,[9] and spread in the 1960s. PARRA-ARANGUREN states "*a dramatic increase in IA which had occurred in many countries since the late 1960s to such extent that IA had become a worldwide phenomenon involving migration of children over long geographical distances and from one society and culture to another very different environment*".[10] Today

---

6 This is the concept of IA taken into account in the main international conventions. The Hague Convention on Protection of Children and Co-operation, adopted on 29 May 1993 and entered into force on 1 May 1995, defines Intercountry Adoption in its Art. 2: *The Convention shall apply where a child habitually resident in one Contracting State ("the State of origin") has been, is being, or is to be moved to another Contracting State ("the receiving State") either after his or her adoption in the State of origin by spouses or a person habitually resident in the receiving State, or for the purposes of such an adoption in the receiving State or in the State of origin.* In the same sense, Art. 1 of the Interamerican Convention on the Conflict of Laws on Adoption, La Paz, Bolivia, adopted on 24 May 1984 and entered into force on 26 May 1988, determines that the Convention will be applied when *"el adoptante (o adoptantes) tenga su domicilio en un Estado parte y el adoptado su residencia habitual en otro Estado parte".*

7 B. TRILLAT, 'Une migration singulière: la adoption international', in *Actes du séminaire Nathalie-Masse 25–27 mai 1992*, (Paris: Centre international de l'enfance de Paris, 1992), 21 ; P. SELMAN, 'The 'quiet migration' in the new millennium: trends in intercountry adoption 1998–2003', Paper presented at the 8th global Conference Manila, 10–12 August 2005.

8 The origin of these population movements were the wars. The Second World War caused many displacements of European and Japanese children to the USA or Sweden; the German case is quite surprising: in 1950, American, Scandinavian or BENELUX families adopted 489 German children, in 1957 2,628 German children were already adopted; M.A. TEXTOR, 'International adoption in West Germany: a private affair', in H. ALSTEIN, R. SIMON (eds.), *Intercountry adoption. A multinational perspective*, (York – Connecticut – London: Praeger, 1991), 119.

9 About 200,000 Vietnamese children left their country because of the war. The USA organised an operation called 'Baby lift' to evacuate between 2,000 and 3,000 Vietnamese orphans; this operation caused many human and legal problems because of its confusion and precipitation; T.E. CARBONNEAU, 'Operation baby lift: the dilemma surrounding child custody controversies', in R. LILLICH (ed.), *The family in international law: some emerging problems*, (Third sokol colloquium, 1981), 87.

10 G. PARRA-ARANGUREN, 'History, philosophy and general structure of the Hague adoption convention', in D. DOEK, H. VAN LOON, O. VLAARDINGERBROEK (eds.), *Children on the move. How to implement their right to family life*, (The Hague–Boston–London: Martinus Nijhoff Publishers, 1996), 63.

it is a phenomenon involving over 40,000 children each year moving between over a hundred countries, and is nowadays in its highest level ever in global terms "confounding predictions from the early 1990s that it was a phenomenon that had peaked".[11]

7. What can be the causes of this increasing international movement of children?

- War: Some wars, for example the Second World War, the civil war in Greece (1946 to 1949), the Korean War (1950 to 1953) and the war in Vietnam (1954 to 1975) explained the very early IA flows in the 1950s and 1960s. However, war and its aftermath are not the only factors leading countries to allow their children to be adopted abroad.
- Economic and demographic background: The flow between the States of origin of IA and the receiving States show the demographic and economic inbalance between the south and the north of our planet. The level of adoption is determined by the demand for children in rich western countries and the availability of children in those countries afflicted by poverty and other ills.
- Different models and resources for child protection.

8. It is however, evident that the major sources have not been the poorest or highest birth rate countries in that patterns persist long past the "crisis" or the war, so there are other factors that may be key factors. Such as the different models and resources of child protection in the origin and receiving countries and the evolution of the motivations of the prospective parents are then the decisive push and pull factors:

- In the receiving countries, low birth rates combined with policies of keeping children at risk in their own families and supporting the families through the social services system, produced a diminishing availability of young children for domestic adoption (the children available are children with *special needs*). In these countries, it is important to mention the "personal motivations" of the adoptive parents as a cause of IA. IA has become a way of creating families not only for sterile couples; the humanitarian motivated adoptions and the new "post-modern" families (IA is sometimes a "fashion") are important pull factors in the receiving countries.[12]
- In some origin countries there are "silent" policies that promote IA as the formula to finance the national children protection system. For example, IA has discouraged Korea from developing an adequate child welfare programme[13] and China's

11 P. SELMAN, supra (note 7).

12 R.A.C. HOKSBERGEN, 'Generaciones de padres adoptivos. Cambios en las motivaciones para la adopción', (1991) 12 *Infancia y Sociedad*, 39.

13 In Korea IA began in 1955 and has placed more than 120,000 children since then, see P. SELMAN, supra (note 7).

"one child policy" has created a crisis in the rejection of girl babies that are adopted by foreign parents.

9. Some authors have affirmed that IA is a cause of child misprotection in the countries of origin: there is a growing demand for young light-skinned healthy babies, which has led to a trade of children from and to countries that discourage some sending countries from developing their welfare system or to change some policies. The demand creates the supply:[14] "Intercountry adoption, therefore, has come to represent in many ways the convergence of 'demand' and 'supply'. One of the more recent concrete expressions of this lie in the use of the internet to promote adoption in ways that often involve the marketing of children – as well as spawning private adoptions and offering 'shortcuts' to the legal adoption process".[15]

2.3. THE BOOM OF IA IN SPAIN

10. The first "adoptive" country in the world was the USA: between 1971 and 2005, US citizens adopted 354,294 children from other countries and in increasing numbers every year with the reduction in children available for incountry adoption.[16] In the USA, the intervention of public authorities in this matter is very little due to the "neoliberal" system, which exists also in matters of family law.[17]

11. Although in the 1990s Spain was a country that did not appear in the international statistics of IA, in 2005 it was the second adoptive country after the USA, the first

---

[14] N. CANTWELL 'La adopción internacional. Un comentario sobre el número de niños adoptables y el número de personas que buscan adoptar internacionalmente', *Protección internacional del niño*, in *Boletín de los jueces V*, <http://www.hcch.net>; N. CANTWELL, 'C'est la demande effective, imbecile!', Colloque Suisse Sur L'Adoption Internationale, Bellinzona, 28–29 Octobre 2004, *Tâches, possibilités et difficultés des pays d'origine* (not published); A. BERÁSTEGUI PEDRO-VIEJO, supra (note 1), 39; A. FERRÁNDIS, 'La adopción internacional', in I.E. LÁZARO GONZÁLEZ and I. Mayoral Narros (eds.), *Jornadas sobre Derecho de menores*, (Madrid: Universidad Pontificia Comillas, 2003), 203–212.

[15] 'Intercountry Adoption', (December 1998) *Innocenti Digest.*

[16] In 1996: 11,340 children; in 1998: 15,583; in 2000: 18,447; in 2002: 21,378; in 2004: 22,884, and in 2005: 22,739. The main origin countries were China, Guatemala, Korea, Philippines and Romania. For Russia and Vietnam see: '*visas issued to orphans, US department of state*, <http://travel.state.gov/family>.

[17] We have qualified the American adoption law as *neoliberal* in other works, see: S. ADROHER BIOSCA, 'Desafíos del Derecho de familia en una sociedad intercultural', in D. BOROBIO (ed.), *Familia e interculturalidad*, (Salamanca, Universidad Pontificia de Salamanca, 2003), 315–264. However, it is easy to deduce it from the web page of the Department of State: "International adoption is essentially a private legal matter between a private individual (or couple) who wishes to adopt, and a foreign court, which operates under that country's laws and regulations. The US authorities cannot intervene on behalf of prospective parents with the courts in the country where the adoption takes place", <http://travel.state.gov/family>.

if we compare the ratio of IA/ population:[18] from 1997–2004 there have been 24,042 IAs in Spain.[19] What can be the reasons for this "family revolution" in Spain? Perhaps the broad legal and social changes in family behaviour after the political transition can partly explain this situation.

- Fewer children to be adopted: Contraceptives, AIDS, legalisation of abortion, destigmatisation of single motherhood, as well as State support for single mothers in some cases, have led to greatly reduced abandonment rates, and consequently the number of children who can be considered for domestic adoption has declined.
- More prospective parents searching to adopt: infertility problems are increasing, partly because of postponement of childbirth to later ages due to higher workforce participation by women. However, not all prospective parents adopt in Spain because of infertility problems. The motivations to adopt have changed significantly: 15% of the solicitants in Madrid in 2002 were single persons, 16% already had biological children (either from both of the prospective parents or from one of them) and 8% were adopted for humanitarian reasons.[20]

In the next figure, the evolution is shown: total number of IAs in Spain, total number per continent of origin of the children and number of the main countries of origin:

Continent/country	1997	1998	1999	2000	2001	2002	2003	2004
ASIA	**241**	**265**	**443**	**686**	**1.107**	**1.586**	**1.196**	**2.577**
China	105	197	261	475	941	1.427	1.043	2.389
India	109	97	163	190	129	109	100	117
Nepal	0	0	18	16	28	35	38	68
EUROPE	**97**	**216**	**645**	**1.439**	**1.569**	**1.395**	**1.913**	**2.111**
Russia	70	91	141	49	652	809	1.157	1.618
Romania	0	84	280	583	373	38	85	48
Ukraine	0	0	116	218	356	358	482	349
Bulgaria	11	27	92	123	172	181	202	57

18 The rates of IA can be referred to three statistic standards: total number of IA, number of IA related to population; number of IA related to number of births, see P. Selman, supra (note 7).

19 We have published the first statistics of IA in Spain (1988–1995) after a research period in the Central Registry office of civil status, see: S. Adroher Biosca, 'La adopción internacional: una aproximación general', in J. Rodriguez Torrente (ed.), *Menor y familia: conflictos e implicaciones*, (Madrid: Universidad Pontificia Comillas de Madrid, 1998), 229–304. From 1997, the Spanish Ministry of Work and Social Affairs publishes the data in its web page: <http://www.mtas.es>. The evolution has been astonishing: in 1990 there were 2,159 incountry adoptions vs. 100 intercountry adoptions. In 1995 there were 1,406 incountry vs. 435 intercountry; in 2000: 964 incountry vs. 3,062 intercountry; in 2004: 5,541 intercountry adoptions.

20 G. Davalos, *Perfil de los solicitantes de adopción internacional en la Comunidad de Madrid*, 2002, (Not published).

Continent/country	1997	1998	1999	2000	2001	2002	2003	2004
L AMERICA	**631**	**960**	**895**	**905**	**721**	**593**	**679**	**585**
Colombia	250	393	361	414	319	271	282	256
Peru	81	151	126	99	71	42	50	50
Mexico	72	90	107	79	92	58	50	31
Guatemala	47	75	70	90	46	28	8	3
Bolivia	18	31	66	66	18	76	126	92
AFRICA	**0**	**16**	**23**	**32**	**31**	**51**	**163**	**268**
Madagascar	0	8	1	10	9	19	24	13
Marruecos	0	3	12	8	5	7	20	21
Ethiopia	0	0	0	0	0	12	107	220
TOTAL	**942**	**1.487**	**2.006**	**3.062**	**3.428**	**3.625**	**3.951**	**5.541**

2.4. THE REGULATION OF IA CENTRED ON THE PRE-ADOPTION PERIOD

12. The regulation of IA in the main international instruments and in many State laws (as the Spanish ones) is focused on the pre-adoptive period. This is the orientation of Article 21 CRC[21] that must inform all the international and State regulations on IA. In this article, "the best interests of the child" is considered as the "paramount consideration" in IA,[22] so the old conception centred on the adults' needs has been substituted by a conception centred on the children's needs: IA is one of the possible

---

[21] State Parties that recognise and/or permit the system of adoption shall ensure that the best interests of the child shall be the paramount consideration and they shall:
(a) Ensure that the adoption of a child is authorised only by competent authorities who determine, in accordance with applicable law and procedures and on the basis of all pertinent and reliable information, that the adoption is permissible in view of the child's status concerning parents, relatives and legal guardians and that, if required, the persons concerned have given their informed consent to the adoption on the basis of such counselling as may be necessary;
(b) Recognise that intercountry adoption may be considered as an alternative means of a child's care, if the child cannot be placed in a foster or an adoptive family or cannot in any suitable manner be cared for in the child's country of origin;
(c) Ensure that the child concerned by intercountry adoption enjoys safeguards and standards equivalent to those existing in the case of national adoption;
(d) Take all appropriate measures to ensure that, in intercountry adoption, the placement does not result in improper financial gain for those involved in it;
(e) Promote, where appropriate, the objectives of the present article by concluding bilateral or multilateral arrangements or agreements, and endeavour, within this framework, to ensure that the placement of the child in another country is carried out by competent authorities or organs.

[22] In relation to this principle, there was a deep modification in the definite text of the Convention proposed by the Finnish observer during the drafting of the CRC, enforcing the child centred conception (Consejo Económico y Social. Cuestión de una Convención sobre Derechos del Niño. Informe del Grupo de Trabajo acerca de un proyecto de Convención sobre Derechos del Niño. Distr. General. E/CN.4/ 1989/48. 2 de marzo de 1989. Español, paras. 362–364).

solutions for children unable to live with their birth families. Another important principle in this article is the *subsidiarity rule.* It is considered best for the child to remain within his original family or within his country of origin being adequately cared for therein. This principle was underlined in the definite text of the Convention because during the drafting of the CRC it was stated that the State Parties must facilitate the IA and this measure is "another measure" for caring for the child. In the definite text, IA is accepted only if the child cannot be placed in foster care or in an adoptive family in his country.[23] The decision whether a child is available for adoption must be made in the child's country of origin.[24] However, it also concerns the receiving countries. If they "promote" IA through their pre and post-adoption measures or they do not control the private promotion of IA (for example through the internet), they contribute to the maintenance in some States of origin of deficient child welfare programmes and they contribute even to the dramatic reality of children being born to be given up for adoption, so sometimes IA creates orphans. Therefore, the subsidiarity principle is also the responsibility of the receiving States, like Spain.

13. The Hague Convention on Protection of Children and Co-operation in respect of intercountry adoption (1993) is mainly focused on the pre-adoption period, and establishes a cooperation system between public authorities of the origin and the receiving country to ensure that the adoption is constituted in the best interest of the child, the process is child centred and the subsidiarity principle is respected.[25]

14. In Spain, there have been broad reforms in the past 10 years that have led to a complex legal framework in IA.[26] Spain has ratified the Hague Convention and bilateral treaties with some countries (Bolivia[27] and Philippines[28]). The Spanish Private international law rules have been modified 5 times over the last 10 years; Spanish substantive family law has profoundly changed, moving from a consideration of the

23 The Venezuela and RFA delegations wanted to define the IA as an "exceptional mean", Ibid, paras. 256 257.

24 Although many times they do not guarantee it at all, see: N. CANTWELL, I. LAMMERANT and L. MARTÍNEZ-MORA, *Assessment on the adoption system in Ukraine,* a Project commissioned by the OSCE.ISS., October 2005.

25 "One of its basic premises is that adoption is not an individual affair, which can be left exclusively to the child's birthparents or legal guardians, or to the prospective adoptive parents or other intermediaries, but rather a social and legal measure for the protection of children. Consequently, procedures for intercountry adoption should ultimately be the responsibility of the States involved, which must guarantee that adoption corresponds to the child's best interests and respects his or her fundamental rights", see: 'Intercountry Adoption', (December 1998) *Innocenti Digest.*

26 S. ADROHER BIOSCA and V. ASSIEGO CRUZ, 'La adopción internacional', in I. LÁZARO GONZÁLEZ, *Los menores en el Derecho español,* (Madrid: Tecnos, 2002), 407–451.

27 Acuerdo bilateral entre el Reino de España y la República de Bolivia en materia de adopciones hecho en Madrid el 20 de octubre de 2001, (20 December 2001) nº304 *BOE.*

28 Protocolo de adopción internacional entre el Reino de España y la República de Filipinas hecho en Manila el 12 de noviembre de 2002, (24 january 2003) nº 21 *BOE.*

adoption as a private civil matter to a regulation of it as a public question, empowering the public administrative authorities at different moments of the process.[29] This philosophical change has coincided with two other "revolutions": the change of the model of State from a centralist to a decentralised model. Nowadays social policy (so also IA) is a competence of the "autonomous communities" rather than a State competence.[30] On the other hand, family law has significantly been modified with regard to different questions, some of them affecting IA, such as the fact that non-marriage couples are capable of adopting in some "autonomous communities" and homosexual married couples can adopt in Spain. All this legislation is also mainly focused on the pre-adoptive period.

3. PROTECTING THE ADOPTIVE CHILD AFTER ADOPTION

15. As noted in the introduction, protection of the adopted child does not end with the adoption; family adaptation and prevention of adoption dissolution must be taken into account by the law. Several problems that the adoptive families must face could be solved by helping the family with adequate post-adoptive policies, some of which can prevent adoption disruption or adoption dissolution.[31]

The average of IA dissolutions (or disruptions) depends on the period studied (before 1970 it was almost unknown), the country of adoption, the characteristics of the children taken into account (children with special needs, age groups, etc.).[32] Although

29 The main state legal framework is the Ley Orgánica 1/1996 de protección juridical del Menor, 15 January 1996, (17 January 1996 nº 15, *BOE*, which states that the public authorities must declare the applicants eligible to adopt; authorise and control the intermediate private agencies (ECAIs); coordinate the adoption with the public authorities of the origin country and send all the information about the progress of the placement to the authorities of the origin country if they demand it.

30 Therefore, the laws regulating the great majority of questions affecting IA are "autonomous".

31 "For children adopted from other countries and other ethnic backgrounds, disruption of this relationship is difficult to conceptualise, since they lose their whole existence. It renders them a stranger in the world in which they find themselves as well as in the world from which they came", see: J. Harper, 'Counselling issues in intercountry adoption disruption', (1993) vol 18 nº 3 *Adoption & fostering*, 20.

32 A. Berástegui Pedro- Viejo, *Las adopciones truncadas y en riesgo en la Comunidad de Madrid*, (Madrid: Consejo Económico y Social, 2003), 30, which summarises the main studies, especially the American studies: in the USA the medium averages are approximately 10%; in the Netherlands 10% and in Great Britain 18.7%. The recent European average is 5%, see: J. Palacios, *Idoneidad en la adopción Internacional*, paper in *VIII Jornadas de Coordinación entre Entidades publicas y Entidades colaboradoras en Adopción Internacional. Corresponsabilidad en la tramitación de las adopciones internacionales*, (Murcia 14–5- mars 2006), Not Published.

the most recent studies in Spain state that it is not common,[33] the adoption disruption generally takes place during adolescence – in this period, some studies suggest a certain risk of maladjustment.[34] Nowadays, the average age of adopted children in Spain is very low. What will happen in 5 or 10 years' time when a great number of adopted children will reach their adolescence?

16. Good family adaptation depends both on the pre and post-adoption measures, as can easily be deduced from the case of Eugenia explained at the beginning of this paper. Nevertheless, the pre and post IA measures must be very careful not to "promote" IA: we must protect the children already adopted in Spain and facilitate their adaptation but we must not "create new orphans" in the origin countries.

This paper will analyse the pre and the post-adoptive measures that can facilitate family adaptation after IA. A recent Spanish study stated that the main circumstances that were conducive to a disrupted adoption are related to public professional intervention: non-preparation of the foster parents, suitability of the foster parents, lack of information about the child and misadjusted assignation, and lack of post-adoptive follow up reports and professional support.[35]

3.1. PREVENTING DISRUPTED ADOPTIONS IN THE PRE-ADOPTIVE PERIOD

17. Several competences attributed to the public authorities in IA before adoption takes place, are essential to guarantee a good family adaptation in the post adoption period. Some of them are the responsibility of the receiving States, others of the country of origin.

3.1.1. Preparation of the foster parents

18. Many countries with broad experience in IA focus their work on the parents with regard to their preparation rather than on the suitability declaration considering the

---

33 The general average in Madrid is 1.5% but it reaches 6.7% in cases of adopted children older than 6 years old. (Ibid) In another study related to the cases in Spain, the total number of cases was 22, see: J. Palacios, Y. Sánchez-Sandoval, E. León, *Adopción internacional en España. Un nuevo país, una nueva vida*, (Madrid: Ministerio de Trabajo y Asuntos sociales, 2005), 184.

34 J.H.A. Van Loon, 'International cooperation and protection of children with regard to intercountry adoption', (1993) VII, 246.229 *Reccueil des Cours de l'Academie de la Haye de Droit International.*

35 J. Palacios, Y. Sánchez-Sandoval, E. León, supra (note 33), 187.

preparation as compulsory.[36] The preparation aims at giving prospective adoptive parents the necessary knowledge and at making them aware of the full scope of adoptive parenthood so that eventually they can make a well-considered choice whether or not to adopt a foreign child. In Spain preparation is not legally compulsory yet (only in four Autonomous Communities and with a diverse duration: 8 to 32 hours), but some "Autonomous Communities" have started offering it and have published some materials to "accompany" the parents' decision.[37] In some Autonomous Communities, preparation is held by the ECAIs because the local legislation states so. In other Communities, different private associations or entities carry out the preparation. Nevertheless almost all the Communities have public information sessions with all the foster parents before the preparation takes place.

3.1.2. Public determination of the foster parents' capability, suitability and eligibility to adopt

19. The laws of the different countries regulate the process to select and to choose the prospective adoptive parents in three different categories:

- Capacity: some countries only grant such capacity to married couples, others to married couples without children, and in some countries single persons can adopt; the difference of age between adoptive parents and the child is not the same in the different State regulations.
- Suitability: the capable applicants must be declared "suitable" to adopt, a suitability that refers to very different questions: affective capacity, family stability, physical and mental health, capacity to accept the personal story of the child and the cultural and racial differences, etc.
- Eligibility: may be there are not enough children to be adopted for all the capable and suitable applicants; the State regulations often establish different criteria to choose the best applicants for abandoned children, to pre-assign and, after the parents and authority consent, assign the parents to the child. The suitability declaration is perhaps the central and most difficult task for the public authorities; they have to examine the foster parents and decide whether they are suited to adopt

---

36 For example in Sweden (MIA. Swedish Intercountry Adoptions Authority. *Adoption in Sweden. Policy and procedures concerning intercountry adoption*, 2005, <http://mia.aopt.se> or in The Netherlands (L. Van Truyll, 'Intercountry adoption in the Netherlands. Compulsory preparation classes for new adoptive parents', (1994) 18 nº 3 *Adoption & fostering* ,16.

37 For example in Valencia, Generalitat Valenciana, Direcció General De La Familia I Adopcions, *Materiales para la preparación de solicitantes de adopción;* In Andalucía, some publications: J. Palacios, Y. Sánchez-Sandoval, E. León, *Adelante con la adopción*, (Sevilla: Junta de Andalucía. Consejería para la igualdad y bienestar social, 2004) and L. Martín Sánchez, *Las diferencias étnicas y culturales. Un reto en la adopción internacional,* (Sevilla: Junta de Andalucía. Consejería para la igualdad y bienestar social, 2004).

after a social and psychological study.[38] In Spain, it is one of the matters that needs broad reform: each Autonomous Community has its own legislation on the matter (some more concrete, others very general) with different criteria mainly centred on the evaluation of the mental health and objective characteristics (age, economic position, etc.) more than on the capacities and attitudes towards the adoptive parenthood.[39] The averages of non-suitable parents differ for geographical reasons.[40] The waiting time for the family study is also different[41] and the "price" of the report is geographically different.[42] The courts that examine the appeals of parents declared non-suitable by the administrative authorities also hold different criteria.[43]

3.1.3. Information on the child

20. The public authorities of the child's country of origin must prepare and send to the prospective parents and the authority of the receiving country a complete report on the child including information about his or her identity, adoptability, background, social environment, family history, medical history including that of the child's family, and any special needs of the child so that the receiving country authorities and the prospective parents agree to the pre-assignation. There is an important lack of information in many of these reports and this is one of the causes of some disrupted adoptions.

---

38 R.A.C. HOKSBERGEN, 'Understanding and preventing failing adoptions', in E. HIBBS, *Adoption: international perspectives,* (Madison: International University Press, 1991). In Germany 1/3 of the prospective parents are declared not suitable. Some studies state that this exigency is the reason for the low tasks, 2%, of disrupted adoptions in this country, see: A. KÜHL, W. WINTER-STEIN, 'Foreign adoption in the Federal Republic of Germany', in R.A.C. HOKSBERGEN (ed.), *Adoption in a worldwide perspective. A review of programs, policies and legislation in 14 countries,* (Berwyn: Swets North America INC, 1986), 173.

39 J. PALACIOS, supra (note 32).

40 In 2003, the average of non-suitable applicants ranged from 15.3% in Valencia to 0% in Cantabria o Canarias (Observatiorio De La Infancia, *Estadística básica de protección a la infancia año 2003,* Ministerio de Trabajo y Asuntos sociales. Secretaría de Estado de Servicios Sociales, familias y Discapacidad. Boletín estadístico 06,83).

41 Coordinadora De Asociaciones En Defensa De La Adopción Y El Acogimiento, *Estudio interautonómico sobre plazos en adopción internacional,* Madrid, 2003 <http://www.asatlas.org/documentos/estudio%20 sobre%20plazos%202000-2003.pdf>. This study stated that the waiting time is very different in the Autonomous Communities and ranged from 16.5 months in La Rioja to 5 in Catalonia.

42 The Special Commission created in the Spanish Senate, which published its conclusions on 13 December 2003, underlined all these dysfunctions, <http://www.senado.es>.

43 M. AGUILAR BENITEZ DE LUGO and B. CAMPUZANO DÍAZ, 'El certificado de idoneidad para las adopciones internacionales desde la perspectiva del Derecho internacional privado español', n° 1888 *Boletín de Información del Ministerio de Justicia*, 5.

3.2. TOWARDS THE PROTECTION OF THE ADOPTIVE CHILD WITH POST-ADOPTION MEASURES

21. Even if, as we have seen, the CRC and the Hague Convention particularly focus on the pre-adoption period, they mention also in some of their articles very important principles concerning the post- adoption period that encourage and justify the necessary implementation of State measures in this matter. The right to an identity is referred to in the CRC[44] (Arts. 7.1[45] and 8[46]) and the Hague Convention (Arts. 9[47], 16[48] and 30[49]); the right (or the "desire") to a family friendly policy in Article 18[50] CRC,

44 M. SANTOS PAIS, 'The CRC and the child's right to an identity', *European seminar on post adoption. Which Approaches, Models, and Support Services to Adoptive Families Relations*, held at the Innocenti Institute on 26 January 2006, supra (note 3).

45 The child shall be registered immediately after birth and shall have the right from birth to a name, the right to acquire a nationality and, as far as possible, the right to know and be cared for by his or her parents.

46 States Parties undertake to respect the right of the child to preserve his or her identity, including nationality, name and family relations as recognised by law without unlawful interference.

47 Central Authorities shall take, directly or through public authorities or other bodies duly accredited in their State, all appropriate measures, in particular to a) collect, preserve and exchange information about the situation of the child and the prospective adoptive parents, so far as is necessary to complete the adoption; e) reply, insofar as is permitted by the law of their State, to justified requests from other Central Authorities or public authorities for information about a particular adoption situation.

48 (1) If the Central Authority of the State of origin is satisfied that the child is adoptable, it shall –
a) prepare a report including information about his or her identity, adoptability, background, social environment, family history, medical history including that of the child's family, and any special needs of the child;
b) give due consideration to the child's upbringing and to his or her ethnic, religious and cultural background;
(2) It shall transmit to the Central Authority of the receiving State its report on the child, proof that the necessary consents have been obtained and the reasons for its determination on the placement, taking care not to reveal the identity of the mother and the father if, in the State of origin, these identities may not be disclosed.

49 (1) The competent authorities of a Contracting State shall ensure that information held by them concerning the child's origin, in particular information concerning the identity of his or her parents, as well as the medical history, is preserved. (2) They shall ensure that the child or his or her representative has access to such information, under appropriate guidance, insofar as is permitted by the law of that State.

50
1. State Parties shall use their best efforts to ensure recognition of the principle that both parents have common responsibilities for the upbringing and development of the child. Parents or, as the case may be, legal guardians, have the primary responsibility for the upbringing and development of the child. The best interests of the child will be their basic concern.
2. For the purpose of guaranteeing and promoting the rights set forth in the present Convention, State Parties shall render appropriate assistance to parents and legal guardians in the performance of their child-rearing responsibilities and shall ensure the development of institutions, facilities and services for the care of children.
3. State Parties shall take all appropriate measures to ensure that children of working parents have the right to benefit from child-care services and facilities for which they are eligible.

and the post-adoption services in Article 18 CRC and in Article 9 Hague Convention,[51] which were qualified as obligations derived from the Convention by the special Commission held in September 2005 in the Hague.[52] This approach is important because of the evolution of IA.

22. It is possible to draw a parallel between IA and immigration movements: depending on the social moment of immigration or IA, the law must face different situations and guarantee progressively new generation rights.[53] In Spain, there are already 25,000 IA children. It is important to protect them and to facilitate their family and personal adaptation. Some of these post-adoption measures, especially in Spanish law will be analysed below.

3.2.1. Family-friendly policies[54]

23. In Spain, there is a general absence of family-friendly policies or family allowances (birth or adoption grants)[55] but in the last years, some reforms have been trying to change this situation, helping the families reconcile family life and work such as maternity and paternity allowances, reduction of the labour time to look after the

---

51 Central Authorities shall take, directly or through public authorities or other bodies duly accredited in their State, all appropriate measures, in particular to c) promote the development of adoption counselling and post-adoption services in their States; d) provide each other with general evaluation reports about experience with intercountry adoption.

52 The Draft Guide to good practice under the Hague Convention drawn up by the permanent bureau, Prel Doc nº 2. August 2005, <http://www.hcch.net/upload/wop/ado_pd02e.pdf> states: "The Convention imposes an obligation on Central Authorities to promote counselling and post-adoption services. When developing a national and intercountry adoption system, States should give consideration to who will provide post-adoption services. The nature and extent of these services is not specified, but States must take all appropriate measures to promote them. This should be interpreted as meaning that States must do everything within their powers and resources to carry out the obligation. The explanatory Report elaborates on the reasons for this provision in the Convention. The words on post-adoption services were added at the suggestion of some origin countries because of the importance of post-adoption services to ensure the child's adjustment to his/her new home or environment and successful outcome of the adoption". See for more information on "implementation measures": J. Degling, 'Post-adoption services as an instrument of implementation of the Hague Convention', *European seminar on post-adoption. Which Approaches, Models, and Support Services to Adoptive Families Relations*, Innocenti Institute on 26 January 2006, supra (note 3).

53 F. Dasseto, 'Pour une theorie des cycles migratoires', in A. Bastenier and F. Dasseto, *Inmigrations et nouveux pluralismes Une confrontation de societés*, (Brussels: Université,1990), 11–40. This author states that the second moment of migration cycle is the time of creating families or regrouping families from the country of origin, so law must guarantee the right to a family life and the integration of the second generation.

54 For a comparative view, OECD, 'Babies and bosses', (2004) 3 *Reconciling work and family life.*

55 M.T. López López Utrilla De La Hoza and A. Valiño Castro, *Políticas públicas y familia. Análisis de la situación en España*, (Madrid: Fundación Acción familiar, Fundación Gondara Barandiarán Ed. Cinca, 2006).

children and so on. These State and local Acts, decrees and programmes affect all the families, also the IA families. One of the factors that contribute especially to good family adaptation is the management of family stress associated with adoption,[56] so it is very important to facilitate conciliation of work time and an increasing family-time demand derived from the new member and his/her necessities (educational, medical, affective, etc.).

Nevertheless, in my opinion, in this context adoptive families must be treated the same as the others – non-justified special allowances can be considered as "promoting measures". However, these families may have special time problems because of the days (almost a month in many countries) estimated to travel to the country of the child. Until now, the regulations only allow the taking into account of the time of travel with regard to maternity; the real advance would be to recognise an independent licence to travel and afterwards the maternity/paternity licence. That is the aim of the Concilia Plan 2006, a national accord between the public administration and workers to facilitate the family life of public workers, i.e. two months of paid work permission to travel to the country of origin.[57]

3.2.2. Economic support: adoption subsidies for IA

24. IA is an expensive way of creating a family. The adoption process generates costs of travel, of a hotel in the country of origin and the costs of all the intermediaries. Some countries ask the foster parents to give a sum of money to the orphan centre through the intermediary agency (obviously the combination of facilitating IA and providing such assistance is a delicate one because the latter activity may easily put the agency in a better position to get access to available children). All these expenses may put some families in a difficult economic position. Must public authorities give special subsidies so that IA is not economically inaccessible for some families? Can the subsidies be considered a "promoting" measure?

In some countries like the USA, family subsidies only cover domestic adoptions. Adoption subsidies, also known as Adoption Assistance Payments (AAP), are offered by all states to assist adoptive parents in managing living and care costs for children with special needs adopted through the US foster care system. Federal subsidies are not available to children adopted internationally. Adoption subsidies are perhaps the single most powerful tool by which the child welfare system can encourage adoption and support adoptive families.

---

56 A. Berástegui Pedro-Viejo, supra (note 1), 240–243.

57 <http:// www.map.es/iniciativas/>.

In other countries, there are also IA grants to cover the expenses due to adoptions from abroad. In Denmark €5,159 per IA, in Finland €1,900 to 4,500 per IA, in Sweden €4,456 per IA, and in Belgium €1,023.45 per adoption. In other countries, there are general birth or adoption grants.[58]

In Spain there are very few general family subsidies for the families (who adopt or not), and almost all the subsidies already existing depend on the family rent, so they are really social subsidies more than family subsidies.[59] Nevertheless, the economic support for adoptive or foster care families shows the existence of some subsidies (in the Autonomous Communities) that promote foster care, helping the families economically, generally without a family income limit.[60] In IA, there is still very little experience. Only two different autonomic Acts helping low-income families have been found: the Decree from Extremadura,[61] which regulates adoption subsidies for the IA process, and the Order from Catalonia approving subsidies of €2,300 in 2006, also conditioned to family rent.[62] These measures help some families to adopt, but do not promote IA.

3.2.3. Post-adoption services

25. Most countries of origin require the submission of follow-up reports to monitor how an adopted child develops and adjusts to the new family and social environment.[63] This requirement is a compulsory obligation of the receiving countries' authorities and if the reports are not sent on time, the origin authorities may paralyse the future adoptions with this receiving country.

Nevertheless, we are not referring now to this post-adoption responsibility of the public administrations. IA is a process in which professional advice is essential, as we have seen already. In conformity with good practice developed internationally, this process begins, in the country of origin where the child's adoptability and the chances of him/her being taken into care in the country of origin are checked (the subsidiarity principle), and it involves informing, selecting and preparing prospective adoptive

---

58 All the data can be verified at <http://ec.europa.eu/employment_social/>.

59 M.T. López López Utrilla De La Hoza and A. Valiño Castro, supra (note 55).

60 There is now a "national problem" in Spain with thousands of children in institutional foster care and very few families ready to receive a child under this protection measure and therefore, there is a "promotion" of family foster care in Spain.

61 Decreto 229/2005 11 October por el que se establecen las bases reguladoras de ayudas para la adopción internacional, DOE 18/10/2005.

62 Orden BEF/74/2006. Prestacions econòmiques per a les famílies amb filles i fills a càrrec (2006) Ajut per adopció internacional, <http://www.gencat.cat>. The condition is: No superar unos ingresos de catorce veces el indicador público de renta de efectos múltiples anual (*€93.903.60), ponderados según el número de miembros de la unidad familiar.*

63 A recent work on this matter is POST-ADOPTION (II): 'Follow-up reports required by countries of origin'. International Reference Centre for the Rights of Children Deprived of their Family (ISS/IRC), Monthly Review n° 3/2006, March 2006.

parents in the receiving country. Then, in cooperation with professionals in both countries, professional matching and the first meeting between the child and adopters follow, preferably within a professional supportive setting.

26. The first stages of IA family life together may also require professional support, in the interests of the completely adoptive family, and particularly of the child who then needs emotional stability and a feeling of integration. Therefore, post-adoption services constitute the last link in the chain of professional and multidisciplinary services that are indispensable in guaranteeing that the global adoption process succeeds in the best interests of the child and out of respect for all interested parties.[64] The Hague Convention does not specify either who will provide post-adoption services or what services will be provided, and considers post-adoption services a good practice rather than a right. Nevertheless, the Convention considers that the purpose of the post-adoption services is to ensure the child's adjustment to his/her new life and the successful outcome of the adoption.[65]

27. In a recent European Seminar on post-adoption,[66] a survey on adoption was presented by PREGLIASCO in which it was concluded that there was an availability of post-adoption services in almost all the 22 European countries studied with the exception of Portugal, Estonia, Hungary and Lithuania, and in Spain only in some autonomous communities. It was stated that "*frequently, post adoptive support is not recognised as a self-standing service but is included among the many other services provided by subjects involved in the adoption process in various ways. Support for the post-adoption phase is generally provided both by authorised private bodies and by the competent public authorities. The modalities of providing services for the post-adoptive period are uniform. The common element is seen in the existence of an authority charged with vigilance over the working and the supplying of post-adoption services, which shows an awareness of the need for these services to be provided in a highly professional manner and with care. This awareness is also seen in the general tendency to set these services within the central structures of government dealing with the protection of children, which almost all countries mention in the questionnaire*".[67]

---

[64] SSI, supra (note 4).

[65] Explanatory report, para. 235.

[66] European Seminar titled: '*Which Approaches, Models, and Support Services to Adoptive Families Relations*' held in Innocenti Institute on 26 January 2006, supra (note 3).

[67] Some examples of the national reports showed different post-adoption practices:
In Austria there are 3 well-known private organisations (they co-operate with the public youth welfare services) supporting adoption procedures and adoptive parents. The government financially supports these organisations. They offer information via websites, brochures, telephone and personal counselling, and help with the bureaucratic necessities, organise pre-adoption groups, write the home-studies for international adoptions to the States of origin, support adoptive-families with different services and support networking between adoptive families (groups, meetings, seminars,

Until now, in Spain, not all the "Autonomous Communities" have post-adoption services (generally consisting of family counselling, psycho-educative intervention, psychotherapy and medical counselling), which the public authorities finance for private associations or companies. Some Communities with post-adoptive services are Madrid, Valencia,[68] Andalusia[69] and Catalonia.[70] Apart from these public initiatives, some ECAIs have post-adoption services and some adoptive parents associations.

In some of the "Autonomous Communities", there are family post-adoption grants covering a percentage of these services. In Madrid, for example 100% of family counselling (between 6 to 10 sessions), 100% of psycho-educational intervention (conferences, formation, workshops, etc.), 100% of medical counselling and 50% of therapeutic intervention are covered. Usually these family subsidies are without a family income limit.[71]

---

lectures with inside information about the sending countries, etc.). The meetings are often organised for families with children from a certain region or continent. They also help adopted children to contact their biological parents or biological parents to find their children.
In the Netherlands the lack of expert counselling on adoption-related family problems was the reason, in 1981, for setting up the Foundation Adoption Aftercare, in Dutch called 'WAN'. WAN is now part of the Foundation Adoption Services. The foundation is subsidised by the Ministry of Justice, has its own Board, and is independent of any adoption agency and works for all the families with inter-country adopted children in the Netherlands. It has a twofold task: 1) to be available for information and consultation in the broadest sense. This means that not only adoptive parents and adopted children can consult Foundation Adoption Services, but also counsellors, teachers, lawyers, physicians, adoption agencies, etc.; 2) to structure the medical and psycho/social counselling for adoptive families by making use of professional organisations that already have a task in youth or adolescent care. In order to meet the wishes of adoptive families, the Foundation Adoption Services stimulate counsellors and physicians to have specific knowledge of and affinity with IA. A wide range of professional consultation, prevention and counselling possibilities were created for the target groups.

68 In Valencia the service is free and is offered by EULEN a private company, <http://www.gva.es>.

69 In Andalusia, the service is free and can be consulted at <http://www.juntadeandalucia.es>.

70 See: <http://www.gencat.cat>, 'El Departament de Benestar i Família, a través de l'Institut Català de l'Acolliment i de l'Adopció, ha posat en marxa el primer programa d'atenció postadoptiva de Catalunya. 'objectiu és garantir un servei de qualitat en l'assessorament i orientació a totes aquelles famílies adoptives que ho requereixen per fer front als reptes que planteja la criança, l'educació i la relació entre pares i mares amb els seus fills i filles al llarg del seu procés evolutiu'.

71 Diario de Sesiones de la Asamblea de Madrid nº 607, 7 February 2006. Comparecencia de la Excma. Sra. Consejera de Familia y Asuntos Sociales, a petición del Grupo Parlamentario Popular, al objeto de informar sobre medidas emprendidas en pro de la política de adopciones. The Consejera informed: "Me proponía también como objetivo contribuir al apoyo postadoptivo, por ello hemos puesto en marcha dos centros de apoyo de los que van a ser destinatarios potenciales más de 5.000 menores adoptados y sus respectivas familias durante todos estos años, y los varios miles de menores adoptados que ya son mayores de edad y que, desde luego, corresponden a adopciones realizadas antes de 1987. Desde dichos centros se dará a quien lo necesite orientación en la fase de adaptación del niño a la familia, consejos sobre peculiaridades o ritmos del desarrollo del hijo adoptado, orientación sobre cómo informar al niño sobre su condición adoptiva, y acompañamiento si desea buscar sus orígenes, complemento este último a las propias iniciativas que está llevando a cabo el Instituto Madrileño del Menor y la Familia. De la misma manera, desde esos centros se dará intervención terapéutica

The little Spanish experience on IA has led to some problems in this field: some "Autonomous Communities" consider that it is better to give these post-adoption services in the general family counselling centres so that the adoptive family is not stigmatised; sometimes some families resist using the services because they feel that it means they recognise that their adoption is problematic; there is a need for well-informed professionals in adoptive matters; ...

3.2.4. Back to the roots policies[72]

28. "*To know one's blood is somewhere else just waiting to be found unless you're lost or in a search you cannot understand.*"[73]

29. The right to an identity is a first generation fundamental right. However, perhaps it is a new generation right because even if some State Constitutions and State laws relating to children recently include it as a fundamental right, there is still very little compromise in the international conventions to define its limits as we have already seen in the CRC and the Hague Convention. The scope of the right differs if the filiation is biological, adoptive or by artificial insemination.

In IA, it is a very important right because it has not only a genetic component (as in the biological filiation) but also a social component, that is, to be able to construct one's identity is essential to know where one comes from, who were one's parents and how one was abandoned. It is of great importance to many people.[74] This "travel to the past" has three steps: the revelation of the adoptive parents to the child of his/her adoptive condition, the legal possibility of knowing the identity and social origin data and finally a meeting with a past life.[75]

This paper will refer to the second step, because it is the one that can be regulated by the law even if the third can be assisted by post-adoption services. The problem of assuring this right in IA is that two State laws, sometimes with different conceptions of this right, may be in conflict. That is the reason why the Hague Convention protects

---

especializada en supuestos de crisis o graves dificultades de vinculación, tanto en sesiones individuales como en terapias de grupo".

72 B. Gómez Bengoechea, *Derecho a la identidad y filiación. Un estudio de Derecho internacional privado y Derecho comparado*, Phd Thesis, Madrid, 2005.

73 M. Hayes, 'Trasracial adopted people's support group', in R. Philips and E. McWilliam (eds.), *Afteradoption. Working with adoptive families*, (London: BAAF, 1996), 188.

74 Y. Baer, 'Adoptees searching for their origins', in J. Eekelaar and J. Sarcevic (eds.), *Parenthood in modern society*, (The Netherlands: Kluwer academic publishers, 1993), 247.

75 In old IA countries like the USA there are social movements called "back to the roots" that organise "motherland tours". Ibid, 245.

this right so weakly – the legal access to origin data depends both on the origin and receiving countries regulations.[76]

30. In Spain, this is a great challenge for the next years when our adopted children reach their adolescence. Until now, Spanish Law and the Decree of the Registry office of civil status guarantee that in the Register of births there appears some relevant information as to a child's origin: name and address of biological parents, date of birth, place of birth, date of adoption, and the name and address of the adoptive parents. The adopted person can ask the Office of civil status for a "Certificate" when she/he is 18 years old and obtain the complete information.

Nevertheless, some problems have occurred in IA cases due to the attitude of the origin country and in other cases the adoptive parents' demands. On the one hand, some origin countries cancelled the biological data in their civil status registry after adoption and made new inscriptions with the adoptive parents' data. When the Spanish consuls had to transcribe this data, they asked the local registrar for information about the original data so that in the Spanish civil status registry the biological data could be registered.[77] But soon cases occurred in which parents asked that their adopted children appear as biological in the "Simple certificate" needed, for example, for a school, although all the relevant biological information can be obtained by asking for a "Complete certificate" available at 18 years of age.[78] Even if the Spanish authorities deny these demands, in the last 7 years broad reforms have taken place in the following sense: the adoptive data must not be public for persons or institutions outside the family, so the simple certificate will "hide" the original data, but the adoptee can obtain the data by asking for the complete certificate.[79] Therefore, in Spain the right of the

---

76 "The right of the child to obtain information about his or her origins derives from the right to know his or her parents as provided in Art. 7(1) CRC. However, this right must be balanced against the right of birth parents not to have their identity disclosed to the child who is relinquished for adoption. For example, in some countries an unmarried mother who had consented to the adoption might be later harmed by the disclosure of her past". See: I. LAMMERANT, 'La post adoption: vers un équilibre des droits et intérêts des adoptés, des adoptants et des familles d'origine', European Seminar in Post-adoption, *Which Approaches, Models, and Support Services to Adoptive Families Relations*, held at Innocenti Institute on 26 January 2006, supra (note 3).

77 Resolutions of the "Dirección general de Registros y Notariado" of 23 April 1993 (Anuario DGRN 1993, 1435) and of 31 December 1994 (BIMJ nº. 1736, 97).

78 For example the case resolved in the Resolution of 17 April 2000 (BIMJ nº 1871, 116) in which the adoptive parents of two Lebanon girls asked that in the simple certificate the place of birth be changed to the Spanish city were they lived so that other people could not deduce the adoptive relationship from this certificate. The Spanish authority denied this demand.

79
- Instruction of the DGRN 15/2/1999 permits substitution of the original birth registration with a new one in which only contains "new" data so that the adoption information is not public.
- Statutory Order 8/7/2005 reforming the Civil Registrar Regalement permitting requests for a change of birth registration to the Registry civil office of the place where the family is domiciled, and in the new registration only the new data will appear (with a reference to the original

IA child to know about his/her origins depends on the decision of his/her parents to reveal the adoptive relationship to her/him, which is evident in an interracial adoption (the main origin country is China) but not always in other cases of IA. If the simple certificate does not give clues, a complete certificate is not always asked for, so it is possible that some of the adoptee(s) will never know their true situation or their biological data. These reforms also encourage the change of the name of the child[80] although all the studies state that it is better to maintain the original name to facilitate the construction of personal identity.[81]

4. CONCLUSION

31. In this paper, there has been referred to two groups of children: the group of children who have not yet been adopted and the group of children who have already been adopted. Rights of both children must be protected in IA. This work has mainly focused on the second group: the case explained at the beginning of this paper, shows that rights can be denied. The pre-adoption period regulations are essential to facilitate good matching and family adaptation but nowadays post-adoption measures are needed also, to avoid disrupted adoptions of maladjustment cases. Different public measures have been underlined: preparation of the foster parents, suitability, post-adoption services, etc. All these services must be coordinated: "the existence of this chain of services constitutes probably one of the best tools in the prevention of adoption failure".[82]

32. These questions have been analysed focusing on the Spanish experience for three reasons. It is the second receiving country in IA in the world, has 10 years of experience and the public social system is adapting very rapidly to this phenomenon. There are already living in Spain many "recent" IA children and the studies on adaptation and disrupted adoptions have started to predict what may happen after a few years when

registration). The Law 15/2005 reforming the Law of the Registry office of civil status is in the same sense.

- Instruction of the DGRN 1/7/2004 permitting that in the birth registration there appears as the place of birth, the domicile if the parents, not the foreign country (with a reference to the original registration). The Law 18/11/2005 reforming the Law of the Registry office of civil status is in the same sense.

80 Advice of the DRGN 19/12/ 2003: If the parents want to change the name of the child they must do it before the birth and adoption registration in the civil register so that only the new name appears.

81 "Le mantien du prénom d'origine affirme la reconnaissance de l'identité premiére; sa disaparition implicitement et concrètement l'annule", see: S. Yakoub, 'Quelques réflexions autour de l'historie des adoptés de l'étranger', *Actes du séminaire Nathalie- Masse* 25–27 mai 1992, (Paris : Centre international de l'enfance de Paris), 133.

82 SSI, supra (note 4).

all these adopted children become adolescents. It is a matter of urgency to implement post-adoption measures, even if the CRC and the Hague Convention mainly design measures in the pre-adoption period, some articles of these international instruments can be the basis for national and local regulations.

SILENT KNOWLEDGE: AN EXPLORATORY STUDY OF THE ISSUES IN ACTIVISM AGAINST INCEST ABUSE IN INDIA

NISHA

1. INTRODUCTION

1. This study focuses on incest abuse of girl children. It also presupposes that any kind of sexual engagement with children is fundamentally abusive. This judgment is made in the knowledge that incest abuse or any form of child sexual abuse, throws up contesting issues of sexual personhood, the consent of the child and morality. The primary condition of consent cannot prevail in a sexual relationship between an adult and a child.[1] Political issues of power and gender embedded in social relationships and cultural practices, variously position women and children as properties of men. The idea of consent is rendered a myth because a child's capacity to resist, stop the abuse and be heard is shaped by the socio-cultural, social policy and juridical contexts.

For the purpose of this study, incest abuse is defined as "any behaviour" by someone in the role of trust as a nurturer, carer, provider, guardian or blood relation in any kind of familial and household setting if the person subjectively experiences that behaviour as such or recognises it as such at a later stage. This definition is rooted in the fact that often children have experienced abuse not through behaviour involving the socially sexualised body parts, rather, through print and electronic media, non-touch and non-penile-vaginal penetration.[2]

---

1 J.L. Herman and L. Hirschman, *Father-Daughter Incest*, (Cambridge – Massachusetts – London: Harvard University Press, 1981), 27.

2 K. Soothill and B. Francis, 'Moral panics and the aftermath: a study of incest', (2002) 24 (1) *Journal of Social Welfare and Family Law*, 15.

1.1. STATEMENT OF THE PROBLEM

2. While sexual violence against girls and women cuts across caste, class, religion and region, the Indian society's response to incest abuse has been one of denial.[3] The silence is particularly noticeable among middle and upper class households.[4] The pattern of reporting incest abuse to the police and by the media has further enforced pervasive stereotypes about the class of families where girls and women are sexually victimised.[5] This has fostered notions that some classes are intrinsically sexually violent and regressive in comparison to the "respectable" classes.[6]

3. In India, there has been very little published on the subject. GUPTA[7] points out that the lack of India specific data has led to incest abuse being thought of as a "Western phenomenon".[8] This myth of a "Western" phenomenon exists in the diasporas as well. POORE[9] observes that such a perception exacerbates the secrecy and silence surrounding the problem. The lack of published data is also used to deny the existence of incest abuse. Off the record, there is both private knowledge as well as extensive tolerance of the abuse. There may be gaps in this knowledge but the knowledge of prevalence is woven so intricately into the Indian mind that women try to maintain subtle vigilance to protect their daughters.[10]

---

3 P. VIRANI, *Bitter chocolate: Child Sexual Abuse in India*, (New Delhi: Penguin Books India, 2000).

4 S. CHANDRAN, *Incest – the most common form of child abuse*, February 2003, at <http://www.the-south-asian.com/Feb%202003/index30.htm>; P. VIRANI, supra (note 3), xv-xvi, 22–23 and 30.

5 H. CHHAPIA, 'Sex at Six', (March 2003) 9 *The Beat: A Monthly Magazine of the Indian Institute of Journalism and New Media* (IIJNM); D. RAO, *Rape: Mostly by kin*, (Hyderabad: Times News Network, 6 November 2003), at <http://timesofindia.indiatimes.com/articleshow/269389.cms> [Accessed 5 October 2006]; and S. JACOB, *Insecure homes: Father rapes daughters* (New Delhi: NDTV, 14 July 2004), at <http://www.ndtv.com/morenews/showmorestory.asp?id=57088&frmsrch=1&txtsrch=sexual%2Cabuse%2Cgirls%2Chome> [Accessed 5 October 2006].

6 S. NELSON, *Incest: Fact and Myth*, (Edinburgh: Stramullion, 1982), 18–19.

7 A. GUPTA is the director of the RAHI Foundation. RAHI is the only organisation in India founded specifically to address incest abuse.

8 A. GUPTA in L. DANIEL (Correspondent), *India's hidden incest*, (London, BBC Online Network, 22 January 1999), <http://news.bbc.co.uk/1/hi/world/south_asia/259959.stm> [Accessed 5 October 2006].

9 G. POORE is the founder and head of SHaKTI PRODUCTIONS. Of 67 organisations approached, this was the only organisation based outside India. G. POORE is one of the first to document incest abuse of children in India in a film – *The Children We Sacrifice.*

10 A. RATNAM GANESH et al.: *How we protect abusers when we actually want to protect our children: Report of a Workshop Series and Survey on Childhood Sexual Abuse of Girls*, (Bangalore: Samvada Publication, 1996), 15.

A few studies have been conducted in the last decade.[11] Based on these and their own experiences some feminists, psychologists, educators, child rights advocates, and the media have begun to raise the "secret crime".[12] These efforts, at best, could be called what HERMAN in her book Trauma and Recovery terms, "episodic amnesia".[13]

1.2. PURPOSE AND METHODOLOGY

4. The purpose of the study is twofold, first, to bring theoretical and feminist perspectives to the subject, and second, to explore the issues that may be hindering feminist and other organisations in challenging incest abuse. Both a feminist standpoint and poststructuralist perspectives has been applied to the study. Taken separately, a feminist standpoint would see incest abuse as a material way in which male domination over women is maintained. Poststructuralist theorising would problematise male domination as a given truth and emphasise the power/knowledge standpoint feminists bring to bear on the construction of this truth. My view is that the work of feminist transformation is a continuing process and it still requires an active political solidarity among feminists. The political solidarity may not be possible without a standpoint. In addition, for this solidarity to be inclusive and relevant to the various contexts, it must be based in a nuanced understanding of the specific socio-cultural circumstances that perpetuate and maintain incest abuse and the different ways in which the abuse affects the survivors in terms of their community relations. I, therefore, feel that the strengths of these two perspectives must be synthesised to take on the issue of incest abuse.

5. Section 2 of the paper includes an analysis of two widely prevalent theories that seem to have influenced the Indian response, their critique and feminist perspectives. Section 3 contains an exploratory analysis of the previous studies in India and the interviews with the fourteen participants. Heads of sixty-seven women's and other organisations were approached on the basis of the leading roles they have played in bringing key issues affecting women and children into the public discourse and policy. The fourteen organisations and their leaders who finally participated in the study have been working on various aspects of women's political and civil rights; violence against

[11] A. RATNAM GANESH et al., supra (note 10); A. GUPTA *et al*, *Voices from the Silent Zone: Women's Experiences of Incest and Childhood Sexual Abuse*, (New Delhi: RAHI Foundation, 1998); A. GUPTA, *The House I Grew Up in*, (New Delhi: RAHI Foundation, 1999); and P. VIRANI, supra (note 3).

[12] A. BHAGAT in L. DANIEL (Correspondent), *India's hidden incest*, (London: BBC Online Network, 22 January 1999), <http://news.bbc.co.uk/1/hi/world/south_asia/259959.stm>[Accessed 5 October 2006]; H. CHHAPIA, supra (note 5), 8–9; A. KRISHNAKUMAR, 'Child Rights: Silent Victims', (11–24 October 2003) volume 20, issue 21 *Frontline*, <http://www.flonnet;com/f12020/stories/200310240 01609000.htm>; V. FARIDI, *Tackling taboos on a new platform*, (HT Media Limited, 23 June 2004).

[13] J. L. HERMAN, *Trauma and Recovery*, (New York: Basic Books, 1992).

women and children, including incest abuse; sexual identity; and sexual health. Incidentally, all fourteen who agreed to be interviewed are women. Some of the participants who did agree wanted their identities to be kept anonymous. Finally, section 4 discusses theoretical and practice implications.

2. THEORIES OF INCEST AND FEMINIST CRITIQUE

2.1. OVERVIEW

6. An overview of the literature on incest abuse suggests that the theories through which incest (abuse) has been approached could be divided into three sets: the first consisting of anthropological, sociological, biological and bio-social theories examining the operations and benefits of incest taboo. They are concerned more with the male informed origin and functions of the incest "taboo" than with incest abuse. The second consists of theories of dysfunctional families, sub-cultural/class patterns, ecology, etc., which present individual and family/environment pathology as explanations for incest abuse. These approaches too are not particularly useful in understanding the gendered nature and incidence of incest abuse. The third set consists of feminist perspectives, which are particularly useful in foregrounding the role power plays in incest abuse. From these three sets, two of the most prevalent theories, the dysfunctional family and psychoanalytical theories together with feminist perspectives, will be discussed in this chapter.

2.2. THE DYSFUNCTIONAL FAMILY THEORY

7. The dysfunctional family theory is premised on pathological family dynamics and carries two main assumptions: one, the incest abuser is not a social threat, which means that the abuser does not act in an abusive manner outside the family;[14] and two, incest abuse is a sexual expression of a nonsexual issue[15] involving three persons – two participants (read the perpetrator and the abused) and a non-participant (read mother).[16] The key dysfunctionality is the mother's failure to live up to the role of a sexual provider and a protective devoted parent. She is seen as pushing for a role

[14] R. Porter, *Child Sexual Abuse within the Family*, (London – New York: Tavistock Publications, © The CIBA Foundation, 1984), 46.

[15] A. Seymour, 'Aetiology of the Sexual Abuse of Children: An Extended Feminist Perspective', (1998) 21 (4), *Women Studies International Forum*, 419–420.

[16] J. Renvoize, *Incest a Family Pattern*, (London – Henley: Routledge and Kegan Paul, 1982), 114.

reversal between the child and herself to evade her sexual role, or as a person placing her material well-being and concerns before her child.[17] In this theory, there is high emphasis on treating the family and on community rehabilitation and an equally high degree of concern for fairness to the perpetrator.[18]

There is little evidence to suggest that family treatment helps family members and reduces recidivism.[19] Still, the dysfunctional family theory remains one of the most widely held explanations for incest abuse and has been used to justify family treatment by State institutions and social workers. While analysing family welfare theorising within the Australian context, PENGELLY argues that the family dysfunctionality approach works against feminist texts by erroneously vesting equal power in the marital pair.[20] In doing so, it suppresses gender as an important factor in incest abuse and non-reporting and empirical findings, which establish power as a male prerogative.

In addition, dysfunctionality is measured against a set system of family norms. Hence this model tends to see gay, lesbian or any other family that does not conform to socially approved goals or values or fails to fit into the normative ideal, as a potential site of incest abuse and therefore a target of reformist attacks. This is best illustrated by the British media's campaign in the post-Cleveland period against "immoral" single mothers in the UK.[21]

This theory completely absolves men of their responsibilities by treating them as persons who resort to incest abuse, as they do not know how to resolve issues constructively.[22] By failing to see incest abusers as capable of extra-familial sexual

---

17 J. RENVOIZE, supra (note 16), 114–119; L. M. CANDIB, 'Incest and Other Harm to Daughter across Cultures: Maternal Complicity and Patriarchal Power', (1999) 22 (2) *Women's Studies International Forum*, 193–199.

18 A.M. SMITH SLEP and R.E. HEYMAN, 'Where do we go from here?: Moving towards an integrated approach to family violence', (2001) 6 *Aggression and Violent Behaviour*, 353–356, R.F. WILSON, 'Recognising the Threat Posed by an Incestuous Parent to the Victim's Siblings: Part I: Appraising the Risk', (2004) 13 (2) *Journal of Child and Family Studies*, 156–158.

19 D. FINKELHOR, 'Abusers: Special topics', in D. FINKELHOR et al (eds.), *a SOURCEBOOK on child sexual abuse*, (Beverly Hills – London – New Delhi: Sage Publications, 1986), 136–137; M.Q. PATTON, 'Patterns, Themes and Lessons', in M.Q. PATTON (ed.), *Family Sexual Abuse*, (Newbury Park – London – New Delhi: Sage Publications, 1991), 233–234; D. GREENBERG et al, 'Recidivism of Child Molesters: A Study of Victim Relationship with the Perpetrator', (2000) 24 (11) *Child Abuse and Neglect*, 1489–1493.

20 B. PENGELLY, 'A Feminist Critique of the Idea of Incest as a Product of the Dysfunctional Family, in P. HETHERINGTON (ed.), *Incest and the Community: Australian Perspectives*, (Perth: Optima Press, University of Western Australia, 1991), 188–189.

21 K. THOMPSON, *Moral Panics*, (London – New York: Routledge, 1998), 89.

22 J.R. CONTE, 'Child Sexual Abuse: Looking Backward and Forward', in M.Q. PATTON (ed.), *Family Sexual Abuse*, (Newbury Park– London– New Delhi: Sage Publications, 1991), 6–9; B. PENGELLY, supra (note 20), 187–188.

abuse, the theory fails to account for child sexual abuse committed by them outside the home.[23] This theory propounds and supports a belief that treatment rather than punishment may make the perpetrator accept his responsibility and that a sentence is destructive for the family, particularly for the non-abused siblings and further harms the child being abused.[24] What gets lost in the process of rescuing the "poor perpetrator" are the experiences of the child who is being abused.[25]

In summary, this theory reinforces some of the myths about incest abuse. Particularly, by blaming mothers for frigidity it strengthens the belief that men have a right to sexual service.

2.3. PSYCHOANALYTIC THEORY

8. Unlike the dysfunctional family theory, the psychoanalytic theory focuses on individual perversion as the cause of sexual abuse. FREUD's psychoanalytic theory was perhaps the first in the West to explain the occurrence of child sexual abuse. He developed what became the classic theory of psycho-sexual development, the "Oedipus Complex" and the "Electra Complex". The crux of this theory is "penis envy" or sexual attraction to fathers among girls. While acknowledging long-term adverse psychological impacts, FREUD posited the daughter as the active desiring agent who seduces her father. He explained the psychological trauma among adult women as arising from incestuous fantasies and the non-resolution of childhood psycho-sexual development.[26] This theoretical framework has also been used by psychoanalysts to explain the behaviour of sexual domination by men as an outcome of castration anxiety or a fear of sexual inadequacy arising from an unresolved "Oedipus Complex". In this theory, the mother holds the key to the psycho-sexual development of the child.[27] Her inability to prevent abuse is seen as transferring her own incestuous desires onto her children. The psychoanalytic theories advocate psychiatric intervention to reduce pathological

---

23 G.G. ABEL et al, 'Multiple Paraphiliac Diagnoses Among Sex Offenders', (1988) 16 (2) *Bulletin of American Academy of Psychiatry and the Law*, 153–168; J.R. CONTE, supra (note 22), 6–9.

24 R. PORTER, supra (note 14), 34–46; N.D. REPPUCCI and J.J. HAUGAARD, 'Prevention of Child Sexual Abuse: Myth or Reality', (1989) 44 (10) *American Psychologist*, 1266–1275; R.F. WILSON, supra (note 18), 152–156.

25 B. PENGELLY, supra (note 20), 193.

26 B.J. VANDER MEY and R.L. NEFF, *Incest as Child Abuse*, (London: Praeger, 1986), 32–37; A. ESTERSON, 'Jeffrey Masson and Freud's Seduction Theory: A New Fable Based on Old Myths', (1998) 11(1) *History of the Human Sciences*, 1–21; A. ESTERSON, 'The Mythologizing of psychoanalytic History: Deception and Self- Deception in Freud's Accounts of the Seduction Theory Episode', (2001) 12 (3) *History of Psychiatry*, 329–352.

27 J.F. CHUSED, 'Male Gender Identity and Sexual Behaviour', (1999) 80 (6) *The International Journal of Psychoanalysis*, 1105–1117.

impacts like distress and depression among abused children.[28] WARD[29] and BELL[30] point out the irony that Western society denies sexuality to children but the moment an accusation of incest abuse is made it brands them as sexually provocative. KITZINGER[31] cautions that child sexual abuse should not be reduced to sexual violence against the nonsexual (innocent child) as it would work against the claims of protection by a "knowing" child. Further, this belief would also make it difficult to understand sexual violence by a child against another child.

9. The victim blame analyses regards that the child, because of long-term psychological impact, grows up to be an emotionally unresponsive mother[32] seeking out abusers as partners/husbands and failing to protect their children, thus creating a pattern of intergenerational abuse.[33] At this point, the psychoanalytical explanations connect well to the dysfunctional family theory. Both accuse the mother of being complicit in abuse and mothers' resistance and attempts to protect their children[34] is judged because of their success rate.

Psychoanalytic theories also tend to be heterosexist insofar that they attribute alternative sexual choices as psychopathological impacts of incest abuse and focus on the "restoration of women's capacity to enjoy heterosexual encounter".[35]

In summary, psychoanalytic theory is an attempt to dismiss the reality of incest abuse. Its penis narcissism makes it a static and single characteristic theory. The emphasis on the abuser's fears and insecurities also work towards his portrayal as a victim.

---

28 J. GOODWIN and J. OWEN, 'Incest from Infancy to Adulthood: A Developmental Approach to Victims and Families', in J. GOODWIN (ed.), *Sexual Abuse: Incest Victims and Their Families* (Second Edition), (Chicago – London – Boca Raton: Year Book Medical Publishers, 1989), 97 104; L.A. MEYERSON et al., 'The Influence of Childhood Sexual Abuse, Physical Abuse, Family Environment and Gender on the Psychological Adjustment of Adolescents', (2002) 26 *Child Abuse and Neglect*, 387–405.

29 E. WARD, *Father-Daughter Rape*, (London: The Women's Press Ltd, 1984), 148.

30 V. BELL, *Interrogating Incest: Feminism, Foucault and the Law*, (London – New York: Routledge, 1993), 86–87.

31 J. KITZINGER, 'Defending Innocence: Ideologies of Childhood', (1988) 28 *Feminist Review*, 79–80.

32 P.C. ALEXANDER et al., 'Adult attachment and Longterm Effects in Survivors of Incest', (1998) 22 (1) *Child Abuse and Neglect*, 47–48.

33 M.Q. PATTON, supra (note 19), 233; J.M. RUDD and HERZBERGER, 'Brother-Sister Incest – Father-Daughter Incest: A Comparison of Characteristics and Consequences', (1999) 23 (9) *Child Abuse and Neglect*, 920.

34 L. ARMSTRONG, 'Making an Issue of Incest', in D. LEIDHOLDT and J.G. RAYMOND (eds.), *The Sexual Liberals and the Attack on Feminism*, (New York– Oxford – Beijing, etc: Pergamon Press, 1989), 45–49.

35 J. KITZINGER, 'Sexual Violence and Compulsory Heterosexuality', in S. WILKINSON and C. KITZINGER (eds.), *Heterosexuality: A Feminism and Psychology Reader*, (London – Newbury Park– New Delhi: Sage Publications, 1993), 220–224; P. REAVEY and B. GOUGH, 'Dis/Locating Blame: Survivor's Constructions of Self and Sexual Abuse', (2000) 3 (3) *Sexualities*, 326.

Simultaneously, it also places a demand on the abused to cope with the abuse by detaching or switching off.[36] Uncritical incorporation of psycho-pathological impacts into research and therapy, into mass media like cinema, further reinforces FREUDIAN myths.[37]

2.4. FEMINIST THEORY

10. Drawing from FOUCAULT's analysis of discourse, BELL points out that feminists have not just critiqued the silence about incest abuse. They have also contested the mythologised ways of talking about incest, which gives the impression that incest is not talked about.[38] She refers to two dominant ways of talking about incest, which have been challenged by feminists. At one end is the "deployment of alliance" or deployment of a system of blood and kinship and at the other, "deployment of sexuality" or deployment of desire and pleasure. The anthropological and sociological theories of incest fall at the end of alliance. The theories of individual and family pathologisation are at the desire and pleasure end.[39]

11. Treading back and forth between these discourses, feminists have questioned the much taken for granted existence of incest taboo and "men cannot control themselves" explanations. Broadly, they focus on two important but previously ignored aspects: unequal power relations between women and men, and male sexual violence in intra and extra familial spaces as a way to dominate women.[40] Feminist perspectives examine complex workings of social structures like family, culture, attitudes and male and female socialisation that reinforce male entitlements and add a sense of "normalcy" to incest abuse.[41] They demonstrate connections between sexual violence and

---

36 J. CAPUTI, '"Take Back What Doesn't Belong to Me": Sexual Violence, Resistance and the Transmission of Affect', (2003) 26 (1) *Women's Studies International Forum*, 1–14.

37 A.J. CURTIS-WEBER, 'Not Just Another Pretty Victim: The Incest Survivor and the Media', (1995) 28 (4) *Journal of Popular Culture*, 37–47.

38 V. BELL, supra (note 30), 79–80.

39 V. BELL, supra (note 30), 112–113.

40 R.E. DOBASH and R.P. DOBASH, *Violence against Wives: A Case against the Patriarchy*, (New York: Free Press, 1979); J.L. HERMAN and L. HIRSCHMAN, supra (note 1); L. KELLY, *Surviving Sexual Violence*, (Cambridge: Polity Press, 1989); L. DOMINELLI, 'Betrayal of Trust: A Feminist Analysis of Power Relationships in Incest Abuse and its Relevance for Social Work Practice', (1989) 19 *British Journal of Social work: British Association of Social Workers*, 295–299.

41 V. BELL, supra (note 30), 176; J.L. JACOBS, 'Victimized Daughters: Sexual Violence and the Empathetic Female Self', (1993) 9 (1) *Signs*, 126–145.

education, customs, media, particularly pornography and so on,[42] which reinforce abusive behaviour as normal and thus perpetuate and legitimise sexual abuse.

Feminists challenge the proposition that incest abuse is about deviant sexuality. They argue that normal masculine sexuality is socialised to seek dominance through sex and is accepted as such.[43] Feminist theorists emphasise incest abuse as one among many ways of exercising male sexual power in a "continuum of violence".[44]

Feminist perspectives do not deny psychological impacts though. They differ on the way the impacts should be addressed and used for intervention. Feminist psychoanalysts have insisted on being aware of male dominance reinforcing patterns of therapy, which by not engaging in analysis of dominance further subjugates survivors.[45]

Some feminists, particularly poststructuralists, allege that the radical and second wave feminist analyses of sexual violence encourage a "victim culture" and give totalising explanations of power and patriarchy.[46] In the context of incest abuse, the basis of this critique may be in the game that feminists have to play in order to produce the "perfect witnesses" in the court battles or to make it to the media.[47] However, this critique cannot be levelled unquestioningly against feminist analyses of incest abuse, which has been reflexive about its knowledge claims and implications of its language.[48] In terms of power and patriarchy, the critique must be taken seriously. The difficult work of feminist transformation will succeed locally only if its socio-political understanding is context specific and nuanced.

12. Further, ASHENDEN articulates that feminists have not engaged critically with social and political theory, which informs the distinctions of public and private and

---

42 D.E.H. RUSSELL, *Making Violence Sexy: Feminist Views on Pornography*, (Buckingham: Open University Press, 1993); C. ITZIN, 'Pornography and the Organizations of Intrafamilial and Extrafamilial Child Abuse: Developing a Conceptual Model', (1997) 6 *Child Abuse Review*, 94–106; C. ITZIN, 'Incest, Paedophilia, Pornography and Prostitution: Making Familial Males More Visible as Abusers', (2001) 10 *Child Abuse Review*, 35–48.

43 S. NELSON, supra (note 6), 63; E.A. STANKO, *Intimate Intrusions: Women's Experience of Male Violence*, (London: Unwin Hyman, 1985), 4; V. BELL, supra (note 30), 74–76; S. WALKLATE, *Gender, Crime and Criminal Justice*, (Devon: Willan Publishing, 2001), 112.

44 L. KELLY, supra (note 40), 74.

45 P. REAVEY and B. GOUGH, supra (note 35), 325–346.

46 C. ATMORE, 'Feminism's Restless Undead: The Radical/Lesbian/Victim theorists and conflicts over sexual violence against children and women', in P. REAVEY and S. WARNER (eds.), *New Feminist Stories of Child Sexual Abuse: Sexual scripts and dangerous dialogues*, (London – New York: Routledge, 2003), 16–33.

47 C. ATMORE, 'Victims, Backlash and Radical Feminist Theory (or The Morning after They Stole Feminism's Fire)', in S. LAMB (ed.), *New Versions of Victims: Feminist Struggle with the Concept*, (New York – London: New York University Press, 1999), 186.

48 V. BELL, supra (note 30), 90.

shapes the relations between the State and family.[49] Both aspects are important in the governance of child sexual abuse. Therefore, the critique is significant, as it points to the need to influence the public practice ideologies, which, as PENGELLY points out, have the capacity to counter the subversive effects of feminist theorising.[50] The issue can be illustrated by the fact that though feminists have sought to place the "subjugated knowledges" of survivors at the centre of their theorising,[51] their absence from policy and juridical formulations has facilitated usurpation of the issue by non-feminist agents. During the 1970s and 1980s, the Anglo-American feminists practice of narration as a political action of consciousness-raising and breaking the silence.[52] However, the emphasis on psychological effects with little engagement with the social and political theory saw the feminist 'speaking out movement' gradually being co-opted by psycho-pathological models of social work, psychiatrists, and State institutions.[53]

13. In summary, feminists have located incest abuse in social practices. Their discursive analyses of the prevailing disciplinary discourses, though a "precarious business",[54] did influence a debate on issue of sexualities and sexual oppression, and social and political contexts.

To sum up this section, the first two sets of theories have implicit and explicit misogynist attitudes. Their major failings are, first, that there is no analysis of gendered socio-political aspects of incest abuse, and second, they are unwilling to hold the perpetrator accountable as a normal, informed and functional individual. The feminist

---

49 S. ASHENDEN, *Governing Child Sexual Abuse: Negotiating the boundaries of public and private, law and science*, (London – New York: Routledge, 2004), 3–4.

50 B. PENGELLY, supra, (note 20).

51 For example, L. ARMSTRONG, *Kiss Daddy Goodnight: A Speak-out on Incest*, (New York: Hawthorn Books, 1978).

52 L. ARMSTRONG, *Rocking the cradle of sexual politics: What Happened When Women Said Incest*, (London: The Women's Press Ltd, 1996).

53 L. ARMSTRONG in S. NELSON, 'Time to Break Professional Silences', (1998) 7 *Child Abuse Review*, 145; H. DANIELS, 'Truth, Community, and the Politics of Memory: Narratives of Child Sexual Abuse', in N.B. MAGLIN and D.M. PERRY (eds.), *"Bad Girls"/"Good Girls": Women, Sex, and Power in the Nineties*, (New Brunswick, NJ: Rutgers University Press, 1996), 150-163; A. LEVETT, 'Problem of Cultural Imperialism in the Study of Child Sexual Abuse' in P. REAVEY and S. WARNER (eds.), *New Feminist Stories of Child Sexual Abuse: Sexual scripts and dangerous dialogues*, (London – New York: Routledge, 2003), 52-54; L. O'DELL, 'The harm Story in Childhood Sexual Abuse', in P. REAVEY and S. WARNER, (eds.), *New Feminist Stories of Childhood Sexual Abuse: Sexual Scripts and Dangerous Dialogues*, (London – New York: Routledge, 2003), 134; L. ARMSTRONG, *Incest : A feminist core issue that needs re-politizising*, (Paris: Les Pénélopes, 2004), <http://www.penelopes.org/Anglais/xarticle.php3?id_article=739>.

54 V. BELL, supra (note 30), 175.

perspectives do not provide an alternative theory of incest or incest abuse; rather, they intervene in the patriarchal theories.[55]

3. CHALLENGES IN WORKING AGAINST INCEST ABUSE IN INDIA

3.1. BACKGROUND

14. This section will place incest abuse of girl children in the context of several barriers and challenges that inhibit the capacity of Indian civil society organisations, especially women's organisations, to act against it. The women's organisations are constituents of the Indian women's movement, which has a long history of struggle against sexual violence in public and private spheres. On the issue of incest abuse, however, women's organisations have rarely acted together as a movement.

15. The first few attempts to map the incidence of incest abuse in India substantiate that neither its extent nor it affects on the already skewed gender relations should be underestimated. A NGO survey in 11 schools and colleges in Karnataka threw up startling data. Nearly 50% of 348 girl participants in the age group of 15 to 21 years were sexually abused by a male relative.[56] Since the sample included both urban and rural participants, it shows that the issue cannot be consigned only to either rural or urban social practices.

16. RAHI Foundation's study among 600 middle and upper middle class women broke the myth of demographic variables with which incest abuse is attributed to the lower economic classes.[57] In this study, 457 (76%) study participants reported being sexually abused of which 181 (40%) reported abuse by a family member. The sample consisted of women who at the time of abuse lived in 50 different cities and towns of India. In another study in Kerala, of the 25 rape cases taken as a sample from the courts in various districts, 5 were perpetrated by immediate and extended male family members.[58] These findings indicate that incest abuse is not confined to a specific geographical region. One of the major findings of RAHI Foundation's study was that 52% of the participants were abused by two or more people.

---

55 B. PENGELLY, supra, (note 20), 184.

56 A. RATNAM GANESH et al., supra (note 10), 41–44 and 48–51.

57 A. GUPTA, supra (note 11), 17–20.

58 U. VENKITAKRISHNAN and S.G. KURIEN, *Rape Victims in Kerala*, Discussion Paper No 52, Kerala Research Programme on Local Level Development, (Thiruvananthapuram: Centre for Development Studies, 2003), 43.

17. This data points to the need to separate incest abuse from stranger child sexual abuse. Otherwise, factors such as proximity, both geographical and social, duration and frequency of the abuse, other socio-cultural factors and child's gendered capacity to resist sexual abuse will be left out of the purview of prevention and advocacy.

18. These studies affirmed that child sexual abuse is much more frequent than previously assumed. This was supported by media discourses on the incidence of incest abuse.[59] In addition, VIRANI cites data from various organisations working on child rights, which puts the average rate of sexual abuse of girls from infancy to 16 years of age at 62.5%.[60] She further quotes unofficial estimates made by the police, which put the average rate of sexual abuse of girls at 40%. Given the findings of the studies of the other studies, it could be assumed that within these general figures nearly 40% to 50% of sexual abuse was taking place at home.

19. In recent years, according to MAITRA,[61] feminist activism along with discourses on HIV/AIDS has facilitated a discussion on child sexual abuse. However, even in HIV/AIDS discourses, the reference to vulnerability is made mostly in terms of children on the street and those forced into sex work. The nature of their "sexual partnerships" is not explored or explained.[62] Reasons, however, are not difficult to find. Any reference to incest abuse causes much public furore and State actions like booking and banning workers and organisations.[63] In feminist activism against child sexual abuse, little acknowledgement of the home as a site of abuse is made. As a result, despite the research findings and efforts of some activists, the public acceptance of the prevalence of incest abuse has not been possible and existence of intervention remains, literally, next to nothing.

3.2. UNCLEAR PROFILE AND OWNERSHIP OF THE ISSUE

20. Based on communication with 53 of the 67 individuals who were initially approached for the interview, two views emerge. First, incest abuse does not have a

---

59 B. SINHA, *Father held for raping minor over two years*, (New Delhi: Times News Netwrok, 14 March 2003), <http://timesofindia.indiatimes.com/articleshow/40207334.cms>.

60 P. VIRANI, supra (note 3), 18–25.

61 From Muskaan and TISS.

62 INDIAN NGOS, *HIV/AIDS Resources: Children, Young People and HIV/AIDS*, (IndianNGOs.com, undated), <http://www.indianngos.com/issue/hiv/resources/children.htm>; HRW INDIA, *AIDS Fueled by Abuses Against Children: Children Affected by HIV/AIDS Face Lethal Discrimination and Exploitation* (New Delhi, Human Rights News, 29 July 2004), <http;//www.hrw.org/english/docs/2004/07/29/india9156.htm>.

63 R. DEVRAJ, *Rights-India: Flak for AIDS program as workers jailed*, (Inter Press Service, 29 May 2000), <http://www.aegis.com/news/ips/2000/IP000510.html>.

clear profile as an issue on it own. It emerges on the peripheries of violence against women and children, and of psycho-sexual problems. Second, in general, there are tensions around its ownership. At one end, nearly 50% of those approached do not regard incest abuse as a women's issue though sexual abuse of vast numbers of girls in their homes perpetuates patterns of gendered violence. SHARMA[64] urges for "... *recognising the issue as an integral concern relating to violence against women, and not as an 'add on' issue which only some "specialised" organisations need to deal with*". At the other end, though sexual abuse by those who are supposed to protect and nurture is an attack at the core of child safety and rights, it fails to stir those working on child rights. Among them, there is a tendency to link the site of the abuse and the fact that the majority of the abused are girls, with the responsibility of women's organisations. Consequently, the status of incest abuse as a private matter gets further reinforced.

3.3. VIEWS OF FEMINISTS AND WOMEN'S ORGANISATIONS REGARDING OWNERSHIP OF THE ISSUE

21. While the participants agree that there is a need to act against incest abuse, on the issue of ownership, three distinct views emerged. The first view, shared by seven participants, saw incest abuse as a social problem with a specific gender dimension, clearly, a feminist issue. The second view, shared by three participants, regarded the issue as a social problem requiring civil society action, not just feminist attention. The third view, held by four participants, saw it as a problem of child protection including boys and girls; certainly not a feminist issue.

The first view is evident in SAKSENA's response: "... *more girls than boys are victims. The "stigma" is more on the female victim and less or non-existent on the male victim.*"[65] Speaking in a similar vein, SHARMA indicates that the nature of families and responses by organisations to the abuse are outlined and acted upon in conjunction with the prevailing discriminatory gender norms. Hence, there is a need for feminist intervention: "*It is certainly a feminist issue since gender dynamics are important in determining the response of family and community to the abuse and the abuser and most importantly the ability to help the survivor*". GUPTA gives a discursive reason for regarding incest abuse of girls as a feminist issue: "*The feminist understanding of the cause of such abuse is also the most comprehensive and it is the feminist movement that has provided the impetus for incest to come to light anywhere in the world, including India*".

---

64 From Nirantar.

65 From Enfold Proactive Health Trust.

This argument for intervention is based on a claim that the knowledge, which feminists have acquired in their struggle against sexual oppression by men, remains relevant in analyses of incest abuse.[66] It corroborates the emphasis in the other two statements on a feminist inspired resistance and practice to support survivors.

BHATTACHARYA[67] and MAITRA's views tended to incline towards action by civil society. At the same time, they saw a need to ensure a feminist engagement with the issue. A few participants clarified that supporting a civil society action does not mean condoning, ignoring or deprioritising incest abuse. The implication of their view is that feminists have a responsibility to counter the silence around incest abuse but it should not become a battle, which only feminists fight. POORE thus remarks, "*It should not be a women's and feminists' issue but by default, the responsibility for education, intervention, prevention and community organising around the issue has fallen mostly on women – and primarily feminists*".

The third view comes from KUSHWAHA,[68] KUMANA[69] and another participant who base their reason for incest abuse not being a feminist issue on the evidence of the sexual abuse of boys and sexual abuse by women.[70]

22. These three views present two parallel perspectives. First, feminism has a specific knowledge, which must be given a space in the discourses and action against incest abuse. Second, feminism is for issues exclusive to women. BELL discusses these perspectives in her analysis of feminist knowledge of incest abuse.[71] According to her, feminist knowledge has grown out of practices of social life and discursive debates, which locate incest abuse in the normal practices of sexuality, power and silence. Feminism, therefore, is not a welfarist institution talking about redressing the sufferings of women. It is a social critique – a fundamental critique of the family, gendered sexualities and power/knowledge networks that produce the silence. Feminism is not a fixed entity; rather, it is a way of analysing and speaking about, and taking action on issues and problems. Sexual abuse of boys, like that of girls, remains marked by a preponderance of male abusers.[72] Feminists have been among those

---

66 J. OKO, 'Towards a New Model of Practice', in P. COX et al. (eds.), *Child Sexual Assault: Feminist Perspective*, (New York: Palgrave, 2000), 163–177.

67 From AIDWA.

68 From Sangini (India) Trust.

69 Aanchal Trust.

70 P. VIRANI, supra (note 3), 36–41 and 54–64; V. PATEL, 'Gender, sexual abuse and risk behaviours in adolescents: a cross-sectional survey in schools in Goa, India', in S. BOTT et al. (eds.), *Towards adulthood: Exploring the sexual and reproductive health of adolescents in South Asia* (Department of Reproductive Health and Research (RHR), World Health Organisation, 2003), 100.

71 V. BELL, supra (note 30), 175–179.

72 D. FINKELHOR, supra (note 19), 126; V. BELL, supra (note 30), 54.

who have tried to analyse and stop it.[73] Application of feminist critiques would reveal the interconnections – how incest abuse of boys interrelates with the abuse of the girls, and it will break the myth of gays as paedophiles to reveal that incest abusers of boys and paedophiles are "heterosexual" men.

3.4. LIMITATION OF CURRENT STRATEGIES USED TO STOP INCEST ABUSE

23. The current ways in which the participants and their organisations are attempting to raise and address the issue of incest abuse are eclectic, with most focusing on school-based sex education and awareness for parents, teachers and children, and therapy. Two of them support survivor groups and provide counselling. Only three have been engaged in direct political and support work.

Networking for advocacy and campaigning on incest abuse is patchy. Even for supporting the survivors, it is usually initiated and maintained on a case-to-case basis. Only three organisations maintain regular communication with psychiatrists and sex educators to support the survivors of incest abuse. Two key problems, which come in the way of networking, as identified by nine participants, are civil society's failure to see incest abuse as a social issue, and gender and rights-based organisations' unwillingness to see the interplay between different forms of violence over a woman's lifespan. POORE explains: "*First, the splits between the movement to end domestic violence, the movement to end rape, and the movement to end trafficking of children needs to be breached … Second, advocates working with survivors and victims of sexual violence must play a greater role in the efforts to hold the sexual violence perpetrator accountable. Otherwise, the voices of survivor advocates and feminists are not heard as loudly in the movements … which has serious implications for how these movements are shaping perpetrator accountability and community safety*".

3.5. LACK OF ADEQUATE RESEARCH & SILENCE ON INCEST ABUSE AMONG ACTIVISTS

24. "*Numbers? What kind of statistics should anyone want as proof that the enemy is within … what numbers would constitute "more" or "too much" so that the so-called*

[73] S. NELSON, 'Time to Break Professional Silences', (1998) 7 *Child Abuse Review*, 144–153; S. NELSON, 'Satanic Ritual Abuse – the Challenge for Feminists', in P. COX et al. (eds.), *Child Sexual Assault: Feminist Perspective*, (New York: Palgrave, 2000), 38–51.

society in India finally agrees …?, angrily asks VIRANI".[74] Her question is valid in view of the knowledge that women's and children's rights activists hold as individuals and the level of "adequacy" which they, as parts of organisations, are seeking. Some participants point out that the issue is not one of lack of knowledge but that of "valid" knowledge –knowledge described and characterised from a male-centred perspective and presented in the form of nationwide crisp statistics. However, the lack of research is not the only barrier to accepting incest abuse as a social concern. Some other participants see the problem of acceptance as part of an overall indifference to women's issues and resistance to women's experiences, especially those that threaten to disrupt the happy family discourses.[75] MENON[76] points to the internalised resistance: "*…it means blaming someone within the family and that is not something we are comfortable with in India. There seems to be a huge need to protect the family and treat it as a sacrosanct institution*". Her analysis could be linked to two of the participants who felt that any punitive action against the perpetrator could destroy the unity of the family and, where the abuser is the father, may deprive siblings of the abused child of fatherly care. These participants suggested "family centred treatment" and "community rehabilitation" to address the issue.

25. Research is needed to influence legislation and policies on women's issues have argued in favour of producing quantitative data.[77] However, data and oral accounts of survivors can be easily disqualified. For example, one of the participants who found 9% of cases of incest (abuse) in research did not explore the issue thinking that women's accounts could be dishonest. However, statistics will not help unless the prevalence of abuse is recognised and the sacrosanct status of the family, particularly the father, is challenged. The personal remains political. GUPTA observes that there is a need for: "*… feminist leaders acknowledging and dealing with their own abuse (if they have been abused) rather than being in denial or undermining its effects and thinking of it as a problem 'out there' …*"

26. The practice of silence over generations makes it easier to delegitimise survivor accounts or to see it as a problem "out there". Challenging incest abuse at social levels may require more personal consciousness and practical shifts than the individuals/activists can bear. While analysing the limited impact survivor narratives have made on the collective consciousness in the UK, COX argues that challenging incest

---

74 P. VIRANI, supra (note 3), 18.

75 P. VIRANI, supra (note 3), 97– 110.

76 From CREA.

77 T. JAYARATNE, 'The Value of Quantitative Methodology for Feminist Research', in G. BOWLES and R.DUELLI KLEIN (eds.), *Theories of women's studies*, (London: Routledge and Kegan Paul, 1983), 140–162; L. GELSTHORPE and A. MORRIS, *Feminist Perspectives in Criminology*, (Milton Keynes: Open University Press, 1990), 86.

abuse at a social level would require greater personal consciousness, and practical shifts in social relations, including re-articulation of relationships with men, and a very strong will to survive that many activists may not be able to bear .[78]

3.6. COMMUNITY REACTION TO FEMINISTS & TRENDS IN PREVENTIVE WORK AGAINST INCEST ABUSE

27. Ten of the participants pointed out that because incest abuse is such a taboo subject in India, concerns about it are nearly always sites of struggle. The resistance, which the activists would like to see, clashes with the male authority in families. Giving examples from cases they have handled or supported or are aware of, the participants point to more than a visible collusion among men to keep the issue under wraps. Most of them mentioned the control of powerful institutions, the internalisation of patriarchal ideologies and the alliances of brotherhood and fatherhood as considerable resources with which men protect their sexual interests and openly attack activists and their organisations. When retaliatory violence and abuse against activists take place, civil society tends to look away. Moreover, CHANDIRAMANI[79] points out: "*In addition, there is general apathy and discomfort among people at large, which makes it difficult to address these issues head-on*".

A situation like this, which enables and shields perpetrators, as MENON-SEN[80] feels, makes feminist solidarity shaky: "*Only organisations that have a clear perspective on violence and are resolutely feminist are prepared to go with us in such cases ... There is a lot of anger and moral outrage but also the recognition that taking up such cases puts the organisation at risk of threat and intimidation by the perpetrator and his supporters*". MENON-SEN's view here is at one with the other participants who feel that the fear of retaliation and the threats to existential stakes are so high that few organisations dare get embroiled in the issue.

28. The current practices of prevention work are influenced by the fear of retaliation and mostly place the onus of preventing the abuse on the child. Child empowerment programmes encompassing a range of approaches from "good, bad and confusing or appropriate and inappropriate touches" to "personal safety" and body awareness are "effective" because they imply recognition of children as sexual beings and impart basic skills to name and identify certain elements of sex and sexuality. Both these aspects

---

78 P. COX, 'Knowledge and Resistance in Child Sexual Assault', in P. COX et al. (eds.), *Child Sexual Assault: Feminist Perspective*, (New York: Palgrave, 2000), 10–11.

79 From Tarshi.

80 From Jagori.

are preconditions if children are expected to talk about incest abuse. However, the knowledge gained by the children and their enhanced assertiveness without paying attention to public attitudes and social structures, which allow abuse to take place, is not going to prevent abuse.[81]

This comment in no way underestimates the challenges in doing preventive work. The retaliatory and dismissive socio-political context has been an influential factor in shaping the nature and approach of the strategy to raise and address incest abuse. According to MENON: "*I think it is wholly possible for women's organisations to work on this issue but it would ... cause activists to have their personal lives discussed publicly ... I don't think a work of this nature can be done without community disapproval, especially if one is looking at holding the perpetrators accountable*".

3.7. LEGAL CHALLENGES IN ACTION AGAINST INCEST ABUSE

29. Attitudinal issues involving the police and judicial systems are seen as major hindrances. In the absence of a law on the sexual abuse of children, within and outside the home, as well as gender-biased guardianship and adoption laws, these two institutions are seen as condoning incest abuse through silence, male prejudice, lengthy and insensitive procedures, and sexism.

The never-ending legal processes, together with social pressures, usually weaken the will and capacity of the supportive family members and the survivor and in most cases result in compromise and acceptance of abuse.

Furthermore, there is insatiable voyeuristic curiosity, which thrives under the guise of legal procedures and which makes investigation and witness examination opportunities and sites of vicarious pleasure. MENON-SEN points out: "*The law is insensitive and the people who enforce it are even more so. Right from the police officer to the judges, there is a lot of prurient interest in dragging out every painful detail, regardless of the trauma of the child. This is nothing new, really, it happens with adult women also, when it's a child it's much worse ...*"

30. Currently there are several demands for the reform of laws related to sexual violence and sexuality. In these discourses, there is no specific focus on incest abuse. The discourses move along several different trajectories – domestic violence, rape,

---

[81] J. KITZINGER, supra (note 31), 85; J. KITZINGER, 'Challenging Sexual Violence against Girls: A Social Awareness Approach', (1994) 3 *Child Abuse Review*, 246–247.

commercial sexual exploitation of children, sexual minority, etc. While targeted vision may improve the visibility of the movements, in terms of analysis and understanding, the overlaps among the issues in such discourses will not achieve much. CHANDIRAMANI points out: "... *some groups are working on expanding the definition of rape under the Indian law; some are looking at the implications of gender neutrality under the law in terms of both the perpetrators and the abused. A dialogue of the implications of changing the law and expanding the present definition is crucial before any change is asked for*".

The expansion of the definition of rape is urgent given that under the Indian law a trace of semen, bruises in the vagina, and the rupture of the hymen are essential to constitute rape. Any other form of non-penile penetration in the vagina or other bodily orifices is not considered rape. The demand for gender-neutral rape laws rationalises the need on the ground of offering greater protection to children. In a context where the majority of the perpetrators – against both boys and girls – continue to be men, this demand may be motivated either by a heterosexist interest to keep the focus off the "normative" family or a sheer lack of understanding of the ways in which these laws could be used against people with same-sex preferences. This dialogue needs to be broadened and made more inclusive. Otherwise the experiences of incest abuse survivors and the children being abused will be excluded.

3.8. POOR SUPPORT SERVICES, SKILLS, INFORMATION AND FUNDING

31. "... *This is very frustrating because we often lose children the moment abuse is disclosed or discovered! ... Health, legal, social and childcare services are often wanting in their ability to deal with the issue in a child-centric manner. We are too preoccupied about maintaining the status quo and keeping the family together, often at the cost of the children's interests*". This comment of MAITRA reflects the problems related to the absence of required provisions and the gaps in the existing services. Participants suggested that the quality of skills is a concern, even in organisations, which are working on the issue. The counsellors, therapists, doctors, social workers, teachers and others who could support the child are either not available, or if available, are not consistent in their approach to the abused survivor/child.

The lack of coordination between them complicates the matter further. According to KUSHWAHA and KUMANA, the lack of refuges or shelters is another issue, which affects the organisational capacity to lend support. According to them for organisations working on issues of sexuality but not necessarily on sexual violence, supporting a survivor gets further complicated by the lack of information, skills and internalised notions.

The participants linked these practicalities with problems related to funding. The influence of liberal and critical political theories, which maintain the public/private distinctions by regarding the private realm as one of freedom and authenticity,[82] is not limited only to the State and its legal and justice systems. The State and its systems may come forward to address sexual violence in the public realm but are unwilling to take up the issue in the private realm. Four of the participants pointed out donor reluctance to support work that intervenes in the private realm. Their statements show that the recognition of violence as a social issue is governed by the public/private dichotomy. Particular behaviour may get criminalised if it takes place in the public realm but an interrogation of the same behaviour in the private realm would be seen as an interference with the autonomy of the family. This may result in the reluctance of various non-profit organisations to take up the issue of incest abuse, and in donor agencies and corporations becoming unwilling to support an intervention that interferes with a widely accepted model of the family.

32. To conclude this section, after nearly a decade since research on incest abuse in India began, the secrecy of abuse continues to be sustained. Among the participants, there was a broad recognition of incest abuse as a social issue. Most of the participants often reflected on this issue and the barriers to any intervention in terms of feminist understanding. Still, this understanding has not taken the shape of a sustained action or a movement because of the gaps in this understanding, high personal stakes, fears of social retaliation, and lack of practical mechanisms.

4. CONCLUSION

33. This study has demonstrated that the complexities of incest abuse must be confronted if this form of sexual oppression is to be addressed effectively. The first part focused on the theoretical landscape in which the issue of incest abuse was shaped. It examined the feminist interventions, which contested the hitherto unchallenged knowledge and sought to give visibility to the linkages between the various forms of men's violence against women. These interventions in the academic theorising, grassroots activism and personal practice levels gave a voice to the adult survivors as well as children who were being sexually abused by the people who they trusted and who were responsible for their care. Analysis of radical and second wave feminist

---

82 S. Ashenden, supra (note 49), 87.

interventions and how these interventions were depoliticised would be useful historical references for India where incest abuse has not yet been politicised.

Equally useful would be to take the poststructuralist emphasis on specificities seriously. Within the Indian contexts, where the adoption of psycho-pathological models poses the threat of the perpetrator going unchallenged well as a rejection of the issue as a "Western" phenomenon, the need for specificities cannot be undermined.[83] WARNER's suggestion of collaboration between poststructuralist perspectives and a feminist standpoint to bring "a focus on situated knowledge that draws on subjugated perspectives" seems relevant.[84] She argues that a poststructuralist framework makes it possible to challenge a given identity while a feminist standpoint allows us to recognise and give privilege to marginalised perspectives. Such an approach leading to localised and experience specific theorisation would be helpful in understanding particular ways in which gendered subjectivities and patriarchal power are maintained and incest abuse is denied. In addition, a feminist standpoint that recognises the differences in positions, circumstances and abilities that affect the opportunity to resist will be strategic in deploying feminist solidarity.

34. The second part of this study explored previous studies and interviews with 14 participants to understand the forces, which deter activists and organisations from owning up to the issue and breaking the silence. The outcome of this exploration suggests that these forces – material and ideological – are embedded in individual as well as social consciences. These forces operate at both personal and social levels to allow incest abuse to take place and maintain conditions which ignore that the perpetrator should be accountable. The connections between the personal and the social must be examined to prevent incest abuse. To recognise incest abuse requires shifts in individual perceptions – at the organisational level a rearticulation of "what is a social issue". It would require self and social critique to understand how the ideologies and practices of the family and society enable men to abuse. In the absence of these, the "merry-go-round-shunning" of responsibility will continue.

35. Research on incest abuse in India is still in its infancy, in volume and in theory. As of now, open, direct and consistent advocacy for services and legislation, and "speak outs" are a distant proposition. The shape that the current level of work will take in future will depend a lot on the nature of research and feminist strategies employed to counter patriarchal discourses. No doubt, the realisation of pragmatic support like refuges and shelters, legal instruments and other forms of assistance remain critical

83 A. LEVETT, supra (note 53), 56–64.

84 S. WARNER, 'Disrupting Identity through Visible Therapy: A Feminist Poststructuralist Approach to Working with Women Who Have Experienced Sexual Abuse', (2001) 68 *Feminist Review*, 119.

in preventing violence against women and girls.[85] However, feminist critique remains crucial to challenge the production and reproduction of patriarchal scripts and complacency by the State. There is another practical reason for proposing a feminist challenge to the sources of abuse: the impossibility of implementing psycho-pathological models in a country like India. Therapeutic approaches may not work in India for two reasons: first, it is doubtful that the State has the capacity to provide services to support such a large number of survivors and abused children, and second, in view of the socio-cultural perceptions and economic factors, therapy and treatment would not be a choice for many. Moreover, an emphasis on dysfunctionality may create a value neutral situation in which incest abuse may become another governance liability – a situation in which both incest abuse and "fixing up of the survivor, perpetrator and family" will be normalised.

---

85 R.E. Dobash and R.P. Dobash, *Women, Violence, and Social Change*, (London – New York: Routledge, 1992).

SYNERGIES AND TENSIONS BETWEEN WOMEN'S EMPOWERMENT AND CHILDREN'S RIGHTS: A CRITICAL ASSESSMENT OF WOMEN'S SELF-HELP GROUPS IN ANDHRA PRADESH, INDIA

NICOLA JONES and MADHURI MUKHERJEE[1]

1. INTRODUCTION

1. Very often policy strategies and government agencies group women's and children's rights together without any critical reflection. Because women assume primary care-giving responsibilities in most societies and children are typically identified as a vulnerable population group necessitating special care and protection, there is undoubtedly an intuitive fit. However, if policy prescriptions are to effectively advance both women's and children's rights, there is a need to explore synergies and tensions between women's empowerment and children's well-being more carefully. For example, child rights proponents generally pay little attention to the potential impact of fulfilling children's rights on other family members. However, calls for improved care of children may fall disproportionately on women rather than men, and on individual families rather than communities and State service providers. In the absence of additional community or State support, costs to family members may be felt in terms of increasing financial, resource and/or time burdens. Similarly, as women are increasingly heralded as the champions of community development, there is often an assumption that by empowering women, children's rights will automatically follow. However, there is a limited understanding of the transmission mechanisms involved, let alone possible conflicts.

[1] The authors would like to acknowledge the helpful comments from S. GALAB and the research support from RAJU SREERAMA. In addition we would like to thank DFID's Central Research Department and UNICEF India for their generous funding of the fieldwork research that underpins this paper.

2. The aim of this paper is to explore the inter-relationship between women's empowerment and children's rights, including differences among different groups of women and children. We explore these broader theoretical issues in the context of the Andhra Pradesh (AP) State in India. The Indian government has endorsed women's self-help groups (SHGs) that focus on credit and savings as a poverty alleviation mechanism since the early 1990s. It established formal linkages between SHGs and the banking system in 1992, and scaled up efforts following the Micro-Credit World Summit in 1997, which called for access to credit for 100 million of the world's poorest. Within India, AP is a key State to assess the efficacy of SHGs in promoting social justice as it has the largest number of SHGs in the country – almost half a million groups with over 5.4 million women members. Moreover, despite being a middle-income State in terms of gross domestic product (GDP), AP has a high level of income poverty[2] and its Human and Gender Development Indices are below the national average,[3] indicating that economic growth alone has been insufficient to address basic socio-economic rights for all. Given strong government and donor support of SHGs as part of a broader poverty reduction strategy, evaluating SHGs from a rights-based approach is urgently needed. More specifically, this paper focuses on whether these efforts are contributing to tackling not only the feminisation of poverty but also childhood poverty.

2. SOCIAL CAPITAL AS A DEVELOPMENT TOOL

3. Our theoretical framework draws on literature on social capital and empowerment. Social capital can most simply be defined as "the institutions, relationships and norms that shape the quality and quantity of a society's social interactions". It encompasses membership in community groups such as women's or peasants' associations (structural social capital), collective action efforts, support from neighbours and family and trust among neighbours (cognitive social capital). The concept emerged as a seemingly magic bullet of development in the mid-1990s, and was embraced by students from multiple disciplines including public health, economics, sociology, political science and so on.[4] Representing a major paradigmatic shift in development

[2] An estimated 30 per cent of households live below the poverty line.

[3] If one examines AP's performance in a broader range of human development indices – life expectancy, literacy and per capita income – the absolute value of HDI is 0.416, which is below the national HDI value of 0.577 in 2002. Like all across India, the GDI value is lower than HDI value at 0.400 (national GDI is 0.560), indicating the persistence of gender inequalities in access to basic needs like health and education.

[4] M.R. Carter and J.A. Maluccio, 'Social capital and coping with economic shocks: an analysis of stunting of South African children', (2003) 31(7) *World Development*, 1147–1163; M. Drukker, N. Gunther, F.J.M. Feron and J. van Os, 'Social capital and mental health v. objective measures of health in The Netherlands', (2003) 183 *British Journal of Psychiatry*, 174; R. Putnam, 'Social capital

thought and practice, civil society participation and empowerment of local communities came to be recognised as key components of sustainable growth and development strategies, as well as an essential feature of good governance.[5]

4. An important manifestation of this emphasis on social capital and community empowerment has been the promotion of women's self-help groups throughout the developing world (especially South Asia, Latin America and Sub-Saharan Africa) by governments, donors and NGOs alike.[6]

Broadly speaking, these initiatives can be classified according to three main paradigms:[7]

- The *financial self-sustainability paradigm* focuses on the entrepreneurial poor and increasing their access to micro-finance services. Women are targeted because their repayment rates are on average significantly higher than those of their male counterparts. This approach also recognises the contribution of women's economic activity to economic growth. Empowerment here is viewed primarily in economic terms and as expanding women's self-reliance.
- The *poverty alleviation paradigm* conceptualises microfinance as part of an integrated poverty reduction programme. Women are targeted due to higher levels of female poverty and because they are viewed as being responsible for household well-being. The assumption is that increasing women's access to micro-finance will enable women to make a greater contribution to household income, which will in turn improve women's intra-household decision-making power.
- The *feminist empowerment paradigm* approaches micro-finance as an entry point for women's economic, social and political empowerment. Women's empowerment is seen as an integral and inseparable part of a wider process of social transformation, which can be brought about by making fundamental changes in the macro level development agenda as well as providing support for women to challenge gender subordination at the micro-level. It is this paradigm that we find

---

measurement and consequences', (2001) 2(1) *Canadian Journal of Policy Research (Isuma)*, 41–51; S. Szreter and M. Woolcock, 'Health by association? Social capital, social theory and the political economy of public health', (2004) 33 *International Journal of Epidemiology*, 1–18.

5 F. Fukuyama, 'Social capital and the global economy', (1995) 74 *Foreign Affairs*, 5, 89–103; N.J.Colletta and M. Cullen, 'The nexus between Violent Conflict, Social Capital and Social Cohesion: Case Studies from Cambodia and Rwanda', *Social Capital Initiative Working Paper*, (Washington D.C.: World Bank, 2000), 23, at <http://www.iris.umd.edu>.

6 N.Craske and M. Molyneaux, (eds.), *Gender and the Politics of Rights and Democracy in Latin America*, (London: Palgrave, 2001); B. Purkayastha, *The Power of Women's Informal Networks: Lessons in Social Change from South Asia and West Africa*, (Lanham, Maryland: Lexington Books, 2004).

7 L. Mayoux, 'From Access to Empowerment: Gender Issues in Micro-Finance', CSD NGO Women's Caucus Position Paper for CSD-8, 2000.

most useful in understanding the strengths and weaknesses of SHGs in Andhra Pradesh.

3. RESEARCH OBJECTIVES

5. The objectives of this paper are twofold. First, we want to assess the impact of women's participation in SHGs on the fulfilment of children's rights. Empirical evidence to date suggests that we should expect both positive and negative effects, and thus we want to explore how these hypotheses play out in the Andhra Pradesh context. Researchers from diverse disciplines have identified a positive relationship between women's empowerment and child outcomes. Feminist economists argue that as household livelihoods diversify due to women's greater access to credit and improved income, women are more likely than their male counterparts to invest in their children. As women's role is transformed from one of economic dependant to an economic actor with greater household-level decision-making power, evidence from multiple countries suggests that women tend to use their income on more and higher quality food for their children, educational expenses and clothing. Men by contrast often use additional income for individual-related expenses such as alcohol, tobacco and the purchase of sex.[8]

Empowerment, particularly through access to education programmes, can also facilitate greater awareness among women about their legal rights, public services for which they and their families are eligible and income-generating opportunities.[9] This in turn may empower women to participate more actively in their communities and the political sphere to demand better government programmes to address women's as well as children's rights. Indeed, there is a well-documented correlation between maternal education and higher levels of child education, physical health and nutrition.[10]

---

8 N. KABEER, *Gender Mainstreaming in Poverty Eradication and the Millennium Development Goals. A Handbook for Policy-makers and Other Stakeholders*, (Ottawa: Commonwealth Secreatariat/IDRC/ CIDA, 2003).

9 M. MOLYNEUX, 'Mobilization Without Emancipation? Women's Interests, State and Revolution in Nicaragua', (1985) Volume 1 *Feminist Studies.*

10 A. BARRERA, 'The Role of Maternal Schooling and Its Interaction with Public Health Programs in Child Health Production', (1990) Vol. 32 *Journal of Development Economics*, 69–91; J. CALDWELL and P. MCDONALD, 'Influence of maternal education on infant and child mortality: levels and causes', (1982) 2(3–4) *Health Policy and Education*, 251–67; P. GLEWWE, 'Why does mother's Schooling Raise Child Health in Developing Countries: Evidence from Morocco', (1999) Vol. 34 No. 1 *Journal of Human Resources*, 124–159; S. MEHROTRA, 'Improving Child Wellbeing in Developing Countries. What Do We Know? What Can Be Done?', *CHIP Report No. 9*, (London: Childhood Poverty Research and Policy Centre, 2004).

6. These positive impacts notwithstanding, other research suggests that women's empowerment may have either a negligible or even negative impact on children or at least some aspects of their well-being. First, a growing body of research on childhood poverty indicates that a reduction in aggregate household poverty does not necessarily translate into an alleviation of childhood poverty.[11] Instead, complementary targeted policy efforts are often required. In the case of Andhra Pradesh, India, for example, while the State is on track for meeting the Millennium Development Goals (MDG) on halving household income poverty, almost all caste and wealth groups are off-track for meeting the MDG with regard to the child-specific indicator for tackling child malnutrition. Unless rising State GDP levels are invested in programmes more aggressively, to address child malnutrition and families avail themselves of these material and informational services, children's right to survival (Art. 6 CRC) and adequate health care (Art. 24 CRC) and standard of living (Art. 27 CRC) are unlikely to be met.

Second, recent research also suggests that we cannot assume an automatic spillover impact from women's involvement in community groups to better child outcomes. GALAB et al.[12] for example found that while participation in SHGs in Andhra Pradesh has been linked to higher school enrolment rates, involvement did not have a significant effect on children's nutritional status. The authors argued that one important difference might be that whereas improving children's education is an explicit aim of many SHG programmes (i.e. school attendance is a non-negotiable condition for SHG membership), there is no comparable focus on child nutrition.

Lastly, if women's empowerment results from improved income-generating opportunities, greater demands on women's time may negatively affect children if alternative childcare mechanisms are not put in place. As women become more involved in productive work, the quantity and/or quality of time they can devote to reproductive activities may be reduced. Moreover, while MOSER[13] has powerfully identified women's triple burden (productive, reproductive and community development activities) in developing countries, evidence increasingly suggests that although women often manage these triple roles, their children, especially daughters,

[11] J. MARSHALL, 'Children and poverty – some questions answered', *CHIP Briefing 1.*, (London: Save the Children UK, 2003).

[12] S.GALAB, A. PIUSH, I. WILSON, N. JONES, A. MCCOYN and R. SREERAMA, 'Exploring linkages between maternal social capital and children's nutritional status in Andhra Pradesh', *Young Lives Working Paper*, (London: Save the Children UK, 2006).

[13] C. MOSER, 'Adjustment from Below: Low-Income Women, Time, and the Triple Burden in Guayaquil, Ecuador', in H. ASHFAR and C. DENNIS (eds.), *Women and Adjustment Policies in the Third World*, (New York: St. Martin's Press, 1992).

often have to shoulder part of this burden through greater involvement in domestic activities (including care of younger siblings).

7. The second major objective of the paper is to evaluate the impact of different SHG institutional arrangements and socio-demographic contexts on women's and children's rights. While some SHGs focus narrowly on micro-finance, others are embedded in broader social development and poverty reduction programmes. We hypothesise that these differences, as well as the socio-demographic make-up (caste and class balance/ urban versus rural location) of the communities in which the SHGs are operational will play an important role in shaping how effective SHGs are as mechanisms for women's empowerment and in turn changes in the fulfilment of children's rights.

4. METHODS AND SAMPLE

8. The research findings presented in this paper draw on both the Young Lives (YL) panel survey from 2002 and in-depth qualitative research from a sub-sample of the YL project sites. The quantitative survey sample comprised 1,996 biological mothers of children aged 6 to18 months (referred to as "one year olds" in the YL survey) sampled across 20 poor communities from the three main agro-climatic regions of Andhra Pradesh (Coastal AP, Rayalseema and Telengana). In examining maternal social capital, the respondents were interviewed by using the shortened version of A-SCAT tool (Adapted Social Capital Assessment Tool) developed by HARPHAM et al.[14] The questions were in a yes/ no format and investigated four main dimensions of social capital typically discussed in the literature. Structural social capital was measured by asking about membership in formal and non-formal groups; social support was defined as material or other assistance received from formal and informal networks; citizenship referred to involvement in collective action initiatives and cognitive social capital assessed on an individual's perception of community belongingness and harmony.

9. The complementary in-depth qualitative research was undertaken in order to gain a better understanding of how child well-being is affected directly or indirectly by mother's participation in community-based processes such as the self-help groups. Research was conducted in four of the 20 YL sentinel sites, more exactly in a rural site from each of the three main geo-political regions in AP and an additional urban site to provide information on urban/rural differences:

---

[14] T. HARPHAM, E. GRANT and E. THOMAS, 'Measuring social capital within health surveys: key issues', (2002) 17 *Health Policy and* Planning, 106–11.

i) Amrabad mandal, Mahaboobnagar District, Telangana region;
ii) Atlur mandal, Cuddapah District, Rayalseema region;
iii) Seetampet mandal, Srikakalum District, Coastal Andhra region
iv) Anantapur mandal, Anantapur District, Rayalseema region.

Specific mandals (villages) from each district were in turn chosen based on a) high or low levels of caregivers' structural social capital (participation in community groups) and b) community caste composition (homogeneous versus heterogeneous). See Box 1 below for further details.

10. The methods of qualitative data collection included semi-structured interviews with SHG members and non-members, and focus group discussions with members, non-members and men (spouses of both members and non-members). In total 64 individual interviews and 28 focus group discussions were conducted involving nearly 300 women and 60 men. The objective was to gather information about the structure and functioning of self-help groups, leadership style, the type of resources and services accessed, the impact of participation in SHGs on women's intra-household status and decision-making power as well as their roles within the community, especially vis-à-vis their interaction with service providers and local authorities. Particular attention was paid to caste, wealth status and urban/rural differences, as well as the impact of women's SHG participation on child well-being.

Box 1: Key characteristics of qualitative research sites

Anantapur is an urban community with a mixed caste composition. Social capital levels are low, at least in part due to a high percentage of migrants from various parts of the State and considerable caste and religious diversity.

Atlur is a rural village, characterised by caste diversity. Maternal social capital is low, perhaps because of large scale out migration and accompanying social upheaval due to frequent droughts.

Seethampet is a rural area where the dominant community is Scheduled Tribes (ST). Social capital is high, partly due to greater group homogeneity and high levels of governmental and non-governmental community organising

Amrabad is also rural and predominantly populated by Scheduled Caste and Scheduled Tribes. Like Seethampet a number of development initiatives have facilitated greater levels of social cohesion and activism.

5. OVERVIEW OF SHGs

11. Andhra Pradesh has approximately half a million SHGs involving almost 7.5 million women.[15] Most participants are from the rural areas and belong to lower socio-

15 See at <www.rd.ap.gov.in>.

economic strata of society (in both class and caste terms). However, although these micro-credit programmes are designed to alleviate poverty, empirical evidence suggests that poorest of the poor are not involved. This is in part because the poorest are typically unable to repay loans and are thus automatically excluded from membership.[16] The majority of groups in AP are affiliated to State-run programmes including Indira Kranti Patham, DWCRA and DPIP. These programmes are implemented in areas with larger impoverished populations. Box 2 below provides a brief description of each programme, highlighting their salient features.

Box 2: Key characteristics of different SHG programmes

Indira Kranthi Patham (formerly known as Velugu): The programme focuses on poverty alleviation, especially for the poorest of the poor in rural communities. It emphasises institution building, social capital through community mobilisation and participation as well as livelihood diversification. The premise is that collective action combined with knowledge and resources will enable the rural poor to overcome high transaction costs, ignorance about markets, prices and products as well as indebtedness.

Swaranajayanti Gram Swarojgar Yojana: Launched in 1999, this programme is implemented through the Development of Women and Children in Rural Areas (DWCRA) scheme and focuses on providing sustainable levels of income through SHG organization. It focuses on mobilisation, and providing training and capacity building for income generation. Members must be below the poverty line in order to be eligible for credit and government subsidies. Most of these groups have federated into Mutually Aided Cooperative Thrift Societies.

SHG's under Bank Linkages: These SHG's are set up by rural banks and belong to the NABARD (National Bank for Agriculture and Rural Development) programme established in 1992. Although, initially small scale, the programme's target is to reach one million SHGs by 2007. Groups are mainly identified through NGOs and are subject to strict lending regulations. The mandate of these SHGs is narrow, focusing on savings and access to credit. Corruption has plagued this model of SHGs as "middlemen" often take a cut from group members' loans.

Independent groups: In some cases, non-registered women also organise into thrift and credit groups. Although not linked to any of the development programmes above, these groups are more likely to be found in programme areas, perhaps due to demonstration effects.

12. In sum, *Indira Kranthi Patham* and *Swaranajayanti Gram Swarojgar Yojana* (SGSY) are underpinned by the poverty alleviation paradigm whereas SHGs linked to banks and independently formed groups are more narrowly focused on financial self-sustainability. None of the programmes are informed by the more holistic gender empowerment paradigm although women's economic empowerment is an explicit concern. Similarly, none of the programmes refer to fulfilling children's rights. However, improving children's welfare is an explicit goal of the SGSY programme – it is assumed that women's access to independent income will spill over into greater household consumption directed towards children's educational and nutritional needs.

---

[16] N.KABEER, 'Money Can't Buy Me Love'? Re-Evaluating Gender, Credit and Empowerment in Rural Bangladesh', *IDS Discussion Paper No. 363*, Institute of Development Studies, Univ. of Sussex, 1998.

6. FINDINGS

13. Our research findings confirmed our hypotheses about four key transmission mechanisms between women's empowerment and children's rights, but also highlighted the need to carefully nuance these assumptions if synergies between women's and children's rights are to be realised through broader poverty reduction and social development initiatives. Before turning to discuss these different pathways in more detail, the discussion begins with a brief overview of the SHG participants in the YL project sample and the structure and functions of the groups.

14. Our quantitative data revealed that women involved in SHGs exhibited higher levels of other dimensions of social capital regardless of caste or wealth category. In particular, SHG members were more involved in collective action than their non-member counterparts and had received support from community and local government leaders.[17] There were marked urban/rural differences: whereas rural women were more likely to be involved in SHGs and to gain support from formal and informal networks, their urban counterparts were more likely to become involved in collective action. There was similarly significant diversity among caste and wealth groups. Whereas lower caste women were more likely to participate in SHGs, the middle poor rather than the poorest participated in greater numbers and also received more support from formal and informal sources alike.

15. In terms of joining an SHG, interestingly informal networks played an important role in women joining SHGs. Regardless of the type of programme, most women joined because they had learned about the benefits of participating from friends, neighbours or relatives. However, once women joined groups, their opportunities for empowerment differed markedly depending on the type of SHG programme they joined. Those with well-regulated leadership were most effective in expanding women's knowledge, networks and asset base, whereas independent groups were most prone to corrupt and disempowering leadership.

6.1. IMPROVED AWARENESS AND ACCESS TO INFORMATION

16. Most women interviewed reported that their awareness of and access to information about child-rearing practices and public services had improved because of their participation in an SHG. Focus group discussions with members' male partners

[17] See Table 1 and Table 2 in the Appendix.

also confirmed this finding, although some noted that women's empowerment had also been enhanced through exposure to media and affirmative action for women in local governments. However, the mechanisms differed depending on the type of SHG and group leadership style. In the case of SHGs, which belonged to broader poverty reduction and social development programmes, the improved awareness and information resulted from formal channels. Informational lectures by community public health workers, enrolment in eye campaigns, vaccination programmes and nutritional supplement programmes as well as home visits to members were organised. However, in the case of SHGs with a narrower mandate on credit and savings only, there appeared to be negligible emphasis on raising awareness. Indeed, a number of women in these groups were even unaware of the loan amounts and terms, suggesting that lending institutions and/or leaders placed little priority on empowerment through imparting knowledge. Nevertheless, some members noted that their awareness about child development and related services was advanced through informal networks with other members who were often immediate neighbours.[18] This finding corroborates other research on the powerful role of informal networking among poor women. Whereas women in developed countries are more likely to participate in organised groups and seek socio-political change through formal channels, women in developing country contexts often rely on support from informal networks to challenge marginalisation and address their problems.[19]

17. Two important limitations should be noted however in terms of the efficacy of this potential synergistic channel between women's and children's rights. First, overall SHG members tend to be mothers with older children indicating that information about early childcare and development is not likely to be reaching the women who need it most. The key obstacle to participation by mothers with young infants is the lack of childcare possibilities to allow these women to attend meetings. As one mother noted: "*If I go out to attend the meeting of the group then who is going to take care of my child; all other women in the group have big children, so they have free time. I may think of becoming a member once my child grows up.*"

Second, although women reported that SHG membership had led to greater awareness and information about children's nutrition, hygiene, health and education, issues about child exploitation and violence were not discussed, largely due to fears of social stigma. For example, one SHG member, SUBHAMMA, who admitted she faced domestic violence, explained that she did not seek support from her group because: "*Women from good families never bad mouth their husbands and if I talk about my problems with*

[18] Due to a spatial clustering of caste groups, SHG members, who tend to belong to the same caste often, reside in close proximity.

[19] B. PURKAYASTHA, supra (note 6).

other women then they might feel that I am not happy with my husband. Moreover all women that I know do face some violence so it's nothing different in my case."

This suggests that while women's involvement in SHGs may advance children's rights to survival and development, to date no positive spillover impact on children's rights to neither protection nor participation (e.g. children's right to have a say in community affairs that affect them) has been identified.

6.2. GREATER HOUSEHOLD DECISION-MAKING POWER FACILITATES WOMEN'S CAREGIVER ROLE

18. Both men and women alike noted that following women's involvement in SHGs, there had been a shift in the intra-household balance of power. Access to credit and/or participation in savings initiatives have allowed women a degree of economic independence and as a result they have been able to assert some decision-making power over issues such as their children's – especially girls' – education, household consumption, access to health services and their children's marriage partners. Although husbands are still reported to have the final say on most matters, participation in decision-making was viewed as a significant change and should therefore not be underestimated. Nonetheless, a number of respondents emphasised that changes in power relations within the family had been short term and superficial. Rather than rethinking gender roles more fundamentally, some male partners appeared to value women's participation in SHGs only for the loan that she might secure. One woman member, LAXMI, for example noted that her husband threatened her ongoing involvement in the group when she was not allocated a loan in the first year of attending SHG meetings. "*My situation at home has not changed at all because I have not yet been able to access credit for my family. Now every time I go to attend the group meeting, my husband expects me to come back with money and when I come back empty handed he threatens me to quit the group.*"

Others similarly explained that their household influence diminished once the loan had been utilised.

19. This finding suggests that an important shortcoming of the SHG approach in AP is the fact that loans are used to satisfy practical consumption needs rather than as seed money for more sustainable income-generating activities. In the three rural communities surveyed, women most commonly used loans and savings to invest in their children's education or to contribute to their children's marriage expenses. For example, one mother explained that only some of her children were attending school due to her lack of access to micro-credit: "*As I have recently become a member I have not yet received any money which I can use for paying the school admission fees.*"

20. While this could be interpreted as a valuable longer-term investment in their children's human capital, the potential benefits are likely to be delayed and the impacts on women's empowerment within the household remain limited. In this case, women are investing in what MOLYNEUX[20] famously dubbed women's practical rather than strategic gender needs. By contrast, women SHG members in the urban site of Anantapur were using their loans and savings as start-up capital for home-based micro-enterprises. As such, the loans were potentially contributing to more sustainable economic empowerment and in turn longer-term household influence.

6.3. LINKS BETWEEN SOCIAL AND POLITICAL CAPITAL

21. One of the postulated benefits of women's participation in SHGs is that it will spill over into broader political participation and that this will result in demands for more and better quality public services. A recent analysis of SHGs in AP has indeed found increased local political participation among women members belonging to the DPIP programme,[21] but our research found only limited evidence of such linkages. Just four of the women SHG members interviewed were members of local village committees or *Gram Sabhas.* A number of respondents pointed out that unlike SHG membership, meaningful participation in local politics is also often hampered by caste and class barriers. ARUNA, an SHG leader summed up her community's reality as follows: "*We are quite happy within our groups because to become a member of the panchayat one needs to have lot of money and contacts with political parties, which is not possible for women like us*".

22. In some cases, SHG leaders had developed linkages with service providers. For example, angawadis/village-level public health officers used their SHG contacts to fulfil their child vaccination programme targets. In Seethampet, an area where the Velugu programme is being implemented, SHGs had also served as a springboard for involvement in a collective action initiative to address a water crisis. One woman, SUBHALAXMI, for example, noted that the help of the SHG was instrumental: "*...we organised a demonstration at the mandal headquarters and eventually the problem was resolved in their village*".

---

20 M. MOLYNEUX, supra (note 9).

21 S.GALAB, A. PIUSH, I. WILSON, N. JONES, A. MCCOYN and R. SREERAMA., supra (note 12).

23. However, mostly this networking did not seem to have penetrated to rank and file members. This is at least in part because decision makers are often located outside the village and thus the opportunities to lobby for change are more limited than in urban contexts. Moreover, in one community due to poorly enforced SHG regulations, SHGs were dominated by two powerful profit-seeking leaders who were in conflict with the local leaders of the government-sponsored Velagu programme. In this case, rather than strengthening women's political capital, fraudulent leadership was actually undermining any potential empowering effects.

6.4. WOMEN'S ACCESS TO INCREASED INCOME FACILITATES INVESTMENT IN CHILD WELL-BEING

24. The hypothesis that women tend to invest in family and child well-being rather than individual needs was borne out. When women did receive loans they invested in their children's education, in accessing private health care services for their children (due to perceptions of superior quality compared to public health providers), and in dowry payments. However, due to limited loan amounts and the infrequency of available micro-credit, the potential for women to make a significant difference to household consumption was relatively limited. As discussed above, the exception was the urban site of Anantapur where a number of women SHG members had used loans to invest in micro-enterprises.

25. Although some researchers have cautioned that women's greater access to economic resources may come at the price of less time for household reproductive activities and a greater work burden for their offspring, this finding was largely unsubstantiated in our research sites. However, this may be because women were using loans for one-off or non-sustainable investments rather than start-up capital for more sustainable and time-consuming enterprises. In the case of rural women, some invested in livestock purchases, especially of milch animals, which did bring in more lasting – albeit unsubstantial – income. In such cases, children were sometimes called upon to take care of the livestock but the time burden was not perceived to be too burdensome. Urban women respondents involved in income-generating activities made the most substantial contribution to household income but they similarly denied that their children had to shoulder any significant additional work burden. This may be because the enterprises were largely home-based and thus facilitated women's ability to balance their domestic and financial roles without major household implications.

7. CONCLUSIONS AND POLICY IMPLICATIONS

26. Our findings indicate that efforts to advance women's economic, social and political rights through community mobilisation in Andhra Pradesh are having limited but positive effects on children's rights. However, in order to maximise synergies and to ensure not only that more children are benefiting (especially the poorest) but also a broader array of children's rights are being addressed through mainstream poverty reduction initiatives, the following policy modifications should be considered.

27. First, given evidence of corrupt and/or disempowering leadership there is a need for tighter enforcement of regulations governing Mutually Aided Cooperative Thrift Societies. Membership alone is not sufficient to empower women—at a minimum SHG members need to be provided with sufficient and accurate information about the loans they can access in order to improve their decision-making power.

28. Second, if women are to be empowered both within the household and within community, programmes with a mandate that goes beyond financial self-sustainability must appear significantly more effective. That is, spillover effects on women's and children's broader well-being should not be accidental but rather derived from deliberate efforts to provide information and foster awareness about citizenship rights and available public services. However, even programmes such as Velagu and DWACRA's SGSY programme could do more to contribute to the alleviation of the multi-dimensionality of childhood poverty if they were to broaden their scope to consider issues of child protection (from exploitation and abuse) as well as participation (in community affairs that affect children's lives). Our findings suggest that issues of family and community violence are still shrouded in silence and that SHGs have not yet emerged as a forum in which to discuss these issues. Similarly, while some members had used participation in SHGs as a springboard for involvement in community politics, there was no mention of a spill-over impact on the importance of children's right to voice their views and to be heard. Taking lessons from and perhaps establishing linkages with the successful local youth parliaments in Karnataka State could be one possible solution here.

29. Third, although the stated purpose of SHGs is economic empowerment through income generation, in the majority of cases loans are being used to cover basic household needs rather than as seed money for more sustainable income generation activities. If women's potential to foster more democratic household and community decision-making processes is to be realised, then more support needs to be provided to women to start up niche micro-enterprises. At the same time, however, it would be important to consider implications on childcare arrangements. The potential negative impacts of exacerbated time poverty among particularly girl children identified in the literature have not emerged to date, but this is at least in part because there have not been major shifts in SHG members' time allocation. Community childcare would also enable more mothers of young infants to participate in SHGs and gain from linkages to public health programmes focused on maternal and child health and nutrition.

30. Fourth, access to credit has equipped women with greater influence within the household but gender relations within the family appear to remain far from equal as men continue to dominate decision-making. Efforts to advance social justice will therefore require that government and non-government agencies involved in community mobilisation also pay attention to changing men's attitudes, including their responsibilities towards their children's well-being.

APPENDIX

Table 1: Composite Measures of Social Capital by Household Location, Caste and Wealth Group (SHG members only)

		Urban N	Rural N	SC N	ST N	BC N	OC N	poor N	Not So poor N	Non Poor N	Total N
1. Formal women's group		84	759	204	136	397	105	274	351	218	843
	%	11.11	33.57	34.99	33.75	28.56	16.41	29.53	34.31	20.47	27.95
	Community leaders	2	47	15	3	24	7	10	22	17	49
	%	2.38	6.23	7.35	2.21	6.09	6.73	3.65	6.34	7.8	5.84
	Politicians	0	14	4	0	8	2	2	7	5	14
	%	0	1.85	1.96	0	2.03	1.92	0.73	2.02	2.29	1.67
2. Support received from formal network	Government sources	1	45	14	4	25	3	10	26	10	46
	%	1.19	5.96	6.86	2.94	6.35	2.88	3.65	7.49	4.59	5.48
	Charities	0	42	16	1	22	3	17	20	5	42
	%	0	5.56	7.84	0.74	5.58	2.88	6.2	5.76	2.29	5.01
	Others	0	5	4	0	1	0	2	3	0	5
	%	0	0.66	1.96	0	0.25	0	0.73	0.86	0	0.6
	Family	52	532	142	72	288	81	183	245	156	584
	%	61.9	70.46	69.61	52.94	73.1	77.88	66.79	70.61	71.56	69.61
	Neighbours	31	420	101	47	240	63	150	199	102	451
	%	36.9	55.63	49.51	34.56	60.91	60.58	54.74	57.35	46.79	53.75

		Urban N	Rural N	SC N	ST N	BC N	OC N	poor N	Not So poor N	Non Poor N	Total N
3. Support received from informal network	Friends (not neighbours)	4	146	41	12	75	22	41	77	32	150
	%	4.76	19.34	20.1	8.82	19.04	21.15	14.96	22.19	14.68	17.88
	Religious leaders	0	5	1	0	1	3	1	3	1	5
	%	0	0.66	0.49	0	0.25	2.88	0.36	0.86	0.46	0.6
	Joinded together with others	37	336	92	82	155	44	125	158	90	373
	%	44.05	44.27	45.1	60.29	39.04	41.9	45.62	45.01	41.28	44.25
4. Citizenship	Talked with local authority	28	186	58	37	81	38	62	89	63	214
	%	33.33	24.51	28.43	27.21	20.4	36.19	22.63	25.36	28.9	25.39
	Majority of people trusted	80	737	194	133	386	103	266	339	212	817
	%	95.24	97.1	95.1	97.79	97.23	98.1	97.08	96.58	97.25	96.92
	Most people get along	76	736	195	133	384	99	267	341	204	812
	%	90.48	96.97	95.59	97.79	96.73	94.29	97.45	97.15	93.58	96.32
5. Cognitive	Feel part of community	81	739	199	133	387	100	269	344	207	820
	%	96.43	97.36	97.55	97.79	97.48	95.24	98.18	98.01	95.95	97.27
	People take advantage	34	311	92	58	149	46	122	148	75	345
	%	40.48	40.97	45.1	42.65	37.53	43.81	44.53	42.17	34.4	40.93

Table 2: Composite Measures of Social Capital by Household Location, Caste and Wealth Group (Non SHG members)

		Urban N	Rural N	SC N	ST N	BC N	OC N	poor N	Not So poor N	Non Poor N	Total N
1. Formal women's group		672	1,500	379	267	991	535	653	671	847	2,172
	%	88.89	66.34	65.01	66.25	71.29	83.59	70.37	65.59	79.53	71.99
	Community leaders	6	42	9	2	24	13	14	19	15	48
	%	0.89	2.82	2.41	0.75	2.44	2.43	2.16	2.86	1.78	2.22
	Politicians	5	18	6	3	9	5	7	6	10	23
	%	0.75	1.21	1.6	1.12	0.91	0.94	1.08	0.9	1.18	1.07
2. Support received from formal network	Government sources	11	51	15	16	24	7	20	20	22	62
	%	1.64	3.43	4.01	5.99	2.44	1.31	3.08	3.01	2.6	2.87
	Charities	1	27	13	2	12	1	8	13	7	28
	%	0.15	1.81	3.48	0.75	1.22	0.19	1.23	1.96	0.83	1.3
	Others	1	5	2	0	3	1	1	3	2	6
	%	0.15	0.34	0.53	0	0.3	0.19	0.15	0.45	0.24	0.28
	Family	415	1,042	248	165	673	371	456	469	531	1,456
	%	61.85	70.03	66.31	61.8	68.39	69.48	70.26	70.63	62.84	67.47
	Neighbours	245	746	186	99	480	226	336	351	304	991
	%	36.51	50.13	49.73	37.08	48.78	42.32	51.77	52.86	35.98	45.92
3. Support received from informal network	Friends (not neighbours)	82	219	61	25	151	64	68	120	113	301
	%	12.22	14.72	16.31	9.36	15.35	11.99	10.48	18.07	13.37	13.95
	Religious leaders	5	8	3	0	4	6	2	3	8	13

		Urban N	Rural N	SC N	ST N	BC N	OC N	poor N	Not So poor N	Non Poor N	Total N
	%	0.75	0.54	0.8	0	0.41	1.12	0.31	0.45	0.95	0.6
	Joinded together with others	160	440	119	113	225	143	171	203	226	600
	%	23.81	29.33	31.4	42.32	22.7	26.73	26.19	30.25	26.68	27.64
4. Citizenship	Talked with local authority	109	243	64	41	142	105	71	132	149	352
	%	16.22	16.2	16.89	15.36	14.33	19.63	10.87	19.67	17.59	16.21
	Majority of people trusted	626	1,,422	357	253	934	504	624	637	786	2,047
	%	93.29	94.8	94.2	94.76	94.25	94.38	95.56	94.93	92.91	94.33
	Most people get along	624	1,448	363	257	947	505	632	647	792	2,071
	%	92.86	96.53	95.78	96.25	95.56	94.39	96.78	96.42	93.51	95.39
5. Cognitive	Feel part of community	640	1,449	362	260	957	510	631	644	813	2,088
	%	95.24	96.6	95.51	97.38	96.57	95.33	96.63	95.98	95.99	96.18
	People take advantage	311	632	179	109	410	245	264	309	370	943
	%	46.28	42.13	47.23	40.82	41.37	45.79	40.43	46.05	43.68	43.44

VIII. JUVENILE JUSTICE

CHILDREN'S RIGHTS IN JUVENILE JUSTICE: A HISTORICAL GLANCE

JEAN TRÉPANIER

1. INTRODUCTION

1. Juvenile justice has existed for slightly more than a century. How did it emerge, and what kind of evolution has it undergone? These questions are crucial if we are to understand how international instruments that concern juvenile justice policies saw the light of day and what orientations were embedded in them. Laws as well as international instruments are the products of societies, ideologies, values and debates that are located in time. This is true for children's rights as much as it is for other social issues. Therefore, we will briefly present the orientations that have shaped juvenile justice policies over the years; secondly, we will try to locate the orientations of the Convention on the Rights of Child and other contemporary United Nations instruments within the context of that evolution.

2. EMERGENCE AND EVOLUTION OF JUVENILE JUSTICE

2. The emergence and evolution of juvenile justice can be divided into following periods: (1) the nineteenth century, where some of its foundations are laid; (2) the emergence of juvenile justice between 1900 and 1930; (3) its consolidation between 1930 and 1960; (4) its partial transformation between 1960 and 1990; and (5) current challenges, since the 1990s.

2.1. THE NINETEENTH CENTURY AND THE LAYING OF FOUNDATIONS

3. The creation of special institutions for neglected and delinquent children remains one of the most important – if not the most important – developments in dealing with these groups of children in the nineteenth century. This must be viewed in a context where incarceration became the main component of penology in the first part of the century. Adults were not the only ones to be subjected to imprisonment: so were children, who were initially detained with adults. Such promiscuity was soon criticised. It was feared that children would be contaminated by the adult criminals with whom they were detained.

Furthermore, as the century passed, reformers put forth the idea that institutions should not serve the sole purpose of detention in the case of children; additionally, they should aim at reforming them through a special regime that would change them. Thus, institutions such as reform or industrial schools, penal or agricultural colonies, houses of refuge and so on, emerged.[1]

4. The legal status of children also changed. For example, one may think about the specific treatment that delinquent children received in some countries, depending on whether they were found capable of discernment or not. Some laws provided for a reduced punishment for discerning children and special measures for non-discerning ones. Some countries also passed laws facilitating the use of summary procedures for children, making it possible for courts to hold separate hearings for minors and reducing sentences of remand in custody in the company of adults. At the end of the century, several countries passed laws for the protection of neglected children. Children's aid societies, *sociétés de patronage* and similar bodies were established to rescue children in danger. The development of such child protection organisations would later prove their importance with regard to the establishment of juvenile courts. Some of their members would become the main advocates of policies aiming at dealing with juvenile delinquents in the same way as these organisations dealt with children in danger, thus proposing the adoption of a child welfare model for juvenile delinquents.

---

1 Various authors have studied the emergence of these institutions. See for example: M.-S. DUPONT-BOUCHAT and É. PIERRE (eds.), with J.-M. FECTEAU, J. TRÉPANIER, J.-G. PETIT, B. SCHNAPPER and J. DEKKER and with the collaboration of S. MÉNARD and V. STRIMELLE, *Enfance et justice au XIXe siècle. Essais d'histoire comparée de la protection de l'enfance, 1820–1914, France, Belgique, Pays-Bas, Canada*, (Paris: Presses Universitaires de France, 2001), Part 1.

5. Key court decisions also helped to pave the way for juvenile courts. One may refer particularly to significant decisions made by US courts to extend the application of the *parens patriae* doctrine to children in danger. In summary, this doctrine was invoked to allow the State to intervene in the lives of some children who were in need of care. Such interventions were not defined as punishments, but rather as being in the interest of the children. Thus, they were not considered as criminal law interventions, which led the courts to decide that the procedures leading to such interventions did not have to include such legal safeguards as were normally provided in the realm of criminal law. Because of such case law, promoters of US juvenile courts would later advocate that such courts as juvenile courts, which aimed at helping and protecting children rather than punishing them, did not have to provide safeguards that were inherent in criminal proceedings. Numerous actors well beyond US borders would share their views. Thus, despite the fact that the creation of juvenile courts would have to wait until the turn of the century, the nineteenth century laid some foundations, which made that creation possible.

2.2. THE CREATION OF JUVENILE JUSTICE (1900–1930)

6. Juvenile courts really emerge at the turn and in the first part of the twentieth century. Legislation enacting juvenile courts (or equivalent bodies dealing specifically with minors) goes back to that period in many western countries. One may find such examples in Norway (1896); Illinois (1899) soon followed by other US States; Sweden (1902); Denmark (1905); England and Wales, Ireland and Canada (1908); Portugal (1911); Belgium, France and Switzerland (1912); Hungary (1913); Spain and Poland (1918); Netherlands and Japan (1922); Germany (1923); New Zealand (1925); Greece (1927); and Austria (1928).[2] The laws of those countries were not all similar. Each of them bore the mark of national or regional legal tradition as well as that of influential

2 The information concerning the various legal systems has been gathered from a number of sources, whose references are too numerous to be listed here and to be repeated constantly throughout the text. Amongst those references, one may quote a few that cover more than one country, such as the following: F. Bailleau and Y. Cartuyvels (eds.), 'Special issue on Juvenile Justice in Europe', (2002) *26/3 Déviance et société*; M.-S. Dupont-Bouchat *et al.*, supra (note 1); H. Kashefi Esmaeil Zadeh, *La protection des mineurs au sein du Conseil de l'Europe*, PhD thesis, (Paris: Université Panthéon-Sorbonne – Paris I, 2005); M.K. Rosenheim, F.E. Zimring, D.S.Tanenhaus and B. Dohrn (eds.), *A Century of Juvenile Justice*, (Chicago – London: University of Chicago Press, 2002); M. Tonry and A.N. Doob (eds.), *Youth Crime and Youth Justice: Comparative and Cross-National Perspectives*, (Chicago: University of Chicago Press, 2004 – Crime and Justice: A Review of Research, vol. 31); J. Trépanier and F. Tulkens, *Délinquance et protection de la jeunesse: aux sources des lois belge et canadienne sur l'enfance*, (Bruxelles: DeBoeck Université, 1995); J.A. Winterdyk (ed.), *Juvenile Justice Systems: International Perspectives*, (Toronto: Canadian Scholars' Press, 1997); J.A. Winterdyk (ed.), *Juvenile Justice Systems: International Perspectives*, 2nd edition, (Toronto: Canadian Scholars' Press, 2002).

persons, pressure groups and political compromises. Yet ideas and models circulated through national borders and contributed to debates. One model stood out as particularly influential: that of US juvenile courts, whose orientation was much in line with the *parens patriae* doctrine. Although some differences could be found between legislation passed by various US States, the first law adopted in that country – the 1899 Illinois law[3] creating the Chicago Juvenile Court – was quite typical and much US legislation that would come in the following years was similar to the 1899 Illinois law. Its last section reflected its orientation: "This act shall be liberally construed, to the end that its purpose may be carried out, to-wit: That the care, custody and discipline of a child shall approximate as nearly as may be that which should be given by its parents [...]".

7. In the latter part of the nineteenth century, the emergence of the positivist school of criminology challenged the assumptions of the classical school, which presented criminal behaviour as the result of free rational choices. Offending behaviour seemed to be associated with factors external to the offender (such as genetic factors, family environment and social surroundings), over which he had no control. If then, as the positivist school argued, the offence is the result of causes over which the offender has no control, punishment therefore becomes irrelevant.

The offender should not be punished for what her/his environment made her/him. Instead, he/she should be protected from those factors that contributed to him/her becoming a delinquent. Child protection was by no means viewed as conflicting with the aim of protecting society, but rather as the best means to achieve this goal, thus blurring the distinction between delinquent children, on the one hand, and neglected or dependent children on the other. A protective approach would be appropriate for both groups.

8. The child welfare model found its way – to varying extents and in different ways – into the legislation of various States in the first part of the twentieth century. Its main characteristics may be summarised as follows. The focus must be primarily on the child, not on the offence. The principle of proportionality and determinate dispositions are deemed inconsistent with this approach and should be eliminated. Aiming at punishment, classical criminal law demands that the nature and duration of the penal sanction be in proportion to the gravity of the offence. This is decided at the time of sentencing, prior to its execution. If, however, the aim is no longer to punish but to protect the child in order to prevent future delinquency, this requirement loses its relevancy. The choice of measure should address the individual needs of the child. The measure should be applied (and prolonged or changed) as long as these needs exist.

[3] *Illinois Juvenile Court Act,* 1899 Ill. Laws 131.

The law should therefore invest the judge with vast discretionary powers, enabling him to choose the nature and duration of the measure in terms of these needs, as well as to adapt the measure from time to time in accordance with their evolution. Once found guilty of an offence (whatever it might be), a youth might become a ward of the court until the age of majority and the judge could take new measures at any time during this period, even in the absence of any new offence. The need to adapt the initial measure or to adopt new measures would be dictated by the evolution of the child's need for protection.

As for procedural safeguards, they appeared inconsistent with the child welfare approach. Why should one grant a child some rights that would enable him to protect himself against interventions that were viewed as required in his own interest? The situation appeared quite different from that which existed under classical criminal law, where the State intervenes to punish the offender. In so doing, the State, in a way, puts itself in the position of an aggressor. The legitimacy of its intervention requires that the limitations of the right to punish be clearly established. This is done by various means, including rules of procedure enabling every citizen accused of an offence to protect him/her against the possibility of an unjust punishment. However, when the State takes the position of protecting the child rather than punishing him/her, the need to guard the child against the intervention of the State through the due process requirements of classical criminal law is viewed as losing its relevance. An informal procedure is preferred, allowing a simple and direct communication between the child and a benevolent judge who is expected to look after the child's interests.

This child welfare approach was viewed as contrary to the practice of ordinary criminal courts, to such an extent that it was deemed necessary to introduce new actors. First, the juvenile court judge should be a fatherly, benevolent and protective figure. He should be selected for his human qualities and his ability to understand children and communicate with them. He should be assisted by a probation officer, whose role would be to carry out assessments and supervise the child in his/her family, in the same spirit as that expected from the judge.

It would be a mistake to assume that this child welfare model was adopted to the same extent in all countries that created juvenile courts. Some legislators endorsed the idea of a separate jurisdiction to hear children's cases, without going as far as introducing the specialised juvenile court judge and his paternal approach. England and France stand as examples of such countries. In contrast, the laws of Canada, Belgium and many US States may be quoted as examples of welfare-oriented legislation. Whether a country opted for the welfare model or not had significant repercussions on the legal rights children were granted.

Those three decades that were the starting point of juvenile justice were followed by three decades of consolidation.

2.3. THE CONSOLIDATION OF JUVENILE JUSTICE (1930–1960)

9. Briefly, the consolidation of juvenile justice in that period occurred in three ways. First, some juvenile courts were effectively put in place in some areas where legislation, passed in the previous period, had given governments the power to establish such courts but where that power had not been exerted and the actual implementation of the juvenile courts was not realised yet.

Second, laws providing for the establishments of juvenile courts were passed in some countries that were still without such laws. One may quote the examples of Czechoslovakia (1931), Hong Kong (1932) and Italy (1934).

Third, some regimes already in existence were changed so as to bring them closer to a welfare approach. For example, the British Parliament passed a law in 1933 that made greater room for the welfare of the child amongst the considerations that English courts had to bear in mind when making decisions. France went further in transforming its regime in 1945 and 1958, as the children's judge became a key actor in cases of delinquent children as well as children in danger. France then joined the ranks of those countries where the juvenile court judge was viewed as a protector of children.

This period was not one of upheavals, but one of consolidation of the trend initiated at the beginning of the century. The following period was to be somewhat different.

2.4. A PERIOD OF TRANSFORMATION (1960–1990)

10. The three decades starting with the 1960s witnessed changes that went in opposite directions. A first trend can be observed in some European countries, where the welfare approach was reinforced. This was clearly the case for the 1965 Belgian Youth Protection Act, where delinquent children would be dealt with as one of the groups of children in need of protection – a regime that would be criticised later in that period. Portugal also strengthened the welfare approach of its legislation when amending its law in 1962 and 1978. In England and Wales, a strongly child welfare oriented White Paper issued by the Labour government in 1965 was confronted with some opposition and was followed by a second White Paper and the adoption of a law in 1969. Despite the fact that it did not go as far as had been proposed in the initial White Paper, the new law gave a considerable role to the social services and strengthened the child welfare orientation of young offenders policies. Scotland went further in that direction with its 1968 Act that replaced juvenile courts with children's panels that were to examine the situation of children first and foremost in the light of their welfare. Due to lack of space it is not possible to describe in further detail the debates and changes that occurred in those and other countries. However, the point must be made that this was a period where some countries provided a new impetus to the child welfare approach.

At the same time, the United States went in a different direction. Decisions made by its Supreme Court[4] reversed the trend whereby the *parens patriae* doctrine had justified denying juvenile delinquents the due process safeguards enshrined in the US Constitution in favour of accused persons. In 1966, delivering the opinion of the Court in *Kent*, Mr Justice FORTAS expressed the view that "*[w]hile there can be no doubt of the original laudable purpose of juvenile courts, studies and critiques in recent years raise serious questions as to whether actual performance measures well enough against theoretical purpose to make tolerable the immunity of the process from the reach of constitutional guaranties applicable to adults. [...] There is evidence, in fact, that there may be grounds for concern that the child receives the worst of both worlds: that he gets neither the protections accorded to adults nor the solicitous care and regenerative treatment postulated for children*".[5] These Supreme Court decisions created a shockwave. They outlawed the informal procedures that the *parens patriae* doctrine had legitimised for over a century, thus compelling the various States to review their laws and the courts to change their practice so as to grant children and adolescents the rights inherent to criminal procedure. More than a mere legal change, this required a change in mentalities. However, these decisions applied only to delinquency cases, not to child protection cases. This resulted in the introduction of a clear distinction between delinquency and child protection cases, a distinction that had remained foreign to juvenile court philosophy until then.

11. Another tidal wave struck in the 1970s, when growing disenchantment with rehabilitation undermined the belief that institutions and other rehabilitation programmes could be successful in preventing recidivism amongst offenders. The image of MARTINSON's "Nothing works" had struck the minds of many.[6] Its impact

---

4 See particularly *Kent v. United States*, 383 US 541 (1966); *In Re Gault*, 387 US 1 (1967); *In Re Winship*, 397 US 358 (1970).

5 *Kent v. United States*, 383 US 541 (1966), at p. 556.

6 Amongst various works, the position of MARTINSON and his colleagues was expressed in: R. MARTINSON, 'What works? Questions and answers about prison reform', (1974) 35 *The Public Interest*, 22–54; D. LIPTON, R. MARTINSON and J. WILKS, *The Effectiveness of Correctional Treatment: A Survey of Treatment Evaluation Studies*, (New York: Praeger, 1975).

could be all the more important since some rehabilitation programmes had often required longer-term placements than would have been justified from a punishment perspective, thus imposing serious restrictions on the freedom of some offenders. The neoclassical ideas put forward by criminologists such as WILSON and VAN DEN HAAG[7] converged with those who thought that justice should punish and deter rather than rehabilitate. Young offenders ought to be treated more like adults. Some proposed to abolish the juvenile court altogether. In the political arena, these ideas found an audience amongst conservatives who wanted more punitive sanctions for offenders and liberals who felt that rehabilitative purposes could lead to abuses. Consequentially, those with a liberal persuasion joined by those with a more conservative critic moved away from the *parens patriae* ideology: the former wanted the legal protections afforded by criminal law, whereas the latter wanted its punitive philosophy. The very legitimacy of the welfare model was challenged.

Reference is often made to the United States when discussing concerns about the rights of juvenile offenders during that period. Similar attention was paid to the same issue in other countries – sometimes fostered by the debates occurring in the United States. This was reflected in the legislation of some countries such as Australia, where laws passed as of 1979 placed a new emphasis on procedural safeguards. This occurred in Canada as well, where the adoption of the Young Offenders Act in 1982 showed a concern for protecting the rights of young offenders while still maintaining their education and rehabilitation as a central goal. Punishment and rights were not linked any more. Like other legally incompetent persons – such as the mentally ill – young people were now viewed as having the right to oppose interventions of the State in their lives, even if this could be construed as being against their interest. Contrary to the view that had prevailed in earlier decades, these two elements were not defined as incompatible anymore. Furthermore, limits were set to the power of intervention of the State through a tempered use of the principle of proportionality and restrictions to the power to increase the degree of intervention in the name of the interest of the young offender;[8] the offence was reintroduced as a significant element in the decision-making process, alongside the offender who remained at the very heart of concerns. In various other ways that cannot be described due to lack of space, this legislation aimed at reaching a delicate equilibrium blending positive elements of the child welfare model and legal safeguards associated with classical criminal law. In a similar way, one could also refer to the case of Spain, where changes introduced in the Constitution in 1978 extended procedural and other legal safeguards to all Spanish people, including

[7] See particularly: J.Q. WILSON, *Thinking about Crime*, (New York: Vintage Books, 1975); E. VAN DEN HAAG, *Punishing Criminals: Concerning a Very Old and Painful Question*, (New York: Basic Books, 1975).

[8] In Canada, the presence of these limits in the Young Offenders Act was clarified by the Supreme Court. See *R.* v. *M.(J.J.)*, [1993] 2 S.C.R. 421.

children. The courts had to apply a welfare-oriented juvenile law while taking into account the new requirements of the Constitution. This led to the adoption of a law that formally introduced procedural safeguards in juvenile law in 1992, without rejecting other aspects of the welfare model. (Other changes would have to wait until 2000).

This period is therefore one of various and partly opposite trends. Whereas some countries strengthened their adhesion to the welfare model, others moved some distance from it, while others stood in between. Safeguarding the rights of children became a major issue in many countries, even when important elements of the welfare model were to be maintained. The major poles of the decision-making process evolved, as the respective weights of the offence and the offender changed – with some significant differences between countries. The legitimacy of the restrictions imposed on the freedom of young offenders was questioned, especially when they involved custodial measures.

2.5. CURRENT TRENDS

12. In his study of the British and the US penal policies of the last decades, GARLAND suggests some indices of the major changes that occurred in that period.[9] Some of them are particularly relevant for us to understand current trends in juvenile justice debates. A summary follows:

- Rehabilitation that has been the overarching ideology of the system has fallen from grace. Punitive sanctions that aim at expressing public anger and resentment towards crime have reappeared both in official discourse and policies, and what purports to be the "expression of public sentiment" has frequently taken priority over the professional judgment of penological experts.
- A change has occurred in the emotional tone of crime policy. Confidence in progressive, humane and rational policies showing compassion for the needs and rights of the less fortunate has given way to a discourse where the fear of crime has come to have a new salience. Crime has been re-dramatised and the background "affect" of policy is now more frequently a collective anger and righteous demand for retribution.
- The victim has returned to centre stage in criminal justice policy. The interests and feelings of victims are routinely invoked in support of punitive measures. The symbolic figure of the victim has taken on a life of its own, and plays a role in

[9] D. GARLAND, *The culture of control: Crime and social order in contemporary society*, (Chicago: University of Chicago Press, 2001), 6–20.

political debate and policy argument that is often quite detached from the claims of the organised victims' movement, or the aggregated opinions of surveyed victims.[10]

- Protecting the public has become the dominant theme of penal policy. Amongst other things, this involves a relaxation of concern about the civil liberties of suspects and the rights of prisoners, as well as a new emphasis upon effective enforcement and control. The call for protection *from* the State has been increasingly displaced by the demand for protection *by* the State.
- The policy-making process has become profoundly politicised and populist. Crime policy has ceased to be a matter that can be devolved to professional experts and has become a prominent issue in electoral competition. Politicians claim the authority of "the people", of common sense, of "getting back to basics". A narrowing of debate and a convergence of the policy proposals of major parties have resulted in a political consensus around penal measures that are perceived as tough, smart and popular with the public, which has moved the centre of political gravity in that direction.
- New management styles and working practices have emerged. For example, probation and parole agencies have de-emphasised their social work ethos and instead present themselves as providers of inexpensive, community-based punishments, oriented towards the monitoring of offenders and the management of risk. Sentencing is less a discretionary art of individualised dispositions and is moving towards a more rigid application of penalty guidelines and mandatory sentences.
- A perpetual sense of crisis has beset the field. The system's failings – such as crime and recidivism rates – are less easily attributed to implementation problems; rather they are interpreted as evidence of theory failure, as signs that crime control is based upon an institutional model that is inappropriate for its task.

GARLAND's examination of penal policies focuses on Britain and the United Sates and is by no means restricted to the field of juvenile justice. Yet, it conveys a general background that exists in other countries as well and against which juvenile justice policies are designed. Perhaps the politicisation of youth crime issues has appeared the most visible of those elements as far as youth justice policies are concerned; this has been a salient trend in France, Canada, the United States and other countries.

13. Just as they had embraced the welfare model with an enthusiasm that went far beyond that of many other countries at the beginning of the twentieth century, the United States seems to have withdrawn its support for it more than several others. A

---

[10] Obviously, GARLAND does not refer here to the restorative justice movement.

review[11] of laws adopted by various US States between 1992 and 1995 shows that more than 90% of them revised their laws concerning juvenile crime, often after a period of intense political rhetoric that compelled action in order to "curb juvenile violence". These laws involved increased transfers to adult criminal courts and a greater use of adult sentences. The underlying intent was to punish, hold accountable and incarcerate for longer periods offenders who have gone beyond a threshold of tolerated "juvenile" criminal behaviour, particularly those convicted of violent offences. In many instances, accountability was defined as punishment, or a period of incarceration, with less attention paid to the activities to be accomplished during that incarceration. Mandatory minimum sentences, sentencing guidelines, and extended jurisdiction were intended not only to hold an offender accountable, however, also to incapacitate an offender for an extended period. Emphasis was placed on residential (often secure) placement of offenders convicted of serious and violent offences, without comparable attention aimed at community corrections. Information concerning some juvenile offenders became less confidential than before. The use of juvenile records for criminal prosecution, information sharing with schools, and public awareness of juvenile criminal behaviour and its consequences were all intended to "tighten the web" of information around some offenders. Judicial waivers, the primary mechanism for transferring jurisdiction of a violent or other serious juvenile case to the criminal courts in the past, was weakened and shared more broadly by the prosecutor and the direct action of the legislature. This shift in authority went with the sentiment (in particular amongst an ill-informed public) that juvenile court judges are too "soft" on juvenile crime and that non-judicial decisions are more likely to achieve the goal of holding serious offenders accountable.

In brief, the trend was to transfer more youths to adult courts and, for those who are not waived, to make juvenile justice more like adult criminal justice. Much of the change resulted from public perceptions of an escalation of violent juvenile crime and the accompanying political reaction to that perception. The necessity was to "do something", and in most instances the changes were not based on evidence that clearly demonstrated the efficacy of the intervention. The assumption is that juvenile justice is not efficient in dealing with serious juvenile crime, whereas the efficiency of adult criminal justice is taken for granted.

This trend is by no means limited to the United States. For example, the Canadian Federal Parliament changed its law relating to young offenders in 2002. This followed

---

11 P. Torbet, R. Gable, H. Hurst IV, I. Montgomery, L. Szymanski and D. Thomas, *State Responses to Serious and Violent Juvenile Crime*, (Pittsburgh: National Center for Juvenile Justice, 1996), 59–61; H.N. Snyder and M. Sickmund, *Juvenile Offenders and Victims: 1999 National Report*, (Washington: National Center for Juvenile Justice, 1999), chapter 4, <http://www.ncjrs.org/>.

a few years of debate that originated in the election campaign of 1993 where right-wing politicians who wanted a tougher law pilloried the 1982 Young Offenders Act. Without going as far as some US laws, the new Canadian Act[12] places the offence and its seriousness at the heart of the decision-making process thus reducing the interest of the offender. Making young offenders accountable for their offences has become central. While it supports rehabilitation in principle, it sets obstacles that are likely to make it more difficult to reach that goal in some cases. The principle of proportionality centred on the seriousness of the offence has precedence over the need for rehabilitation and some other considerations. A distinction is made between violent offences (not violent offenders) and other offences to lead to different treatments for the two groups of offenders. Reparation and restitution to the victim are encouraged. Adult sentences for young offenders are facilitated, particularly through a presumption that an adult sentence should be imposed upon offenders aged 14 or over who are charged with very serious offences or were found guilty of certain offences in the past.

In brief, this Act retains a law that is specific to minors, but it makes it more akin to adult criminal law than was the case before. The child welfare model is clearly kept at distance.[13] The very title of the Act is a good indicator: *Youth Criminal Justice Act.*

14. Recent debates and revisions of youth justice laws are by no means limited to North America. In England, for example, the dual care/crime jurisdiction of the juvenile court that dated back to the early twentieth century ended in 1991 when the Children Act of 1989 entered into force. A separate care jurisdiction was created in the family proceedings court, leaving the juvenile court (later renamed as Youth Court) to deal exclusively with criminal cases. The orientation of the youth justice system has fairly changed, particularly by the Crime and Disorder Act of 1998 and the Youth Justice and Criminal Evidence Act of 1999, under the impulse of a Labour government that meant to be "tough on crime and tough on the causes of crime". This orientation included the following four key principles highlighted by BOTTOMS and DIGNAN.[14] The principal aim of youth justice is the prevention of offending by children and young persons, notably through effective early intervention and the intensive supervision of persistent offenders. Greater attention must be given to reparation in sentencing. Greater efficiency must be pursued in the use of the resources of the youth justice

---

12 *Youth Criminal Justice Act*, Statutes of Canada, 2002, Chapter 1.

13 For more information on the Canadian 2002 Act, see for example J. TRÉPANIER, 'Les transformations du régime canadien visant les jeunes contrevenants: les frontières de la justice des mineurs en mutation', (2005) 85 *Revue de droit pénal et de criminologie*, 559–602; A.N. DOOB and J. B. SPROTT, 'Youth justice in Canada, in M. TONRY and A. N. DOOB (eds.), supra (note 2), 185–242.

14 A. BOTTOMS and J. DIGNAN, 'Youth Justice in Great Britain', in M. TONRY and A. N. DOOB (eds.), supra (note 2), 21–183, at 41–43. For more information on the English and Scottish systems, one may consult this excellent presentation by BOTTOMS and DIGNAN.

system, including by the speeding up of case processing. New emphasis on responsibilisation means that young offenders must not be excused but rather take responsibility for their actions and that parents must face up to their responsibilities for their children's offending behaviour. In contrast to what occurred in England, the evolution of the children's hearings in Scotland has led to no major change; Scotland can be seen as an example where the welfare model has remained constant for several decades.

15. Other countries from outside the realm of the common law also carried out revisions of their legislation. The most recent case is that of Belgium, where the long lasting review of the Youth Protection Act of 1965 led to the adoption of an Act by the Belgian Parliament in May 2006. One may also quote the case of Portugal, where a review of the two laws dealing respectively with children in danger and young offenders were reviewed in the last few years with a restraint and an equilibrium from which other countries might very well draw some inspiration. In France, the adoption of new legal provisions has occurred in the context of highly politicised debates on security (which are still going on), where youth – often immigrant youth – and violence are very often associated.

16. One of the changes that are present in a number of countries is the new emphasis placed on reparation. This trend should attract attention for it may help juvenile justice to leave behind such debates where the poles of discussion are too often defined in terms of repression and welfare. In the same way as adult criminal justice, juvenile justice has tended to consider that the cases that were brought to its consideration involved essentially an individual actor – the offender – and a collective one, society. In that context, victims were forgotten except when the justice system needed them as witnesses to help in condemning the offender. Emerging from experiments in the 1980s, the restorative justice movement expanded in the 1990s, largely due to the crisis of legitimacy of the rehabilitation ideal and the incapacity of punishment to fill the resulting gap.[15] Restorative justice proposes to re–introduce the victim as one of the principal actors in defining what the solution ought to be to the problem created by the offence. Emphasis is no more on the offence as a symptom of an underlying pathology or as the violation of social norm that would require a punishment, but on the harm caused by the illegal act, that must be repaired. Mediation and conciliation appear the processes that ought to be privileged to reach that aim, although there may also be some room for the judicial process. Various possible forms of reparation must be considered, including the expression of excuses. The goal of restorative measures is not as such to educate the youth with regard to their responsibilities; however, it may nonetheless carry this result. In that sense, these measures can be viewed not only

[15] See for example L. WALGRAVE, 'Restoration in Youth Justice', in M. TONRY and A. N. DOOB (eds.), supra (note 2), 543– 597.

as a way to hold youths accountable for their acts – a way that appears far more positive than punishment – however, also as a way to induce greater responsibility in youths, to educate them to become more responsible people. So far, the extent to which restorative justice has been integrated in national legislation is somewhat limited and varies from one country to another. New Zealand stands amongst the pioneers with its 1989 Children, Young Persons and Their Families Act, which formally introduced family group conferences that may not have been planned as a restorative justice experiment in the first place; however, that "is now commonly presented as an example of restorative justice in practice".[16]

However, promising restorative justice may be positive, if it is used as extensively as it should be. One should be sensitive to the need to ensure proper legal safeguards. Such processes as conciliation and mediation lead to negotiated justice, where the parties must reach an agreement about the solution to their problem. The protection of rights has to be viewed differently from the way it is approached in a judicial setting and it must be adapted accordingly. This dimension should not be forgotten.

Therefore, even though one may not conclude that present times witness trends that all go in the same direction, it remains that their most striking features are characterised by a greater detachment from the welfare approach and a return to orientations that are more akin to those of classical criminal law. In the context where youth justice issues are politicised more than ever, simple solutions that appeal to public feelings are likely to lead to greater re-penalisation of youth justice. One of the results of this re-penalisation is that it should involve ensuring the legal safeguards of criminal law for accused and condemned persons. However, it should be kept in mind that, as was seen in the previous period, such re-penalisation is by no means a condition for granting such safeguards that can be offered in the context of other orientations.

3. THE CONVENTION ON THE RIGHTS OF THE CHILD AND OTHER UNITED NATIONS INSTRUMENTS

17. United Nations instruments aimed at children have been in force for a long time. As early as 1924, the League of Nations adopted the Declaration of Children's Rights that can be viewed as the ancestor of the Convention on the Rights of the Child. It was followed by the UN Declaration of the Rights of the Child in 1959. Yet, the period 1985–1990 was more important than any other was as far as instruments relevant to

[16] A. Morris, 'Youth Justice in New Zealand', in M. Tonry and A.N. Doob (eds.), supra (note 2), 259.

juvenile justice are concerned. Besides the Convention itself, adopted in 1989 and entered into force in 1990, we must note the Minimum Rules for the Administration of Juvenile Justice (the Beijing Rules, 1985), the Guidelines for the Prevention of Juvenile Delinquency (the Riyadh Guidelines, 1990) and the Rules for the Protection of Juveniles Deprived of their Liberty (the Havana Rules, 1990). More recent guidelines issued by the Economic and Social Council complement these instruments, whose orientation they share: the Guidelines for Action on Children in the Criminal Justice System (1997) and the Guidelines on Justice in Matters involving Child Victims and Witnesses of Crime (2005).

Thus, the major instruments were prepared and adopted between 1985 and 1990, at a time when juvenile justice was being repositioned in a number of countries; the welfare model still had its place but was tempered by a clear concern for the rights of young persons. The impact of the politicisation of issues that has been present in more recent times was little felt. Then a question that may be asked is whether these instruments are a reflection of the times in which they were produced, that is the period when juvenile justice underwent important transformations, before the presence of recent trends could be felt however. This question may be examined by having a look at some of the most significant provisions that are likely to provide relevant indices: procedural safeguards, protection against restrictions to liberty and the major criteria against which juvenile justice decisions must be made. Other aspects would have been both relevant and interesting to take into consideration; however, space limitations do not allow us to discuss them here.

3.1. PROCEDURAL SAFEGUARDS

18. As mentioned above, the welfare model questioned the relevance of granting children procedural safeguards that would enable them to protect themselves against interventions that were viewed as required in their own interest. By the 1980s, the legislation of a number of countries had put into question that approach and granted children due process rights, while still retaining some of the key elements of the welfare model. The Convention on the Rights of the Child and the other UN instruments share that orientation. However benevolent the motivations leading to interventions may be, the latter can be legitimate only if their necessity is established in a process where the youth is granted normal procedural rights. Granting such rights does not require the State to take a punitive stance. The mere fact that the State intervenes in the lives of youths – and possibly their family – is sufficient to require such safeguards. The rights to freedom and privacy are values that must be protected, even against benevolent interventions.

19. The principle of procedural safeguards is established in the Convention (Art. 40) and the Beijing Rules (Rule 7.1). The Convention embodies such specific rights as those for the youth or child:

- not to be accused of having infringed the penal law by reason of acts or omissions that were not prohibited by national or international law;
- to be presumed innocent until proven guilty according to law;
- to be informed of the charges against him or her;
- to have legal or other appropriate assistance in the preparation and presentation of his or her defence;
- to have the matter determined without delay by a competent, independent and impartial authority or judicial body in a fair hearing according to law, in the presence of legal or other appropriate assistance (including his or her parents);
- not to be compelled to give testimony or to confess guilt;
- to examine adverse witnesses and to obtain the participation and examination of witnesses on his or her behalf under conditions of equality;
- to have the decisions as to conviction and disposition reviewed on appeal;
- to have the free assistance of an interpreter if needed;
- to have his or her privacy fully respected at all stages of the proceedings.

The Beijing Rules add that the proceedings should be conducive to the best interests of the juvenile and be conducted in an atmosphere of understanding, to allow the juvenile to participate and to express her or himself freely (Rule 14.2).

20. Thus, in line with national legislation adopted at the same time in some countries, the UN instruments aim at ensuring for children normal procedural safeguards, while at the same time adapting the procedure to create a climate allowing children to express themselves and participate, without the publicity existing in adult cases.

3.2. PROTECTION AGAINST RESTRICTIONS TO LIBERTY

21. Some of the measures that courts can impose may involve significant restrictions on the liberty of children and youths. Custodial measures are the most symbolic and most effective in that respect. In the pure welfare model of the first part of the twentieth century, limiting the powers of the courts to impose measures restricting children's freedom did not appear desirable. Such measures were defined as helping children, not as restricting their liberty. They were less viewed as interfering with the value of freedom than as serving another value – the interests of the child. The latter was the dominant value, to which freedom had to yield. As the ability of rehabilitation measures to prevent recidivism was contested in the 1970s, the legitimacy of such measures was even more questioned as they involved deprivations of liberty. Thus, it was felt that restrictions to freedom had to be limited to the minimum. The UN instruments were designed precisely at the time of those debates and they bear the mark of those concerns. They affirm the value of liberty much more clearly than would have been the case some years earlier.

Such affirmation is at the foundation of various provisions. It touches upon Rules regarding the detention of juveniles awaiting trial. The Rules for the Protection of Juveniles Deprived of their Liberty provide that, as juveniles are presumed innocent at that particular stage of the proceedings; their detention must "be avoided to the extent possible and limited to exceptional circumstances". All efforts must "be made to apply alternative measures" and proceedings must be expeditious "to ensure the shortest possible duration of detention" (Rule 17). At the stage of disposition, restrictions on liberty should "be imposed only after careful consideration and [should] be limited to the possible minimum". Placements in institutions should "always be a disposition of last resort and for the minimum necessary period" (Beijing Rules 17.1 and 19.1). Another rule points to the same direction: that which requires that no juvenile should "be removed from parental supervision [...] unless the circumstances of her or his case make this necessary" (Beijing Rule 18.2). Placements must be limited not only because they involve restrictions to freedom, but also because they are likely to sever the links between children and their families, a situation that must be avoided as much as possible.

This way of approaching restrictions to liberty is consistent with the vision that prevailed in the 1980s. The welfare model was questioned in as much as it had been used to justify interventions in the lives of children and families that, sometimes, were abusive. In the wider context where many raised the question as to whether it was legitimate to deprive minors of rights that were granted to adults, it was felt that an educative or welfare approach could be endorsed only if it were not used to justify excessive interventions. Limiting measures through the concept of minimal intervention seemed to be an acceptable way to reconcile the educative or welfare approach with the concern for the rights of children that characterised that period. The earlier conception of the welfare model where the concern of protecting children overrode that of protecting their rights was abandoned. Moreover, today's trends that lead some to support a re-penalisation of juvenile justice policies had not gained yet the strength they have now. Thus, the orientation of UN instruments seems to bear the mark of the era during which they were conceived.

3.3. CRITERIA FOR THE CHOICE OF DISPOSITIONS: THE OFFENCE, THE OFFENDER, THE VICTIM AND SOCIETY

22. It is generally admitted that, amongst the factors that courts must consider in sentencing adult criminals, the seriousness of the offence is by far the most important. The principle of proportionality according to which "the punishment must fit the crime" is a cardinal principle in criminal law. With the advent of the welfare model at the beginning of the twentieth century, juvenile justice changed the balance between the factors the courts had to consider. The offender and his or her situation moved to the forefront of attention, in the perspective of better protecting society. In this context, little space was left for the offence and the victim. In the 1970s, as the capacity of rehabilitative measures to prevent recidivism was challenged, the weight of the offence as a factor influencing decisions increased. For some, the doubts cast on rehabilitation led to the position that juvenile offenders had to be punished, and this was to be in proportion to the seriousness of the offence, as in adult criminal law. For others, welfare-oriented measures had to be retained, but the degree of intervention (not punishment) was not to exceed what could be justified based on the seriousness of the offence. The principle of proportionality could be used to limit the degree of an educative or welfare intervention – and it could be applied with lesser rigour than was the case in adult criminal law. This latter position meant that educative and welfare measures could be encouraged, however their use had to be tempered through limits borrowed from criminal law. Recently, this hybridisation of welfare and criminal justice approaches would see its importance reduced. Making young offenders accountable for their offences would become paramount. This would make juvenile justice policies more akin to those of adult criminal justice. Where do the UN instruments stand in that respect?

Beijing Rule no. 17.1 provides that dispositions must "always be in proportion not only to the circumstances and the gravity of the offence but also to the circumstances and the needs of the juvenile as well as to the needs of society", and that the "well-being of the juvenile [must] be the guiding factor in the consideration of her or his case". This Rule, which is part of a specific section on "Guiding principles in adjudication and disposition", is a re-affirmation of another disposition entitled "Aims of juvenile justice", according to which the "juvenile justice system shall emphasise the well-being of the juvenile and shall ensure that any reaction to juvenile offenders shall always be in proportion to the circumstances of both the offenders and the offence" (Rule 5.1). Two observations emerge from these provisions. First, The Beijing Rules define the principle of proportionality not only in terms of the seriousness of the offence, but also according to the circumstances and needs of the juvenile and the needs of society.

This involves a re-formulation of the principle of proportionality with three poles instead of one. First, the offender and society are added to the offence. Second, the well-being of the juvenile is presented as "the guiding factor in the consideration of her or his case". Therefore, it is clear that the underpinning model is one that leaves considerable space for the welfare of the youth, and where the offender's accountability for his or her act(s) is not the paramount consideration. Here, we have a hybrid model that retains essential elements of the welfare model while granting the offence a weight that the same welfare model used to reject. Clearly, the UN instruments do not endorse the most recent trends that go in the direction of a greater re-penalisation of juvenile justice policies; instead, they appear much more in line with the views that prevailed in the 1980s, when they were adopted.

What about the victims? Are they part of the picture? The answer is yes. Beijing Rule 11.4 encourages the use of restitution and compensation of victims in diversion practices. The commentary on Rule 5.1 mentions the youth's endeavour to indemnify the victim amongst the factors to be considered when deciding on a case. Furthermore, the UN Declaration of Basic Principles of Justice for Victims of Crime and Abuse of Power (adopted in 1985) emphasises the need for ensuring proper compensation and redress for victims, as well as adequate processes to reach this aim.[17] Victims are presented as being entitled to reparation, not as claiming vengeance and more punishment for delinquents. Clearly the UN instruments bear the mark of that movement that re-affirmed actively in the 1980s the need for the justice system to take into account the rights and needs of victims and to repair the consequences of delinquent acts. This movement gained further notoriety in the 1990s with the development of restorative justice. It can offer a positive version of making offenders accountable for the consequences of their acts – certainly more so than by punishing them.

4. CONCLUSION

23. After a journey of over a century, juvenile justice is now different from what it was at its inception. Even when taking into account the diversity of national legislations, it remains that the welfare model was very influential in shaping juvenile justice in most countries at one time or another. Yet the criticisms this model met with led many countries to temper its potential abuses, especially through reintroducing into juvenile justice some protections and safeguards traditionally offered by criminal

---

[17] See in particular sections 4, 5 and 7–9 of the Declaration. In the absence of any indication that it should apply only to cases involving adults, this Declaration must be interpreted as applying to juvenile cases as well.

law. These changes, characteristic of the 1970s and 1980s were followed by more recent trends that go in the direction of greater re-penalisation of juvenile justice policies. Some questions were asked throughout the whole century and they are still present in today's debates: should we be more concerned with the welfare of young offenders, their rehabilitation, their education or their punishment? Should we aim at deterring, incapacitating or repairing the consequences of offences? How should the rights of the parties involved – notably offenders and victims – be safeguarded?

The orientations of the UN instruments bring a qualified answer to these questions. They aim at reconciling perspectives that were viewed as irreconcilable during several decades; however, as the legislation of some countries showed in the 1970s and 1980s, such perspectives can be brought together. According to the initial welfare model, juveniles could not be granted rights that were perceived as undesirable obstacles to interventions that those juveniles needed for their own interests. The perspective endorsed in the UN instruments is one where a person should be given the means to oppose an intervention that he or she does not want, even if that intervention is perceived as being in his or her own interest. Such interventions should occur only to the extent they are actually necessary, and the rights of juveniles should be restricted as minimally as possible. There is no need to re-criminalise juvenile justice orientations and punish offenders to grant rights to those who are subjected to its interventions.

The main instruments of the UN relevant to juvenile justice bear the mark of a vision that prevailed in the 1980s, that is, when they were designed and adopted. Then, perhaps, it could be asked if these instruments should not be updated in order to reflect recent trends that were observed in some of the debates and national legislation over the last few years. We would suggest that the answer to that question should be negative. Certainly current trends do not include only setbacks. The progress of restorative justice is an important achievement that should be consolidated and amplified. Already present in the previous period, the concern to restore and repair the consequences of the offence is now affirmed with greater strength. This offers juvenile justice a path other than those between which it has wavered over the years, that is the welfare/educative and the criminal justice models. On the other hand, the re-criminalisation of juvenile justice and the increased blurring of the border between the juvenile and adult criminal justice systems offer no useful avenue for juvenile justice, especially when they occur in a context where issues are politicised and where privileged solutions are brought into line with a populist discourse. One does not have to be anti-democratic to observe that election campaigns are not the best of all forums to make choices about penal policies. The public is all too often deluded by persons who hold up the bogeyman of crime waves (without demonstrating their existence) and make them believe that fast and simple solutions exist for problems that are as complex as crime and delinquency. A balanced approach such as adopted in the UN instruments is by far preferable. Perhaps – and hopefully – it may provide a model whose inspiration might provide some counterbalance to some of our current fads.

BUILDING A BRIDGE BETWEEN PSYCHOLOGY AND LAW: THE CRIMINAL AND CIVIL LIABILITY AGE LIMITS AND THE CHILD'S COGNITIVE AND MORAL DEVELOPMENT

NUNO FERREIRA

1. INTRODUCTION

1. Article 3(1) of the United Nations Convention on the Rights of the Child elects the *best interests of the child* as (at least) one of the main and more important criteria to be used whenever deciding a measure regarding a child. Most important is also the fact that this criterion should be followed by the *courts of law* as well, which is not at all meaningless: courts of law should not be blind to the special conditions of the person sitting behind the bench, namely and more importantly, their *age*. Children are a kind of defendant whose age demands for a particular consideration for his/her present childhood conditions and future perspectives. Besides that, Article 40 of the same convention states that when a child is accused of having infringed the *penal law*, the following priorities should be observed (which, we believe, are *equally valid*, with the necessary adaptations, for the infringement of *civil law*):

i. promote the child's sense of dignity and worth;
ii. reinforce the child's respect for human rights and fundamental freedoms of others;
iii. take into account the child's age;
iv. promote the child's reintegration and assumption of a constructive role in society.

These standards of protection are further supported by other international human rights documents, among which, the Universal Declaration of Human Rights (Article 25(2): the entitlement of childhood to "special care and assistance"), the UN Standard Minimum Rules for the Administration of Juvenile Justice ("The Beijing Rules"), and the UN Guidelines for the Prevention of Juvenile Delinquency ("The Riyadh Guidelines").

Despite these internationally recognised and consensual rules, the sanctioning or compensatory aims of the legal systems of many countries still disregard them and stipulate very low ages for standing criminal charges or even no age limit whatsoever for the duty of civil compensation, which undoubtedly is not up to the requirements set in the above rules. The practice of a criminally punishable or civilly wrongful act by minors can, in many countries, lead to their condemnation to several years of imprisonment beside adults or to the payment of high amounts of damages, leading to their life-long lack of professional training and education, psychological and social ineptness, as well as economic plight and premature financial indebtedness.

2. Repressive tendencies and security trends very often overshadow sensible and adequate social, educational and legal policies. Youth justice has followed different models since it was created. From a retributive model, which aimed at penalising the child for what he/she had done, we moved to a re-educational model, which tried to re-socialise the child. More recently, youth justice systems have been adopting a new model, the reparation-reconciliation (or mediation) model: the focus is now placed on giving the child the possibility to repair and solve the conflict caused and the damage provoked.[1] Which option better promotes the voluntary and spontaneous respect for the norms by children? What can justify one perspective or the other? What can give sufficient grounds to a legislator to lower the criminal or civil liability age? What constitutes a good argument for children's rights activists to claim for the increasing[2] of such age limits? If law is supposed to regulate people's lives in society, in order to render them the most peaceful and fulfilling as possible, then lawyers should be able to leave their own complex and intricate small world and investigate the object of their work: people's lives themselves. Only in that way is one able to actually make valid and meaningful proposals for improving the law. Therefore, we tried to find some answers in the children's lives, more precisely, in their psychological development. When do children truly gain awareness of the consequences of their acts? When do they become able to make valid, long-term judgments and analysis? When do they grasp such concepts as 'guilt', 'punishment', 'shame' and 'conformity'? Several authors have studied the moral development of children, among whom we can point out ERIKSON and KOHLBERG, experts of the child's different moral stages and sense of justice. More recently, other authors have disputed the accuracy of these theories and have suggested some changes thereto or completely new ones. This area of knowledge is immensely precious to allow us to understand how a child's cognitive

---

1 S. ABBRUZZESE, 'Un giudice del cambiamento', (1996) 4 *Minori Giustizia*, 69–75, especially 73–74.

2 Curiously enough, children's rights activists in Thailand have contested a governmental bill which aimed at increasing the criminal age from 8 to 13, claiming that it could encourage children to commit crimes (knowing that they would not be punished) and adults to exploit children in criminal activities. See A. CHAROENPO, "Analysis/ Crime and youth – Coming of criminal age", <http://www.bangkokpost.com/ /270104_news/27jan2004_opin25.html>.

and moral development may influence their ability to stand responsible before the law.

In this search for precious contributions from psychology and sociology to this legal field, one cannot lose sight of the fact that jurists should be critical in accepting the results of scientific research as having universal validity. In fact, there has been an abusive use of scientific research, namely in the USA, in order to support results that the legal policy-makers identify themselves ideologically with, even if other plausible interpretations could have been deduced from the data.[3] Since much research is not entirely neutral, its use by commentators is not either. But although social sciences cannot offer all the answers, they can, nevertheless, help in discussing the limits and contents of legal regulation or the good sense of a political option. We will then take psychological and sociological research as an additional material to be carefully used in conjunction with other data, to model or question the legal policy in this field.[4]

2. CONTRIBUTION FROM TWENTIETH CENTURY PSYCHOLOGY

3. The main issue that we will concentrate on in this paper is how the psychological evolution of minors relates to the possibility of holding them liable for the damage they may cause. This amounts to assessing how the capacity of a minor of *consciously* and *willingly* committing a wrongful act changes throughout his/her development. When does the child acquire the capacity to *understand* and *want* a certain act?[5] We aim at taking into account what psychology and sociology have studied, researched, discovered and concluded in the field of child development. This can prove to be essential to us, as far as it can provide us with many interesting and crucial answers. When do children start realising the danger of their behaviour, be it in general terms, and be it in specific situations? When do they acquire the ability to adjust their behaviour?

---

3 M.L. FINEMAN and A. OPIE, 'The uses of social science data in legal policymaking: Custody determinations at divorce', (1987) 1 *Wisconsin Law Review*, 107–158, especially 124–125, 156–157.

4 Ibid.

5 Traditionally, to consider someone liable for the damages caused for fault, it has to be proved that he/she acted consciously and willingly. The specific importance of distinguishing both elements of fault in our subject theme lies in the fact that very often adolescents are conscious of the act (as well as its wrongfulness), but are not able to determine their behaviour so as to avoid it. See, in this sense, L. PEPINO, 'Chi ha paura della non imputabilità minorile?', (1996) 4 *Minori Giustizia*, 45–53, especially, 47–48.

2.1. THE CONCEPT OF MORAL RESPONSIBILITY

4. Although it may seem an obvious truth, it seems to be forgotten that in many places and occasions children and adults cannot be held responsible in the same way. Responsibility implies freedom and children and adults are not equally free. Freedom and duties mutually determine each other. Furthermore, since there are different degrees of freedom, there have to be different degrees of responsibility. The degree of freedom of children and adults is closely linked with the notions of ability, control, knowledge and autonomy.[6] As the intensity of these elements increases in the personality and behaviour of a person, the degree of freedom that one enjoys increases too. Moral freedom, in particular, can be defined as "the power or ability to form a judgment of the relative goodness and badness of the alternatives possible and of acting in accordance with that judgment".[7] Moral development has, therefore, to do with normative issues concerning what "should be", and not with factual issues concerning what "is".[8] However, authors disagree on how what is fair or not should be defined, what criteria should be used to asses moral development, what are the psychological processes involved in the moral functioning of people and what are the best ways to promote it.

Children have been compared to intuitive moral philosophers.[9] In fact, they develop moral concepts within a process of active search and construction, not simply disclosing previously existing static meanings of ordinary moral language. In fact, "ordinary moral language" simply does not exist.[10] Several psychologists have attempted to elaborate theories which explore the concept of moral responsibility and the development of conceptions of justice. PIAGET worked on the progressive capacity of producing subjective responsibility judgments, whereas HEIDER researched on the attribution of responsibility and KOHLBERG on the theory of moral development. While moral responsibility already answers the question of what it should be, in regard to legal responsibility one can distinguish what it is from what it should be. Therefore,

---

6 K. HELKAMA, *Toward a cognitive-developmental theory of attribution of responsibility – A critical review of empirical research and some preliminary data*, Annales Academiae Scientiarum Fennicae, Dissertationes Humanarum Litterarum 27, Helsinki 1981, Suomalainen Tiedeakatemia, 24.

7 M. GINSBERG, 'The nature of responsibility', in *Essays in sociology and social philosophy*, (London: Penguin, 1968), 344, quoted in K. HELKAMA, supra (note 6), 30.

8 O. M. LOURENÇO, 'Psicologia de desenvolvimento moral – teoria, dados e implicações', 3rd edition, (Coimbra: Almedina, 2002), 37.

9 Research carried out by TURIEL, SCHWEDER and MUCH, quoted in O. M. LOURENÇO, supra (note 8), 74.

10 K. HELKAMA, supra (note 6), 10.

priority should be given to the concept of moral responsibility in determining what legal responsibility should be.[11, 12]

2.2. PIAGET AND THE COGNITIVE DEVELOPMENT OF CHILDREN

5. PIAGET, one of the most renowned psychologists of the twentieth century, constructed what is arguably the most influential theory of child development and learning. PIAGET's theory revolves around the idea that, during the development of a child, he/she builds cognitive structures. These structures consist of networks of concepts, which allow the child to understand and respond to external stimuli provided by the surrounding environment. These structures become increasingly sophisticated throughout the child's development, going from a mere cry to highly complex operations. PIAGET identified four main stages of cognitive development:[13]

1. *Sensorimotor stage (birth – 2 years old)*: The child begins to process the information he/she receives and builds a set of concepts about reality and how it works. He/she does this through physical interaction with his/her environment. During this stage, the child plays with physical objects, but does not know that they remain in existence even when out of sight. Towards the end of this stage, the child gains the capacity for maintaining the mental image of an object or person, even without its actual presence (object permanency).
2. *Preoperational stage (ages 2–7)*: The child does not conceptualise abstractly yet and needs concrete physical situations. He/she develops language rapidly and uses words and images to interact with the environment. The child believes that everyone sees the world the same way that he/she does (Egocentrism). Furthermore, he/she is still unable to understand that quantity does not change if the shape changes (reversibility) and focuses on only one aspect of a stimulus (centration). Towards the end of this stage, the child understands reversibility and already understands that quantity does not change if the shape changes (conservation).

---

11 Ibid., 2.

12 Attention has been drawn to the fact that normative concepts inevitably influence the design and interpretation of the results of the empirical research on children's development of justice conceptions. K. KRISTJÁNSSON has pointed out that research in this field has taken as assumptions normative consideration regarding what is a valid conception of justice or not and which one is better or worse. The author also proposed an alternative research programme that aims at overcoming this problem. See: K. KRISTJÁNSSON, 'The development of justice conceptions and the unavoidability of the normative', (June 2003) 32 (2) *Journal of Moral Education*, 183–194.

13 We follow the text published on the website <http://www.funderstanding.com/piaget.cfm>, which states: "The content on this page was written by On Purpose Associates".

3. *Concrete operations (ages 7–11)*: Thanks to the physical experience that the child collects, he/she starts to conceptualise. He/she creates logical structures that explain his/her physical experiences. The child also gains the capacity to solve abstract problems, such as solving arithmetic equations with numbers instead of objects, but their thinking is still mainly connected to objects rather than abstract ideas. The child has gradually less centristic thinking and increasingly focuses on more than one aspect of a stimulus.
4. *Formal operations (beginning at ages 11–15)*: The cognitive structures of the child are similar to those of an adult, including conceptual reasoning, such as the idea of cause and effect. The child develops a more abstract view of the world and can apply reversibility and conservation to both real and imagined situations.

Throughout the development of the child, he/she uses the mental structures that he/she possesses in order to cope with the experiences offered to him/her by the environment. When the experience is not new, the child fits it into the already existing cognitive structures and maintains a balance. However, if the experience is new, this balance is harmed and the child has to alter the existing cognitive structures in order to fit the new experience. This process enables the child to construct increasingly satisfactory cognitive structures. Although PIAGET believed that all children, from different cultures, went, in the same order, through these stages, he also admitted that the age range from each stage could vary from child to child.[14]

6. Taking this framework as a starting point, PIAGET elaborated a *theory on the development of moral judgment* in his book "The Moral Judgment of the Child", in 1932. The judgment at stake here has morality as its object, morality being understood as the social, prescriptive and normative rules and principles whose respect is asked from everyone. Based on stories which concerned clumsiness, stealing and lying, PIAGET assessed the degree of development of moral judgment in children of different ages. He concluded that[15]:

a) Young children adhere to a notion of *objective responsibility*, which means that they evaluate acts according to their exact material conformity to rules and material consequences and, not to the motives or intentions behind them. This notion of responsibility is characteristic of *moral realism*, i.e. seeing duty as self-subsistent and imposing category, to which individuals have to abide no matter what the circumstances are. These notions fit in the *heteronomous morality* of young children: the moral notions of young children are a product of their submission

14 C. L. HEFFNER, 1 April 2001, <http://allpsych.com/psychology101/development.html>.
15 We follow K. HELKAMA, supra (note 6), 38–39.

to adult authority.[16] This is a morality based on fear of punishment and strict obedience to authority. According to these children, punishment should be immediate, retaliatory and exculpatory.

b) After the *age of seven*, children increasingly acquire the capacity for making moral judgment based on intentions and motives. They then enter the stage of *subjective responsibility*, developing an *autonomous morality*.[17] Cognitive moral development does not, however, stop this early. The child slowly develops towards a morality based on equality, reciprocity and agreement. Punishment should have a didactic aim, be reciprocal and contribute to the improvement of the person.

Although children may become aware of their own intentions as early as at the age of three, it seems that the constraints imposed by adults in the lives of young children prevent them from using intentions as a moral criterion at an earlier age than seven years old.[18] The shift from the phase of objective to subjective responsibility is slow and gradual, and depends on the:

- General intellectual development (cognitive growth and transition from egocentrism to decentrism);[19]
- Social relations (transition from submission to adult constraint to co-operative social relations with peers).

The content area in which children seem to be able to produce subjective responsibility judgments at an earlier age is in lying, most likely because this is also the content area where the notion of intention is acquired earlier. It has also been suggested that children attain subjective judgment earlier when situations involve human beings (as opposed to objects) and, in particular, when acts are committed towards peers/familiar people (as opposed to adults/strangers).[20] Methodological improvements incorporated

---

16 Some authors, such as LAUPA and SMETANA, questioned the degree to which there is, in fact, such submission from children to authority. They based their criticism on the observation that children do refuse to obey adults when ordered to commit immoral acts. However, PIAGET had mostly in mind submission to adults in everyday relationships between adults and children, not particular moments of committal of unfair or immoral acts. See O. M. LOURENÇO, supra (note 8), 81.

17 Later research conducted by SHAW, SULZER, BRISCOE, GARCIA-ESTEVES, REITAN, SCHNEIDER and IWASAKI, has indicated that children of 7 and 8 years old can sometimes even consider extenuating circumstances in their judgments of attribution of responsibility. See K. HELKAMA, supra (note 6), 134–137

18 Findings of MINTON, KAGAN and LEVINE, and HOFFMAN, quoted in K. HELKAMA, supra (note 6), 40–41.

19 Confirmed by revision of studies performed by M.L. HOFFMAN, LICKONA and SHANTZ, quoted in K. HELKAMA, supra (note 6), 98. However, although intelligence remains a very relevant variable, it is not strong enough to prevail over the importance of age.

20 See research carried out by MCKECHNIE and IMAMOĐLU and RUFFY, quoted in K. HELKAMA, supra (note 6), 55.

by later studies have indicated that children can make subjective responsibility judgments at an earlier age than seven.[21] Still, there is "ample evidence for the fact that the more refined psychological distinctions of motivation develop rather slowly", mostly concerning a satisfactory understanding of the concept of "good intentions".[22] Furthermore, it has been found that young children have severe difficulties in understanding complex sequences of actions involving hierarchical means-ends relations and older children frequently consider intentional injury accidental.[23] Moreover, it has been advanced that adolescents *up to the age of thirteen* could "lack a clear conception of a moral agent as an independent centre of distinct personal causality, capable of resisting provocation or temptation and making decisions independently of the social environment. This lack might partly reflect their lack of moral independence from adults and peers."[24] Most importantly, it has been proved that, up to the *age of at least seventeen*, there is a systematic development in the ability to produce subjective responsibility judgments and to understand intentionality.[25]

Despite the focus on the developmental trends of the acquisition of moral judgment of children, PIAGET's theory also pays consideration to those social psychological factors that may be relevant thereto. Furthermore, the research that has been carried out subsequently tends to confirm the developmental sequence proposed by PIAGET. Even though some criticism is valid, many authors (DEAN & YOUNISS, KURTINES & PIMM, LICKONA, SHANTZ, VANDENPLAS-HOLPER) consider that most elements that contradict PIAGET's theory can be explained without discarding the whole theory.[26]

2.3. THE SOCIAL LEARNING CRITIQUE

7. The understanding of PIAGET of the moral judgment stages has been the object of modifications and has been harshly criticised by the social learning theorists ever since the 1960s.[27] While PIAGET sees the evolution of moral judgment in children as a pre-defined path to be followed and makes it depend on the (cognitive) development

---

21 K. HELKAMA, supra (note 6), 86–87.

22 See, for example, the study conducted by VON WRIGHT and NIEMELÄ in 1966, attesting to how exceptionally slowly and gradually children understand motives as a moral criterion in situations that offer other criteria besides motives and material consequences, quoted in K. HELKAMA, supra (note 6), 61, 87, and 94.

23 See studies conducted by COLLINS, BERNDT and HESS, FLAVEL, and BERNDT, quoted in K. HELKAMA, supra (note 6), 95.

24 K. HELKAMA, supra (note 6), 96.

25 Study conducted by KUGELMASS and BREZNITZ in a large sample of Israeli youth, quoted by K. HELKAMA, supra (note 6), 90–91, and 94.

26 K. HELKAMA, supra (note 6), 66; O. M. LOURENÇO, supra (note 8), 91.

27 BANDURA and MCDONALD, quoted in K. HELKAMA, supra (note 6), 42–43.

of children, social learning theorists do not support that moral development should be conceptualised in stages. They accept the existence of developmental trends, but believe that stages overlap and objective and subjective judgment exists simultaneously at all ages.[28] Children acquire moral judgment mainly through *modelling*, but modelling can have no or limited effects in moral reasoning if the cognitive skills or the performance preferences of the children do not allow for a stronger evolution. So, cognitive skills and performance preferences of the children have, according to these authors, a stronger role in the acquisition of moral judgement than any fixed sequence of development stages. Specific socialising and environmental effects have more weight than the active construction of the child.

Another common critique to PIAGET is that his research on moral judgment is middle-class and culturally biased.[29] However, there is no conclusive proof thereof. On the one hand, it is true that some research including different social classes indicates that the ability to employ language independently of the immediate context, as required in verbal moral judgment, is not favoured by the common forms of socialisation used in the lower social classes. Consequently, children from these classes limit themselves to a local and personal perspective and are hardly capable of analysing situations from the perspective of others, i.e. have difficulties decentrating. But on the other hand, the existence of the objective and subjective responsibility stages in PIAGET's theory has withstood the cross-cultural consistency test.[30]

2.4. KOHLBERG AND THE MORAL DEVELOPMENT STAGES

8. In 1963, KOHLBERG advanced his theory on moral development. For KOHLBERG, morality has its essence in the sense of justice. The sense of justice is more important than the respect for social or moral norms. Therefore, consideration for equality, equity, social contracts and reciprocity in human relationships is more important to KOHLBERG than obeying or disrespecting certain social or moral norms. Justice should not only be the rule for the action, but also the reason for the action itself.[31] According to KOHLBERG, moral development goes through six main stages, divided into three

---

28 K. HELKAMA, supra (note 6)., 42–43.

29 K HELKAMA, supra (note 6), 53–54.

30 Ibid., 115.

31 Inherent to this understating is the idea of hierarchy between moral rules and moral principles. Several psychologists and sociologists, such as MANCUSO & SARBIN, DURKHEIM, BERKOWITZ and EYZENCK, have expressed serious doubts in regard to this understanding, laying instead more importance on the social context or conditioned reflexes than on reason. See, on this debate, O.M. LOURENÇO, supra (note 8), 29–30.

levels, each stage corresponding to a specific *socio-moral perspective* and *concept of justice*, which is, a different moral orientation or philosophy and a particular way of coordinating and prioritising conflicting perspectives and values:[32]

A. First Level (Pre-conventional) – justice and morality are a group of external norms which are respected in order to avoid punishment or to satisfy concrete and individualistic desires or interests:
   1. Heteronomous Morality (obedience and punishment are most valued);
   2. Individualism, Instrumental Purpose and Exchange (individualist, concrete perspective);
B. Second Level (Conventional) – social norms and expectations have been interiorised, people fulfil their duties and claim their rights as established by the social order:
   3. Mutual Interpersonal Expectations, Relationships and Interpersonal Conformity (interpersonal, relational morality);
   4. Social System and Conscience (respect for law is the highest value);
C. Third Level (Post-conventional) – people value universal ethical principles and determine their action in respect to these principles; the law is worth less than moral imperatives:
   5. Social Contract or Utility and Individual Rights (social and common good; rules yield to principles);
   6. Universal Ethical Principles (ethical principles and the principle of justice command action).[33]

These stages were defined based on the kind of arguments advanced by subjects of different ages when presented with moral dilemmas. Immediately relevant to our discussion is that:

- At stage 1, "what is right" already includes "avoiding physical damage to persons and property";
- By stage 4, "what is right" implies upholding the laws, "except in extreme cases where they conflict with other fixed social duties";
- At stage 6, self-chosen ethical principles take priority and one disregards laws if these do not respect those principles.

---

32 L. KOHLBERG, 'Child Psychology and Childhood Education – A Cognitive-Developmental View', (New York – London: Longman, 1987), 259–324; O. M. LOURENÇO, supra (note 8), 96–121.

33 This stage was later withdrawn by L. KOHLBERG from his theory as an empirical stage, but has been kept as a mere ideal of moral development, O. M. LOURENÇO, supra (note 8), 96 and 114.

Each stage forms a complete autonomous unity and integrates the previous stage(s). In addition, stages form a universal and fixed sequence. In order to attain a certain stage of moral development, one has, among other things, to:[34]

- Possess a certain level of logical thought;
- Possess a certain level of role-taking or social perspective;
- To a certain extent, closely relate his/her behaviour to that moral stage;
- Have developed certain features of his/her ego.

KOHLBERG attempted an indication of which ages usually reach each stage. Although such ages are merely approximate, it is extremely relevant to the aims of the subject-theme of this article to make a reference to them:[35]

A. Pre-conventional level (Stages 1 an 2): Children *until around nine years old*, as well as some adolescents and adults;[36]
B. Conventional level (Stages 3 and 4): *Adolescents between 10 and 20 years old*, as well as *some adults*;
C. Post-conventional level (Stages 5 and 6): *Some adults*, usually older than 20–25 years old.

Development can stop at any stage. Although the majority of adults most likely reason from stage four structures, some stop at stage two or three and others evolve to stage five or six.[37] KOHLBERG's view of moral judgments as both cognitive and developmental has later been further developed and updated, as well as consistently reaffirmed, by the Minnesota approach to research in moral development.[38]

---

34 K. HELKAMA, supra (note 6), 6–7.

35 O. M. LOURENÇO, supra (note 8), 96–101.

36 Nevertheless, according to research carried out by TURIEL and his collaborators, children of 3 or 4 years old are already able to distinguish morality from social conventions, morality being obligatory, general and inalterable, and social conventions being dependent from social organisation, existing practices, rules and authority. These authors attribute children a high level of moral autonomy and an overtly generous moral competence. This has been criticised, namely the methodological and conceptual inaccuracies pointed out by LOURENÇO, FOWLER, GLASSMAN and ZAN. See O. M. LOURENÇO, supra (note 8), 75.

37 R. DUSKA and M. WHELAN, *Moral Development: A guide to PIAGET and KOHLBERG*, (Dublin: Gill and MacMillan, 1977), 102 and 105.

38 See S.J. THOMA, 'An overview of the Minnesota approach to research in moral development', (September 2002) 31 (3) *Journal of Moral Education*, 225–245. See also L.J. WALKER, 'The model and the measure: an appraisal of the Minnesota approach to moral development', (September 2002) 31 (3) *Journal of Moral Education*, 353–367, identifying contributions and limits of the Minnesota approach.

2.5. SOME INTERMEDIATE REMARKS

9. The theories of both KOHLBERG and PIAGET have in common the developmental dimension. Although this implies a considerable degree of cultural universality, these authors have integrated the relevance of cultural factors into their theories. It has also been shown that KOHLBERG's levels of morality are confirmed in people from very different cultures.[39] It has been shown that it is possible to induce durable developmental changes through teaching programmes.[40] Still, the developmental dimension seems to be mainly influenced by the forms of inter-individual interaction (general socialisation), not by specific cultural traditions or forms of education.[41] Furthermore, experimental research has failed to prove social learning theorists right and to accurately question the cognitive-developmental theory. It is still judicious to believe in the existence of a universal developmental trend in children, which includes the evolution from objective to subjective responsibility in moral judgment, even if the emergence of the latest can vary considerably depending on several factors. Development is not solely influenced by age. However, age remains the most important indicator of moral development of a human being, mostly during adolescence.[42] As ERIKSON puts it: "*It often takes considerable time – well into the early twenties – before an adolescent can make a workable whole out of all that became distinctive of him in the years of childhood. For what once was play and pretense, in adolescence becomes rehearsal with different ways of living until the main life performance, namely the individual's lasting identity in the adult world, is established.*"[43]

While the social learning and psychoanalytic perspectives should be given due consideration, the cognitive-developmental approach subsists as the most convincing and solid theory in this field. It refuses to classify an action as moral or immoral without first knowing the reasons that structure that action and it accepts that someone's moral development is the construction of a person in interaction with the environment surrounding him/her, not just the mere result of the influences exercised

---

39 Research carried out by COLBY, in the USA, NISAN and KOHLBERG, in Turkey, SNAREY, REIMER and KOHLBERG, in Israel, and BIAGGIO, in Brazil. See O. M. LOURENÇO, supra (note 8), 96–97.

40 See studies carried out by CROWLEY, GLASSCO, MILGRAM and YOUNISS, JENSEN and HAFEN, and JENSEN and LARM, quoted in K. HELKAMA, supra (note 6), 120–121. See also, on the teacher's role in the creation of the conditions that stimulate maximum development for each individual, R. DUSKA and M. WHELAN, supra (note 37), 103.

41 K. HELKAMA, supra (note 6), 113.

42 See R. DUSKA and M. WHELAN, supra (note 37), 103. The authors refuse that development is governed by age, but recognise that certain ranges of age are "good predictors" of stages of moral development, mostly between the ages of twelve and twenty.

43 E. H. ERIKSON and K. T. ERIKSON, 'The confirmation of the delinquent (1957)', in S. SCHLEIN (ed.), *A way of looking at things: Selected papers from 1930 to 1980 Erik H. Erikson*, (New York – London: W. W. Norton & Company, 1987), 622.

on him/her.[44] All things considered, the cognitive-developmental theory offers the most exhaustive answers, effectively combines philosophical arguments, psychological research and educational purposes, proposes the most rational criteria in regards to morality and moral development, better assumes the idea of one's development and is most committed to the construction of a fairer society.[45]

3. A SOCIOLOGICAL PERSPECTIVE

10. Children seem increasingly self-confident and in control of their lives. They seem to grow in a very independent way, are given much freedom and are given access to a number of activities and opportunities that their parents at that age were not. This may be, at least partially, the result of the strongly urbanised western societies in which so many children grow up nowadays. However, experts have alerted to the fact that present day youths are, in fact, more protected, less autonomous, emotionally less mature and more subordinate and susceptible of being manipulated than before.[46] Furthermore, youths enter the labour market later than before and become responsible later too. Experts also defend that this should have consequences, for example, in the field of sexual self-determination.[47]

The concept of *maturity* has increasingly gained relevance in the legal field too. Several studies have pointed out the importance of maturity as a key concept in determining the capacity of discernment[48] of children. Therefore maturity should be used as a corrective tool for the concept of discernment, defining this in reference with the "'evolutionary dynamics' experienced and expressed during adolescence".[49] An individual can be considered mature when he/she is autonomous both in the affective-

44 O. M. LOURENÇO, supra (note 8).

45 Ibid., 37–38. This author also analyses post-KOHLBERG critiques and proposals. In particular, he considers the contextual and post-modern perspectives (e.g. BROWN, DEBOLD, TAPPAN, GILLIGAN and PACKER) epistemologically contradictory, nihilistic and opportunistic. Furthermore, the behaviourists, in particular SKINNER, do not pay enough attention to cognitive elements, nor assume any basic moral principle (justice, for example).

46 M. GUERREIRO, 'Jovens mais manipuláveis', (17 November 2005) *Correio da Manhã*, interview to psychologist Luís Reto, <http://www.correiomanha.pt/noticia.asp?id=179761&idselect=181&idCanal=181&p=0>.

47 Ibid.

48 This concept ("capacity to discern") is described by a different word in the southern European legal systems which use romance languages: "imputabilità" (Italian), "imputabilidade" (Portuguese) and "imputabilidad" (Spanish). In French, although the word "imputabilité" exists, this concept is more often translated by the word "discernement" in legal writings.

49 A. CERETTI, 'Il concetto di maturità del minore. Alcune proposte per la sua valutazione dal punto di vista dello scienziato dell'uomo', (2002) 3–4 *Minori Giustizia*, 272–299, especially, 277.

emotional-instinctive sphere and in regard to his/her social integration.[50] The necessary requisites to be a mature and normal person acquire a predominant role in determining responsibility. Besides that, responsibility is *ontologically* understood, that is, in considering if an individual is responsible or not one has to individualise and measure all elements that may be relevant in that *concrete* situation (level of education, dynamics of interpersonal relationships, reasoning capacity, susceptibility, infantile characteristics, deficit in structuring the personality, etc).[51] Since the 1970s, external factors, such as the socio-cultural context surrounding the child, have been incorporated in the analysis of discernment of the child: individual-psychological factors are nowadays inseparable from the social-environmental factors in the determination of the personality development of the child. Furthermore, in the 1980s several studies concluded that youths who can be considered mature but have grown up in an underprivileged environment might not be able to interiorise adequate models of behaviour and of social valuation.[52]

The considerations produced by scholars regarding discernment in the criminal field are *mutatis mutandis* applicable to the civil field. In fact, the exam of the physical and mental maturity should be carried out having close regard to the wrong committed and all its surrounding circumstances. Accordingly, a child should only be responsible when he/she is in possession of a range of capacities and competences, which vary from individual to individual and depend on several factors (age and psychological conditions determined by endogenous and exogenous conditions).[53] Moreover, the discernment of the minor is to be assessed in connection to the specific (wrongful) act, since to understand the consequences of certain behaviour, the minor needs a greater deal of maturity than for other behaviour.[54] So, for example, anyone understands the value of life and the immorality of attempting to work against it. Although this approach certainly makes sense, it also raises an important problem: should adopting a behaviour that violates the most basic values and rules (which even a person with low discernment would grasp) not indicate that that person possesses a strongly unbalanced or disturbed personality? The same data may, then, give origin to opposite judgments and, therefore, create conflicts between psychological and legal approaches. In any case, maturity and discernment cannot be objectively analysed in an isolated situation. This normative analysis requires a comparison with other similar situations. This means that one has to take into consideration what another child of normal development of the same age would do in the same situation. Despite all efforts to ground scientifically this assessment, legal certainty inevitably allows for some

---

50 A. Ceretti, supra (note 49), 279.
51 Ibid., 279–280.
52 Ibid., 283.
53 Ibid., 279.
54 Ibid., 277.

flexibility in the court, since the judge has to deal with a complex multiplicity of factors.

Lastly, it is relevant to point out that a rigorous exam of the child's maturity in court would undoubtedly lead to fewer condemnations in court.[55] Too often, judges and other judicial operators take legal ages of liability as the definitive element in the determination of the discernment of the child. If the assessment of the maturity and discernment of a child is carefully done in every individual case, as it should happen, courts' decisions would most likely be less grave for children above the legal age of liability. It may be argued that considering a child immature and without enough discernment to be held liable for his/her doings is tantamount to harming his/her self-esteem and confirming his/her role of wrongdoer. This argument forgets that a punishment or condemnation only makes sense for a child if it is proportionate. Furthermore, not punishing or condemning a child to pay damages in a specific case does not mean that the child is irresponsible in general, it just means that the child should not be held responsible under particular circumstances.[56]

4. LEGAL IMPLICATIONS OF THE CONTRIBUTIONS FROM PSYCHOLOGY AND SOCIOLOGY

11. As pointed out at the beginning, the "vision of reality that is given to us by the empirical science is a partial vision", so the "research on empirical sociology cannot discharge us from deciding based on judgments of value".[57] Still, we absolutely cannot disregard the importance of the findings in the psychology and sociology fields mentioned until now. We will then attempt to draw some relevant implications to the legal field of liability of children.

Some kind of age framework is essential, in order to provide a minimum degree of legal certainty to children. As we have seen, children only start acquiring the capacity for making moral judgments based on intentions and motives at the *age of nine*. This allows us to include under this age limit all children under PIAGET's stage of subjective responsibility and KOHLBERG's stages 1 and 2. Therefore, until this age children should undoubtedly be exempted from any kind of criminal or civil liability. From the age of ten years old on, children gradually develop a moral reasoning more centred on

---

55 L. PEPINO, supra (note 5), 48.

56 Ibid., 50–51.

57 B. MACHADO, 'Introdução ao Direito e ao Discurso Legitimador', (Coimbra: Almedina, 1997), 47 and 49.

others and on society as a whole (KOHLBERG's stages 3 and 4). Furthermore, up until the age of thirteen children very often lack moral independence from adults and peers and up until the age of seventeen children's discernment is still developing.[58] Consequently, during an intermediary age span *between ten and seventeen years of age* some form of civil liability could be allowed, but it should be especially attenuated. Criminal liability should still be excluded, taking into account the risk of the labelling effect that it could have on such young children. Thirdly, and finally, a last stage *between the age of seventeen and twenty-one* is justified in light of the findings that the cognitive and moral development continues to take place into the early twenties. Therefore, young adults should enjoy some kind of privileged form of liability regime as well.

12. Whatever the legal framework may be, the correct reading of all the relevant elements concerning the maturity and discernment of a child has to be *integrated*.[59] This means that the judge cannot exacerbate the value of individual elements. He has to give due value to each of the relevant aspects: psychological and physical development of the child, his/her family life, social integration, education, nature of the wrongdoing, procedural behaviour, cultural and ethnic origins and characteristics, etc.[60] Secondly, the role and importance that each one of these elements concretely (and not abstractly) has on the child's development have to be assessed. Thirdly, special attention has to be given to problematic conditions of the child's life (regarding personal, family or other social or environmental elements), and to the resources he/she can access (any means available to the child which can provide him/her with support in any sense). Fourthly, when determining the degree of *fault* or *guilt* of the child, one also has to take into account the cognitive and social competences of the child and the capacity of the child to determine his/her own behaviour in face of an act that can be perceived as wrongful. Fifthly, the age groups above proposed could be used as mere *presumptions* of development, meaning that judges could rebut such presumptions and place the child in question at a higher or lower level of cognitive and moral development in comparison to the average child of the same age, consequently increasing or diminishing his/her degree of liability.[61] Finally,

---

58 See the study conducted by KUGELMASS and BREZNITZ in a large sample of Israeli youth, supra (note 25), as well as HELKAMA's opinion: K. HELKAMA, supra (note 6), 90–91, 94 and 96.

59 We here follow A. CERETTI, supra (note 49), 286–288.

60 See A. CERETTI, supra (note 49), 286, referring to Cass. Pen., sez. 1, 19 May 1989. See also, in Italy, Art. 9 of the Minors Procedural Law 1988, which foresees the valuation of the maturity of the minor.

61 Judges can obtain this information through expert opinions of psychologists trained in the field of assessment of moral development. The methods of assessment of moral development are quite varied: psychoanalytic methods focus on emotion-related elements (fear, shame, guilt, sadness, empathy, selfishness), social learning methods measure the occurrence and frequency of moral and immoral behaviour of the individual (through direct observation, interviews with third persons or submitting the individual to tests), cognitive developmental theorists use cognitive tests to assess the moral

experts and judges should work together in using all opportunities available to them to:

- Make the child aware of the meaning of his/her acts (help him/her interiorise and gain conscience of the negative value of his/her action through an ongoing communication process with reality);
- To promote responsibility as a connection between the norms and values of the child's culture and his/her expression through behaviour.

Indeed, these functions fit well in the importance of the development of empathy, something highly valued by authors such as HIGGINS, YEATES & SELMAN, and RAWLS. Developing empathy and other affectional factors helps children, as well as any other human being, to expand their perspectives, allowing them to put themselves in others' positions, and, consequently, better develop their moral judgments.[62] Furthermore, if judges and experts, working in a multi-disciplinary team[63] in the interest of the child, perform their duties with this in mind, the fight against repressive tendencies can be more successful.[64] This does not mean transforming the judge into a social worker; it simply means giving back to justice its primordial social function. Criminal and civil aspects of justice affecting children are ever more intertwined, and should complement and strengthen each other. The aim is only one: to prevent any further wrongdoings and protect and make the child a responsible member of society.

5. CONCLUSION

13. Children's criminal and civil liability age limits, as crucial as they are for the life of any child, should be given very close attention. General prevention and special

reasoning of individuals. The latest were developed by several psychologists throughout time, such as PIAGET, DAMON, KURTINES & PIMM, COLBY & KOHLBERG, REST, and GIBBS, BASINGER, FULLER & WIDAMAN. From these, those most commonly used and considered most reliable are the KOHLBERG methodology, the Rest methodology (also known as Minnesota test or DIT – Defining Issues Test), as well as the Social Reflection Questionnaire, created by GIBBS. The KOHLBERG method is defended as the one which allows the deepest analysis of moral reasoning, although it is also considered the most complex to carry out. In any case, the methods for assessment of moral development are instruments to assess the moral reasoning of individuals, not their moral value. Although this implies that people should not be treated differently depending on the stage of moral reasoning they fit in, it should not prevent us from drawing elements from the moral development theories to ground a proposal of legal framework which better protects children's interests in the field of civil and criminal liability. In fact, as long as this use is made in the promotion of the well-being of individuals and of justice, it is completely justified. For a discussion on all these methods, how they work, and the advantages and disadvantages of each one, see O. M. LOURENÇO, supra (note 8), 123–155.

62 R. DUSKA and M. WHELAN, supra (note 37), 106-107; O. M. LOURENÇO, supra (note 8), 82.

63 S. ABBRUZZESE supra (note 1), 69–75.

64 L. PEPINO, supra (note 5), 53.

positive prevention theories have already convincingly demonstrated that the wisest reaction to wrongdoings places emphasis on relational-consensual, responsibilisation, educational and re-socialisation dimensions of public policies.[65] Nevertheless, only a trans-disciplinary perspective can aspire to understand and contribute properly to improving the legal framework applicable to children, including all the rights and duties that it includes. This text attempted at building a bridge between, on one side, the results produced by psychologists and sociologists' research, and, on the other, legal concepts such as "discernment" and "competence". This bridge can lead us to a better understanding of where we should set the age limits for criminal and civil responsibility and how we can better advocate their change.

It should be clear by now that, under certain circumstances, not considering a child liable for damages he/she caused is not the result of any benevolent, voluntary or altruistic gesture of the legislative or judicial power. Indeed, it is merely the result of the due recognition of a natural fact: the ability to consider legal and social norms, as criteria for moral behaviour and judgment progresses slowly and gradually through childhood and adolescence. Besides that, the recognition of such fact has found echo in legal systems since the Roman XII Tables, throughout the Middle Ages, until modern times.[66] Children only integrate conscience and legal and social rules as determinants of responsibility at a more advanced stage of development.[67] There are undeniable age-development trends in the acquisition of moral behaviour and judgment skills and competences. The exact evolution depends on the cognitive and role-taking stages attained by each individual. The psychopathologic paradigm no longer provides a sufficient and accurate image of the child's discernment for legal purposes. On the contrary, a broader view is required to grasp the complexity of the elements which form part of the child's development and personality. Although age remains an *indicator*, as opposed to evidence, of cognitive and moral development, *legal certainty* requires the definition of an *age-liability framework*. This framework needs, however, to be used in a flexible and reasonable way, taking into account all possibly relevant elements and circumstances of each case in particular.

65 A. Ceretti, supra (note 49), 299.
66 L Pepino, supra (note 5), 49.
67 K. Helkama, supra (note 6), 165.

RIGHTS BASED RESTORATIVE JUSTICE: TOWARDS CRITICAL PRAXIS WITH YOUNG PEOPLE IN CONFLICT WITH THE LAW

SHANNON A. MOORE and RICHARD C. MITCHELL

1. INTRODUCTION

1. This paper examines rights based restorative justice[1] (RBRJ) in the context of contemporary Canadian social policy and practice for young people. Conceptualised through the United Nations Convention on the Rights of the Child (CRC) and international standards[2] that reflect principles of restorative justice, the authors argue that RBRJ has the potential to contribute to ethical democratic practice with young people in conflict with the law. In addition, adopting such practices will enhance Canada's accountability with regard to longstanding commitments made within international law. Until recently, literature linking child and youth human rights with restorative justice practices in Canada was rare.[3] In addition, a restorative justice program for young people currently being piloted in southern Ontario is conceptually framed by the core principles and provisions of the CRC.[4]

Accordingly, this paper aims to contribute towards critically conscious practice with young people in conflict with the law through an exploration of the links between CRC

---

1 S.A. MOORE, 'Making It Right: Inciting a Rights Based Restorative Justice Dialogue in Canada for Young People', in R. B. HOWE and K. COVELL (eds.), *The Rights of the Child in Canada*, (Waterloo, ON: Wilfred Laurier University, in press).

2 J. BRAITHWAITE, 'Setting Standards for Restorative Justice', (2002) 42 *British Journal of Criminology*, 563–577.

3 S.A. MOORE, W. TULK and R.C. MITCHELL, 'Qallunaat Crossing: The Southern-Northern Divide and Promising Practices for Canada's Inuit Young People', (2005) 2(1) *First Peoples Child and Family Review*, 117–129.

4 M. VANDER VENNEN, 'Directors Corner', (2005) 22:2 *Salem Digest*, Retrieved from <http://www.salem.on.ca/html/pdf/autumn05.pdf> and accessed 14 October 2006.

principles and those found within restorative justice discourse. This will be achieved by first discussing Canada's unique social-historical and political contexts and the current state of youth justice. Then an overview of restorative justice practice and how CRC principles are philosophically congruent is taken up. Finally, a model based upon an integration of human rights meta-narratives is presented that accounts for power relations between adults and young people within restorative justice programming.

2. CANADIAN CONTEXT FOR YOUTH JUSTICE

2. Canada's social fabric has been woven through historical contexts that include centuries of European colonisation, the resultant devastation of Indigenous cultural systems and contemporary social policies related to multiculturalism – the first among three officially multicultural states in the world. Indeed, Canada is described as having three distinct cultures supporting her poly-ethnic landscape: Aboriginal, English and French Canadians.[5] It is imperative that discussions of multiculturalism include the recognition of millennia of Aboriginal (or Indigenous) history[6] underpinning the Multicultural Act of 1988 – created in the context of Eurocentric ideologies that shaped the colonisation of Canada is the first instance.[7]

Moreover, the culture of Aboriginal communities in Canada prior to colonisation was imbued with vibrancy, spirituality and social order.[8] This reflection is of particular salience while discussing youth justice since it is well recognised that modern interpretations of restorative justice are informed by Indigenous social processes the world over. Nonetheless, disproportionate numbers of Aboriginal young people and adults are found in Canadian justice systems as well as being disproportionately represented as victims of crime.[9] The recognition that Indigenous peoples around the world are over-represented in prisons and courtrooms is well documented.[10]

Furthermore, Canada's formal justice system is historically based upon retributive principles inherited from 17th and 18th century French and English colonists noted previously. Indeed, the structures and processes embedded in the contemporary

---

5 S.A. MOORE, 'Transdisciplinary Approach to Critical Multicultural Pedagogy in Canadian Higher Education', in D. ZINGA (ed.), *Navigating Multiculturalism: Negotiating Change*, (Newcastle: Cambridge Scholar's Press, in press), 129–145.

6 E. NEEGAN, 'Excuse me who are the First Peoples of Canada? A Historical Analysis of Aboriginal Education in Canada then and now', (2005) 9 *International Journal of Inclusive Education*, 3–15.

7 S. A. MOORE, supra (note 5).

8 G. RADWANSKI and J. LUTTRELL, *The Will of a Nation: Awakening the Canadian Spirit*, (Toronto: Stoddart, 1992).

9 S.A. MOORE, supra (note 1).

10 E. ELLIOTT and R. GORDON (eds.), *New Directions in Restorative Justice: Issues, Practice, Evaluation*, (Devon: Willan, 2005).

criminal justice system took shape two centuries ago as Canadian civil law is based upon both English common and statutory law in all provinces. The notable exception, of course, is Quebec where civil law is based upon the Napoleonic Code.[11] Informally, Aboriginal systems of justice, which existed prior to colonisation, continue to prevail within many First Peoples communities.

3. Over the past forty years significant social movements have impacted Canada's formal system of justice. For instance, diversion and community mediation emerged as an alternative option through the informal justice movement of the 1970s and set the stage for more organised restorative justice processes to be developed through the 1980s and 1990s. Namely, worldwide it is acknowledge that the first restorative justice program, in the contemporary sense, started in Ontario Canada. This organisation, known as Community Justice Initiatives, began in 1994 and continues to thrive today.[12] Currently, "the most extensive application of restorative justice in the criminal justice system has been court-based victim-offender mediation programs and police-led Community Justice Forums".[13] Although focused on minor offences in Canada these processes are often modelled from international examples provided by countries such as South Africa, Scotland and in particular New Zealand and Australia where restorative justice is fully integrated into correctional services for young people and adults.[14]

It is also noteworthy that recent changes within Canada's youth justice legislation reflect an effort to integrate restorative principles further broadening our vision of justice beyond punitive and retributive responses to crime. This development epitomised by the integration of principles of restorative justice as well as children's human rights under the CRC within the Youth Criminal Justice Act (YCJA) of 2003. The Canadian YCJA..."*Contrasts sharply with the orientation of the previous legislation (the Young Offenders Act...) in several ways. Among these are the institutionalisation of a police officer's discretionary power, the increased participation of victims and families, the assumption that extra judicial measures are effective in improving the levels of responsibility among youth, and the use of the civil community through justice committees and consultative groups.*"[15]

---

11 S.A. MOORE, supra (note 1).

12 G. NYP, *Pioneers of Peace: The History of Community Justice Initiatives in the Waterloo Region 1974–2004,* (Kitchener: Community Justice Initiatives, 2004).

13 T. RUGGE and R. CORMIER, 'Restorative Justice in Cases of Serious Crime', in E. ELLIOT and R. GORDON (eds.), *New Directions in Restorative Justice: Issues, Practice, Evaluation*, (Devon: Willan, 2005), 266-277.

14 E. ELLIOTT and R. GORDON (eds.), *New Directions in Restorative Justice: Issues, Practice, Evaluation*, (Devon: Willan, 2005).

15 S. CHARBONNEAU, ' The Canadian Youth Criminal Justice Act 2003: A Step Forward for Advocates of Restorative Justice?', in E. ELLIOT and R. GORDON (eds.), *New Directions in Restorative Justice: Issues, Practice, Evaluation*, (Devon: Willan, 2005), 75.

Although the Youth Criminal Justice Act demonstrates changes that make it significantly distinct to previous legislation and presents opportunities to explore rights based restorative alternatives within criminal justice, cautious optimism about this progressive shift is warranted. Canada's political system leaves interpretation of legislation to the governance of Provinces and Territories within the Canadian Federation. The result of this Federalist system is inconsistent and sometimes non-existent implementation of child rights and restorative justice programming across the country.[16]

In addition, the effect of restorative programming may 'widen the net' if the focus becomes increased social control and heightened intolerance. Also, restorative justice processes are, by their nature, community centered and reliant of citizen volunteers to support programming. This in turn creates a dependence on a critical mass of investment, interest and knowledge of these alternative approaches in order for programs to be sustained by individual communities. In the final analysis, the YCJA is likely to reflect a bifurcation of youth justice such that restorative justice will continue to be advocated for minor offences while principles and processes of the traditional justice system will likely be engaged for more serious offences.[17] Let us now turn to a more in-depth consideration of the principles of restorative justice and its contrast to traditional criminal justice.

3. UNDERSTANDING RESTORATIVE JUSTICE

4. As the introduction to this paper indicates, restorative justice is sourced in ancient indigenous epistemologies found the world over that pre-date the violent colonial social-political foundations that shaped traditional retributive systems of justice in countries such as Canada.[18] Aboriginal dispute resolution is built on communitarian values, an ontological standpoint of interconnectedness and a focus on full participation of all impacted parties. Processes promote oral expression, emotional responses and community based interventions that are non-hierarchical, non-linear and strongly contrast the Canadian and British formal legal systems.[19] Restorative justice ranges vastly in its complexity and formality and may include information, dialogue between

16 S. A. MOORE, supra (note 1).

17 S. CHARBONNEAU, supra (note 15).

18 H. BLAGG, 'Restorative Justice and Aboriginal Family Violence: Opening a Space for Healing', in H. STRANG and J. BRAITHWAITE (eds.), *Restorative Justice and Family Violence*, (Cambridge: Cambridge University Press, 2002), 191–205.

19 L. BEHRENDT, 'Lessons from the Mediation Obsession: Ensuring that Sentencing 'Alternatives' Focus on Indigenous Self-determination', in H. STRANG and J. BRAITHWAITE (eds.), *Restorative Justice and Family Violence*, (Cambridge: Cambridge University Press, 2002), 178-190.

impacted parties, mutual resolution of conflict between victim and offender, restitution, reduction of fear, heightened sense of safety, acceptance of responsibility, and/or renewal of hope.

5. To clarify the contrasts between Aboriginal and retributive systems of justice, the following table summarises six core distinctions:

Table 1: Comparison of principles of retributive & restorative justice

JUSTICE	RETRIBUTIVE	RESTORATIVE
EPISTOMOLOGY	Individualistic	Communitarian
ONTOLOGY	Punitive	Capacity building
PROCESS	Adversarial	decrease antagonism
FOCUS	Single act	disharmonies in relationships
VICTIM'S ROLE	not meaningfully involved in the solution	central to the solution
OFFENDER'S ROLE	alienated & isolated	opportunity to be accountable

Table 1 demonstrates how the epistemological and ontological distinctions between retributive and restorative justice impact the process and the focus of programming as well as the roles of victims and offenders. In addition, restorative justice themselves demonstrate a variance of processes and goals as do processes related to Aboriginal justice more specifically.

Consequently, notwithstanding the connection between Aboriginal and restorative justice it is essential to reinforce distinctions between these systems in the Canadian context.[20] The reasoning for highlighting distinct qualities is found in the following: "*If the cause of Aboriginal over-representation [in the justice system] is colonisation, the solution to the problem will have to be found by Aboriginal communities themselves- it is not possible for colonial structures to remedy the problems that they have created. For this reason, one of the cornerstones to addressing the problem of over-representation must be the development of restorative justice responses to criminal behavior by Aboriginal people*".[21]

In essence, Aboriginal justice travels a path towards decolonisation through community building. In contrast, non-Aboriginal restorative justice processes may find

[20] J. Rudin, 'Aboriginal Justice and Restorative Justice', in E. Elliot and R. Gordon (eds.), *New Directions in Restorative Justice: Issues, Practice, Evaluation*, (Devon: Willan, 2005), 89–114.

[21] Ibid., 95.

communities strengthened as a result of programming, but community building is not an essential indication of success for any such program.

6. Moreover, restorative justice processes are co-constructed within social worlds of those impacted by crime, harm and conflict and are context bound whether they take place in Aboriginal or non-Aboriginal communities. Thus, it is difficult to offer a single definition for restorative justice. Philosophically, restorative justice consistently reflects a set of principles that guide processes and facilitate resolution, restoration and transformation. As central features of these practices, the following principles emphasise accountability, respect, honesty and the importance of human relationships:

1. The perpetration of crime and infliction of harm are fundamentally the violation of a human being or human relationships as they rupture the well-being of individuals, societies and communities.
2. The goals of restorative process include repairing harm done and restoring relationships between individuals and community as they aim for transformation of all parties towards greater equilibrium.
3. All restorative processes are voluntary and respect individuals' right to choice with sensitive consideration of power relations within systems and society.
4. Victims of crime must always be of central concern and given free choice to participate.
5. Perpetrators of hurt or crime are given opportunity to accept responsibility for the harm they have caused and a choice to participate in a restorative process.[22]

Therefore, restorative justice has many forms and is conducted in a variety of contexts while being connected within a single policy arena by the principles described above. Importantly, these principles are congruent with the United Nations basic principles of restorative justice, which have been adapted by Canada to guide this nation's unique programming needs: "*With the adoption of UN basic principles, the issues facing restorative justice will not evaporate. Finding a place for healing in a system that is fundamentally punitive will continue to challenge policy makers and practitioners. There will continue to be concerns regarding the application of restorative justice. Nevertheless, internationally accepted principles will assist by providing guidance that, if followed, will help to prevent the misinformed and inappropriate activities that may be under-*

[22] S. A. Moore, 'Towards an Integrated Perspective: Restorative Justice, Crosscultural Counselling and School-based Programming', in M. Honore France, M. Carmen Roderoguez and G. Geoff Hett (eds.), *Diversity, Culture and Counselling: A Canadian Perspective*, (Calgary, Alt: Detselig 2004), 347–355.

taken under the rubric of restorative justice but do not conform to its philosophy and values."[23]

These fundamental UN principles of restorative justice also offer a yardstick for evaluation programming, a concern taken up in the last section of this paper.

4. RIGHTS BASED RESTORATIVE JUSTICE: AN ANALYSIS OF POWER RELATIONS

7. The intention of a rights based restorative justice (RBRJ) is to broaden understanding of justice within a human rights framework while deepening an articulation of principles already embedded in these processes. In the first instance, a rights based approach for working with young people in conflict with the law is guided by Article 40 (1) of the CRC, which asserts that all young people are to be: ..."*treated in a manner consistent with the promotion of the child's dignity and worth, which reinforces the child's respect for human rights and freedoms of others and which takes into account the child's age and the desirability of promoting the child's reintegration and the child's assuming a constructive role in society*".

In addition, restorative justice and children's rights similarly encourage the voice of victims, offenders and young people to be heard through non-discriminatory, safe, authentic and full participation in matters that impact them. Such an approach emphasises the four core principles of child rights articulated within CRC Articles 2, 3, 6, 12[24] while reinforcing the following basic principles of restorative justice:

1. **Non discrimination, Equality and Mutuality: CRC Article 2**
   All young people have the same human rights regardless of social-cultural context or whether they are victims or perpetrators of harm; processes address the balance between equality and mutuality among stakeholders.
2. **Best Interests, Well-Being and Restoration: CRC Article 3**
   For all young participants involved there is a concern for their best interests, their well-being and a restoration of equilibrium for all stakeholders. The aim is to heal harm done in the context of human relationships.

---

[23] R. B. CORMIER, *Restorative Justice: Directions and Principles-Developments in Canada* (2002), Retrieved from <http://www.psepcppcc.gc.ca/publications/corrections/200202_e.asp#Restorative>, accessed 14 October 2006.

[24] R.C. MITCHELL, 'Postmodern reflections on the UNCRC: Towards utilising Art. 42 as an international compliance indicator', (2005) 13 *International Journal of Children's Rights*, 315–331.

3. **Survival, Development and Safety: CRC Article 6**
   For young participants there is an appropriate consideration for the healthy development especially in the context of vulnerabilities and power relations typical in circumstances of victimisation. All stakeholders must feel a sense of safety throughout the process.
4. **Participation, Voice, and Volunteerism: CRC Article 12**
   All stakeholders must have an opportunity to fully participate and experience their views being meaningfully heard. All processes must be voluntarily engaged in by all stakeholders.[25]

8. It is argued that to achieve effective outcomes for young people in conflict with the law a delicate balance that protects human rights, well-being and welfare through accountable justice is necessary. This is an expression of youth justice that repairs harm, empowers participants and reintegrates individuals back into their communities.

In the authors' experience, such a rights based approach to restorative justice is not established in integrated practice with young people in conflict with the law within Canada. This may largely be attributed to the ongoing lack of accurate knowledge to which Canadians have been exposed under the CRC in the first instance.[26] Nonetheless, the current authors have recently linked the CRC and restorative justice in Canadian academic discourse.[27] In addition, the authors' are participating in a pilot project launched within five regions in province of Ontario building explicitly upon a rights based restorative justice framework to guide policy and practice for young people. This "Hosting Restorative Justice Project" is sponsored by Salem Christian Mental Health and the Ontario Multi-faith Council on Spiritual and Religious Care, and is in response to recent changes in the Canadian Youth Criminal Justice Act discussed earlier. The aim of this multi-site project is to engage a broad range of spiritual and faith-based centers within local communities to act as 'hosts' for restorative justice processes for young people. In this manner, the focus is on community-based and multicultural contexts, making things right for all stakeholders, mental health and well-being of young people, in addition to young peoples' human rights. This grass-roots project is guided by international leaders in rights based approaches to restorative justice found in such countries as Australia, New Zealand and South Africa.[28] Moreover,

---

25 S.A. MOORE, supra (note 1).

26 R.C. MITCHELL, supra (note 24), 317.

27 S.A. MOORE, supra (note 3).

28 J. SLOTH-NIELSEN, 'The Juvenile Justice Law Reform Process in South Africa: Can a Children's Rights Approach Carry the Day?',(1999) 18 *Quinnipiac Law Review*. Available from <http://www.restorative-justice.org/articlesdb/articles/3102> and accessed 14 October 2006. Also, A. SKELTON, 'Juvenile Justice Reform: Children's Rights and Responsibilities Versus Crime Control', Paper presented at the Children's Rights in a Transitional Society Conference, Centre for Child Law, University of Pretoria (October 30, 1998). Available from <http://www.restorativejustice.org/articlesdb/articles/313> and accessed 14 October 2006.

standards of practice such as those articulated by criminologist BRAITHWAITE[29] account for the exercise of power within systems impacting the lives of young people.

5. STANDARDS OF PRACTICE, POWER RELATIONS AND RIGHTS BASED RESTORATIVE JUSTICE

9. Straightforwardly, accountability within justice is guided by clear standards of practice that promote equality and mutuality within the overarching context of personal and community safety. Of course, this type of praxis is also dependent upon thought and action working together towards social change in our traditional legal processes.[30] This arguably feminist approach towards social justice encourages critical reflection on the source of authority that sets said standards. Through an analysis of power relations within Canadian socio-political systems we readily find top-down power structures shaping grassroots processes like restorative justice, adultist views conflicting with child-centred philosophies and victims' needs being over shadowed by offending behaviours in our youth justice system. Given these caveats, tensions arise when notions of child rights, restorative justice and traditional legal systems attempt to merge mandates.

Philosophically and practically speaking, restorative justice requires a transparent and accountable use of power that is best guided by clearly articulated standards – yet such benchmarks are most often set by "top-down manergerialist" structures within the traditional legal system which contradict the democratic ethos of this emergent, global social movement.[31]

As discussed, youth justice policy has historically been shaped by philosophical standpoints that are the antithesis of egalitarian. Thus, within youth justice arenas we fide a milieu in which: "*adult power… is a power readily and systematically abused. It is a dangerous and debilitating power, capable of stunting the personal development and potential of even the most resilient children… What is so difficult for adults, as power-brokers, to accept is that the 'crisis' is not of childhood' but one of adultism.*"[32]

Consequently, paramilitary structures within both policing and custody procedures are often ill-equipped to engage restorative processes that focus on voice and full participation of young people. Instead, adultist goals of power and control can

---

29 J. BRAITHWAITE, supra (note 2).

30 J. PENNELL and G. BURFORD, 'Feminist Praxis: Making Family Group Conferencing Work', in H. STRANG and J. Braithwaite (eds.), *Restorative Justice and Family Violence*, (Cambridge: Cambridge University Press, 2002), 108–127.

31 J. BRAITHWAITE, supra (note 2), 563.

32 P. SCRATON, 'Whose "childhood"? What "crisis"?', in P. SCRATON (ed.), *Childhood in 'Crisis'?* (London: UCL Press, 1997).

overshadow the search for deeper understanding regarding the meaning of behaviours that are in conflict with the law.[33] This problem of adultism is reflected in viewing young people as victims or offenders, or citizens in becoming that must show respect before they are granted human rights.

10. In spite of these systemic barriers to rights based youth justice an opportunity is presented in theory. This is illustrated in Canada with the passing of the Youth Criminal Justice Act and the formal acknowledgment of the CRC and restorative justice principles, as discussed previously. Next, what is needed is social action that reinforces young peoples' citizenship rights. For instance, to make… "*children central to development and social analysis requires a person–centred rather than category-centred approach [that] recognises the fundamental importance of relationship to peoples' actions, entitlements and well being.*"[34]

A young person-centered approach is congruent with the basic principles of restorative justice and the principles and provisions of the CRC. The challenge is to deploy human rights meta-narratives, such as the UN Declaration of Human Rights and the CRC, in a manner that reframes top-down human rights discourse to the level of local, lived experiences in transformative ways for young people.[35] Recent research by MITCHELL comparing educational policies in Scotland and Canada found that such meta-narratives also straddle the modernist/postmodernist divide when applied according to local culture.[36] Thus, it is fundamental that minimum standards and expected outcomes of restorative justice practice with young people are clearly articulated and framed by human rights in order to inform practice-based local experiences. Such standards also need to create space for criticality to be voiced, for young people to be authentically heard, for victims' needs for equality of power relations to be safeguarded, and for offenders to have opportunities for accountability. Such a transparent approach in which power is exercised with accountability in mind may be more easily achieved in theory than in practice. Nonetheless, the suggestion here is to forge a way forward in practice by understanding that: "*Policy texts are sites of power…by establishing narrative conventions, authoritative repertoires of interpretation and frameworks of argumentation and communication, they confer power upon preferred modes of speaking and judging, and upon certain ways of expressing moral and political subjectivity.*"[37]

---

33 G. BAZEMORE and C. GRIFFITHS, 'Restorative Justice and Restorative Policing', (2003) 4 *Police Practice and Research Police Reform,* 335–346.

34 S. WHITE, 'Being Becoming and Relationship', (2002) 14 *Journal of International Development,* 1095–1104.

35 J. BRAITHWAITE, supra (note 2).

36 R.C. MITCHELL, supra (note 24).

37 S. SEVENHUIJSEN, *Citizenship and the Ethics of Care: Feminist Considerations on Justice, Morality and Politics,* (London: Norton, 1999).

The current authors argue that the Convention on the Rights of the Child may be fully integrated with restorative justice processes to become the 'preferred mode' of engaging young people in conflict with the law. Subsequently, a tentative proposal for standards of rights based restorative justice is offered along with the intention to encourage further rights based practice without being prescriptive. As BRAITHWAITE astutely cautions: "*We must be careful in how we regulate restorative justice....unthinking enforcement of standards is a new threat to innovating with better ways of doing restorative justice....we can craft open textured restorative justice standards that allow a lot of space for cultural difference and innovation while giving us a language for uncontroversially denouncing bad practice.*"[38]

11. Accordingly, Table 2 demonstrates the integration of core principles from UN human rights meta-narratives and restorative justice processes for praxis with young people in conflict with the law.

Table 2: Standards of Practice for Rights Based Restorative Justice

STANDARDS & EVALUATION FOR RIGHTS BASED RESTORATIVE JUSTICE				
United Nations Human Rights Meta-narratives: UN Declaration of Human Rights, UNCRC, UN Basic Principles of Restorative Justice				
I **Minimum Standards** **Guided by** CRC ARTICLE 40 Safety, equality, mutuality, citizenship		II **Maximising Values** **for** RESTORATION Wholeness, well-being		III **Emergent Standards** **for** TRANSFORMATION Emotional gifts
CRC Article 2	CRC Article 12	CRC Article 3	CRC Article 6	
• Non-domination • Honouring legally specific upper limits on sanctions • Equal concern for all stakeholders	• Empowerment • Respectful listening • Accountability, 'appealability'	• Human Dignity • Property Loss • Safety, injury, health • Damaged human relationships • Communities • Environment • Compassion, caring • Prevention of future injustice	• Emotional • Freedom • Peace • Citizenship • Social Support to develop human capabilities	• Remorse over injustice • Apology • Censure of the act • Forgiveness of the person • Mercy

[38] J. BRAITHWAITE, supra (note 2), 565.

Table 2 also demonstrates the interconnected, interdependent relationships among UN human rights meta-narratives as articulated by BRAITHWAITE,[39] as well as the core principles of the CRC as discussed by MITCHELL,[40] within this integrated, rights based restorative justice approach.

The intention of this synthesis is to show the relationship among United Nations meta-narratives and rights based restorative justice praxis. Thus, the aim is to support Canadian social policy to transcend theory towards more ethical democratic practice with young people. When stakeholders are clear about the principles guiding practice philosophy justice will be more accountable as the yardstick for evaluation is made clear.[41] Importantly, the starting point for standards of Rights Based Restorative Practice is found in United Nations Human Rights meta-narratives such as UN Declaration of Human Rights and more specifically the CRC in the case of young people in conflict with the law. Although, "UN Human Rights instruments give quite a good guidance on the foundational values and rights restorative justice processes to observe",[42] in Canada barriers to rights based practice have impeded local implementation of CRC principles. Hence, Table 2 illustrates a proposed relationship among CRC Article 40, core principles of the CRC and restorative justice in a way that simplifies tenants for basic practice, articulates maximising values that are the foundational goals of restorative practice, and emergent gift that have been identified as transformative outcomes of some restorative justice practice.

5.1. MINIMUM STANDARDS

12. Minimum standards of practice are guided by the legal statutes and upper limits of sanctions, and center on the principles of non-domination (for instance, young people have a right to speak and be heard in all matters that impact them). If these processes reflect rights based approaches then they would also be guided by the provisions within CRC Article 40 in the first instance.

Certainly, these minimum standards are not consistently reflected in mainstream justice systems yet, and the CRC may even be contradicted in both policy and practice through the lack of basic knowledge in Canada and elsewhere. For example, under Canada's Youth Criminal Justice Act young people may be charged as adults in cases

---

39 J. BRAITHWAITE, supra (note 2), 565.

40 R.C. MITCHELL, supra (note 24).

41 H. ZEHR, 'Evaluation and restorative justice principles', in E. ELLIOT and R. GORDON (eds.), *New Directions in Restorative Justice: Issues, Practice, Evaluation*, (Devon: Willan, 2005), 296–303.

42 J. BRAITHWAITE, supra (note 2), 257.

of violent crime,[43] which is a direct contravention of CRC Article 40, as well as the four core principles of the CRC. More importantly, in Canada the disproportionate number of Aboriginal young people found within youth justice systems has come to the attention of the Committee on the Rights of the Child upon their review of Canadian reports.[44]

The suggestion here is to engage reflective practices and to consider how such minimum standards might consistently reflect the provisions of CRC Article 40 (as well as Article 30 and its cultural considerations) with the expectation that young people are referred to extrajudicial measures such as restorative justice. In addition, these measures must reflect CRC Article 2 principle of non-discrimination and Article 12's participatory goals more specifically. This in turn will lead us to question whether restorative processes are child and youth rights based, and actually empowering young people to be heard respectfully while addressing the endemic racism within Canadian social, political and justice systems.

5.2. MAXIMISING VALUES FOR RESTORATION

13. Within Table 2 the column, so labelled lists principles associated with restorative justice processes, and encourage change towards greater well-being and wholeness in all facets of life including mental health. Striving to bring individuals back into balance within their communities, within themselves and within their interpersonal relationships is a consistent quality of restorative processes. Certainly, individuals involved in restorative processes may not have experienced well-being in their lives prior to engagement in restorative justice. The aim then would not be to restore an individual back to a state of imbalance but to aim for transformation, which is reflective of Emergent Standards articulated within the next section. Thus, it is possible to link both CRC's Article 3 best interests and Article 6 maximum development principles with these restorative values. Accordingly, when a loss is encountered as the result of a serious crime the aim is to restore the whole person back to their environment and community with a focus on safety, dignity and the prevention of

[43] For example, in April 2006 a twelve-year-old girl along with her twenty-three-year-old companion received three charges of first degree murder in connection to the for the deaths of that young girl's parents and brother in the province of Alberta. For more information see <http:www.ctv.ca/servlet/ArticleNews/story/CTVNews/20060424/medicinehat_murders_060424?s_name=&no_ads= >, retrieved 14 October 2006.

[44] CRC Committee, *Concluding Observations on: Canada*, 1995; and CRC Committee, *Concluding Observations on Canada*, 2003, both available at: <http://www.pch.gc.ca/progs/pdp-hrp/docs/crc/crcconc_e.cfm>, retrieved 14 October 2006.

future harm. A sense of peace can result from this restoration as well as the freedom to experience fuller developmental capacity.

5.3. EMERGENT STANDARDS

14. Emergent Standards are not expected outcomes of restorative justice as it would be unreasonable to assume such inward-looking emotional transformation would be available from the outset of these processes by stakeholders.[45] These are, however, outcomes attributed to restorative justice processes by many within the literature and indeed set these processes apart from other forms of dispute resolution. They are indicative of a transformational change process in which individuals may experience a sense of completion that positively impacts them psychologically, socially, behaviourally and contextually.

As previously highlighted, accountable restorative justice practices are guided by basic standards of practice. These standards need to form a clear reference point for evaluation while being flexible enough to respond to culturally diverse local practice that is young person-centered. By utilising the Convention of the Rights of the Child as a conceptual framework for good practice with young people in conflict with the law, we are empowering new modes communicating moral and political subjectivity. In brief, rights are connected to the lived experiences of young people through focusing upon the values and standards charted above. This is of great importance as children's and young peoples' human rights are too often abstracted from reality or moral purpose as we focus on "rights without specification of what human goods the rights are meant to safeguard".[46] Further, as restorative justice is found to be practiced in over one hundred countries[47] and the CRC has been ratified and implemented throughout a globalised world, it appears a trustworthy framework for rights based restorative justice praxis is readily at hand.

---

45 J. Braithwaite, supra (note 2).

46 D. Smith, 'Contemporary Youth Justice Systems Youth Policy and Social Inclusion: Critical Debates with Young People', in M. BARRY (ed.), *Youth Policy and Social Inclusion – Critical Debates with Young People,* (Oxfordshire: Routledge, 2005), 211–225.

47 D. Van Ness, '*An Overview of Restorative justice around the world*', paper presented the *United Nations 11th congress on Crime Prevention and Criminal Justice*, (Bangkok,Thailand, 22 April 2005). Available from: <http://www.pficjr.org/programs/un/11thcongress/danspaper/download > and retrieved 14 October 2006.

6. CONCLUDING REFLECTIONS: RIGHTS BASED RESTORATIVE JUSTICE PRAXIS

15. This paper presented an exploration of rights based restorative justice in the context of contemporary social policy and practice for young people and the implementation of the Convention on the Rights of the Child in Canada. By providing an overview of historical and contemporary themes impacting the lives of young people in conflict with the law, an effort was made to move from theoretical discourse to practice-based action that boasts greater systemic and international accountability.

Hence, in relation to restorative justice processes the entry point for paradigmatic change typically presents itself at the grassroots community-based level where we are asked: "*To think about… how to make the quality assurance processes and accountability work well. We don't have to wait for the United Nations for this. A local restorative justice initiative can take a very broad list of values… and use them as a starting point for debate on what standards they want to see accomplished in their programme. A few discussion circles with all stakeholders in the programme may be enough to reach a sufficient level of shared sensibility to make quality assurance and accountability work.*"[48]

Indeed, the "Hosting" restorative justice initiative discussed in this paper contributes towards rights based restorative practice. For instance, although early in its inception this initiative has engaged in a cross-systemic dialogue about how the CRC may be seminal to achieving program goals while sustaining criticality and socially conscious action. This program (2005–2006) has supported a rights based restorative justice approach while focusing on bringing young people in conflict with the law back to their communities, families and themselves. Moreover, the authors' earlier research linking restorative justice and children's rights with indigenous epistemologies aimed at improving practice with Inuit young people in Canada's North furthers the discourse on this holistic, innovative approach.[49] Accordingly, rights based restorative justice also aims to transcend the types of deficit labelling[50] associated with mainstream justice and psychiatry by considering young peoples' mental health, well-being and wholeness in the context of local communities.

48 J. BRAITHWAITE, supra (note 2), 572.

49 S. A. MOORE, W. TULK and R. C. MITCHELL, supra (note 3).

50 See R.C. MITCHELL, 'Ideological reflections on the DSM-IV-R (or Pay no attention to that man behind the curtain, Dorothy!)', (2003a) 32 *Child and Youth Care Forum*, 281–298; and R.C. MITCHELL, 'Canadian health care and child rights – what are the links?', (2003b) 94 *Canadian Journal of Public* Health/Revue Canadienne de Santé Publique, 414–416.

16. Similarly, upon reflection on the basic principles of restorative practice and children's rights it seems straightforward to identify the congruence of these constructs within many theoretical frameworks. To move forward in praxis we must engage in critically conscious dialogue about the meaning and impact of such integrated approaches, and discover how newly emergent standards may guide best intentions while at the same time being responsive to the unique needs of young people and diverse community cultures. In practice, rights based restorative justice advocates full voluntary participation by all individuals impacted by crime without discrimination and in consideration of evolving capacity.

17. In brief, rights based restorative justice strives to overcome the systemic discrimination, overt racism and adultist myopia characterising contemporary justice systems for young people through its analysis of power relations. Furthermore, rights based restorative justice calls adults in authority to transcend the habitual deficit labelling of young people with its commitment to improving psychological, behavioural, social and cultural well-being. In the authors' views, such transdisciplinarity[51] – discussed in detail in this volume – also reflects a vision of justice that is at once holistic and accountable to both local and global expressions of praxis.

[51] B. NICOLESCU'S definition of this concept is based upon quantum physics and is found within his *Manifesto of Transdisciplinarity* (New York: State University of New York Press, 2002) as well as being the focus of a paper by R.C. MITCHELL in this volume.

THE RIGHT TO BE TREATED WITH HUMANITY: IMPLICATIONS OF ARTICLE 37(C) OF THE CRC FOR CHILDREN IN DETENTION

TON LIEFAARD

1. INTRODUCTION

1. Many children all over the world are deprived of their liberty. The exact number is not clear; however an estimation of Defence for Children International – the Netherlands shows that, worldwide, at least one million children are detained, imprisoned, incarcerated or placed in institutions, police cells, remand homes, prisons, mental health clinics, treatment centres or other closed facilities.[1] The reasons for incarceration vary from those derived from the criminal justice system (arrest, pre-trial detention and imprisonment), the immigration system (detention of immigrants or aliens) or the mental health system (placement in psychiatric hospitals), to reasons of child protection (placement in treatment centres or temporarily placement in remand homes as an emergency measure) and reasons related to public safety or politics (arrest and detention of vagrants, political prisoners).[2] Not infrequently, deprivation of the liberty of children is related to other major issues, such as poverty or health care. Deprivation of liberty affects a large number of children worldwide and it links up to many different (political and legal) aspects of society. Therefore, it must be considered as a large issue. The issue is actually even larger because too often the

1 S. MEUWESE (ed.), *Kids behind bars. A study on children in conflict with the law: towards investing in prevention, stopping incarceration and meeting international standards*, (Amsterdam: Defence for Children International, 2003).

2 Sometimes (very young) children are detained with (one of) their imprisoned parents. This group of children does not fall within the scope this paper. *Cf.* e.g. <www.eurochips.org>.

rights of these children are denied, being infringed upon, not well developed or not recognised at all. Children are often incarcerated under hazardous conditions.[3]

2. Every form of deprivation of liberty limits one's right to liberty of person. This right of every human being is acknowledged by Article 9(1) of the Covenant on Civil and Political Rights (CCPR) and can be considered as one of the oldest, fundamental human rights. However, it is not absolute. Article 9(1) CCPR allows deprivation of the right to liberty of person under the condition that this is neither unlawful nor arbitrary. In other words, the grounds for and procedures regarding deprivation of liberty must be embodied in domestic (statutory) law and the application may not be arbitrary. The UN Convention on the Rights of the Child (CRC) contains an equivalent to Article 9(1) CCPR in Article 37(b) that prescribes that "[n]o child shall be deprived of his or her liberty unlawfully or arbitrarily" and more in particular that "[t]he arrest, detention or imprisonment of a child shall be in conformity with the law (...)".[4]

3. This paper focuses on deprivation of liberty as part of the (juvenile) criminal justice system only, although much of the content would apply to all other forms of deprivation of liberty as well. The objectives of the different forms of deprivation of liberty may (and will) differ; still there are many similarities, particularly regarding the application of deprivation of liberty.

Deprivation of liberty means, "any form of detention or imprisonment or the placement of a person in a public or private custodial setting, from which this person is not permitted to leave at will, by order of any judicial, administrative or other public authority".[5] Regardless of the reason for deprivation of liberty, it results in the child being placed in a setting that is designed to avoid the child running away. Therefore it often is a closed, prison-style setting, that lacks transparency and that makes the child particularly dependant upon the institution's administration and its regime.[6] Subsequently the child will be particularly vulnerable to abusive practices. It is

---

[3] See e.g. S. Meuwese (ed.), supra (note 1); G. Cappelaere, A. Grandjean and Y. Naq VI, *Children Deprived of Their Liberty, Rights and Realities*, (Paris: Éditions Jeunesse et Droit, 2005), in particular part three.

[4] This paper will not discuss the implications of these provisions thoroughly. For more info see M. Nowak, *U.N. Covenant on Civil and Political Rights. CCPR Commentary, 2nd revised edition*, (Kehl: N.P. Engel Verlag, 2005), 210; and S. Detrick, *A Commentary on the United Nations Convention on the Rights of the Child* (diss. Amsterdam VU), (Dordrecht: Kluwer Law International, 1999), 629

[5] Rule 11(b) of the UN Rules for the Protection of Juveniles Deprived of their Liberty (JDLs; GA Res. 45/113 of 14 December 1990). Due to the fact that JDLs define deprivation of liberty this broadly, this UN resolution covers all forms of institutionalisation on behalf of a public authority that results in a child being placed in a setting from which he cannot leave at will.

[6] Although the setting is not necessarily closed, it can be (semi-)open as well. *Cf* Rule 30 JDLs.

important to stress these characteristics of deprivation of liberty of children for the purposes of this paper.

This paper addresses in an overview the implications of international human rights law for the arrest, detention and imprisonment of children as part of the (juvenile) criminal justice system (para. 2). Subsequently this paper will elaborate more in detail on Article 37(c) CRC's requirement that "[e]very child deprived of liberty shall be treated with humanity and with respect for the inherent dignity of the human person, and in a manner which takes into account the needs of persons of his or her age" (para. 3). What are the implications of this requirement? What does this requirement mean in more concrete terms? Moreover, how can this requirement be implemented into the domestic legal system? In order to answer the latter question this paper will also discuss the implementation of Article 37(c) of the CRC into the domestic legal system, by presenting an example from the Netherlands, the Youth Custodial Institutions Act (para. 4). This paper will end with a conclusion (para. 5).

2. DEPRIVATION OF LIBERTY OF CHILDREN UNDER THE (JUVENILE) CRIMINAL JUSTICE SYSTEM

2.1. THREE FORMS OF DEPRIVATION OF LIBERTY; ARREST, DETENTION AND IMPRISONMENT

4. The common three forms of deprivation of liberty as part of the (juvenile) criminal justice system are *arrest*, *detention* and *imprisonment*. The Body of Principles for the Protection of All Persons under Any Form of Detention or Imprisonment (Body of Principles)[7] provide for definitions of arrest, detention and imprisonment. Arrest means "the act of apprehending a person for the alleged commission of an offence or by the action of an authority", while detention covers the condition of any person deprived of personal liberty except as a result of conviction for an offence (pre-trial phase), and imprisonment: the condition of any person deprived of personal liberty as a result of conviction for an offence.[8] In other words, arrest is the act that leads to deprivation of liberty, detention is the situation in which persons awaiting trial are incarcerated, and imprisonment is meant for the group of persons that have been convicted and sentenced.

---

7 GA Res. 43/173 of 9 December 1988. The JDLs explicitly refer to the Body of Principles in their preamble; G. VAN BUEREN, *The International Law on the Rights of the Child*, (Dordrecht: Kluwer Academic Publishers 1995), 206.

8 See respectively Body of Principles (a), (d) jo. (b), and (e) jo. (c).

2.2. PRECONDITIONS OF DETENTION UNDER THE (JUVENILE) CRIMINAL JUSTICE SYSTEM

5. Due to the fact that these forms of deprivation of liberty fall within the (juvenile) criminal justice system, the implications of international human rights law for (juvenile) criminal justice must be taken into account.

This means, first of all, that arrest, detention and imprisonment must meet the requirements of Article 40(1) of the CRC which stipulates that State Parties must "recognise the right of every child alleged as, accused of, or recognised as having infringed the penal law to be treated in a manner consistent with the promotion of the child's sense of dignity and worth, which reinforces the child's respect for human rights and fundamental freedoms of others and which takes into account the child's age and the desirability of promoting the child's reintegration and the child's assuming a constructive role in society". Deprivation of the liberty of children, being part of the juvenile justice system must, in other words, have the child's reintegration as the primary objective and therefore the child must be treated, and this includes the treatment during detention, in a way that takes into account the age of the child, that promotes its sense of dignity and worth and that reinforces its respect for human rights and fundamental freedoms of others. This can be seen as the pedagogical character of the juvenile justice system, which stretches out to arrest, detention and imprisonment as well.[9]

Secondly, there are some preconditions that must be taken into account. As mentioned in the introduction of this paper, deprivation of liberty limits one's fundamental right to liberty of person. Like Article 9(1) of the CCPR, that unlike Article 37 of the CRC explicitly acknowledges this fundamental right, Article 37 (b) of the CRC prohibits unlawful or arbitrary deprivation of liberty. *A contrario*, the fundamental right of liberty of person is not absolute and may be limited, provided that this does happen based on and in accordance with the law and not in an arbitrary way. This affects both the legal grounds for deprivation of liberty and the legal procedures that lead to this situation.

Thirdly, Article 37 (b) of the CRC prescribes that "[t]he arrest, detention or imprisonment of a child (...) shall be used only as a measure of last resort". The UN Standard

---

[9] *Cf.* S. DETRICK, supra (note 4), 682–683 and Art. 14 CCPR. Obviously other relevant requirements of Art. 40 CRC should be met as well. E.g. Art. 40(2)(b)(i) CRC's requirement that every child must be presumed innocent until proven guilty according to law has implications for the treatment of children in pre-trial detention. However it goes beyond the scope of this paper to discuss this more thoroughly.

Minimum Rules for the Administration of Juvenile Justice (Beijing Rules)[10] set out in Rule 17 "guiding principles for adjudication and disposition". Rule 17(b) states that "[r]estrictions on the personal liberty of the juvenile shall be imposed only after careful consideration and shall be limited to the possible minimum." Furthermore in paragraph (c) the rules prescribe that "deprivation of personal liberty shall not be imposed unless the juvenile is adjudicated of a serious act involving violence against another person or of persistence in committing other serious offences and unless there is no other appropriate response".[11] Finally, according to Rule 17(c) "the well-being of the juvenile shall be the guiding factor in the consideration of her or his case".

Thus, deprivation of liberty must be limited to the possible minimum and must only be imposed after careful consideration has taken into account the well-being (i.e. best interests of the child – Art. 3 CRC) of the child as the guiding principle.[12]

6. Regarding pre-trial detention, this implies that if it is not necessary to detain an accused child or there are other options to avoid him/her fleeing or in any way obstructing the criminal proceedings (i.e. the most common, justified reasons for pre-trial detention), the child must not be detained or the detention should be suspended. Regarding imprisonment, CRC Article 37(b) implies that those responsible for the juvenile justice system should try to avoid the use of imprisonment as a sentence, by providing for other reactions to criminal behaviour, like alternative sanctions, for instance within the community.[13] Moreover, Article 37(b) prescribes that arrest, detention or imprisonment must be only for the "shortest appropriate period of time".[14]

---

10 GA Res. 40/33 of 29 November 1985.

11 R. HODGKIN and P. NEWELL cite a member of the UN Committee on the Rights of the Child that pointed out, during the discussion of Nigeria's Initial Report, that the expression 'as a last resort' in Art. 37 of the Convention was often misunderstood as referring to children guilty of serious crimes; in fact, it meant that prison could be resorted to only if there was no other way of giving the child the protection it needed. The phrase 'for the shortest appropriate period of time' implied that other measures than prison sentences should be sought' (for the precondition 'for the shortest appropriate period of time' see further below); R. HODGKIN and P. NEWELL, *Implementation Handbook for the Convention on the Rights of the Child. Fully revised edition,* (New York – Geneva: UNICEF 2002), 550.

12 *Cf.* regarding detention Rule 17 JDLs that states that '[d]etention before trial shall be avoided to the extent possible and limited to exceptional circumstances' and that '[t]herefore all efforts shall be made to apply alternative measures'. See also Rule 2 JDLs.

13 See e.g. the commentary of Rule 19 Beijing Rules that elaborates on the advocacy for the use of non-institutional over institutional treatment. See also the commentary of Rule 17 Beijing Rules. *Cf.* UN Standard Minimum Rules for Non-custodial Measures (Tokyo Rules), GA 45/110 of 14 December 1990 and G. VAN BUEREN, supra (note 7), 209.

14 Life imprisonment without the possibility of release for children, who have committed crimes, while they still were below the age of eighteen, is prohibited under Art. 37(a) CRC. *Cf* Rules 13.1, 17.1(b) and 19.1 of the Beijing Rules and Rule 2 JDLs. The wording 'shortest appropriate period of time' is often confused with the wording 'shortest *possible* period of time', which means something

The requirements of Article 37(b) fit in the pedagogical rationale behind Article 40 of the CRC, designed for the administration of juvenile justice, as described earlier above. In addition and more in particular with regard to the sentencing of children State Parties must, according to Article 40(4) of the CRC, "ensure that children are dealt with in a manner appropriate to their well-being and proportionate both to their circumstances and the offence". To reach this objective "[a] variety of dispositions" must be made available, "such as care, guidance and supervision orders; counselling; probation; foster care; educational and vocational training programmes and other alternatives to institutional care".

Thus, arrest, detention and imprisonment are not banned from being part of the juvenile justice system, but should nonetheless be avoided as much as possible and must – in any case – not interfere negatively with the objectives of the system, as prescribed in Article 40 of the CRC. In this regard, it is interesting to take a closer look, in the next paragraph, at the international legal implications for the treatment of detained or imprisoned children.

3. THE RIGHT TO BE TREATED WITH HUMANITY – ARTICLE 37(C) OF THE CRC

3.1. CORE ARTICLE FOR CHILDREN IN DETENTION

3.1.1. Introduction

7. If a child is arrested, detained or imprisoned[15], he/she must be treated with "humanity and respect for the inherent dignity of the human person, and in a manner which takes into account the needs of persons of his or her age". This "right to be treated with humanity" is stipulated by Article 37(c) of the CRC and can be considered

different. The confusion is most likely caused by the Rule 13.1 Beijing Rules that speaks of pre-trial detention used only 'for the shortest possible period of time'. However, the wording of the CRC should be followed. There arrest, detention or imprisonment of the child must be used 'for the shortest *appropriate* period of time', which means that the length of the period of time may not interfere negatively with the 'best interests of the child' (Art. 3 CRC). *Cf* G. VAN BUEREN, supra (note 7), 214. Obviously, for a proper implementation of Art. 37(b), the right to challenge the legality of the deprivation of liberty before a court and the right to a prompt decision on any such action, as enshrined in Art. 37(d) CRC (Right to *Habeas Corpus*), are of the utmost importance.

15 From now on, if not explicitly stated otherwise, the term 'detention' will be used for these three forms of deprivation of liberty together.

as the core article regarding children in detention.[16] "In particular, every child deprived of liberty shall be separated from adults unless it is considered in the child's best interests not to do so and shall have the right to maintain contact with his or her family through correspondence and visits, save in exceptional circumstances", adds the second part of Article 37(c). These aspects can be considered as elements of the requirement of humane treatment as stipulated in Article 37(c). This paragraph addresses these and other implications of Article 37(c)'s right to be treated with humanity.

3.1.2 Article 10 of the CCPR – the fundamental part of Article 37(c) of the CRC

8. Article 37(c) of the CRC embodies a positive obligation for State Parties to ensure minimum guarantees for the humane treatment of detained children and is mainly based on Article 10 of the CCPR.[17] In its first paragraph, Article 10 uses similar wording and stipulates, "[a]ll persons deprived of their liberty shall be treated with humanity and with respect for the inherent dignity of the human person". According to NOWAK "*[a]rt. 10 establishes a relationship between the rights to liberty of person (Art. 9) and personal integrity (Art. 7)*".[18] Article 9 of the CCPR, as addressed earlier, embodies everyone's right to liberty of person and allows limitations only if these are not unlawful or arbitrary, but does not contain any requirements regarding the treatment of persons deprived of their liberty. Article 7 CCPR prohibits torture or cruel, inhuman or degrading treatment or punishment.[19] However, it is formulated negatively, as a prohibition, and does not provide for positive obligations to guarantee humane treatment. Article 10's value is that it prescribes minimum guarantees of humane treatment. Taking into account everyone's (other) fundamental human rights, as *inter alia* the right to life and to physical integrity, and the right to privacy, the prohibition of discrimination, the right to education and the freedom of religion, Article 10 provides more precisely for the permissible limitations of these rights.[20]

16 Art. 37(c) CRC explicitly addresses '[e]very child deprived of liberty'. Therefore the requirement of treatment with humanity is not limited to arrest, detention or imprisonment under the (juvenile) criminal justice system only.

17 S. DETRICK, supra (note 4), 633.

18 M. NOWAK, supra (note 4), 241.

19 Medical and scientific experimentation without free consent is prohibited by Art. 7 as well. *Cf* Art. 37(a) CRC.

20 M. NOWAK, supra (note 4), 242 with further reference to the HRC case *Angel Estrella v. Uruguay* (no. 78/1980) in which the HRC found that limitation of a prisoner's correspondence may very well amount to violation of Art. 10(1) besides a breach of Art. 17's prohibition of arbitrary or unlawful interference with one's correspondence. The American Convention on Human Rights contains a similar article, Art. 5, but the European Convention on Human Rights lacks one.

The specific characteristics of detention show the importance of this requirement. Persons in detention find themselves in a specific situation, that is characterised by three elements: (I) it is designed to avoid the person leaving, fleeing or running away, (II) it lacks transparency, and (III) it makes the person particularly dependant on the institution's administration. Subsequently, the detention makes the person particularly vulnerable to abusive (or hazardous) practices.[21] Obviously, children in detention are even more vulnerable. According to NOWAK, "experience has shown that precisely the situation of 'special power relationships' within closed facilities often occasion massive violations of the most diverse human rights".[22]

3.1.3. Relation between Article 10 and Article 7 of the CCPR

9. Article 7's prohibition of torture, cruel, inhuman or degrading treatment or punishment and Article 10's requirement of treatment with humanity are closely related, as are Article 37(a) and (c) of the CRC. The question can be raised when inhuman treatment constitutes merely a violation of Article 10 or when it amounts to torture or cruel, inhuman or degrading treatment (as well). The Human Rights Committee (HRC) has not always made a sharp distinction between the two articles in its jurisprudence under the CCPR's first optional protocol[23] and it shows some inconsistencies in this regard. However, it is assumed that inhumane treatment under Article 7 has a higher threshold than under Article 10. Article 10 seems to be meant to ban less serious forms of inhuman treatment than those prohibited under Article 7.[24]

In addition, it is important to distinguish the objectives of both articles. Article 7 is primarily designed to prohibit "specific, usually violent attacks on personal integrity", while Article 10's requirement of treatment with humanity implies "a positive obligation to ensure human dignity".[25] Article 10, therefore, must be seen as a positive obligation for State Parties to guarantee minimum conditions of detention in order to meet the requirement of treatment with humanity. In other words, State Parties must provide for a certain *legal status* for persons deprived of their liberty.

---

21 *Cf* e.g. General Comment 21/44 of 6 April 1992, para. 3 in which the HRC refers to *inter alia* persons in detention as 'persons who are particularly vulnerable because of their status as persons deprived of their liberty'.

22 M. NOWAK, supra (note 4), 242.

23 This protocol regulates individual communications of individuals against State parties. For more information see S. JOSEPH, J. SCHULTZ and M. CASTAN, *The International Covenant on Civil and Political Rights Cases,Materials and Commentary. Second Edition*, (New York: Oxford University Press Inc. 2004), 16 and 22.

24 M. NOWAK, supra (note 4), 172, 245, 249; S. JOSEPH, J. SCHULTZ and M. CASTAN, supra (note 23), 277, 280, 292 and 293.

25 M. NOWAK, supra (note 4), 250.

This can be confirmed by linking up to the HRC's General Comment No. 21. The HRC therein states that "[A]rticle 10, paragraph 1, imposes on State Parties a positive obligation towards persons who are particularly vulnerable because of their status as persons deprived of their liberty, and complements for them the ban on torture or other cruel, inhuman or degrading treatment or punishment contained in Article 7 of the Covenant. Thus, not only may persons deprived of their liberty not be subjected to treatment that is contrary to Article 7, including medical or scientific experimentation, but neither may they be subjected to any hardship or constraint other than that resulting from the deprivation of liberty; respect for the dignity of such persons must be guaranteed under the same conditions as for that of free persons. Persons deprived of their liberty enjoy all the rights set forth in the Covenant, subject to the restrictions that are unavoidable in a closed environment".[26] Thus, persons deprived of their liberty are in principle entitled to all rights under the ICCPR. These rights may only be restricted if "unavoidable" with regard to the special condition they are in (i.e. a closed environment). Other or further restrictions of their human rights are not permitted.

3.1.4. Needs of a person of his or her age – special features of Article 37(c) of the CRC

10. Due to the fact that Article 37(c) of the CRC is based on Article 10 of the CCPR, the explanation of the previous paragraphs, applies to Article 37(c) in conjunction with Article 37(a) of the CRC as well. However, Article 37(c) adds to the requirement of treatment with humanity, that every child, deprived of liberty, must be treated "in a manner that takes into account the needs of persons of his or her age". This requirement fits into the CRC's concept of the evolving capacities of the child.[27] In CCPR Article 10, the special status of the child has been acknowledged in paragraphs 2(b) and (3).[28] The HRC has elaborated a little bit on the content of the special approach regarding juvenile offenders in General Comment 21. It has stated *inter alia* that 'under Article 10, paragraph 3, juvenile offenders shall be segregated from adults and be accorded treatment appropriate to their age and their legal status in so far as conditions of detention are concerned, such as shorter working hours and contact with relatives, with the aim of furthering their reformation and rehabilitation'.[29]

---

26 General Comment 21/44, supra (note 21), para. 3; S. Joseph, J. Schultz and M. Castan, supra (note 23), 277.

27 G. Van Bueren, *The International Law on the Rights of the Child*, (Dordrecht: Kluwer Academic Publishers 1995), 219. *Cf* Art. 5 CRC and G. Van Bueren, *The International Law on the Rights of the Child*, (Dordrecht: Kluwer Academic Publishers, 1995), 32 (Chapter 2).

28 S. Detrick, supra (note 4), 633. Although Art. 10 (3) CCPR aims at imprisonment of juveniles after a conviction and does not include pre-trial detention of juveniles. Art. 37(c) CRC affects all forms of deprivation of liberty.

29 General Comment 21/44, supra (note 21), para. 13.

3.1.5. *Conclusion – Three elements of the legal status of a child in detention*

11. Thus, Article 37(c) of the CRC embodies a positive obligation for State Parties to guarantee minimum conditions, which guarantee that children in detention are treated with humanity and with respect to the inherent dignity of the human person. As pointed out earlier, CRC Article 37(c), like its "predecessor" Article 10(1) of the CCPR, prescribes minimum guarantees of humane treatment of children in detention. Together with the child's fundamental rights, embodied in the CRC, it provides more precisely the permissible limitations of these rights. Therefore, State Parties must provide for a *legal status* for children in detention that consists of the following three elements:

1. Every child in detention must be recognised as rights-holder entitled to all rights under the CRC;
2. the enjoyment of these rights may only be limited if required by the special condition (i.e. detention) the child is in, and
3. with full implementation of the principle that the best interests of the child shall be a primary consideration (Art. 3 CRC).[30]

12. The child's entitlement to all rights raises the question whether the child is entitled to all rights, civil, political, social, economic and cultural. The answer should be positive due to the holistic approach of the CRC, which means that there is no distinction between the different children's rights and that they are interrelated.[31]

This is slightly different with regard to Article 10(1) of the CCPR. The CCPR contains civil and political rights, while the economic, social and cultural rights are embodied in the Covenant on Economic, Social and Cultural Rights (CESCR). As pointed out before, the HRC observed in General Comment 21 that persons deprived of their liberty should be entitled to all rights 'under the Covenant', which aims at the CCPR. However, NOWAK argues that in order to achieve the objectives of the penitentiary system (i.e. social rehabilitation) this cannot happen without a proper enjoyment of human rights, like the rights to work, food, shelter, clothing, health and education.[32]

It is important to note that the HRC has considered that the requirement of treatment with humanity is "a fundamental and universally applicable rule" and that "[c]onsequently, the application of this rule, as a minimum, cannot be dependent on the

30 For an effective application of these elements, it is essential that the child has the right to remedy violations of his legal status. See further below. *Cf* the HRC's comments regarding the effective application of Art. 10(1) CCPR, in General Comment 21/44, supra (note 21), para. 7.

31 *Cf* S. DETRICK, supra (note 4), 22.

32 M. NOWAK, supra (note 4), 250.

material resources available in the State Party".[33] The HRC does not seem to make a distinction in this regard between civil and political rights on the one hand, and economic, social and cultural rights on the other, while Article 4 of the CRC seems to allow a limited implementation of economic, cultural and social rights, depending on (i.e. to the maximum extent of) the available resources.[34]

The enjoyment of the rights of the child in detention may only be restricted if required by the child's special condition and may only take place with full implementation of the best interests of the child principle. This implies that limitations of enjoyment of CRC rights may only be imposed if necessary and proportionate in light of the (objectives of the) detention, and only after assessing the interests of the child, which includes a duty to consult the child.[35] An example of further limitations of the child's rights is provided by Rule 64 of the UN Rules for the Protection of Juveniles Deprived of their Liberty (JDLs) that stipulates that "[i]nstruments of restraint and force [i.e. limitation of rights to privacy and physical integrity] can only be used in exceptional cases, where all other control methods have been exhausted and failed, and only as explicitly authorised and specified by law and regulation".

3.2. WHAT SHOULD BE INCORPORATED IN THE LEGAL STATUS?

3.2.1. *Introduction*

13. Provided that Article 37(c) of the CRC places State Parties under a positive obligation to provide children in detention with a legal status that acknowledges the child as a rights-holder entitled to all rights under the CRC and that allows limitations of the enjoyments if required by the state of detention the child is in, with full

---

33 General Comment 21/44, supra (note 21), para. 4. *Cf* HRC case *Mukong v. Cameroon*, No. 458/1991, para. 9.3 in which the HRC observed that 'certain minimum standards regarding the conditions of detention must be observed regardless of the State Party's level of development'. *Inter alia*, the HRC refers to Rules, provided in the UN Standard Minimum Rules for the Treatment of Prisoners (ECOSOC Res. 663 C (XXIV) of 31 July 1957 and 2076 (LXII) of 13 May 1977) regarding minimum conditions of accommodation, clothing, food and health. The HRC adds that 'these [Rules 10, 12, 17, 19 and 20] are minimum requirements which the [HRC] considers should always be observed, even if the economic or budgetary considerations may make compliance with these obligations difficult'; S. JOSEPH, J. SCHULTZ and M. CASTAN, supra (note 23), 250.

34 The latter approach – unfortunately - seems to be more realistic than the observations of the HRC. In addition, improving conditions of detention, while not taking into account the developmental level of a State Party, may lead to problematic differences between life outside the detention facility and life inside. Unfortunately, it goes beyond the scope of this paper to elaborate more on this.

35 G. VAN BUEREN, supra (note 7), 222; General Comment 21/44, supra (note 21), par. 3 in which the HRC speaks of 'restrictions that are *unavoidable* in a closed environment'.

implementation of Article 3 of the CRC, the question raises what this means in more concrete terms. What should be incorporated in this legal status? This paragraph will address the content of the legal status of children in detention and can be divided into three parts, namely separation from adults, contact with the family and minimum standards for detention provided by the JDLs.

3.2.2. Separation of children and adults

14. As mentioned before CRC Article 37(c) explicitly provides two elements of the requirement of treatment with humanity. The first one is that a child shall be detained separately from adults, unless it is not in the child's best interest to do so. Similar requirements can be found in Article 10 of the CCPR. In paragraph 2(b) Article 10 stipulates, "[a]ccused juvenile persons shall be separated from adults" and according to paragraph 3 "[j]uvenile offenders shall be segregated from adults".[36]

Separation of juveniles and adults is not only important in light of the protection of the child. It also helps to create an environment that has been specifically designed for children and meets their special needs.[37] It furthermore implies that juveniles and adults should be housed in different institutions or in separate facilities within the same institution.[38]

Both provisions of CCPR Article 10 can be considered as absolute, due to the absence of possible exemptions. This has led to many reservations, mostly by Western

[36] The term 'juvenile persons' is not defined. The HRC has suggested 'that all persons under the age of 18 should be treated as juveniles, at least in matters relating to criminal justice' and the HRC has explicitly invited 'State Parties [with regard to their indication about the age groups of persons treated as juveniles] (...) to indicate whether they are applying the United Nations Standard Minimum Rules for the Administration of Juvenile Justice, also know as the Beijing Rules (198[7])'; General Comment 21/44, supra (note 21), para. 13. It goes beyond the scope of this paper to elaborate on this. Furthermore, Art. 10(2)(b) and (3) apply to persons detained under the criminal justice system only, while Art. 37(c) CRC applies to all forms of deprivation of liberty of children. Art. 10(2) CCPR also prohibits detention of accused and convicted persons together. This applies to detained juveniles as well.

[37] *Cf* Art. 24 CCPR and Preamble and Rule 28 JDLs. Regarding detention and imprisonment under the juvenile criminal justice system a legal basis for this 'special treatment' can be found in Art. 40(3) CRC.

[38] G. Van Bueren, supra (note 7), 220–221. *Cf* the HRC case *Pinkey v. Canada* (No. 27/1978) in which the HRC found that the 'requirement of article 10(2)(a) of the Covenant [segregation of pre-trial detainees and convicted detainees; *Cf* Rule 17 JDLs – tl] (...) means that [accused and convicted persons] shall be kept in separate quarters (but not necessarily in separate buildings)'. The HRC allowed (under Art. 10(2)(a)) an arrangement in which a remand prisoner, although placed in a cell in an area separated from the area of convicted persons, got his food served from a convicted prisoner, and in which convicted persons worked as cleaners in the remand unit.

(European) Countries, who believed that an absolute prohibition was inappropriate.[39] The drafters of the CRC considered among other things these objections and added the words "unless it is not in the child's best interest to do so". This implies that the child's best interests must be assessed when a State Party is not willing or not able to live up to requirement of separation. VAN BUEREN argues that "[a]n example of non-separation in the best interests of the child is where there are inadequate facilities for detained children and to detain a child separately may be tantamount to solitary confinement". She adds that "[w]hen assessing the child's best interests the State Party is under a duty to consult the child' and that the CRC in this regard "provides a State with an impetus to admit to the existence of child prisoners in adult institutions and to recognise their entitlements".[40]

Rule 29 of the JDLs has worked out this requirement of Article 37(c) of the CRC.[41] According to this rule "[i]n all detention facilities juveniles should be separated from adults, unless they are members of the same family".[42] Juveniles may be brought together, but under strict conditions. Rule 29 demands "controlled conditions", "carefully selected adults" and the placement must be "part of a special programme that has been shown to be beneficial for the juveniles concerned".

3.2.3. *Contact with family*

15. The second element of the requirement of treatment with humanity, that has been highlighted explicitly in Article 37(c) CRC, is that the child deprived of liberty "shall have the right to maintain contact with his or her family through correspondence and visits, save in exceptional circumstances". Although the CCPR, obviously, does not entail a similar provision, the HRC has commented that "[a]llowing visits, in particular by family members, is also such a measure, which is required for reasons of humanity".[43] Again, this requirement is not absolute. On the initiative of the representative of the Netherlands, the phrase "save in exceptional circumstances" has been added.[44] The rationale behind this was that a State Party should have discretion to leave the principle, that a child must be able to maintain contact with his family, if his best interests requires to do so, for example to avoid that the child will be exposed to bad influences.[45] VAN BUEREN argues that "*[i]t is clear that it is an exception, which*

---

39 M. NOWAK, supra (note 4), 243 and 252 and G. VAN BUEREN, supra (note 7), 221.
40 G. VAN BUEREN, supra (note 7), 222.
41 *Cf* Rule 8 (d) UN Standard Minimum Rules for the Treatment of Prisoners.
42 For more information on children detained together with imprisoned members of their family see, e.g. G. VAN BUEREN, supra (note 7), 226–227.
43 General Comment 9/16 of 30 July 1982, para. 3. The HRC has deleted this phrase in General Comment 21/44, supra (note 21), which has replaced General Comment 9.
44 S. DETRICK, supra (note 4), 636; G. VAN BUEREN, supra (note 7), 220.
45 G. VAN BUEREN, supra (note 7), 219.

should be exercised only in accordance with the child's best interests and not imposed as a disciplinary measure or as a means of securing the child's cooperation".[46] It needs no explanation that the maintenance of contact between the child and his/her family is of the utmost importance for the reintegration of the child, one of the main objectives of the juvenile justice system, stipulated by Article 40(1) of the CRC.

3.2.4. Minimum Standards for Detention

16. Besides the specific elements of the CRC itself, the implications of the requirement of treatment with humanity affect the general state of the detention facilities or the minimum conditions of detention. Where, *inter alia*, the UN Standard Minimum Rule for the Treatment of Prisoners (1957/1977) should be used for the interpretation of Article 10(1)[47], the JDLs contain rules regarding the fulfilment of the requirement laid down in Article 37(c) of the CRC. This UN resolution, although considered as so-called soft international law, gives content to the requirement of treatment with humanity of children in detention. It is worthwhile taking a closer look at the JDLs, although it goes beyond the scope of this paper to discuss them in detail.

The purpose of the JDLs is "to [counteract] the detrimental effects of all types of detention and to [foster] integration [of the child] in society" by establishing minimum norms for children deprived of their liberty, that are accepted by the United Nations and that are "consistent with human rights and fundamental freedoms".[48] According to O'DONNELL one of the principles underlying the JDL's is "the principle of incompleteness", which means that the JDLs do not proclaim that institutions should be designed to meet all the requirements under international law.[49] Instead, the use of community facilities should be stimulated in order "to foster integration and minimise stigmatisation".[50] An example of this principle is Rule 30 which prescribes that open institutions for juveniles should be established. Another principle of the JDLs is that they intend to promote a greater respect for the dignity of the juvenile, "building on the widely accepted tent that self-respect is essential for the healthy development

---

46 G. VAN BUEREN, supra (note 7), 220 with further reference to Art. 12(1) and 9(4) CRC. *Cf* Rules 59ff JDLs that work out this requirement and Rule 67 JDLs that prohibits the denial of contact with the family as a disciplinary measure.

47 General Comment 21/44, supra (note 21), para. 5ff; *Cf* S. JOSEPH, J. SCHULTZ and M. CASTAN, supra (note 23), 283–285 and S.M. BERNARD, 'An Eye for an Eye: The Current Status of International Law on the Humane Treatment of Prisoners', (1994) 25 *Rutgers L.J. (Rutgers Law Journal)*, 759–798.

48 Rule 3 JDLs.

49 D. O'DONNELL, 'The UN Draft Standard Minimum Rules for the Protection of Juveniles Deprived of their Liberty. A Legal Revolution', (1988) 22–23 *Children's Rights*. O'DONNELL has been involved in the drafting process of the JDLs.

50 D. O'DONNELL, ibid, 23. See Rule 8.

of the child".[51] In addition, it is important to stress that many rules use "rights terminology" which has been done to emphasise that disregard of these rules may very well amount to violation of human rights embodied in hard international law instruments. The child is recognised as a rights-holder, which has been acknowledged by Rule 13 which states that "[j]uveniles deprived of their liberty shall not for any reason related to their status be denied the civil, economic, political, social or cultural rights to which they are entitled under national or international law, and which are compatible with the deprivation of liberty". O'DONNELL stresses furthermore that a couple of fundamental rights that are enshrined in (different rules of) the JDLs, namely the right of the juvenile to understand the process of institutional treatment, which has been considered by the experts during the drafting process as to be of "fundamental importance in the process of rehabilitation", the right to have contact with the family and the right to protection against arbitrary treatment.[52]

17. The JDLs contain a preamble and five sections. The first section (I) embodies "fundamental perspectives", one of which is the objective of the JDLs as described earlier and the second section (II) the scope and application of the rules, including the definitions of the terms 'juveniles' and 'deprivation of liberty' (Rule 11). A special section (III) has been designed for juveniles under arrest or awaiting trial and entails a few extra requirements, above those contained in section (IV), which should be applicable to this group of juveniles, taking into account their special status as non-convicted persons within the (juvenile) criminal justice system (Rule 18). The fifth and final section (V) contains rules regarding the (training of) personnel working in juvenile institutions.[53]

The fourth and largest section (IV) aims at the management of juvenile facilities and covers many different aspects of detention of juveniles. These rules can be divided into three groups. The first group of rules concerns aspects of the administration and organisation of the institutions and includes rules regarding records (Rule 19ff), admission, registration, movement and transfer (Rule 21ff), classification and placement (Rule 27ff), and rules regarding the notification of family members in case of illness, injury or death of a juvenile, or *vice versa*, of a family member (Rule 56ff).

The second group can be characterised as the group with rules regarding *substantive rights*, including physical environment and accommodation (Rule 31ff), education, vocational training and work (Rule 38ff), recreation (Rule 47), religion (Rule 48),

---

[51] D. O'DONNELL, ibid, 23. See e.g. Rule 31.

[52] D. O'DONNELL, ibid, 23. See e.g. Rules 59ff (contact with wider community) and 66ff (disciplinary measures).

[53] See also Art. 3(3) CRC that provides for a hard international legal fundamental requirement for, *inter alia*, suitable staff.

medical care (Rule 49ff), contact with the wider community (Rule 59ff) and rules regarding the child's return to the community (Rule 79ff). This group of rules reflects the child's right to civil and political rights, as well as economic, social and cultural rights, which fits into the Article 37(c) CRC's implication that every child must be entitled to all rights under the CRC.[54]

The third group of section (IV) of the JDLs contains rules regarding the *procedural rights.* These include rules regarding limitations of physical restraint and the use of force (Rule 63ff), regarding disciplinary procedures (Rule 66ff), and rules for inspection and complaints (Rule 72 ff). This group of rules is of significant importance for the protection of the child against arbitrary and unlawful treatment inside the detention facility. As mentioned before the legal status of a child in detention contains three elements, entitlement to all rights under the CRC, limitations of the enjoyment only if required by execution and objectives of detention and full compliance with the best interests of the child principle. For an effective legal status, it is of the utmost importance that it contains a specific set of rights and duties meant to protect the child against unlawful and arbitrary treatment, including the right to file complaints.[55]

4. IMPLEMENTATION ON THE DOMESTIC LEVEL

4.1. IMPLEMENTATION IS A DOMESTIC MATTER

18. In order to implement the right to be treated with humanity and, therefore, strengthen the legal status of the child in detention it is important that it is concretely elaborated and included in national law, as part of the national statutory law. Implementation of international law is primarily a domestic matter. Based on for example Article 4 of the CRC, State Parties are under the obligation to translate human rights guarantees into domestic rights for individuals.[56] Subsequently, the JDLs invite States to adopt legislation and regulations that establish the norms provided in the rules.[57]

---

54 *Cf* Rule 13.

55 *Cf* Art. 2(3) CCPR that prescribes that State Parties should ensure an effective remedy to every person whose rights have been violated, before a competent authority. See also General Comment 21/44, supra (note 21), para. 7.

56 S. DETRICK, supra (note 4), 100; *Cf* Art. 2 CCPR; S. JOSEPH, J. SCHULTZ and M. CASTAN, supra (note 23), 14.

57 E.g. Rule 68 states that competent administrative authorities should adopt legislation or regulations regarding the conduct of juveniles that constitutes a disciplinary offence, the type and duration of disciplinary sanctions that may be inflicted, the authority competent to impose such sanctions and the authority competent to consider appeals, 'taking full account of the fundamental characteristics, needs and rights of juveniles'. *Cf* General Comment 21/44, supra (note 21), para. 5.

4.2. DUTCH YOUTH CUSTODIAL INSTITUTIONS ACT

4.2.1. Domestic legislation specifically designed for children in youth custodial institutions

19. This paragraph presents – in an overview – an example from the Netherlands that has the potential to strengthen the legal status of detained children; the Youth Custodial Institutions Act (YCIA).[58] The YCIA came into force on 1st September 2001. It was drawn up as a framework Act on the execution of deprivation of liberty in Dutch youth custodial institutions.[59] The most important objective of the YCIA is to strengthen the legal status of children in youth custodial institutions. To this end, the YCIA contains clearly defined and verifiable rights and duties. The rights and duties concern the most important objectives of the deprivation of liberty (and thus the functions of a youth custodial institution): security, upbringing and (social) rehabilitation. Treatment can be an objective, too. Based on these objectives (i.e. grounds) the civil rights of children can be restricted.

The YCIA provides for minimum rules with regard to placement, replacement, to register a complaint against placement, and the possibility to request (re)placement (e.g. in the vicinity of the family). It entails also provisions with regard to (obligatory) education, upbringing and (personal, health, spiritual) care and provisions for leave arrangements, contact with family through correspondence, telephone (two times 10 minutes per week) and visits (1 hour minimum; parents and lawyers may have a meeting in private if this is not against the best interests of the child), and contact with for example the mass media. Furthermore, the YCIA embodies rules regarding a so-called Training and Schooling programme, as a form of placement outside the institution to help the child reintegrate into society.

With regard to the child's procedural legal status in particular, the YCIA prescribes in detail on what grounds and by whom the child's civil rights may be restricted. In essence, these restrictions must be based on the grounds of the deprivation of liberty as mentioned before (security, upbringing, rehabilitation and treatment). Furthermore, these restrictions may only be imposed by the administration of the institution. The child needs to be heard in advance and he/she must receive a written copy of the decision. Some forms of restriction are: inspection and screening, use of force, measures to restore the order or safety in the institution or to protect the child, and

[58] This example is not meant to be the only possible example. However there is not much legislation known –worldwide – that is specifically designed for children deprived of their liberty.

[59] In the Netherlands children can be placed in youth custodial institutions on different grounds. Besides detention or imprisonment under the juvenile justice system, children can be placed in institutions on the basis of a court order under child protection law, mental health law or immigration law.

disciplinary sanctions, like placement in solitary confinement. Every youth institution must have its own independent supervising committee that can visit the institution at any time and should do this at least twice a month according to the YCIA.

The YCIA provides for the right to file a complaint against individual decisions taken by, or on behalf of, the administration of the institution. An independent complaint commission of the supervising committee hears the complaints. There is also an appeal procedure at the Council for the Administration of Criminal Justice and Youth Protection (a national independent supervising committee). Furthermore, the YCIA provides for the right to an interpreter and the right of (legal) assistance.[60]

The evaluation of the YCIA, published in 2004, concluded that in general the YCIA is working reasonably well and that it has improved the legal status of the children in youth custodial institutions.[61] The following paragraph will address some of the benefits and the challenges of legislation, like the YCIA, that incorporates, *inter alia*, the international legal requirement that children in detention must be treated with humanity.[62]

4.2.2. Benefits and challenges of domestic legislation

20. One of the biggest problems the YCIA is confronted with is that it applies to institutions based on a welfare approach where the best interests of the child are the leading objective, which in essence is good in light of Article 3 of the CRC. However, staff (team leaders and group workers) of the Dutch institutions find the strong emphasis on the legal position of the child to be a barrier to their pedagogical tasks. Although they are not squarely against it, they expressed the experience that the emphasis on the legal status of the child can frustrate, infringe or limit the process of upbringing and rehabilitation (e.g. by filing complaints). This had also something to do with the fact that the YCIA explicitly made the administration of the institution responsible for decisions with regard to the restriction of the civil rights of children. Furthermore, the YCIA is a complex legal instrument and because of that group workers had to become part-time lawyers.[63] One of the big lessons learned is the vast

---

[60] T. LIEFAARD, *Toegang tot de Beginselenwet justitiële jeugdinrichtingen,* (Amsterdam: SWP, 2005).

[61] M.R. BRUNING, T. LIEFAARD and L.M.Z. VOLF, *Rechten van jongeren in justitiële jeugdinrichtingen. Evaluatie Beginselenwet justitiële jeugdinrichtingen,* (Amsterdam: Amsterdam Centre for Child Studies / Vrije Universiteit Amsterdam, 2004), 75–76.

[62] Obviously, legislation like the YCIA can be used to implement the other relevant provisions of Art. 37 and 40 CRC as well.

[63] Or at least they had the feeling they had to become part-time lawyers. Another point is that the emphasis on legal status is now and then experienced, unrightfully, as inappropriate, because it effects juvenile delinquents or children accused of delinquent behaviour, in essence 'no sweeties'.

importance of educating (in a broad sense) all the staff involved as the legislation enters into force.

Another important aspect is that a legal instrument like this can be ineffective by the fact that the children are not aware of their legal position. One of the questions should be: How can we increase the awareness of children's legal position among the children themselves? One might think of some kind of education, an intake conversation (a counterargument would be that this would overemphasise legal status), an hour's consultation with a lawyer or legal aid service, a regular meeting with the independent supervising committee, etc. Although the YCIA prescribes that, a child should be informed about his/her rights when he/she enters the institution, the evaluation shows that children are aware of the fact that they have rights, but they seem to experience their rights without having really been aware of them in advance. In general, the children themselves find a strong legal position of great importance.

More in general it can be said that legal instruments like the YCIA cannot work (or can be very much ineffective) without sufficient resources[64] and (political) will to implement them; the (infamous) gap between "the law in theory and the law in practice".

Nevertheless, a legal framework, as the YCIA, meant specifically for children deprived of their liberty, provides for legal standards, legal principles that a country accepts with regard to this group of children. It gives content to the provisions of international legal instruments as the legally binding but broadly formulated CRC, and can help to provide the more detailed JDLs with a more legally binding effect. It can be used as a framework of reference, as a tool for advocacy on the national level. That is to say: "These are the principles we have agreed upon. We are willing to protect the fundamental rights of children deprived of their liberty." Finally yet importantly, it shows that a country in essence respects the rights of the child and acknowledges the child as the holder of these rights.

5. CONCLUSION

21. Many children, worldwide, find themselves in detention, a (closed) environment that lacks transparency and that makes them particularly vulnerable to abusive practices. Therefore, it is of great importance to acknowledge that every child in detention has the right to be treated with humanity and respect for the inherent dignity

64 Although, this cannot be used by the State Party as an argument for not implementing international legal standards in this regard. See earlier above para. 3.1.5.

of the human person, and in a manner, that takes into account the needs of persons of his or her age. This paper has tried to address the implications of this requirement laid down in Article 37(c) of the CRC.

State Parties are under the positive obligation to establish minimum conditions of detention and provide all children in detention with a legal status that guarantees that a child is treated with humanity and with respect for his human dignity. By implication, every child must, first, be recognised a rights-holder entitled to all rights under the CRC. The enjoyment of these rights may only be limited if required by the (execution of) the detention and with full implementation of the best interests of the child principle of Article 3 of the CRC. Subsequently, the legal status of the child in detention must be concretely elaborated on and included in domestic (statutory) law, and embody at least the rights of the child to be separated from adults and to maintain contact with his family, unless it is not in the child's best interests to do so. In addition, the legal status should meet the minimum requirements provided by the JDLs, and include, besides substantive rights, a specific set of rights meant to protect the child from arbitrary and unlawful treatment, including the right to file complaints.

Obviously, the requirement of treatment with humanity is not the only requirement regarding children in detention. This paper has left aside, for example, the prohibition of torture or cruel, inhuman or degrading treatment (Art. 37(a) CRC) and the rights of the child to have legal or other appropriate assistance and to *habeas corpus* (Art. 37(d) CRC), which are of significant importance for children in detention as well.

This paper has tried to address the implications of the right of every child in detention to be treated as every other child and with respect for its human dignity. An attempt that is based on the conviction that lives up to this requirement, will serve Article 40(1) CRC's objective that every child within the juvenile justice system will be reintegrated, in order to be able to play its constructive role in society.

RESTORATIVE JUSTICE IN BELGIUM: FROM DREAM TO REALITY

Isabelle Delens-Ravier

1. INTRODUCTION

1. The restorative justice model certainly influenced the debates on the reform of the 1965 Act on the Protection of Young People, which governs the judicial response to infringements of the law committed by minors. However, the new law recently adopted by Parliament falls far short of establishing a new justice model for minors. This paper will analyse the "alternative" restorative measures set down in this new law from the point of view of the experience of young delinquents.

2. THE IMPACT OF THE UN CONVENTION ON THE RIGHTS OF THE CHILD

2. The idea of alternatives to a delinquency management model and to detention and imprisonment is not set down as such in the Convention on the Rights of the Child. Although, the latter does clearly state that the detention and imprisonment of children and young people shall be used only as a measure of last resort as it is "harmful to the child's physical, mental and moral development".

The principles it lays down do not claim to establish any particular model of justice for minors, but rather make it necessary to ensure a variety of social reactions to juvenile delinquency[1] in order to achieve the objectives laid down in the Convention. This is done by introducing a range of measures relating in particular to care, guidance, supervision, counselling, probation, foster care, education and vocational training programmes and other alternatives to institutional care. Article 40(3)(b) states similarly that precedence should be given to measures other than judicial proceedings. The framework laid down is thus extremely broad.

---

1 UN Convention on the Rights of the Child, Art. 40(4).

While the Council of Europe guidelines are based on the Convention itself, they have evolved in line with the debates under way in society. Thus, while in 1987[2] the recommendations by the Council of Europe ministers concerned the gradual elimination of imprisonment and the need for particular attention to be paid to probation assistance, intensive education, repair of damage, community work, etc., by 2003 the scope had become considerably reduced, and the recommendations were then confined to the gradual abolition of imprisonment, but with rehabilitation programmes in the event of imprisonment.[3]

3. A NEW MODEL OF RESTORATIVE JUSTICE?[4]

3. As a new paradigm, the restorative justice model seeks to reconcile the interests of the community, the victims and the young delinquent with a view to achieving social rehabilitation in which the repair of the damage caused to the victim satisfies the objective of social pacification and hence the interests of the community. It is no longer a question of "punishment" by inflicting one wrong in exchange for another wrong, but of repairing the damage and rehabilitating the offender in society. The restorative justice model supports the ideal of justice that is "participatory, softer and closer to citizens, and which endeavours at their level to combat the breakdown of social links".[5] It shifts the perspective from the minor to the damage as an expression of the disruption of social links. Thus, according to WALGRAVE, the question is no longer, as in protective justice systems, what to do with the delinquent, but rather what to do to repair the damage. "As a new paradigm, restorative justice adopts a "participatory democracy" perspective based on a socio-ethical approach which encourages all citizens to actively take their responsibilities and to show solidarity in order to contribute constructively to community life. This position runs counter to "consumer democracy" in which citizens consume the services supplied by social institutions without worrying about the consequences on social life in general. Each citizen is required to participate in social functioning and hence to contribute to peace and to

[2] Recommendation R (87) 20 of the Committee of Ministers to the Member States on social reactions to juvenile delinquency.

[3] Recommendation R (2003) 20 of the Committee of Ministers to the Member States concerning new ways of dealing with juvenile delinquency and the role of juvenile justice.

[4] See I. DELENS-RAVIER, C. VANDRESSE, 'La réforme de la protection de la jeunesse: quelles alternatives ?', in J. CHRISTIAENS, D. DE FRAENE, I. DELENS-RAVIER (eds.), *Protection de la jeunesse, formes et réformes – Jeugdbescherming, vormen en hervorming,* (Bruxelles: Bruylant, 2005), 195–196.

[5] Y. CARTUYVELS, F. DIGNEFFE, D. KAMINSKI, 'Droit pénal et déformalisation', in J. DE MUNCK and M. VERHOEVEN (eds.), *Les mutations du rapport à la norme,* (Paris – Bruxelles: De Boeck & Larcier, 1997), 232.

good relations in the community. Even victims of crime are still citizens responsible for the collective well-being".[6]

The damage is remedied by restorative action and by the process which precedes this. There are a number of direct and indirect, practical and symbolic types of restorative action, aimed at the actual victim, his or her family and/or a specific community or society in general: restoration of goods, compensation, repair of damage, reconciliation, apologies and so on. Repairing damage/compensation of victims and community service are archetypes with many variants. Priority should be given to a process of deliberation to ensure greater motivation by the delinquent. That is why the process leading to the restorative action itself is extremely important, as it is through this process that a situation of frank and informal exchanges is created between the victims and the delinquent. The delinquent's motivation is of vital importance in ensuring a restorative effect. The "restorative power" of compensation will be greater if the delinquent wholeheartedly agrees to do it than if he/she is resigned to it only to avoid the consequences of his/her actions. By agreeing to community service, a young person begins to understand his/her accountability in terms of the damage and suffering caused by his/her behaviour".[7]

The current attachment to more humane, negotiated justice, the concept of repairing damage is "fashionable" and, while it encompasses a number of different practices, it represents one of the most important changes in criminal law.[8] It comprises the idea of "a different kind of justice" and the hope that it is possible to humanise the criminal justice system. It embodies the wish of a number of actors to work towards rehabilitation and building relations even in a prison situation. The concept of restorative justice has given rise to debates and discussions about the reform of the protection of young people in Belgium although the model has not really changed.

4. LEGAL BACKGROUND IN BELGIUM – RESTORATIVE MEASURES

4. The current government has decided not to choose a new, alternative juvenile delinquency management model. The agreement it has reached explicitly provides

---

6 I. Delens-Ravier, 'La réforme de la protection de la jeunesse, vue de Flandre ; Synthèse de l'intervention de L. Walgrave', in *La réaction sociale à la délinquance juvénile, Questions critiques et enjeux d'une réforme, Revue de droit pénal et de criminologie,* Dossier n° 10, (Bruges : La Charte, 2004), 42.

7 L. Walgrave, 'La justice restaurative et la justice pénale: un duo ou un duel', in R. Cario (ed.), *Victimes : du traumatisme à la restauration – œuvre de justice et victimes vol. 2,* (Paris : l'Harmattan, 2002), vol. 2, 281.

8 Y. Cartuyvels, F. Digneffe, D. Kaminski, supra (note 5).

for the "modernisation of the law on the protection of young people by establishing in law a series of practices to be developed by the public prosecutor and by juvenile judges, and by introducing certain innovations into the treatment of a minor who has committed an offence".[9] The reform is not really intended to change the paradigm. While endeavouring to "ensure better protection for young people and give them every opportunity and assistance to rehabilitate in our demanding society", the new regulation is aimed at establishing a restorative approach to delinquency by emphasising the assumption of responsibility by the young person and the development of awareness of victims' rights. This is to be done by introducing alternative measures to imprisonment, as well as by a system that penalises.

Thus, the new law governing the treatment of minors who have committed offences supplements the "welfare state" approach to juvenile justice by establishing a series of practices based on restorative justice and by reforming the treatment of offending minors. For instance, by means of "more appropriate responses in situations where the welfare approach has turned out to be ineffective, such as in the case of persistent offenders or minors who have committed a serious crime. The response by society to a minor who has committed an offence must be educational, preventive, rapid and effective, and must involve protection, education and restraint".[10]

It provides juvenile courts with a series of measures, which judges can use with respect to these minors, ranging from a reprimand to imprisonment, measures to support these young people in everyday life,[11] the possibility for young people to submit a personal commitment project, restorative measures, mediation and restorative conferences ("family group conferences").[12] Judges can also, in certain precise circumstances, decline jurisdiction and send a minor over the age of 16 before a special chamber of the juvenile court consisting of two juvenile judges and a criminal judge who will apply criminal law.

---

9 Bill amending the legislation concerning the protection of young people and the treatment of minors who have committed offences, *Doc. Chambre,* 2004–2005, 1467/001, 4.

10 Ibid.

11 These measures include the obligation to attend school, to do a maximum of 150 hours of community service, to do a maximum of 150 hours of paid work, to attend an educational guidance centre or to follow instructions issued by a mental health centre, to take part in modules to raise awareness of the acts carried out and the consequences for the victims, to engage in specific supervised activities, bans on frequenting or exercising certain professions or "any other conditions ordered by a court".

12 The aim of these conferences is to allow the perpetrator of an offence, the victim, the social circle involved and any other persons who might be useful to discuss, in a group situation and with the assistance of a neutral moderator, agreed solutions as to how to solve the conflict arising from an offence. The conference consists essentially of a meeting between the victim and his relatives, the delinquent and people he trusts (family members or others) and the police, assisted by a professional moderator.

The new law contains restorative measures including mediation and "Family Group Conferences" or "restorative conferences" already tested in the Flemish Community,[13] as well as a range of other measures. These diversionary measures all introduce a form of negotiation into conflict management, recommended by some in order to solve the problem of overcrowded courts and above all, to allow the parties to deal with the conflict themselves. The restorative philosophy is found in a quite particular material form in the "personal projects": the young person can submit a personal commitment project, which comprises a series of non-restrictive commitments.

This set of measures is presented as a mean of educating minors, getting them to assume responsibility, and allowing them to become aware of the consequences of their acts. Therefore, restorative measures can, following the same protective logic, be superimposed over other measures such as surveillance or imprisonment, without abolishing the latter and without guaranteeing that the "restorative" approach undertaken by the young person will be enough. The law thus allows all these measures to be cumulated and combined, without ruling out the ultimate decision of removing the minor from the juvenile justice system by declining jurisdiction.

5. THE EXPERIENCE OF COMMUNITY SERVICE

5. Our analysis refers to the comments[14] of young people placed in "specialised" institutions, in an open or closed community home, as well as those of young people doing community service. The experience of providing an educational or philanthropic service is recounted by two types of young people, based on very different experiences. Those who were ordered to carry out community service, who completed it and who were positively evaluated by the social workers and host environment, and those who were placed in specialised institutions, in an open or closed community home, but who were confronted with this type of service in one way or another, with some simply refusing to do it.[15]

13 I. VANFRAECHEM, 'Herstelgericht groepsoverleg: een project voor ernstige jeugddelinquentie', in J. CHRISTIAENS, D. DE FRAENE, I. DELENS-RAVIER (eds.), *Protection de la jeunesse, formes et réformes – Jeugdbescherming, vormen en hervorming*, (Brussels: Bruylant, 2005), 229–238.

14 The comments were gathered in the course of qualitative research concerning the experience of judicial measures. They were gathered during semi-guided interviews with young people in specialised institutions or who were doing community service.

15 I. DELENS-RAVIER, C. THIBAUT, 'Du tribunal de la jeunesse au placement en IPPJ: la parole des jeunes', (January 2003) *Revue de Droit Pénal et de Criminologie*, 22–69; I. DELENS-RAVIER, 'Juvenile offenders' perception of community service', in L. WALGRAVE (ed.), *Repositioning Restorative Justice*, (Devon : Willan publishing, 2003), 149–166.

5.1. THE CONCEPT OF "REACTION STRATEGIES"

6. Young people develop different "reaction strategies" to a court decision on restorative measures. The term "strategy" does not indicate a conscious and rational will, but rather a way of reacting to the situation created by the judicial decision, and a way of adapting to the consequences of having their actions submitted to the judicial process.[16]

An analysis of the comments has brought to light various reaction strategies developed by these minors, which indicate the complexity of the elements to be taken into account in order to understand the path taken during their life. The different themes which emerged as "discriminatory" when identifying the various reaction strategies to judicial orders included the social environment (family and school), the delinquency, the judicial aspects, the experience of delinquency, the perception of the judge's decision, the perception of the relationship with the judge, and lastly the perceived role of institutional players involved in dealing with the minor.

We will briefly mention the social and judicial aspects as well as the social, cultural and school profile of these young people subject to a court order, before going on to explain the different reaction strategies, understood as methods of adapting to the consequences of a judicial process and in particular to the restorative measure. We will endeavour to understand, from the subjective point of view of the actor, in this case the young person, how the various "key elements"[17] are linked to the different strategies identified.

5.1.1. Adaptation and rationalisation strategies

7. For these young people, the restorative measure is seen as a way of paying for their "fault". The punishment is perceived as logical and fair. The meeting with the judge and/or the other parties involved is seen as a way to establish relations. Implementation of the community service measure gives rise to a feeling of social usefulness and the repair process allows the young person to rebuild his/her personal image and to re-establish social links.

---

[16] I. DELENS-RAVIER, 'Paroles de jeunes délinquants et stratégies de réaction aux mesures judiciaires', in N. BRUNELLE, M-M. COUSINEAU (eds.), *Trajectoire de déviance juvénile, Les éclairages de la recherche qualitative,* (Québec: Presses de l'Université du Québec, 2005), 179–202.

[17] These key elements refer to the experience of delinquency, the perception of the judge's decision and of the relationship with the latter, the meeting with the institutional players, and the overall assessment of the measure based on their perception of the institutional regime.

5.1.2. *Strategy of indifference*

8. This type of young person is characterised by imperviousness. They try above all not to expose themselves to the social workers by conforming as little as possible. For them, community service is an unavoidable punishment that is less onerous than imprisonment. The evaluation of the community service is generally positive, but these young people do not make an effort as regards the restorative process. It can be said that the immediate effects of the offence are repaired, but social links are not restored.

5.1.3. *Strategy of withdrawal-rejection*

9. For these young people, the judicial measure is an unbearable punishment. The young delinquents refuse to participate and to contribute in providing the service, which is why the judge then decides to place them in a specialised institution. The penalty is perceived as deeply unjust and the community service is experienced as an additional humiliation: "don't expect me to work for this f... society, to give it my time and my energy when it has never given me anything!" is the type of comment heard from this type of young person.

6. CONCLUSIONS

10. The very different comments made by the young people on community service provide grounds for the hypothesis that the reaction strategy is linked to the relations that the young person maintains with social workers in terms of integration or exclusion. Thus, the measure may be perceived as a penalty that enables them to turn the page, as an unavoidable penalty that is less bothersome than imprisonment or as an additional, unbearable humiliation.

Not all the young people concerned experience restorative measures as restorative. In this respect, the reform adopted in Belgium does pose some questions as regards the counterproductive nature of placing restorative measures within the framework of the youth welfare system as being possibly punishing. Thus, the accumulation and possible gradation of court decisions have every chance of being perceived by a young person as an accumulation of punishments, which will certainly arouse a strong feeling of injustice that will undermine the reparative effect.[18] The various reaction strategies show that the same restorative measure can produce very different reparative effects, and even have no reparative effect at all for some young people because of their

[18] J. Christiaens, D. Defraene, I. Delens-Ravier (eds.), supra (note 4).

perception of the justice of the decision and because of their social position. Reaction strategies are linked to social relationships based on integration and exclusion.

The legitimacy and feeling of justice regarding the decision, which triggers the reparative process of the young people, the victim and the social link, depend on whether the judicial response is perceived as fair and proportionate, and whether there is a feeling of social inclusion, which can be established or even reinforced through community service. However, if the young person has the impression that the judge is imposing penalty upon penalty, does not know him/her and is not considering him/her, then the judicial reaction is seen as unjust. For these young people characterised by a lack of connections with any socialisation institution, and living in marginalised, unstable families, restorative measures are not perceived as an educational penalty or as an alternative to a more severe measure, but as an unfair penalty highlighting their exclusion. Thus, social, family and school exclusion results in exclusion from these restorative measures because these young people actually exclude themselves by refusing to become involved.

The quest for recognition is at the core of strategies of adjustment to the judicial process. It is by establishing a relationship of trust between a young person and an adult, which will enable the young person to reform himself/herself and restore or create a social link. The experience of the judicial process can permit this reciprocal recognition since the underlying logic repair is not a one-way process, from the young person to the victim and society, but must be a process of joint construction of a social link. It is not so much the measure itself as what it permits in terms of an encounter that is important in the restorative process. Therefore, we think that it is important to examine this in order to find out in which framework and under which conditions these measures can effectively perform the function of restoration of the social link. The comments and practices that emerge from the idea to give children and young people more rights should not become a concealed method of making them depend on themselves and leaving them on their own to rebuild their social integration. The restorative method is primarily interactive.

IX. IMPACT OF THE ECONOMIC, POLITICAL AND CULTURAL ASPECTS ON THE APPLICATION OF THE CRC

THE CONVENTION ON THE RIGHTS OF THE CHILD PUT TO THE TEST BY POWER RELATIONS AND SOCIAL NORMS IN RURAL WEST AFRICA

GUY MASSART

1. MULTI-SITED[1] ETHNOGRAPHICAL RESEARCH

1. Plan International is a child-centred, international, non-governmental organisation,[2] working in eleven countries in West Africa. Plan's West African Regional Research and Evaluation Unit is currently conducting action-research into the daily experiences of children and youths so that their daily experiences can better inform future Plan interventions. This project, entitled "*Listening to the Experiences of Children and Young People: Agents of our Contemporary World*", is being carried out in collaboration with five African research centres, in Benin (LASDEL), Guinea (University of Kankan, Department of Sociology), Guinea Bissau (INEP), Niger (LASDEL) and Senegal (IFAN, University Cheikh Anta Diop).

2. The present article is based on rural realities in four of the five countries involved. The data from Senegal being from urban settings will not be taken into account here. Ten African researchers (ethnographers) speaking the local languages will soon produce eight ethnographies based on five to six months of residential fieldwork in villages. The fieldwork itself has now been finished. The feedback and validation of the main findings with the youths, children and their communities has already taken place. However, the final reports and transcription of data have not yet all been completed. Nevertheless, the benefit of sharing this process and preliminary results justifies this deviation from the methodology and political stance it strives to materialise.

---

1 G.E. MARCUS, 'Imagining the Whole', (1989) 9 *Critique of Anthropology*, 7–30.

2 <www.plan-international.org>.

2. METHODOLOGICAL OPTIONS

3. Solid research rests on the active involvement of the children and youths. Therefore, particular attention was given to using child-friendly methods of data collection to encourage their free expression. Affinity groups of children and youths (constituted spontaneously by the children before the study) were invited by the ethnographers to dramatise themes of their own choice. Community of inquiry[3] exercises were also implemented by affinity groups. Children and youths also produced photo-reports on their daily activities, during which one child followed another during a whole day. This activity was called "on the heels of...". It allowed the researcher to record the daily activities of the children. Finally, children interviewed each other about their aspirations for the future: taking the roles of interviewer and interviewee in turn, they imagined themselves five and ten years from today. All the material gathered was fed back to the children and their communities during village feedback sessions that took place in each fieldwork site. The research aimed to give the children and the youths a central role in the elaboration of the data and its interpretation. Thus, one of its specific objectives was to ensure the effective participation of the children in the production and interpretation of the data.

4. No specific theme was selected for this research, as it was expected that themes would emerge naturally from the children's different forms of expression. Once the themes had emerged, the children were then encouraged to reflect upon them. This reflexivity was facilitated through the specific tools mentioned above. During this process, the ethnographers were encouraged to concentrate on what the children were trying to communicate. Conscious that making sense of the world is a power issue,[4] the research was looking for child-authored, folk sociologies. It would be misleading to assume that all children and youths share the same sociology, as this varies with age and gender as well as other important characteristics. Their immediate interests, their roles and preoccupations change according to a combination of the factors such as age, gender and access to exogenous knowledge, socio-economic position and their status in the kinship group they live in. This research shows clearly that girls are an oppressed group at the bottom of the social ladder. For example, the status of their own mother in polygamous society is very important to their own position, whereas, young men perceive that their coming of age brings them closer to the positions of power held by the elders, as they grow out of adolescence. However, changing social conditions render the reproduction of the hegemonic masculine positions held by their fathers and ancestors nearly impossible for them.

---

[3] See M. SASSEVILLE (ed.), *La pratique de la philosophie avec les enfants*, (Québec: Les Presses de l'Université Laval, 1999).

[4] H. WHITE, 'The Value of Narrativity in the Representation of Reality', (1980) 7 *Critical Inquiry*, 5–27.

All of them share the consciousness of these changes. From their point of view, the most significant change that is taking place nowadays is certainly the process of individualisation.

3. THE QUESTIONS

5. This paper is driven by two general questions based on children's voices and practices. Firstly, what are the limits to the applicability of the CRC in the research sites? From this first question, two sub-questions follow: to what extent do the rights and norms of the Convention form part of the children's own expectations? What are the main constraints in applying the CRC in those contexts?

6. The second question is what should be the priorities in terms of intervention in favour of children, of an institution such as Plan International, which shares the values and norms of the Convention? The aim is to get beyond generic explanations, largely phrased in terms of culture, traditions and economy … and take into account the everyday social relations.

4. INDIVIDUALISATION

7. Other empirical and review studies[5] support our findings, not only that the rights of the child are well known to the children, but also that children and youths (at least during interactions with their peers and the researchers) desire that their life choices are respected. They appeared very keen to be themselves and develop their own individuality. In fact, during these exchanges they revealed strong individual identities. This individualisation brings them into conflict with the local leaders and authorities whose expectations of young people are based on their gender, age and religious and political roles. The most sensitive sphere being the basic kinship groups run by "fathers".

This critical assessment of constraints at the local level is only possible when alternative positions can be taken. In fact, such a critique requires the mental capacity to consider alternative identities. This implies the existence of other vantage points and of other narratives. There are many links between community logics and structures and the

[5] G. Bonati, 'Baseline Study on Child Rights, Participation, Protection and Communication- Guinea Conakry', (2006) Plan Guinea; C. Norris, 'Analysis of some major child protection issues', Research project, *Listening to the Experiences of Children and Young People: Agents of our Contemporary World*, (2005) Plan International - WARO.

wider world, even in these rural settings. Migrants, students, traders and civil servants move (physically) in and out of the village, and such links have become even more powerful as a result of the growing access to various media, radio, video (video clubs are very common and valued spaces by children and youths), religious institutions and their networks, as well as other sources of social capital, such as non-governmental organisations. The availability of new consumer goods in the villages, including the ever-present drugs, such as alcohol, marijuana and amphetamines, supports this movement between alternative worlds. Therefore, local markets provide essential spaces and occasions which nurture interactions with other worlds and hence, the construction of individual identities.

The quest of the self, or rather, as KAUFMAN puts it, the invention of the self,[6] that is, the construction of identities through different interactions, in dialogue with different realities, people, objects and narratives is a particularly intense activity during adolescence. The specificity of our times seems to rest in the multiplication of the agencies with which the children are in contact.

5. SOCIETAL CONTEXT

8. In this section, a few relevant norms and local practices concerning childhood are described and interpretations of the conditions of their reproduction are suggested.

9. In all the research sites, work appears an essential element in the education of children. From the age of approximately 7 years old, both boys and girls are supposed to accompany adults from their kinship unit (fathers, mothers, elder siblings, uncle, aunts, etc.) in their activities. Children as young as 5 years old carry out domestic chores (laundry, fetching water, sweeping, cooking, retail sales of local products, etc.). These domestic chores are locally considered the least-valued activities necessary to daily life. In fact, children have a very effective role in the reproduction of the basic social unit at a very early stage of their life.

10. When they reach the age of 12 to 13 years, adults consider that children should become autonomous producers in their own right. Besides participating in the works of the larger unit, they are also given means of production that they may partially manage at their own discretion. Their main responsibilities, however, lie in contributing to the well-being of adults. In fact, adults have the power to demand from them whatever they have produced to secure their own survival.

---

[6] J-C. KAUFMAN, *L'invention de soi. Une théorie de l'identité*, (Paris: Armand Colin, 2004).

11. This relationship appears particularly heavy in these mainly polygamous societies where mothers often rely on their children to secure their own means of survival. In the rural communities studied, young adolescent girls form the weakest group, and the one most exposed to violence and exploitation. Rather than as individuals, they are dealt with as extensions of a hegemonic elder, who manages his dependents as extensions of himself. This fact is easily observable in every matter touching upon the reproduction of society. Seniority, gender and caste define the local hierarchy. The management of his dependents by a hegemonic elder actually assimilates them to objects he manipulates to secure his prestige, family honour and wealth, but also to secure the reproduction of a social order resting on social cohesiveness characterised by authoritarianism. Again, girls are the most exposed in this patriarchal system. "Bride wealth", often negotiated without the knowledge of the woman or girl concerned also shows that children's bodies are considered as objects under the control of adults. Control is a constant preoccupation of adults towards children. Girls' bodies, being a central material element of the exchanges and reproduction in these societies, are treated as dangerous and potent objects. Mothers are held responsible for the conformity of their daughters to the order as defended by the male elders. In this sense, the identity quest of the children and the youths stands in direct contradiction with the shaping of the bodies current in these groups. This observation helps to understand the reproduction of female genital cutting (FGC) still very widespread in villages in both Guinea Conakry and Guinea Bissau.[7] In Niger, the young wives of migrants are entrusted to the vigilance of their mothers-in-law and popularly referred to as "pounders" (referring to the laborious task of pounding cereals). The use of this identification reduces their identity to their role as producers at the service of their in-laws.

Where hegemonic masculinity reigns, women and, *a fortiori*, girls are physically constrained to specific spaces under adult control where social order is the strongest, that is, the domestic space. Therefore, markets, school, the bush and video clubs are seen as threatening to social order. The girls' husbands, mothers-in-law or mothers are in charge of policing girls' movements. In fact, mothers in the patriarchal and largely polygamist societies in the research sites are held responsible for girls' conformity. Mothers hold intermediate positions, balanced between their daughters' promotion (for example to support them to go to school or to escape from their fathers' marriage diktats) and their responsibility to ensure their conformity. They

---

7 A. Behrendt, *Les déterminants socio - culturels de la pratique de l'excision en Guinée forestière*, (Dakar, Senegal: Plan International West Africa Regional Office, 2005) ; A. Behrendt, *The practice of excision in Guinea Bissau: Perceptions, attitudes and practices in five regions of the country*, (Bissau: Plan Guinea Bissau, 2006).

oscillate between supporting and reprimanding their daughters in the face of regular feuds with their husbands and co-wives.

In all the research sites, girls interpret the increase of divorce and conjugal violence as the source and proof of their weak position and as constant threats that structure their experience, expectations and tactics. The weakening of their mothers' status in a polygamous household exposes them to dangers. They then respond to the dire need to assure their mothers' survival, by limiting their own efforts to promote their own interests.

Girls understand forced marriage as stemming from the above-described phenomena. On the one hand, the marrying of young girls by elders is a commonly used strategy to maintain social order (delegating the responsibility for controlling girls to the in-laws and husband) and securing the social status of the elders' families, as they understand it. Marrying off daughters is also a way to control girls' individuality and to gain personal, economic and prestigious benefits. On the other hand, becoming pregnant outside marriage often allows girls to counteract the elders' plans while contributing to their stigmatisation and physical reprimand. Risky abortion practices are understandably very common in this context.[8]

12. Children's work is locally seen as having an educational role and as a legitimate participation in the reproduction of the household. Children coming from other households and integrated into local families (whether disciples studying in a Koranic school (*talibé*), orphans or simply children entrusted to wealthier or less impoverished households) are always in weaker positions. Children do not discuss the fact that they have to work; they complain about the workload, and the lack of leisure time.

13. Corporal punishment is seen by all as a legitimate education method. Moreover, in all sites, a strong culture of endurance is found. The capacity to endure suffering and deprivation is put forward both by adults and by children. This culture of endurance is clearly very functional in contexts heavily stigmatised by poverty. In all the situations considered, all social groups convey a deep sense of being poor. This permanent discourse of lack puts real pressure on social relations and helps to reproduce the existing social order, in which, as seen above, a few male elders especially, objectively enjoy a much more comfortable position than other categories. The enjoyment of this hegemonic position is legitimised through the endurance discourse insofar as patience, submission to elders, God's favours (being born a male), and passing time all concurred to bring the elders into the position they now enjoy.

---

[8] The above three paragraphs are drawn from G. Massart, *Violence against girls: their experience and protection in West Africa*, paper presented at the ACPF conference, Addis Ababa, 2006.

14. Children see fear as a very violent and powerful instrument to constrain and to control them. Fear is generated through direct physical violence, spiritual forces, witchcraft activities and isolation from one's peers. Powerful adults exclusively control witchcraft. In their dramatisations, children and youths desperately called on the leading elders to defend and protect them from such harm. During the feedback sessions, where the dramatisations were presented, adults were irritated by the children displaying this in public; just as they were by the children acting out of a forced marriage ending in the death of the young wife (Guinea Bissau, Niger and Benin). Children and youths point to witchcraft's close connection to envy, or in other words, egalitarianism. Discursive egalitarianism, hegemonic leadership and the capacity to endure both psychological and physical suffering significantly shape norms and relations.

15. The instrumentalisation of "tradition" in daily life is patent.[9] The very vagueness of the notion epitomises its uses in stating the opposition being constructed in the villages between the social order defended by adults (especially by religious leaders) and modernity characterised by an anomic and permissive society. Therefore, tradition appears as a central element in a specific form of resistance to neo-colonialism, albeit a form based on the defence of a collective order whose reproduction constrains the aspirations of children and youths to develop and promote their individual identities, in line with the spirit and values conveyed in the CRC. A common trait of both attitudes is the consciousness of living in a society going through a fundamental process of change.

16. Most striking in the communications of the children and adults is the lack of relevance of external agencies, such as the State, local government and international non-governmental organisations. Service providers are mainly referred to in terms of their failure to provide infrastructure, health and education services, and create adequate markets.

Communities are well informed about the rights of the child, but, the institutions, the institutional spaces, the psychosocial services where these rights can be claimed are painfully lacking, leaving children and youths feeling frustrated. This being the case, it is quite understandable that children and youths are very keen to abandon their villages and to find themselves in contexts where they can develop their individual identities and escape from the control of the "community".

---

9 E. Hobsbawm, 'Introduction: Inventing traditions', in E. Hobsbawm and T. Ranger (eds.), *The Invention of Tradition*, (Cambridge: Cambridge University Press, 1983).

6. RESPONSES

17. The tactics, strategies and reactions of children and youths are explored in this section. A general observation is the importance of affinity and peer groups, which allow children and youths to develop collective endeavours to face challenges. Firstly, these groups are instrumental in responding to economic challenges. Secondly, they are often used as platforms where children and young people can express themselves, principally through dance and rap. Furthermore, peer groups are also the privileged loci where children and youths can exchange and bounce ideas and be listened too. Their need for expression and individual attention significantly contrasts with the silence traditionally imposed on youngsters in communities. The development of listening capacities is essential to the effective development of one's self. Among peers, it allows children to make sense of their situation and the world they are living in: the pursuit of making sense is a constant practice. Thirdly, peer groups carve out spheres in which they can develop their own sociability through leisure (gambling, video watching, etc.), and collective work arrangements.

18. Again, the girls, considered as precious objects, central to the reproduction of society, enjoy much less freedom to engage in these activities. From the age of 12 to 13 years, large numbers of both boys and girls develop group economic activities. Although they feel obliged to contribute to their household needs, they are allowed to use the revenues gained at their own discretion. These are principally used to buy clothes and food, pay for school fees, and in a few instances, to constitute informal mutual systems, to pay for literacy courses. These economic activities usually take the form of agricultural services to adults for which they are paid. In Niger and Guinea Bissau, migration strategies by boys are very common. The revenue gained is used to acquire modern consumer goods for themselves and family members, as well as to pay bride-wealth. For all children and youths, the main aim rapidly becomes to acquire resources to express themselves; in fact, these two are often interlinked, and developing one's own identity is generally synonymous with securing a livelihood.

19. As a central theme in these villages, behaviour relating to reproduction and sexuality is usually at the centre of the conflictual relationships between children and adults. In a way, the youths and children replicate the collective norms defended and enforced under the control of elders in the same idioms: the management or use of their bodies and their reproductive potential. On the one hand, early marriage is a declared strategy of elders to maintain the social order and to avoid the shame and the economic loss of having a daughter or a son that becomes involved in a relationship they do not want, or even worse a daughter who becomes pregnant before marriage. This logic is pursued even in extreme cases where the girl has been abused, or forced into intercourse. On the other hand, youths themselves use their bodies to escape from the choices imposed on them by elders: by becoming pregnant, girls lose their exchange value. In any case, this situation puts young girls especially at risk. It also reflects the risky context in which they are growing up. Early pregnancies, beatings and abortions are very common.

In these circumstances, one can conform to the socially imposed norms and endure suffering as a collective destiny, or flee physically or as in several cases witnessed in Benin, even commit suicide to escape from undesirable pressures.

7. LIFE OPTIONS

20. What are the options for children in those village settings? The first is to engage in agriculture, a traditional and necessary activity to secure a living. Another option is school. A third combined or not with the previous is to attend Koranic school led by a master called a *marabout*. As a fourth option, one may have the opportunity, depending on his/her caste, to follow an apprenticeship in the village, or in a town or city. This fourth option leads to the importance of mobility. Mobility is an option open to the young men and boys. Migration can be seasonal or itinerant. Migration is based on the capacity of youths and children to rely on themselves and enhance their social capital,[10] through their use of diverse networks. Migration is an empowering process, insofar as developing social capital is a source of prestige as well as of resources, but is of course littered with risks of exploitation and suffering. In those mobility projects, peer groups based on age, common geographical or ethnical origins are precious. The role of the local *marabout* is very significant in these matters, as they often provide networks and coverage for the mobility of children. Again, depending on the age of the children and their capacity to rely on peers, more experienced migrants and existing remunerated mediators, the *talibés* (disciples of a *marabout*), are often shamelessly used to provide resources for their masters by begging in large cities of the region. Nonetheless, mobility is on the increase, both in numbers and diversity, and is a relevant individually empowering strategy for the children.

21. Although they largely value school for the acquisition of literacy and connections to the outside world, it appears to both the children and their parents as just another option in their survival tactics. And a worse one, in some cases, where school is seen as a dangerous option, especially for girls as it exposes them to the look and lust of others (both peers and teachers); in other words, it removes them from the control of the adults responsible for them. School is also considered critically as it exposes

[10] R. Bekkar-Lacoste and P. Demba Fall, 'Les Sahéliens à l'assaut de la forteresse européenne : de la *patera* marocaine à la pirogue artisanale au départ du Sénégal', (2006) 47 *Zénith Hebdo*, 14–16.

children to values alien to those defended by the "community" (whose agency is embodied by its ruling group), while nurturing their individual aspirations as well as unacceptable behaviour. School is costly for families and hardly prepares the children to earn a living. These local perceptions of school highlight not only the ineffectiveness of the rural education system, but its lack of relevance to the actual milieu, including the local economic situation.

22. Ultimately, from their perspective, children and youths are constantly exposed to a double discourse: the conservation of their "tradition" and of a broad collective identity in which roles are strictly assigned, and to narratives of individual self-fulfilment, in an ever-changing world, whose rhetoric and ideals inspire them and enhance their reflexivity. This realisation implies the construction of a new sociability, which they strive to explore. In fact, one can only lament the almost complete absence in their daily lives of anything to support them in their struggle to be considered as individuals with rights common to all.

23. It was painful to realise that despite all the declarations in favour of participation and the focus on the poorest of the poor and the most vulnerable, by all kinds of agencies, from government to NGOs and the so-called civil society systems, this research revealed that the children and youths in the areas studied were experiencing enormous isolation.

Where are the new social alliances necessary to support their legitimate rights? Where are they to find relevant social spheres to be listened to, to test their own reflexivity? They are all cruelly lacking. No services seem readily available to children and youths beyond their local social networks to help with their initiatives, to support their claims or ease their suffering. Unfortunately, this is a clear negative evaluation of the justice systems and social services, whether delivered by the States or the civil society systems. To presume that awareness raising and advocacy will pressure States to assume "their" responsibilities, not only leaves children and youths in their actual predicament but also reflects a naïve analysis of the actual political systems prevailing in Africa,[11] and of the links of the contemporary governance systems to global factors and actors.[12]

In this sense, raising awareness, as a single strategy to enhance rights, not only falls short of its objective but also is illusionary and reflects an unacceptable distance from the actual experience of children. The problem of transformation of the notion of the individual, is not only a problem of information, but requires profound social changes;

---

[11] A. MBEMBE, 'Du gouvernement privé indirect', (1999) 73 *Politique Africaine*, 6–15.

[12] M. TROUILLOT, 'The Anthropology of the State in the age of Globalization', (2001) 42 *Current Anthropology*, 125–138.

this entails power struggles in which the oppressed need allies and the means to realise their utopia.

8. SOCIAL CHANGE

24. Humans are by nature conservative and reluctant to push for social change.[13] Finally, the complexity of social change must be recognised; social change is not a linear process.[14] The nineteenth century metaphor of the mechanical model of change in which actions have effects resulting in a desired new situation appears epistemologically laughable now. However, this belief seems very prevalent indeed, when observing institutions engaged in social change (NGOs, States). Led by their own accountability and management models,[15] they are compelled to embrace practices dictated by this naïve illusion. Serious consideration of the endeavours of contemporary youths and children compels us to recognise the material and conflictive reality of social change. Much more so when this social change occurs in a situation where wealth is scarce and the struggle over resources between different social actors is fierce. Likewise, it is an illusion to believe that social change will only come about through enhancing reflection and knowledge of the oppressed's own predicament. Power is about constraints and the capacity to gather resources and impose one's will. It is about building social and economic capital.

In such difficult times, anomy is looming at every corner, in every experience. Many people despair of reaching their goals and objectives to know the world, to form a family and to be able to offer one's children a better life. The consciousness of rights without justice and resources enhances the quest for order, meaning and justice. Many popular religious movements offer this kind of meaning as well as material and imaginary support. Rebellion can be looming as well.[16]

25. Although it appears clear that children and youths are developing stronger individual identities, a process that can be summarised under the general term of individualisation; this situation should not conceal the fact that the pursuit of their

---

13 W. JAMES, *Lecture II. What pragmatism means*, 1906,<http://www.marxist.org/reference/subject/philosophy/index.htm>.

14 R.L. STIRAT, 'Cultures of Consultancy', (2000) 20(1) *Critique of Anthropology*, 31–46.

15 J. DE CONINCK, *Current procedures and policies dominating aid: building strong relationships and enabling NGOs meet their stated aims?*, A summary report on research carried out in Uganda, 2000–2004, <http://www.ngopractice.org/casestudies.htm>.

16 I. ABDULLAH, "I Am a Rebel': Youth Culture and Violence in Sierra Leone', in F. DE BOECK and A. HONWANA (eds.), *Makers & Breakers: Children & Youth in Postcolonial Africa*, (Trenton, N.J.: Africa World Press, 2005).

individual rights cannot be supported exclusively through enhancing their rights among the actors with whom they interact daily.

Their participation in this research has shown clearly that the main constraints on the realisation of their individual rights are largely influenced by issues relating to their restricted citizenship and therefore to the forms of government and the general economic situation of their countries, itself related to unequal trade relations, as well as to the power structures active in their communities of origin. In other words, it appears clear that these youths and children cannot obtain their individual rights without action on the global conditions of today's world.

26. It is also erroneous to stick to a common vision of West African societies as structured by a succession of sovereign political entities vertically organised with clear responsibilities – from families, to schools, to local government, to national government, to regional bodies and universality. This framework just does not reflect the actual situations in which these children evolve. The governmentality[17] of youths and children in contemporary Africa must be contemplated from its actual reality and this entails transnational dimensions.[18] The relevance of actors to children's well-being cannot be classified according to their level of theoretical – ideal – responsibility, to the spatial realm of their competence, to their declared functions.[19] For example, international non-governmental organisations, international financial organisations, regional and local religious networks, affect, as seen above, the living conditions of children. Actions based on an erroneous representation of the power affecting children cannot bring satisfying and lasting responses and interventions in their favour.

Furthermore, one can point to a certain level of dysfunctional behaviour when observing that the very elders striving to constrain the movements of their own offspring, for example to safeguard the virginity of their daughters, might be the ones abusing others' daughters. In these impoverished and rapidly changing societies, the interstices where widely accepted values are trampled on are multiplying.

27. No matter how appealing we find our ideal representations of an ordered society and world, with specific institutions having specific responsibilities over specific spaces, they are inoperative in the light of the actual constraints affecting children.

---

17 M. Foucault, 'La "gouvernmentalité"', in Dits et Ecrits, III, (Paris: Gallimard, 1994), 635–657 ; D. Mitchell, *Governmentality. Power and Rule in Modern Society*, (London: Sage, 1999), 229.

18 J. Ferguson and A. Gupta, 'Spatializing states: toward an ethnography of neoliberal governmentality', (2002) 29 (4) *American Ethnologist*, 981–1002.

19 R. Botte, 'Economies trafiquantes et mondialisation. La voie africaine vers le « développement » ?', (2002) 88, *Politique Africaine*, 131–150.

In other words, the strategy of enforcing the respect of universal rights through aiming at specific institutions, however desirable, lacks realism. This implies that actions, advocacy and pressures, from the local level to the global level, should address a very wide range of actors, individual and institutional, all with roles and responsibilities affecting youths and children.

These endeavours require the active participation of children and youths in the fight for their rights. Youths and children experience clear limits to the spaces in which they can evolve and the actual alliances on which they can count. Not only is the children's outreach very limited, as they have few opportunities to link up with progressive forces, but even their mobility takes place in the impoverished spaces to which they are actively restricted. This notion of spaces refers not only to the boundaries resulting from the actual socio-economic structures, but also to their confinement to subordinate positions, and to spheres marked by precariousness (in wealth, knowledge and services).

9. ACTIONS

28. Going back to the initial question of this paper on the directions for intervention, recommendations are presented below:

- Support the economic initiatives that both girls and boys develop to generate income.
- As peer and affinity groups are key resources for youths and children of both genders, their actions in the social and economic realm as well as activities to promote learning and reflection should be supported.
- Intra and inter-group dialogues, relating to their specific situations, should be encouraged, to help people articulate common visions and strengthen their abilities to decide on actions to face today's challenges.
- The products of the reflexivity resulting from discussions within the peer groups should be spread beyond the peer groups themselves. In addition, the formation of new links between the groups should be supported.
- Access to quality information and knowledge should be facilitated, and exchanges between different agencies and groups should become more frequent.
- It is obvious that if advocacy and concrete efforts in terms of providing basic services should be pursued, participation should also be encouraged.
- The development of pressures on duty bearers through advocacy from different actors concerned by the future and actual conditions of contemporary children and youths should be continued by large and diversified alliances.

- All those measures require human resources; the intensification of the contacts between different spheres is essential and entails exchanges between different social groups, and the development of an empathetic attitude.

10. THE APPLICABILITY OF THE CRC

29. From the evidence presented, one can say that the CRC presupposes conditions that do not exist in the contexts of this research. Nor do the developments observed in the region suggest that they will be a reality in the near future. This point of view must not be reduced to a relativistic position, but rather considered a pragmatic and realistic approach based on the actual experiences of youths and children. Moreover, the CRC assumes definitions of categories irreconcilable with local practices[20] (in many societies in West Africa, a mother is no longer considered a child, even at the age of 14), including practices developed by youths to enhance their rights. Therefore, the established facts leave us with the questions of the utility of the CRC in such contexts. Considering the CRC as a fruitful framework accepted by almost all States allows its use as an advocacy instrument. It has been very useful in crystallising energies and attention, in spreading information and in reinforcing the legitimacy of the claims of children.

30. In the end, the CRC remains a driving utopia for some and a post-colonial ideology for others. The danger of being misled looms if we, as fundamentalists, consider the text of the CRC, as an immutable reality to be put in place at all costs, and not as a norm of reference. The CRC was produced from a specific vantage point, as a leverage instrument. It becomes prejudicial when our consideration for it leads us to be distracted from the necessary accompanying actions grounded in local realities. Yes, universal texts have their relativity, but deep desires for recognition, dignity and being true to the self are universal. Texts can feed ideas of utopia and utopia can feed resistance[21] to injustice and oppression, and as a result support endeavours to change society for the better.

---

[20] F. De Boeck and A. Honwana, 'Introduction: Children and Youth in Africa', in F. De Boeck and A. Honwana (eds.), *Makers & Breakers: Children & Youth in Postcolonial Africa*, (Trenton, N.J.: Africa World Press, 2005).

[21] P. Ricoeur, *L'idéologie et l'utopie*, (Paris: Editions du Seuil, 1997).

REFERENCE POINTS IN THE LEGAL DISCOURSE ABOUT THE SEXUAL ABUSE OF MINORS

ISABELLE WATTIER

1. INTRODUCTION

1. Article 34 of the Convention on the Rights of the Child provides that "States Parties undertake to protect the child from all forms of sexual exploitation and sexual abuse. For these purposes, States Parties shall in particular take all appropriate national, bilateral and multilateral measures to prevent: the inducement or coercion of a child to engage in any unlawful sexual activity; the exploitative use of children in prostitution or other unlawful sexual practices; the exploitative use of children in pornographic performances and materials".

2. In Belgium, children are protected against sexual exploitation and assault by criminal law in particular. The government also adopted an Act of 28 November 2000 on the criminal protection of minors. Belgian criminal law, like the law of the State Parties to the Convention, punishes various forms of sexual evocation, exploitation and assault against minors and sets different age thresholds below which the consent of a minor to a sexual act has no legal standing. However, our purpose is not to detail the entire Belgian criminal law, but to look at some of the points of reference in the criminal law discourse about the sexual abuse of minors. This discourse is based in particular on interpretations of the field of decency and sexuality, on assumptions of non-consent in favour of minors and, finally, on the evolution of morals, the collective consciousness and the norms on the subject.

2. THE FIELD OF SEXUALITY AND DECENCY: VARIABLE REFERENCE POINTS

3. In Belgian law, rape and indecent assault come under the category of "crimes and offences against the order of the family and public morality".[1] Separate legal provisions cover these two offences, although rape is seen as a specific form of indecent assault.[2] The law,[3] unlike indecent assault,[4] defines rape.

Assault conventionally requires the conjunction of the following elements: physical or psychological sexual duress presenting a degree of severity, the absence of consent by the victim and guilty intent on the part of the perpetrator of the offence.[5] The Criminal Code (Art. 375, para. 1) defines rape as "any act of sexual penetration, of any type and by any means whatsoever, committed on a person without their consent". Insofar as the question of consent only arises when a minor is over 14, for rape proceedings, or over 16, for indecent assault, the question of knowing what rape or indecent assault is in the eyes of the criminal justice system becomes all the more acute. If, below these age thresholds, the lack of consent of a minor is assumed absolutely, one still has to establish what, in the field of sex, is censurable as rape or indecent assault committed against a minor.

Actual cases of rape, despite the legal definition, lend themselves to judicial and theoretical interpretation just as much as cases of indecent assault. Thus, acts of penetration committed by a 14-year-old minor on a person of full age, for example sodomy, or acts of fellatio carried out by a person of full age on a minor are sometimes classified as indecent assault, for example by the Court of Appeal in Brussels,[6] and sometimes as rape, for example by the Principal State Prosecutor's Office of the Court of Appeal at Liège.[7] Amongst legal theorists, there is a controversy over the classification of a forced French kiss, with some feeling that it amounts to penetration of a

1 Code pénal, Livre II, Titre VII [Criminal Code, Volume I, Title VII].

2 A. DE NAUW, *Inleiding tot het bijzonder strafrecht*, (Mechelen: Kluwer, 1981), 81; 4de Herwerkte uitgave, 2002, 93 ; Cass., 13 mai 1942, *Pas.*, 1942, I, 125 and Cass., 8 décembre 1981, *Pas.*, 1982, I, 476 ; Cass., 3 octobre 2001, P010537F, unpublished ; Cass., 16 juin 2004, RG P040595F, <www.juridat.be>.

3 Code pénal, Art. 375, para. 1 [Criminal Code].

4 Code pénal, Art. 372, para. 1 [Criminal Code]: "*Tout attentat à la pudeur commis sans violences ni menaces sur la personne ou à l'aide de la personne d'un enfant de l'un ou de l'autre sexe, âgé de moins de 16 ans accomplis sera puni de la réclusion de cinq à dix ans*".

5 I. WATTIER, 'Etat du droit pénal des mœurs après la loi relative à la protection pénale des mineurs et questions critiques', (2002) 1–2 *Annales de droit de Louvain*, 84–96; L. STEVENS, *Strafrecht en seksualiteit*, (Antwerpen-Groningen: Intersentia), 2002, 467–481.

6 Bruxelles, 30 April 2003, RG 478, unpublished.

7 Discussion with a member of the Principal State Prosecutor's Office of Liège. However, currently judicial ruling confirms that another interpretation is untraceable.

sexual nature due to the sexual intent of the perpetrator[8] and the state of the collective consciousness,[9] and others feeling that such acts, in view of their low level of seriousness, fall outside the scope of criminal law.[10]

In legal practice, the decision to classify acts as indecent assault depends on a series of variables that are applied unequally: the private, family, professional or police context of the acts; the assessment of the seriousness of the acts; the characteristics of the victim; the drive and motives of the perpetrator; and public morality, good morals and the state of the collective consciousness. Thus, for example, the kisses on the mouth forced on a 10-year-old minor by her uncle were not deemed to constitute indecent assaults[11] due to the lack of sexual intent on the part of the perpetrator of the acts. In another case, the classification of indecent assault was dismissed because the fact that advances or propositions of sexual contact were accompanied by physical closeness in the cramped quarters of a tent meant that the Court was unable to attribute sufficiently serious physical conduct to the accused for it to constitute indecent assault. This was particularly because the advances had been rejected, and the accused had not persisted. However, he was sentenced on grounds of indecent exposure in public, as provided by Article 385 of the Criminal Code, for having exposed himself fully naked, several times, in front of minors whom he was responsible for supervising. The Court of Appeal in Brussels justified its ruling upholding that "*such exposure is the act of a person responsible for supervising young people who have had a particularly strict moral education*".[12] In a ruling given on 6 October 2004, the Court of Cassation judged that "*indecent assault presupposes sexual duress, carried out on a living person or with their help, without necessarily requiring physical contact with that person*".[13]

4. It has been observed that during the 1990s, the notion of the "general feeling of decency at a given time in a given society" on which the conventional approach to this offence is based gave way to the notion of "sexual inviolability as conceived of by the collective consciousness in a given society at a given time".[14] However, as STEVENS points out, this is merely a change of formulation, and the assessment criterion remains similar, which is, the reference to the collective consciousness in given society at a given time. It seems to us that it is even less a change of formulation than a

---

8 Y. DE BROUWERE, 'Antwoord op de anotatie 'Over de tongkus en de seksuele penetratie'', (1998–99) *Rechtskundig weekblad*, 791.

9 L. STEVENS, supra (note 5), 486.

10 A. VANDEPLAS, 'Over de tongkus en de seksuele penetratie', (1998–99) *Rechtskundig Weekblad*, 505; ' Wederantwoord van de annotator op de reactie van Y. DE BRAUWERE', (1998–99) *R.W.*, 791.

11 Brussels, 14 February 2002, (2002) *Journal des Tribunaux*, 342 and note.

12 Brussels, 19 March 2003, (2003) *J.T.*, 486.

13 Cass., 6 octobre 2004, RG P040665F.

14 L. STEVENS, supra (note 5), 467.

terminological variant. Contemporary precedent still always refers expressly to "good morals", "decency" and "public morality". Thus, for example, the Court of Appeal in Brussels recently proclaimed that "*decency is related to propriety in its sexual sense, and this notion – which is constantly evolving – is assessed depending on the values that come under public morality protected by the law, as they are perceived, at a given time by the collective consciousness; this collective consciousness must be understood by reference to the average man's perception of it; this perception is different depending on whether it relates to an adult or an adolescent, even aged over 16; the context in which the alleged act is placed is vitally important*".[15]

There is therefore a relative vagueness with regard to the offences of rape and indecent assault committed against a minor. This uncertainty of the law must doubtless be related to the legislative discourse itself with regard to sexual exploitation and abuse of minors. The notions of paedophilia[16] and perverted offences[17] are frequently used without ever being made explicit or even established by the law, although some members of the Belgian Parliament are clearly in favour of this.[18]

The debate about the notion and offence of child pornography[19] reveals a certain degree of confusion between sexuality and perversity, leading to passages such as the following: "*Sexual acts is given to mean all acts that might constitute indecent assault, even if the minor has freely consented to them, under influence or constraint, or acts that artificially excite the senses of the person watching them and offend the decency of the average citizen due to the depraved or perverted attitudes or behaviour that they depict*".[20] Finally, the harmful influence of images of degrading and humiliating sexual acts on the intellectual development of young children and adolescents is regularly highlighted.[21]

---

15 Brussels, 19 March 2003, (2003) *J.T.*, 487. This saturating accumulation of criteria is a singularity of this legal discourse.

16 'Projet de loi contenant des dispositions en vue de la répression de la traite des êtres humains et de la pornographie enfantine', Report of P. CAHAY-ANDRE and S. VERHOEVEN, *Doc. parl.*, Sén., s.o. 1994–1995, n° 1142–3, 53–57.

17 Proposition de loi de répression de la traite des êtres humains, Report of M. LANDUYT, *Doc. parl.*, Ch. Repr., sess. ord. 1993–1994, n° 1381/6, 3.

18 Report of P. CAHAY-ANDRE and S. VERHOEVEN, supra (note 16), 53.

19 Code pénal, Art.385bis, para. 1 [Criminal Code].

20 Proposition de loi de répression de la traite des êtres humains, Commentaire des articles, *Doc. parl.*, Ch. Repr., sess. ord. 1993–1994, n° 1381/1, 19

21 Proposition de loi de répression de la traite des êtres humains, Développements, *Doc. parl.*, Ch. Repr., sess. ord. 1993–1994, n° 1381/1, 16.

3. THE ASSUMPTION OF LACK OF CONSENT: SHOULD THE LEGAL REFERENCE POINT ITSELF BE CALLED INTO QUESTION?

5. Under Belgian criminal law, the provision relating to the offences of indecent assault and rape involving minors is based on a system of irrefragable assumptions of lack of consent founded sometimes solely on the age of the minor victim, and sometimes both on the age of the victim and on the position of the perpetrator of the abuse. The question of the consent of the minor is in these cases, on principle, disposed of by the legal fiction. The incontestable nature of the assumption of lack of consent deprives both the perpetrator and the victim of the right to provide proof to the contrary, that is, to demonstrate that the acts were committed consensually. Until recently, acts of sexual penetration committed on a minor aged under 14 were classified as rape with violence due to an irrefragable assumption of lack of consent on the part of the minor. Similarly, acts of a sexual nature committed against minors aged under 16 were, depending on their severity, classified as indecent assault.[22] Thus, a sexual relationship involving penetration is not assumed to constitute rape with violence if the minor involved is 14, but the acts nonetheless remain punishable as indecent assault if the minor has not yet reached the age of 16.[23]

However, on 30 October 2003, a trial court, the Criminal Court of Liège, gave a ruling that overturned the assumption of lack of consent by the minor involved. The Court ruled: "*given the evolution of morals, sexual relations freely consented to between a young man of 21 and a girl of 15 does not necessarily constitute indecent assault*".[24] This judgment was surprising because it holds in check the legally incontestable nature of the fiction of lack of consent by a minor aged under 16 in sexual matters. Thus, the *de facto* consent of the minor and the evolution of morals enabled the courts to deem the consent of a minor aged under 16 admissible, and thus frustrate the fiction of the law.

6. In particular, this ruling raises the question of the purpose of the age thresholds of the assumptions relating to them raised by criminal law. Is it to protect the minor? From whom? From what? The position that states that one must take into

---

22 Code pénal, Art. 472 et 475 [Criminal Code]; Cass., 14 décembre 1971, *Pas.*, 1972, I, 367 ; M. RIGAUX and P.-E. TROUSSE, *Les crimes et délits du Code pénal*, t.V, (Bruxelles–Paris: Bruylant), (1968) *L.G.D.J.*, 304; A. DE NAUW, *Inleiding tot het bijzonder strafrecht*, 4de herwerkte uitgave, (Mechelen: Kluwer, 2002), 95.

23 Cass., 5 février 1985, RG 8743 ; Cass., 30 novembre 1988, *Pas.*, 1989, I, 190 ; Cass., 3 octobre 2001, RG P010537F ; Cass. 16 juin 2004, RG P040595F.

24 Corr.Liège, 30 octobre 2003, (2004) *J.L.M.B.*, 1385.

account the "reality" of the consent of the minor for the sake of her/his right to self-determination, rather than the fiction of the lack of consent, is based on a series of debatable postulates. Firstly, it postulates that the law is devoted to finding a match with "reality", at least with the subjective reality of the individuals. Secondly, it associates the expression of consent with the hypothesis of genuine freedom, which is debatable to say the least. IACUB and MANIGLIER expose the full ambiguity of the very principle of "consensualism" in intimate matters insofar as passionate love and sex drive are likely to render the requirement for reasoned consent incongruous.[25]

More fundamentally, the placing in check of the legal fiction by the courts should call our attention to the sense of the legal fictions, and more generally to the fiction of the law. It could be maintained that the general and abstract nature of the law, in other words the fact that it is decidedly arbitrary but applies equally to all, constitutes a guarantee against the arbitrariness of the ruling.[26]

Finally, it must be observed that the placing in check of the legal norms in the name of the evolution of morals brings us to the ambivalence of the philosophy of the rights of the child itself. Sometimes liberating, it talks of making children free citizens in the same way as adults, and freeing them from the burden of parental and State authority; sometimes protective, it talks of providing specific legal protection in favour of children due to their vulnerability. THÉRY feels that, at the risk of rendering the child responsible for her/his own protection, the reforms in favour of the rights of the child are only meaningful if they respect the fundamental principles of the law,[27] which is with its categories and fictions.

7. If we turn once again to the parliamentary debates on the subject, it can be seen that the absolute assumptions of lack of consent (legal fictions) of minors have been discussed several times, both with regard to the principle and to the related age thresholds. However, there has been no legal change to either of these. With regard to the principle of the fiction, in the end it is always concluded that although some minors are in fact capable of discernment, they are nonetheless less well armed than adults are against seduction.[28] With regard to the critical age threshold, it is easy to acknowledge that not all young people reach sexual maturity at the same time, and that one could endlessly debate the age from which a person can validly consent to

---

25 M. IACUB and P. MANIGLIER, *Antimanuel d'éducation sexuelle*, (Paris: Rosny,Bréal, 2005), 152– 161.

26 I. THÉRY, *Le Démariage. Justice et vie privée*, (Paris: Odile Jacob, 1993) in (2001) 418 *Poches*, 436–437.

27 Ibid., 399–414.

28 Proposition de loi abrogeant les Articles 372bis et 377, 3e alinéa, du Code pénal, Report of M. SUYKERBUYK, *Doc.parl.*, Ch., sess. 1981–1982, n°349/5, 11.

sexual relations.[29] This reminds us that the rule of law never reflects anything other than an arbitrary choice and not any obvious fact, nature or ontology. When the bill on the criminal protection of minors was tabled in 1998,[30] there was talk of firstly, no longer conferring an absolute nature on the assumptions of the lack of consent of minors, and secondly, of adopting a single age threshold for all sexual abuse, which is the age of 14.[31] However, in the end the government abandoned the bill, feeling that the debate had not yet ended. This justification is paradoxical to say the least as it takes place in the very heart of the space within which political debate in principle should occur in a democratic state.[32]

4. MORALS, THE COLLECTIVE CONSCIOUSNESS AND THE "NORMS ON THE SUBJECT"

8. In 1998, the Court of Appeal in Brussels handed down a decision in which it refused to confer a sexual nature on forced kisses. There was fierce controversy amongst legal theorists about the decision. On the one hand, one author considers that, based on the *ratio legis*, it is difficult to see forced kisses as sexual duress. He thus compares a forced kiss to inserting a pencil in someone's ear or putting a vibrator in someone's mouth. He feels that if one sticks to the word of the law, someone who inserts a stick into a person's ear or rummages about in her/his nose, or someone who brushes against her/his belly button or tickles her/his armpits, should be seen as guilty of rape subject to proof that he committed such acts with sexual intent. He thus appeals to good sense and the role of criminal law to reflect our values.[33] Reacting to this theory, another author feels, on the contrary, that forced kisses undeniably constitute an assault of a sexual nature.[34] This is a view shared by STEVENS, who believes that this type of act falls within the sphere of physical sexual inviolability in the eyes of the current state of the collective consciousness.[35]

Several observations can be made on this controversy. Firstly, it bears witness to a frequent confusion between on the one hand, the scope of the field of sexuality, and

29 Report of M. SUYKERBUYK, supra (note 28), 2; Proposition de loi relatif à la protection pénale des mineurs, Exposé des motifs, *Doc. parl.*, Ch., s.o. 1998–1999, n° 1907/1, 18.

30 Projet de loi relatif à la protection pénale des mineurs, supra (note 29), 18.

31 Ibid.

32 I. WATTIER, 'Responsabilité et responsabilisation du législateur. Le cas de l'irrecevabilité du consentement des mineurs et la notion de " majorité sexuelle"', in TH. MOREAU and FR. DIGNEFFE, *La Responsabilité et la responsabilisation dans la justice pénale*, (Brussels: Larcier – de Boeck, 2006), 387–396.

33 A. VANDEPLAS, supra (note 10).

34 Y. DE BRAUWERE, supra (note 10) .

35 L. STEVENS, , supra (note 5), 579.

on the other, the scope of the field of punishment in sexual matters within the legal discourse. Secondly, the controversy demonstrates that neither the criterion of the seriousness of the acts nor the criterion of the state of the collective consciousness eliminates the divergence of opinions on what merits description as sexual or criminal. These criteria inevitably lead interpreters of the law to express an opinion on the scope of the field of sexuality sometimes as a function of their own perceptions (of sexuality, seriousness or the collective consciousness) and sometimes as a function of the micro-systemic precedents[36] of their jurisdiction. The appeal to "good sense", as made by one of the protagonists in the theoretical controversy over the forced kiss, and his conception of the role of criminal law, are also debatable for the same reasons. Finally, more fundamentally, the interpreters of the law, the judiciary or the legal theory act as though they were clearly the depositaries of the state of the collective consciousness. Although a judge has to rule one way or another, failing which he is in denial of justice, nothing but a certain degree of tradition obliges commentators on the law to do the same.

9. We noted above that the criteria of the "collective consciousness" and "the evolution of morals" constitutes regular points of reference in the legal discourse with regard to sexual offences. The first criterion, which is sometimes combined with "public morality" relates in substance to the moral norm, whilst the second relates to the social norm. The ruling handed down by the Criminal Court in Brussels on 5 July 1999 is entirely emblematic of the confusion between the normative registers on the subject. In sentencing a man for incest with his minor daughter, the Court declared that this was "*an opportunity to reaffirm the consensus enjoyed by the criminal norm*".[37] However, about which criminal norm are we talking? The Criminal Code does not make incest as such an offence, and consensual sexual relations between a parent and a child of full age are not punished under criminal law. So, to what does the consensus relate? "On the condemnation of incest!" we hear you cry. Maybe, but that is not strictly speaking a criminal norm. Legal discourse thus slides from one register to another without anyone necessarily noticing or worrying about it.

Similarly, parliamentary discourse keeps between on the one hand, social, moral or statistical norms, and on the other hand, legal or criminal norms, without making much distinction between them.

---

36 By "micro-systemic", we mean the immediate institutional territorial level, i.e. the legal canton *in specie*, while "macro-systemic" means the criminal institutional system *in globo*.

37 Corr. Bruxelles, 5 janvier 1999, (1999) *J.T.*, 627.

10. In the 1980s, the offence of homosexual indecent assault on a minor was criticised in the light of the evolution of morals and serious scientific work.[38] It was acknowledged that the criminal provisions themselves sometimes encourage blackmail and perversity such as the assumptions of abuse of power between a master and a servant, a major and a minor,[39] and that prejudices and hostile and punitive attitudes with regard to sexual behaviour create anxieties and difficulty in accepting oneself.[40] It was also said that certain sexual practices are condemned in the name of suppositions.[41] Moreover, members of the Belgian Parliament observed, "*that it is generally accepted that at the age of 17, sexual relations are not an act of debauchery.*"[42] At the time, however, voices were raised asserting that "*homosexuality is a fashion that presents dangers for society*"[43] and opposing the "*gay trend*".[44] The danger identified is that of having to acknowledge sexual tendencies such as paedophilia, sadism, exhibitionism, etc., as well. The partisans of the bill won out however and the "homosexual offence" was finally revoked. In the context of the debate on rape (1982–1989), the legislator noted the liberalisation of sex.[45] It must be noted that we now have difficulty sharing this analysis.[46] The political majority is generally in favour of the easy adaptation of the norm to the evolution of morals, and as a result, of conferring on the judge broad powers of assessment on the subject. Some however criticised the fact that in certain hypotheses, the courts are called upon to define the boundary between "normal" and "abnormal" sexual behaviour.[47] About which normality are we talking? Statistical, social, moral or other? Confusion reigns. Towards the middle of the 1990s, the tone changed, in the context of the debate about the sexual exploitation of children (1993–1995); although members of parliament repeatedly declared that there had been a change in social norms with regard to sex,[48] they also targeted "*the perverted shifts to which the permissive climate of the last decade may give rise*".[49] One can thus see a

---

38 Proposition de loi abrogeant les Articles 372bis et 377, 3e alinéa, du Code pénal, Développements, *Doc. Parl.*, Ch. sess. ord. 1981–1982, n° 349/1, 6.

39 Proposition de loi abrogeant les Articles 372bis et 377, 3e alinéa, du Code pénal, Amendement au texte adopté par la commission, *Doc. parl.*, Ch.., sess. ord. 1981–1982, n° 349/6, 1.

40 Proposition de loi abrogeant les Articles 372bis et 377, 3e alinéa, du Code pénal, Développements, supra (note 38).,3 et 5.

41 Ibid., 2.

42 Report of P. Cahay-André and S. Verhoeven, supra (note 16), 41.

43 Report of M. Suykerbuyk, supra (note 29), 4.

44 Ibid., 4.

45 Ibid., 8.

46 M. Foucault, *Histoire de la sexualité*, volume I (La volonté de savoir), 1976, volume II (L'usage des plaisirs), 1984, volume III (Le souci de soi), 1984, (Paris: Gallimard, 1984); M. Bozon, *Sociologie de la sexualité*, (Saint-Germain-du-Puy: Nathan, 2002), 128; M. Iacub and P. Maniglier, supra (note 25).

47 Projet de loi modifiant certaines dispositions relatives au crime de viol Mme Merckx-Van Goey, *Doc. Parl.*, Ch., s.o. 1988–1989, n° 702/4, 6.

48 Report of M. Landuyt, supra (note17), 41.

49 Ibid., 34.

"lowering of the norms on the subject" in pornographic publications that aim specifically to pass off sexual relations with children as normal.[50]

11. Here is what can be said of the norms on the subject: "In the same way as the family, the neighbourhood and school, the media, and in particular television and video, have taken an extremely important place in education. Due to the lack of any appropriate regulation, pornographic films are exposed, deliberately or otherwise, to the gaze of an ever-growing number of children. The renting of violent pornographic films is generating a new problem. Certain families use these films in order to give their children "sex education", or allow them to watch them in their company. In some cases, the children are even forced to watch; this type of situation often occurs in the context of the sexual abuse of minors. The children therefore acquire an abnormally broad knowledge with regard to sexuality, which can seriously interfere with their sexual development."[51]

12. Some less "politically correct" Congressmen however questions the appropriateness of punishing a paedophile, even if he is aware of possessing images of child pornography: "*Paedophilia is a pathology that cannot be remedied by criminalisation, but by understanding and management. The prison environment is not a solution to the problems of paedophiles, just as it does not provide a solution to the problems of drug addicts*".[52] Another member leaves the problem to the judge's discretion: "*It must be hoped that the judge will also pay attention to corrective measures. This bill must not lead to the purely punitive treatment of paedophiles*". The Minister of Justice adds that a judge can always order probative measures. He makes a comparison with exhibitionism, which continues to be prohibited but which, in practice, very rarely leads to charges being pressed, or gives rise to alternatives to imprisonment.[53] At the end of the 1990s, according to the bill on the criminal protection of minors, "the desire for modernisation of the criminal code is reflected not only by the highlighting of the values that are recognised by contemporary society, in the structure of the code[54] and the content of its provisions, but also by the revoking of certain provisions that have become outdated or show an unacceptable inequality (...)".[55] It adds, "For the sake

---

50 Proposition de loi insérant un Article 383bis dans le Code pénal et un Article 82bis dans la loi du 8 Avril 1965 relative à la protection de la jeunesse, en vue de réprimer la production, la diffusion et la possession de représentations pornographiques impliquant des enfants, Développements*, Doc. parl.*, Sén., sess. 1993–1994, n° 992–1, 2.

51 Proposition de loi de répression de la traite des êtres humains, Développements, *Doc. parl.*, Ch., sess. ord. 1993–1994, n° 1381/1,16–17.

52 Report de P. CAHAY-ANDRÉ and S. VERHOEVEN, supra (note 16) , 52.

53 Ibid., 52.

54 The Bill initially intended to classify all sexual abuses under Crimes and Offences against individuals.

55 Projet de loi relatif à la protection pénale des mineurs, Exposé des motifs, *Doc. parl.* Ch., sess. ord.1998–1999, n° 1907/1, 3.

of consistency, the bill groups together the different offences in accordance with the interests protected as they are currently conceived".[56] In the context of the original version of the bill on the criminal protection of minors, the government felt that "beyond fourteen, the sex life of young people outside situations of duress must no longer be in principle governed by the criminal system as it comes more within the educational sphere, the ethical sphere and the protective sphere". At the end of the legislative process, these draft amendments were sent to the parliamentary archives. Since 1867, sexual abuse, rape and assault have been classified as crimes and offences against the order of the family and public morality.

13. It is interesting to observe that, in the context of this debate, the criminal approach itself to the phenomenon of sexual abuse of minors has also been explicitly called into question by an expert psychiatrist: "*The situation of battered children in Belgium, in which she includes sexual assault committed against children, is not at all characterised by a legislative deficit, but rather by a lack of real priority given to the needs of children in all areas. She emphasises the fact that the question of knowing how to bring parents round to taking a different attitude towards their children is never debated*".[57] This expert bravely questions the punitive approach to the sexual abuse of minors, and when she states, "*this question is never debated*", the very quality of the parliamentary debate is called into question.

5. CONCLUSIONS

14. It can be seen that the legal discourse on this subject slides almost systematically into the register of social events, the norms on the subject, the evolution of morals and the collective consciousness. This quite obviously bears witness to the "internormativity"[58] of the law, or the fundamental triangle of criminal law of morals, the three sides of which are morals, morality and the law respectively. Nowadays, we can add to these ethical, educational, scholastic, familial, pedagogical and televisual norms.

Of course, the problem lies elsewhere. Perhaps we should ask more strictly in what direction social, moral, educational, etc., but also criminal, sexual norms have evolved. The legal discourse implies that the criminal norm has to steer a course close to the

56 Ibid., 4.

57 Report of N. de T'Serclaes, Audition du Dr. C. Marneffe, *Doc. parl.* Sén., sess. ord. 1999–2000, n° 2–280/5, 37.

58 J. Carbonnier, *Les phénomènes d'internormativité, in Essais sur les lois*, (1979)*Répertoire du notariat Defrénois*; Ph. Robert, Fr. Soubiran-Paillet and M. van de Kerchove, 'Normativités et internormativités', in *Normes, normes juridiques, normes pénales. Pour une sociologie des frontières*, (Paris: L'Harmattan, 1997), 7–31.

other norms, without these being clearly identifiable. One can clearly detect greater suspicion with regard to the "norms on the subject" in the 1990s than in the 1980s, but the question of identifying these "norms on the subject" remains open.

15. Secondly, we must ask to what extent and with what consequences we can move from one normative register to the other, whilst running the risk of weakening the plurality of normative orders.[59] The risk of diluting normativety in social, moral or statistical normality is clearly present.[60] This question of the inspiration and relative autonomy of the legal norms is obviously fundamental if we want to confer any sense on the criminal laws that claim to protect children. Paradoxically, there is also without doubt an overinvestment of the legal norm, or the criminal norm in any case, compared with the other means of social regulation in favour of the protection and welfare of children with regard to sex. If the law is applied to the letter, the law on the criminal protection of minors does not lie. It does not claim to protect minors by anything other than criminal means, which is by the application of a sentence to child abusers. It could be asked whether Article 34 of the Convention on the Rights of the Child can provide no more than similar protection and similar effectiveness.

---

59 M.-L. DELFOSSE, 'Normes juridiques, normes non juridiques dans le domaine biologique. Expérimentation médicale sur l'être humain et comités d'éthique', in *Normes, normes juridiques, normes pénales. Pour une sociologie des frontières*, (Paris: L'Harmattan, 1997), 211.

60 D. ALLAND, 'Les mœurs sont-elles solubles dans le droit', (1994) 19 *Droits*, 9 ; I. THÉRY, 'le droit et les mœurs, un enjeu politique, (1993) *L'Année sociologique*, 85–124 ; J. COMMAILLE, I. THÉRY, CHR. BIET, Introduction à ' La famille, la loi l'Etat. Débats révolutionnaires, problèmes d'aujourd'hui', (1993) 14 *Droit et société*, 8–12.

WORLDS APART FROM THE CRC: "THE TALIBÉ CHILDREN ON THE STREETS OF DAKAR"

AHMADOU TALL

1. INTRODUCTION

1. Generally portrayed as the "window to French-speaking Africa",[1] Senegal, like the other countries on the black continent, is facing the social consequences of the structural adjustment programmes imposed by lenders for over twenty years. This comes on top of the deterioration in terms of international trade, the oil crisis and the drought in the seventies in the Sahel countries, which have generated a severe economic crisis.

According to a source[2] at UNDP Senegal, 65% of the population is living below the poverty line. In twenty years, society has suffered several profound impacts: the application of the structural adjustment programme at the end of the 1980s, the emergency plan (an austerity plan imposed by the government to reduce public expenditure), the devaluation of the CFA franc in 1994 and the intensification of the rural exodus in the 1980s and 1990s.

2. As found by sociologists DIOP and DIOUF, this has resulted in "widespread impoverishment"[3] that has been followed by blatant begging in the streets.

Begging is a highly developed phenomenon in Senegal. There are two explanations for this. Firstly, 95% of the Senegalese population is Muslim, and charity is an obligation in the Islamic tradition. Secondly, in order to have an income and not depend on their families, which are often very poor themselves, poor people are forced to beg in the street.

1 (February 2002) *Le Monde Diplomatique*, 18–19.

2 'Le Sénégal au défit de l'ajustement structurel', (October 1998) *Le Monde Diplomatique*.

3 M.C. DIOP and M. DIOUF et al., 'Le baobab a été déraciné', (June 2000) *Journal Politique Africaine*.

There are countless child beggars on the streets of Dakar. Almost every street has a group of children whose main activity is no longer attending school, but holding out their hands. In 1990, the NGO Enda Tiers Monde estimated that there were 20,000 of such children. Today, the phenomenon continues to take on ever greater proportions. According to the United Nations Children's Fund (UNICEF), in 2000, between 50,000 and 100,000 children were conducting "professionalised"[4] begging in Dakar.

3. Yet Senegal is a signatory of the International Covenant on Civil and Political Rights, which was adopted by the United Nations on 16 December 1966 and entered into force on 23 March 1973. Article 24 of the Covenant states that "every child shall have, without any discrimination..., the right to such measures of protection as are required by his status as a minor, on the part of his family, society and the State".

Senegal was above all one of the first countries to ratify the Convention on the Rights of the Child adopted in New York on 20 November 1989. This international convention enshrines the right of children to enjoy benefits appropriate to their needs. They should receive proper food, accommodation and decent clothing. They have the right to live in a healthy, danger-free environment, receive social security, medical care and education, and enjoy leisure activities. They have the right to be protected against all forms of exploitation. These two international instruments are obligatory with regard to the signatory States.

Finally, Senegal ratified the African Charter on the Rights and Welfare of the Child, adopted in Addis Ababa on 11 July 1990. The preamble of the Charter recognises "that the child occupies a unique and privileged position in the African society and that for the full and harmonious development of his personality, the child should grow up in a family environment in an atmosphere of happiness, love and understanding."

4. This being the case, how have we come to a situation in which the number of talibé children has increased fivefold, their living conditions have become more poverty-stricken and society has fallen into a sort of passive tolerance? The phenomenon of the talibés certainly raises many questions and alarmingly brings up the issue of the effectiveness of the relevant provisions of the 1989 International Convention on the Rights of the Child. This is undoubtedly the reason why, after reading the initial report submitted by the State of Senegal, the Committee on the Rights of the Child clearly stated, that it was "seriously worried at the difficult living conditions faced by a great number of talibés, who are deprived of the enjoyment of their fundamental rights under the law."[5]

---

4 'Profession: mendiant', (24 April 2003) *Journal Jeune Afrique L'Intelligent.*

5 Concluding Observations of the CRC Committee, <http://www.unhchr.ch/tbs/doc.nsf/>.

5. In order to define this scourge, which has moved both the domestic and international community, this paper will first examine the social situation of talibé children with regard to their fundamental rights, and secondly, this paper will look at the question of the responsibility of the various actors involved in the phenomenon.

2. THE SOCIAL SITUATION OF TALIBÉ CHILDREN AND THEIR FUNDAMENTAL RIGHTS

2.1. TALIBÉ CHILDREN AND THEIR LIVING CONDITIONS

6. Previously (as is the case today in the countryside), the talibés were children from Muslim families who were placed by their parents with a marabout.[6] The role of the marabout was to provide the child with education and instruction (teaching of the Koran), and meet their social, physical and emotional needs.

Children were sent to a marabout to receive Koran education as well as a practical initiation into community life and to acquire a sense of humility, the ascetic life and unfailing endurance. In exchange, the marabout received material goods and money, both from the parents and from practising Muslims, services and the potential help of his pupils, particularly with domestic chores.

7. Today, the talibé are nothing more than street children. There are thousands of them in Dakar, generally in the age group of 4 to 17 years. They assail, on a daily basis, drivers in the numerous traffic jams in the city. They can be seen early in the morning, shivering in shop doorways, at traffic lights or walking barefoot in the blazing sun or in the freezing cold, the empty tomato can that they use as a begging bowl in hand, roaming the city looking for alms.

Certain marabouts house several dozen children, sometimes as young as 4 or 5, in their daara.[7] These children are often badly treated, poorly looked after (if looked after at all) and malnourished. They have to beg seven days a week, all day and sometimes even at night.

8. The talibés roaming the streets of Dakar mainly come from the regions of Senegal, which are stricken by a crisis (drought, rural exodus and underemployment). They also come from the neighbouring countries such as Mali, Guinea Bissau, Mauritania and so on. The conflicts erupting in many places have accentuated the cross-border

6 Confer conceptual definition.
7 Traditional school for Koranic education.

migration of street children. According to a study,[8] non-immigrant talibés in Dakar only represent 3.11% of all of the talibés in the city.

9. Due to their difficulty accessing water, they do not wash regularly. Some can go for over a month without washing, especially in cold weather. Their basic clothes are very often in very poor condition and always dirty. In short, they live in the most wretched state. In order to eat, they go from house to house and collect leftovers in their begging bowls, which contributes to their precarious state of health. They are the section of population most exposed to various diseases such as scabies, malaria and cholera.

10. Currently, the status of the phenomenon leads to the statement that the main activity of the talibés is begging. Children who do not bring back the amount set by the marabout at the end of the day (generally 300 CFA francs)[9] are subjected to beatings, cruelty and physical ill-treatment, and even torture. Most talibé children bear the scars of the harsh punishments that they have undergone. This situation constitutes a serious violation of the rights of the Child.

2.2. CLEAR LACK OF RECOGNITION OF THE RIGHTS OF THE CHILD

11. The situation described above forcefully raises the thorny question of the implementation of several provisions of the 1989 International Convention on the Rights of the Child (CRC).

Article 7 of the Convention recognises that the child has "the right to know and be cared for by his or her parents." One of the first consequences of the talibé phenomenon is that the child is separated from his parents. In most cases, contact and personal relationships are rare or even non-existent.

Under Article 19 of the CRC, the child must be protected "from all forms of physical or mental violence, injury or abuse, neglect or negligent treatment, maltreatment or exploitation, including sexual abuse". Talibé children suffer each of these failings constantly and regularly. The case of a child named Siléye Ba recently stirred national opinion. Just seven years old, he was bound, beaten, deprived of food and locked up for forty hours in a dark, dilapidated, unsafe abandoned room. His Koran teacher, to whose care he was entrusted and who was the perpetrator of these indescribable acts, was arrested by the police and brought to justice.

[8] See: <http://membres.lycos.fr/talibes/>.

[9] Around 0.45 euro, 1 euro is equivalent to 655.957 CFA.

Generally, talibé children, even though they are deprived of their family environment as set out in Article 20 of the CRC, receive no protection or special help from the State. They are left to their own devices and to the terror and greed of their teachers.

The worst thing is that talibé children are exposed to all sorts of disease. They are often forgotten in vaccination programmes. Their state of health is very precarious and they only receive very few of the existing medical services; it must simply be said that there is a lack of recognition of the right of the talibé child to "enjoy the highest available standard of health" as stipulated in Article 24 of the CRC.

There are many questions with regard to the right to education (Art. 29 CRC). In principle, the daara is supposed to provide the talibés with a certain level of religious education. The talibés should receive an education that prepares them for community life through the acquisition of essential virtues, particularly humility. Today, it is easy to see that the activity of begging easily has the upper hand over the education which the children should receive. Compared with a child who has had the good fortune to go to a French school, there is clearly a breach of equality of opportunity, especially with regard to preparing them to "assume the responsibilities of life in a free society".

These children cannot claim to enjoy the "right to rest and leisure", or "engage in play and recreational activities appropriate to the age of the child", or "participate fully in cultural and artistic life". Instead, these children are through the begging that forms their main activity, subject to abject "economic exploitation" (Art. 32 CRC), which clearly violates their "human dignity" (Art. 28(2) CRC), seriously compromises their education and hinders their "physical, mental, spiritual, moral or social development".

The situation experienced by talibé children can be likened to cruel, inhuman or degrading treatment and in many cases they are simply subjected to torture, notwithstanding the clear and relevant provisions of Article 37 of the CRC. The picture is gloomy and the responsibilities of those involved must be identified.

3. THE RESPONSIBILITY OF THE ACTORS INVOLVED IN THE PHENOMENON

3.1. EXPLOITATION BY THE MARABOUT

12. In Africa, and particularly in Senegal, the term "marabout" is slightly ambiguous. It is used to denote a pious, virtuous man with great spiritual knowledge. He acts as a model and guide for his community. In another sense, marabout denotes a Koranic teacher. He gathers children at his home in order to teach them the Koran. It is in the latter that we are interested here.

Previously, the Koran was taught more in the villages. The teacher took into his daara children who, for the most part, lived with their parents or were entrusted to a tutor, close relative or friend of the family because they came from an urban centre or a neighbouring village. The village community met the material needs of the marabout, who also received support from his adult disciples in the form of agricultural work. The talibés were subjected to acceptable study conditions. If they were made to beg, it was only within the village and with the sole aim of instilling a sense of humility into them.

13. This balance was soon disrupted. Successive droughts led to poverty in the countryside, which resulted in a massive rural exodus to the large towns. The marabouts who had thrived in the urban areas were forced to find a new strategy for survival.

The emergence of the consumer society, which brought about changes in behaviour, customs and social relationships, led the marabouts to use their activity to turn it to good account. As they have no trade, they take advantage of the children entrusted to them to gain resources for themselves. The money that the marabout demands from the talibés varies depending on the location of his daara. In the suburbs of Dakar, a child under 10 has to pay between 250 and 400 CFA francs. In the city centre, the daily payment can be as much as 3,000 CFA francs. This makes the business very profitable for the marabout.

If each child brings in around 300 CFA francs to a daara with between 30 and 45 children, that gives the marabout a daily income of 9,000 to 13,500 CFA francs, and a monthly income of 270,000 to 450,000 CFA francs. The size of these amounts must be assessed in relation to the minimum wage, which is just 36,000 CFA francs in Senegal. Many marabouts have no hesitation in piling dozens of children into their concession in order to guarantee higher incomes, without any consideration for their health or their future.

14. In truth, the establishments in Dakar and the other urban centres are no longer daaras. In most cases, the talibé children on the streets of Dakar are not learning anything and are not receiving any education whatsoever. Their only activity is begging and adults driven only by a taste for lucre are exploiting them. These children are victim to physical and mental violence, injury and abuse, neglect and negligent treatment, maltreatment and exploitation as set out in Article 19 of the CRC.

3.2. ROLE AND RESPONSIBILITIES OF THE PARENTS

15. Article 18 of the CRC states: "States Parties shall use their best efforts to ensure recognition of the principle that both parents have common responsibilities for the upbringing and development of the child. Parents or, as the case may be, legal guardians, have the primary responsibility for the upbringing and development of the child. The best interests of the child will be their basic concern."

There is great difficulty in fully applying this principle, which is apparently so simple and is common sense, in a rural African environment. Marrying young, polygamy and high fertility levels mean that in rural surroundings, families are often very large. The great number of dependent children means that the head of the family is unable to assume his responsibilities. In addition, the scarcity of resources means that the State is unable to render "appropriate assistance to parents… in the performance of their child-rearing responsibilities". Sending a child to a daara is therefore a way of reducing the parental burden.

16. A distinction can be made between two types of parents:

- Parents who remain attached to the culture. They are generally former talibés themselves, who served their apprenticeship in the daaras. They remain convinced that suffering is the best way of learning how to overcome life's difficulties. The differences are that during their apprenticeship the talibés did not beg much, and only for the purposes of teaching asceticism and humility. It took place in rural surroundings that do not pose the same dangers as the urban centres. They did not therefore suffer the living conditions of the contemporary talibé.
- Then there are parents who do not have the means to look after their children. These families are from a modest social background, are generally large and cannot meet their needs, and therefore send their children to learn the Koran with a relative who is a marabout. Because of this, they do not have to pay the consideration that should represent their contribution to their child's education.

In addition, very few parents of talibés go back to see their children and talk to the marabout. Talibés unfailingly complain about their "familyless" state.[10]

---

10 Y. Marguerat and D. Poitou (eds.), *A l'écoute des enfants de la rue en Afrique Noire*, (Paris: Fayard, 1994).

3.3. ACTION BY THE STATE AND CIVIL SOCIETY

17. When it signed the 1989 International Convention on the Rights of the Child, the government of Senegal freely undertook to "respect and ensure the rights set forth in the Convention to each child... without discrimination of any kind". As such, the State must "ensure the child such protection and care as is necessary for his or her well-being" (Art. 3); it must ensure as far as possible that the child's right "to know and be cared for by his or her parents" (Art. 7) is implemented, and that "the child shall not be separated from his or her parents against their will". Furthermore, the State guarantees to take "all effective and appropriate measures with a view to abolishing traditional practices prejudicial to the health of children" (Art. 24(3)) and "to ensure that school discipline is administered in a manner consistent with the child's human dignity" (Art. 28(2)). In addition, the State undertakes to protect the child against economic exploitation and from performing any work that is likely to be hazardous or to interfere with his or her education or be harmful to his or her physical, mental, spiritual, moral or social development (Art. 32).The implementation of these legal obligations by the State should not permit the spread of the phenomenon of talibé children.

18. Firstly, it could be thought that the Senegalese government is not greatly in favour of the phenomenon as it currently exists, and thinks that ways should be found to adapt the daaras to modern society, which Senegalese society has become. It has expressed its intention to eliminate begging through Article 245 of the Criminal Code, which formally prohibits begging. The same law punishes "those who allow minors under twenty-one in their care to beg" with a three to six-month prison sentence. However, the prohibition is greatly attenuated by the provision in the law that "asking for alms on the days, in the places and under the conditions set out by religious traditions does not constitute begging."

Despite a stated intent, the government means to go softly so that its actions are not perceived as an infringement of religious practice and customs. Furthermore, the political authorities prefer not to clash with the marabouts, some of whom are very influential. During elections, their voting advice is generally followed. This means that politicians make particularly sure that they maintain good relations with these major "vote carriers".

19. In addition, the State's inability to provide a concrete response to the phenomenon means that it is turning away from the fate of the talibés. Despite the relevant provisions of the Senegalese Criminal Code, which advocate measures of educational support for children whose health, safety, morality or education are being compromised, indifference seems to have moved in.

20. However, on a legislative level, there is cause for hope. Recently, the Senegalese government, with the support of the US State Department, adopted a special law on the fight against slavery and similar practices and the protection of the victims.[11] The law formally prohibits "the exploitation of another's begging" and sets out severe penalties (2 to 5 years imprisonment and a fine of between 500,000 and 2,000,000 CFA francs) for "any person who organises the begging of another person with a view to profiting by it, recruits, trains or leads a person astray with a view to sending them out to beg or exerts pressure on them to beg or continue to do so". The law specifies that when the offence is committed with respect to a minor, there will be no reprieve for the guilty party, and the judge will apply a firm penalty.

The fantastic new feature is that the 2005 law authorises associations and public services, which look after victims, to represent them in legal proceedings. This is an excellent opportunity for NGOs that so wish to fight effectively against the exploitation of children.

21. In May 2006, during the 25th national women's fortnight, AÏDA MBODJ, minister for Women, the Family and Social Development, denounced this "atrocious begging" and vehemently lamented the fact that "children of all ages, wearing rags, with a desperately empty begging bowl in their hand, barefoot, roam the streets and crossroads of the city from dawn to dusk looking for charity that no sharia law recommends".

The minister also emphasised that "these innocent children, unjustly described as talibés, usually exploited by dubious adults, need our help to escape from the worst forms of work and slavery to which they are subjected. All of society must condemn it and must take action so that this begging, which is nothing less than exploitation of children by adults, ceases".[12]

22. Artists and actors, social commentators, humanitarian organisations and NGOs have become involved in finding solutions to the social phenomenon of the talibés. Awareness campaigns have been developed, targeting both the authorities and the public. Some are taking action on the ground. One of the most remarkable initiatives is one by an association named "DAARA". The association was created by a group of women who were shocked by the young talibés begging in the streets of Dakar, and because of a great surge of solidarity, in 1980 it opened the first home for the rehabilitation of the talibés.

---

11 Law no. 12–2005 of 29 April 2005.

12 (8 May 2006) n° 1939, *Le Populaire*.

4. CONCLUSIONS

23. In traditional society, the daara was almost a traditional rite. Even children from rich families went to daaras, which were a place to learn the Koran and to build character in the face of the vicissitudes of life. The sole aim of making a child beg was to teach him humility, and begging consisted of going to get their daily food, which was provided by the community.

Today, demographic growth, poverty, the monetarisation of the economy, the rural exodus, and in particular the transfer of the daaras to Dakar, has severely corrupted the tradition. Children are shamefully exploited by so-called marabouts in conditions that are inconsistent with human dignity and seriously endanger their education, their health and even their lives.

24. An analysis of the social phenomenon of the talibé children lays open the paradoxes that exist between the State's stated intent to provide children with legal protection, education, leisure, the best possible health and a sufficient standard of living, as demonstrated by the ratification of the New York Convention on the Rights of the Child of 20 November 1989, and the pitiful, inhuman, degrading fate that awaits these children.

25. In its concluding observations when examining the initial report from the State of Senegal, the Committee on the Rights of the Child, having expressed its concern about the situation of the talibé children, made the following recommendation: "*The Committee recommends that in the implementation process of the Convention the State Party pay special attention to the situation of talibés. Further measures should be adopted to ensure the effective enjoyment of their fundamental rights and that they are protected against any form of discrimination. Efforts should be made to ensure an effective monitoring system of their situation by the State Party, in close cooperation with religious and community leaders.*"[13]

This recommendation is still burningly topical, as now more than ever before, the talibé children "live in particularly difficult conditions" and it is time that they were "paid... special attention."

[13] Concluding Observations of the CRC Committee, <http://www.unhchr.ch/tbs/doc.nsf>.

X. CONCLUDING REMARKS

DOES PRACTICE ALSO WORK IN THEORY?

Karl Hanson

INTRODUCTION

1. In many fairy tales, it takes seven of a kind to assure a happy ending to exciting adventures. Here, seven questions will assist in structuring the concluding remarks for the interdisciplinary conference aimed at evaluating how the UN Convention on the Rights of the Child (CRC) has furthered children's rights (or not), and to explore the challenges we still face in realising children's rights. In so doing, I will build upon the conference papers and discussions that were presented and held in the plenary and workshops sessions,[1] as well as upon results obtained in the phase of the interdisciplinary research network on children's human rights that lies at the basis of this conference.[2] The congregation of child rights practitioners and academics around the achievements and challenges of the CRC offers a distinctive opportunity to ask questions on the relation between child rights rhetoric and reality. We are concerned, not only to better understand how CRC principles work out in implementation practice, but also to consider the theoretical basis of these practices.

1. CAN ONE STAND ON THE BALCONY AND IN THE SCENE AT THE SAME TIME?

2. During the conference, 15 different workshops have been held, during which about 70 papers have been presented. Given the conference format and timeframe, including

---

1 A selection of the conference papers are published in the present volume; for an overview of the full conference programme, see: <http://www.law.ugent.be/pub/iuap/c_welcome.html> (Visited: 25 September 2006).

2 The IAP (Interuniversity Attraction Poles) project concerns a joint interdisciplinary research on children's rights between three Belgian universities. Through interdisciplinary dialogue, jurists, criminologists, sociologists and pedagogues examine the role of human rights instruments for the emancipation of children. The IAP-project is financed by the Belgian Federal Science Policy Office. See: <http://www.law.ugent.be/pub/iuap> (Visited: 25 September 2006).

parallel sessions and informal gatherings, it is beyond my capacity to give in these concluding remarks a full account of all the papers and discussions. Hence, my impressions and observations cannot possibly be exhaustive. What I can do is present some critical reflections and personal comments based on a subjective interpretation of the many abstracts, papers, PowerPoint presentations and discussions. The answer on the first question, if one can be on the balcony and in the scene at the same time, is a short one: no. It is impossible to look as a complete external observer from the balcony at what is happening in the scene, and stand in the scene at the same time.

3. The same question can be asked in relation to interdisciplinary research, where it deserves a more nuanced answer. Lawyers, educationalists, psychologists, social workers, sociologists and persons with yet other disciplinary backgrounds have addressed a varied set of topics and questions, ranging from education to juvenile justice and children in armed conflict. In such a setting, adopting an interdisciplinary approach seems a good option. It enables us not only to approach children's rights from different scientific disciplines, but also to examine interdisciplinarity itself. The interdisciplinary approach can be understood as a special form of dialogue between several scientific disciplines,[3] which respects the specific identity of each discipline. This interdisciplinary process implies the willingness to listen and an open-mindedness with respect to other points of view and ways of thinking. It requires spontaneous attention and an open dialogue in order to attain an honest and critical intellectual reflection of one's own points of view and those of other people. Interdisciplinary work takes time.[4]

4. Until now, I have taken part in this conference as a spectator who was observing from the balcony the play being performed on stage. However, I have never been a complete outsider: the balcony where I had my seat is located in the same theatre as where the play was being performed. My move from the balcony to the stage is a fit metaphor to clarify my particular role during this closing session, as well as my perspective on interdisciplinary children's rights studies. In attempting to describe from an external point of view the internal viewpoint of participants in this conference, I will adopt a "moderate external point of view".[5]

---

[3] F. Ost and P. Gerard, 'Congrès et colloques – Conference on critical legal scholarship, University of Kent, 30 mars-3avril 1981', (1981) 7 *Revue Interdisciplinaire d'études juridiques*, 151–162.

[4] L. Cattrijsse, I. Delens-Ravier, K. Hanson, T. Moreau, A. Vandaele, T. Vanthuyne and M. Verheyde (eds.), *From standard setting to implementation…and vice versa? Towards a coherent analytical framework for the interdisciplinary research 'Human rights of children. Implementation and monitoring through participation*, (Brussels: Belgian Federal Office for Scientific, Technical and Cultural Affairs, 2002).

[5] F. Ost and M. Van de Kerchove, 'De la scène au balcon. D'où vient la science du droit?', in F. Chazeland and J. Commaille (eds.), *Normes juridiques et régulation sociale*, (Paris: LGDJ, 1991), 67–80.

2. WHAT IS AT STAKE WHEN THEORY MEETS PRACTICE?

5. I have subsequently attended the workshops on "critical reflections on children's rights" and on "poverty and children's rights", which were very dissimilar. The critical reflections workshop was theoretical in nature and scholarly in approach; the poverty workshop included presentations exclusively from a field perspective with speakers all working either for Save the Children or for UNICEF. Furthermore, the people taking part in each workshop were very different. On both occasions, there was only very little time for discussion.

Albeit I heard echoes from other workshops with more time for discussion, I am not absolutely sure whether the past days' theory and practice have really met – both approaches were present and have been on stage. Maybe there has been more time in the foyer, and we will engage further one with another during the closing reception, as well as back home, where we promise to read and digest theory and keep in touch with practice. Sufficient time is needed not only when disciplines come together, but also when theory and practice meet.

6. An important issue, which is at stake when theory meets practice is finding the right balance between "enlightenment" and "engineering". Is child rights research sufficiently theoretical, and not too practical? Conversely, is field work in children's rights sufficiently practicable and not too abstract, existing only in the minds of programme designers and presenters?

A consensus on the extent, priorities or even precise content of children's rights is not readily available: children's rights are a moral sensitive domain having to deal with strong and often competing normative and ideological perspectives. One speaker who took a strong stance against a legal ban on corporal punishment has different viewpoints compared to the CRC Committee's most recent General Comment that urges States Parties to ban all corporal punishment, including within the family.[6] In addition, children's rights, as is the case with human rights in general, are permeated with high ideals of social justice, making children's rights an arena perfectly fit for social change and advocacy.

For researchers, such a context poses some particular challenges. Doing scientific research on a subject that has been pushed forward far and foremost from an activist's

[6] CRC Committee, *General Comment No. 8: The right of the child to protection from corporal punishment and other cruel or degrading forms of punishment (articles 19, 28(2) and 37, inter alia)* (UN Doc. CRC/C/GC/2006/8, 2006).

perspective is not an easy undertaking, as it catches many a human or children's rights researcher between their role of a distant scientific observer, and the role of a human rights advocate wishing to contribute via research findings to make the realisation of children's rights come closer to reality. As said, it is difficult to stand in the scene and on the balcony at the same time.

7. While acknowledging the tension between advocacy and research, we consider interdisciplinary children's rights research primarily as a scientific undertaking and suggest adopting a reflexive perspective on the subject. Such a stance lies at the heart of our "moderate external point of view": standing on the balcony to comment on what happens on stage. The overall objective of scientific research in children's rights is to foster social enlightenment aimed at describing, understanding and evaluating children's rights. Albeit research *can* have a positive impact on furthering respect for children's rights, in my opinion its key objective is not to implement the CRC or to change the world into a better place for children. These are the primary objectives for child rights advocates and policy makers. Research findings can of course be used for legislative changes, social policy or programming. However, it is up to advocates and policy makers to make use (or not) of research findings. For instance, a national government is perfectly apt and quite often does prefer fixing it's minimum age of criminal responsibility in response to a tragic event rather than on development psychological research findings that can give nuanced insights into children's ability to stand before the law. Conversely, researchers can direct their research interests to issues proposed by advocates and practitioners. However, if they prefer to invest their research time in issues that seem less urgent from a child rights practitioner's point of view, for example looking into philosophical theories on natural law theory or questioning whether there is a legal obligation for international co-operation regarding economic, social and cultural rights in the CRC, then researchers do have that liberty. Moreover, curiosity is their social responsibility, i.e. they get paid for being curious and asking all kinds of questions, even those that seem less relevant from a practitioner's point of view.

3. CAN THEORY HELP HOLD THINGS TOGETHER?

8. In his novel *Sabbath's Theatre*, Philip ROTH describes the simple pleasures of Gus, a very ordinary man who loves telling jokes. For Gus, jokes give sense to the world and hold together anything that is not explained on TV. For us, theory functions like telling jokes for Gus, since theory can give sense and holds together the complicated, fragmented world. Can theory also help hold together the numerous approaches on children's rights that were presented during this conference?

9. The IAP research network on children's human rights elaborated a common reference framework that makes a distinction between three clear-cut research fields and their mutual interaction: the standard setting field, the implementation field and the social reality. Figure 1 provides a pictorial representation of this framework, stressing both the three separate phases as well as their mutual interaction.

Figure 1: Three interrelated research fields[7]

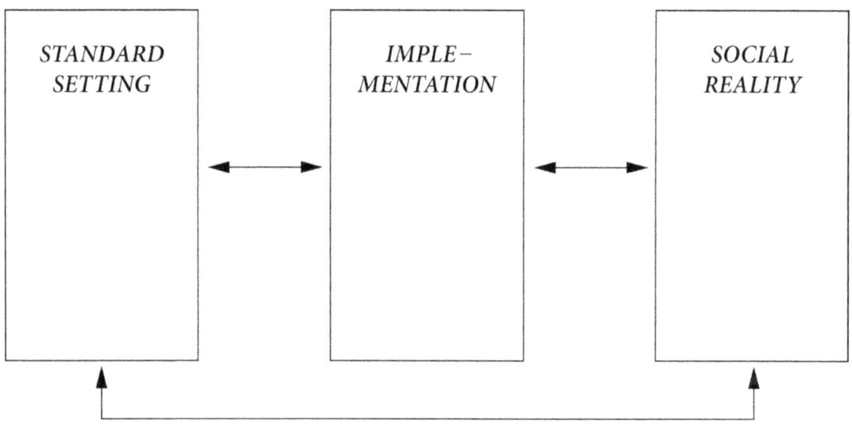

The first, *standard setting* field refers to the process of the creation, the drafting, and the formulation of legal norms and rights. Research demands a thorough analysis of the legal texts and of the "*travaux préparatoires*". Legal rules that establish children's rights can be questioned with respect to their normative value, to their objectives and their objective logic. Children's human rights are guaranteed in a variety of instruments on the national, regional and international level. For instance, the legal status of refugee children is not only dealt with in the CRC, but also in EU law. Together they constitute the normative legal framework of children's rights. These different standards present themselves as an overlapping tangle of standards with different legal capacities and diverse objectives, rather than as a coherent and logically structured whole. Hence, it is important not only to disclose the normative value of the rules in a legal sense, but also to identify the different interests they might serve. During his plenary speech RAOUL KIENGE-KIENGE for example addressed the differences between the CRC and the African Charter on the Rights and Welfare of the Child.[8]

---

7 L. CATTRIJSSE, I. DELENS-RAVIER, K. HANSON, T. MOREAU, A. VANDAELE, T. VANTHUYNE and M. VERHEYDE (eds.), supra (note 4).

8 See R. KIENGE-KIENGE in the present volume.

Many papers discuss how to better translate the CRC in national policy, for instance inquiring on how to implement child-focused budget analyses; whether reporting makes sense; analysing the national and international jurisprudence on children's rights; or asking how to implement a rights-based approach to de-institutionalisation. These studies can be clustered under the second field of *implementation*, which refers to all the actions that can be or are undertaken in order to secure the correct application and monitoring of human rights standards. From a legal point of view, special attention is paid to the solutions proposed by international monitoring mechanisms or by national jurisprudence. How is the legal standard put into practice? What are the available monitoring and enforcement mechanisms? Which institutions exist and what are their tasks? From a policy standpoint, the analysis of implementation also comprises empirical studies, for example, on how governments put the CRC principles and rules into practice (or not). We have heard many criticisms of the divergence between international child rights standards and national policy and practice, which are often formulated in terms of the now famous "gap" between the rhetoric and reality. How can we close this gap?

The third field concerning *social reality* refers to the actual daily situation of people and the way they experience the standards and their implementation. Within the social reality field, the focus is on the one hand on the social consequences of the standards and on the way in which these standards are experienced and lived out by the actors. What are the problems, the paradoxes and the possibilities involved in the standards? The key question is: "What consequences did the actors, which are the children, the young people themselves and their environment (family, social environment, school environment, etc.), experience following the implementation of the standards?" Regarding the right to education, young people in Northern Ireland have drawn visual metaphors on real school life. One of the images that was presented shows a bird in a cage – standing for a pupil in school – shouting "Let me out of here!" The field of the social reality on the other hand also comprises research on the way in which the social actors influence the creation of new standards or the interpretation and implementation of existing standards. Quite some lobby work has been done to introduce children's rights in the EU Charter on Fundamental Rights and in EU policy.

Finally, we can also look at the permanent and mutual *interaction between these three fields*, standard setting, implementation and social reality. Changes in one field may generate effect in the other fields.

In this sense, it is entirely possible to describe positive as well as negative outcomes; intentional as well as unexpected effects; emancipatory as well as conservative processes in the area of human and children's rights. The interaction between legal and social norms thus becomes obvious and constitutes one of the most central research issues, for example, raising awareness in the social reality field to make more acceptable standards and implementation of standards. At the same time, the implementation of standards is expected to help change mentalities in social reality.

4. CAN CHILDREN'S RIGHTS CHANGE SOCIAL REALITY?

10. An underlying aspiration of many papers presented during this conference – or even of the conference itself – seems to be, ultimately, to bring about social change, even if the findings as a whole are ambiguous. However, can children's rights actually enhance children's lives? Three different positions can be discerned.

11. A first set of papers leaves this question open, or just takes it for granted; they merely call to strengthen implementation and monitoring, for example:

- On the international level CRC monitoring should be strengthened by introducing an individual complaints procedure;
- On the national level CRC implementation can be strengthened via the constitutionalisation of rights, as has been the case for education rights in the South African constitution;
- What are common points in the CRC Committee's Concluding Observations concerning EU-countries, in order to give guidance to an EU children's rights policy?
- What can be done to render existing legal protection mechanisms more *de facto* effectiveness?

12. A second set of papers gives a realistic/pessimistic view as to the actual effects of CRC implementation. For instance:

- Regarding Uganda, one paper describes the country's commitment to the CRC by domesticating it in key national legislations, formulating policies based on it and by submitting three periodic reports to the Committee on the Rights of the Child. The paper nonetheless notes that despite this progress made, many Children in Uganda still live in conditions that place them at the risk of not developing their potential as healthy, social and active citizens.
- Another paper comments that, despite the signing and ratification of the CRC, the enactment of national child rights legislation and the institution of mechanisms to protect children's rights at the national level, the realisation of these rights for children in especially difficult circumstances is still far away;

- Regarding participation, one paper contains the warning not to conflate changes in discursive practices about listening to children's views with policy change itself. The question is whether the taking on board of children's views has also actually been transmitted into child-sensitive policy actions and related budget allocations.

13. A third set of papers has serious doubts about the capacity of children's rights to enhance children's lives, for example:

- One paper has reservations about child labour abolition programmes, and particularly questions the extent to which grandiloquent programmes such as the Indian child labour abolition programme will actually have a positive impact on working children's lives. Referring to the high prevalence of child labour, the author comments that the legislator's intentions (i.e. adopting laws aimed at child labour abolition) are mistaken;
- Finally, one would like to understand why more and more children are begging in the streets of Dakar, whereas more and more national and international legislation has been adopted that is against it.

This last question is quite puzzling, especially when posed during a conference that devotes a great deal of attention to learning how the realisation of children's rights can be furthered. It raises important questions on the very possibility of an international, almost universally ratified international human rights document to further respect for children's rights. The example makes two apparently contradictory observations. One, more and more national and international legislation has been adopted aimed at doing away with child begging. Two, more and more children are found begging in the streets of Dakar. We can suggest at least three different hypotheses that all might explain this contradiction:

Hypothesis A: Without the CRC and subsequent national legislation, the rise of begging amongst children in Dakar would have been even higher.
Hypothesis B: Because of the CRC, more children need to beg for their subsistence. Here, the children's rights discourse is applied against children's interests.
Hypothesis C: There is no direct link between the CRC and the magnitude of begging in a country. The number of children found begging is due to poverty and the rise of inequalities amongst populations, within and amongst countries.

Hypothesis A is an optimistic one, but quite impossible to verify. One can always find examples of instances where the CRC has had some impact, where there has been no impact, or where the situation has worsened. In this respect, the UNICEF study on the implementation of the CRC,[9] that was discussed in a workshop presentation, only studies half of reality. When one looks for examples where the CRC has had a positive impact on children's lives, one is very likely to also find them. However, imagine a study looking for the negative impact of the CRC – the chance is high that such a study would also be able to prove it's point of departure, and conclude that the CRC has a negative impact. To empirically verify the totality of both positive and negative impacts of the CRC seems fairly unrealistic.

Hypothesis B is all too cynical. It might of course be true that the CRC is partially used and misused to serve interests other than that of children, for instance by employing the emphasis on children's participation as an argument to scale down public services ("they can do it themselves"). However, it is an oversimplification to just point the finger at a children's rights document or at international human rights legislation to explain why children's living conditions deteriorate.

My preference goes to Hypothesis C, which refutes that there would be any necessary or essential link between the CRC and the situation of children in a given country. A case study from Peru that was presented during the workshops illustrates this hypothesis. Albeit greater trade openness has generated a decrease in the demand for child labour in Peruvian urban areas, it also has augmented children's involvement in the mining industry and in some agricultural sectors. Connections between trade openness, its consequences for vulnerable social groups, including children, and the impact of the CRC need to be more carefully scrutinised if we wish to understand the precise role of the CRC and its implementation efforts within permanently changing political, social and economic contexts. The advent and development of children's rights coincided with a period of intense global expansion. Both the inspiration and the pressure to make particular children's rights real, including child soldiering, working children and children living in poverty, do not as such stem from an international human rights document, but were pushed on the agenda as a result of challenges facing children that made a "decent" childhood out of reach. Children, especially in the developing world, were fully part of the globalisation process.[10]

---

9 UNICEF, *Summary report of the study on the impact of the implementation of the Convention on the Rights of the Child*, (Florence: Unicef Innocenti Research Centre, 2004). The study documents the process set in motion by the CRC across regions and aims to consider the changes the CRC has promoted, with particular emphasis on national legal and institutional reforms. UNICEF presents its findings to encourage cross-fertilisation of experiences and the replication of good practices, as well as *to advance the cause of children's rights* (emphasis added). The publication of the first phase full report and the second phase preliminary findings are announced by the end of 2006, see: <www.unicef-icdc.org>.

10 P. Reynolds, O. Nieuwenhuys and K. Hanson, 'Refractions of children's rights in development practice', (2006) 13 (3) *Childhood*, 291–302.

This also implies that the CRC does not provide a universal remedy for curing all adverse consequences of macro policies for children. This might seem a rather disappointing hypothesis, especially for child rights advocates who put so many efforts into strengthening the implementation and monitoring of the CRC. Their play would just serve to amuse the people on the balcony, with no effects in real life outside the theatre? Let us explore this last hypothesis a few steps further.

5. IF THE CRC IS NOT THE PANACEA TO CHANGE THE WORLD, THEN WHAT IS IT?

14. From a non-essentialist approach to children's rights, we see that human rights and children's rights are not a metaphysical abstraction of moral norms, but are social constructions. Rather than asking ourselves whether the CRC is correctly applied or whether children's rights are compatible with local cultural values, we contend that they can be made to carry many, even contradictory meanings.[11] In this sense, the human rights discourse may provide children a powerful tool for social change in view of their emancipation as social actors deficient in power. Human rights, however, do not act by definition as a tool for social change. The social world is not solely shaped by high ideals of empowerment, but is also taking form as a consequence of pragmatic policies, that might even make use of human rights discourses, not to alter but to sustain extant power relations.[12]

15. Research of children's rights has to empirically investigate the social consequences of children's rights. In which contexts and on what conditions do they function as an effective tool for change? And in which contexts and on what conditions are they expressing pragmatic policies? Seemingly well intentioned attempts at addressing the admittedly pressing needs of children *in abstracto*, may turn into an entirely different affair when put into practice in local contexts. For example, the use of children's rights in development practice not automatically leads to empowering children, but can also turn out to belittle children's autonomy and chances, as has been demonstrated via certain interventions towards street children that ended up marginalising street children rather then providing them the necessary support to enhance their street life.[13] Consequently, we should not only look at the high ideals of child rights policies and norms, but also try to understand the social effects of child rights implementation. What are in turn the effects of the distance between high ideals of change and

---

[11] Ibid.

[12] N. STAMMERS, 'Social movements and the construction of human rights', (1999) 21 *Human Rights Quarterly*, 980–1008.

[13] P. REYNOLDS, O. NIEUWENHUYS and K. HANSON, supra (note 10), 291–302.

pragmatic policies for the children concerned? Are children not getting frustrated because the promises of emancipation and improvement in the CRC is not realised?

16. The presented papers and the discussions held during this conference illustrate that there is more critical awareness around children's rights than 15 years ago. Children's rights are no longer solely seen as the panacea to change the world into a better place for children.

17. There has been discussion on the instrumentalisation of the CRC. Of course, we all instrumentalise the international instrument. What else is it there for? Although, we do not agree on the purposes of its instrumentalisation, many people using the CRC as a tool indeed utilise it for distinct objectives, or have different preferences. The CRC is used to raise awareness, as an instrument of foreign policy, and so on. Both extremes on the continuum of conceptions of children's rights, which is, those who see them either as entitlements that can empower the powerless or as mere tools in the hands of the powerful, share a naïve instrumentalist view of children's rights that is highly problematic.[14] The instrumentalist view distorts reality and hides complexity; it fails to take into account variations and commonalities in local contexts. Rights are brought into effect through social practices in particular contexts and time frames and do not necessarily always carry the same meaning, nor do the consequences of particular usages of children's rights necessarily coincide with their initial objectives.[15]

18. There are detectable, strategic configurations in the game between different social groups around children's rights. Competing or complementary strategies are generally deployed together, so that no person or group can claim ownership. Large development agencies, grass-root children's rights groups, international organisations and local governments make use of children's rights to support their claims. In the debate on child labour, both the International Labour Organisation (ILO) and organisations of working children refer to children's rights in defending contrasting positions on child labour. The ILO refers to children's rights to advocate the effective abolition of child labour as their ultimate goal; organisations of working children make use of children's rights in support of their claims for recognition of their right to work in dignity, as well as to participate in forums regulating child labour.[16] Both African

---

14 R.S. Summers, 'Naïve instrumentalism and the law', in P.M.S. Hacker and J. Raz (eds.), *Law, Morality, and Society. Essays in Honour of H.L.A. Hart*, (Oxford: Clarendon Press, 1977), 119–131.

15 M. Foucault, 'Qu'appelle-t-on punir?', in F. Ringelheim (ed.), *Punir mon beau souci. Pour un raison pénale*, (1984) 1–3, *Reveu de l'Université de Bruxelles*, 35 – 46.

16 K. Hanson and A. Vandaele, 'Working children and international labour law: A critical analysis', (2003) 11 (1) *The International Journal of Children's Rights*, 73–146.

governments and local NGOs make use of children's rights language for gaining access to scarce and much needed resources.[17]

19. Not only nobody owns children's rights, but we should also be wary of claims that children's rights would be an invention of western society. If children's rights are made into what they are, it might also be because, in all their imperfections, they are alive in the minds and hearts of children in the world. Some obvious dangers in proclaiming children's rights lie in the possibility that they may obscure the politics of poverty or give false promises. On the other hand, there is the possibility that in not declaring rights and implementing them we perpetuate or encourage calm neglect, or the expansion of abuse, or entrench a global disregard of children's interests.[18] Children are not passive recipients of ideas that come "from above" and that, if children's rights are to be entrenched, children should be party to their shaping and implementation – many of you indeed expressed their concerns about participation rights – and they should be actively concerned with their rights.

20. Strategic configurations of the game between different social groups around children's rights generate competing or complementary strategies at work simultaneously, so that no one can claim ownership. International organisations, NGOs, local governments, village and neighbourhood groups and children make use of children's rights to support their claims. Rights have come to take a prominent – albeit not the only – place both in policy-making and in public discourse in part because they express concerns about the place of children in a globalising world.

6. WHAT SHALL WE DO WITH OUR DARLINGS?

21. Alongside the maturing of the children's rights field also our darlings are growing older. I am happy that the abstracts, papers and discussions can affirm and complement my small collection of child rights phrases:

- A new popular introduction to conference presentations has appeared, which seems to be becoming the number one argument to sustain that a particular topic is important. It goes as follows: "I have typed in 'child soldiers' / 'violence against children' / 'child rights policy', etc. in Google, and I have found 1 million / 25 million / 1 billion, etc. matches".
- We are all convinced of "The need for a holistic approach to children's rights"
- "Children's rights are a slogan in search of a definition"

---

17 R. Kienge-Kienge, supra (note 8).

18 P. Reynolds, O. Nieuwenhuys and K. Hanson, supra (note 10), 291–302.

- "It is time no longer to consider children as becomings but to see them as beings"
- The CRC includes a revolutionary concept, which changed the view of children "from objects to subjects of rights"
- "A lot has been accomplished, but still much needs to be done".

I wonder if it would be possible to show the deepest respect for our ancestors by reiterating these beloved aphorisms, and at the same time constantly reinterpret their meanings for the changing environments.

Not only our slogans, but also the very concepts with which we work need to be constantly updated and reconceptualised. Much used and abused concepts such as exploitation, participation, survival or socialisation need to be carefully reconsidered. Also the child, the family and the more recent "child-rights based approach to development" are concepts that can use much more clarification. I suggest to invite the darling "Children's rights are a slogan in search of a definition"[19] to stay with us for some time to come.

7. SHOULD WE DISTINGUISH DIFFERENT SCHOOLS OF THOUGHT IN CHILDREN'S RIGHTS?

22. Finally, I would like to raise the question on the need to distinguish between different schools of thought in children's rights, or to at least acknowledge the plain existence of different approaches to the CRC. Within the children's rights field there is not only agreement but also disagreement, and we should more clearly reflect on the lines of disagreement, not in order to work on a new compromise but to better equip the children's rights field with general analytical tools.

23. The *kiddielibbers* and *welfarists* have found a compromise in the CRC, that acknowledges a holistic, comprehensive way for both children's autonomy and welfare rights. With that compromise, the analytical and pedagogical useful distinction between both approaches has disappeared. Now, we are all in children's rights. Furthermore, the holistic character of the CRC also pushes to the background the distinction between civil and political rights versus economic, social and cultural rights. Those who distrust States – the civil and political rights approach – and those who call upon States for the fulfilment of their rights see their antagonism disappearing and are more and more obliged to work together. With the CRC we now indeed have

19 H. Rodham, 'Children under the law', (1973) 43 (4) *Harvard Educational Review*, 487–514.

a common language. It is the Esperanto for people working and studying the human rights of children. However, speaking a common language does not imply that we also have to agree on the things of which we speak.

24. The variety of papers and the contrasting viewpoints discussed during this conference call for distinguishing at least the following two approaches to children's rights:

- Those who see the CRC primarily as a policy instrument, which is used by international organisations, NGOs and State actors to push (or hamper) the development of genuine child-sensitive social policies.
- And those who see the CRC as a human rights document, to be subdivided in civil and political rights on the one hand, and economic, social and cultural rights on the other hand, who see it as a legal tool to further the respect, protection and fulfilment of children's individual human rights.

Other divisions can be proposed, for example taking the degree of adherence to children as special or separate human rights holders. Should we highlight differences between children and adults, or, on the contrary, stress that children's human rights are very similar to human rights in general, and hence associate the cause for children's rights more closely with the advancement of human rights in general?

25. The discussion of analytical categories, which can take into account not only our similarities but also our differences in approaching children's rights could be the subject of a new conference where we can try to find agreement over the points we disagree on, and over the lines of our disagreements. The call to distinguish schools of thought in children's rights hence wishes to contribute to a better understanding of the diversity of child rights approaches and of the various uses and consequences of the CRC in practice. The ambition is not to dictate social actors in the children's rights field what they ought to do or think, nor to assess the degree of conformity of their position with a particular child rights approach. On the contrary, to ask if the practice also works in theory is an appeal to theorists to more actively develop heuristic second-level constructs[20] that can modestly be put at the service of a prolific and wide-ranging child rights practice.

---

20 B.Z. Tamanaha, 'A non-essentialist version of legal pluralism', (2000) 27 (2) *Journal of Law and Society*, 296–321.

BIOGRAPHIES

Eva Brems (° 1969) studied Law at the universities of Namur (candidat en droit, 1989), Leuven (licenciaat rechtsgeleerdheid, 1992), Bologna (exchange student 1991) and Harvard (LL.M 1995). She obtained a Ph.D. in Law from the University of Leuven (1999), with a dissertation on "Human Rights: Universality and Diversity" (Martinus Nijhoff, 2001). Before joining Ghent University, she was a researcher at the University of Leuven (1992–1994 and 1995–1999) and a lecturer at the University of Maastricht (1999–2000). In Ghent, she is a Professor of Human Rights Law and non-Western law. Her research in the human rights field covers most areas of human rights law (in Belgian law, European law, international law, and comparative law). She is the author of numerous publications in this field in Belgian and international journals and books, and a member of the editorial board of several law journals. She is the chair of the Flemish section of Amnesty International and an activist in several human rights organisations.

Lina Hammad is an Assistant Project Officer and currently holding the Officer in Charge responsibility of the Planning section at UNICEF Iraq Support Centre in Amman, Jordan. Before that, she worked for UNICEF Middle East and North Africa Regional Office in the Monitoring & Evaluation unit, and has previously held several management/coordination responsibilities, research, consultancies and field-based work in different UN organisations, NGOs and research organisations. A Palestinian-Jordanian, her professional experience has primarily been focused in the area of social development and human and children's rights. Lina received her master's degree in Development Management from the University of Wales, Swansea with distinction, and has been awarded the Andrew Lochhead award for outstanding performance in Development Studies.

Raoul Kienge-Kienge Intudi studied Law at the university of Kinshasa and the university of Nantes. He obtained a Ph.D. in criminology from the Catholic University of Leuven (2005). He is a Professor of Law the university of Kinshasa and a Visiting Professor at the Faculty of Criminology at the University of Lubumbashi and at the Faculty of Law at the Catholic University of Bukavu (R.D. Congo). He is also a lawyer at the Bar of Kinshasa/Gombe. His research covers the area of criminology, Penal Law, Juvenile Justice and Children's Rights.

Aye Aye Tun, from Myanmar, is Deputy Director for Health, HIV/AIDS, Nutrition and Economic Opportunities Programmes in Save the Children in Myanmar. Her previous work supported sectoral programmes in applying child rights programming.

Guy Cave, from the UK, has worked for Save the Children for three years, currently as Director of Programmes (Education & Child Protection) in Myanmar (Burma). He has a Masters in Social Work, and a Masters in Children's Rights.

Duncan Trotter is Child Rights Programming Adviser at Save the Children UK with whom he has worked for fifteen years. British, he has a background in community social work, human resource and organisational development.

Bill Bell is Head of Protection at Save the Children UK. British, he has been involved in the development of child rights programming for several years and has been active in advocacy through the NGO Group on the CRC, CRIN, and the Child Rights Caucus for the UN Special Session on Children and EURONET.

Laura Lundy is a Reader at the School of Education, Queen's University Belfast (Northern Ireland). She has researched and published extensively in the area of education law and human rights, with a particular focus on children's rights.

Ursula Kilkelly is a Senior Lecturer at the Faculty of Law, University College Cork (Ireland) where she researches children's rights with a focus on their enforcement and effective implementation. Laura Lundy and Ursula Kilkelly are co-authors (et al) of 'Children's Rights in Northern Ireland' (2005), research commissioned by the Northern Ireland Commissioner for Children and Young People and undertaken by a research team based at QUB in 2004.

Julia Sloth-Nielsen is currently a professor in the Law Faculty at the University of the Western Cape. She holds the degrees BA, LLB, LLM and was awarded a LLD in 2001 for a thesis entitled "The influence of International Law on South Africa's Juvenile Justice Reform Process". She has published extensively on children's rights related issues in South African and international context, and has served as a member of the editorial board of the International Journal on Children's Rights since 1995. She was appointed to the South African Law reform Commission Project Committee on juvenile justice which prepared the Child Justice Bill 49 of 2002. She also served on the South African Law reform Commission Project Committee on the Review of the Child Care Act, which drafted the Children's Act 38 of 2005. She has consulted extensively on child law reform in Africa (in Sudan, Zambia, Mozambique and Lesotho, for instance), and prepares a manuscript for a book entitled /Children's Rights in African Context, due to be published by Ashgate Dartmouth in early 2007.

Mieke Verheyde is a Belgian researcher at the Human Rights Centre of Ghent University (Belgium). She is one of the researchers of the interdisciplinary inter-university research network on the UN CRC that organised the conference. Her research focuses on the protection of children's rights by the European Court of Human Rights. She is the editor and co-author of the series *A Commentary on the United Nations Convention on the Rights of the Child- CRC Commentary* (Martinus Nijhoff Publishers, Leiden/Boston, 2005-ongoing). She is currently also involved as international children's rights expert in a project regarding an education campaign on children's rights in Romania (EU Phare Programme). Previously, she worked for two years as a researcher on women's rights issues in the Cabinet of the Belgian federal minister of employment and labour, and as a member of the Equal Opportunities Department of the Belgian federal ministry of employment and labour. She studied law at the University of Leuven (Belgium), obtained an LL.M. at the University of Stellenbosch (South Africa) and a European Master's Degree in Human Rights and Democratisation at the University of Padova (Italy).

Joost Van Haelst is since 1995 an official of the Flemish Government (Belgium). Until 1997, he was a legal advisor at the section of special assistance to the youth. In 1997, he became Children's Rights Co-ordinator. As co-ordinator, he set up a network of contact points for children's rights in the different administrations for the follow-up of the implementation of the CRC in nearly all competences of the Flemish Government. This includes, inter alia, the Flemish contribution to the Belgian periodic report on the CRC, the follow-up of the Child Impact Reports for Flemish Parliament draft Acts, the annual governmental reports on children's rights, subsidies for the Centre for the Rights of the Child, and collaboration with the NGO's in a Reflection group.

Laurencio Essewegnon Akohin is a lawyer/publisher, specialised in children's rights, particularly in the area of juvenile justice. He is a founding member of the DCI section in Togo and has been the president of the section since 1993. He was also involved with the creation of the center for social and legal assistance and defense for children in conflict with the law at Lomé, Togo. He is a member of DCI's International Executive Council and Vice president of the Africa zone. Mr Akohin has taken part in several studies on incarcerated children in Paraguay, Bolivia and Brazil. In 1989 he was enrolled in the International Interdisciplinary Course on Children's Rights, Ghent (Belgium). He is now in the process of completing a Master's degree (DESS) in Paris (France) in Family Counselling.

Bernard Boëton is working with the Foundation Terre des hommes since 1980, first as a Delegate in Bangladesh, in Africa, and so on; then as Director of Fund-Raising and Communication (1986–1996), and from 1997 till now as Head of the Children's Rights Department. He is working, as a resource-person of the Foundation programmes on the following issues: Juvenile Justice, Sexual exploitation of Children, Child Trafficking and the general issue of "Consequences of Globalization on Children's Rights", through trainings and workshops with children's rights activists, Magistrates, Police, Social Workers, and so on.

Katarina Tomaševski (1953–2006) obtained degrees from Harvard Law School (LL.M., 1977) and the University of Zagreb (Ph.D., 1980). Her professional activities comprised university teaching, human rights training, consultancies, applied research as well as voluntary public interest work. In 2006, she was a Visiting Professor at the Peking University Law School, teaching human rights at the masters' programme, previously she was a Professor of International Law and International Relations at Lund University. Human rights training includes strategic planning, knowledge acquisition and management, operational procedures in casework, domestic and international litigation, and training of trainers, especially the interface between development and human rights. Cross-national research projects include the first global survey of imprisoned children, a cross-national study into prison health, a global survey of HIV/AIDS-related travel restrictions, or human rights impact assessment in international development cooperation. Consultancies for a range of intergovernmental organisations, donor agencies and NGOs span mainstreaming human rights in development and elimination of gender discrimination. Her previous appointments included, *inter alia*, the Special Rapporteur on the right to education of the United Nations Commission on Human Rights, senior researcher at McGill Centre for Medicine, Ethics and Law (Montreal), and human rights officer of the Global Programme on AIDS of the World Health Organization (now UNAIDS). She is the founder of the Right to Education Project (www.right-to-education.org) established in 1999. She published extensively in internationals journals and books. She was a member of governing or advisory bodies of a variety of public interest, professional and academic organisations and networks. She lived and worked in more than a dozen countries and carried out academic and professional assignments in all regions.

Richard C. Mitchell is an Assistant Professor in the Department of Child and Youth Studies, Brock University, Ontario, Canada. A graduate of the University of Victoria, British Columbia, he completed his Ph.D. in Sociology and Social Policy with the University of Stirling, Scotland. His dissertation is entitled 'The UN Convention on the Rights of the Child in Postmodernity: A Grounded Systemic Analysis of Children's Rights Educational Policies in Scotland and Canada'. He has taught courses on young people's rights and equity issues within childhood and youth studies, social work, social policy and qualitative research methods. In a previous career, he worked as a counsellor within British Columbia education, mental health and specialised foster-care. His research and consultancy focus upon interdisciplinary and transdisciplinary approaches to implementing the human rights of children and young people within institutional and community-based settings.

Haina Lu is from the People's Republic of China. She is currently a Ph.D. candidate in law and researcher at the Institute for Human Rights of the Catholic University of Leuven (K.U.Leuven) in Belgium. Her dissertation examines the right to work in China. She holds an M.A. in the theory and practice of international human rights from the University of Oslo, Norway, and a DES in international law from the Free University of Brussels (ULB). She is also a researcher at the Centre for Ethnic and Migration Studies of the University of Liège, Belgium. She was a guest lecturer at the Law School of Suzhou University in China in 2004

Aoife Daly has a degree in Applied Psychology from University College Cork. Her thesis examined the effect of peer pressure on the eyewitness testimony of young children. After studying psychology she went on to do a Masters in International Human Rights Law at the Irish Centre for Human Rights, National University of Ireland Galway. After an internship with Palestinian human rights organisation Al-Haq in Ramallah, West Bank, she wrote her thesis on the right to education of Palestinian children in the Occupied Palestinian Territories. She graduated from N.U.I. Galway in 2003. She currently holds the position of Research Fellow at Children's Research Centre, Trinity College Dublin. At the Centre, she has researched issues ranging from education for children with disabilities to inter-country adoption. She also lectures on the International Law on the Rights of the Child at the Irish Centre for Human Rights. She is currently doing a Ph.D. at Trinity College Dublin on the participation rights of children. She also sits on the Executive Committee of Amnesty International, Irish Section.

Paulí Dávila Balsera is a professor of History of Education at the University of the Basque Country (EHU-UPV). His research work focuses on the history of education in the Basque Country (Euskal Herria), and he takes part in a number of diverse themes in the educational sphere: educational policy, literacy, teacher education (training), national curriculum, text books, professional training, schooling, childhood, etc., topics about which he has published a number of books, chapters within books and articles in specialised journals. He has also conducted research on the development and application of the Convention on the Rights of the Child and international bodies, highlighting the educational role underpinning the CRC, as well as the study of the history of childhood.

Luis María Naya Garmendia is a Senior lecturer in Comparative Education at the University of the Basque Country (EHU-UPV). He is the author of numerous publications amongst which we can make special mention to the editorial coordination of the series of books by the Donostia-based Erein publishing house: El derecho a la educación en un mundo globalizado (2006) [The Right to Education in a Globalised World}, La Educación y los Derechos Humanos (2005) [Education and Human Rights], La infancia en la historia: Espacios y representaciones (2005) [Childhood throughout History: Spaces & Representations]; or the chapter "Comment et à quelles conditions, l'éducation comprarée Peut-elle faire avancer l'Europe de l'éducation?", in the book *L'Éducation comparée un outil pour l'Europe* (Paris, L'Harmattan) edited by P. Laderrière and F. Vaniscotte (2003) *[Comparative Education – a tool for Europe]*. He also edited the monograph on Childhood and Rights (2003) for the Spanish Journal of Comparative Education. Mr Naya's main lines of research focuses on the use of ICTs, minoritised languages and the rights of children.

Joost Kooijmans works as a legal officer in the International Program on the Elimination of Child Labour (IPEC) of the International Labour Organization (ILO). He is responsible for monitoring the application by member states of the ILO Conventions relating to child labour. Prior to his work in IPEC he has worked for the ILO in Southern Africa and has been involved in many technical human rights and social development in Europe, Asia, and Africa.

Antonella Invernizzi is a Swiss social scientist. She studied and taught at Fribourg University (CH) where she was awarded a Ph.D. for a study of street working children's experiences in Lima, Peru (1999). Whilst based at the University of Cambridge (England) between 2001 and 2004 she carried out research on children's work in Southern Portugal. Both studies are referred to in her contribution to this book. Since 2004, she has worked on children's participation and citizenship. Her most recent publication is a collaboration with Henk van Beers and Brian Milne (eds.) *Beyond Article 12. Essential Readings in Children's Participation*, Knowing Children, Bangkok. She has been based at Swansea University since 2004. Dr Invernizzi is Senior Lecturer within the Department of Applied Social Sciences.

Maria-Carmen Pantea is an International Policy Fellow of the Open Society Institute and a Ph.D. candidate in Sociology at "Babes Bolyai" University, Romania. She has an MA in Gender Studies from Central European University and a background in Educational Sciences. Her research explores the issue of child labour and education in Romania, with a focus on ethnicity and gender. Currently, she undertakes an MA in Evidence Based Social Work at the Department of Social Policy and Social Work, University of Oxford.

Aoife Nolan is a Lecturer in Law and Assistant Director of the Human Rights Centre at Queen's University, Belfast. She has previously worked as a part-time Lecturer at Trinity College, Dublin, and as a Senior Legal Officer with the Economic, Social and

Cultural Rights Litigation Programme at the Geneva-based Centre on Housing Rights and Evictions. Her Ph.D. focused on the judicial treatment and enforcement of children's socio-economic rights. Her primary areas of research are children's rights, socio-economic rights, international human rights law and public interest law. She has written and been published on these topics. She has been a Visiting Research Fellow at Columbia University School of Law, New York, and has spent time as a Visiting Student at the University of Cape Town. She is Coordinating Editor of the Housing & ESC Rights Law Quarterly.

Jan Van Gils (° 1950) is a doctor in pedagogic sciences and currently the director of the Research Centre Childhood and Society in Belgium. He is an expert on qualitative research projects in which children themselves voice their experiences and ideas and an expert on children's play in several contexts. He is strongly involved in several international projects and organisations that intend to promote the child's right to play. He is the former president of IPA (International Play Association for the Child's Right to Play), 1999 – 2005. Currently, he is the president of ICCP (International Council for Children's Play) since 2005; the president of ECFCN (European Child Friendly Cities Network) and he is a member of the EPSF (European Play Safety Forum).

Fiona Ang is a Ph.D. candidate at the Catholic University of Leuven (K.U.Leuven, Belgium). She is involved in an interuniversity and interdisciplinary project on the UN Children's Rights Convention and conducts Ph.D. research on the human rights framework applicable to children with a psychiatric disability. Previously, she studied law at the Catholic University of Leuven and Northwestern University (Chicago, USA) and fulfilled internships with Amnesty International (Geneva, Switzerland) and the International Labour Organization (Jakarta, Indonesia), where she participated in the International Programme on the Eradication of Child Labour. She is co-editor of the international series "A Commentary on the UN Convention on the Rights of the Child" (Martinus Nijhoff, 2006) and is actively involved in various organisations such as Amnesty International (Flemish section), the Children's Jury for Children's Books (Sint-Niklaas), and the High School Students' Parliament (Leuven).

Nigel Cantwell began working on international children's rights issues in the late Seventies with the International Union for Child Welfare. In 1979, he founded Defence for Children International, and throughout the Eighties, he coordinated international NGO input into the drafting of the Convention on the Rights of the Child. He was also active in the development of the 1990 UN Rules for the Protection of Juveniles Deprived of the Liberty and, subsequently, the 1993 Hague Convention on Intercountry Adoption. He joined UNICEF as a consultant in 1994, and then as Senior Project Officer at UNICEF's Innocenti Research Centre in Florence until 2003, heading the unit on implementation of international standards. He is now a Geneva-based child protection consultant specialising in juvenile justice, responses to children without parental care, and rights and protection issues arising from intercountry adoption and other forms of cross-border movement of children.

Ruth Farrugia is an advocate and Senior Lecturer in the Faculty of Law at the University of Malta. She studied at the University of Malta, the University of Strasbourg, the Mediterranean Academy of Diplomatic Studies and the Metropolitan Ecclesiastical Tribunal. She was the first woman deputy registrar at the Courts of Justice, worked in the Attorney General's Chambers, and was acting Director of Welfare. She has been a consultant to the deputy Prime Minister and Minister for Social Policy, Minister for Family and Social Solidarity, the Social Affairs Committee in Parliament, UNHCR and the Commissioner for Children, defending Malta's report before the UN Committee on the CRC. She was the chairperson of the Children Care Orders Board and drafted the Children Act, Commissioner for Children Act and Gender Equality Act. She is a member of the International Society of Family Law and has numerous publications on Family, Child and Refugee Law.

Meda Couzens is a Romanian national, currently living in Durban, South Africa. She graduated in July 1997 the Faculty of Law, Babes-Bolyai University, Cluj-Napoca, Romania. From September 1998 until September 2004 she has been working as a prosecutor in Bucharest, dealing with a significant number of children in conflict with the law. From 2002–2004 she studied towards an MA at the Faculty of Sociology and Social Work, Bucharest. In 2004, she was awarded a Chevening (British Council) Scholarship, which funded her LL.M studies at University of London, Queen Mary College. Her main areas of focus during this LL.M have been children's rights and child law. Currently she lives in South Africa, where she is studying towards an LL.M in Child Care and Protection (University of KwaZulu-Natal, Durban, South Africa), she is a part-time Lecturer in Law at Durban University of Technology, and involved in NGO work in the field of children and refugees' rights. Her main research areas are child participation, international children's rights, child-headed households and juvenile justice.

Salomé Adroher Biosca (°1961) is the chair of the Private International Law Department at the Pontificia Comillas University of Madrid. From 1997 to September 2004 she has also been director of the University Family Institute and since January 2005 she is Head of the Department of Private Law at the same university. Besides teaching migration and familiar mediation at the Faculty of Law and at the masters of the same university, she is a lecturer at different courses organised by public administrations (Ministries, Autonomous Communities and Town councils), professional colleges, juridical schools, and others. She has directed different individual and collective research projects, has published more than 40 studies in books and reviews and has presented almost 50 lectures, papers and communications at conferences, and symposiums, particularly in matters related to the regulation of migration and family law.

Nisha is an Indian women's rights advocate and a development worker with experience in gender and community based programming, advocacy and campaigning. Gender equity has been the mainstay of all her work. She is particularly interested in the analysis of gender dimension of development programmes; policy analysis for gender equality issues; campaigning for women's rights especially to stop violence against women and girl children; and gender mainstreaming into development programmes. She also holds experience in planning and conducting training in gender equality issues, programme assessment and evaluation, and process evaluation. Nisha has worked with different national and international NGOs in India and outside. Currently she is heading the country programme of an international NGO in Afghanistan.

Nicola Jones has a Ph.D. in Political Science from the University of North Carolina at Chapel Hill. She currently works as the Policy Research Manager for Young Lives, a DFID-funded research initiative on childhood poverty in developing countries led by the University of Oxford and Save the Children UK. Previously, she was the project manager for an 8-country Asian network on gender studies and policy; worked as a consultant for the Ministries of Foreign Affairs and Gender Equality in South Korea and was actively involved in advocacy work with various civil society coalitions in East Asia (1998–2003). She is the author of Gender and the Political Opportunities of Democratization in South Korea by Palgrave Macmillan, New York, 2006, as well as a number of articles and working papers on gender relations, comparative policy processes, poverty reduction and child well-being.

Madhuri Mukherjee based at Hyderabad (India) is presently working as the policy research coordinator, with Young Lives- an international study on childhood poverty in Andhra Pradesh, India. At Young Lives, she is involved in various research studies focusing on child rights and policy advocacy for children. She previously worked with Oxfam GB in India, responsible for management and implementation of the gender programme in North India. She has also worked with other national level advocacy organisations working on gender. She has co-authored a number of publications on various aspects of girl child prostitution in India. Her doctorate on development communication focused on developing an alternative model of communication for women's development by analysing the impact and affectivity of the existing and predominant forms of development communication as used in the Indian context.

Jean Trépanier is a professor at the School for Criminology of the University of Montreal (Quebec, Canada) and has conducted various researches on juvenile justice systems and juvenile delinquence. His publications include (in English): "Network, lobbies and pressures: Children's aid societies, and the adoption of the Canadian Juvenile Delinquents Act of 1908", *Paedagogica Historica, International Journal of the History of Eductaion*, 2002; "Juvenile delinquency and youth protection: The historical foundations of the Canadian Juvenile Delinquents Act of 1908", *European Journal of Crime, Criminal Law and Criminal Justice*, 1999; Juvenile courts after 100 years: past and present orientations", *European Journal of Crime, Criminal Law and Criminal Justice* 1999; "Young offenders and their families", in *Young Offenders and their Families: The Human Rights Issue* 1998.

Nuno Ferreira graduated from Law School, University of Coimbra (2000). He is a member of the Portuguese Law Bar Association (since 2002) and he was a legal consultant at the Portuguese Securities Market Commission (2001–2003). Currently he is a doctoral research fellow at the Centre of European Law and Politics at the University of Bremen (ZERP) and a young researcher of the Research Training Network "Fundamental Rights and Private Law in the European Union" (2003–2006). Since 2006, he is a lecturer in law at the University of Manchester. He participated in courses on medical law (Helsinki University, 2000) and children's rights (Ghent University, 2004). He is a contributor to the Common Core of European Private Law/Trento Project on "Personality Rights and Tort Law in Europe". He is the author of articles on organised crime, international responsibility and euthanasia. He speaks Portuguese, English, Italian, French, German and Spanish.

Shannon A. Moore is an Assistant Professor at Brock University, Canada, in the Department of Child and Youth Studies. She holds a Ph.D. in counselling psychology and is an applied social scientist. Her research interests focus upon community-based social justice with young people and qualitative methodologies. The intersection among restorative justice, children's rights, diversity, mental health, and exceptionalities are her current research interests. As a registered Canadian counsellor, Dr. Moore has practiced privately and as a consultant within education, social service, mental health and correctional service contexts in Canada and the United Kingdom.

Ton Liefaard (LL.M) is a lecturer in Juvenile Law, and a Ph.D. researcher at the Faculty of Law and the Amsterdam Center of Child Studies of the Vrije Universiteit in Amsterdam, The Netherlands. Previously he worked as a senior judicial clerk at the Amsterdam Criminal Court of Appeal. In 2003 and 2004, he conducted, together with two colleagues, the evaluation of the Dutch Youth Custodial Institutions Act, commissioned by the Dutch Ministry of Justice. Currently he is preparing a dissertation on deprivation of liberty of children in light of international human rights standards. Ton is a member of the editorial boards of the Dutch Journal for Family and Juvenile Law and the Dutch Journal for the Rights of the Child. He has published a law book called *Toegang tot de Beginselenwet justitiële jeugdinrichtingen* (Amsterdam: SWP 2005) and several articles, in the Netherlands and abroad on juvenile (criminal) law and children's rights.

Isabelle Delens-Ravier is a doctor in criminology and a sociologist. Her Ph.D. thesis focused on the issue of placement of children. She is currently a guest lecturer and researcher at the Department of Criminology and Penal Law at the Catholic University of Louvain-La-Neuve. Her main research interests are the development and incidence of children's rights in the area of family aid and youth protection. She has participated in numerous research projects relating to family support, particularly regarding poverty situations and situations where a parent is in prison, and the social reaction to juvenile delinquency. She is particularly interested in the experiences of the social "actors": families, young people and intervening professionals, when they are dealing with social, judicial and penitentiary institutions.

Guy Massart is a Belgian social anthropologist, he holds a Ph.D. in Communication Sciences from the Ecole Normale Supérieure – Lyon. Currently he is the Regional Research and Evaluation Advisor for Plan International in West Africa based in Dakar, Senegal. He is the coordinator of a regional ethnographical research project entitled: "Listening to the Experiences of Children and Young People: Agents of our Contemporary World". His work focuses on pursuing experimental ethnographical projects, both in terms of communication (multimedia, website, arts, events), and in terms of participatory research methods, namely with children and youth. His specific research interests focus on the impact of contemporary social changes on the daily experience and identities of men in Portuguese speaking Africa.

Isabelle Wattier is an assistant at the Thomas More College, Law Faculty of the Catholic University of Leuven, Belgium (since 1995). She was lawyer at the Brussels Bar for several years and was researcher for the Ministerial Commission for the reform of the Belgium Criminal Procedure from 1995 to 1999. She was also parliamentary attaché from 1999 to 2003. She published several contributions on criminal procedure, negotiated justice and criminal protection of children. She is currently Ph.D. Candidate in Law at the Catholic University of Leuven.

Ahmadou Tall is a Senegalese magistrate and is a practising judge at the Regional Court of Dakar (Country Court). He is a lecturer in juridical sciences at the faculty of law at the University of Dakar where he obtained his master's degree in private law in 1992. After a certificate at the Senegalese National School of Administration and Magistracy (ENAM) of Dakar, he was appointed as a judge. In 2004, he obtained, with distinction, a specialised studies degree in human rights at the Catholic University of Leuven (UCL), Belgium.

Karl Hanson is a Doctor of Law and Senior lecturer and researcher at the Children's Rights Unit, University Institute Kurt Bösch (IUKB) in Sion, Switzerland. He is programme coordinator of the Master of Advanced Studies in Children's Rights, an interdisciplinary postgraduate programme jointly organised by IUKB and the University of Fribourg Switzerland (www.iukb.ch/emcr). He has previously worked as a senior researcher at the Children's Rights Centre and at the Human Rights Centre of Ghent University in Belgium, where he has extensively been involved in an interdisciplinary research network on children's human rights. His publications and main research interests include children's rights as human rights, juvenile justice and the debate on working children and child labour.

www.ingramcontent.com/pod-product-compliance
Ingram Content Group UK Ltd.
Pitfield, Milton Keynes, MK11 3LW, UK
UKHW051924100926
8556IPUK00022B/1361

9 789050 95640